Marina and Lee

Also by Priscilla Johnson McMillan

Khrushchev and the Arts:
The Politics of Soviet Culture, 1962–1964

Marina and Lee

Priscilla Johnson McMillan

HARPER & ROW, PUBLISHERS

NEW YORK, HAGERSTOWN, SAN FRANCISCO

LONDON

Portions of this book previously appeared in *The Ladies' Home Journal.*

The lines from "I Have a Rendezvous with Death" on p. 462 are reprinted from Alan Seeger's *Poems* by permission of Charles Scribner's Sons. Copyright 1916 Charles Scribner's Sons.

FIRST EDITION

Designed by Lydia Link

Library of Congress Cataloging in Publication Data

McMillan, Priscilla Johnson.
  Marina and Lee.
  Includes index.
  1. Oswald, Marina, 1941–   2. Oswald, Lee Harvey.
3. United States—Biography. 4. Kennedy, John Fitzgerald, Pres. U.S., 1917–1963—Assassination.
I. Title.
CT275.0737M32 1977   973.922'092'4 [B]   76–26238
ISBN 0–06–012953–0

77 78 79 80 10 9 8 7 6 5 4 3 2 1

For George
and
For my parents

Contents

"I want to give the people of the United States something to think about."

Lee Harvey Oswald to the author,
Moscow, November 16, 1959.

Prologue

It was the last sweltering evening in August of 1964. We had come to the lake set in flat clay country carpeted by pine trees to do the work that had eluded us in Dallas.

After supper Marina insisted on giving the floor a scrubbing, Russian-style. This she accomplished bent forward nearly double, like a jackknife, fingers to the floor, swaying from side to side in a graceful, dancelike movement that ended in a triumphal backward swish of Ajax and hot water. It was easier that way than with a mop, she declared. Besides, that's how she had done it while she was married to Lee.

Afterwards she lay prone on the sofa in front of the massive stone fireplace. The evening's reminiscences—the work we had come for— were about to begin. Suddenly we were caught in the glare of headlights as a long white Cadillac swung to a stop before our glass door. The tall, pot-bellied man who clambered out had a fringe of white hair and a slight forward slouch. He was clad in khaki from head to toe. I slurred my words a little as I told him our names, mine and Marina Oswald's, and asked him to join us for a beer.

Our caller, Mr. Cope, was night watchman at the private lake where we had been loaned a cabin for a few days. Tomorrow, he informed us as he settled in a leather armchair, was the opening of the dove-shooting season in Texas. The woods would be filled with hunters. I translated his remarks, and upright now on the sofa, Marina came to in sudden animation. "Why," she exclaimed in Russian, "it's like a scene from Turgenev! Some hunters are alone in a tiny cabin. A passer-by notices a light quite by chance, knocks at the door, and comes in for a long

1

evening's talk. Strangers meet, and for no reason. Except that they're alone in the woods at night!"

Marina's sally in a strange tongue brought Mr. Cope upright in his chair, too. Perhaps he had never heard Russian before, for he entered on a painful guessing game, and several times he tried to guess her nationality. Each time he was mistaken. Finally it came, incredulous. "You're not from Russia, are you?" Marina nodded, Yes. She was kneading her hands now, and I noticed that they were covered with sweat. He stared at her, through steel-rimmed glasses. "You didn't bring a guy named Oswald here, the guy who shot President Kennedy?" Her hands shaking a little, Marina lit a cigarette. "Tell him," she turned to me, "that my name is Marina Oswald."

The stranger continued to stare. He asked Marina to stand, so that he could see her, all of her, with his own eyes. After everything he'd read about her, he said, after the way he'd followed her in the papers and all the times he'd seen her photograph, he couldn't believe that he had failed to recognize her. Pained and self-conscious, Marina demurred. All the same, the rest of the conversation was a kind of recognition.

If she really *was* Marina Oswald, Mr. Cope assured her in a polite Southern way, then he was *proud* he had come by tonight on his rounds.

"I am nothing to be proud of," Marina responded softly in Russian.

Anything he could do for her, Mr. Cope went on, he would do. He wanted her to know that she had nothing to be ashamed of. Even so, Marina answered as she lit another cigarette, she and her children would feel the weight of guilt for the rest of their lives.

Mr. Cope was very serious now. He understood how she felt, he told her. He had lost his wife because of mental illness. He had taken her to a succession of doctors and watched over her day and night. All the same she had killed herself. Afterwards he had been tortured by doubts. What had he failed to do that he might have done if only he'd understood? Marina mustn't feel that way. What had happened wasn't anybody's fault.

Then he asked her how much she weighed. A hundred pounds, she told him. "I'm twice as big as you are," he remarked as he prepared to leave. "I weigh two hundred and twenty-five. Now listen here, little girl. Don't you feel bad about anything at all. I have a boat. Will you come with me for a ride?" He turned to her again when he was halfway out the door. "I want you to know that the American people have feelings."

Next day Marina was on a boat. Not with Mr. Cope, but with some well-to-do Dallas realtors who had found us trespassing on their part of the lakefront. They had not been very friendly when they first came upon us sunbathing on the beach. So when they returned a little later we expected to be shooed away. But apparently one of them had recognized Marina and they asked us to come boating instead. It was sticky at first, as they and their young wives put on water skis. With all their good will, they had not reckoned on what we would talk about. Marina was nervous, too, smoking one cigarette after another. To break the silence and make sure they had a good time, she gave them a drinking demonstration, tossing down a swallow of Seven-Up, a quick gulp of vodka and, finally, a chaser of Seven-Up. That way, she explained in her accented English, "you will never be T-R-O-O-N-K."

At sundown, trudging home, Marina was thoughtful. "All day," she remarked, "I am saying, 'Thank you, thank you, thank you.' "

I was thoughtful, too. I wondered how, if I had been Marina, I would have responded to the kindness of Mr. Cope, to the curiosity of the realtors and their wives. I wondered what Marina thought of me, there to dredge up everything she could remember of her life. I spoke Russian, and had lived and worked in Russia. Otherwise we had had very different lives. Yet as we entered the cabin to spend another evening together, I wondered if our meeting had been inevitable. By a curious coincidence I had met her husband, Lee Harvey Oswald, in Moscow in 1959. And I had known John Fitzgerald Kennedy, the man he shot four years later in Dallas on November 22, 1963.

Like many idealistic young people right after World War II, I was a World Federalist and hoped that the Soviet Union could be persuaded to join a world government. Because of this interest, I majored in Russian at Bryn Mawr and in 1953 received an M.A. in Russian Studies from Harvard. My first job was in Washington as a researcher for the newly elected senator from Massachusetts, John F. Kennedy.

Oddly, it was in New York, where I later went to work as a Russian-language translator, that I got to know Senator Kennedy. I saw him there occasionally during the winter of 1954–1955 when he was undergoing two operations on his spine. Doctors at the hospital said that the danger did not come from his back, but from a form of Addison's disease, a disorder of the adrenal glands which produce hormones that enable the body to deal with stress. Kennedy could survive a major operation, and was one of the very first to do so, because of cortisone and other artificial substances that were used to combat shock and infection.

One of the doctors I knew begged Kennedy not to go through with the first operation. And Kennedy, about to be wheeled into surgery, said simply: "I'd rather die than go around the rest of my life on crutches."

That winter he did almost die, several times. I went to see him, posing as one of his sisters, whenever he asked me to come or whenever I heard that he was better. Each time I went I was sad because I thought he was going to die. But within a few minutes I would be laughing and incredulous at the scene in his hospital room. One Saturday I found him with a Howdy-Doody doll as tall as he was lying under the covers beside him. He had a tank of tropical fish at the foot of his bed and a lifesize cutout of Marilyn Monroe tacked upside down on his door. On the floor at the head of his bed were three tall stacks of books and I noticed that many of them were about how this or that politician had become President, or how some other politician had won his party's nomination for the presidency. On this particular afternoon, the room was also filled with a gaggle of gum-chewing bobby-soxers, "cousins from New Jersey," Jack said, every one of whom was treating him with the most ebullient irreverence. A nurse came in and raised her hand to her head in dismay. "He's supposed to see no one but family," she moaned. "But he has such an *enormous* family—especially sisters."

Sometimes I brought him a copy of *The New York Post* in an effort to make him more liberal. Once he hurled it across the room and it hit me with a force that belied his weakened state. "You liberals," he shouted, "you liberals," and went on to excoriate half a dozen Harvard professors and experts on Russia whom I admired. All were to become well-known advisers of his once he was in the White House. Jack had not come on his liberal days yet.

When he got out of the hospital he came across my path once in a while, lit it up briefly, then disappeared, very often for months at a time. I was one of hundreds of friends in his life; he was unique in mine. Because he was unique, I thought about him a good deal. Aside from his humor and his Irish irascibility, the characteristic of Jack's of which I saw most was his wide-ranging curiosity. He was forever bombarding me with questions. Should we give aid to Yugoslavia? With whom was I going skiing that weekend? Why had So-and-so been defeated for state office the week before? At what age did I expect to get married? He treated everyone to an endless flow of questions, and I imagine that they, too, were as amused and flattered as I was.

But in spite of all the questions, I noticed that Jack held his curiosity within limits. Even in the hospital, when he had plenty of time and no certain future at all, it seemed to me that he did not allow his questions to roam freely, wherever they might lead. He kept them on a fairly tight course, to those whose answers might help him—in his very next telephone call. Eager as he was for information, he did not allow himself the luxury of genuine intellectual curiosity. He did not think he had time.

Kennedy had a rebellious streak, and it showed through in many delightful and eccentric things he did. But he had on the whole accepted the ambition his father thrust upon him, the ambition to become President of the United States. Only, I thought, he had done it at a cost to his capacity for empathy and imagination. He had a candor and a breathtaking detachment about himself, but I wondered how well he understood other people, especially those who lacked his kind of ambition, or those who happened to be failures.

I saw little of Kennedy after the mid-1950s. I went to Russia whenever I could, and in 1955 got a job as a translator for the Joint Press Reading Service, run by the British, American, and Canadian embassies in Moscow to provide English-speaking diplomats with Soviet newspaper translations. Then I worked as a translator for *The New York Times,* but I had to leave in 1956, with great regret, when my succession of visas ran out. I was in Moscow again from 1958 to 1960 as correspondent for the North American Newspaper Alliance and *The Progressive* magazine. And it was in 1959 that I interviewed a young American who was defecting to the U.S.S.R. His name was Lee Harvey Oswald.

We met in my hotel room, and I wrote a feature story about him. I thought he was very, very young and touching in his eagerness to stay in Russia, but afterwards I did not think a great deal about him. Except for one thing. Oswald said that he was a Marxist and was defecting because of his beliefs. In Moscow we thought we had seen everything, but we had never seen anyone like this.

The time for ideological defectors had been the 1930s. Then, blacks, Communists, women who were eager for sexual liberation, flocked to Russia from all over the globe to help build the socialist paradise. No more. Stalin, the purges, and the war intervened. Russia had lost the old élan. The outsiders of the 1950s—newspapermen, diplomats, itinerant American politicians—were there because Moscow was a great dateline, a place from which to launch a career. Yet here was this boy who was prepared to take a very drastic step because of his political convictions. I remembered Lee Oswald because he was the only one who did not seem to fit.

I returned to Russia in 1962 to write a series for *The Reporter* magazine, and in the fall of 1963 I was a visiting scholar at the Russian Research Center at Harvard. On November 21 I drafted a letter to President Kennedy, whom I had scarcely ever approached in his new eminence. My letter was a plea for Olga Ivinskaya, a woman who had been loved by the poet Boris Pasternak and was said to be the model for the heroine, Lara, in his novel *Dr. Zhivago*. Soon after Pasternak's death in 1960, Mrs. Ivinskaya was seized by the Soviet authorities and shipped to a prison area in the desolate Mordovian Autonomous Republic, where she was going blind. Her friends in Moscow were afraid that she was going to die from cold and lack of medical care. I wrote President Kennedy to ask if he would intervene for Mrs. Ivinskaya should he meet with Soviet Premier Nikita Khrushchev at a summit conference the following spring.

I asked a friend, Rose di Benedetto, with whom I worked at the Russian Research Center, to type the letter. I addressed it to the President in care of his private secretary, Mrs. Evelyn Lincoln, because I had known her and thought she would see to it that the letter got through to him. Rose and I mailed the letter on the night of November 21.

Harvard Square was in chaos the next afternoon. President Kennedy had been murdered in Dallas. People wandered up the subway stairs looking dazed, with tears streaming down their faces. Men and women who had not seen one another in years fell into each other's arms. Like every other place in America, we were a community pulled together by shock.

By chance I met Rose in front of a florist shop. "Isn't it awful?" she said. "He'll never see our letter. He'll never get to help that lady."

For a second we were too stunned to think beyond our letter.

Then I asked: "Do they know who it is? Have they caught anybody yet?"

"Yes. His name is Lee Harvey Oswald."

"My God," I said. "I know that boy."

Two days later, on November 24, Lee Harvey Oswald was dead, himself the victim of an assassin's bullet. On November 29, Lyndon Johnson created the President's Commission on the Assassination of President Kennedy, and for ten months the Warren Commission, as it came to be called, probed into the tragic and bizarre events in Dallas. Witness after witness was called, including Oswald's widow, Marina, who scarcely spoke any English and had to testify through an interpreter. The Commission was able to establish *what* happened in Dallas. But it was unable to give a clear answer to the most intriguing question of all, the question that puzzles many people even today. *Why?*

During the early months after the assassination, I was worried about President Kennedy. He, too, would want to know why he had died. I could see him meeting Oswald somewhere and peppering him with questions. What put it into your head? Was it something about me personally, or did you do it out of principle? Is it hard to kill someone you have never met? He would not have had the slightest malice, only that astonishing curiosity.

I wondered what Kennedy would make of Oswald. As inquiring as Kennedy had been, he shied away from probing too deeply into other people—or himself. He had disciplined himself sharply, worked desperately hard, even put his life at hazard, all to achieve what he wanted. Would he, who had curbed even his ability to enter into the feelings of others lest it slow his race to the top, be able to understand a man so unlike himself?

There was another thing that I needed to settle for myself. I needed to reconcile the quiet, rather gentle "Lee," the boy whom I had met in my hotel room and who told me he was "unemotional," with the dangerous "Oswald," the man who shot the President. I was not at all sure how they fitted. I wanted to understand why "Lee" did it—first of all for myself and then, even though he was dead, for President Kennedy.

If there was an answer to the question, I thought that Marina Oswald might be the one who could help find it. And so, through the offices of my publisher and her lawyer, I arranged to meet her with a view to writing a book.

As I came up the drive of her small ranch house in Richardson, Texas, outside Dallas, she ran over from a neighbor's house to greet me. She was tiny, she looked like a child, and she had very large, light blue eyes.

"You met Lee?" It was the first question she asked.

"Did you meet him once or several times? Did he speak Russian then?"

It came up again and again in our conversations. "Was he wearing his gray suit when you met him? His dark red tie? Didn't he look nice in that suit? He was good-looking then, wasn't he?" One day, when a neighbor came on us working at the dining table, Marina simply nodded in my direction and said by way of introduction: "She knew Lee in Moscow."

Marina's life had been turned upside down. First there were the numbing events themselves, the assassination and Lee's death. Immediately afterwards she was placed in protective custody and sequestered in a hotel. She was in the care of two organizations which were competing with one another and whose treatment of her was at cross-purposes: the Secret Service and the FBI.

The Secret Service was made responsible for her protection because it occurred to the Attorney General, Robert Kennedy, and the new President, Lyndon Johnson, that Marina might meet the same fate as her husband. Later, the Secret Service was kept on because it occurred to the newly created Warren Commission that Marina held a Soviet passport, might be a Soviet agent, and might try to flee the country. Marina did not mind. She liked the Secret Service. She enjoyed the company of the agents, who babysat and burped her baby and regaled her with stories about President and Mrs. Kennedy and their children, whom they had also guarded.

But the FBI was another matter. Marina instinctively mistrusted the FBI, equating it with the secret police in Russia. In addition, Lee had hated and feared the FBI, and Marina had taken over his attitude wholesale. As if that were not enough, a few days after Lee died the FBI brought down an immigration official from New York who insinuated that unless Marina cooperated fully, she might be deported from the United States.

And so Marina was being manipulated by two sets of officials: one afraid that she might leave the country, and another threatening to throw her out. On every side she encountered suspicion that she might be a Soviet agent and might have been Lee's accomplice. Apart from the Secret Service men, no one treated her as if she had feelings, as a woman who had just lost her husband and had lately given birth to a child. No one realized that as a Russian she was especially frightened of having government agents all around her and was secretly terrified of being sent to some American equivalent of Siberia. Because of the language barrier, she had no one in whom she could confide. She had only her husband's brother, Robert Oswald, to turn to. From him, in spite of the fact that they could barely communicate, she was able to draw a good deal of comfort.

From the very first days her greatest dilemma lay in her loyalty to Lee. She was subjected to searching interrogations. Lee was dead, she could not help him, and in a way her instinct was to tell the truth. But she had another instinct, and that was not to inculpate Lee, outside the bare fact of the assassination, any more than she could help. She resolved her dilemma imperfectly, telling the whole truth in response to some questions, holding back for a time in response to others, and, about one question, Lee's trip to Mexico, she claimed at first that she didn't know about it and then later said that she did. In a word, she created suspicions about her truthfulness that endure to this day.

The problem of loyalty to Lee that came up during her interrogations by day also came up in her dreams at night. Again and again she had a nightmare that she was rushing Lee away from an angry crowd, running, running, running from a mob that would kill him. And there was another in which she screamed to an accuser: "Say what you like. Only, don't say it to me. I am not guilty. Lee did it, not me!"

The problem of guilt was always with her, and again and again she asked the question: Is it a sin to have loved a criminal? It was to be a long time before she could begin to come to terms with the fact that she had indeed loved Lee and yet at the same time accept what he had done.

By the time I met Marina, she was out of protective custody and was living in the ranch house she had managed to buy. But she had two tiny children to care for, business and legal headaches, and was still spending many hours a week answering the questions of a by now polite and rather charming FBI man who kept showing up in her dinette. With so much to worry about and hundreds of hours of questioning behind her already, I wondered why it was worth it to her to collaborate on a book that would dig even more deeply into her private life. One night after we had been working late, she explained in a small, sad, tired voice that she was doing it to find out the truth. "The truth is in Lee," she said, "and Lee is dead." I noticed that the word she was using for "truth" was not the everyday Russian word *"pravda,"* but rather, *"istina,"* a word that has a holy ring to it, God's truth, gospel truth.

Marina was speaking at that moment of the truth about Lee and the assassination. But she cares about another truth, too—the truth about herself. She had been asked thousands of questions about Lee, his maps, his guns, his movements, but she had been asked surprisingly little about herself and nothing at all about her feelings. In spite of the hysterical bustle all around her, Marina never once, to her credit, lost sight of the fact that the thing that meant most to her was the truth about herself and her emotions.

I suspect that may be one reason why she was willing to work on this book. Throughout our collaboration she spoke to me with complete honesty about herself and demanded equal honesty from me. I found it hard to match her candor. I was anxious, moreover, not to influence her recollections and I tried, mistakenly, I now think, to appear neutral and neither approve nor disapprove what she was saying. But some of my feelings came out. "You know," I said cruelly one night, as we were working together, "I don't know if I can write this book. Your husband killed a friend of mine."

Marina was shocked and hurt. But she will accept any frankness and I guess she accepted mine. Perhaps it even cleared the air, for we spent seven humorous and tempestuous months together after that. I came to like Marina very much and, what is more, to respect her. I respect her most for being open to all of the truth about herself.

She for her part has been loyal. After having done everything she could to enable me to write truthfully, she has waited thirteen years for me to finish this book.

For the problem of which I spoke cruelly that night came back to haunt me. If my friendship with Kennedy had been my youth, then his death marked the end of it. During the years after he died, I suffered long periods in which I was unable to write at all. Where did all the words lead, if not to death?

Because of her aliveness and her remarkable memory, Marina has not been hard to write about. Lee is another matter. Even though I met and talked with him, I have found a deadness in him that has made it difficult to bring him alive again, on paper. Still, I hope I have found the answer to my question: *Why?* If so, the answer begins where I began. With Marina.

PART ONE

Russia, 1941–1961

1

Archangel

IN THE PRE-DAWN HOURS of Sunday, June 22, 1941, the dive bombers of Adolf Hitler swept down savagely on the sleepy, utterly unprepared Soviet fortress at Brest, on the border between Russia and Poland. So, abruptly, the war began, and for millions of men and women living in Russia at that time, as well as for millions yet unborn, life was destined to become the sprawling panorama of tragic suffering that is the shape of the country itself. Countless thousands were swallowed up as Hitler's greedy divisions pounded across the plains and marshlands of western Russia. In the four cold, hungry, disease-wracked years that followed, thousands more were caught at random, seized and spun in the cyclone of war. For those who survived, life was never to be the same again.

A few months before the war began, Klavdia Prusakova, a twenty-three-year-old laboratory worker in Leningrad, found herself in a classic predicament. She was pregnant and unable, for reasons that are obscure to this day, to marry the father of her child. She packed up her bags that spring, said goodbye to the uncle whose apartment had sheltered her, and hurried home to her mother in Archangel. She found work in the nearby village of Molotovsk (now Severodvinsk) on the White Sea, and there, on July 17, 1941, two months prematurely and less than a month after the outbreak of war, Klavdia gave birth to a girl weighing little over 2 pounds. Miraculously, the child survived, and when the doctors pronounced her strong enough, Klavdia bundled the baby up and took her the 30 miles to her mother's apartment in Archangel. That apartment was to be the child's home until she was almost six years old.

The mistress of the apartment was the baby's grandmother, Tatyana Yakovlevna Prusakova, a member of the former landowning class and a straitlaced woman of the old school who was steeped in the religious values of the Russian provinces. The child herself never learned exactly the circumstances in which she happened to be conceived. Perhaps it was an age-old story of seduction. But perhaps, as the child herself hopes, it was one of the innumerable sad stories of Russian life in the 1930s and early 1940s—purges, the Finnish war, the conflict with Germany, a time when men frequently vanished into the night as victims of political disfavor.[1] Whatever the circumstances of Klavdia's pregnancy may have been, Tatyana Yakovlevna found it in her heart to forgive her favorite daughter. She took the baby and consented to bring it up. But first, she insisted on a christening. Religious observances of any kind were frowned on, if not actually forbidden, by Stalin himself. But Tatyana Yakovlevna, as usual, had her way. At the age of two months the child was christened in the living room of her apartment by a priest of the Russian Orthodox Church. She was immersed in warm water in the family's most treasured ornament, a bowl of green porcelain and mother-of-pearl. The child was named Marina.

Tatyana Yakovlevna was apparently glad to have a child to take care of. The war had scattered her large family to the four winds. Her husband Vasily Prusakov, a lanky, mustachioed man, had worked for a British shipping company before 1917. So valued were his services that his employers had offered to move the whole family to London to escape the Revolution. But Tatyana had flatly refused to leave Russia, and Vasily was now the captain of a Soviet commercial vessel plying the northern seas and was seldom at home. One of their seven children, the youngest son Nikolai, had gone straight to the army from school, and had been killed on the Leningrad front soon after the war broke out. For years Tatyana refused to admit that he was dead and expected him to return at any moment.

Klavdia went back to her job in Molotovsk, and Marina was left in her grandmother's care. The only other member of the household was Klavdia's sister Lyuba, a flirtatious young woman who worked for a restaurant trust. Tatyana Yakovlevna disapproved of Lyuba, whom she considered too easily deceived by men. With a shake of her head, she sometimes called her "my wayward daughter" or "my bad girl." Free to devote her formidable energies to bringing up her granddaughter, Tatyana Yakovlevna was determined that Marina would be a good girl.

In spite of the war, it was a peaceful, even privileged home. Marina, her grandmother, and her aunt Lyuba shared a three-room apartment with a kitchen and bath. Marina remembers it, even during Archangel's endless Arctic winter, as a place filled with warmth and sunshine, with rubber plants, geraniums, flowering tearoses, and mimosa. There was a row of copper pots in the kitchen and a heavy brass samovar, polished to shine like gold.

Then there was Tatyana Yakovlevna herself, an altogether commanding presence. Tall and dark-haired still, clad in a long dress with flowers embroidered on the front, she moved unhurriedly through the day's tasks, propelled by some invisible list of chores in her head. Every morning, no matter how cold it was outside, she threw open the windows to air out the apartment. Each day she scrubbed the floors, did the washing, and polished the copper, brass, and silver. She pressed clothes the old-fashioned way, with hot coals inside a heavy iron. She made clothing and bed linen on an old Singer sewing machine purchased before the 1917 Revolution when the company had a factory in Leningrad.

If Tatyana Yakovlevna was scrupulous to keep the apartment clean, she was no less scrupulous about her grandchild. Every night she heated water on the stove, bathed her, and then tucked her into the bed the two of them shared in the living room. Marina said her prayers, and the last sight she saw as she dropped off to sleep was her grandmother sitting by the samovar, stirring jam into her evening tea.

In spite of the unyielding ways that made her a figure of awe to nearly everyone, Tatyana Yakovlevna bent a little when it came to Marina, whom she called "little daughter" or "little granddaughter." Marina was said to be her favorite. Marina, for her part, admired her grandmother's pale skin and her unvarying fragrance of kindling and soap and perfume. She loved nestling next to her in bed at night. "Grandma," she would say, "you smell so sweet. May I kiss you?" Her grandmother never turned her away.

Their apartment building, a sprawling L-shaped structure of whitewashed stucco close to the heart of Archangel, had a courtyard to play in. Marina was also allowed to play in a little park across the street where there was a merry-go round and a zoo with seals cavorting in a fountain, rabbits, foxes, a wolf, and a big brown bear. As she grew older, she got to know more of Archangel. She became aware of cobblestone streets and of sidewalks paved, after the fashion of the cities of the Russian north, with wood. She became familiar with the smell of birches—the birches of the park, the birches of the woods outside the city and, above all, the birch smell the sidewalks gave off whenever they were wet with rain. On the outskirts of the town there were wooden houses so close to the edge of the sea that they had to be set on stilts. Beyond the town lay frozen Arctic tundra and thick virgin forest where wolves and bears had their lairs.

Archangel was a busy port in wartime, one of the principal cities in Russia where the Allies could land supplies. Unlike almost any other provincial Soviet city at the time, Archangel was filled with sailors and foreigners from every nation. There were Englishmen, Chinese, and Americans, even Negroes, whom few Russians had ever seen. With so many foreigners, with foreign music and foreign cloth and foreign canned goods to buy and sell, Archangel had a muffled wartime lilt and, in its own gray, Soviet way, a little of the feel of an icebound honkytonk town.

All of this spelled privilege. One of Marina's early recollections, for example, is of eating American Spam. Another is of the green and red striped peppermint sticks that arrived in a tin box at intervals from her Aunt Taisya, an accountant who traveled back and forth on a Soviet ship between Russia and America. Each time a new box came, Marina thought: "What a lucky country!" To her, America was like a big box of candies. Or a gingerbread house in the forest, filled with good things to eat while Russia had almost nothing.

In spite of the terrible wartime shortages, Marina never went hungry, for her grandmother was an ingenious cook in the old Russian style, skilled at making the most of fresh fish, and mushrooms and berries from the outlying forest. Nor did Marina have to wear the shabby, somber ready-made clothes that were all the stores of Archangel had to offer. Her grandmother sewed her full smock-dresses and a dark blue coat with a white fur collar and cap. She also had a half-dozen bright, flowered dresses bought by her Aunt Taisya in America.

Marina's clothes nearly brought her to grief. One day she was playing alone in the park when a strange woman promised her a mechanical toy if she would come with her. Marina trotted after her, but on the street she became frightened and burst into tears. A passer-by noticed her, managed to get her away from the woman, and took her home by the hand. When Tatyana Yakovlevna heard what had happened, she told Marina that she must never listen to the stories strangers told. So difficult were conditions during the war that there were people who roamed the streets kidnapping children for their clothes. They would sell the clothing and leave the children to starve in the woods.

As World War II came to an end in 1945, Marina's life began to change. It is difficult to fix with precision the sequence in which hitherto unknown relatives appeared in the Archangel apartment. But the sheltered life Marina had known with her grandmother became less tranquil and the cast of characters whose lives touched her own grew larger.

One of those who appeared was Alexander Medvedev, the man whom Marina's mother had married during the war. So far as is known, they had met in Leningrad before the war. But the romance occurred afterward, when Marina was a baby, in a hospital somewhere in western Russia where Alexander was a wounded soldier and Klavdia a laboratory worker. They were married in September 1942, when Marina was fourteen months old. Alexander Medvedev, then, was Marina's stepfather. She was told, however, that he was her real father, who had been away at the front.

She met him for the first time in the early spring when she was not yet four years old. She remembers it as if it were a fairy tale. Early one morning she was on her way to the park to ride on the merry-go-round. But when she got there the gate was still locked and she reached up as far as she could, trying to undo the latch from inside. Suddenly a stranger appeared. He had on civilian clothes and was carrying a suitcase. "Will you open the gate for me, please?" Marina asked.

"Do you want to get in very much?" the man said.

"Yes!" she replied.

"And what will you do there?" he asked.

"I want to ride on the merry-go-round," Marina said.

"Where do you live?"

"In that house," Marina said, pointing to the apartment building.

"What is your name?"

"Marinochka."

"And is your mother called Klava?"

"Yes."

"Where's your papa?" the man said.

"Papa's at the front," Marina replied. "He's coming home soon."

"Do you want him to come very much?"

"*Very* much," Marina said.

"Well," the man said, "he's here."

Marina buried herself in his arms and kissed him. Then she raced across the street to the courtyard of her building shouting: "Papa's here! Papa's here!" She was overjoyed to see her father at last. He had dark hair and blue eyes, and she thought he was wonderfully handsome. He had been wounded in the leg by a bullet, and he showed Marina the scar and the place where his toe was missing. She lifted her dress and showed him *her* scar that had been left by a childhood infection.

Alexander Medvedev did not stay in Archangel long. About a month later, he vanished to Murmansk, taking Marina's mother with him. Marina was left behind, but a short time later her grandfather, Vasily Prusakov, came home from sea for the last time, fatally ill with cancer of the throat, and Marina went to stay in Murmansk.

Her recollection of this first visit alone with her mother and stepfather is a happy one. Marina thought that her mother, with her soft, brown hair and huge, sad green eyes, was the most beautiful person alive. She remembers the leather smell of Alexander Medvedev's windbreaker as he took her, perched on his shoulders, coasting downhill on a toboggan. She remembers that he warmed her cot with an electric heater before she went to bed at night and wrapped her up in a scarf whenever she went outdoors to shield her face from the wind.

On September 3, 1945, Klavdia gave birth to a son, Pyotr (called Petya) Medvedev. While her husband remained in Murmansk, Klavdia returned to her mother's apartment in Archangel, bringing Marina and the new baby with her. Pyotr was christened, as Marina had been, in Tatyana Yakovlevna's green porcelain bowl. Marina no longer had her grandmother all to herself.

Soon other members of the family began to appear. In December 1945, Tatyana Yakovlevna's oldest son, Ilya, came back from the war, his tour of duty with the Soviet army in Germany at an end. Tall, slender, about thirty-seven years old, with a tired smile and a face like a kindly eagle, he brought candy and toys and dresses from Germany. He also brought his wife Valya, a jolly, good-looking woman in her early twenties.

Marina's grandmother did not approve of Valya. Tatyana Yakovlevna considered her son a paragon, and pretty and kind-hearted as Valya was, Tatyana thought she was too simple, too poorly educated—in short, not good enough for Ilya. And so she was treated as an inferior member of the household. She scrubbed floors and polished copper and did as she was told. But she always found time to sing to Marina, tell her stories and help her draw pictures. Despite his mother's attitude, Ilya was devoted to his wife and they were destined to play an important role in Marina's life later on.

With so many of the family at home, the three-room apartment was very crowded. Marina still slept with her grandmother in the living room, Aunt Lyuba was alone in the second room, while the third was jammed with Klavdia and Petya in one bed, and Ilya and Valya in the other. Privacy was impossible, and disagreements inevitable. But there was no question of who had the final say.

When Valya read aloud to the family in the evenings, the only writers Tatyana Yakovlevna consented to hear were pre-Revolutionary writers like Pushkin, Lermontov, and Leo Tolstoy. What she really wanted was to have the same passages in *War and Peace* read aloud to her again and again. She refused to have the names of Soviet writers even mentioned in her presence.

Tatyana Yakovlevna hated everything modern and called airplanes "the devil's own handiwork." She had a lofty contempt for her country's Communist overlords and nursed a certain nostalgia for the Czar and his family. "Poor souls," she said. "The brutes killed them all. For nothing. They turned everything upside down. What for? It's all for the worse! It was better under the Czar." With a majestic disdain for the all-powerful Stalin, she called him a "demon let loose on earth," and could never hear his name without giving a little spit of derision.

She often lost patience with her son Ilya, a rising member of the Communist Party. Still, she respected his convictions and his Party membership, remarking that Ilya alone knew what was best for him. But when it came to her own old-fashioned ideas and religious beliefs, she would yield no quarter, not even to her favorite son. "I'm an old woman," she would say. "It's too late to make me over. You young people may live any way you please. But leave me in peace." She would not give up her Bible, her visits from black-bearded Orthodox priests, nor her ikons and the holy lamp that burned night and day in a special corner of the apartment where they were only too likely to be noticed by Ilya's Communist Party friends.

Tatyana Yakovlevna always had time for her granddaughter. She was a stern disciplinarian, but she called Marina a "genius" and a "marvel of intelligence." She took her to church, and like so many Russian grandmothers, kept her at home long past the age when most children were in kindergarten. She did not want her granddaughter subjected to the influence of the Soviet system a single moment before the age of seven, when it became legally imperative that she go to school.

Many years later, her Aunt Valya told Marina that she had been "spoiled" by her grandmother. It was true. As early as Marina can remember, her grandmother had made her feel special. And as long as she, her grandmother, and her Aunt Lyuba were the only ones who lived there, she felt that she was the center of affection in the household and had no sense of deprivation at its incompleteness.

Now things had changed. The apartment was filled with adults, as well as the new baby Petya. Marina used to go to bed early in the living room, and sometimes during the evening she would wake up and hear sounds of merriment in the kitchen, sounds from which she was excluded. The grown-ups were drinking tea from the samovar and listening to American records. Marina heard music, songs like "Blue Moon" and "Who's Afraid of the Big Bad Wolf?", and the tears would come streaming down her face. For the first time in her life five-year-old Marina was beginning to feel alone.

She was not sure to whom she belonged. She hardly knew Alexander Medvedev, the man she supposed to be her father, and she saw little of her mother. Marina loved her mother, whom she remembers as a wistful-looking woman and very loving. But Klavdia was away all day at work, her health was frail, and much of her time at home was devoted to the new baby. She loved her bright and pretty little daughter and called her a "wunderkind." But even in her mother's behavior, there was something that made Marina feel different.

Afterwards, long afterwards, Klavdia was to say to her: "If I had known what you were going to grow up into, I wouldn't have taken such good care of you. I'd have just let you die."

2

Moldavia

In the early spring of 1947, Alexander Medvedev appeared in Marina's life again. He left Murmansk, came to Archangel, and then he and Klavdia went away, evidently in search of a job. When they returned a few weeks later, they had found one in Moldavia, over 1,000 miles from Archangel. They packed their belongings, got Marina and Petya ready for the long journey, and said their goodbyes. It was the beginning of their life together as a family.

Tucked between Rumania and the Ukraine, in the southwestern corner of the U.S.S.R., Moldavia was then a primitive agricultural area. Most of the countryside still had no electric power or light. It appeared quite natural and in the order of things that Alexander, a skilled electrical technician, should have found a job in the tiny village of Zguritsa setting up an electric power station.

With its mild winters, long, hot summers, and fertile black earth, Moldavia was one of the richest sections of the Soviet Union. Taken over from Rumania on the eve of the war and quickly overrun by the Germans, it had not yet been organized into collective farms. The peasants were free to buy up land, to till their own soil and hawk their produce to the highest bidder at the bazaar. Private initiative flourished and with it, the countryside. Wartime rationing was still in force, but food was plentiful. Marina's mother used to say that they went to Moldavia "to eat our fill" after the rigors of war.

There may, however, have been another reason why the Medvedevs went to an out-of-the-way place like Moldavia. Marina later recalled something she scarcely noticed at the time. Countless wives and children of political prisoners were in rural Moldavia, trying to blend into the landscape and hoping the authorities would lose sight of them. Apparently Alexander, too, was in trouble and in need of a quiet spot where he could wait for the dust of disgrace to settle. Marina recalls that her stepfather had snipped the officer's insignia off his uniform and seldom spoke of his years in the army. When he did, it was to describe the terror he felt in shooting his first German and the psychological attacks that had caused his hair to go gray. She surmises that he must have committed some offense, such as a self-inflicted wound or refusal to obey an order, for which he had been broken in rank, sentenced to serve in a penal battalion in Murmansk, discharged in dishonor, and then required to "disappear" in a rural backwater for five years or so. It was a frequent form of punishment in the Soviet Union.

The family made the five-day journey by train to the Moldavian border, and then by horse-drawn cart, over muddy roads, to the tiny village of Zguritsa. They set up housekeeping in a single rented room in a thatched, one-story farmhouse. The walls, the floor, and the yard outside were of clay. Sweet-smelling grass covered the floor and, over it, a rug woven with the bright geometric designs favored by the Moldavians. The walls were covered with native rugs, too, and the room was heated by an old stove, fed with a rapidly burning peat made from sunflower seeds. In the yard there were an outhouse and a shed for corn and hay which also sheltered an old sow and her litter. Whenever Alexander wasn't looking, Marina rode the sow around the yard, her legs sticking straight out at the sides.

She came to love Zguritsa. She loved watching the birds glide over the low hills and the trees. She loved the fields of tall grass and wildflowers, dotted with white acacias and fruit trees of every variety. She liked the pungent aroma of smoking fuel from the outdoor stoves that had been dug into the ground in nearly every yard to use when it was too hot to cook indoors. It was the special smell of straw and cow manure. She loved going with her mother to the bazaar in the center of town where the Moldavians in colorful native costumes spread their rugs on the ground and sold live chickens and geese, cackling ducks and turkeys, goats and the sheep cheese called Brynza, milk, melons, and butter, grapes and fruit of all kinds, corn, wine, and sunflower oil, and herbs that could cure any illness. It was a noisy spectacle, loud with the sounds of pigs screeching and hawkers trying to outshout one another.

Moldavia, unlike Archangel with its cold and rigorous climate, was a place where Marina could spend most of her time out of doors. One of her favorite games was suggested by the Tarzan films that had been captured by the Russian armies in Germany and were being shown all over the Soviet Union. After the movie was over, Marina and her friends would race to the orchards that studded the village and hang from the trees screeching: "Me Tarzan, you Jane!" The Tarzan-boys, in noisy pursuit of the Jane-girls, would run from orchard to orchard, stealing apricots and cherries and apples and devouring them whether they were ripe or green. The children tied ropes to the trees and spent whole days swinging back and forth like their hero.

A summer's day seldom went by without Marina and her playmates spending hours splashing in the river, the muddy, meandering Kainar. They wore undershirts which had been resewn at the bottom by their mothers into the shape of modest one-piece bathing suits. In the river they would cover themselves with mud from head to toe to look like Negroes—an exotic race that they had heard about but never seen. Another pastime was exploring the meadow on the far side of the river where the gypsies had come to camp. There they found children dirtier than any they had ever seen before, and the music of drumbeats could be heard day and night. Of all the inhabitants of Zguritsa—Ukrainians, Moldavians, Russians, Jews—the gypsies were the most notorious. None of them worked; they made their living by stealing. Plainly, they did not think that Marx's commandment—"He who does not work shall not eat"—applied to them. The Soviet authorities thought otherwise. In an attempt to tame the gypsies, the militia descended upon them and took away the internal passports of the few who happened to possess them. No longer were the gypsies free to steal anything they could lay their hands on, then slip away under cover of darkness to another campsite. From now on, it was thought, they would stay in one spot and work. But the gypsies went on living exactly as before. In Zguritsa, it seemed, not even pigs and horses were safe from the gypsy stealth.

In the postwar effort to clean up the loose ends of Soviet society, the gypsies were by no means the only ones whom the authorities attempted to chasten. A few months after the Medvedevs came to Moldavia, in December 1947, the government devalued the currency in a sudden move to combat inflation before wartime rationing was ended. It was the peasants in places like Moldavia who were hardest hit. They had been free during the war to produce all the food they could and sell it on the open market. They had profited from the war and kept their bundles of rubles not in the banks, but in their mattresses or some other spot at home where they thought they would be safe from confiscation. But now the old rubles had no value. The peasants were forced to turn them in at the rate of 10 old rubles for 1 new one. Hardworking, industrious farmers were wiped out overnight. There was literally wailing and gnashing of teeth.

It was not the end of their troubles. Early one morning in the summer of 1949, Marina and her family were awakened by the sound of shrieking in the street. They ran out of doors to find women weeping and tearing their hair. "What kind of kulaks are we?" the women wailed. "Everything we had, we earned by our own sweat." The Medvedevs did not know what had happened. Then they learned that trucks full of Soviet soldiers had rumbled into the village during the night. Moving with unerring accuracy, the soldiers had stalked into the houses of the richer peasants, arrested all the men, seized the pigs, cattle, and household chattels, and told the women that the houses were no longer theirs. Some of the soldiers found it hard to carry out their orders in the face of so much misery, for they were from peasant families themselves. Marina heard one of them tell a weeping woman with sympathy in his voice: "Little mother, we're not to blame. They told us to do it. We're only following our orders." However the soldiers may have felt, it was a fact that the long-dreaded dispossession of the kulaks, or rich peasants, had begun.

No one in Moldavia was unaffected, not even the Medvedevs. By this time they had moved to a bigger and better place, a solid house of stone with a wooden floor. Their landlord was a kulak. Both he and his son, the miller of Zguritsa, had been arrested and carried off in the night. Their house was converted into a health center for the district, their lands confiscated and turned over to a collective farm, or *kholkhoz*. To Marina it seemed unjust because she had loved their landlord and was sure the charges against him were untrue. Her mother agreed with her. The Medvedevs had to find another place to live, and Marina remembers that there was no gaiety in the village any more, only sadness.

She learned a lesson about another form of injustice in Zguritsa. The Russian residents of Moldavia, her own family among them, enjoyed privileges that were not granted to the natives. When Moldavia belonged to Rumania, everyone remembered life as rich and happy. Having seized the area on the eve of World War II, the Russians were there as colonists. They were on the top and Moldavians were on the bottom. Nostalgia for the old order was keen and resentment of the Russian overlord deep.

The position of the Russians was less enviable than that of the Moldavians in only one way. They held most of the responsible jobs and were therefore much more exposed to political disaster. The fate of a Russian who fell out of favor was even more swift and brutal than the arrest and deportation of the Moldavian kulaks. A neighbor or a friend might suddenly disappear for no apparent reason. Some were exiled, some were shot in the rising tide of political purges of the late 1940s, just as the nightmare memories of the war were beginning to fade.

To the eyes and ears of a child, it was very puzzling. It had to do with "politics," Marina learned at a very early age, and politics was something that was discussed only in whispers. If a child ran into the room during talk with even the faintest political overtones, he was told to go out and play. No one dared take a chance of being overheard. Even the most innocent rumors could spell arrest and exile. In Archangel, Marina had listened to angry words between her grandmother and her Uncle Ilya about politics. There was something mysterious, something political, about her stepfather's past and the family's move to Moldavia. Now she witnessed the unjust treatment of the Moldavians and saw Russian friends and neighbors sent to prison—all for politics. She grew to fear and hate the very word.

In one respect only were the horrors of politics mitigated, and that was because they were living in a provincial backwater. When someone was caught in the cruel fate—arrest, exile, even execution—which was becoming a more and more common occurrence, the rest of the community, far from shunning the children and relatives of the victim, pitched in and did what they could to help. The atmosphere of fear that was causing a kind of numbness among educated people and Communist Party professionals in the larger cities had not seeped down to out-of-the-way places like Zguritsa. Each time the blind mechanism of terror struck, the first thought was not, as it tended to be in the cities, "Next time it may be me." People did not turn their backs out of fear of contamination. They still were human to one another, very often in touching ways. And whenever such misfortunes did occur, Marina's mother was one of the kindest and most decent.

Marina was not yet six when she also became aware of injustice in her own home. Perhaps because of his old troubles in the army, or simply because he found life difficult, Alexander Medvedev started to drink. And his attitude toward Marina changed. She was expected to take care of Petya while her parents were at work, and one day she took him by the hand and led him to the kindergarten she was to attend that fall. The teacher allowed them to stay, and Klavdia was frightened when she came home to find her children missing. She soon traced them to the kindergarten, but that night Alexander struck them both as punishment. Marina remembers it as the first time Alexander ever hit her, and the last time he was to treat her equally with her brother.

Alexander grew increasingly critical of Marina. If she toyed with her food, he said harshly, "Who do you think you are—a princess? You'll eat what's set in front of you!" When she fell ill with whooping cough one winter, Alexander, annoyed by her constant bark, would snap: "For God's sake stop that." They all slept in the same room, and when Marina coughed at night, Alexander scolded: "Be quiet. You're not letting anybody get any sleep." Alexander was afraid she would infect Petya, who shared the bed with her, and Marina at last realized that her father was drawing a line between her and Petya. For some reason that she did not understand, Petya meant more to him. And when Petya finally did catch whooping cough, Alexander made no secret of his anger. "*You* gave it to him," he accused Marina.

Alexander clearly favored Petya whenever he and Marina had some childish dispute. He began to strike Marina more often now, and once when she failed to weed a corn patch to his satisfaction, and lost his knife besides, he grew red with fury. He marched Marina home and beat her ten strokes over the backside with his leather belt. Her mother was powerless to protect her.

Marina did not know it, but Klavdia was pregnant again. She was often sick in bed and Marina, who was only seven, was expected to help with the household chores, washing dishes and laundry, grazing the pig, and drawing water from the village well. If she neglected her chores to run outdoors and play games with her friends, Alexander was there to punish her when she returned.

Then one afternoon when Klavdia was lying sick in bed, Marina's grandmother, Tatyana Yakovlevna, suddenly appeared. She had come from Archangel to spend the summer with her daughter and son-in-law, Musya and Vanya Berlov, who had moved to Moldavia soon after the Medvedevs. Tatyana Yakovlevna visited for a while, and when Alexander thought she had left, he shouted to Marina: "Why haven't you shined my shoes yet?" Marina, thinking she was safely out of earshot in the kitchen, grumbled: "All day long it's Marina this and Marina that. The others are all out playing and I'm supposed to be pasturing the pig. Your Petya doesn't have jobs to do. Polish the shoes yourself!"

Alexander heard her. "I'll show you," he shouted, and hurled his shoe at Marina's head.

At that moment Tatyana Yakovlevna reappeared in the doorway. "I'm taking Marina with me," she told Alexander firmly. "You have no idea how to treat children. She isn't a hired hand. She's not big enough to work in a cornfield. I won't let you hit her."

She took Marina by the hand and led her away, without so much as asking Klavdia. Marina spent the rest of the summer with her grandmother and her Aunt Musya and Uncle Vanya. Each day at lunchtime or after work, her mother came by to see her. She wanted to take Marina home, but Tatyana Yakovlevna would not hear of it. Marina was grateful to her grandmother for defending her, yet she wanted to be home with her mother. Then August came and Tatyana Yakovlevna announced that she intended to take Marina back to Archangel with her. Klavdia, in tears, saw them off at the station.

And so the next year, when she was eight years old, Marina was again in Archangel with her grandmother and her Uncle Ilya and Aunt Valya. She was in the second grade and spent the greater part of each day in school, but once again she was "spoiled" by Tatyana Yakovlevna and exposed to her grandmother's old-fashioned views and her outspoken dislike for the Communist system. Tatyana still took her granddaughter to church, and there, one afternoon, they met Marina's teacher, a graying woman in her fifties. The three of them walked home together and Tatyana remarked that she was glad to see a teacher in church. At least a few people still believed in God. The teacher sighed: "In school, you have to tell the children there isn't any God. But in your heart, you believe otherwise."

To Marina, the encounter seemed to prove the truth of what her grandmother had been saying, that in school she was taught nothing but lies. And if her teachers lied about God, were they telling the truth about Stalin? At school she was taught that Stalin was a good, kind man who loved little children. But at home her grandmother told her, with every bit as much assurance, that he was a demon let loose among men. What was she to believe?

Marina was plagued by another uncertainty. Nearly every schoolchild belonged to the Pioneers, the Soviet organization for children. But since she hated everything about the Soviet system, Tatyana Prusakova told Marina not to join. The child did not know what to do. She felt that she would be betraying her grandmother if she joined. On the other hand, it was hard to refuse.

Marina found an alibi; she would join when she returned home to Moldavia. But there, too, she kept on stalling until the end of her third-grade year. Even though she had hardly any choice by then, she still felt that she had betrayed her grandmother. When Tatyana Yakovlevna came to Zguritsa that summer, Marina hid her red neckerchief, the badge of the Pioneers, in shame. At last the old lady caught sight of it and said just one thing: "Humph! Is that a devil's tongue they've stuck on you?"

When she returned to Moldavia after the year in Archangel, Marina found a new child in the family, a chubby little girl called Tanya. From the outset Alexander was devoted to the baby, who strongly resembled Klavdia. The family alignment had changed again. Petya was no longer the favorite, and was now in the same boat as Marina when it came to punishment.

Marina had more chores than ever. As always, she had to pick up Petya at kindergarten, but now she had to fetch Tanya at the public nursery, too. She had to help with the ironing, the bed-making and floor-washing, help make pelmeny (jam or meat dumplings), peel potatoes, and draw heavy bucketfuls of water from the well. If something she did displeased Alexander, she received a cuff on the face or backside with a remark like, "It's all your grandmother's doing," or, "A fine young lady *she* wanted you to be, you and your lily-white hands!"

Then, one spring day just before her tenth birthday, Marina made a startling discovery. It was a holiday and the village streets were deserted. Marina and a classmate called Emma were off to school for the celebration. On the way, Emma turned to Marina and said: "Guess what? My mama was talking to your mama last night. And your mama said your papa isn't your real papa at all!"

Just then they came to Emma's house, and she went in to pick up something she had forgotten. Marina did not wait for her. She ran away. Stunned, she did not want anyone to witness her turmoil. She came to a wide dirt road and followed it. There was a meadow with bluebells and yellow dandelions on one side and a cornfield stretching into the forest on the other. Marina walked and walked. She cried until she was tired of crying. She was hungry, but she did not want to go home. She found a clump of cherry trees and climbed one of them. There she lay on a branch, plucked green cherries, and ate them. Gazing up through the branches at the sky, she thought, "Other children are happy and play." But she had no right to be happy. She did not have a father.

Finally, it was time to go home for supper. Marina found her mother in the kitchen and started peeling potatoes. She worked in silence for several moments. Then she could not stand it any longer. "Mama," she asked, "where is my real papa?"

"Who told you?" Klavdia inquired with a startled expression.

"One of my friends," Marina replied.

"Your papa died at the front," her mother answered simply.

"Why didn't you tell me before?" Marina said.

Her mother spoke hesitantly now: "You were too little to understand."

Even today Marina thinks that her discovery changed her outlook forever. Now she understood why Alexander treated her differently; he was not her father. She could no longer feel affection for the man she had once been proud to call "Papa," even though she bore his patronymic and surname, Marina Alexandrovna Medvedeva. Nor could she feel the same way about her mother. She continued to love her, but she became more critical of her with every passing day. She blamed her mother for marrying Alexander, and begged her to leave him. "You silly," her mother would smile, "where could I go all alone with three children? You're only a little girl. You don't understand."

Klavdia was in anguish over the change in her daughter's behavior. Whenever Alexander was not looking, she kissed Marina and tried to reassure her. But Marina avoided her caresses, much as she longed for them, because she was hurt that her mother dared kiss her only on the sly. When she was punished by Alexander, she blamed her mother for failing to stand up for her. Where once she thought her mother the most beautiful person on earth, now she considered her sloppy, even dirty. She was even annoyed by her mother's poor health. Marina knew that her mother loved her, perhaps even better than Petya and Tanya, but she wanted her to prove it again and again.

Marina's rudeness toward her mother angered Alexander even more. He treated her as if she had no feelings and were a servant who had to earn her every crust of bread. The line he drew between her and the other two children became clearer with every passing day. Trying to avoid him whenever she could, Marina took refuge in the nearby home of her Aunt Musya and Uncle Vanya. There she knew she was welcome. And it was from Uncle Vanya that she acquired the bookishness that was to be her other escape.

Marina became a relentless reader. She read Dreiser's *Sister Carrie* and Jules Verne's *Around the World in Eighty Days* in Russian translation. She overstrained her eyes from reading and had to have an operation. But after her recovery, she went on reading as before. She read Dumas's *Three Musketeers* and Tolstoy's *Anna Karenina*. But her favorites were the novels of Turgenev, with their splendidly idealistic young women and their stories of life in the Russian countryside. These books stimulated her imagination and sharpened her perceptions, and that, in turn, increased her awareness that she was somehow different from her brother and sister, somehow different from her friends.

Marina's closest friend was a Jewish girl named Beatya Roitshtein. Anti-Semitic feeling was high in Moldavia, but Marina insisted that she respected Beatya and preferred her over anybody else. That was no doubt true; yet as a child, and later as she was growing up, Marina deliberately chose outsiders for her friends, boys and girls who were different, as she considered herself to be different.

When they were ten, Beatya informed Marina that she had witnessed love-making between her parents. She refrained from describing the dreadful scene. But she wondered whether the same thing went on at Marina's house. Although all her family shared the same room, Marina found that she did not know. But the thought of such a thing added to her dread of her stepfather, and her scorn for her mother.

By the late winter of 1952, when Marina was ten, Alexander Medvedev's five-year term of exile, if that is what it was, was over. The electric power station, whose construction he had come to supervise, was now a going concern and he was offered a job in Kishinev, the capital of Moldavia. Klavdia wanted him to take it, but Alexander declared that he had had enough of what he called "gypsy civilization." He took Petya with him to Leningrad, the city of his birth, the city where his mother was living, in search of a job. Marina, Tanya, and Klavdia stayed behind in Zguritsa, waiting to join him.

Marina's last memory of Zguritsa is of the kind of neighborly solicitude that she had often seen in Moldavia. Her mother, Tanya, and she were packed and ready to set off for Leningrad. But there had been a heavy snowfall, the last of the winter, and the tiny houses of Zguritsa were smothered to the rooftops in snow. It would be two or three days before they would be able to leave and they had used up all their fuel. They sat on their suitcases and shivered, waiting for morning to come. Suddenly they heard a knock at the door. Marina opened it to find her friend Beatya outside. Behind her was a sled loaded with wood and coal that she had dragged all the way from her home in the winter twilight.

3

Death of Klavdia

OF ALL THE CITIES of the Soviet Union, Leningrad was probably the hardest to get to live in. During the heroic 900-day siege of 1941–1943, Nazi shells had razed whole districts. Even when the Medvedevs came in 1952, seven years after the war's end, the rebuilding was only getting under way. Yet such was the boredom and lackluster quality of life in the provinces, so suffocating the absence of horizons, that a torrent of men and women streamed in from all over Russia, seeking to wrest permission from the militia to live in a city that was already unbearably overcrowded.

On his arrival that winter, Alexander was immediately offered a highly skilled job as an electric repair technician at the First Coke and Gas Plant. But neither the offer of a job, the possession of desperately needed skills, nor even the fact that he was a native of the city, guaranteed that the militia would permit him to register. He had to find a place to live. Here, he was fortunate. His stepfather had died a few weeks before and space was available in his mother's apartment. Still, the militia was free to assign that space to somebody else. By resorting to the magic of bribery, Alexander was finally allowed to register.

When Klavdia arrived, she, too, resorted to bribery. She had set aside for this purpose two woven rugs she had brought all the way from Moldavia, and four new ladies' furpieces. She carried her tribute to the housing office, where the woman responsible for passports took the booty to the district militia headquarters and somehow brought off the miracle. Thus, all the Medvedevs were finally registered as occupants of an apartment at No. 86 Obvodny Canal.

Conditions in their apartment were typical. Alexander, his mother, his wife, and three children lived in a single room in what had once been a three-room apartment. Each of the other rooms was also occupied by an entire family, making a total of twelve people who shared the front door and hallway and the communal toilet and kitchen. They had to go to the public baths to bathe.

Her new home was more cramped than any she had lived in, but Marina did not give it a thought. She shared a bed, as she always had, with either Petya or Tanya, unaware that people could live in any other way. She missed the meadows and low hills of Moldavia, but she was overwhelmed by a feeling of privilege to be living in a city once again. Soon she considered Leningrad—an island city of bridges and canals, with its cluster of magnificent baroque buildings at the center —the most beautiful place on earth.

The family quickly settled into a new routine. Alexander went to work at the gas plant and Klavdia found a job not far from home in the laboratory of a medical clinic for railway personnel. Tanya and Petya went to kindergarten, and Marina set off each morning for a nearby school of 800 or 900 girls, where she was in the fourth grade. Marina liked the new school, but conditions in her new home were hard. In Moldavia, the Medvedevs had at least had a place of their own; here, they were squatters in the apartment of Alexander's mother, Yevdokia Yakovlevna Medvedeva.

She was a diminutive woman, immensely fat, with a large hooked nose and tiny, shrewd black eyes. Marina liked her well enough at first, although she noticed with the sharp eyes of a ten-year-old that her step-grandmother was taking every stick of good furniture she owned and shoving it into an adjoining room which belonged to her daughter-in-law Musya. Marina soon came to realize that while Yevdokia tried to appear generous and open-hearted, she was, in reality, greedy and hypocritical. Her hypocrisy went so far that she insisted that she and all her family were of pure Russian stock. Actually, as Marina found out, Yevdokia herself was half-Jewish. Because the subject was not openly discussed, it is not clear that Alexander himself realized that he was partly Jewish, a distinction of great importance in Russia. As for his mother, she was a woman who judged others solely by appearances, by the scope of their money and possessions, not by what they were underneath. And it was obvious that she disapproved of Klavdia.

Yevdokia was not the only source of poison in the atmosphere. Her qualities were carried to an extreme by her porcine and acquisitive daughter-in-law, Musya. Marina calls this Musya, the widow of her stepfather's brother, "bad Aunt Musya," to distinguish her from her mother's sister, "good Aunt Musya," whom she had been close to in Archangel and Moldavia. Musya lived with her two sons in the next room. And, like her mother-in-law, she strongly disapproved of the woman Alexander had married.

Both of them were at their worst when Alexander was not there to protect his wife. If Klavdia was tired and lay down to rest, they acted as if she was a criminal. When Alexander came home drunk, it was Klavdia who was to blame and not he. It was *her* fault, for giving him money to buy vodka. She did it, they hinted, only so he would continue to love her. Any token of tenderness between Alexander and his wife, as Marina describes it, was "like a bomb" to his mother and sister. If he put his arm around Klavdia, or if Klavdia sneaked him a kiss, they would say, "How disgusting!" or, "Have they no shame?" and storm out of the room. One morning the old lady went about her chores with an air of particular fury. "Humph," she snorted, "they won't even let me sleep with their noises." To which Musya added, "She only holds him because she never turns him away." Marina had never witnessed the act of which they were speaking, but she guessed from their tone that it was something dirty. She felt ashamed for her mother.

Klavdia turned the other cheek. She took it all as her due, as though she were to blame for daring to exist at all. Did someone wound her feelings brutally one day? Very well, she would work her fingers to the bone for him the next. It was obvious that she and Alexander were devoted to one another. But their love, the only cohesive and happy element in the household and one that might have been a source of strength for Marina, had its outcome in unhappiness for her instead.

Alexander hated to share Klavdia with Marina or with anyone, and no matter how Marina behaved, it only made the situation worse. If she called her mother "mamasha," after the French novels she read, and showed the love she truly felt for her, Alexander was enraged. If, on the other hand, she was rude or disobedient, Alexander punished her for being "spoiled." Either way, Klavdia failed to defend her. Marina continued to reproach her mother for having married him. Curiously, Klavdia did not even defend Alexander. "You're too little," she would say to her daughter. "You don't understand. I couldn't live my whole life alone. You hope things are going to turn out better, but you never know."

Marina did understand—in her own way. To her, Klavdia's inability to stand up to Alexander when he was cruel to her could mean only one thing, that her mother did not love her. Afraid to kiss Marina in front of her husband, Klavdia showed her affection for her daughter only on the sly. And Marina resented it so much that she became unable to allow her mother to kiss her at all. "I bristled like a little porcupine," she says.

Looking back on it later, Marina said, "My mama was happy in only one respect. She loved her husband and he loved her. It was just 'Sashenka, Sashenka' all the time. I think she loved him more than her children. She showed her weak side too much. My mama wasn't smart. She let everyone trample on her. She didn't dare stand up for her children. She wasn't sensible in her love; she was like a blind mother hen. I don't like weak people. I can't bear it if a mother doesn't stand up for her children."

In accented, slightly ungrammatical English, she continues: "I am so sorry, but this make me mad. I had reached a difficult age, an age at which children begin to judge. A child looks at her mother, hoping to find an ideal to make part of herself. If a child looks at her mother and doesn't find an ideal, then it hurts her spirit for the rest of her life."

Eyeing herself in the mirror, Marina says, "Everything I dislike in my looks comes from my mama." She remembers lying awake at night clutching her nose to keep it from growing long like her mother's. She was ashamed of her mother's tall, angular build, even embarrassed to be seen with her on the street. And at home, in a turmoil of love and resentment, Marina behaved toward her mother with a sort of involuntary cruelty. In that household, with its multiple possibilities for treachery, she found her own torn-up emotions fitting all too neatly into the designs of Yevdokia and Musya, who used Marina as a "blind weapon" to wound her mother. Witnessing her mother's suffering, Marina felt unspeakable love and sorrow. She was tormented by remorse over her behavior. And yet she was powerless to change it.

The conflict with her mother that had begun in Moldavia grew sharper in Leningrad, and in the highly charged atmosphere of that crowded apartment, Marina detected something new—she was her mother's Achilles heel. Klavdia felt guilty for having her at all. This, and Alexander's harsh treatment, imbued Marina with a conviction of her own abasement, a feeling that she was worse than other people, although she had no idea why. That conviction, and the memory of her mother's many failures to stand up for her, ricochet through Marina's recollections of her childhood like a cruel and obstreperous echo.

Only one member of the family understood. She was Maria Yakovlevna Arsentyeva, Alexander Medvedev's aunt. A rotund and tiny woman, she had alert brown eyes and silver hair, gathered in a severe bun at the nape of the neck. She always wore an old-fashioned dark dress with a single piece of jewelry, a round ornament of Estonian silver which hung on a chain around her neck. But Maria Yakovlevna's real adornment, Marina thought, was her air of openness and kindness, which contrasted sharply with the mean and suspicious manner of her sister Yevdokia.

The children were overjoyed whenever Maria Yakovlevna came to the apartment. She took them on outings: to children's concerts or the ballet, to the zoo and the botanical gardens, to Pushkin's *Dubrovsky,* staged to all appearances with real fire and smoke, and to the great museums of Leningrad. Together they saw the magnificent buildings of the czars, and she instilled in the children a love of the city that had been the capital of Imperial Russia. She taught them to venerate works of genius and to distinguish such works from the ugliness and mediocrity of the modern city.

Maria Yakovlevna had been born to the middle class, but because of her keen intelligence she had been selected to attend the Smolny School for young ladies of noble birth in St. Petersburg, as Leningrad was called before the Revolution. The school was under the personal patronage of the Czar. Maria Yakovlevna described to Marina the great occasions when Nicholas II—young and handsome he was, too—visited the school for lunch. She had been part of the choir that sang for him. Marina listened with fascination to stories about the glittering balls Maria Yakovlevna had attended, and about the decorous way young ladies and gentlemen behaved—"So different from the behavior of young people today."

On the heels of the Revolution, Maria Yakovlevna, a devout believer in the tenets of the Russian Orthodox Church, had met and married a man whose faith in the new religion of communism was every bit as fervent as her own faith in God. He was a Communist in the best and most idealistic spirit of those Revolutionary times, and she, too, became an atheist and enthusiast of Communist power. Their marriage was a happy one, although only one of their four children survived. Maria Yakovlevna's husband did well. He was an engineer, and rose to become head of an institute in Leningrad. Then came the purges of 1936–1937.

Like so many other true believers who had survived the early days, Maria Yakov-levna's husband was swept away.

The arresting officers came under cover of night, but one of them took pity on Maria Yakovlevna. "Hide your treasures, little mother," he whispered. She owed her life to his advice. She salvaged some bracelets of pearl and some antique jewelry of rubies and gold before being dispatched, with her little son, to cold and lonely exile in the southwest Urals. It was only by selling off the jewelry, piece by piece, that they were able to survive. Maria Yakovlevna never heard from her husband again. She knew only that he died, innocent of the charges against him, a victim of torture in a barren prison somewhere.

After the war, mother and son returned to Leningrad. As a victim of political misfortune, she could find work only as a janitor in a large factory on the Neva River. It was hard work for a lady of distinguished upbringing, but Maria Yakov-levna never complained. She had recovered her religious faith. "Life," she would say, "gave me back my faith in God and now no one will ever make an atheist of me again."

Perhaps it was because her existence had been such a memorably difficult one that Maria Yakovlevna met life with such candor and openness. She had touched bottom already and nothing now could make any difference. She had no fear of anyone, certainly not Alexander Medvedev. He had only to speak unkindly to the children for her to answer him in his own rough coin. And when he hit Marina in her presence or when she heard about his treatment of her from others, she scolded: "You cannot treat her that way, Sasha. Have you forgotten that *you* had a stepfather, too?"

She stood up for Klavdia, too. When Musya, who was very fat, asked mockingly: "What is there to love in *her?* She's nothing but a bag of bones!" Maria Yakovlevna retorted tartly that "elephants aren't to everyone's taste." Sometimes Musya boasted, in one of her jealous asides, that *she,* unlike Klavdia, was perfectly able to get along without the love of a man. "Has it never occurred to you," Maria Yakovlevna inquired, "that it's not *you* who can get along without a man, but *men* who can get along without you?"

Maria Yakovlevna urged Marina to be more loving and thoughtful of her mother, and Marina promised to try. It meant a great deal to her to feel that she had been weighed in the esteem of so just a woman and found worthy. "She helped me," Marina recalls, "because I knew that there was one person who loved me and trusted me, and looked on me as a human being." It was not to Klavdia, not even to her beloved grandmother in Archangel, but to Maria Yakovlevna that Marina believes she owes "nearly all the good" that is in her. "It was she," Marina says, "who taught me to love truth and hate lies, to value people for their real worth and not for their money."

Maria Yakovlevna also added to Marina's growing distrust of politics and the "truths" of the Communist system. Everyone was told that Stalin loved the people. But how could anyone who loved the people, Marina wondered, allow them to live in the squalor that afflicted them all? Housing was wretched, there was not enough food, everyone was poor. These thoughts, half-thoughts really, were tucked away so unobtrusively at the back of Marina's mind that she was almost unaware that she had them.

Suddenly, when Marina was nearly twelve, Stalin fell ill. Over the somber midnight airwaves came tidings that the mighty ruler of all the Russias had been struck down, just as an ordinary man might be, by a hemorrhage of the brain. From the moment of the announcement, the men and women Marina knew behaved as though they, too, were stricken. Many would neither eat nor drink. An entire people were frozen in a state of sorrowful suspense. Marina knew only one exception—Maria Yakovlevna. "Let him," she announced, "die as quickly as possible." And when news came that Stalin was indeed dead, Maria Yakovlevna remarked: "Thank God for delivering the people from Judas!" Marina could hardly believe her ears. Yet, as young as she was, she knew that, as always, Maria Yakovlevna was speaking the truth.

Marina was growing up a skeptic and a rebel. At school, she looked on political subjects with distaste. She preferred history and literature. She gobbled up stories by the great Russian writers, Gogol, Chekhov, and Pushkin. And she was engaged, as the innocently flirtatious Princess Mary, in an imaginary love affair with Pechorin, the fatalistic and self-pitying central figure of Mikhail Lermontov's story "A Hero of Our Time." Vengeful and cold, Pechorin is forever spinning webs of intrigue that destroy all those whose lives touch his own. As the ideal man of her imagination, Pechorin was to cast a very long shadow over Marina's future.[1]

At home, Marina read Russian translations of Jack London, Mark Twain, and Thomas Hardy, and she often forgot her homework. In spite of her lack of preparation and her mischievous behavior in class, she got good marks in school. The teachers viewed her as a wayward prodigy. And when the girls' school she attended became co-educational, the boys quickly found a nickname for her. It was "Spichka" or "Matchstick," first because she was thin, and second because she would flare up in an explosion of words whenever anyone addressed her.

Marina had an especially close friend at school, Nina Samilyuk, a girl with lucent hazel eyes and hair the color of a sheaf of wheat. Nina had no father and no idea who her father might have been. She was ashamed of her own illegitimacy and of her mother's poor reputation. Marina believed that her situation was not like Nina's since she had both a stepfather and a real father who had died "at the front." Yet it was plain to her all the same that she and Nina had common ground. Both of them were "different."

In the summer of 1954, the Medvedevs moved from their apartment on the Obvodny Canal to a large new building on the outskirts of Leningrad. The authorities were opening their assault on the housing shortage by repairing the decrepit buildings in the heart of town, and, accordingly, the occupants were emptied, like objects from a cornucopia, into a new, four-story apartment complex called Sosnovaya Polyana. Two years later, the repair of the old building was completed and its former residents were allowed a choice of moving back or remaining at Sosnovaya Polyana. The Medvedevs returned to the Obvodny Canal. But after the "repair" and "redecoration," Marina recalls, the pipes leaked worse, the floors sloped more, and the place was darker than before.

During this time, Marina's mother became seriously ill. Klavdia had always been frail, and for a woman with three young children and uncertain health, her existence was a taxing one. She was up every morning by 7:30 A.M. and left almost immediately for work. After a ten-hour day, she went shopping every evening, never arrived home before seven, and then had to cook supper for her husband and children. She was always limp and worn out by ten, ready to drop into bed.

When Marina was about twelve, Klavdia began coming home at night white with exhaustion. Alexander would turn down the sheets of their bed and beg her to lie down. But fearful of what her mother-in-law might say, Klavdia at first would demur. Her husband refused to take No for an answer, and listened to the taunts of Musya and his mother as he cooked supper. He treated his wife, as always, with the utmost tenderness. But as time went by, Klavdia started running a temperature of 99 or 100 degrees nearly every day, and finally became too weak to climb out of bed.

Klavdia had been ill for two years when Marina completed the seventh grade. It was the end of her compulsory schooling, and Klavdia hoped that her eldest and cleverest child would finish the full ten-year course that comprises a Soviet high-school education. Attracted by drawing and the arts, Marina planned to study fashion design, which would require the ten-year diploma. But one afternoon in the early summer of 1955 she came home, perched on her mother's bed, and suggested another idea. A friend at school, Nina Samilyuk, was about to take examinations for pharmacy school and Marina wanted to try, too. All her life, she told her mother, she had admired the white coats pharmacists wore and the spotless cleanliness of apothecary shops. To Marina's surprise, her mother was enthusiastic.

Uncertain of her own health, Klavdia was evidently anxious that her daughter be able to stand alone. She got up from her bed and accompanied Marina to school to obtain the documents she would need for her examinations. The school officials tried to dissuade them. Too many of the more promising boys and girls were leaving for work or vocational schools after the seventh grade, they grumbled. If this kept up, there would soon be hardly any of the better students left to go on to the university. But Klavdia and Marina had their way.

Marina entered the examination with a light heart and a total absence of preparation. If she failed, she said to herself, she could always go back to school. She was entering the competition, after all, mainly to keep her friend Nina company. In the end, she passed with 23 of 25 possible points. The decision was made for her. She was going to pharmacy school. Nina, who had inspired the decision, failed. She went to work in a chocolate factory and eventually studied to be a nurse.

Marina had another close friend, Tamara Kumilan, who lived with her aunt and uncle in the apartment building on the Obvodny Canal. One cold afternoon in November of 1956, when Marina was in her second year at pharmacy school, she and Tamara went to the public baths as they did every week. They shivered a little as they hurried home, for a wintry wind was blowing along the canals and bleak-looking patches of snow dappled the ground. Rather shyly, Tamara opened up an unexpected topic. Marina's mother had been talking with Tamara's aunt about the atmosphere at the Medvedevs' apartment. She was distressed by the way Alexander's mother and sister were treating Marina. And all, Klavdia said, because Marina was illegitimate. "Let's be sisters," Tamara said. "You have no one. And neither do I."

Marina was shocked. She had always believed that her father died at the front during World War II. She dared not ask any questions, and Tamara, anxious not to wound, spoke only allusively, in quick, shorn-off sentences, as she repeated Klavdia's story. From her Marina learned virtually all she has ever found out about her father. He had been an engineer, and in the course of his work, he had drawn up a blueprint for a bridge or some other public project. In a mysterious effort to frame him, someone—nobody knew exactly who—tampered with the calculations on the blueprint and rendered it defective. He had been blamed, of course, and arrested as an "enemy of the people." And he had vanished forever.

Marina refrained from asking anyone at home about Tamara's revelation. The truth of it was only too plain. Now that she had the key, the pieces of the puzzle fitted together. At no time in her life had Marina felt equal to Petya and Tanya. Now she understood Alexander's cruelty, the taunts of his mother and Musya, the guilt her own mother seemed to feel in loving her. Under the circumstances by which she had come into being, she *was* of less value than other people.[2]

From the moment of her discovery, Marina spent a good deal of time wondering who her father might have been. What had happened between her mother and him? It was of crucial importance to her that their relationship had been a serious one. If it were only a chance affair, a seduction, then how could the child conceived in it be of any worth? She consoled herself with the thought that her father might have been a foreigner, a general, or somebody else of importance who had been carried off as "an enemy of the people." She even dared hope that her mother and he had actually been married, and that after his arrest Klavdia, fearful that she, too, might be arrested, had managed to destroy the marriage documents and conceal her identity.

Marina looked to her stepfather for proof that her birth had not been a shameful accident. He treated her badly, but unlike his mother and sister, he never once reproached Klavdia for anything in her life before she met and married him. To Marina, that seemed to indicate that her mother and father had been in love. Finally, she cast back for reassurance to her upright old grandmother in Archangel. Surely so straitlaced a lady would not have forgiven her daughter and consented to bring up a child who was merely the result of a short-lived attraction. Yet one thought always returned to haunt Marina. From the beginning, no one had wanted her.

Klavdia's illness was growing even more grave. One afternoon when she was lying sick in bed, Marina entered the room unexpectedly and caught a sudden change in her mother's expression. "You reminded me so much of your father just now," Klavdia sighed. Marina wanted to know how. Her eyes and her mouth and the gesture she had just made, her mother replied. "Tell me about my father," Marina begged. "Not now," Klavdia said. "I'll tell you when you've grown up a bit."

Marina did not tell Klavdia that she had discovered the secret of her illegitimacy. But just as she had turned against her mother years before on learning that Alexander was not her real father, so she now found new reason to hate Klavdia. She could not even sympathize with her mother's illness, and although her feelings were in guilty turmoil, she could neither conceal her hardened attitude nor change it. While the fact of Marina's illegitimacy was never made explicit between them, Marina believes her mother saw the change in her and realized the secret was out.

During Klavdia's long illness, Alexander was more difficult to get along with than ever. A good deal of the time he had his lips pressed tightly together and he refused to speak to anyone at all. And he drank. Sometimes he came home from work silent and morose, only to slip into the toilet, take a nip of vodka, and come out singing. Sometimes he appeared at the front door with a bottle in his hand. Klavdia or Yevdokia would quickly snatch it away and hide it. Often Klavdia gave it back, but if she did not, he would look for it himself, or jog little Tanya on his knee, kiss her, and ask in a whisper where it was hidden. Such scenes occurred every week. But even when Alexander was drunk, he did not change toward Marina—"I made him mad any time."

But for his drinking the family would not have been poor. Alexander gave his earnings to Klavdia every pay day. Later, he would have second thoughts and beg to have some of it back for vodka. Klavdia invariably obliged, and the family had to live the second half of each month on what it could manage to borrow. Marina resented her stepfather for "drinking up" the rubles he and her mother worked so hard to earn.

Ill as she was, Klavdia became pregnant once more in the spring of 1956, and that summer she had an abortion. Again, Marina was sorry for her, yet angry as well. "Why," she asked, in a question that was by now a refrain, "does she live an immoral life and then complain?" She was sure the abortion was a judgment of her mother's relationship with Alexander.

After the abortion, Klavdia went to the city of Kharkov, in the Ukraine, to spend her vacation with her sister Polina. But her health failed to improve. When she returned to Leningrad, she was sent to the Academy of Military Medicine, and spent the fall and early winter there. She had a series of operations, the latest treatments, the most promising new drugs—the best care the city could provide. But when she finally came home, she could get out of bed only with her husband at her elbow to support her.

Marina knew that her mother was dying, and so acutely painful were her emotions that she tried to pretend she was someone else, living in some other time. She lived as far away from home as her imagination could carry her. She began doing poorly in her heavy load of courses at pharmacy school, and she endured the perpetual cruelty of her step-grandmother and step-aunt. One day Yevdokia invited a radiant and handsome woman to the apartment. They sat together in the one room they all had to share, with Klavdia lying ill on the bed. The moment Alexander came home and saw the caller, he held a whispered conference with his wife and quickly left the apartment. He stayed away for two hours. When he returned, the strange lady had gone. Tears were rolling down Klavdia's cheeks. Alexander ordered the children to leave the room while he tried to comfort their mother.

Yevdokia later told Marina who the strange lady was. She was Anna, a woman Alexander had courted before he married Klavdia, and Yevdokia had invited her to call with no other thought than to let Alexander see with his own eyes the contrast between the blooming and well-dressed visitor and the failing creature he had married. Marina overheard Yevdokia tell her son: "You ought to have married *her* and not that frivolous woman who had a child and is sick all the time."

Klavdia had been home only a fortnight when she started running a high fever. At night she moaned pitifully so that none of the others could sleep, and it was decided that she would have to go back to the hospital. Exhausted from lack of sleep and from the very odor of illness, Marina made a remark she has never been able to extinguish from her memory. "First to the hospital," she announced to her mother, "and then the cemetery!" Marina was thinking of her mother's trip to the hospital for an abortion the year before. Now it would be her punishment to die.

Klavdia was taken to a hospital in Leningrad on what is called the "Vyborg Side," an island on the opposite bank of the Neva River from the Obvodny Canal. Because of the city's web of bridges, rivers, and canals, the journey to the hospital was circuitous, requiring several bus and trolley changes and the better part of an hour. Marina dreaded the long, cold pilgrimages to the hospital, but she tried to visit her mother as often as she could. During her first visit, Klavdia reminded her daughter of what she had said. "It made me very sad," Klavdia told her. "Probably I *will* go from here to the cemetery. Some day you'll understand that life is complicated. All your life you'll remember your sad mama." In tears, Marina sat on her mother's bed and protested that she did not want her to die.

On later visits, Marina tried her best to be cheerful. Klavdia laughed and smiled. She promised she would be home soon and they would all be happy again. But behind her effort at gaiety, Marina could see only the sorrow and pain. She was unable to hold back her tears. "Don't cry, Marisha," her mother said to comfort her. "Everything will be all right." But one day a nurse drew Marina aside. "Let's talk like grown-ups," she said. "Get hold of yourself. You're a big girl now. Your mama has less than a month to live." The name of the illness was cancer.

Even now, the merciless women at home kept up their persecution. Yevdokia and Musya urged Alexander to seek the company of other women. Alexander refused. One day, however, Musya asked Marina to inform her mother, untruthfully, that Alexander was seeing another woman. Marina, to her lasting sorrow, complied. To this day she remembers her mother's wistful reply: "He is not the only man who has been capable of loving me."

On April 8, 1957, Klavdia died. Marina was to have gone to the hospital the day before. But it was rainy and cold. She had only thin shoes, her clothes were not warm enough to withstand the wind, and she did not have the heart for the trip. The following day she arrived home from school to find Petya sitting by the door with tears streaming down his cheeks. To Marina's questioning look, he said simply: "Mama's dead." Fifteen-year-old Marina gathered together the clothing for her mother's burial and accompanied her stepfather to the hospital.

Later, an uncle told Marina that Klavdia's last words were of her. "I don't want to die," she had said. "I have little children at home. Where is Marina? Where is Marina? I have to see her. I have something to say to her." Then she lost consciousness and died. Marina believes that her mother intended to tell her who her father had been.

Klavdia's mother, Tatyana Yakovlevna, the magnificent old matriarch who had given Marina her first home, came to Leningrad all the way from Minsk, where she now was living, for the burial. It was she who insisted upon the two-hour funeral service in the Russian Orthodox church. After the service, Musya was taken by a sudden and belated seizure of remorse. Beside the open coffin she fell to her knees and wailed: "Forgive me, Klava! Forgive me!" Up marched the redoubtable Maria Yakovlevna. She drew Musya away from the coffin, admonishing her firmly and quite audibly to everyone, "This is no place to put on an act. You ought to have thought of it before."

Yevdokia did not attend the service. She lay moaning in bed at home, summoned a doctor, and complained of how ill she was feeling herself. She refused Alexander the thing he wanted most—to escort his wife's body home and hold the final leavetaking there. She refused even to allow the coffin to be carried upstairs for a momentary gesture of farewell.

It was Maria Yakovlevna who uttered the final judgment on them all. To her sister, Yevdokia, she said with majestic scorn: "It was you who killed Klava, not the cancer. You gave her not a life, but a hell. A healthy person couldn't have stood it, much less a sick one. You had no heart." Before all of them, this veteran of Stalin's wrath pronounced an epitaph for the woman who had died at the age of thirty-nine. "Klava," she said, "was a golden human being. I could not have lived with you a single hour."

4

Farewell to Leningrad

WITH KLAVDIA, the single bond between them, gone, relations between Marina and her stepfather took an immediate turn for the worse. It was the day after her mother's funeral, she recalls, that Alexander said: "And when will you be taking yourself out of here?"

Stunned, Marina ran from the apartment and spent the rest of the day pacing the wintry canals near home. She had no other thought but: "Mama's gone. He can do as he likes with me now." This thought, this fear, grew louder and louder until it became a sort of ringing in her head like the insistent clanging of a bell. Dazed by the sound, Marina looked up and was startled to see a streetcar screaming to a stop in front of her. A volley of profanity by the driver brought her to her senses. Crossing the street like a sleepwalker, she had narrowly escaped being hit by a passing trolley.

Marina spent many hours walking along the canals as winter gave way to spring that year and the bare branches became filigreed with the first shoots of green. Rather than go home after school, she would make her way into one of the countless little parks with which the city is studded to sit by herself on a bench. She thought mostly of her mother, who now seemed to her an injured and blameless being, a Christian figure of forbearance. Marina could see her mother only through a blur of remorse. She felt that it was she who had killed Klavdia by her lack of love and, at the last, by those searing words: "First to the hospital, and then the cemetery!" Marina could not forgive herself. Often she entered the flickering half-darkness of the Nikolsky Cathedral, lit a candle, and prayed.

But solitude seemed to add to her sadness. And so she forsook the lonely parks, the desolate back streets, the empty cathedral, and began to direct her footsteps to the most crowded thoroughfares of the city, and above all, to the Nevsky Prospekt. She found herself lingering by the music counters of department stores, listening to the popular rhythms of the West, which were just beginning to be heard in Russia. For a full year after the death of her mother, Marina could not bear to take a novel in her hand. Her feelings were too raw, and the contrast between her own sorrowful surroundings and the glittering world of her imagination was too abrasive. It was music that brought solace to her now.

When school was out that summer, Marina journeyed to Minsk to visit her grandmother, Tatyana Yakovlevna, now an old lady in her sixties, who was living there with her eldest son Ilya and his wife Valya. Marina's Aunt Musya and Uncle Vanya Berlov, whose home had been her refuge in Moldavia, were also living in Minsk. They were the only family she had left, and Marina was glad to be with them, especially her grandmother. Tatyana had old-fashioned, even crotchety, ways. She did not allow Marina to dress in slacks, and insisted that she wear her hair long as in Russia nice girls—and little girls—did. But Marina accepted her strictness. With her mother gone, she knew that her aged grandmother was probably the one person on earth who genuinely loved her.

That summer, Marina for the first time met a young man who caught her fancy. His name was Vladimir, and he took her to the movies and the park, played French love songs to her on the guitar, and taught her how to kiss. He was twenty-two and she was barely sixteen. She wished she were more grown up. Then one afternoon, as she was trying on a new dress, Marina was incredulous that the vision she beheld in the mirror was herself. She *had* grown up. But another vision intruded. She imagined that she saw a man standing behind her. He was gazing at her image in the mirror with approval, even admiration. She had never seen the man before. He was a stranger. But she knew who he was. He was her father.

They held a long and fanciful conversation. "What a splendid daughter I have!" she imagined him exclaiming. "So pretty and so grown up!" He begged her to come and live with him as his daughter. But with that, Marina grew stern and reproving. "You ought to have thought of it before," she said. "You're not my father at all. I grew up without any help from you. You made Mama and me very sad. Another man brought me up. He is my father now."

But in her loyalty to her stepfather, Marina soon suffered a cruel disappointment. At the time of her sixteenth birthday while she was in Minsk, Tatyana wrote the registry office at Severodvinsk, Marina's birthplace, requesting copies of her birth certificate and other documents. She also wrote Alexander to ask for copies of the papers he had signed upon his formal adoption of Marina. For it was known among Alexander's and Klavdia's relatives alike that he had adopted his wife's oldest child. Marina herself had been informed of it as a matter of certainty. In fact, she carried Alexander's surname, Medvedev, with his first name as her patronymic, Alexandrovna. Neither in school nor anywhere else had she been known by any other name. But the formal documents—the birth certificate and the adoption papers—were needed now so that Marina could receive the internal passport for identification and travel within the country that is issued to every Soviet city dweller on reaching the age of sixteen.

All of them, Marina, her grandmother, and the rest of her relatives in Minsk, were thunderstruck by the answers Tatyana received. From Leningrad, Alexander wrote denying that he had adopted Marina. And from the registry office at Severodvinsk came the reply that there was no birth certificate or other documents for a Marina Alexandrovna Medvedeva, only for a Marina Nikolayevna Prusakova. (Marina's real father had been named Nikolai and her mother's maiden name was Prusakova. If the father does not claim, or the mother prove, paternity, a child born to an unmarried Soviet mother is given his father's first name as his patronymic and his mother's maiden name as his surname.)

Together, the two replies converging from different corners of the country confirmed Marina's worst fears. Not only had she been abandoned by her own father, she had also been repudiated by the man who had taken his place. It was a cruel blow. To this day Marina refuses to accept it fully, clinging still to the idea that she was, in fact, Alexander's adopted child, that he was lying when he denied it, and that he had merely hidden the documents of adoption. But whatever she made of his denial, she had still to face the terrible fact of his rejection.

This new discovery had humiliating consequences for Marina. Legally she had to take the name inscribed on her birth certificate—Marina Nikolayevna Prusakova. Teachers and older friends of the family who had always addressed her as Marina Alexandrovna now had to call her Marina Nikolayevna. She had to change her pharmacy school registration from "Medvedeva" to "Prusakova" and endure the teasing of the other girls. As if this were not embarrassment enough, the space on her new passport for her father's name was left blank—to any Soviet child the ultimate token of illegitimacy, carrying a stigma of which he or she is painfully reminded on the innumerable occasions when the passport is presented as identification.

When Marina returned to Leningrad that autumn for her third and final year at pharmacy school, she found matters in her stepfather's household in no way improved. Not that Alexander interfered with her freedom or tried to dictate what she should do. On the contrary, he ignored her, at least at first. Mourning for Klavdia, he spent hours at her grave, his dark skin darker still from the sun, building a little monument and creating a flowerbed there. Neither he nor his mother gave the slightest sign of caring at what hour Marina came home at night. To a sixteen-year-old girl, living in a large and rather rough city, this indifference to the hours she kept could mean only one thing. It was the ultimate token of abandonment. Marina knew that she was utterly alone.

Then one day soon after she came back from Minsk, Alexander informed her through his mother—he did not bother to tell her himself—that he would no longer tolerate her presence at meals with the rest of the family. "You're grown now," Yevdokia said. "You have relatives of your own. Let them look out for you." Later, Alexander put it more bluntly. "You're not my daughter," he said. "I'm under no obligation to feed you."

Marina did not know how she would eat. Luckily, someone told her that she was entitled to an orphan's pension of 16 rubles a month. She was already receiving a student stipend of 18 rubles a month, and on the combined sum of 34 rubles (about $34) a month, plus small sums her grandmother in Minsk was able to scrape together and send her, she tried to feed and clothe herself.

Unwelcome at home, Marina was exposed as never before to the temptations of the city of Leningrad. She was exposed, moreover, at an age when she was exceptionally vulnerable and almost wholly inexperienced. Her distractions were innocent enough at first; she went to the movies or sat in a cafeteria by the hour, chatting with friends from pharmacy school. But it was a struggle just feeding and clothing herself, to say nothing of paying for tickets to the movies. And so during the New Year holiday, Marina found a job delivering telegrams through the wintry streets of the city. Cold and often hungry, she was made even more miserable by the sight of gaily ornamented New Year's trees winking behind warm, curtained windows.

Like any sixteen-year-old, Marina craved gaiety. She started going to student dances on Saturday nights at the University of Leningrad. On other nights she went to mixers and get-acquainted dances at the Technological Institute and the Institute of Railway Transport. She never had an escort. She went, as Soviet girls often do, with a friend or two from school. But even at these casual get-togethers, Marina was painfully self-conscious about her unbecoming hand-me-down dresses. On several poignant occasions she was passed over in favor of girls who were not as pretty as she, but who had blouses of German nylon or shoes of Czechoslovak make to give them a look of prosperity or glamour.

A young man named Leonid invited her to attend the New Year's Eve dance in his dormitory at the University of Leningrad. Of all the schools in the city, the university was the most prestigious. Its students were the finest in the country. In the competitive scramble of Soviet student life, they were the élite. Marina accepted Lonya's invitation with alacrity.

Ordinarily, the ramshackle university dormitory buildings were brilliantly lit in what Marina calls an effort to "guarantee the morality of Soviet youth." On New Year's Eve, however, the ingenuity of the students proved equal to the occasion. Every light bulb that could be reached had been twisted from its socket; the rest had simply been smashed. The corridors and rooms were dark and crowded with couples, and phonographs played music of a sort Marina had never heard before. There were the strains of rock 'n' roll, newly fashionable in the West but still virtually unknown in Russia. There was the "Lullaby of Broadway," which Marina was later to hear so often that she calls it the "theme song" of her youth. There were the unfamiliar voices of Eartha Kitt, Louis Armstrong, and Nat King Cole, all of them banned under Stalin but by this time recorded on the sly from broadcasts of the Voice of America. Marina's enthusiasm for this new music was wholehearted. She considered it, and the young men who were its possessors, to be the last word in sophistication.

But her date Lonya was just an uncouth boy. He got Marina alone in a bedroom, locked the door, switched off the light, and tried to force himself on her. Marina succeeded in wrenching herself free, but the incident was a revelation nonetheless. This was not the kind of "love" she had read about in books. She had supposed that love and sex were identical. Now, in real life, it turned out that they were quite different. She was frightened and repelled.

Even while Marina was fighting Lonya off, another thought had crossed her mind: "How will I face Mama in the morning?" But her mother was dead. Later, when she had time to reflect, she realized that it had been not fear of her mother, but fear of being *like* her, that had caused her panic. She must stop herself before it was too late, or she would end up doing the same terrible thing for which she had so long condemned her mother.

As far as Yevdokia and Musya were concerned, Marina's late hours meant that she was already a fallen woman. Meanwhile, her bitter quarrels with Alexander continued. He reminded her again and again that he did not want her living at home after she had finished school. Often he threatened: "If you won't go of your own free will, I'll find a law to make you go!"

Marina answered weakly that if he tried to make her leave, she would appeal to the police or to a court.

"Just try it," Alexander said. "I know all about you. I'll tell them who your father was and they'll listen to me."

"Who *was* my father?" Marina asked.

Alexander spat out her father's name—Nikolai, and a surname that Marina would not remember until years afterward. "He was a traitor!" Alexander shouted.

Touched at her weakest, most vulnerable spot, Marina sobbed. "I never saw him. I never knew him. Children aren't responsible for what their parents do." She crumpled up on the sofa and cried.

Marina had no idea that there could be any family secrets left for her to discover. Then one day she came upon one that cast new light on her stepfather's behavior. Rummaging through an old suitcase of her mother's, she found a set of legal documents about a court case for child support. They showed that Alexander himself had had an illegitimate daughter in Moldavia before he and Klavdia were married. The child's name was Alla, and she was only a year younger than Marina.

Marina came across another set of documents in the suitcase. They were papers filed by Klavdia with the Inquiry Bureau in Leningrad in what had almost certainly been an effort to find her real father. With her own life fading, and little hope that her daughter would be treated gently by the Medvedevs when she was gone, Klavdia had evidently tried to find him—if he had survived his sentence in Siberia or the Far North—so that he could help Marina after she was dead.

Neither of these discoveries gave Marina any comfort at all. The realization that Klavdia at the time of her death had been searching for her father only seemed to prove to Marina, probably erroneously, that what she had been dreading was true—she was the child of a casual liaison after all and her father had simply abandoned her. The discovery deepened Marina's curiosity about herself, while at the same time deepening her conviction that the further she tried to dig, the greater the likelihood that what she might find out about herself would be the very truth she feared most.

As for the discovery that Alexander had a daughter of his own who was nearly the same age as she, it failed to soften in any way the harsh facts of his treatment of her, and it never occurred to Marina that perhaps it was not she, but that other little girl who was at the heart of his anger toward her.

Taken together, both discoveries deepened Marina's skepticism about the truth of things as they are presented on the surface. She had grown up in a household which was electric with lies, reticences, and outspoken brutality. Yet the outspokenness had failed to guarantee that what was being said was true.

At last Marina's troubles caught up with her. With barely enough money for food and clothing, and with no one to love or care for her, she became passive and apathetic. She lost the will to shoulder her heavy load as a third-year pharmacy student: six hours of classes a day, plus four hours' training in a pharmacy. She started cutting classes, ignored her homework, and embarked on an orgy of moviegoing. By the middle of the school year, her marks had dropped so sharply that she lost her stipend and had to get by on her orphan's pension plus whatever her grandmother happened to send from Minsk. For a while she had only 18 rubles a month to live on, and with nothing to eat but rice kasha, she quickly contracted a disease of malnutrition that caused abscesses to erupt all over her body. She went regularly to a medical clinic for shots of penicillin, glucose, and vitamins, and for treatments from an ultra-violet lamp. Venereal diseases were also treated there, and Marina was deeply embarrassed by the disapproving glances she received.

At school Marina's classmates did their best to cover for her absences. Even the teachers and administrators tried to make allowances for her. The elderly professor who was in charge of the students in the third and final year was especially kind. Boris Zakharovich, whose initials had been transformed by the girls into the nickname "Bizet," bent all the rules for Marina. Not only did he mark her "present" at classes she had cut, he also repeatedly gave her a B for recitations she had not given. Gently, tactfully, with endless patience, he took her on, she says, "like a nanny," and tried to wheedle her through school.

"Marina Nikolayevna," he told her, "you're one of the finest students in the class. I think very highly of you. You can become a brilliant pharmacist if you'll only try. You're having a hard time, I know, but keep trying just a little longer. Graduate, and I'll find you one of the best jobs in the city."

Marina did not respond. In May, only two weeks before the final examinations which might have entitled her to graduation, a job and a room in a young people's hostel, she was expelled for "academic failure and systematic non-attendance at class."

She was far more upset at being expelled than she was willing to show. She knew she had to find a job, but she tried only lackadaisically to look for one. Why bury herself in a factory or pharmacy all summer when her student friends were enjoying themselves without a shadow of self-reproach? Marina thought she could get by somehow.

Everyone at home knew that she was virtually penniless, and when some silver disappeared from the cupboard, Alexander, Musya, and Yevdokia accused her of taking it. They locked up their possessions and kept a careful watch on even the food, down to the last crust of bread. The silver later reappeared, and this time, Marina was accused of having pawned it. She suspected that it was

Alexander who was guilty, but she had no way either of proving her suspicions or of clearing herself.

Treated like a criminal at home, liberated by the casual atmosphere of summer, and without even the requirements of school or a job to restrain her, Marina stayed out later than ever and started to make friends quite different from her classmates. One was a girl named Lyuda, three years older than Marina and bold as brass. She had a job as deputy director of a commission shop that dealt not in the shoddy, mass-produced goods turned out by Soviet factories but in items that were old or unusual: clothing and cosmetics from abroad or finely wrought jewelry and porcelain that had been changing hands ever since the Revolution. It was thanks to her job in the commission shop that Lyuda could deck herself out, to the envy of all her friends, in Czechoslovak handbags and English lipsticks.

Marina created a home for herself, of sorts, at the commission shop, helping Lyuda fill out invoices and keep books, or fixing herself a new hair-do at the back of the shop while Lyuda dealt with customers out front. It was a lively place, a headquarters for sailors of the Soviet commercial fleet, mainly Latvians and Estonians, who came in with foreign shoes, cigarettes, or cloth to sell at bloated prices. Most of them were mere boys, poorly educated boys at that, who asked nothing better than to take pretty girls like Lyuda and Marina to the best restaurants in town and spend stacks of rubles treating them to caviar, shish-kebab, and champagne. Marina remembers one two-week period during which she never missed an evening in the restaurants of the Astoria or the Evropeiskaya hotels. She had no respect for these young sailors because of their poor education; and because she went out with them just to get a free dinner, she began to lose respect for herself.

Marina was attracted by foreigners. For one thing, she sometimes imagined that her father had been a foreigner. Besides, foreigners behaved with a politeness she liked much better than the rough and casual ways of Russian boys. In addition, she acquired a collection of Georgians and Armenians, lean, dark-eyed young men from the southern republics of the U.S.S.R. whose Mediterranean looks gave them some of the exotic appeal of the foreigner and whose jealous and possessive ways she liked. Most of these young men were in Leningrad on vacation, and Marina and her friends often met them on the beach by the Petropav-lovsk Fortress. Marina did not swim; she was too conscious of her "bony, grace-less" figure to do that. Then they all went to the movies or a restaurant, where they made sure that Marina had enough to eat, since she was so emaciated that she aroused the protective instincts of everyone she met. That summer, the summer of 1958, she says, "I simply lived off chance acquaintances."

It was not a happy summer. Alexander had started locking her out of the apartment at midnight. With the rest of the family at their dacha in the country, there was no one at home to let her in, and she spent many a night nodding on the staircase outside the apartment. She often found herself in compromising situations. One night she, Lyuda, and a boyfriend of Lyuda's were walking in the woods along the Neva River when they stumbled on an all-night drinking party of the kind Russians call a *bardak* (as distinguished from an "orgy," at which intercourse is expected of the girls). Marina was shocked to see so many drunken forms on the ground. Inexperienced in matters of sex, she was frightened—and fascinated.

Then one evening, a foreigner she had met—a diplomat from Afghanistan —lured her to his hotel room on the assumption that she was not a virgin and tried to make love to her. Again Marina was shocked. If a stranger from abroad could so easily mistake her for something she was not, what was she in danger of becoming?

She began to feel guilty and ashamed of the life she was leading. After the first excitement had worn off, Marina realized that she was bored by the young men she was seeing. She went out with them to avoid going home, and because they enabled her to eat. She had allowed a few of them to kiss her in return. But how, she wondered, did that differ from being a prostitute? It was a harsh word to use. But sexual standards at that time were strict. Most unmarried girls were either virgins or prostitutes; there was not much in between.

The Medvedevs did not hesitate to call her names. Musya accused Marina of trying to ruin the family's reputation. Alexander said: "Don't come to *me* bringing a baby in your skirts. Go to Minsk. You're in my way. I don't want any prostitutes around *me!*" Having concluded that the law would not support him in an attempt to get rid of Marina on the grounds that her father had been an "enemy of the people," Alexander may have been trying to drive her at least into the appearance of prostitution, since Leningrad by now had laws allowing the deportation of "parasites," as those who did not have jobs, including prostitutes, were called. He also wrote to Marina's relatives in Kharkov, implying the worst about her and begging them to come and get her. From Kharkov, the word spread to her relatives in Minsk.

It was the most degrading time of Marina's life. She "went around in a fog," trying not to think what she was doing, or what she could easily become. She tried to avoid Maria Yakovlevna, her stepfather's aunt and the beloved counsellor of her earlier years. She felt she "could no longer look Maria Yakovlevna in the eye" because she was "not so pure as before, not the person Maria Yakovlevna wanted" her to be. As for Maria Yakovlevna, she said to Marina: "Of course I don't believe the slander they're dredging up about you, but I can see you're not what you were. But you're a big girl now. Live your own life. I won't interfere." To Marina, the words meant that even Maria Yakovlevna no longer cared about her. And if nobody cared, then she was past salvation, and there was no depth to which she did not deserve to sink.

It was Lyuda's mother who helped break the vicious circle. Sometimes Marina spent the night at Lyuda's when she was locked out at home. One morning, Lyuda's mother said: "Marina, I don't want you here any more. I don't want a girl of light conduct in my home. I don't want to feed you and I don't want trouble with your family. Really, you ought to get a job." Marina was stung, but she knew Lyuda's mother was right. It was what she had been waiting for —someone who cared enough about her to crack down on her.

It was August, summer was ending, and Marina knew that she had to find work. She was leaving a cheap cafeteria one day when she spotted a "Help Wanted" sign. "A princess like me," she said to herself wryly, "won't lose her crown if she washes a dish or two." She went back and applied. The manager, a gray-haired man in his fifties, examined her documents and asked her a great many questions. Then, with a thoughtful look, he turned her hands over in his. They were soft, white hands, not the hands of a girl accustomed to heavy work. "My dear child," he said, "this is no work for you. It'll land you in the hospital in a day." But he gave her the job. "You won't earn much," he said, "but at least you can eat for free."

Marina became a cleaner-up in the cafeteria of a large boys' school. The boys were a rough lot, and they made no secret of their raucous delight at having a pretty new face around. But the supervisor, an officious woman, disliked Marina and soon lodged a formal complaint that she was too slow at scrubbing floors and ought to be fired. A special commission arrived to investigate and Marina was transferred to a new school and a new cafeteria.

Marina was happier there. She still had heavy work to do, but her new supervisor was a compassionate woman who treated Marina like a daughter. After the first snowfall, she presented Marina with a pair of mittens she had knitted specially for her.

The academic headmaster, Robert Neiman, gave Marina something she needed even more, encouragement to believe in herself. He was a gifted, outgoing man of twenty-eight or twenty-nine with dark hair and swarthy skin that were tokens of mixed Russian, Polish, Jewish and gypsy ancestry. When he learned Marina's story, Robert spent hour after hour with her, cajoling her, teasing her, reasoning with her, and above all, reassuring her, in an effort to induce her to go back to pharmacy school. "You're young. You like your work now," he told her. "But this is no life for you."

Instinctively Marina agreed, but she was held back by fear—fear that she might be turned away, or else that she might be readmitted, only to fail once again. It was Robert who helped her surmount her fear. He told her that when she was ready to reapply, he would see to it that she got in. And it was Robert who made Marina feel that she could make something of herself if she would try. Finally, in December, after three months of work in cafeterias, Marina decided she was ready. With misgivings, and without a word to Robert, she went to the Pharmacy Institute and asked to be taken back. The school officials did not accept her right away. Instead, they gave her a job at the Central Pharmacy on the Nevsky Prospekt, the main thoroughfare of Leningrad. Marina knew she was being tested, but she was only too grateful to exchange the white coat of a cafeteria helper for the white coat of a pharmacy worker.

Robert Neiman was not the only man who influenced Marina's decision. That autumn she had started seeing a good deal of Oleg Tarussin, a blond, curly-headed philology student. Ambitious to enter the Soviet diplomatic service, Oleg had a reputation at the University of Leningrad as a hardworking young man of promise. Marina had lied to Oleg when they met. Implying that she already had her degree, she told him she was working in a pharmacy, and he was under that misconception when he took her to meet his parents.

Oleg was the only son and, Marina suspected, the adopted son of Ekaterina Nikitichna Tarussina, a fine-boned woman with warm blue eyes, and a slender, retiring father. The mother, Marina gathered, worked in a factory or a hotel, and the father was a highly skilled plumber. Although the jobs they held were modest, they enjoyed exceptional good fortune: they had a one-room apartment for just the three of them, to say nothing of a dacha outside the city and, almost unheard of, a small private car—a Moskvich.

Marina met the Tarussins when Oleg invited her to spend the November 7 holiday, the anniversary of the Bolshevik Revolution, at their apartment. From then on, she was a frequent visitor. She quickly came to love the Tarussins' airy apartment with its cozy, overstuffed Victorian furnishings. This was as much of a home to her as any place she could imagine. She even loved the sprawling, rundown old dwelling in which the apartment was situated, reachable, just as in a rabbit warren, only by a succession of inner courtyards and corridors. It was not long before it was comfortably taken for granted that she and Oleg would one day be man and wife. In a word, Marina became a daughter of the house. "They were," she says, "too good to me. Better than I deserved."

But close as they all became, Marina still had not confessed that she was a cafeteria worker, not a pharmacy graduate. Her fear of losing Oleg was one reason she decided to go back to the Pharmacy Institute and actually earn her diploma. But in December, when Marina, unknown to her family, had started working in a pharmacy but had not yet been admitted to the institute, the truth came out. She fell ill, and lay for three days on the Tarussins' sofa, shaking with fever. Ekaterina Nikitichna went to the Medvedevs' to let them know where Marina was staying. When she returned, she said, "My dear child, I know all about you. Why didn't you tell me before?"

Marina acknowledged everything.

"Don't worry, my dear," Ekaterina Nikitichna soothed her. "You have nothing to be ashamed of." She promised to say nothing to Oleg.

When Marina heard in January, 1959 that she had been readmitted to the Pharmacy Institute, it was not to her home that she went with the news but to the Tarussins'. It was an occasion of family rejoicing. Marina asked Oleg to forgive her for not telling the truth. Oleg answered that she had been a "little goose" to think that he would break off with her because she worked in a cafeteria. He had known all along, it turned out, and had merely been waiting to hear it from her.

Oleg depended on Marina and wanted to have her near him when he was studying, but he considered her "bourgeois." He thought that she would never understand him or his world. His world was politics—already he was in trouble over a minor political incident at a student party—and he acted as if, compared with important things like politics, his personal life did not matter at all. He seldom took Marina on a date, and such money as he had, he spent on books for himself, not on her. When they were with outsiders, he spoke of Marina as his "fiancée." Yet he had never even told her that he loved her, much less asked her to marry him.

The prospect of marrying Oleg and moving in with him and his family was an appealing one. "Where else," Marina asks, "could I have found such a mother-in-law?" It was her feelings for Oleg that she doubted. She felt as if he had suffered an inner hurt of some kind and that she ought to take care of him. He was not the "knight from a bygone century" she was looking for. They gradually subsided into a sort of brother and sister relationship, with an occasional flareup of romantic feeling on one side or the other. Marina did not marry Oleg, but remembering him now, she is aware of similarities between him and a man with the same nickname, "Alik," whom she did marry two years later—Lee Harvey Oswald.

By the end of January, Marina was back at the Pharmacy Institute, attending classes from nine in the morning until three in the afternoon, and working at the pharmacy from four to eleven at night. It was a grueling schedule. But her colleagues at the pharmacy were what Marina calls "a wonderful collective. They made allowance for everybody's difficulties." At the institute, too, the teachers went out of their way to help. They were aware that Marina, unlike most of the other girls, had to work full time for a living.

Now that Marina was both working and going to school, the disfavor of the Medvedevs was muted a bit. She was allowed to take meals with the family again, and when Alexander locked her out at night, his old mother, Yevdokia, got up and let her in. Marina knew that Yevdokia was a hypocrite and a grasping woman, who contributed her share to the mean and miserly atmosphere of the household, but she came to feel sorry for her. There was even a momentary break in the hostility between Marina and Alexander. Nine-year-old Tanya, his favorite child, was lying ill with a high fever, and after all his efforts to fill a prescription for her had failed, Alexander appealed to Marina for help. She immediately went to the pharmacy and made up the prescription herself. Later, she and Alexander were standing by Tanya's bed. Suddenly, to her astonishment, she felt her stepfather's hand on her shoulder. She heard him say, as if thinking aloud: "Our Marina is a good girl after all. Thank God she's grown up at last!"

Marina could not endure the touch of his hand. She ran away to the toilet and there gave way to tears. Why had he spoken to her like that? Could it be sex that he wanted? She was more frightened than if he had hit her.

Yet Marina had sympathy for him, too. She suspected that Alexander had a greater share of inner refinement than he was able to show in the squalid atmosphere of that apartment. She sensed in him somewhere a kindred spirit, a man who longed to rise higher and was forever held down by his surroundings. She thought that he was a gentler, more chivalrous man than he would let her see, and that he, like herself, had dreams of a more gallant and courtly life. And it was an idea that would not go away. After Klavdia died, Alexander eventually took a mistress. He dressed up for her, took her to the best restaurants in town, and treated her with more respect than many men treat their wives. His mother and his sister taunted him for it, but Marina stood up for him. "We hated each other, he and I," she says, "but I felt sorry for him, too. I knew that he needed someone."

In April, Marina quit her job at the pharmacy. Boris Zakharovich or "Bizet," the kindly teacher who had helped her the year before, came to her rescue once again and had her stipend restored so that she could devote all her time to studying for the approaching examinations. Midway through June, she took the exams. In her appearance before the oral examiners, Marina was able to answer only two of four questions in chemistry, and she all but ran from the room after the ordeal, convinced that she had failed again. But to her astonishment, she learned that she had passed everything but chemistry, and thanks to the compassion of one of the examiners, she was allowed to appear again. This time she was asked pointedly easy questions. The examiners even coached her. Marina protests a trifle indignantly that "I didn't need all the help they tried to give me." She passed and was awarded her diploma.

The Tarussins held a banquet in her honor, but by this time Marina had a new boyfriend. The White Nights had descended upon Leningrad, the period from late May to July when the city is cloaked in midnight sun and, scorning sleep, young and old alike stroll night after night along the canals and embankments. One evening when she was supposed to be studying, Marina slipped out to a movie, and there she met a dark-haired stranger of about thirty who escorted her back to the trolley. Marina liked his sleek, self-satisfied good looks and his humorous and sophisticated conversation. He was Armenian, and his name was Eddie.

Before long Oleg was forgotten, and Marina and Eddie were together constantly. Early in July, with her diploma miraculously in hand and the White Nights beginning to wane, they went on half a dozen all-night boat trips around the city, dancing and talking until six in the morning. Eddie informed Marina that she did not know how to kiss, and he proceeded to teach her. To measure her progress as a pupil, he gave her a mark with each kiss.

Eddie was very generous, and when Marina's eighteenth birthday came around on July 17 he took her to a restaurant, treated her to dinner, and presented her with a ring. Unlike Oleg, he made her feel cherished and desired. He lavished rubles upon her, and presented her with flowers and even nylon underclothing from East Germany. Moreover, Eddie, a documentary film operator associated with one of the big Leningrad studios, had an apartment to himself for the summer.

On evenings when they were alone in the apartment, Eddie and Marina danced to the music of Lolita Thorez, an Argentine singer who was then the rage. Later, Eddie would play "Scheherezade" softly on the Victrola, turn down the lights, and spread pillows on the floor. He and Marina would lie there by the hour, watching shadows from the fire. Then he would kiss her, long kisses that made her head reel. Soon, Marina says, everything had happened between them except the final act of sexual intercourse. Even that, she would not have refused. It was Eddie who refused. Marina likes to believe that he was so experienced, so "delicately depraved," that he simply preferred hours and hours of "petting" to the sexual act itself. But Eddie explained that she was too young, that she had too many troubles already, and he did not want to add to them.

Marina trusted Eddie, even when she pieced together from an odd fact here and there that he was married and had a wife and small son at a dacha in the country. He made her feel wanted, and for the first time Marina lost her shyness and shame. She was in love, or at least infatuated, with Eddie. Yet, at the same time, she was disappointed in herself. She knew Eddie was not free to marry her, and she was afraid that she was capable of arousing only sexual desire, not love.

Reality, meanwhile, was forcing her to make choices. As a final act of kindness, "Bizet" and the other teachers at the institute helped Marina get one of the best job assignments available to a member of the graduating class. She started in on the usual two-week trial period at the Central Pharmaceutical Warehouse, but soon began to skip work. She wanted to spend all her time with Eddie. Finally, she told her superiors she did not want the job. It was a risky decision, for Alexander had given her an ultimatum. She could go to a hostel in Leningrad for which her job had qualified her, or to her mother's family in Minsk. It made no difference to him, just so long as she left his roof.

Marina had been saying goodbye to Leningrad for some time. But she could scarcely endure the thought. She loved the city—the whole miraculous expanse of it. She loved the wind and the falling snow, the smell of the trees, even the sound the trolleys made. Looking at the shadows of the willows in the Griboyedov Canal, at the maples and oak trees in the Summer Garden, at the sunset glowing over the Neva River, she wondered sorrowfully how she could bear to go. One evening when she and Eddie were out walking, she caught sight of the red sky behind the Nikolsky Cathedral, the spot where Czar Alexander II had been murdered. The tears started streaming down her cheeks. "Must I really leave all this?" she asked.

Eddie knew of her dilemma and decided to take a hand. He advised her to go to Minsk. "Marina," he said, "I don't want you to go. I want what is best for you. It's your choice whether you go or stay. But I'm older than you and I have more experience. I don't take advantage of you, but other men may. You fall for men very easily. I'm afraid you'll be ruined here. With all the temptation in this city and no one to control you, it may be too much for you." It was this Eddie feared for Marina, and this Marina feared for herself.

A few nights later, an episode occurred that crystallized her fears. She and another girl were on their way home from a movie when they were picked up by a pair of young men, one of whom turned out to be a well-known soccer player. They ended up in an apartment, and Marina's friend went to one of the rooms with her young man, leaving Marina in the other room with the soccer star. Carefully closing the door, he took off the bracelet he was wearing—a gold bracelet with a little watch inside that he had won in competition in Finland—dangled it in front of Marina, and said it would be hers if she would have intercourse with him. Marina refused, and in the struggle that followed she hit him with all her might. The couple next door were roused by the scuffle and came to her rescue.

Marina left the apartment and went home alone on the trolley. She still looked so disheveled and upset that a man who was seated nearby asked if there was anything wrong. Did she need someone to see her home? Shaking with fright, Marina rose from her seat and moved to the other end of the trolley, certain that the man was trying to take advantage of her, too. "Good God!" she wondered. "Is *everyone* beginning to take me for a prostitute?"

She arrived home at six or seven in the morning. Still trembling, she packed everything she owned in a suitcase and sat down to await Alexander's return from the midnight shift. When he came in, she told him: "Papa, I'm going away. But I need 10 more rubles to get to Minsk." Without a word, he gave her the money. The rest of the family was at the dacha in the country, and Marina left without saying goodbye to any of them, not even her beloved Petya and Tanya.

She spent the day at the Tarussins' with Oleg's mother. She refused to accept any money or let Ekaterina Nikitichna come to the station to see her off. Oleg's mother would not let her leave, however, without a stack of sandwiches, a whole chicken, cheese, chocolate, and a jar of jam—enough food to keep her going for a fortnight.

Throughout the three-day train trip to Minsk, Marina sat by herself. Only too happy to talk to strangers as a rule, she could not bear to speak to anybody now. She was filled with sorrow at leaving Leningrad. Whatever the future might hold, she was sure that happiness would be no part of it. Not one of her relatives in Minsk even knew that she was on her way.

5

Meeting in Minsk

IT WAS early August 1959 when Marina arrived in Minsk, at two o'clock in the morning, with 60 kopeks (60 cents) in her pocket. The railway station was shrouded in darkness, the trolley stop dark and deserted. Fortunately, a pleasant-looking young man—a violinist, it turned out—came to the rescue by lending Marina a few rubles and carrying her suitcase straight to the apartment building where her Uncle Vanya and Aunt Musya Berlov lived.

Although she was completely unexpected, Musya, her mother's youngest sister, welcomed Marina joyfully. But Marina detected misgivings—and soon found out why. Musya explained that Alexander had written to Marina's aunt in Kharkov the year before, complaining of her late night hours and suggesting that she had become a prostitute. Clearly, Marina could not expect much of a welcome in Minsk.

Musya tried to reassure her. "Don't worry," she said. "I'll telephone Uncle Ilya tomorrow and see how the land lies." If Marina was to stay in Minsk, it was Ilya, her mother's eldest brother, who would have to take her in. Musya and Vanya had four children and lived in a small apartment; Ilya and his wife Valya possessed a three-room apartment and had no children.

Musya telephoned Ilya the next day and received an ungracious response. Why had Marina arrived "like snow off the roof," without letting anybody know? "It was *you* she came to," he said to Musya. "*You* look out for her."

Reluctantly, Ilya invited them to tea, and on a hot midsummer Sunday, Marina, dressed as demurely as she knew how, went with her Aunt Musya to his apartment. She received a chilly reception. She had no job and, her uncle told her, without one she would be unable to obtain a residence permit. When Musya asked Ilya to help, he replied: "Let her do it herself."

Musya rose, her eyes brimming with tears. "Come on, Marina. It's no use our staying *here!*"

Marina spent the next two or three weeks with Musya and Vanya. They were a loving pair, loving of one another and of their niece. Marina would happily have stayed on, but August was coming to a close and their children were due back from camp. Once again Ilya was approached. "Tell her to come on over," he said with resignation.

Ilya's reluctance was understandable. Only the very privileged had as much space as he did, but until recently he had been forced to share it. Tatyana Prusakova, Marina's grandmother, had lived with him and Valya until her death the year before, and his sister Lyuba and her husband had only just moved out. Ilya was still savoring his privacy, and he had no desire to be overrun by another relative, above all not a marriageable girl who might soon acquire a husband and, with a new family of her own, gain the right to live with him indefinitely.

Ilya also had his official position to consider. Not only had he risen to become a high-ranking member of the Communist Party, he was also a lieutenant colonel and head of the Timber Administration of the Belorussian Republic's Ministry of Internal Affairs, known by its initials as the MVD. He was an engineer and Marina believes that he supervised the use of convict labor in the timber industry of the area. He held a sensitive post, therefore, although not nearly as sensitive as if he worked in the secret police ministry, the KGB. But Ilya had to be careful, even if it meant closing his heart to a relative in need.

The neighborhood in which Ilya and Valya lived was also charged with political vibrations. Their apartment building was set aside specially for high officials. The Suvorov Military Academy was just across the street. Also across the street was a wooden dwelling with a stockade that had once belonged to Marshal Timoshenko, one of Russia's great heroes of World War II, and had just been taken over by Kirill Mazurov, head of the Belorussian Communist Party. It was an area that must have been carefully watched, and if Marina was the kind of girl her stepfather said she was, she could jeopardize the career to which Ilya had dedicated his life.

Marina had doubts of her own about going to live with the Prusakovs. She knew that she was unwanted. Moreover, she was fearful they would clip her wings and force her to live "like a nun." Her fears were justified, at least at first. Life at Valya and Ilya's was "just like a corrective labor colony." One evening when two young men who happened to be her only friends in Minsk dropped by to take her out, Ilya exploded, "You're not to give people your address. I don't want your friends coming here." Like many other members of the Soviet élite, he was afraid of losing his privileges if outsiders saw the way he lived.

Marina found Minsk a polite enough place, but she was lonely and so homesick that night after night she went to the terminal to wave off the 9:30 bus for Leningrad. One night when Ilya was out of town, Valya woke to a stirring in the living room, where Marina was supposed to be asleep. She found her niece in tears, packing to go back.

Valya sat down and the two had a long talk. Marina told her of the way she had been treated by her stepfather and Valya wept. "My poor child," she said. "I want you to feel this is your home. We never had children. We love you like our own. You must understand Uncle Ilya. He loves you and worries about you. But he's a man. He can't show how he feels." For the first time in her life, Marina began to feel that perhaps she was wanted after all, perhaps she was not "in the way."

Ilya was still stern and aloof, but for Valya having a niece in the house was the next best thing to having a daughter of her own. Marina trusted her aunt and confided in her as she had in no one before. She even asked Valya the story of her father and mother. Who had her father been? Valya could not help. She had tried to pry the story from Ilya, but he had declined to tell her anything.

When Marina set out to obtain a residence permit to remain in Minsk, she had not only a rigorous set of housing regulations to contend with but the requirement that she show proof that she already had a job. Here she came up against the rock-ribbed character of her Uncle Ilya. He was what Russians call *poryadochny,* a person who prefers to go through regular channels or do without rather than use his official position to seek privilege, even so minuscule a one, in his case, as obtaining firewood. But he finally unbent a little for Marina. He took what was for him the precedent-shattering step of having a *spravka,* or job permit, made up at the MVD. Armed with Ilya's document and a written statement from the manager of the apartment building that her uncle had room for her, Marina went to the city and district militia headquarters to fill out countless questionnaires. After a suspenseful wait of two weeks, she received a permit to reside at her uncle's address, Apartment 20, No. 38–42 Kalinin Street. Without knowing it, Marina had vaulted from the middle to the upper class.

Her next task was to find a job. She had left Leningrad without the proper documents from the Pharmacy Institute, and even though trained pharmacists were in great demand in Minsk, she could not be hired. Finally, luck came to her rescue, and through a friend of her Aunt Lyuba's, she was given a job at the Third Clinical Hospital. She became one of four pharmaceutical assistants, all girls, who filled prescriptions for doctors and nurses in the hospital.

Marina loved the work. She loved mixing powders and pills, and she enjoyed the easygoing spirit of the place. She especially liked the head of the pharmacy, Evgenia, a radiant, handsome, magnificently garbed woman, whose special genius lay in wheedling and politicking scarce supplies out of warehouses all over town. Evgenia was lenient in the extreme, and even Marina's habitual lateness failed to get her in trouble. If she fell behind in her work, the other girls pitched in to help her catch up.

Marina wanted to be liked by her co-workers, but most of all she wanted their attention. They might all be seated at a table, filling prescriptions, and Marina would entertain them by recounting some of her escapades in Leningrad, usually those that involved smoking, wearing slacks, and going to restaurants with men—things that "nice girls" did not do. Her co-workers decided that she was "fast," and that she was judging them as provincial. Marina did think they were provincial, and she was at war, too, with the hypocritical "brother's keeper" mentality that she found on every side. But before long she realized that the other girls considered her a snob. "Look," she said. "I'm just homesick. That's why I talk about Leningrad." Nevertheless, as Marina describes it, not without a certain pride, her colleagues "looked on me ironically, askance, like a creature from another planet. We had different interests and different ideals. We inhabited different worlds." Her reaction to the suggestion that she join the Komsomol was typical. In theory, at least, the Komsomol was the flower of the Soviet younger generation. But Marina doubted that the description fitted her, and joining would not alter that fact. She had learned to hate the hypocrisy of her elders. It was no better among the young. "I thought 'Komsomol' ought to mean the 'best,' " she says. "I knew I wasn't the 'best,' and someone just sticking a label on me wouldn't make me so."

Eventually Marina joined, but only after pressure from her peers and a good deal of passive resistance. As a first step, she had to memorize the Komsomol Charter and answer a number of questions about the organization, Soviet policies, and herself. Marina got by on the coaching of friends. Then at a solemn meeting staged in the headquarters of the Belorussian Communist Party Central Committee, she had to answer questions put to her by the "big wheels" of the Belorussian Komsomol. The hardest question was the last: Why did she want to join? Marina, like everyone, said that she "wanted to be in the front rank of Soviet youth." The truth was that it would have been awkward to refuse.

The formalities over, she was told to fill out a questionnaire and return a week later, bringing a photograph for her membership card. Marina filled out the questionnaire but forgot the photograph. Rather, she put it off from week to week and as a result never received a membership card. But she paid the monthly dues of 30 kopeks (30 cents), and from time to time put in an appearance at meetings of the Komsomol *aktiv,* or cell, of the hospital. The meetings were usually devoted to disciplinary matters or boring lectures on foreign affairs. Occasionally, there were picnics or dances, but Marina considered them dull and avoided them whenever she could.

As the months went by, Marina made many friends. Because of them, and because of her uncle and aunt, it was the happiest time of her life. She soon had an assortment of admirers, one of them a good-looking young man by the name of Sasha Peskaryov. A medical student, Sasha came from what was considered a "good family," and Ilya made him an exception to the rule that his niece was not to bring young men to the house. Sasha put Marina on a pedestal, where she felt distinctly out of place. "He thought I was an angel," she recalls. To cool his ardor, she told him that she had a lover and a child back in Leningrad, but Sasha assured her that he would cheerfully marry her anyway. He was Marina's faithful standby, the doormat she trampled on and broke dates with whenever someone more interesting came along.

Marina had met Misha Smolsky on one of her summer visits to Minsk years before, and it was through him that she was introduced to a new group of friends. Misha was not Russian at all, but half-Tartar and half-Pole, a tall, heavy-set, red-haired young man who was the scion of a distinguished father and grandfather both and somewhat oppressed by his heritage lest he fail to match their achievements. He was a flashy dresser, and one day he stopped by the pharmacy to pick up Marina wearing a hip-length overcoat, a pair of pointed English shoes, and a towering karakul cap. He was smoking a pipe and, as he led Marina off, he draped his arm casually over her shoulder as if he had proprietary rights. The other girls were horrified and were bristling with questions the next day. "Are you his mistress?" one of them asked.

Misha was the presiding genius of a circle of young people who were both unconventional and irreverent toward the values of their elders. And yet they were also well educated and took a serious interest in music and literature. When *Dr. Zhivago* became the scandal of the day because the author, Boris Pasternak, was awarded a Nobel Prize for a book that had been forbidden in Russia, one of the members of Misha's group got hold of a Russian-language edition printed in Paris and each patiently waited his turn to read it.

The group's "all for one, one for all" cameraderie was rather like the spirit of the characters in Ernest Hemingway's *The Sun Also Rises,* the novelist most of them preferred over all others at that time. His books were just then beginning to appear in superlative Russian translation, and Hemingway's staccato style had an enormous appeal compared with the wooden dialogue and the longwinded, moralistic tales of Soviet writers.

Marina's favorite novel, as it happened, was not by Hemingway but was Erich Maria Remarque's *All Quiet on the Western Front.* The "tomorrow we die" outlook of Remarque's characters, the anti-war spirit, the author's sympathy for the common soldier whose fate is determined by the forces of history and the self-deluded leaders above him, all struck a sympathetic chord among millions of Soviet young people. But Marina has another explanation for the rage that swept the Soviet Union for Remarque and Hemingway. The level of sexual morality among her contemporaries was "not very high," she says, and in the novels of these writers they found the moral sanction they were seeking. Hemingway and Remarque gave sex an explicit quality the younger generation was longing for, and pointed the way toward reconciling reality with romance.

Since foreign writers and foreign ways meant so much to them, and since all of them knew foreign languages, it was hardly surprising that foreign words crept into the slang of Misha Smolsky and his friends, words like "Broadway" for the main street of Minsk, "pad" for Misha's family's apartment, and "do" or "carouse" for an ordinary evening get-together. At these gatherings of the group, the boys would exchange tidbits of news from abroad which they had gleaned from the Voice of America or the BBC. The girls would huddle over a French fashion magazine, and they would dance to the music of Elvis, Eartha Kitt, or Louis Armstrong. "A thing had only to be forbidden," Marina recalls, "for us to get hold of it somehow."

Her favorite escort among the young men in the group was Leonid. Lonya was an architect, and to Marina, everything about him was darkly appealing, from his dark lashes and hair to his black eyes and swarthy skin. Lonya was a Jew—once again Marina had chosen an outsider. As the winter of 1960 faded into spring, she was often in Lonya's company, and in June he asked her to live with him. Marina was horrified. When a man and woman wanted to live together, she pointed out in an injured tone, they usually talked about getting married. Lonya could not consider it. He was poor. He did not have an apartment. And he had thought that Marina was above such bourgeois ideas. They saw less of one another after that. But the attraction did not wear off.

If Lonya's appeal was exotic, Marina faced another threat to her peace of mind that summer, and it came from inside her own family. In August, her cousin Valentin arrived to spend his holiday at the Prusakovs'. He was the son of Klavdia's younger sister Polina and her husband Georgy Alexandrov, who was head of the building trust in Kharkov. The legend of Valentin's noble looks had preceded him, and Marina found that the handsome reality very nearly lived up to the legend. They were soon deep in a clandestine and, to Marina, sinful romance, of which one of the chief delights was being seen with Valentin on the street.

Strangely enough, Valya, who could be a zealous chaperone when the occasion, or her husband, required it, had not the slightest suspicion of the flirtation that was blossoming under her very roof. She even let Valentin sleep in the living room, which was also Marina's bedroom. Marina for once was in a quandary that she dared not share with her aunt. She enjoyed Valentin's kisses by day, but at night she curled up in her bed like a frightened rabbit and refused to allow him near her. When Valentin left after his two-week visit, he swore he would never forget her, and asked her to wait for him. She even had a passionate love letter from him which she hid at the pharmacy. But she made herself forget Valentin, for she considered her feelings for him incestuous and she was frightened by them.

In October, Marina went to Leningrad on vacation and stayed at a government Rest House. She had been there a week before she even dared to venture back to the Medvedevs' apartment. When she did go, laden with gifts for everyone, Petya and Tanya were overjoyed. Even Alexander seemed glad to see her, although he behaved in his usual gruff manner and before long excused himself and went to bed. Marina promised to come again, but somehow she failed to get around to it.

She spent part of her vacation in Leningrad with the Tarussins, the parents of her old suitor, Oleg. Marina had written to them regularly from Minsk, and Oleg's mother still treated her as a prospective daughter-in-law. But when she and Oleg were reunited, it was clear that his feelings had changed. The day before her return to Minsk, Marina told his mother that the romance was over—Oleg did not love her any more. She did not love Oleg either. But it hurt her to be unwanted again.

The faithful Sasha was there to console her on her return from Leningrad. She consented to be his date for New Year's, but she promised herself that she would dance with anyone who came along, to torment the hapless Sasha and seek revenge on the entire male species. That evening she found herself in the arms of Anatoly Shpanko, a lanky fellow with unruly, dark blond hair and a wide, appealing smile. Tolya, as she soon called him, was a twenty-six-year-old medical student who had already served his term in the army. He was whimsical, yet deferential, to Marina, and from the moment of their first kiss—they were standing in a dimly lit courtyard, with snow swirling all around them and a lantern creaking in the doorway—she was deliriously in love with him. "He was a rare person," Marina recalls. "He was honest in everything he did."

There was only one drawback. Attracted as she was to Anatoly, Marina did not think he was handsome. Nor did she like the way he dressed. He simply did not fit the image she had created for herself of a girl who goes out only with handsome men. Not wanting to be made fun of, fearful that her friends might think less of her, she steered Anatoly along back streets when they were together as surreptitiously as if they were engaged in a clandestine affair. But she forgot her calculations when he kissed her. His kisses made Marina's head spin. Finally he proposed, but there were obstacles. Anatoly had two or three more years in medical school, no money and, even more important, no apartment. Marina consulted Valya and Ilya. "No, my girl," Ilya said. "Let him finish the institute first. He can talk about getting married then."

Marina was not surprised. It was what she had expected, after all. But there was something in her uncle's words that hurt her deeply. He would not consent to her marrying anyone, no matter how superior a human being, who did not have a place of his own. It was not Anatoly, whom he had never met, he was rejecting. It was Marina herself.

In later years, Anatoly's broad grin and unruly hair would return to haunt Marina. She knew she would be lucky to have him. She admired him, she was attracted to him sexually, he had a fine future as a doctor, and he loved her. He came, moreover, with a pair of adoring parents who would have been good to her. What more on earth could she want? But Marina was having a good time, and as yet she did not feel quite ready to settle down. Or perhaps she did not feel ready for someone who treated her with Anatoly's decency. She and Anatoly kept on seeing each other, and Anatoly kept on proposing. Marina simply shelved his proposals. "Let's wait and see how our feelings develop," she said. And she would see, perhaps, whether anybody else came along.

On Friday, March 17, 1961, Marina went to a medical students' dance at the Palace of Culture, a huge building in the center of Minsk. Both Sasha and Anatoly had asked her to go with them and Marina could not make up her mind. She preferred Anatoly, of course, but Marina, as she often did, decided to let fate take a hand. If she arrived early, she would go with Anatoly. If late, it would be Sasha. She told both of them to wait for her outside.

Marina was late. That evening, she spent a long time in front of the mirror doing and redoing her hair. Wearing her very best, a dress of red Chinese brocade with a tiny bodice and a bell-shaped skirt, she did not arrive at the Palace of Culture until ten o'clock. Sasha had been waiting outside for nearly three hours. Anatoly was somewhere inside, alone.

The Palace of Culture contained within it a vast, impersonal hall with immense white columns and several glittering chandeliers. It was not a place for intimacy. The orchestra was deafening and brassy. Dancing with Sasha, her eyes sweeping the floor for Anatoly, Marina was approached by another medical student, an acquaintance of hers and Sasha's by the name of Yury. He had a dark-haired stranger in tow, and as Yury began the introductions, the stranger stuck out his hand to Marina, grinned, and said simply: "Alik." A moment later, he asked Sasha for permission to dance with her.

Marina could not have cared less. They had been dancing in silence a minute or two when the stranger said, "I'm sorry, but I didn't catch your name."

She told him.

"What a pretty name!"

Marina thought he was giving her a line. Still, he was a good dancer and he was very well dressed. He was wearing a gray suit, a white shirt, and a white tie of some funny foreign material. The tie and his accent told her immediately that he was not a Russian. He must be from Latvia or Estonia.

"It's not just your name that's pretty," the stranger continued. "You're pretty, too. I saw you when you came in. I was trying to figure out how to meet you, but you had a crowd around you. I'm glad we finally met."

Alik danced with her again and again, as if he could not bear to lose her for a moment or let her dance with anyone else. The second the music stopped, he asked for the next dance, and Sasha barely had a chance. When she did dance with Sasha, Alik did not dance with anybody else. He waited for her to be free. That was all right with Marina. This Alik was a good dancer. He was clean and polite. And his accent amused her.

But she still was looking for Anatoly, hoping to make him jealous. To teach him a real lesson, she suggested to a group of young men, all standing around waiting to dance with her, that they go to the bar. "It's boring here. Let's get some champagne!"

It was the climax of Marina's career as a single girl. She felt like a princess, resplendent in her red brocade and her elaborate hair-do. Never had she looked so pretty. Never had she had so many admirers. They all drank champagne and were on their way back to the dance floor when Marina finally saw Anatoly. "You go on back," she said to her entourage. "I'll catch up with you later."

Her performance had had the desired effect. Anatoly was angry and insisted on taking her home. Marina refused. She returned to Sasha and her other admirers, and when the dance was over, she brushed past Anatoly, who was waiting for her at the door, with five young men in tow, the stranger Alik among them. All six of them set off down the street. A few paces behind, to Marina's intense satisfaction, was Anatoly. He called out to her twice. Marina paid no attention. He caught up with her, put his hand on her shoulder, and pleaded: "Marina! I've got to talk to you."

"I can't talk now. Can't you see? Go away!"

Alik was a witness to the scene, Alik, the stranger with the funny accent. Long afterward he told Marina that he had made up his mind that night. "I got what I wanted," he boasted. "I got you away from them."

The group of young people went to Yury's apartment, where his mother, who was a professor of microbiology, was waiting up for them. That night, before the dance, she had given a lecture on America, which she had just visited as part of a delegation. Suddenly, Marina realized that Alik was American. Yury had asked him to the lecture, hence the dance, to hear his mother talk about America.

They all sat together in the living room asking Yury's mother questions. Alik listened carefully but did not say anything. Finally, Yury's mother went to bed and the boys turned to Alik. They wanted to know what was right and what was wrong in Yury's mother's description of America.

Marina remembers his tone. He was pleasant and self-confident. He dismissed some of her remarks as "propaganda." The rest, he said, was fair enough. Yury's mother had been struck by the absence of lines in American stores. She attributed it to those two vices of the capitalist system, unemployment and overproduction, and concluded that Americans were too poor to buy. Alik politely disagreed. The stores seem empty, he said, because there is plenty for everyone at a price each can afford. "Your mother is right, though," he said to Yury. "Unemployment is a problem."

Marina liked the way he talked. She especially liked the way he stuck up for his country. She asked him if he loved America. He did, he said, but he did not love everything about it. He disliked unemployment and racial discrimination and added that education and medical care cost far too much. But he noted that housing was better than in Russia and that the ordinary apartment was bigger. Of the two countries, Russia and the United States, he thought America was more democratic because everyone can say what he thinks.

For a while Alik and two of the boys spoke English. Marina, who had seldom heard it spoken before, was enthralled. When it was time for Sasha to take her home, he offered to drop Alik off afterward. The three of them left the apartment together.

When she reached home, Marina rang the doorbell and called out excitedly: "I'm not alone, Aunt Valya. Sasha's here." Properly warned, Valya unlatched the door in her nightgown and quickly scuttled back to bed. Marina followed her into her room.

"Aunt Valya," she whispered, her eyes very large. "Sasha's in there. Sasha and another boy, an American. He's really nice. Come in and I'll introduce you."

"Are you out of your mind?" Valya said. "Bringing an American here and the place in such a mess?" She was afraid to meet him. "I look too awful," she said, and then groaned, "Oh, my God, an American was the only thing lacking in your collection."

Before he left, Alik asked Marina if he might see her again. He begged her to name the time and place, adding that he seldom missed a dance at the Palace of Culture.

"Maybe I'll go there next week," she said.

With that the young men said good-night, and as Marina closed the door behind them, she tried to remember Alik's name. It had a German-Jewish sound to her, something like "Oswald."

Interlude

The path that led Lee Harvey Oswald to the Palace of Culture in Minsk in 1961 had opened up seven or eight years earlier when, as a very young teenager, he was handed a pamphlet on the streets of New York about Julius and Ethel Rosenberg, the two Americans who were convicted of and executed for betraying atomic secrets to the Russians. Next, when he was fifteen and was looking for what he later called "a key to my environment," he borrowed books by Marx, Engels, and American Communist writers from the New Orleans Public Library and began to consider himself a Marxist.[1]

Only a few days after reaching the eligible age of seventeen, he joined the U.S. Marine Corps. His half brother, John Pic, had chosen the Coast Guard for a career, and his full brother, Robert Oswald, had recently completed a tour in the Marines; both assumed that Lee enlisted to get out from under the "yoke of oppression" of their mother, Marguerite, who sought to control the lives of all her sons in every way. The older boys had entered the armed services to get away from her, and that was largely Lee's motive as well. But he had another motive, too. Lee's father, Marguerite's second husband, had died before Lee was born, and Marguerite had raised the boy almost single-handedly. Lee desperately wanted to be a man, to learn a man's skills and be part of the world of men. He idolized his older brother Robert, and he knew no better way than to follow where Robert had led.

Lee's three-year term of enlistment began on October 26, 1956, in San Diego, California. He underwent the rigorous Marine Corps basic training, including use of the M-1 rifle, both at San Diego and at Camp

Pendleton, California. At the Naval Air Station in Jacksonville, Florida, and then at Keesler Air Force Base in Biloxi, Mississippi, he was trained in aircraft surveillance and the use of radar. Six months after joining the service, he was granted low-level clearance to deal with material up to the "confidential" (as distinguished from the "secret" or "top-secret") level. He was simultaneously promoted to Private First Class. Lee had a higher than average I.Q., 118 on the Wechsler scale, and during his training he scored well, both in proficiency and in conduct. But he was unpopular with his fellow Marines. He kept to himself, preferred reading to the company of others, and spent his weekends alone.

Lee was next assigned to the Marine Corps Air Station at El Toro, California, and, in the late summer of 1957, he shipped out to Japan, where he joined an air control squadron at Atsugi, outside Tokyo, as a radar operator. The squadron's job was to direct American aircraft to their targets by radar and to scout for such Chinese or Soviet planes as might stray into the area. It was while he was at Atsugi that Lee may first have become aware of what was perhaps the most highly prized secret in all of U.S. aerial reconnaissance, the U-2 aircraft.

During his early months in Japan, Lee Harvey Oswald began to blossom. He lost the meekness that had caused the men to christen him "Ozzie Rabbit," and he became more manly and assertive in standing up for his rights. He had his first experiences with women and, like many of the men, was said to be keeping a mistress. Feeling free in a way he had not felt at home, he told one friend that he did not care if he ever went back to the United States.

But a curious episode occurred on October 27, 1957, six weeks after Lee's arrival in Japan and only a few days after his eighteenth birthday. One of his buddies, Paul Edward Murphy, heard a shot in the cubicle next to him. He rushed in to find Lee sitting on his footlocker, looking in a bewildered way at his left arm. Murphy asked what had happened and, "very unemotionally," Lee replied, "I believe I shot myself."[2] The wound, inflicted by a .22 caliber pistol Lee was not authorized to possess, was in his left elbow, and he spent the next two and a half weeks in a naval hospital. It may have been a clumsy accident, but Lee was not a novice when it came to handling guns.

Just after Lee left the hospital, his unit was sent on maneuvers to the Philippines. It remained at Subic Bay, on Bataan, across Manila Bay from Manila, for three months, and it was at Subic Bay, Lee was to say later, that he learned to sympathize with local Communists and conceived a hatred for U.S. "militarist imperialism" for exploiting the Filipino natives.[3]

While Lee was stationed in the Philippines, a second curious episode occurred. Private First Class Martin E. Schrand was found shot to death one night while on guard duty outside a hangar that could have been sheltering a U-2. Lee knew Schrand well. They had been part of a small group of men who started radar training in Jacksonville the year before, and had been together most of the time since. A Marine Corps investigation in 1958 established that Schrand's death was accidental and self-inflicted, and yet a rumor arose among the men that Lee Oswald was responsible.[4]

The rumor is notable for two reasons. Lee had considered himself a Marxist for two years. And at Subic Bay he had become sympathetic to what he called "Communist elements" among the Filipinos. Afterwards, speculation arose that Lee wanted to break into the hangar and learn something about the U-2 so that he could use the information later on.[5] Although the speculation appears to be groundless, the rumor is still notable as a measure of Lee's unpopularity among his fellow Marines.

When Lee returned with his squadron to Japan in the spring of 1958, he was court-martialed for the offense that had led to the wound in his elbow. The court decided that the wound was accidental, but for unauthorized possession of the pistol Lee was reduced in rank to private and sentenced to a forfeiture of pay and confinement at hard labor for twenty days. His confinement was suspended for six months.

Two months later, in June of 1958, Lee was court-martialed again. While drunk in a café, he had spilled a drink on a sergeant and abusively challenged him to a fight. Such episodes often occurred in after-hours drinking places, but the sergeant brought charges, another measure of Lee's unpopularity. This time he drew a second forfeiture of pay and a twenty-eight-day sentence of confinement at hard labor. The earlier, suspended twenty-day sentence was invoked as well, and during the summer of 1958 Lee spent seven weeks in the brig. Further, his request for extended overseas duty was denied.

Lee's two courts-martial, his being broken in rank, his time in the brig, and now the refusal of his request for extended duty overseas, all were keen disappointments. But he had a new enthusiasm. In Japan, he was again exposed to Communist propaganda, this time to Soviet magazines and to individuals who were fanatically pro-Soviet. "Soviet propaganda works well," he was to say later, referring to his time in Japan.[6] He made up his mind that he would go to the U.S.S.R.

After a brief tour in the South China Sea, he returned with his unit to the United States and, in November 1958, was assigned to the Marine Air Control Squadron at El Toro, California, another base at which U-2 aircraft were stationed. Again he was part of an aircraft surveillance crew, and one of his superior officers, Lieutenant John E. Donovan, has said that Lee was "competent, very competent," on the job. He took orders willingly and was cool in assessing emergency situations.[7] Donovan urged him to go to noncommissioned officers' school.

Nevertheless, it was clear that Lee's enthusiasm for the Marine Corps had eroded, and at El Toro he began to flaunt his enthusiasm for the U.S.S.R. He acquired a Berlitz phrase book and started to study Russian ostentatiously in the barracks. He subscribed to a Russian-language newspaper, and when he and his roommate played chess, he always chose the red chessmen because he liked the "Red army." He played Russian songs so loudly that they could be heard outside the barracks. He asked to be called "Oswaldskovich," used words like *"da"* and *"nyet,"* called some of the men "Comrade" and was pleased when they called him "Comrade" in return. It was the behavior, one would guess, not of a spy but of a slightly egregious schoolboy hungry for attention. Nonetheless, some of the men did call him, jokingly, a "spy"—and Lee loved it.

From a lieutenant named Nelson Delgado, Lee also learned a few words of Spanish. With Delgado and some of the other men he followed the ups and downs of Fidel Castro, who came to power in Cuba on January 1, 1959, while Lee was at El Toro. He talked enthusiastically of going to Cuba and fighting for Castro. But his talk about Castro had nothing like the shock value of his talk about Russia because Castro had not declared himself a Communist yet, and the United States had not made up its mind whether he was an enemy or not.

Lee had other characteristics, besides his interest in Russia, that set him apart from his fellow Marines. He had completed only the ninth grade, but he listened to classical music, read books like George Orwell's *1984* and *Animal Farm,* and tried to appear more intellectual than the other men. He loved to lure his officers into discussions of foreign affairs to show off his superior knowledge, and then, when he had outshone them, he treated them as if they were unfit to be in command over him. Lee apparently had a very high opinion of himself. One friend said that he liked to "come out top dog."[8] He seldom went out with girls following his return to California, explaining to a roommate that he was saving money and would one day do something that would make him famous.

With less than a year left of his enlistment, Lee was promoted, for a second time, to Private First Class, and took and passed a series of high-school equivalency tests. He did "poorly" on the Russian-language tests he had asked to take. And he made no plans to reenlist.

He wrote to his brother Robert that once he was out of the Marine Corps, "I know what I want to be and how I'm going to be it, which I guess is the most important thing in life."[9] He applied and was accepted for the spring 1960 term at Albert Schweitzer College, a liberal arts school in Switzerland, stating that he hoped to study philosophy, broaden his knowledge of German (a language he did not know), and live in a "Good moral atmosphere."[10]

By his last summer in the Marine Corps, the summer of 1959, Lee was taken off radar duty and assigned to clerical and janitorial jobs. He was considered to be deficient in discipline, sloppy in his personal habits and in barracks inspection, and it was said that the sergeant major was going to take steps to "straighten him out." It was even rumored, falsely, that he had lost his security clearance.

Lee was anxious to get out of the Marines. In August of 1959, he saw his opportunity. Marguerite had sustained a slight injury to her nose while working in a candy store the previous Christmas, and Lee, with four months left to go in the Marine Corps, applied for an immediate hardship discharge on the grounds that he was his mother's sole source of support. Marguerite, who in the past had supplied her sons with false documents so that they could enter the service before they were of eligible age, now supplied documents attesting that she was disabled and unable to support herself. Less than a month later, Lee was released from active duty and transferred into the Marine Corps reserve. On September 4, 1959, as soon as he knew that his release would be coming through, he applied for a passport, stating that he planned to study at Schweitzer College and at the University of Turku, Finland, and would be traveling to Cuba, the Dominican Republic, England, France, Germany, and Russia.

He did not tell his mother about his plans. But he quickly disabused her of her hopes that he would live with her. He stayed with her in Fort Worth for two days and then left abruptly for New Orleans, telling her that he was going to get a job on a cargo ship and would send her "big money." In a letter just before his departure, he wrote to her that "my values are very different from Robert's or yours. I did not tell you about my plans because you could hardly be expected to understand."[11] And on September 20 he was aboard a freighter, the S.S. *Marion Lykes,* bound from New Orleans for Le Havre, France.

Lee landed at Le Havre on October 8, and left for England the same day. The following day he flew to Helsinki, applied for and was granted a tourist visa to the Soviet Union, crossed into Russia by train on October 15, and arrived in Moscow on October 16. His visa, good for only six days, would expire on October 20. But the day after his arrival, Lee told his Intourist interpreter, Rimma Shirokova, that he wanted to give up his American citizenship and become a citizen of the U.S.S.R. It was October 17, the day before his twentieth birthday.

Rimma reported Lee's desire to her superiors and helped him draft a letter to the Supreme Soviet requesting citizenship. She was uneasy about the strange fish she had on the hook, but she befriended Lee, continued to guide him around Moscow, and presented him with a copy of Dostoyevsky's *The Idiot*, perhaps as a warning, on his birthday.

On October 19, Lee was interviewed in his room at the Hotel Berlin by a correspondent for Radio Moscow, Lev Setyayev, who was ostensibly seeking his impressions as a tourist to use in propaganda broadcasts overseas. Whatever Lee may have said—and he felt guilty about it long afterwards—his remarks were not used on the air, and part of Setyayev's job almost certainly was to gather impressions of Oswald for the KGB, the Soviet secret police.

On the morning of October 21, Lee reported for an interview with an official of the Ministry of Internal Affairs, the MVD. The official was not encouraging. That afternoon Lee was informed that his visa had expired and he had to leave Russia that night. A few hours later Rimma found him locked in his hotel room, bleeding badly. He had slashed his left wrist.

Lee described his suicide attempt in a handwritten account of his experiences in Russia which he called his "Historic Diary."[12] In it he wrote that he had soaked his left wrist in cold water to numb the pain, slashed it, and then plunged it in a bathtub full of hot water in order to make it bleed more. He knew, however, that Rimma would be coming within the hour. After she found him, he was rushed to the Botkin Hospital, where foreigners are frequently treated, and placed in the psychiatric ward. He had recovered enough by the next day to complain about the poor food and about being in a ward for the insane. A psychiatrist examined him, decided he was not dangerous, and transferred him into a new ward, where he enjoyed a more or less happy, attention filled week. Rimma came to see him often and he noted in his Diary that she was "preety."

Lee was released on October 28 and moved from the Hotel Berlin to the Hotel Metropole, two blocks away. That afternoon he was driven to OVIR, the Soviet visa office, and interviewed by a new set of officials, who appeared to know nothing about him or his earlier interview. They asked if he still wanted citizenship and he said he did. They told him that a decision would be forthcoming, but "not soon." He was to return to his hotel room and wait.

After three days, Lee was wild with impatience. He decided that a "showdown" might convince the Russians of his earnestness and so, while Rimma was briefly absent—she was watching him closely—he took a taxi to the American Embassy. There he told a receptionist in the consular office that he wished to "dissolve his citizenship." She summoned Richard E. Snyder, the U.S. consul, and he took Lee into his office, where his assistant, John A. McVickar, was also present. Lee repeated his desire to renounce his citizenship, affirmed his allegiance to the U.S.S.R., and announced that he had applied to become a Soviet citizen. He slapped his passport down on Snyder's desk and demanded to take the oath renouncing his American citizenship that very moment. And he handed Snyder a letter formally requesting that his American citizenship be revoked and affirming his allegiance to the U.S.S.R. He added that he had been a radar technician in the Marine Corps and would make available to the Soviet government such knowledge as he had acquired.

Richard Snyder was in a dilemma, for Lee Oswald appeared to be sane and he was within his rights. But Snyder was newly stung from handling the cases of two would-be defectors, one of whom had quickly changed his mind. If only from a humanitarian point of view, Snyder thought, glancing at Oswald's passport and noting that he was still a minor, the boy ought to have time to think it over. The step he was proposing was irrevocable, for if he were granted Soviet citizenship he would never be allowed to leave Russia. Snyder decided to put Oswald off, telling him that he could not administer the oath because it was a Saturday and he needed time to prepare the papers. But Oswald was free to appear two days later, on Monday, he said, and take the oath then if he chose. Snyder suggested, however, that Oswald wait until he was assured of Soviet citizenship, or he would have no citizenship at all. Lee stalked out, leaving his passport and his letter behind.

The exchange lasted less than an hour, but it had so nasty a tone that it was remembered long afterward by three Americans, besides Snyder and Oswald, who were present during parts of it—John McVickar, the vice-consul, Marie Cheatham, the receptionist, and Edward L. Keenan, a graduate exchange student down for the weekend from Leningrad.

Lee returned to his hotel greatly pleased with himself and confident the Russians would accept him after his bravura display of good faith. That day and the next he was besieged by members of the American press corps in Moscow, who had been told by the embassy about his attempt to defect. Lee confided to his Diary that the attention made him feel "exhilarated and not so lonely." But, fearful lest he prejudice his case, he turned every one of them away. He repeatedly refused long-distance telephone calls from his mother and his brothers and spent two weeks in "utter loneliness."

On November 3, Lee wrote Llewellyn Thompson, the American ambassador in Moscow, again asking that his citizenship be revoked and complaining about his treatment by Snyder. Snyder replied by mail that he had only to appear at the embassy to renounce his citizenship. But Lee did not stir from his hotel. On November 8 he wrote to his brother Robert: "I will never return to the United States, which is a country I hate."[13]

On November 13 Lee telephoned Aline Mosby, a reporter for United Press International; she came to see him, and he talked to her "non-stop" for two hours. And, on November 16, a Soviet official came to his room and informed him that he could remain until a decision had been made what to do with him. It was virtually a promise that he could stay, and Lee was vastly relieved.

I happened to be the beneficiary of his relief. I was a newspaper and magazine reporter in Moscow in 1959. I had just returned from a visit to the United States and, on November 16, I went to the consular office of the American Embassy, as the American reporters did, to pick up my mail. John McVickar welcomed me back with these words: "Oh, by the way, there's a young American in your hotel trying to defect. He won't talk to any of *us,* but maybe he'll talk to you because you're a woman."

McVickar turned out to be right. At the Hotel Metropole I stopped by Oswald's room, which was on the second floor, the floor below my own. I knocked, and the young man inside opened the door. Instead of inviting me in, he came into the corridor and stood there, holding the door open with his foot. I peeked into his room, and saw that it was exactly like mine, right down to its shade of hotel blue. To my surprise, he readily agreed to be interviewed, and said that he would come to my room at eight or nine o'clock that evening. Good as his word he appeared, wearing a dark gray suit, a white shirt with a dark tie, and a sweater-vest of tan cashmere. He looked familiar to me, like a lot of college boys in the East during the 1950s. The only difference was his voice—he had a slight Southern drawl.

He settled in an armchair, I brought him tea from a little burner I kept on the floor, and he started talking fairly easily. He spoke quietly, unemphatically, and only rarely betrayed by a gesture or a slight change of tone that what he was saying at that moment meant anything special to him. He began by complaining about Richard Snyder and his refusal to accept on the spot his oath of renunciation. I had no idea what he was talking about, since I had not discussed him with Snyder or McVickar, nor heard about the stormy scene at the embassy two weeks before.[14]

During our conversation Lee returned again and again to what he called the embassy's "illegal" treatment of him, which he termed a "prestige and labor-saving device." He spread out two letters on my desk: one his letter of protest to the American ambassador, Llewellyn Thompson, and the other his letter from Snyder, which said that he was free to come to the embassy at any time and take the oath. Well, I said, all you have to do is go back one more time. He swore he would never set foot there again. Once he became a Soviet citizen, he said, he would allow "my government," the Soviet government, to handle it for him.

Lee's tone was level, almost expressionless, and while I realized that his words were bitter, somehow I did not *feel* that he was angry. Moreover, he did not seem like a fully grown man to me, for the blinding fact, the one that obliterated nearly every other fact about him, was his youth. He looked about seventeen. Proudly, as a boy might, he told me about his only expedition into Moscow alone. He had walked four blocks to Detsky Mir, the children's department store, and bought himself an ice cream cone. I could scarcely believe my ears. Here he was, coming to live in this country forever, and he had so far dared venture into only four blocks of it.

I was astounded by his lack of curiosity and the utter absence of any joy or spirit of adventure in him. And yet I respected him. Here was this lonely, frightened boy taking on the bureaucracy of the second most powerful nation on earth, and doing it single-handedly. I wondered if he had any idea what he was doing, for it could be brutal to try to stay if the Russians did not want you—futile and dangerous. I had to admire Lee, ignorant, young, and even tender as he appeared, for persisting in spite of so many discouragements.[15]

I was sorry for him, too, for I was certain he was making a mistake. He told me that he had been informed that morning that he did not have to leave the country. So I supposed that he would soon be granted citizenship, vanish into some remote corner of Russia, and never be heard from again. He would not be allowed to see any Americans, much less reporters, and he would be unable to signal his distress. Like every Westerner in Moscow, I had heard innumerable tragic stories about foreigners who had come to Russia during the 1930s, crossed the Rubicon of Soviet citizenship, and never been allowed to leave. I assumed that Lee would regret his choice and that he, like the others, would be trapped. As young as he was, he would have a lifetime to be sorry.

Our evening was like a seesaw, with me trying to get Lee to talk about himself and Lee trying to talk about his "ideology." I would say that Lee won. But occasionally our purposes coincided, as when he spoke of "exploitation" in the United States. His mother, he said, had been "a worker all her life, having to produce profit for capitalists," and I thought I heard his voice tighten. I supposed he must love his mother very much.

What about his father, I asked. Lee said that his father died before he was born. I asked what his father's work had been. "I *believe* he was an insurance salesman," Lee said, and his "believe" had a cold sound indeed. I wondered if he was angry at his father, ashamed of him, or what.

Lee made it clear that he would not be talking to me or to anyone, except that the American Embassy had told the press of his defection and he wanted to give his "side of the story." Now that he had been informed that he did not have to leave Russia, he supposed it was "safe" to speak out—he would not be endangering his chances of remaining. He told me repeatedly that his decision was "unemotional," and this seemed important to him. But he added—a hint, perhaps, that he felt he was unusual—that he did not recommend defection for everyone. It meant coming to a new country, adjusting, and "always being the outsider." But at least he would never have to go home, and that was the big thing to him. "I believe what I am doing is right," he said. He also said that he had talked to me because he wanted to give the American people "something to think about."

Before he left, at two o'clock in the morning, he told me that he had never talked so long about himself to anyone. I felt another twinge of pity, for if this was his idea of openness, then I thought that he must never have talked about himself to anyone at all. As for me, I felt that I had failed. I had reached out, and my fingers had not touched anyone.

"Look," I said, "I'll be writing my story about you tomorrow. Do you want to come up and look it over? There might be some mistakes you'll want to correct."

"No," he said, "I trust you. It'll be okay."

I made him promise that before he left the Metropole to be swallowed up in Soviet life forever, he would at least come up to say goodbye.

The following night I had supper with John McVickar. We talked about Oswald, of course, and McVickar told me a little about the angry scene at the embassy. As vice-consul, McVickar daily saw former Americans who were fruitlessly trying to go home. He thought that if someone at the embassy had had time to listen to Oswald, it might have helped defuse him. He was afraid that, instead, the encounter had pushed him further toward the tragic step—Soviet citizenship—that would make it impossible for him ever to go home. I was puzzled over Oswald's refusal to return to the embassy. If he had come 5,000 miles just to renounce his citizenship, why allow pique to stand in his way? Partly to comfort McVickar, I wondered aloud whether Oswald might be leaving himself a loophole, a crack in the door, just in case he decided some day to go home.[16]

Years later I asked McVickar if he had told me about Oswald in the hope that I would try to talk him out of defecting. That, in a bugged hotel room and with my own visa hanging by a thread, would have been risky indeed. "Oh, no," McVickar laughed. "I hoped you would *listen* him out of it."

I made one more effort to see Lee. Later in the week, with my story about him written and on its way to New York, I was trudging upstairs in my hotel and found myself on the second floor, Lee's floor. I went up to the *dezhurnaya,* a tiny woman in white who sat on the landing and presided over a huge desk filled with keys. "How about Number 233?" I asked. "Is he in?" She inspected her drawer of keys and her arms flew into the air. "Out!" she said.

Lee forgot his promise to say goodbye, and I never saw him again.

Why was Lee Harvey Oswald permitted to remain in the Soviet Union? Was he the pitiful, slightly unbalanced boy Soviet officials had at first taken him for, or was he a determined and single-minded individual who would go to any lengths to get what he wanted? The question was a crucial one, and the answer Soviet officials seem to have reached may have determined the outcome of his case. Oswald's suicide attempt was proof that in order to get what he wanted he would stop at nothing—he would even try to take his own life. And his willingness to talk to reporters showed that he would not hesitate to embarrass either the Russians or the Americans publicly.

Oswald told me that Soviet officials had warned him that his case would be decided according to the "international atmosphere." In that sense he could hardly have timed his arrival more propitiously, for on September 26 and 27, while Oswald was on the high seas on his way to Russia, Premier Khrushchev and President Eisenhower were meeting in the Maryland woods to christen what became known as the "Spirit of Camp David." After Khrushchev's return to Moscow, even minor questions affecting Americans in the U.S.S.R. began to be decided, to a greater degree than before, according to whether they would help or hurt Soviet-American relations.

Yury Nosenko, a Soviet secret police officer who later defected to the West, told the CIA and FBI that the initial decision to expel Oswald was taken by the KGB, working through Intourist, the agency which handles travel by foreigners inside the U.S.S.R.[17] Nosenko was unable to say who reversed that decision, although he speculated that it was overruled by the Soviet Red Cross or Foreign Ministry. The speculation appears poorly founded unless one of these organizations was fronting for another that was politically more powerful, either the KGB at a very high level, or some special Party body or official whom Khrushchev entrusted with overseeing implementation of the Spirit of Camp David.

Thus Oswald's suicide attempt appears to have been pivotal. First, it came at a moment, late in October, when the new policy began to be effected. Second, it appears to have altered the Russians' estimate of Oswald's character and of the damage he could do. Evidently they decided that it would be less harmful to their image abroad to accept this young American who claimed to be motivated by Marxist ideals, than to reject him with the risk that he might embarrass them with a very public suicide. During the long weeks he was kept in limbo, until after the first of the year, they no doubt hoped that he would become disenchanted and would quietly go away.[18]

But Lee, by his self-imposed sequestration in the Metropole, avoided any confrontation with reality that might conceivably have caused him to change his mind. Instead, he spent his emotions writing angry letters to his brother Robert. He told Robert that he "would like to see the capitalist government of the U.S. overthrown," and "happiness is taking part in the struggle." He added that Robert and Marguerite were *"not objects of affection"* and he had to come to Russia in order "to find freedom." And in December, even before he had been told what his future would be, he wrote Robert that he chose to break all ties with his past and would not be writing to him or to their mother again. "I am starting a new life," he said, "and I do not wish to have anything to do with the old."[19]

On January 4, 1960, he was informed what his new life would be: He could stay in the U.S.S.R., not as a citizen, but as a "stateless person." He was to be sent to Minsk, capital of Belorussia, where he would be a metalworker at the Belorussian Radio and Television Plant. Through the Soviet Red Cross he was given 5,000 old rubles, or $500, with which he was able to pay his hotel bill, his train fare to Minsk, and still have some rubles left.

Lee started his job in Minsk on January 13, and in March he was awarded a pleasant one-room apartment with a view overlooking the river. His financial situation was superb. He earned $70 to $90 a month at work and received an additional $70 a month in the form of a Red Cross subsidy. He had as much monthly income as the director of his factory. Lee did not particularly like his job. It was mere manual labor, while he had hoped for a place in an institute and a chance to study full time. But as the object of much attention and the recipient, like every foreigner, of many favors, he was at first reasonably content.

Lee made friends at the factory, and in his free time he studied Russian and went to the opera with Rosa Kuznetsova, an Intourist interpreter. He bought a 16–gauge single barrel shotgun that summer, joined a hunting club, and went on hunting trips in the countryside. His fellow workers, who called him "Alik" because "Lee" sounded Chinese, peppered him with questions about America, and Lee liked that. And, in the fall, he began to have love affairs. He soon discovered that some of the girls cared passionately about him because he was an American, the only one in Minsk, and he had an apartment. Others, however, seemed to care about him for himself. But the woman he wanted turned him down. She was Ella Germann, a dark-haired Jewish girl whom he had met at the factory. They saw each other for a few months and Lee celebrated the New Year of 1961 with Ella and her family at their apartment. He decided that he was in love with her and, more or less on impulse, proposed to her the following evening. To his astonishment Ella rejected him, first, because she did not love him and, second, because relations between Russia and America might some day grow worse and he would be arrested as "an American spy."

Lee was stunned. Ella's refusal helped to crystallize the many criticisms—the provincial drabness, the cold climate, the officiousness of the Party secretary in his workshop—that had been quietly taking shape in Lee's mind ever since his arrival in Minsk. He no longer considered Russia a paradise. On January 4, two days after Ella's refusal and a year to the day after he had been assigned to Minsk and given his documents as a "stateless person," the visa authorities in Minsk inquired whether he still wanted Soviet citizenship. It was not an offer, simply a pulse-taking. Lee replied that he did not, and asked merely to have his documents extended for another year. And he confided to his Diary, "I have had enough." In February he wrote the American Embassy in Moscow asking to have his passport back. He rudely reminded the embassy that he was still an American citizen and said he would like to go home.

It was in such a mood of disappointment in love and with Russia that Lee Harvey Oswald met Marina Prusakova.

PART TWO

Russia, 1961–1962

6

Courtship

ON SATURDAY NIGHT, March 25, 1961, Marina and a girlfriend from the pharmacy went to another dance at the Palace of Culture. Wearing a simple gray dress and her best Czechoslovak shoes, Marina was walking down the stairway to the dance floor when she met Alik coming up.

"Hello," he said, grinning happily. "I'm very glad you came. I was afraid you might not be here."

He was dressed differently from the last time she saw him. He was wearing black trousers, a blue button-down shirt without a tie, and a charcoal gray V-neck sweater. Marina noticed that his eyes were a deep blue. She was pleased that he had been looking for her.

They danced and talked all evening long. Strolling home together down Ulitsa Kalinina, the broad thoroughfare on which Ilya and Valya had their apartment, Alik pointed out the building in which he lived. It was on the same street, about a seven-minute walk away. Outside Marina's building, Alik asked: "May I see you again?" She agreed to a date on the following Thursday. He asked for her phone number, "just in case."

Three days later, on Tuesday, when Marina came home from work, Valya informed her that a young man had called, not once but twice, and said he would call again the next day. He had a "nice, polite voice," Valya remarked, "but I couldn't understand him very well. It's probably your American." On Wednesday he called again. This time, Valya reported, he sounded upset. He was in the hospital and unable to meet Marina the next evening.[1] Would she come to see him in the hospital? Valya had written down the address.

On Friday, Marina appeared at the Fourth Clinical Hospital, unannounced, bearing a jar of apricots. Alik was overjoyed. He exclaimed that apricots were his favorite dessert. He was wearing hospital pajamas and flushed with embarrassment when Marina arrived. Both were uneasy as they sat talking in the corridor for about an hour. Alik was to have an operation on his adenoids the next day, and the prospect made him so nervous that he was scarcely able to speak of anything else. As Marina got up to leave, he begged her to visit him again. He looked so pale and seemed so lonely that she agreed. In her pharmacist's coat, she explained, she could pass for a nurse any time. She could come and go as she pleased.

Marina came again the next day. The operation was over, his adenoids were out, but Alik complained of pain and the absence of anesthetic. Marina felt sorry for him and started coming to see him nearly every day. She noticed that as a foreigner he got a good many favors from the hospital staff. She herself was allowed long after visiting hours. Had she been seeing anyone but a foreigner she would, she knew, have been shooed summarily away.

One day as they were walking down the hospital stairway, Alik suddenly asked if he might kiss her.

"If you ask," Marina said, coquettishly, "I'll have to say No."

And so he kissed her.

Marina cringed. The whole thing—Alik, his asking for the kiss, the fetid hospital air—repelled her. She felt averse to herself and to him, and left abruptly.

Marina resolved not to see him again. She had liked Alik at first, and when her co-workers at the pharmacy learned that she had an American boyfriend, they were intrigued and envious. But now Alik was pale and unattractive. He was not a boyfriend, anyway, just a foreigner she felt sorry for. But she was anxious not to hurt his feelings. So when he called from the hospital a day or so later and asked her to come again, Marina reluctantly consented. As long as he's sick, I'll go, she said to herself, but the moment he's out of the hospital I'll refuse to see him any more.

He had a hangdog look that first visit after the kiss. Marina sensed that he wanted to say something, and this time, as he walked her down the staircase, he took her two hands, kissed them, and said: "I want you to be my own girl [he used the Russian for "fiancée"]. I don't want you going out with anybody else."

Was it a proposal of marriage, or had Alik merely chosen the wrong word? Marina was surprised, but she replied as she usually did. She promised him that she would think it over—promising herself, meanwhile, that she would go serenely on seeing her other boyfriends, especially Anatoly, whose kisses were still making her head spin. Marrying Alik was the last thing in her mind.

Easter was approaching, and Aunt Valya was overflowing with sympathy for Marina's new American friend. "It's bad enough to be in a hospital in your own country," she said. "But he has nobody here. We can't let him feel all alone." So on Easter Sunday, Marina turned up at the hospital bearing an Easter egg dyed specially by Valya, as well as candies and *kulich,* a sweet Russian Easter bread with raisins, donated by Aunt Lyuba.

When Marina returned home, she told Aunt Valya that Alik had loved the egg. She also confessed that he had asked her to be his fiancée. In Valya's eyes, that meant he was an honorable young man, and she urged Marina to bring him to supper as soon as he left the hospital. On Tuesday, April 11, the day of his discharge, he came. It was his first meeting with Marina's aunt and uncle. Marina felt shy about the "fiancée" business and asked Valya not to bring it up.

At dinner Ilya quizzed their guest about how he happened to be in Russia and whether he was happy there. Alik answered that he had come as a tourist, and had found it difficult to get permission to stay. But he had been eager to live and work in Russia and learn the truth about it, not just the "truth" that is shown to tourists. He told Ilya that he worked at the Minsk Radio Plant and had his own apartment. He said he had made friends and was happy in Russia.

At the end of the meal, Ilya proposed a toast. He raised a glass of cognac to "the health and happiness of Americans in the U.S.S.R." Then he excused himself to go to work. As he rose from the table, Alik stood up, too, a polite gesture that endeared him to Valya and made an impression on Marina. Ilya put an arm around Alik's shoulders. "Take care of this girl," he said. "She has plenty of breezes in her brain."

When Valya and Marina got up to do the dishes, Alik, in another welcome and unfamiliar gesture, followed them into the kitchen to help. Then he and Marina went for a walk and she agreed to go out with him two evenings later. When Alik kissed her that night for the second time, it seemed to Marina that the aversion she had felt in the hospital was gone.

The next evening Sasha and Yury came by. Alik had invited them to his apartment and they asked Marina to come along. She hesitated and then agreed. Alik might as well know that there were other men in her life. Let him feel a pang of jealousy or two. But she insisted on taking Lyalya Petrusevich, a close friend who lived in her apartment building. She and Lyalya had strolled past Alik's building a year or so before, admiring the balconies that overlooked the river. Now she wanted Lyalya to see the building—and meet her new American acquisition.

Alik was surprised to find not only Yury and Sasha but Marina and Lyalya at his door. He gave them wine and chocolates and they danced. Marina noticed that Alik's collection of classical records was poorer and reflected a good deal less musical knowledge than the collections of other boys she knew. Alik wanted to walk her home. But she went with her friends instead.

Lyalya was lyrical about Alik. "Good God!" she exclaimed. "That boy is really great! He's so neat and polite and good-looking, and he keeps his apartment so clean! I'd throw everybody over for a chance at a man like that! You're too choosy, Marina."

Marina asked Lyalya whether Alik was better than Anatoly? "Of course," she said. "If I had a boyfriend as good-looking as that, and an American besides, I'd marry him blindfolded!"

Her Aunt Valya's approval, and now Lyalya's, raised Alik in Marina's esteem. Not everyone could have an American boyfriend; he was the only American in Minsk. He could probably have any girl in town, and it occurred to her that if she wanted to keep him, even as a curiosity in her collection, she had better watch out.

When he came for their date the next evening, Marina's feelings had undergone a full revolution from what they had been in the hospital. They strolled along the frozen river, and Alik politely cleared the snow off a bench so that Marina could sit down. Soon he confessed that he was cold and led her back to his apartment. He played a record, the theme song from the film *Around the World in Eighty Days,* and they danced. They did the samba, the cha-cha-cha, and a little rock 'n' roll. And Alik kissed her again.

From that evening on, Marina's dates with Anatoly were infrequent. All she wanted was to go to Alik's apartment and dance, to kiss and drink tea and talk. He was more gentle, tender, and affectionate than anyone she had known. His caresses seemed different somehow, because they were the caresses of a foreigner. Furthermore, it was the first time she had enjoyed the luxury of a man's kisses without the fear of interruption. With the brief exception of Eddie in Leningrad, she had never before known a man with an apartment of his own.

There were other things that attracted her to Alik, little things, like his accent and his voice on the telephone. And bigger things, too. One evening as they were walking near the opera house, she asked about his family in America. He told Marina he did not have a mother. Was she dead? Marina asked.

"I don't want to talk about it—it's too painful." Later he said that his mother was dead and that he had been raised by an aunt. And to Marina, the fact that they were both orphans, above all the fact that they had both lost their mothers, was a significant bond. She told Alik that her parents were dead, too, but said nothing about being illegitimate. After that, they scarcely ever spoke of their pasts.

Alik told Marina that he was twenty-four, almost as old as Anatoly, and Marina found that attractive, too. He also told her that he had renounced his American citizenship and could never go back to the United States. But that revelation in no way diminished his appeal. It was flattery enough that he was an American and that, for the moment at least, his choice seemed to have fallen on her.

One evening toward the middle of April, Alik took Marina to his apartment and began to kiss her until he reached such a point of desire that he said, with "madness in his eyes," as Marina describes it, that she must go home immediately or he would compel her to stay with him until morning. Terrified and delighted, Marina grabbed her coat and ran home. When she told Valya what had happened, she smiled and said, "I see."

After that, Alik did not call for a couple of days. The next time they saw each other was April 18, only a month and a day after they had first met. Alik took her hands, looked gravely into her eyes, and said to her quietly, "Marina, I'd like you to be my wife. I've no idea whether you'll agree. I don't make much, but I have a little saved up. You'd have to go on working. Are you afraid of marrying a foreigner?"

"You silly," Marina replied. She was willing to marry him, she said, but she wanted to wait a bit. Alik wanted to get married in May.

"What will other people say?" Marina exclaimed. "We've known each other such a short time. Besides, my mama said May is an unhappy month. You should never get married in May."

Alik said her mother's superstitions were nonsense. He refused to wait until June. They must marry right away or they must part. Not, he added, that it would be easy for him to part. But he could not bear to go on seeing her and not having her.

Marina went home that night and told Valya that the American had asked her to marry him. She begged Valya to prepare Uncle Ilya for an interview with Alik.

The next day Alik put on his holiday best: a black suit, a white shirt and tie, even a dark blue hat. As he and Marina climbed the three narrow flights to Ilya and Valya's apartment, he stopped at nearly every step. "Oh, my God, what will I say?" he groaned. "Please help me out." He was pale and his knees were shaking as he waited on the landing, summoning courage to ring the bell.

"My heart is pounding," he said.

"Mine too," Marina replied.

"He'll probably chase me away."

"I don't know what he'll do." They felt like a pair of conspirators.

Ilya met Alik in the living room and Marina went apprehensively into the kitchen with her aunt. Her cheeks flushed with embarrassment, she asked: "Aunt Valya, is Uncle Ilya in a good mood today?"

Valya nodded in the affirmative.

"Do you know what he's going to say?"

Valya had no idea.

Ilya, meanwhile, was asking Alik a battery of the usual questions. He said that Marina was still very flighty. She was fickle and immature, and she wasn't ready to get married. Then he asked Alik if he had the proper papers. Although he was an official of the MVD, Ilya, as he examined Alik's documents, overlooked a fact that might have been critical in giving his consent. Alik did not have a regular Soviet passport, but a special document for the so-called stateless person, the foreigner who does not have Soviet citizenship and may or may not have retained citizenship of another country. Ilya later explained that he was not expert in that type of document.[2] He thought it was a special residence permit issued to a foreigner during his first three years in Russia, and he believed that Alik was already a citizen of the U.S.S.R. Had he had any other impression, he said, he would have withheld his consent to the marriage. As it was, he took the precaution of asking: "And what about America, Alik? Do you intend to go back?"

Alik swore that he did not, and Ilya took him at his word.

After twenty minutes or so, Ilya called Marina in from the kitchen. "So it's getting married you lovebirds have in mind. Alik, here, asks if he can marry you. I told him what kind of little bird you are and he has promised to reform you. Do you consent to marry him?"

Marina answered that she did.

"Marriage is a serious thing," Ilya said. "Personally, I think it's too soon. But if I say No, Marina will blame me if her life is unhappy later on. If you think you'll be happy together, then it's not for me to refuse. Only, live with one another in peace. If you fight or if anything goes wrong, settle it yourselves. Don't come to me with your troubles."

Marina broke in like a little girl. "Does that mean you are saying Yes, Uncle Ilya?"

"I am. Let's drink to it." The four of them went into the kitchen and sat at the table, drinking cognac.

During their lunch hour the next day, April 20, Marina and Alik went to ZAGS, the bureau where Soviet citizens go to register birth and death, marriage and divorce. The two old biddies who presided over the front corridor said, "Which did you come for, to be married or divorced?" Alik announced they had come to be married and produced his residence permit. The unfamiliar document puzzled the old ladies. When Alik told them that he was a foreigner, they instructed him to proceed to another ZAGS office and painstakingly wrote out the address.

A gray-haired gentleman greeted Marina and Alik pleasantly at the second ZAGS and motioned them into a chair. There they made out separate applications and the old man promised to relay the papers higher up. He suggested that they come back in a week, but was unable, in response to their questions, to reassure them or give them any notion whether their application would be approved.

That evening, Marina and Alik planted seeds in the window boxes on his balcony. His thoughts on the future, Alik said he hoped they would have a son.

Marina reproached him gaily: "We're not even married yet, and already you're dreaming of a son!"

"Do you solemnly promise me a son?" he asked.

She giggled, "I promise."

They decided to name him David. Marina knew the name from a novel by Theodore Dreiser, and she liked it. Alik went into the kitchen and came back with a sheet of paper. He placed it in front of Marina and instructed her to write: "I promise that we will have a son. We will call him David. Marina Prusakova, April 20, 1961."

The next evening they went window shopping for furniture and had supper with Ilya and Valya. As always, Alik got along splendidly with them. Later, as they were sitting in a little park near her apartment house, Alik was rather downcast. He asked Marina to come home with him for the night. "You always tease me so. We've applied to be married now. What are you frightened of? Please, Marina."

Marina rose and walked away, tears streaming down her face. "They're all just alike," she thought. "They all want the same thing. What do they take me for—a fool? They think I'm not even worth marrying."

Alik caught up with her. "Forgive me, Marina. I didn't mean to hurt your feelings. But really it is a strain. I didn't know you cared so much about a ceremony."

"It's not the ceremony," Marina replied. "I'm hurt because you're just like all the others. I don't ever want to see you again."

She went home in a fearful cacophony of feelings. She had meant it when she said that she never wanted to see him again. Applying at ZAGS had been nothing but a trick. He did not want to marry her at all. "What does this

American take me for—a fool?" she asked herself again and again.

She was angry at Alik. If he wanted her that badly, he would have to ask to be forgiven and marry her. Before, she had wanted to marry him because she cared for him. Now she would make him marry her on principle. But in the morning when she woke up, she felt that she did, in fact, love him.

At lunchtime the next day, Alik appeared at the pharmacy to apologize. He refused to go back to work unless Marina forgave him, and she did. She even agreed to phone ZAGS for news of their application. But the following week was a long one for both of them. Sometimes she telephoned ZAGS and there was no news. Other times the telephone rang and rang, and no one answered. Each evening when he arrived at the Prusakovs' for dinner, Alik scanned Marina's face anxiously. "Do you think they'll let us get married?" he said again and again. Marina asked what he would do if they were refused? Go to Moscow, Alik insisted, and appeal to the Foreign Ministry. What, Marina wanted to know, did the Foreign Ministry have to do with marriages? He said only that he would go to the "very highest" level.

Finally, Marina was asked to appear at ZAGS in person on April 27. When she got there, she was told that permission had been granted. "Why are you marrying him?" the gray-haired man asked. "Really and truly, couldn't you have found yourself a Russian?"

"I've plenty of Russians to choose from," Marina answered. "It's just that I like him and want to marry him."

"Well, it's none of my business," the old man said. He told Marina to come back with Alik on Sunday, April 30, at eleven o'clock in the morning for the wedding ceremony.[3]

News spread like a brush fire that Marina had been given permission to marry "her American," and by no means everyone was pleased. The girls at the pharmacy were in high excitement, but Tamara, a slightly older woman in whom Marina confided, had doubts. She was convinced that of the two men Marina had been seeing, it was Anatoly whom she loved.

"But what would other people say?" Marina objected. "He's so gangling and tall, and he isn't the least bit handsome."

"And who would you be getting married for?" Tamara asked. "Other people —or yourself?"

Anatoly, too, reacted quickly. He asked Marina to meet him in a café, and there he wished her the best of luck. But he remarked that "no one falls in love in two weeks." It was his opinion that Marina had chosen Alik "because foreigners have such privileges here." Marina was stung, partly because it was Anatoly who was accusing her, and partly because there was truth in what he said.

Marina is the first to say that "I married Alik because he was American." It was almost as if, being the only American in Minsk, he had the right to pick anyone he pleased. It would have been an act of lèse-majesté to refuse. But Marina adds, "I married him because I liked him. He was neat and clean and better looking than Anatoly. I was more in love with him than with anybody else at the time."

She also concedes that his apartment played a role in her decision and that she might not have married him without it. For Marina had always felt unwanted and "in the way." All her life she had dreamed of having a room of her own. She had seen many a marriage turned into a nightmare of animosity for lack of a decent place to live, and for her, as for many girls she knew, the great lottery of Soviet life was to find a man you loved—who had an apartment.

The apartment also played a role in guaranteeing the consent of her Uncle Ilya. For Ilya wanted his own apartment to himself. He may, moreover, have wanted Marina married so that he could once again enjoy the full-time attention of his wife. How else explain the fact that Ilya, a Russian chauvinist and a xenophobe, quickly gave his consent to his niece's marriage to Alik, a foreigner and a factory hand, and discouraged her interest in Anatoly, a Russian with a much better future? Ilya himself called Marina "flighty," and he knew that he could influence her choice. Yet he never bothered to meet Anatoly and see with his own eyes who was the better man and who would give Marina a better life. For Ilya there was no comparison. The difference lay not in the qualities the two men possessed, but in the apartment one of them possessed.

But there were other currents stirring, emotional currents, and they, too, powerfully affected Marina's choice. Because of her illegitimate birth, she had felt like an outsider all her life. From her earliest years she showed the way she felt in her choice of friends, in her reluctance to join the Pioneers and the Komsomol, and in her long string of alien and exotic beaux. Marrying Alik, for her, was the culmination of a lifelong flirtation with the outsider.

For all these reasons, and possibly because of what she considered "incestuous" attractions to her first cousin Valentin and, perhaps less consciously, to her harsh stepfather Alexander Medvedev, Marina felt impelled to marry "out," just as far out as she could go. And who could be farther out than an American, a native of her country's feared and admired enemy, the United States?

There was something else about Alik that attracted her, a kinship they shared. He, too, obviously felt "outside" and alone in Minsk, but it went further back. Marina believed that he was an orphan, and that made her feel enormously sympathetic toward him, as if they were brother and sister. Both obviously felt the same way about their early lives. Both rejected their past so completely that they did not tell each other anything about it—ever. Because he was older than she was, Marina could look up to Alik. They would support and take care of each other. Alik was exotic—yet somehow familiar.

There is one other way in which Marina was nearly fated to marry Alik. He brought her the attention she craved. They had only to walk down the street hand in hand for heads to swivel and eyes to pop. It was unimaginably gratifying to her. For at a deeper level, Alik's choice of her and the attention it brought, confirmed the feeling she had always had that she was different and special. The mere fact of being married to him would mean that for the rest of her life she was going to be singled out as someone special. Such outer recognition was in profound correspondence with the inner feeling she had had all along.

Marina had no thought of leaving Russia. In spite of his other attractions as a foreigner, she did not marry Alik for his passport. She believed him when he said that he did not want to go back to America, that, in fact, he could not go back. It was only one of several lies he told her. She did not know that, even before they met, he had written to the American Embassy in Moscow to request his passport and help in returning to the United States. Nor did she know that he had lied about his age. He was twenty-one, not twenty-four. And he was not an orphan—his mother was alive.

And so Marina made the choice she was bound to make. "Maybe I was not in love with Alik as I ought to have been. But I thought I loved him." And perhaps she did, for she made her decision with few regrets and surprisingly few backward glances. She had an instinct that she was doing what was right for her, the thing ordained by her destiny to be special. The step she was taking was in harmony with so many of her needs, both inner and outer, as to have been almost inevitable. What, after all, was "love" compared to the forces that were carrying her toward Alik? And were those forces not also love?

What of Alik? Why did he marry Marina? He acted for a variety of reasons, of which he himself appears to have been aware of only one. He confided to his Diary that he was still in love with Ella Germann, the dark-haired Jewish girl at the factory who had rejected his proposal of marriage three months before. He was, he wrote, marrying Marina "to hurt Ella."[4]

Of course, Marina herself played a part in his decision. She set her cap for Alik and she won. From the outset, she showed just the right blend of eagerness and hesitation. She made him feel jealous with her many boyfriends; she made him feel wanted with her sympathetic visits to the hospital. Then, too, she came as part of a package, a family who made Alik feel welcome, and especially an aunt who may have reminded him of his own aunt in New Orleans, a female relative whom he genuinely cared about. Finally, Marina teased him sexually, exactly as an American girl of her age might have done. She led him on, made him desire her, then refused herself unless they were married. Alik could have searched the length and breadth of Russia and not found a girl as American in her sexual behavior as Marina. He, too, may have felt that she was exotic—yet somehow familiar.

But there were other, deeper reasons that enabled Alik, for the first time in his life, to think about marriage at all. Emotionally, he was freer than he had ever been before, free, that is, of his mother and the inner conflicts she incited in him. Thousands of miles from home, he had not written her in more than a year. Apparently, it was only at such enormous distance from Marguerite, emotionally as well as geographically, that he was able to summon up the strength to marry, that is, to replace her in his life.

While Alik's distance from his mother may have been the principal key to his emotional wholeness at this time, it was not the only one. He was, in Russia, receiving tremendous support from his environment: a job from which he could not be fired, an apartment, his "Red Cross" subsidy. And in addition to the government's munificence, he was on the receiving end of a great deal of generosity from the men and women he met. Left to themselves and unafraid, Russians are extraordinarily hospitable. They go out of their way to help the foreigner.

Thus, in Russia, Alik was liberated a little from the American myth of independence, the idea that it is a sin to be weak and in need. Russians do not feel that
way. Their history has been far too studded with catastrophe, each family has
suffered far too many random disasters, for people to cherish such illusions.
Dependence is a reality of life—the weak simply accept succor from the strong.
There is a huge amount of cheerful give and take.

Alik was deeply dependent—and he was ashamed of it. It was something he
tried to deny, but in Russia he hardly had to bother. There, this quality of his
received protective coloration—from his special needs as a foreigner, from the
naturalness of giving and taking and from the generosity of nearly everyone
around him. And, being camouflaged on the outside, his need was very nearly
masked from Alik himself. Cradled and buttressed by Mother Russia, he was on
more gracious terms with himself than he had ever been before.

Marina says that Alik was happy in her country, happier than he had ever
been before and was ever to be again. He was receiving an enormous emotional
subsidy from everything and everyone around him. But for all that Mother Russia
was giving him, it was not enough, for his dependence was bottomless. He disliked
his job as a manual laborer, he disliked the dull provincial city of Minsk. He
wanted to continue his education, but thus far Soviet authorities had taken no
action on his request to attend the Patrice Lumumba University of Friendship
of Peoples in Moscow to study as a full-time student—not technical subjects, but
economics, philosophy, and his real forte, so he believed, politics. He was no
longer interested in Soviet citizenship and had already made the opening moves
in his campaign to return to the United States. It is paradoxical that just as he
was courting Marina, preparing to accept her as his future wife and acting
positively to meet his needs, he was also planning to reject her homeland, the
country that had given him the energy and inner coherence to marry in the first
place.

For more than a year, no one at the American Embassy in Moscow had
known the whereabouts, or the fate, of Lee Harvey Oswald. Then in February
of 1961, the embassy received a letter from him postmarked Minsk.[5] Oswald
accused the embassy first of ignoring an earlier letter, which he had in fact not
written; then he stated his desire to return to the United States, "that is if we could
come to some agreement concerning the dropping of any legal proceeding's
against me"; and reminded the embassy of its obligations toward him as an
American citizen, although it was by no means certain that he was one. Despite
his attempt to renounce his citizenship, and his fear that he might have committed
some crime for which he could be prosecuted, he acted as if he expected the very
best from the embassy and the American government.

Oswald also stated that he was applying by letter rather than in person
because he could not leave Minsk without permission. That permission might
easily have been obtained, but the authorities would have been alerted that he
intended to visit the American Embassy. Oswald preferred not to tip his hand to
the Russians until he was certain of his reception by the Americans. Actually the

letter did alert police officials in Moscow of Oswald's intention, and his subsidy from the Red Cross was stopped immediately. But it was many months before the authorities in Minsk became aware that their American wanted to go home.

The embassy's reply, dated February 28, 1961, asked Oswald to appear in person for an interview.[6] But, puzzled by Oswald's reference to "legal proceeding's," the American consul, Richard Snyder, in a dispatch to the State Department the same day, inquired whether Oswald might have to face prosecution on his return and, if so, could Snyder be frank and tell him so? If it became clear that Oswald had committed no expatriating act, Snyder added, he would be inclined to return the boy's American passport to him through the open mails.[7]

Since the case was not an urgent one, Snyder had to wait for a reply. The answer, when it came, was that the Department had no way of knowing whether Oswald might have violated some state or federal law and was in no position to issue guarantees. Nor was the embassy under any circumstances to return Oswald's passport to him through the Soviet mails.[8]

Oswald was overjoyed by the embassy's reply, and on March 12, five days before his first meeting with his future wife, he wrote a new letter.[9] It was quite as impertinent as the first. "I find it inconveniet to come to Moscow for the sole purpose of an interview," he wrote. Requesting instead that the embassy send him a questionnaire, he ended the letter petulantly. "I understand that personal interview's undoubtedly make to work of the Embassy staff lighter, than written correspondence, however, in some case's other means must be employed."

Snyder's reply, dated March 24 and carefully drafted to enable Oswald to use it to obtain the necessary permission to travel to Moscow, again requested that he appear in person.[10] And there, for the moment, the matter rested. Alik Oswald was caught up in his courtship and forthcoming marriage, a marriage that appears to have been incompatible with any firm desire to leave Russia. He was happier now and not so lonely. Perhaps he was wavering in his plan, but he had not forgotten.

7

The Wedding

SUNDAY, April 30, was sunny and clear. The drip, drip, drip of thawing icicles was forgotten, but the wind was icy and a lingering hint of winter hovered in the air. Marina rose early in the morning to find that her aunt had been up nearly all night putting the finishing touches on her wedding dress, a short white gown with a tiny green pattern, like miniature blades of grass.

At ten o'clock Alik arrived, rather pale. "You look so pretty today!" he exclaimed at the sight of his bride. He urged Aunt Valya to come to the registry office, but she, in high spirits, declined; she had a wedding feast to prepare. And so, accompanied only by their witnesses—Lyalya Petrusevich, who lived across the hall, and her current boyfriend, Valentin—the pair set off in a taxi.

At ZAGS they were received by the same old man who had handled their request to be married. Seated behind a large desk he greeted them gravely, with fatherly familiarity. The only ceremony was the signing of his registry book. Afterward he shook both of them by the hand. "It won't be easy," he told them. "Anything can happen in life, but it's better if you support one another. You're young, you're high-spirited, but in marriage you must give in a little and make allowances for each other's characters." Then, in a lighter mood, he added: "Next year, if there's a baby, come back and register *it*. A baby, by all means. But a divorce, no! I don't want you back here for that!"

He turned with a solicitous air to Alik. "Do you really love this woman? Do you want to marry her? It's for the rest of your life, you know."

Alik emitted a nervous "Yes," and with a bit of a flourish, the old man placed the marriage stamp in Alik's passport. Then he admonished the bride: "Be a good wife to him, now. No looking at the other boys!" With that he affixed the stamp to her passport.

They departed in a lighthearted mood, and as they went out the door, Marina peered over Alik's shoulder to inspect his marriage stamp. She noticed, with vague surprise, that his date of birth was 1939. Out on the street, with no one in earshot, she turned to him. "Why did you lie? You are only twenty-one. Why did you tell me you were twenty-four?"

"I was afraid you wouldn't take me seriously," Alik said. "You made fun of Sasha. You said he was only twenty and you'd never marry such a baby."

It was true she had wanted someone older. But the pang of learning that her bridegroom had lied to her and that he was, after all, only two years older than she, was buried in the excitement of her wedding day. "You *are* a baby," she said to him. And she let the subject drop.

There were peals of laughter from the wedding party as they reached the Svisloch River. The bride and groom stood hand in hand on the bridge staring down at the water below. Alik picked a few narcissi from Marina's bouquet and dropped the petals, one by one, into the sun-streaked river.

By the time they returned to the Prusakovs', the early guests had arrived. Many brought gifts for the newlyweds. But before the celebration could begin in earnest, there was a job to be done: the bride and her belongings had to be moved to her new home. So Lyalya and Valentin gathered up Marina's clothing, along with pillows and the homemade feather mattress which was Valya's wedding gift to the couple, and bundled the whole lot, with the bride and groom, into a taxicab.

Marina blushed as they pulled up in front of Alik's building. The mattress and pillows, to say nothing of her entire wardrobe, tumbled out of the cab, proclaiming to all the world that this was to be her wedding night. She was embarrassed, too, as Lyalya and Valentin placed flowers all around the bed in Alik's apartment and, with a final loving pat, laid her nightgown on the pillow. At this, even Alik flushed. Then he joined the others in laughter. "Never mind," he said. "When you get married, I'll fix *you!*"

Back at the Prusakovs', they quickly found that Valya and her sisters-in-law had outdone themselves. The dining table was piled high with a great variety of Russian *zakuski,* or hors d'oeuvres: red and black caviar, pâté, crab salad, and salami in a sauce of pepper and wine. There were stuffed Bulgarian peppers and a shimmering fish in aspic. There was fruit, of course. And towering over all was the wedding cake. It had many layers, pink and yellow buttercream roses, and an inscription to the bride and groom: "To Alik and Marina—A Happy Life." It had been made at the bidding of Aunt Lyuba in the kitchen of the Belorussian Council of Ministers where she worked.

As for the celebrants, they included Marina's three aunts and their families —Valya and Ilya, of course, Lyuba and Vasily Axyonov, Musya and Vanya Berlov and their four children—and several of the Prusakovs' neighbors. Marina had invited several colleagues from the pharmacy, but they all found an excuse not to come, apparently because the groom was a foreigner. Two friends of Alik's were on hand: Erich Titovyets, whom Marina had already met, and curly-headed Pavel Golovachev, whom she was meeting for the first time.

The guests soon were seated before the table. Vanya Berlov struggled to his feet. "Valya," he admonished his sister-in-law. "Have you forgotten how to cook? Things are usually tasty at your house but suddenly, today, they're bitter." The other guests took up the chorus, *"Gorko, gorko"* ("Bitter, bitter"), in keeping with the Russian custom that the wedding wine is bitter until sweetened by the kisses of bride and groom.

Marina reddened with embarrassment. At length, after much shrinking on her part and much shouting by the others, she relented. She and Alik stood in full view of the company and he kissed her firmly on the lips. Only then did the guests resume their feasting. But every few minutes the raillery was renewed. Someone would shout: *"Gorko!"* The chorus would grow louder, the bride and groom kissed, and the guests once again fell to feasting.

Before long, drinking gave way to dancing. Uncle Ilya, as always on such occasions, danced with all the ladies and gaily kissed every one. The bride, by contrast, was an enigma even to herself. She succumbed to some nameless confusion while dancing with Ilya and left him standing on the dance floor. "My God!" he groaned. "My own niece, and she won't even dance with me!"

Marina played a trick on Alik. Because she wanted to flirt with the men at her wedding, she told him it was the Russian custom for the bride to dance with everyone. It was her last chance, after all. One by one the men politely asked Alik for permission. He very affably smiled and nodded his assent. Marina danced with all of them, while Alik spent most of his wedding party standing by himself in a corner.

Feeling pity for her new nephew, the kind-hearted Valya took him in hand and taught him how to waltz. The wedding guests then raised a chorus for Alik to dance with his bride. With his cheeks pink and his eyes glowing, he did a few turns with Marina as if he had been waltzing all his life.

When the guests asked him to sing an American song, Alik obliged with a Russian song instead, the popular "Moscow Evenings," of which he had memorized every verse. Then he and his friends Erich and Pavel sang a trio, "Chattanooga Choo-Choo." Finally he sang his favorite, an Armenian drinking song with Russian words:

> Where can I find the sweet words?
> How can I say that I love you?
> You have brought me so much happiness in life
> I sing to you and share with you my life.[1]

Soon it was approaching midnight. Valya led Marina into the kitchen and gave her a glass of vodka—"for courage." Marina then vanished into the bathroom to dress, and when she emerged, she and Alik said their goodbyes. "Good luck, my boy!" Ilya said, giving his own brand of gruff encouragement. The guests gathered on the stairway and waved to the bride and groom.

Alik and Marina walked the few blocks to his apartment. Suddenly, as they reached the door of his building, he swept her up in his arms, told her to hang on for dear life, and carried her the four flights upstairs. On his own threshold Alik paused, then gently lifted her across. He never told Marina that it was an American custom.

The two of them stood there bewildered. "Are we really married?" Alik said.

"Take a look at our passports," Marina replied.

"You're a sly one," he said to her. "I didn't mean to marry you—you tricked me into it."

"Yes, I *am* clever," she agreed. "But we'll divorce tomorrow if you like."

"You're tricking me again," he said. "Tomorrow's May Day and all the offices are closed." Then, catching sight of her nightgown, neatly folded on the pillow, Alik said: "It's awfully pretty. I've never seen you wear it."

"Oh—there's plenty of time," Marina said. And she insisted on dancing to the phonograph.

When it came to it, she knew nothing about sex after all. She tried to lie still and be quiet. "Careful," she kept whispering and he, who was very gentle, would stop.

Finally he said to her: "If we stop each time you tell me to, it'll be a year before we get anywhere. Just close your eyes and try to get through it!"

When it was over and the first light was coming through the window, he kissed her and remarked, very thoughtfully: "Thank you for saving yourself for me. Frankly, I didn't think you had."

Later, they were awakened by a knock at the door. Alik opened it and there, to his utter bewilderment, stood Aunt Valya holding a white plate in her hand. Suddenly she lifted the plate and hurled it to the floor.

"What's that about?" Alik asked in astonishment.

"It's for luck," Valya said. "The two of you pick up the pieces."

They dressed and went to Valya's for breakfast. It was May Day, a gray, drizzly morning, and Ilya was on duty in Stalin Square checking passes for the big parade. In a buoyant mood the newlyweds decided to try to find him. They were going to pay a call across town, and maybe he would let them by without a pass. Ilya was easy to pick out. He was in uniform, eagle-like and very tall. To their great disappointment, he was abrupt with them and refused to allow them into the square. "But I'm your niece," Marina pleaded with him.

"At home you're my niece," he corrected her. "Here, I'm on duty."

Crestfallen, the bride and groom walked away. "What a bureaucrat he is!" Alik grumbled.

When they reached their destination, they received a warm welcome from Marina's friends, an older woman and her husband. They plied the newly married pair with vodka, and the husband ran out several times for reinforcements. All day the four of them talked politics, an unlikely pastime for the bride. The hosts asked many questions about America, and Alik was happy to oblige. But what he really wanted to talk about was Russia. The older couple recalled the hardships of the German occupation of Minsk, and the terror and injustice of the Stalin years. But critical as they were of their country's faults, they were utterly loyal to the Soviet Union.

Marina was pleased by this first day of her married life, grateful for her friends' welcome and their open-hearted cordiality to her American husband. As for Alik's steering the conversation toward politics and his rapt attention to everything that was said, she saw nothing surprising in that. She was not interested in politics herself. Politics were in the masculine sphere, and it was to be a long time before she woke up to the fact that her husband's interest in politics was anything out of the ordinary.

The next evening, the evening of May 2, they paid a call on friends of Alik's. They were Alexander Ziger, his wife and two daughters, Eleonora and Anita, who had been like a family to Alik from his earliest days in Minsk. Ziger, a black-haired, bushy-browed man of somewhat spherical shape, was deputy chief engineer at the Minsk Radio Plant. He had met Alik nearly a year and a half before, during his first visit to the plant on January 12, 1960, and they had seen each other frequently ever since, both at the plant and in Ziger's home. As the weeks and months went by, Alik had courted both daughters, especially the younger and livelier, Anita. Now, he wanted to introduce them to his bride.

At first, only Eleonora and Anita were at home. They greeted the newlyweds warmly, sat them down, and plied them with coffee. Marina took an immediate liking to Anita, a spirited girl who was constantly erupting into peals of laughter. But she detected something else in the dark and sultry Eleonora. That something was jealousy. When she asked Alik about it later, he conceded that Eleonora had wanted to marry him, but Mrs. Ziger warned him against her elder daughter on the grounds that she might try to use him. His choice then fell on the mettlesome Anita. But she rejected him in favor of a Hungarian.

When the Zigers returned, Mrs. Ziger, a short, plump woman, greeted Marina with great warmth and kissed her tenderly. "My dear child," she said almost immediately, "consider yourself lucky to have married an American!" Thus, on only the second evening of her marriage, did politics again intrude on Marina's life.

The Zigers' story was an extraordinary one. Neither of them was Russian; he was a Pole and a Jew, she a Belorussian and a Catholic. Both had grown up in eastern Poland, a territory annexed by the Soviet Union in 1939, but by that time the Zigers had abandoned their native land and settled in Argentina. There, in Buenos Aires, Mr. Ziger won an engineering degree and went to work in a factory. There, too, his daughters grew up, proved talented, and acquired musical educations. Only Maria Ziger, the mother, was unhappy. She was homesick for her native land, longed to hear the sighing of the birch trees, longed to be laid to rest in the Polish earth. But that soil was not Polish any more. It was Russian, and going home was out of the question.

Then, in the 1950s, everything changed. Stalin died and Khrushchev, with aggressive acumen, launched a campaign to persuade people like the Zigers to return to Russia. His blandishments fell on credulous ears. The Zigers believed —and came home.

They bitterly regretted their decision. Everyone in Khrushchev's country was watched, they discovered, and none more closely than those who had chosen to live abroad. Eleonora and Anita suffered most. Both passed the examinations for the renowned Music Conservatory in Moscow. Yet neither was accepted— because they had lived abroad. A ceiling had been set on the Zigers' lives, and, whatever their talents, they could have no hope of going higher. Disillusioned, they applied again and again for visas to leave Russia. Their applications were ignored.

Mr. Ziger refused to give up. He told Marina and Alik: "In a year, or two years, or five, or ten, I believe I'll get what I'm hoping for. Of course it's going to take time. But we'll get our visas some day."

To Marina his remarks, and indeed the entire evening, were a revelation. Here was a family who had lived in the West and had concluded that life there was incomparably better than anything Russia had to offer. It was an idea contrary to everything Marina had been taught. She was startled, moreover, when Mrs. Ziger led her into the kitchen and said to her pointedly: "My dear child, if Alik ever has the slightest chance of leaving, you must by all means go too."

Astonished, Marina assured Mrs. Ziger that Alik had no thought of leaving her country. But later, it occurred to her that, at the time of her marriage, Mrs. Ziger already knew what she herself did not: that Alik Oswald intended to go home.

Oswald's Diary confirms not only that the Zigers were aware of his intention, but that Mr. Ziger had had a hand in shaping it. From the very beginning of their acquaintance, he had warned Oswald against taking Soviet citizenship, an act that would forever close the door on his leaving the U.S.S.R.

May 1, 1960: At night I visit with the Zegers daughters . . . Zeeger advises me to go back to U.S.A. It's the first voice of oppossition I have heard. I respect Zeeger, he has seen the world. He says many things, and relats many things I do not know about the U.S.S.R. I begin to feel uneasy inside, its true!

Jan. 4–31, 1961: I am stating to reconsider my desire about staying The work is drab the money I get has nowhere to be spent. . . .

Feb. 1: I make my first request to American Embassy, Moscow . . . I stated "I would like to go back to U.S."

March 1–16: I now live in a state of expectation about going back to the U.S. I confided with Zeeger he supports my jugement but warnes me not to tell any Russians. . . .[2]

The May Day holiday over, on Wednesday, May 3, Marina and Alik went back to work and their everyday married life began. Each day, six days a week, the alarm clock went off and Alik rose at seven. He dressed quietly and fixed his breakfast, which was invariably the same: coffee, a hard-boiled egg, and four tiny sweet rolls. Then he sat on the bed beside the sleeping Marina. He kissed his bride and told her, "I hate so much to go off and leave you here." After a few minutes he would tear himself away. "Look out, now. Don't oversleep," he would call as he went out the door. At 9:30 the alarm went off again. Marina struggled out of bed, sipped the coffee he had left her, pulled on her clothes, and dragged herself off to work.

Alik met her every evening outside the pharmacy at 5:30. They would stroll for a bit, nod to friends on the street, window shop, and then repair to the cafeteria opposite their apartment house for dinner. It was a dingy, bare place called the "Café-Avtomat," which was staffed not by vending machines but by tiny, officious waitresses swathed in white who were forever shouting "Next!" and "Hurry up!" to those who were standing in line. The food was not very good, but Alik preferred it to Marina's cooking.

By the time they reached home, sunset would be flooding the apartment with a reddish glow. Alik would vanish onto the balcony to weed and water the flowers. Then he loved nothing better than to sit outside with his feet propped against the window boxes, leaning back in his chair and gazing out at the night sky and the river. Sometimes he used his binoculars to scan the horizon and in particular, the main street of Minsk to his left, to see what was playing at the movies. The evening was over when, in the concluding phase of his ritual, Alik tuned in to the Voice of America at ten to listen to the English-language news.

Money burned a hole in Marina's pocket, so she was only too happy to turn over to Alik what she earned and allow him to take charge. He paid for everything, from the groceries they shopped for together to the ice cream and halvah they carried home every night as a concession to his sweet tooth. The first few weeks they spent a good deal on records—classical for him, popular for her—and furniture: a low Georgian bed, or *takhta,* a tiny child's bureau, and four chairs.

Marina was proud of their apartment, of the spare, modern, uncluttered look they had given it, and of her own sprightly touches of color—a spray of birch leaves here, a bouquet of flowers there. But she quickly discovered that her husband had a domestic streak, too. Only a few nights after they were married she came home to a surprise: a new kitchen table and tablecloth and a new set of silverware. Not only had he bought the table and set it, he had decorated it with a bunch of spring flowers he had stolen in a public park. But it was not, as some brides might suppose, a hint that he would like to start taking his evening meal at home. "Better the cafeteria," he said to her, "than what you fix."

He bought her another surprise—white lace curtains. When he got them home, they were the wrong length; his solution was manly and straightforward. He took a pair of scissors and sheared them off around the bottom. At woodworking he was more accomplished. He made little legs for their bed and fashioned a rod to hang their clothes on in the closet.

But Alik's main concern was washing and cleaning. If he did not meet Marina at the pharmacy, the first thing he did when he arrived home was wash the breakfast dishes and mop the floor. Then, on the days when they had hot water, he did the laundry. When Marina came in the downstairs door, she could hear her husband, four flights up, singing the Volga Boatman's Song or some other Slavic melody. Entering the apartment she would be greeted by a cloud of steam.

"My girl is home, is she?" Alik said, bent over the bathtub.

"She is."

"I'm doing the laundry."

"So I see."

Alik was ashamed of the fact that he did manual labor. He did not want Marina to see his grimy work clothes. When she offered to do them herself, he snatched them away from her and said, "I don't want you washing my dirty clothes!"

If Marina for any reason came home late, she would find Alik waiting at the top of the stairs with an angry, mistrustful look that she was soon to know very well. "Where have you been?" he would ask. "I called the pharmacy and they said you had already left."

"I was shopping with Sonya," Marina might answer truthfully.

"Sonya—or who?" he would ask.

"In a half hour I couldn't do much," Marina said, "no matter who I was with."

Alik was extraordinarily jealous. Even if she was only a few minutes late, he demanded a full explanation of where she had been, with whom, and what she had been doing.

The first few weeks of their marriage, Marina and Alik spent most of their free time by themselves. On weekends they often went to one of the two large lakes outside Minsk for a picnic. Both lakes were in marshy areas surrounded by birch groves, clumps of aspen, and clearings with tiny daisies in bloom. Alik would take a boat and row Marina out to an island in the middle of the lake. There they picnicked and he lay in the sunshine by the hour trying to get a tan, usually ending up with a sunburn instead. Marina liked to lie on her stomach in the grass, watching the minnows and the baby frogs darting in the shallow water. Once, using his T-shirt as a net, they spent a long time splashing in the water in a futile effort to snare some fish.

A week or so after their wedding, they spent an evening with Marina's Uncle Vasya and Aunt Lyuba Axyonov. In an attempt to keep up with Uncle Vasya, Alik downed four shots of vodka. He was not used to it, and was soon drunk. They brewed some coffee to sober him up and he fell asleep on the sofa. But on the way home he was still tipsy and burst out with "Chattanooga Choo-Choo." "Hush," Marina told him. "The police will arrest you for being noisy." "Hell," he shouted, "it's a free country. No one will arrest a man for singing."

Another night they went to a movie, a Polish thriller about a stealthy Nazi spy who got off scot-free, unlike Soviet movies in which the enemy spy always got caught.

"I'd love a life like that," Alik commented as they came out of the theater.

Marina felt a stab of anxiety. Was it possible, she wondered for a fleeting second, that her American husband might be a spy, like the German villain of the movie? "Are you mad?" she inquired.

"I'd love the danger," came the spare rejoinder.

One evening, Alik took Marina to see his friend Pavel Golovachev, with whom he worked at the factory. With his fair hair, snub nose, and open, peasant features, Pavel was easy to write off as a hick from the country and Marina had done precisely that when she met him at her wedding. But when she saw his apartment, she realized that she could not have been more mistaken. Pavel occupied three rooms with the most sophisticated decor she had ever seen. He had fashioned a tape recorder and a television set of his own, and he had a vast collection of foreign tapes. Pavel, it appeared, was the son of a general, one of the great Russian air aces of World War II and a man who had twice received the highest combat award: Hero of the Soviet Union. The general was allowed to keep apartments in various parts of the country, and Pavel occupied one of them. By virtue of his father's position he qualified as a member of the Soviet aristocracy. Marina soon came to believe that he was an aristocrat in the Greek sense as well, one of the very "best." Open, friendly, frank, Pavel, or "Pavlik," was a "golden human being."

Because of his father's virtually invulnerable position, Pavel had grown up open and unafraid. He was not afraid, for example, to make a friend of the only American in Minsk, Lee Oswald. Nor was he afraid to talk to him frankly both about his country's virtues and shortcomings. But it soon became clear to Marina that her husband's liking for Pavel went well beyond the fact that he was one of the few people who could talk to him intelligently about politics. There was a small gadget on the wall of Alik's and Marina's apartment that had no apparent use. They supposed it to be a listening device, which led them to speculate about their friends and who might be informing on them. Marina asked about Pavel. Alik looked at her a long, meaningful second, and delivered a devastating answer. "I'd trust him," he said pointedly, "a whole lot sooner than I'd trust you."

Marina soon came to trust him, too. Pavel had many faults, but he was incapable of calculation and was, as the Oswalds were to learn, an utterly disinterested friend. In fact, Marina believes that Pavel was far and away her husband's closest friend in Russia, and probably the closest friend he ever had.

As for Pavel's opinion of Alik, he appears to have had his eyes open. Either on this first visit to Pavel's apartment or another very shortly thereafter, Marina found herself alone with her husband's friend, in the bathroom hunting for a towel. "What's Alik like at the factory?" she asked. "Do the other men like him?"

"They like him," Pavel replied, "but he's not quite one of them. You sense that he's reserved—that he holds himself a little bit aloof. Somehow he's different from the others."

"What do you mean?" Marina asked.

"Well," Pavel's eyes grew wide and thoughtful, "maybe it's that he's not completely open. He isn't straight from the heart, the way we Russians are."[3]

Alik had an unhappy experience at the factory only a fortnight after he was married. A special outing was planned, a weekend excursion by chartered bus to Riga and Leningrad. Alik knew his bride's love of Leningrad and wanted to give her a surprise. He signed up for the trip and said nothing to her about his plan. A day or so later he was given his money back and told that the trip was off. Alik thought no more about it until one Saturday when he went to work and noticed that a couple of his friends were missing. They had gone on the trip to Leningrad. Alik was furious at the deception. "Why couldn't they tell me to my face?" he fumed, when Marina finally pried it out of him. "This way it's so underhanded."

Still angry, he asked the Party organizer at the plant if he had been denied permission to go because he was a foreigner.

"Yes," the Party organizer said. "*You* have to have permission to go out of town, and that's usually a matter of days. I couldn't let you go on my own hook and I didn't want to keep everyone else waiting while the militia was making up its mind."

Alik never forgot. He never forgave the Party organizer and refused to have any more to do with him.

Marina also had an unpleasant experience, and it, too, had to do with Alik's being a foreigner. A week or two after she was married, a rumor swept the hospital and the pharmacy that she had been a prostitute. That, it was said, was why she had had to leave Leningrad. The rumor was traced back to her old beau, Sasha, now an intern in one of the wards. With Sasha known to be a disappointed suitor, the rumor would not have taken hold had Marina not married a foreigner. Her colleagues at the pharmacy were incensed. They had declined to come to the wedding because Alik was a foreigner, but this was another matter. They took Marina to the headquarters of the Komsomol and made her file a complaint that she had been unjustly slandered, which all of them signed as witnesses. Sasha was, in fact, issued a "warning" that he had behaved in a manner unworthy of the Komsomol. When Marina told Alik about the incident, he growled: "If you see Sasha, tell him not to show himself in front of me. I'll bash his head in." For good measure he added: "I'll break both of his legs."

Despite these ripples on the surface of their tranquility, the early weeks of their marriage were happy ones. But there was one thing that troubled Marina. Alik had never actually said that he loved her. Once when she asked him if he loved her, he replied impatiently, "You ought to know how I feel from the way I act." He seemed content, it was true, especially when they were together. But sometimes when he was sitting by himself Marina noticed that an enveloping thoughtfulness settled over him, as if he were unhappy or uncertain in some way. She suspected that he might be thinking about another woman.

Marina's suspicions were correct. Alik was still thinking about Ella Germann. In the early weeks of his marriage to Marina, he confided to his Diary:

May—The transistion of changing full love from [Ella] to Marina was very painfull esp. as I saw [Ella] almost every day at the factory but as the days and weeks went by I adjusted more and more my wife mentaly. . . . She is maddly in love with me from the very start.

June—A continuence of May, except that; we draw closer and closer, and I think very little now of Ella. . . .[4]

There was another woman in Alik's life whom Marina did not know about —his mother. Alik had told her that his mother was dead and she had no reason to doubt him. But a few weeks after they were married, she saw him reading a letter from home with such a thoughtful expression that she asked whether it contained bad news. An hour or so later he glanced up from the book he was reading and said: "Forgive me, Marina. That letter isn't from my aunt. It's from my mother."

Marina was startled. "Why didn't you tell me your mother was alive?"

"I didn't know we were going to get married. If people had known I had a mother, I was afraid it might cause her some unpleasantness."

After that Marina noticed that the arrival of a letter from his mother never seemed to raise her husband's spirits. "Don't you love her?" she asked.

"No. It's a long story," he explained. "We had a fight when my brother Robert got married. I didn't like her treatment of his wife." He told Marina to ask no more about it.

The pain of learning for a second time that her husband had lied to her was blunted by Marina's discovery that she was pregnant. From the moment they were married Alik wanted a child. When the first weeks went by with no sign, he suggested that he might have something wrong with him. "Maybe it's my fault. If there's no sign in another month we'll go to the doctor to be checked."

Marina was by no means so eager. She mixed herself some chemical contraceptives at the pharmacy. But she found them painful, and a week after they were married Alik hurled them across the room: "We won't use *those* any more." He offered to take precautions himself if she wanted to avoid a child. (Condoms are known in Russia as "galoshes.") But Marina was fatalistic, and they took no more precautions. She'd have an abortion (legal in Russia since 1955), she vaguely thought, if it came to that.

Then one day on a picnic they made love. It was a luminous day in June, cloudless and hot, with daisies and wildflowers in bloom. Alik was certain there would be a child after that. And a week later, standing at one of the marble-topped tables in the Café-Avtomat, Marina crumpled to the floor in a faint. It was the signal he had been waiting for. When they got back to their apartment building, he carried her tenderly upstairs and lowered her gently onto the bed. Sitting beside her, the tears streaming from his eyes, he told her for the first time that he loved her.

The next day he made her go to a doctor for confirmation. But the doctor threw up his hands and said it was too early. Shortly afterward, however, when he learned that Marina's menstrual period was overdue, Alik took her in his arms and danced gleefully around the room. "My girl is pregnant. I told you so. I promised. I'll be a father now."

Marina did not know it, but her husband had been twice treated in the Marine Corps for gonorrhea.[5] Perhaps that is why he suggested it might be his fault when she showed no sign of pregnancy in the early weeks of their marriage. Perhaps, too, the fear that he might be unable to have a child played a part in his elation.

Once she knew that she was pregnant, a change came over Marina. She had enjoyed making love before, but now she was repelled by it. When Alik approached her for a kiss, she had to summon up strength in order not to push him away. She thought she had made a mistake getting married. By this time she had learned about the existence of Ella, and all her confused emotions burst out in their first serious quarrel.

It was an evening later in June, and Marina and Alik were strolling through the park. A band was playing. They were standing beneath a tree, and Alik asked for a kiss. She refused. He wanted to know why.

"I don't know, Alka," she said. "Maybe I made a mistake. Maybe I don't love you after all."

"Do you want a divorce?" he asked.

"Maybe," she replied noncommittally.

"I ought to have married Ella after all," Alik said. "She at least loved me. Do you remember the morning after we were married—May Day? I went out on our balcony, and there was Ella on the street outside. She was crying. She left as soon as she saw me."

"A fine proof of love she gave you," Marina taunted. "Between you and her parents, she chose them. Poor Jewish girl. She was only crying out of jealousy, because someone took her little American away. She thought no one would have you."

Marina sat on a bench, shaking with sobs, while Alik went off by himself and paced among the trees. When he returned, he said: "Look, it's too late now. Suppose we *did* want a divorce, we've still got the baby to think of. Come on now. Let's go to a movie. That's enough of making each other miserable."

But the movie was sold out and they ambled home through the park. People were dancing in a pavilion. "Let's dance," he suggested. Marina refused.

"You don't know what you want," Alik said, trying to reason with her. "People get that way when they're pregnant. You're not used to it yet. Things look bad to you right now. But you'll get over it."

Marina was unmollified. "You're not even pregnant, and you think you made a mistake, too. You're sorry you didn't marry Ella."

"I don't care about Ella," he said.

"Then why did you say you saw her from the balcony that day?"

"You hurt me, and I wanted to hurt you back."

He spent the rest of the evening placating her. "I told you before that I used to go out with her. I even asked her to marry me. But she was scared. She hurt my pride. But I'm not in love with her. She's gotten so fat it's awful. She'd have gotten fat as a barrel if I'd married her."

Marina was ready to make up. All she wanted was reassurance. "How did you know I wouldn't get fat?" she inquired as she tumbled into bed. He reassured her and the two of them made up.

8

Journey to Moscow

LESS THAN THREE WEEKS after his marriage, in a letter postmarked May 16, 1961, Lee Harvey Oswald wrote for the third time to the American Embassy in Moscow.[1] ". . . I wish to make it clear," he said in the demanding tone of his earlier letters,

that I am asking not only for the right to return to the United States, but also for full guarantee's that I shall not, under any circumstance's, be persecuted for any act pertaining to this case. . . . Unless you think this condition can be met, I see no reason for a continuance of our correspondence. Instead, I shall endeavour *to use* my relatives in the United States, to see about getting something done in Washington.

Oswald repeated his reluctance to come to Moscow for an interview: "I do not care to take the risk of getting into a awkwark situation unless I think it worthwhile." And he informed the embassy that he had got married. "My wife is Russian . . . and is quite willing to leave the Soviet Union with me and live in the United States." He said, moreover, that he would not leave Russia unless arrangements were made for his wife to leave at the same time. "So with this extra complication," he wrote, "I suggest you do some checking up before advising me further."

At least two events may have crystallized Oswald's resolve to return to the United States. Early in May, just after his marriage, he received a letter from Patrice Lumumba University in Moscow rejecting his application for admission. It meant to Oswald that the road to a higher education in Russia was closed to him. It spelled the end of his hopes of escape from the dreary, provincial town of Minsk. He was doomed to remain a factory worker forever. So keen was Oswald's disappointment that he did not tell Marina about the rejection until months later and, when he did tell her, he was still so disappointed that she got the impression that the wound was fresh.

On May 5, probably on the same day he learned that his application to attend

Lumumba University had been denied, Oswald wrote a letter to his brother Robert in Fort Worth. He announced matter-of-factly that he had married, but said nothing about wanting to come home. Nevertheless, Robert rightly took the letter as a signal that his brother had tired of life in Russia. He wrote a letter in reply and they resumed their correspondence. In a later letter Oswald confided that he wanted to return to the United States, but doubted that it would be possible. He also wrote a letter to his mother, the first in a year and a half.

A second disappointment came two weeks after his marriage when Oswald was excluded from the bus excursion to Leningrad. He often complained to friends about the lack of freedom in the Soviet Union. Apparently he now felt that the many privileges he received as a foreigner were outweighed by the restrictions that were placed on him. For only a day or so later, he resumed his correspondence with the American Embassy. As in the case of Ella Germann, a rejection seemed to demand an act of rejection in return. It was a response by Oswald that was to recur again and again.

Alik still had said nothing to Marina about his desire to return to the United States, despite the statement in his letter to the embassy that she was willing to leave Russia with him. It was, under the circumstances, an irresponsible statement for him to make. Fearful of what the Soviet and the American reactions to his request might mean for *him*, he was unconcerned about what such a declaration, made through the open mails where it could be seen by Soviet officials, might mean for Marina—pressure on her and perhaps even danger for her family. In fact, he did not tell Marina of his intentions until five or six weeks after he wrote to the embassy.

It was an evening late in June, and Marina and Alik were taking a walk after dinner. They passed several lighted store fronts and saw nothing they wanted to buy. "In America," Alik said tentatively, "the store fronts are huge. They're all lit up and you can find anything you want inside. If I were able to go back, would you come?"

"But you told me you couldn't," Marina said.

"If I tried?"

"No."

"Why not?"

"You're trying to trick me," Marina said. "You want to see if I married you to go to America. That's enough of your nonsense now."

But that was not the end of it. In bed that night, gazing up at the ceiling, Alik asked, "You mean that if I go, you'll stay?"

Marina sat upright in bed. "Are you kidding?"

"I'm not kidding, Marina. I'm serious."

"I'm not going anywhere," Marina said. But he persisted and she promised to think it over.

Next morning he asked if she was afraid of going?

"I don't know the language, Alka," she said. "I don't know what your family will think of me. They won't like me, maybe. And then you won't love me any more."

"I've seen your country, Marina," he said. "Now I'd like you to see mine. Please, please come with me."

For three days he begged her. He showered her with kisses and affection. Marina says that "he literally stood on his knees." Finally she agreed. He made her sit down at once and write a letter to the American Embassy asking to go to the United States.

The next day he told her he had mailed the letter. But he never did, and his motive in making her write it is obscure, unless he was trying to commit her so that she would not change her mind. Or perhaps he wanted to keep it in reserve, to send to the embassy if it became necessary. A week or so after "mailing" her letter, Alik told Marina that he had received a "reply" inviting the two of them to pay a visit to the embassy. There had been no such reply. In fact, he had not yet received a reply to the letter he had written more than a month earlier.

Oswald's threat to invoke his relatives "to see about getting something done in Washington" led the embassy to seek advice from the Department of State. But there were other causes for delay, for technically, Oswald's situation was a tricky one. The embassy first had to ascertain whether or not he was still an American citizen. His citizenship had not been revoked in 1959, embassy officials knew, but they had to make sure that Oswald had not taken any action in the U.S.S.R., such as assuming Soviet citizenship, to forfeit his standing as an American. Despite the fractious tone of his letters, the embassy sympathized with Oswald's desire to leave Russia, and with the difficulties he might have in obtaining permission from the Minsk authorities to travel to Moscow. But it had to insist upon a personal interview and answers to questions about his status in the U.S.S.R. Then, and only then, could his American passport be returned to him. After that, he would be free to apply for a Soviet exit visa and, as an American citizen, he had at least a chance of receiving it.

Whether or not Oswald would be able to get one for himself—and for his Russian wife—was a question for Soviet authorities to decide. During the Stalin era, defectors to the Soviet Union who desired to return to their homelands invited, at best, refusal and, at worst, imprisonment or even death, whatever the status of their citizenship. But this was the Khrushchev era and no new policies had yet taken shape. There were no precedents, although there was a fair possibility that someone who had not assumed Soviet citizenship, was not needed in the U.S.S.R., and was not in a position to know secrets or possess particularly sensitive information about Soviet life, might well be permitted to leave.

Oswald's concern at the moment, however, was not with the Soviet reaction to his request, but with the American. To him, the embassy's delay in responding to his application and its insistence on a personal interview meant only one thing. A trap was being laid for him, and he would be arrested the moment he passed through the embassy gates. Hence his insistence in all his letters that the embassy guarantee he would not be "persecuted," i.e., prosecuted. The embassy could make no such guarantee. Its officials knew nothing of Oswald's history in Russia, or, for that matter, of his history in the United States before his defection. But they were required by rules of the Department of State to resolve any doubts about reentry in favor of an American citizen. Moreover, American embassies abroad have no procedure for arresting anyone. Oswald who, a year and a half before, had known in detail the procedures for swearing an oath renouncing his citizenship, was ignorant of the facts that now concerned him most. Thus he was fearful and suspicious, but the tone of his letters was also full of bravado, as if he expected the embassy to give him everything he asked.

During the first week of July, just after he learned of Marina's pregnancy, Alik still had no word from the embassy and his fears gave way to impatience. He decided to take his vacation and fly to Moscow.[2] He did not inform the embassy that he was coming.

Before he left, Alik told Marina that he would telephone to let her know if she was needed. But on no account was she to say a word to Ilya or Valya about his absence. Above all, not a word about his going to the embassy. "If they find out and nothing comes of it," he said, "they'll only make fun of me." Marina was baffled by her husband's desire for secrecy since she supposed they had nothing to hide. Later, she realized that he was wary lest her uncle forbid her to go to the American Embassy.

Alik made no secret of his fears. He told Marina that the embassy was "entitled" to arrest him and might do so. Why? "I threw my passport on the table and said I didn't want to be a citizen any more." Thus their journey to the airport in the dawn hours of Saturday, July 8, was an anxious one. They ordered breakfast while waiting for his flight to be announced, but both were too nervous to eat. Alik was afraid he might never come back, might never see her again. But he tried to keep their courage up: "Don't worry. Everything will be okay." Incongruously he added, "I'll let you know if anything goes wrong."

Breakfast forgotten, Alik took Marina to a deserted corner of the waiting room, clutched her apprehensively by the hand, and kept repeating: "My God! It's the first time we've ever been apart." He was the last to board the plane. He led her to the gate, kissed her, to her great embarrassment, in full view of the woman dispatcher, then begged Marina to wait so that he could see her from the plane. He glanced back several times as he strode to the waiting aircraft, and Marina saw tears in his eyes. "He loves me," she thought. "It's hard for him to go."

"Is he your husband?" the dispatcher inquired.

Marina nodded.

"Is it the first time you've been apart?"

"Yes."

"I thought so."

At two o'clock that afternoon Richard Snyder was eating lunch in his apartment in the American Embassy. A 41-year-old, bespectacled Foreign Service officer with sharp, pointed features and an inquisitive air, Snyder had spent most of his career overseas and was known for his fluency in Russian. Like most members of the embassy staff, he lived as well as worked in the tight little compound on the Sadovoye Ring, Moscow's biggest thoroughfare, which was forever reverberating with the traffic of heavy trucks. His apartment was on the second floor, directly over the consular office. The duty of a diplomat was literally never far away. But Dick and Anne Snyder were at the end of their two-year tour of duty. In three days, on July 11, they would be sailing from Leningrad for home.

Suddenly, the telephone rang. Lee Harvey Oswald was calling from downstairs. Snyder remembered him immediately; he was one of the most obnoxious young men he had ever met. Snyder was not surprised that Oswald had tired of life in his adopted country, and the embassy was currently awaiting an opinion on his case from Washington. In keeping with the State Department's recommended procedure of giving a possibly angry or unbalanced defector time to cool down before taking the irrevocable step of renouncing his citizenship, Snyder had put Oswald off during their stormy interview in November 1959, and Oswald had been so furious at the delay that he refused to set foot in the embassy again. Now he was back and, ironically, it was due to Snyder's tactics, and the fact that Oswald had never officially renounced his citizenship, that he owed whatever chance he still had of returning to America. Yet Snyder had rather hoped, if he thought about it at all, that this particular "bad penny" would not turn up again until after the 11th.[3]

With a vague feeling of annoyance, Snyder stepped into the elevator and rode the single flight down to the lobby. He greeted Oswald with precisely calibrated coolness and led him directly to his office. There they chatted for a few minutes, and Snyder noticed that the young man seemed chastened compared to his behavior during their earlier encounter. He asked Oswald to return on Monday. Oswald left the embassy, and Snyder went back to his lunch. Once again, Oswald had chosen to appear unannounced on a Saturday, when the consular office was closed for business.

Marina, meanwhile, was facing a dilemma of her own in Minsk. Although she had been married more than two months, some of her old beaux continued to call her at work, and she permitted it. Sasha, who had branded her a prostitute, had the nerve to telephone her there. So did Yury, the young man who had introduced her to Alik. Even Anatoly Shpanko called to ask if he might see her. But Marina had refused. With a pang of disappointment she felt that Anatoly had given her up too easily. He must not have loved her after all.

Yet Marina had her regrets. Since her pregnancy she had felt a strange sexual aversion to her husband and she wondered if she had made a mistake. During the third month of her marriage it was not Anatoly on whom her doubts converged but Leonid, her Jewish suitor of the summer before.

On the morning of July 8, she went straight to the pharmacy after seeing her husband off. There she received a phone call from, of all people, Leonid, asking if he might see her. How on earth, she inquired, had he known her husband was out of town? "Sheer intuition," he replied enigmatically. Marina agreed to meet him that evening. Half-hoping something might come of it, she went home after work and washed her hair. She took a nap, then rose and carefully put on her best dress. Perhaps the evening would show whether she had made a mistake getting married or not.

Lonya certainly knew the script. He had an empty apartment at his disposal; he even had a bottle of French apéritif. Once they were in bed, however, his sophistication proved to be a matter of appearances only. He was making love to a woman, or trying to, for the first time. It was all over before it had begun. Marina was furious. She insisted on walking home by herself—at two o'clock in the morning.

The following evening, Sunday, she went to the central post office to receive a long-distance telephone call. It was from Alik in Moscow. "I went to the embassy," he told her with a breathless, conspiratorial air. "It was okay. They didn't arrest me." He wanted her to fly to Moscow the next morning. She was to call him at his hotel the moment her plane touched the ground.

Marina now faced a new dilemma. She would have to get out of work for several days, and must explain the reason for her absence, or, under the regulations, she would be fired. Yet Alik had commanded her to tell no one where he had gone. What excuse could Marina give? She decided to tell the truth. "Evgenia," she told her supervisor over the telephone, "Alik's been called to the embassy. He wants me to join him there."

Marina boarded the plane to Moscow on Monday morning, July 10.[4] It was her first flight, and she was deliciously apprehensive. She threw up twice on the plane. From Sheremetyevo Airport in Moscow she took a bus to Sverdlov Square, in the heart of town. Alik was there to meet her. "I missed you so!" he greeted her. "I had no idea I'd miss you so much in two days." He rushed her to the Hotel Berlin, only three blocks away. Their room was filled with blue cornflowers which he had bought to welcome her. They made love right away. "I feel as if we'd been apart for a year," he said. There was a mirror at the foot of the bed, and he liked that very much indeed. Later he often said that he wanted a bedroom with mirrors on every side.

Alik had an appointment that afternoon at the embassy.[5] He was nervous as they careened up to the big, boxlike fortress in a taxicab, for despite his easy reception by Richard Snyder two days before, he still thought he might be arrested. Marina had cause to be nervous, too, for without being aware of it, she, as a Soviet citizen, was forbidden to enter a foreign embassy without permission from her country's authorities that was practically unobtainable. Even though she was unaware that what she was doing might be dangerous, she was nonetheless apprehensive as they approached the building. What was her astonishment, then, when uniformed militiamen, far from stopping them to examine their papers, actually snapped to a stiff salute as they sauntered through the embassy gates. It was like going to a palace to be decorated, Marina thought, when you had done nothing to deserve it.

Marina was wearing her best cotton dress and her wedding shoes, made in England, and the militiamen apparently took her for American. Indeed, whenever she saw anyone in the offices and corridors of the American Embassy that afternoon, Marina's eyes traveled as if magnetized to their feet. For no matter how clever a Soviet girl might be at procuring things from abroad, her shoes, her heavy Russian clodhoppers, seldom failed to give her away. The first person she saw was the pretty young receptionist who greeted them as they walked in the front door. The girl was so poised in manner and her hair so neatly done that Marina was thoroughly awed.

She was gratified and intrigued by something else. As they were walking down the hallway to the consular offices, she saw a whole row of glassed-in cubicles with Russian girls seated at the desks inside. Marina felt distinctly relieved. If anything went wrong here, if she was kidnapped or forced to sign some paper she did not understand, one of these girls would help her. Besides, it was good to see Americans and Russians working together in this fashion. But then another thought struck her. If those girls were working for the Americans, they must also be working for the KGB. Marina did not like that at all. Disgusting as it was for a man to be a spy, it seemed even worse for a girl. The very thought made Marina's flesh crawl.

When they reached the large office shared by the consul and vice-consul, Marina sat in the waiting room while Alik went inside. He was gone a long time and Marina was able to compose herself and look around. She found the place a revelation. It was filled with gadgets, for one thing, and all of them seemed to work. Out on the street it was hot, but there was something whirring in the window, a fan or a ventilator or something, and inside it was practically cold. Everything seemed designed for simplicity and convenience: even the telephone wires appeared to be laid out differently from those she was accustomed to in Minsk.

But the best was still to come. During her husband's long absence, Marina had to go to the toilet. On the way she paused at the water cooler and had only to press a knob and cold water came cascading out. But the washroom itself— that was a work of art! It was immaculate and as fragrant as a garden. There was even real toilet paper. Marina had seen that, instead of small squares of newspaper, only once in her life before, at the Hotel Metropole in Leningrad. There were paper towels, too, and green liquid soap. Again, she had only to press a knob.

The girl who took her to the toilet was also a revelation. She was one of the Soviet girls who worked at the embassy, although she was all dressed up like an American and might not be taken for Russian at all. Marina had been fearful that the girl would be suspicious of her motives or reproach her for wanting to leave Russia. But the girl chatted pleasantly with her and never once alluded to the touchy subject. Marina returned from the toilet in much better spirits, reassured that nothing bad would happen to her. Yet she was still stunned to think that she was here at all.

Alik emerged from the consul's office chewing gum and well pleased with himself. Since his case involved a decision by the State Department as to whether he had forfeited his American citizenship, his interview had been conducted by Snyder, the senior consular officer. Once it was over, Alik and Marina sat in the waiting room and Alik began to fill out a long questionnaire. He was relaxed and playful. "I wish I could make the Zigers my relatives and take them out with me, too!" he commented as he pored over the questionnaire.

Marina's reply was tart. "Okay. Divorce me and marry Eleonora if you like!"

Alik had done a favor for the Zigers when he entered the embassy. He had carried with him to Moscow a letter from Alexander Ziger to the embassy of Argentina, presumably a request to the Argentine government to bring pressure on the Russians to grant him an exit visa. Either Ziger was afraid to write the Argentine Embassy through the open mails, or he had already done so and because he had dual citizenship—Soviet citizens are forbidden even to have contact by mail with a foreign embassy—his letters had been intercepted. On a table downstairs in the American Embassy there were two wooden boxes, one for outgoing and the other for incoming diplomatic mail of a routine nature, such as invitations. Alik dropped Ziger's letter into the outgoing box. In a day or so it would be picked up by a U.S. Embassy chauffeur and delivered to the embassy of Argentina. It was one of the few occasions Marina remembers when Alik did a favor for somebody else.

Elated by the way things were going for him at the embassy, Alik inquired about the fate of a young man named Webster who had come to the Soviet Union shortly before he did, fallen in love with a Russian waitress, married, and gone to work in Leningrad in a glassworks or plastics factory. He, too, was trying to go back to America, and was having a difficult time.

After he had completed the questionnaire, Alik handed it to an embassy typist, one of the Russian girls Marina had noticed earlier in the afternoon, so that she could fill out an application to renew his American passport which, even if he received it back that day, was still due to expire on September 10. He then returned to Snyder's office with the questionnaire and the renewal forms.

Snyder inspected the questionnaire. Oswald's responses were routine. The two of them had already had a long talk and it appeared to Snyder that Oswald had done nothing to forfeit his citizenship. His Soviet passport, for one thing, was of the type issued to "stateless" persons. That, on the face of it, was evidence that he was not a Soviet citizen. Moreover, Oswald's letters from Minsk had been delivered to the embassy; had he become a Soviet citizen, the letters would not have gone through. Oswald had also responded to Snyder's queries with an air of frankness. He appeared to have nothing to hide.

There was, however, one concern that seemed uppermost in Oswald's mind. He confessed to Snyder that he was worried that he might face several years in prison in the United States for having chosen to live in Russia. What was Snyder's view? Snyder advised him, as he later phrased it in a dispatch to the State Department, that he knew no grounds on which Oswald might have to face "punishment of such severity as he had in mind." Oswald answered that he realized Snyder could make no promises, but he was reluctant to return home if it might mean going to jail. He had refrained from approaching the Soviet authorities about letting him go until he "had this end of the thing straightened out."[6]

Oswald had not been arrested the moment he set foot inside the embassy, as he had feared. His fear was probably the reason why he had appeared, unannounced, on a Saturday and why he had today taken the precaution of bringing Marina, although the embassy had not suggested it, nor was it essential for her to appear so early in the proceedings. But if Oswald was reassured by his reception at the embassy, he was still afraid that he would be arrested when he returned to the United States. In his own mind, he had committed a catalogue of crimes against his country by coming to live in the U.S.S.R.[7] and accepting a job in a Soviet factory (working for a foreign state);[8] and he was under the illusion that he had taken a formal oath of allegiance to the U.S.S.R.[9] Moreover, he had offered the Soviet government any radar secrets which he might have learned in the Marine Corps, and he had granted an interview criticizing the United States to Radio Moscow for use in its propaganda transmissions abroad. Finally, from January 1960 until his desire to return to the United States became known to the Soviet authorities, he had received a subsidy from the Soviet Red Cross, which he believed had been arranged by the secret police as payment for the interview denouncing his country.

Oswald had all of this very much on his mind. Nevertheless, up to this point every one of his fears was groundless, since they were based on acts he had either not committed or that were not crimes under United States law. As of lunchtime on July 10, he had done nothing for which he could reasonably expect to face prosecution on his return to the United States, much less arrest in the American Embassy. The fears that haunted him, motivated by feelings of guilt and perhaps by his attributing to the government of the United States the anger toward him that he had felt toward it, were altogether unrealistic.

But on this very day, Oswald altered his condition of juridical innocence. For the first time he did, in fact, commit what could have been construed as a crime. Several times that afternoon, he knowingly lied to Richard Snyder. He claimed that he had at no time applied for citizenship of the U.S.S.R., yet he had done so on October 16, 1959. He stated that he did not belong to the trade union at his factory when at that very moment he was carrying a membership card in his pocket, and could not have been employed without one. He claimed that Soviet officials had never questioned him about his life before his arrival in the U.S.S.R., and that, too, was probably false. Finally, he dismissed the significance of his Radio Moscow interview and claimed that he had "made no statements at any time of any exploitable nature concerning his original decision to reside in the Soviet Union."[10] His own notes written later make perfectly clear that in giving the interview, and accepting his subsidy, he believed that he had "sold himself" and betrayed the interests of the United States.[11]

The irony was that all his falsehoods were unnecessary. Even had he told the truth on every point, he would not have been subject to prosecution. Nor, apparently, would the truth have affected the ultimate finding that he was still an American citizen, for he had not crossed either of the Rubicons: he had not renounced his U.S. citizenship, nor become a citizen of the U.S.S.R. By telling these falsehoods he had, however, laid himself open for the first time to a criminal charge: that of knowingly lying to an official of the United States. And on the next day he would persuade his wife to do the same. But there is not a shred of evidence that he ever realized that these were crimes—and the only ones he had committed.

Snyder, of course, did not know that the young man sitting opposite him was lying. Snyder had no sympathy for communism or the Soviet Union, and very little sympathy for those who were taken in by either. On their first meeting almost two years before, he had taken a harsh line, some said too harsh, toward this very same young man; he had even poked fun at his Marxist convictions.[12] Still, Snyder's record was replete with evidence that he had compassion for anyone unfortunate enough to be trapped in this inhospitable land. He had found Oswald "aggressive," "overbearing," "insufferable" during their initial interview; but now, as he would report to the State Department:

Twenty months of the realities of life in the Soviet Union have clearly had a maturing effect on Oswald. He stated frankly that he had learned a hard lesson the hard way and that he had been completely relieved of his illusions about the Soviet Union at the same time that he acquired a new understanding and appreciation of the United States and the meaning of freedom.[13] Much of the arrogance and bravado which characterized him on his first visit to the Embassy appears to have left him.[14]

Snyder reread the answers on the completed questionnaire which Oswald brought in to him. He glanced at the application for renewal of Oswald's American passport. Carefully, he signed both copies, and placed a stamp, "Valid only for direct travel to the United States," in the green document which Oswald had left with him nearly two years before.

Then, in what must have been almost the last official act of his two long years in Moscow, Richard Snyder leaned across his desk and handed back his American passport to Lee Harvey Oswald.

As he led her through the embassy gate back to the street, Marina could see that Alik was elated by their visit. He was overjoyed that Snyder had received him, welcomed him back to the fold and even returned his passport. Alik was so reassured by his visits to the embassy that the following day, Tuesday, July 11, he and Marina returned, this time to initiate the steps that might enable her to enter the United States. Nevertheless, he was nervous as they again approached the building, and he coached Marina on what *not* to say. She was not to admit that she was pregnant; that could cause a delay. If anyone asked, she was to say that she did not know. Above all, on no account was she to admit that she belonged to the Komsomol. That might ruin things for good.

They walked through the embassy gates without hindrance and headed for the consular office. "Go on in," Alik said to Marina when her turn came. "Only don't say anything about the Komsomol."

"How can I lie?" Marina said. "They'll find out anyway. They'll say I can't have a visa for lying."

"It'll help your visa if you shut up," he replied.

Marina was received by John McVickar, the vice-consul, whose job it was to handle applications by foreigners seeking to enter the United States. McVickar had brown hair, a round face, a gentle manner. Marina sat in front of him shaking like a leaf. He sat very straight in his chair, she noticed, and offered her chewing gum.

"I don't speak Russian very well," McVickar began, smiling at her. "Please correct me if I make a mistake."

Here she was, Marina thought, talking to practically an ambassador or a minister of the American government and he was asking her to correct his Russian! It was in keeping with the rest of this whole incredible journey. Marina liked McVickar immediately. He was simple and direct, and she was grateful for his lack of airs. The office, too, was wonderful. It was neat, compact, convenient. But Marina was feeling unwell. If she had one thing on her mind, apart from her extraordinary surroundings, it was the fact that she was pregnant.

"Excuse me, are you feeling all right?" McVickar asked.

"Oh, oh, yes!" she stammered, terrified that she had given her secret away.

McVickar asked her to take an oath promising to tell the truth. Then he asked a whole string of questions: where was she born, where had she lived as a child, where did she go to school, were her parents alive, and so forth? Do you belong to the trade union, he asked, and Marina answered that she did. Finally, the question she was dreading: "Are you a member of the Komsomol?" Lying, she told him that she was not, trying to comfort herself, meanwhile, with the thought that she had, after all, never bothered to pick up her membership card. If there was one thing she did not like, it was Alik's forcing her to lie. You have to support a husband and back him up, she knew, and Alik wanted to go home. But Marina would have preferred to tell the truth and take her chances.

McVickar was having trouble understanding her, for she spoke rapidly, out of one corner of her mouth, allowing the ends of words and even sentences to trail away. He went to the waiting room door and asked her husband to come in to translate.

"Have you relatives in the United States?" the questioning proceeded.

"Oh, no," Marina protested. It was a frightening thought.

"She doesn't understand," Alik interrupted quickly. "She has a mother-in-law and a brother-in-law there."

Marina was puzzled, to say the least. For a Russian it could be a calamity to have a relative abroad. It was always cause for suspicion and sometimes even for arrest. Naturally, she had been quick to deny it. How could she know that for Americans it was just the opposite? It not only helps to have a relative in America, the authorities practically require it. Without one, you may fail to get into the country.

Marina's interview was satisfactory. McVickar filled out a visa petition for her to be allowed to enter the United States, and Alik signed it.[15]

Afterwards, happy and hopeful, they returned to the Hotel Berlin and spent the next day enjoying Moscow. On Wednesday night or Thursday, they returned to Minsk by air.

9

Marina's Ordeal

ON HER FIRST DAY back at the pharmacy, Marina was greeted by icy silence. Word had spread that she had visited the American Embassy in Moscow with her husband. That could mean only one thing, and the girls parted like a wave as she walked in, leaving her face to face with their superior.

"Marina," Evgenia Ivanovna said coldly, "you're a foolish child. If I were your mother I'd take down your pants and spank you."

The next day Marina was called to the office of the head of the hospital. Assisted by the Communist Party organizer of the hospital and two junior doctors, he conducted a virtual inquisition. "You're so young," one of them said to her. "You hardly know your husband at all. Yet here you are, trying to go to a strange country with a man you scarcely know." Urging her to do nothing hasty, her inquisitors suggested that she think it over, and Marina agreed.

A day or so later she had a visit from the Party organizer, a woman. Had Marina changed her mind? If not, the woman said, she would regret it the rest of her life. Next, a Komsomol organizer appeared at the pharmacy and told her that she would be summoned to Komsomol headquarters. Her colleagues at the pharmacy continued to treat her with such suspicion that finally, her temper growing short, Marina said. "Girls, don't worry about a thing. There's a big corridor in the embassy and nothing but Russian girls on one side. Our government knows every move I made. I didn't do a thing, I didn't sign a single piece of paper that isn't legal. I'm a big girl. Maybe I'm ruining my life, but at least I'm not ruining yours!" The only note of sympathy and understanding came from two elderly cleaning women. "Where your husband goes, you go," one of them told her. "Fish go where water's deeper, man goes where life is better," said the other. "Your husband has seen both. He can compare. He knows which is better."

At home, Marina had never been so close to Alik as she was now. Never before had she needed him so much. After each of her ordeals he was eager for every detail. When she told him of her session with the head of the hospital, Alik vowed: "If he calls you in one more time, I swear I'll go talk to him. I'll make him leave you alone." Trying to encourage her, he said: "You're very brave. Remember when you answer them back, I'm with you in spirit every second."

Marina felt he was proud of her—and he was. Two or three days after their return, he wrote the embassy about the pressures to which she was being subjected. Like a little boy boasting, he concluded: "My wife stood up well, without getting into trouble."[1]

To his brother Robert, he wrote:

You don't know what a trial this is. . . . The Russians can be crude and very crude at times. They gave a cross-examination to my wife on the first day we came back from Moscow, they knew everything because they spy, and read the mails, but we shall continue to try and get out. We shall not retreat. . . . I hope someday I'll see you and Vada [Robert's wife] but if and when I come, I'll come with my wife. You can't imagine how wonderfully she stood up.[2]

They had their lighter moments, too. There was a raft of forms to fill out for the authorities in Minsk. Marina had to apply for a Soviet foreign passport, good for travel abroad, and an exit visa. Alik needed only an exit visa, but every form had to be filled out at least in triplicate, each with photographs attached. Alik insisted on doing them all, even hers. He told Marina that she would never get around to doing them herself. But he had great difficulty with the forms because, without knowing it, he suffered from a reading disability called strephosymbolia. The condition, also known as dyslexia or "word blindness," is caused by what doctors term "mixed lateral dominance of the brain." A person suffering from this condition is not predominantly left- or right-handed, but for genetic reasons displays the characteristics of both. Thus Alik read not only from left to right but also, part of the time, from right to left, and when he wrote he often reversed letters and punctuation marks. Filling out forms was laborious for him, and Marina recalls that he had to bring five or six blanks home for every form he managed to complete successfully. He was in rollicking good spirits nonetheless.

When they were faced by Marina's biggest ordeal, a full-scale meeting of the Komsomol *aktiv* of the hospital, Alik wanted to go with her. "You don't need to," Marina said. "In fact, you can't. You're not a member."

He tried to support her anyhow. "I won't let them hurt my little girl." He took her in his arms. "I want you to show you're your own person. You've a right to go abroad if you want. It's they who are wrong to meddle. I'll be thinking about you the whole time. Maybe that'll help."

The chairman of the meeting was a leader of the city-wide Komsomol organization. Representatives of every department of the hospital appeared as witnesses, as did two girls from the pharmacy. Looking very solemn, they were seated around a long table draped in red, with a red flag furled to one side and an attentive-looking portrait of Lenin peering down from the wall. Only Marina was standing, her pregnancy not yet apparent.

She was not intimidated by their questions. The Komsomol had not cared about her in the least, she said, until she went to the American Embassy. She knew she was being rude, but she was bitterly offended by their questions. She had done nothing to harm others. This was her private life, and she hated having it raked over the coals. When one of the members suggested that her husband might be a spy, she quickly found her reply: "So my husband was right after all. He said you people think there's a spy under every pillow. Actually what he does every night is tap out messages in Morse code about how the Komsomol is trying to brainwash me."

The chairman told her that the Komsomol knew everything about her and her husband. "We knew each time you had a date. We knew when you applied for your marriage license. We knew the date of your wedding," he said. Marina was chilled but not surprised. She had long been aware that the Komsomol was a tool of the police. Its members were often assigned to report on the activities of their friends.

Finally, the chairman again warned that her husband might be a spy. "You're young," he said. "We wouldn't expect you to find out right away. One doesn't wake up to such horrible things overnight." Marina refused to believe it. "So I don't know my husband well yet," she said. "But one thing I can assure you. He's not an American spy. On that score you can set your minds at rest."

When the meeting ended she was told that another meeting would be called with representatives from every hospital in Minsk to decide whether to expel her from the Komsomol.

"Go ahead and expel me if you like," Marina said. "But don't expect me to come to the meeting. I've told you everything I know."

Out on the street afterwards, the chairman drew Marina aside and warned her that she had behaved so egregiously it might now be necessary to make a public example of her. Marina knew a threat when she heard one—a full-scale attack in the press.

Alik was waiting anxiously at home. Had they "tormented" her long? he wanted to know. The meeting lasted two hours, she told him. "They said you were a spy," she said with a weary smile.

"I expected it," he answered. "That's what Ella's family thought."

A week or so later, the girls at the pharmacy went off to the meeting on Marina's case. She waited behind at work. She expected the news they brought: "You were expelled today." She took it with a touch of bravado. "Fine! Now I'll have money for the movies."

Alik's response echoed her own. "Fine! Now you won't have to go to the meetings." The few times Marina had gone to them, he accused her of using them as a pretext to slip out with old boyfriends.

Her expulsion was, in reality, a blow to Marina, as if the Komsomol were a mother who had pushed her out in anger. Her world was collapsing beneath her. It was the sort of thing that often happens to a girl *before* she marries a foreigner, not after. Marina had been spared before her marriage because every-one, even the Komsomol, assumed Alik was a Soviet citizen and could not go back to America even if he wanted to. Few people had seriously supposed that Marina was marrying Alik for a foreign passport. Now the accusation was heard often. "You ought to have married Anatoly," Marina's best friend at the pharmacy said. Then she added: "Forget it, Marina. You'll never be allowed to go."

The official pressure, as it happened, was over. But Marina had yet to endure other, personal pressures. Her most painful rebuff came from Aunt Valya and Uncle Ilya. On Sunday, a few days after their return from Moscow, Alik went off to visit the Prusakovs. In a matter of minutes he was home again. Valya had answered the bell and said, "I'm sorry, Alik, we don't want to see you any more." Valya, the warm, approving Valya, had shut the door in his face.

Alik was crushed, and he begged Marina to find out why he had been turned away. He had repaid the Prusakovs' kindness by taking a step in secret that was bound to affect them all, perhaps disastrously. But, Marina recalls, "Alik just didn't understand that you don't do things that way."

After a week or so Marina finally telephoned the Prusakovs: "Aunt Valya, I want to see you."

"Good," she said. "Come on over, only don't bring Alka."

Valya greeted her at the door. "Uncle Ilya is very angry and he wants to talk to you," she warned.

"A fine niece you are," Ilya began. "You're here all the time. Then you fly off to Moscow without a word and leave me to hear it from others." He grilled Marina about the visit to the embassy. He wanted to know every detail. "You ought to consult your family before you do a thing like that," he said finally, and with that, he picked up the newspaper and disappeared into his study.

Ilya had spent a lifetime in a special part of the Soviet bureaucracy. At stake for him in Marina's application to go abroad, although he never said so, were the pension he had earned by a lifetime of labor, his friends, his apartment, his position of dignity, his way of life. Ilya would soon be retiring. He was looking forward to the peace he had earned.

Marina and her aunt withdrew as usual to the kitchen, and Valya, too, began to scold her. Marina knew that her criticisms were just, but she wanted them all to make up. "Well, what can we do about it now?" Valya said. "It's too late. All right, bring him over."

Marina and Alik came together, and this time it was Alik whom Ilya subjected to cross-examination. Once again he went through every step, every nuance of the visit to the embassy. Ilya said that he thought Alik had not only given up his American citizenship but had become a citizen of the U.S.S.R. He added that he would never have consented to the marriage if he had known that Alik was not a Soviet citizen. Alik was truthful but vague in his answers to Ilya's questions. He conceded that he had asked for his American passport back, omitting to mention that he had received it. Marina believes he was ashamed. "Don't worry, Uncle Ilya." Alik tried to end the interview on a soothing note. "It's nothing but a first step. I have no idea whether we'll even be allowed to go back."

On the way home, he exploded in anger at Marina. "I wasn't ready for a grilling like that. I had no idea you'd told them everything."

"They're my family," Marina said. "They took me in and gave me a home. I can't keep things from them."

"You could have waited awhile," he said. "We don't know anything anyway."

"Alik," Marina complained. "You force me to lie. I can't live like that. I can't open my mouth without giving you away as a liar. You lied about your mother and your age. You lied when you said you couldn't return to America. Now you're making me lie. When will there be an end to it?"

There were more questions to come, not only from family and friends, but from Marina herself. A few days after their return from Moscow, she observed Alik, for the first time, writing on a yellow pad at home, seemingly lost in thought. Then she noticed that he had photographs and a ground plan of the radio plant. Marina was horror-stricken. So Alik was a spy after all. To make matters worse, he would not let her near the papers and refused even to say what he was doing. Marina was nearly in a panic.

Finally, Alik relented. "I'm writing my impressions of Russia," he told her. "What for?" she wanted to know.

"Maybe there are people in America who will want to read them. Maybe I'll publish them and maybe I'll keep them for myself."

Marina sighed with relief. She thought how foolish she had been. Yet, one day when she returned home from work before Alik, she raced upstairs and ransacked the apartment, looking for what he was writing. All she found was a litter of unsuspicious-looking papers covered with her husband's scrawl.

She did her best to compose herself after that. But then she made another discovery. Alik had a shocking sum of money saved up, the small fortune of 500 rubles ($500), which he said was from the Soviet Red Cross. Again, Marina's suspicions were aroused. Alik had lied to her in the past. Was he lying again now to conceal the fact that he was a spy?

Marina came to a different conclusion. She had grown up in a country where informing is a way of life. Eyes and ears are everywhere. A trusted friend often turns out to be an agent of the police. It is vital to keep secrets, your own and those of others, merely to have a quiet life. Discretion is, indeed, the better part of valor. But Marina soon realized that her husband's secretiveness was of another kind entirely. He told lies without purpose or point, lies that were bound to be found out. He liked having secrets for their own sake. He simply enjoyed concealment. For him it was not a matter of life and death but a matter of choice. In a Russian setting that must have seemed like frivolity indeed.

For Marina to perceive, at the youthful age of nineteen, that her husband told lies as a matter of character rather than of necessity was a feat of mature intuition. Still, she trusted him—she had nobody else. All day every day she held back her tears at the pharmacy. But when she came home each night, she broke down. "Alka," she cried, "don't leave me. Don't give me up. You see I have no one but you. No one at work. No Ilya or Valya. I have no family now."

"My poor little girl," he said to comfort her, taking her in his arms and kissing the nape of her neck. "Cry as much as you like. It'll be easier that way." Then he added, as if to himself, "I never thought it was going to be so hard."

It was hard, and Marina had moments of vacillation. But she felt from the outset that she had a right to be with her husband, to go where he went, and that she was not doing anything wrong. The opposition she encountered served only to stiffen her resolve. From time to time she wavered, but she did not give up. She was committed to Alik now, and she was sustained by his patience and understanding and by the certain knowledge that he was proud of her.

Somehow, after the initial turmoil, their lives returned to normal. Marina's pregnancy progressed without incident, but in early August she underwent a special medical examination at the hospital because of "unpleasant sensations in the heart region,"[3] probably a result of the pressures she had been under. There was nothing seriously wrong, however, and she was not hospitalized.

Little change took place in their schedule. Marina went to work at the pharmacy; Alik went to the radio plant. Their evenings and weekends were spent in a variety of ways. Sometimes Alik rented a boat and paddled along the Svisloch River. When he found himself alongside their apartment building, he would shout and wave, "Mama! Marina!" Marina would run out onto their balcony and wave back.

They went on picnics in the woods, sometimes with Alik's friend Erich Titovyets and sometimes with Marina's friends Misha Smolsky and his crowd. On one of their picnics, Alik did the hulahoop to amuse the others. And the Oswalds often entertained friends at their apartment. From time to time Erich came by to give Alik a lesson in German. Pavel Golovachev came, Anita Ziger came, and so did Marina's old friends. There was one item of the Oswalds' decor that always aroused their comments: Alik's shotgun. It occupied a place of honor on the wall above the sofa, which was also the Oswalds' bed. Each week Alik took the gun down and oiled and polished it with the utmost care. He oiled, polished, squinted, and then oiled, polished, and squinted some more. The spot on the wall where he hung the gun was stained with oil. From the devotion he lavished on this ritual, it occurred to Marina that her husband was like a mother with a little child. "He's lonesome for America," she thought. "He had more amusements there." He had fewer hobbies, fewer diversions he really enjoyed, than anyone she knew. So, seeing him happy with his gun, she did her best to leave him in peace.

Her friends had no such compunctions. They urged him to bring it with him the next time they all went to the country, and he did. The day was dull and overcast, and although it was not yet the end of August there was a hint of autumn in the air. The birches and aspen were turning yellow; the pine trees whispered overhead. The girls picked mushrooms and hazelnuts, and built a fire under a canopy of pines. The boys went off in search of doves. There was a crack of rifles, and when they returned they were empty-handed, but joking and in obvious good spirits. Halfway through the shoot they had given up doves and looked for squirrels and rabbits. They claimed to have hit a few, but no one had been able to locate his prey. None of the boys mentioned whether Alik was a good or a poor shot.[4]

He did, in fact, belong to a gun club, a necessity to possess a gun in the U.S.S.R. And before he met Marina he had gone on a few outings. But he complained that the club held more meetings than outings, and after their marriage, their expedition to the country was the only time he used his gun. Marina thought little about her husband's having a gun; she supposed merely that it was one of those things men do.

When Alik and Marina were alone in the apartment, he spent a good deal of time on his writing. Marina calls everything he wrote his "Diary," but actually, in addition to the Diary proper, he wrote letters home, a memo on his love affairs in Russia, and two essays which he called "The Collective" and "The New Era." When Marina first noticed that he was writing, in mid-July soon after their return from the American Embassy, Alik was furtive and uncomfortable about it. The moment she came in the door, he snapped his folder shut and put the writing away. As time went on he grew accustomed to writing with Marina in the room, but continued to show the old uneasiness if any of their friends came by. He would close his folder and quickly hide it, and Marina sensed that he was shifting uneasily in his chair, waiting for the visitor to go.

He wrote on a large pad and the pages were carefully numbered. The pad was in a yellow folder, which he kept on the topmost shelf of the kitchen, at the very back, behind a stack of suitcases and well out of Marina's reach. Once she suggested that he keep it in a place that was easier to get at. Marina promised not to touch it. He refused: "You'll give it to someone else to translate."

Marina was, indeed, a little curious. She did not know English but she was familiar with Latin script and had spotted her name and the names of other girls in the Diary. "I hope you're writing nice things about your old girlfriends," she teased. "It's none of your business," he snapped. Another time she asked him to translate a little of the Diary aloud.

"I write in English so you won't be able to read it."

"Is it secret?" she asked.

"No. I just don't like people reading my things."

Marina decided to study English at the Institute of Foreign Languages. But Alik was not enthusiastic about the idea, and refused to help her learn. "Study by yourself," he told her. "Or study if we go to America." Once she asked why he had not found a wife who knew English. He replied that he much preferred a wife who did not.

Alik's Diary sprawled over twelve large, handwritten pages, but he lavished much of his attention on "The Collective," an ambitious fifty-page essay.[5] On the surface the essay is a description of the Minsk Radio Plant, loaded with facts and figures. At a deeper level, however, the radio plant is a metaphor for the whole of the Soviet Union, and the major theme is political control and how the Communist Party runs the country. The essay does not come off. It is not well organized and the analogy between country and factory on which it depends breaks down. It is also biased by a rather special insight, the kind that is born of hostility. But although the handwriting is almost illegible and the spelling and punctuation erratic, it is thorough and thoughtful, and it reflects a good deal of work—by no means the work of someone stupid. The message that emerges is clear: Alik felt suffocated by the rigid controls that the Communist Party exercised over Soviet life.

While he was working on "The Collective," Alik pelted Marina with questions: the retail prices of countless items, as well as details of Komsomol meetings she had been to. He also wanted to know the salary and rank of her Uncle Ilya, both of which, since Ilya held a sensitive post, were something of a secret to her. However, by discreet questioning of her Aunt Valya and the neighbors across the hall from the Prusakovs, she learned that Ilya was a full colonel of the MVD, to which rank he had only recently been elevated, and that his salary was nearly 300 rubles ($300) per month, though Valya claimed it was only 200.

Alik was probably planning to use Ilya's salary, rank, and the size of his apartment in "The Collective," to illustrate wage differentials and the role of privilege in the U.S.S.R. But Marina was apprehensive. She knew that her husband hoped to publish what he was writing, and she was afraid of the repercussions on her family. She asked Alik not to write about her or her relatives and he complied.

In spite of his difficulties in expressing himself in his own language, due in part to his lack of education and in part to his reading disability, Alik's spoken Russian was good. Before he came to the Soviet Union, he had studied the language by himself for two years with the help of a Berlitz grammar and he was still at a loss. But by the time he met Marina, a year and a half later, his Russian was colloquial and idiomatic. He used, more or less correctly and with apparent ease, words she herself avoided because she thought them obscure. From this and from his conservative way of dressing, Marina, who is something of a language snob herself, inferred that he was better educated and from a higher social class than in fact he was.

Marina learned that her husband's mastery of the language was largely due to the help of his co-workers at the radio plant. From the day he first appeared among them in January 1960, they took him into the courtyard after lunch and started in on his Russian. Seated in the sun in their shirtsleeves, they would pick up an insect and point to it. "Come on now, Alka," they encouraged him, "what's this little fellow here?", and he would commit to memory the word for "ant."

"They were really great," he told Marina. "Each day they taught me a new word and went over the ones I'd learned already. They even taught me to swear." Meanwhile they laughed and joked with him and asked him questions about America. Since they had no English, he had to answer in Russian. It gave him the push he needed. He came home at night after that, took up his grammar books again, and really began making headway. He had other help, too, from his friend Erich and from a girl at the Foreign Languages Institute who helped him in Russian in return for his help with her English. But it was the men at the plant who got him going.

Marina was impressed by Alik's Russian. What she liked best was his concision. He could say in three words what she would say in six. Both of them spoke in shorn-off, staccato phrases; Alik spoke English the same way, suggesting ideas rather than completing them. And while his English sounded abrupt and un-schooled, perhaps, such speech in Russian was the fashion among the young.

Although she was proud of the way her husband spoke, Marina noticed weaknesses, too. She observed that he never read Russian for pleasure, and when he went to the public library, with the whole of Russian literature before him, he never took out a volume in Russian. Every day he bought a newspaper, *Pravda* or *Izvestia* or the Belorussian Communist Party paper. But he said they were boring—"They always say one and the same thing"—and most of the time he merely glanced at them. The only thing he claimed to read were the speeches of Nikita Khrushchev, which were colorful, frequent, and entertaining. They were a great source of knowledge about the country and were given, no doubt to Alik's delight, to flaying one of his favorite enemies—the Soviet bureaucracy.

Marina thinks he read so little Russian because he was lazy. Neither he nor she knew that he had a reading disability that must have made it tedious and frustrating to wrestle with the strange Cyrillic symbols. Alik was not lazy. He struggled to improve his Russian, and his efforts represent a strenuous attempt to compensate, even overcompensate, for the difficulty with his own language he at most only sensed that he had. When they were at home, for example, Marina used short, simple phrases to be sure he understood. But he asked her to speak normally so that he could keep on learning. When she was angry, on the other hand, Marina expressed herself in abstruse words and long-drawn-out sentences. The words simply flooded from her tongue. "Wait, wait," Alik would cry out in anguish, not at her anger but at her syntax. "What does it mean? Say it again from the beginning." Marina found her anger beginning to ebb. "Poor boy," she would think, "he doesn't understand." And her fury would give way to pity.

Unmarried friends of Marina's often dropped by to seek advice in some matter of the heart. They purposely spoke in synonyms, difficult, unfamiliar words so that he would not understand. But they were reckoning without Alik. He listened raptly and wrote down every word he did not know. He was not prying; he was trying to enlarge his vocabulary. Before long, curiosity got the better of him and he interrupted the conversation: What did *this* mean, what did they mean by *that*? The girls had forgotten. They peered at his sheet of paper, trying to decipher what they had said. The words he had written down bore only a coincidental resemblance to the words they had actually spoken. Alik had a good ear and he had heard accurately enough. But because of his language difficulty, he was unable to reduce to written symbols what his ear had heard.

Alik owed more to the other men at the factory than his proficiency in Russian. So open were they, so easy and frank in his presence, that he felt like one of them. "They tell stories and criticize the foreman and Partog in front of me as if I wasn't a foreigner," he boasted to Marina. He soon came to share their attitudes about the Party organizer and the deputy director of the factory, and like the other men, he despised the hypocrisy and favoritism on every side. But while he liked his fellow workers, he was not really a part of things at the plant and Marina knew it. At lunchtime, he nearly always sat by himself, or at a table of men he did not know, rather than with the men he worked with. He did not join the other men on drinking sprees, or go to see them at their homes. He was considered antisocial, and with some of them he was actually unpopular because he had been given an apartment of his own without doing anything to deserve it. They would have forgiven him quickly had he been either a congenial fellow or a good worker. But his work, if anything, was below average. He did only what he had to do and no more. It is ironic that Alik grew to dislike the Soviet system, in part, because of the restrictions it placed upon him, while his colleagues disliked him because of the privileges he received.

Yet Alik was as well liked in Russia as he had ever been before or was ever to be again. At the plant he was the object of a good deal of teasing, much of it with sexual overtones. Was he sorry he had married a Russian girl? Was she pregnant yet? So many and so personal were the matters discussed at the plant that Marina felt acutely self-conscious. "For heaven's sake, Alka," she would exclaim, "don't tell them about our lovemaking!" For her husband would come home with the most intimate details of the others' sex lives, together with suggestions that they try some new sexual technique he had heard about. Marina enjoyed his tales about the sex lives of others but had no wish for Alik to reveal their own.

The truth was that the Oswalds were having difficulty in sex and they were worried about it. They could not reach a climax together; in fact, Marina failed to have an orgasm at all. Whether it was three, five, or ten minutes after they started making love, Alik ejaculated too soon, before Marina was ready. It made her so furious that at times she could have hit him.

"I'll do anything you want, only please, please don't be angry," he would beg.

Sometimes he pretended that he had not had an orgasm yet. "Who are you trying to fool," Marina said, "me or yourself?" She would slap him on the rear end. "Go and wash yourself off. And don't show your face in here again." Half an hour later she was remorseful at being so sharp with him. There were moments, nonetheless, when she thought there was nothing so hateful as the sight of a man who has been satisfied. To her it was the sight of a "dead bird in a bush."

They tried all sorts of distractions—talking about something else, for example—while they were making love, hoping that he could go on longer, until she was ready for him. Nothing helped. Sometimes in the early months of their marriage she refused sex altogether: "I'd rather you didn't touch me. You finish too soon. It makes me sick."

"*All* men are like that," Alik said. Or, "With *you*, what man could wait more than five minutes?" Or, "It would take five men to satisfy *you!*" Marina began to think it really was her fault. Then one day he suggested something new, a variation he had heard about at the factory. It involved some oral sex, or what they were to call "French love."[6]

Marina was greatly embarrassed. But Alik assured her that "between husband and wife everything is good and pure," and she consented to try it. It became a frequent way of making love, although Marina never felt right about it, and Lee evidently preferred normal intercourse most of the time.

Marina was ashamed of her body. She was acutely self-conscious about it. All through the sexual act she would be thinking how sinful she was, how thin she was, and wondering what Alik must think of her. He took endless pains to reassure her. Again and again he said that she was "the best woman" in the world for him, sexually and in every other way. He made love to her at all times of the month, even when she was menstruating, and this signified to Marina that he accepted her just as she was. Another sign of his acceptance concerned a scar on her lower back, the remnant of a childhood operation. Never in all their married life did Alik mention the scar or ask Marina how she got it. She considered his reticence a mark of the most exquisite tact. As she grew to realize that her husband was not critical of her body in any way, Marina eventually came to feel freer with him.

Alik appears to have been proud of his body. Marina sometimes teased him about his shoulders, which were sloping or, as she put it, "weak" and "womanly." But she was overcome with joy when, after they were married, she caught her first glimpse of Alik naked below the waist. She considered his legs, his back, and his thighs objects of real beauty, and was gratified to think that her children might inherit such marvelous features. He was soon aware of her admiration and, on occasion, when they had quarreled, he would sit with one leg draped over the arm of a chair, displaying his most perfect features. More than once this was an invitation to reconciliation.

Marina was gratified, too, by his cleanliness. She would not have gone near the handsomest man on earth were he not also immaculate. In this respect, Alik left nothing to be desired. He was as obsessed as she by the notion of cleanliness. Invariably, no matter how late at night it might be, he bathed, shaved, and brushed his teeth before they made love, singing or whistling and looking forward happily to what was ahead of him. When he was through he would call out, "I'm ready, Mama," and after sex he washed again. He was, Marina says, "a hundred times cleaner" than she was. It pleased her that while she demanded perfect cleanliness from him, he liked her and accepted her however she happened to be.

Her feelings had changed a good deal since the days when she had been repelled by her husband, repelled by sex, and finally, two months after they were married, spent a brief, unhappy night with someone else in a forlorn effort to discover whether her marriage had been a mistake. She continued to feel an underlying disappointment with the sex act. But as time went on, their sexual relationship grew more harmonious, and eventually Marina came to consider her husband a tender and accomplished lover. "The longer I lived with him, the more I felt attracted to him," she says, adding that he could be "quite a seducer" when he wanted to be. "He was willing to do anything at all to give me satisfaction." She was touched by his efforts. They increased the tenderness she felt for him. All through their marriage, sex, despite its discontents, made for much greater closeness between them.

Alik was extremely jealous of Marina. He allowed no former boyfriend of Marina's ever to set foot in the apartment unless he was now married. He would not permit her to dance with anyone but him. He was, moreover, very much a

Puritan about sex. He hated divorce and he hated infidelity, especially on the part of a woman. When he heard of a case, he would say: "Women are all alike." He also disapproved of abortion. People, he said, "ought to pay for their mistakes." He never sought out anybody else and neither, after that one night in July, did Marina. He never blamed or reproached her for his sexual difficulty—or theirs. He blamed himself for reaching climax too soon, while Marina blamed herself for her inability to reach climax other than through a form of sex of which she felt ashamed. They both enjoyed sex. It made up many a battle between them and was one of the best things in their life together. But because of the form it took, Alik thought that he was less than he should be as a man, and Marina thought she was less than she should be as a woman. Even though their sexual relationship got better as the months went on, each felt that he or she had something still to prove.

10

The Long Wait

ALIK LOVED to sing. He sang Harry Belafonte in the bathtub, Rimski-Korsakov while mopping the floor, Rachmaninoff while washing dishes. He whistled or sang Russian folk tunes, and when he played opera on the phonograph, he sang and pantomimed as if he were on stage. His favorite singer was the incomparable Russian bass, Chaliapin, and when he sang along with a Chaliapin recording, he would turn red as a beet trying to hit the low notes. When he made it, he would shout: "Look at me. I sing as well as he does!" At the end of an especially taxing passage he would call out in triumph to Marina: "Mama, I love you!"

One Sunday in early September, when the leaves were turning yellow out of doors, they were sitting together in the apartment, Marina sewing and Alik bending over his Diary. He was singing as usual, and Marina noticed that nearly every line ended with the same words—"oh my darlin'." They were English words, but she understood them and hoped they might refer to her. After a while she grew tired of hearing the same song over and over. "Put on another record now," she said. "You've been singing that one thing all day."

"I'm sorry," Alik apologized absent-mindedly, and after a brief pause started singing it again.

Marina was to hear the song often, and always, it seemed, when Alik was working on his Diary. It was not until years later that she found out it was the title song of the movie *High Noon,* the story of the sheriff of a small Western town who, against the wishes of his wife and without any help from the townspeople, is brave enough to stand up to a band of outlaws who are out to take over the town. Alik saw the movie in Fort Worth in 1956 on the enthusiastic urging of his brother Robert, and they loved to sing the song together.[1] He may also have seen it again while he was in the Marine Corps, and it is apparent that the theme of the movie and its title song, the conflict between love and duty, made a deep impression on him.

Alik's favorite opera was Tchaikowsky's *The Queen of Spades,* based on a short story by Pushkin. He saw the movie of the opera countless times and played it on the phonograph again and again. One aria, in particular, he played as many as twenty times a night:

> I love you. I love you beyond measure.
> I cannot conceive of life without you.
> I would perform a heroic deed of unheard-of prowess
> for your sake . . .[2]

Marina suspected that her husband associated the aria with some former love, and she grew jealous. She must have shown it, for Alik began to play the record only when she was out, and changed it quickly the moment he heard her footstep on the stair. Marina soon found a name to attach to her jealousy. They had received postcards from someone vacationing in the south, and Alik explained that they were from an Intourist interpreter who had helped him a great deal when he first arrived in the Soviet Union. A week or so later the front door opened and in she walked. It was Rimma Shirokova.

Alik looked pleased but ill at ease as he made the introductions. Rimma, about twenty-seven, was blond and tastefully dressed, and was plainly a person of education. Marina liked her right away.

Alik and Rimma began to talk in English until Rimma tactfully suggested that they speak Russian so Marina could understand. Marina noticed that the visitor addressed her husband as "Lee," a name she had rarely heard him called before. Rimma laughed and joked a good deal as the two of them sipped coffee and talked over acquaintances they had in common in Moscow. She asked "Lee" if he was going to continue his education. He told her, untruthfully, that he had applied for Friendship University but had not yet received a reply. "You must study," Rimma said firmly, and he agreed. She stayed about an hour—she was catching a night train for Moscow—but before she left, Rimma said to Alik: "You have a good wife. Take care of her."

"What a nice-looking girl!" Marina exclaimed, as soon as she had gone. "How on earth can you love me when you might have had someone like her!"

"I was in love with her," Alik admitted. "I wanted to marry her. But she is older than I am. She thought I was just a little boy, and she wouldn't have me." He assured Marina that she was every bit as good for him as Rimma, and a good deal younger besides. In spite of his reassurance Marina continued to feel inferior; Rimma was prettier and better educated than she was. "Rimma was too good for him—I wasn't," she thought.

Marina remembers more about the visit than her feelings of jealousy. Soon after Rimma arrived, Alik came into the kitchen and said to her in a low voice: "Don't tell Rimma that we're trying to go to America!" Rimma had gone out of her way to help him when he was trying desperately to stay in Russia two years before. He must have felt that he would cut a ridiculous figure if she learned that he was now trying, almost equally hard, to get out.

Marina also remembers that Alik was nervous throughout the visit. At the time she supposed that it was because of their former relationship. But years later, when she learned that it was Rimma who had discovered him that day in 1959 when he slashed his wrist in his hotel room in Moscow, she realized that Alik must have been afraid that Rimma would mention his suicide attempt.

Indeed, Marina would have been very shocked had she known of the episode. Yet she suspected something. A few weeks after she was married, she noticed a small scar on Alik's left wrist. She asked if he got it in a fight over a girl and was surprised when he at first refused to answer. She was more surprised still when he snapped: "Don't ever ask me again."

"Was it your first love?" Marina persisted.

Visibly upset, he replied, "I was young and foolish then."

After that Marina noticed, out of a corner of her mind, that Alik kept the scar hidden. He wore a watch on his left wrist and once, when it broke, it was months before he would take it to be fixed. Later, when he broke it again, and again had to take it to be fixed, he covered his wrist with an identification bracelet even though he hated jewelry and knew that Marina, too, hated jewelry of any kind on a man.

Marina never asked him about the scar again. But when she learned that it was the result of a suicide attempt, her thoughts again fastened on Rimma. She believes that her husband attempted suicide not only to put pressure on the Soviet authorities to permit him to stay in Russia, but to impress Rimma. "I would perform a heroic deed of unheard-of prowess for your sake."[3]

About September 20, very soon after Rimma's visit, Marina was on her way to work on the bus one morning when she was overcome by gas fumes. She stepped off to buy a glass of carbonated water and crumpled to the street in a faint. A passer-by rushed her to the Third Clinical Hospital, right above the pharmacy where she worked. When Alik returned to the apartment that evening, he found a message and rushed to the pharmacy. Marina crept down the back stairs of the hospital to see him.

"Did you lose the baby?" he asked, pale and upset. Marina assured him the baby was all right. He told her to do anything, have an abortion even, but be sure no harm came to *her*.

The doctors found Marina run down, and deficient in vitamins and iron. Then they discovered that her blood type was Rh-negative and, fearing complications in the pregnancy, kept her in the hospital about five days. Later, at Alik's suggestion, they tested his blood. Marina was with him during the test and she had never in her life seen anyone so afraid of pain and the sight of blood. He nearly fainted twice and was very peevish and cross. "Can't they dig up a better nurse than that?" he complained. When it was over, it turned out that his blood type was Rh-negative, too.[4]

Marina was overcome. Fate had, indeed, taken a hand in her life. Throughout her marriage she felt certain that no other husband could have given her a child; no one else would have had the same blood type. It meant that they had been truly destined for one another. Somehow, across an ocean, he had found her.

Marina felt the same way about the scars both of them had on their arms.

Skin had been removed from her right arm during an eye operation in childhood. Alik had the scar on his left elbow from the accidental discharge of a pistol while he was in the Marine Corps in Japan, although he told Marina, falsely, that he had been wounded in action in Indonesia. The scars were the same size and looked identical. To Marina, the similarity was another sign that she and Alik had been destined for each other by fate.

Marina's illness was not serious and she had a good time in the hospital. Nurses came from all over to have a look at the "marvel" who had married an American. She had visits from two or three old beaux, but since husbands were not permitted, she had to steal downstairs to the pharmacy at night to see Alik.

One evening just after she left the hospital, Alik came home in a special hurry. "President Kennedy is going to speak tonight," he said. He closed the balcony doors to shut out noises from the street, or perhaps to keep the neighbors from hearing. A series of announcements came over the radio, the first in a Baltic tongue, then Russian, then Ukrainian. Next, they heard a voice in English.

"Is it him?" Marina asked.

"Not yet," Alik answered impatiently.

At the beginning of the year 1961, the year the Oswalds met and married, the new young President of the United States had stood in icy sunshine half a world away and taken the oath of office. "Let every nation know," he said, "whether it wishes us well or ill, that we shall pay any price, bear any burden, meet any hardship, support any friend, oppose any foe to assure the survival and success of liberty." Less than three months later, a band of Cuban exiles armed by the United States landed at the Bay of Pigs in Cuba. Khrushchev and Kennedy met somberly in Vienna. A summer of crisis followed. Khrushchev threatened to end Western access to Berlin. Kennedy called out reserves. A wall went up in Berlin. At the end of August, Russia announced that it was resuming atmospheric nuclear testing. Three H-bombs of unprecedented megatonnage were detonated in Central Asia. The cold war entered a dangerous new phase as Khrushchev tested the mettle of the new President.

Alik recognized Kennedy's voice the second it came over the air. He had apparently heard Kennedy before while he was in Russia, as the result of scores of Kennedy speeches or excerpts broadcast by the Voice of America and Radio Liberty, another station to which he listened. This speech was being broadcast live and in its entirety by the Voice. It was Kennedy's address of September 25, 1961, given at the United Nations General Assembly, announcing the end of the Berlin crisis.

Alik was rigid with attention as Kennedy spoke for about an hour. The voice was wavy and distorted, and now and then a word was lost by jamming. "Oh, *chort*" ("damn"), Alik swore each time it happened. Once, when Marina made a slight sound, he waved her in irritation into the kitchen. After that she sat motionless beside him.

The moment the speech ended, Alik bounded into the kitchen to make tea. What was it about? Marina asked. "About war and peace," he told her, and quoted a few of the President's phrases.

"That's funny," said Marina. "Everybody wants peace here. They want peace there, too. So why do they talk about war?"

"Politics," Alik grinned.

A day or so later, Alik defended the President's speech in a discussion with Uncle Ilya. He thought the Soviet government was "sneaky," since it had attacked the speech without publishing it or printing a fair account. Sipping tea in the kitchen with Aunt Valya, Marina heard her husband speak up stoutly for the United States. Uncle Ilya was equally staunch in his defense of the Soviet Union. But on one thing they both agreed—the Bay of Pigs. Alik roundly deplored American policy toward Cuba and Fidel Castro.

Marina did not know it, but her husband had long been enthusiastic about Castro. That autumn he took her to see a movie about the Cuban leader by the illustrious Soviet film director, Roman Carmen. Alik loved it and he started calling Castro "a hero" and "a man of talent." And at about this same time, he began to seek out the Cuban students in Minsk, 300 or so strong, to learn what he could of Castro's revolution.

The Cuban students were a lively lot, who found Soviet communism a drab disappointment. They loved singing, dancing, and playing the guitar, but no matter what amusement they thought up, the militia quickly forbade it. They were even discouraged from going out with Soviet girls, and they hated the cold weather. The Cubans were in dread that the Americans would invade their country and overthrow Castro, lest they be doomed to stay in Russia forever. Looking at the dreary, colorless city around them, they asked—was it for this we built a revolution?

Alik shared their disappointment in Russia, but he had believed in communism for six years now, and it was hard to give up the dream that somewhere a perfect society was coming into being. Was it not sensible to suppose that the clumsy, stolid Russians, who had never done things right anyway, had merely fumbled the chance history had given them, and that in the hands of a livelier, more talented people like the Cubans, and with a heroic leader like Castro, communism might yet yield its promise? And so, perhaps seeking a cushion against his disenchantment, Alik turned again to Castro, who might truly achieve an egalitarian society and whose communism, Alik was certain, would be of a gaudier feather altogether than the drab thing Russia had created.

In October, three months after their visit to the American Embassy, Marina and Alik still had no word from the Soviet authorities on their application for permission to leave Russia. It had to be assumed that such an application would be considered at a very high level, adding weeks, or even months, to the bureaucratic process. Alik sought to speed things up by putting pressure on the American Embassy. He had written to the embassy at least once a month since his trip to Moscow, complaining of the difficulty he was having in obtaining Soviet exit visas, and the harassment he and Marina were being subjected to. Now, in Marina's recent illness, he saw another opportunity to enlist sympathy for his cause, and on October 4 he wrote Ambassador Llewellyn E. Thompson, asking him to make inquiries on his behalf at the Soviet Ministry of Internal Affairs in

Minsk. He said that his wife was still under pressure to withdraw her visa application, and because of that she had been hospitalized for nervous exhaustion. Like many of Alik's lies, there was a germ of truth in his claim. (Marina had been hospitalized, but not for nervous exhaustion.)[5] He also inquired about the status of his passport renewal, and whether or not Marina's application to enter the United States had been approved.

The embassy was not encouraging. Oswald's passport renewal had been approved, but the embassy had been instructed to validate it only when his travel plans to return to the United States had been made, and when he reappeared in person at the embassy. Marina's status with the American government was still pending, the embassy wrote; finally, Oswald was informed that the embassy had no way of influencing Soviet authorities to act upon applications for exit visas.

Marina was due for a three-week vacation in October. Alik, who had had his vacation, urged her to get away for a change of scene, and after a few days sitting at home she decided to go to Kharkov, nearly 500 miles to the southeast, to stay with her mother's sister Aunt Polina and her husband Uncle Georgy (Jorya) Alexandrov. Another sister of her mother's, Aunt Taisya, also lived in Kharkov, and Marina discovered, to her surprise, that none of her relatives there knew that she had married an American. They were even more shocked when she told them that she had applied for permission to go to America with her husband. Uncle Jorya hardly spoke a word to Marina after that. He stopped laughing and joking, and abruptly ceased being the uncle she had known. For Georgy Alexandrov was head of the Kharkov Building Trust, one of the most important jobs in the city, and he, like her Uncle Ilya in Minsk, had every reason to suppose that Marina's decision to go abroad could affect him disastrously.

Aunt Polina and Aunt Taisya begged Marina to change her mind. They told her horror stories about poverty and unemployment in the United States. "You'll cry and no one will hear you," Aunt Polina said. Because of her, Uncle Jorya and Uncle Ilya might lose their jobs. "I'm sorry if I've upset you in your condition," Aunt Polina said, "but I can't stand silently by while my niece in her inexperience makes such a mistake. Stay here. Let your husband go back by himself. We'll all help you. You're young—you can marry again."

A few days of this and Marina was sorry she had come. She went back to Minsk a day sooner than planned—and with new doubts about leaving Russia.

The anxious wait for word on their visas and her advancing pregnancy made her nervous and depressed. Night after night, in tears, she would seek reassurance from her husband, and in the mornings she would play "Peer Gynt" on the phonograph, sob a little, eat breakfast by herself, stare out the windows, and trudge off dully to work. Her mood was a match for the gray skies of autumn. But eventually the crying spells ceased. "Alik stopped paying attention," Marina recalls, "so I stopped crying."

Meanwhile everyday life went on. Alik took Marina to a dance at the factory. His friends were eager to have a look at her and he could not refuse any longer. But there was another motive. All evening long Alik twirled Marina purposefully on the dance floor, grinned at her as contentedly as a Cheshire cat and generally played the part of the blissfully married man. It was a performance for the benefit of Ella Germann, the girl who had turned him down. "Phi, how ugly and fat she's gotten," Alik said. "It's lucky I married a thin girl."

The subject of obesity was to come up constantly in their conversations. If Alik said of a woman, "Oh, she's so thin," it meant that he liked her. Walking down the street one day, he spotted a girl he knew slightly. She was flat-chested, bony, and tall. "She'd suit me fine" was his comment. "I could feel all her bones." He once told Marina that he had slept with a girl named Nella. "She was a peasant girl from the country. But there was so much of her in all directions it made me sick. I felt as if I'd overeaten. I had a date with her but I stood her up." Marina, always self-conscious about her own thin body, came to realize that it was one of the reasons Alik had married her. Only later, after she had met Marguerite Oswald did she conclude that Alik's aversion to plump women had something to do with his feelings for his mother.

Marina and Alik continued to spend a good deal of time at Ilya and Valya's. Ilya was hospitable, for he had long ago concluded that they would never be allowed to leave the Soviet Union. He spent long, patient hours playing chess with Alik. An experienced player, Ilya nearly always won, and Alik took his losses hard. Ilya would pat him encouragingly on the back and say that his game was getting better. But just as Alik was misleading Ilya by allowing him to suppose that he had abandoned his efforts to return to America, so he was misleading him about chess. He told Ilya that he was just learning to play. In truth, he had been playing since he was about thirteen years old.

Gruffly kind as Ilya was, it was Valya who made Alik a special favorite, and in ways that were telling to one who knew him, he returned her affection. He was obsessed by cleanliness, refusing, for example, to kiss any woman wearing lipstick or to eat food that had been touched by anyone else. For Valya, and Valya alone, Alik made an exception. He allowed her and no one else, not even Marina, to pick up tidbits in her fingers and pop them into his mouth. Once, before Marina's unbelieving eyes, he went so far as to take a morsel from Valya's plate and eat it.

Finicky as he was about food, Alik was more finicky still about smoke. He tried to get Marina, a chain smoker, to stop, claiming that it was bad for the baby. He cut her down to three, then two, then one cigarette a day. But Marina was expert at evading him. She had cigarettes hidden all over the apartment and she smoked on the sly, even in the bathtub. Alik had a poor sense of smell and rarely noticed.

And he was parsimonious, always saving for something. When they were first married he was free with their money, buying records and furniture. Then, when he was thinking of returning to America but had not yet said anything to Marina, he put her off. "Later—we'll see what we need." Finally, after he had told her of his plans and convinced her to come with him, it was: "Why buy a whole lot now? We'll only have to sell it when we go." Marina turned over her salary to him. He doled out money for groceries and saved up the rest for their trip.

All through the fall, America was very much on Alik's mind. He poured through copies of *Time* magazine that began to arrive in bundles from his mother in Texas, issues that were full of stories and pictures of the Kennedys, and of another public figure who was to become important in Alik's life, Major General Edwin A. Walker. Still there was no word from the Soviet authorities, and Alik made visits to three Soviet government offices in Minsk to inquire about the progress of their visas: the Ministry of Foreign Affairs, the Ministry of Internal Affairs, and the Office of Visas and Registration (OVIR) of the Ministry of Internal Affairs. They could tell him nothing. He began to complain in letters to his brother Robert about the slothfulness of Russian bureaucrats, suggesting that his rights under international law were being violated, protesting the American Embassy's lack of interest in his case, and stating his determination not to stay in the U.S.S.R. a single moment beyond the first of the year (his Soviet residence permit was due to expire on January 4). His complaints were designed not so much to impress Robert as the Soviet officials whom he presumed to be reading his mail. But there were signs of uncertainty and hints in his letters that Alik was aware that life would not be so easy when he got back home. On one occasion he wrote Robert: "Its not going to be to convient to come back to the States and try to start life over again."[6]

Meanwhile, an event of great public magnitude had occurred, an event which Alik soon saw was to have a bearing on his life. While Marina was on vacation in Kharkov, the Twenty-second Congress of the Soviet Communist Party opened in the Kremlin in Moscow, and a new wave of "de-Stalinization" got under way. Stalin's body was removed from its marble mausoleum on Red Square, and Khrushchev began to move away from the alliance with China toward better relations with the United States. As his friends Pavel and Ziger probably suggested to Alik, it was a hopeful omen as far as his and Marina's visas were concerned.

A week or so after her return from Kharkov, Marina was trudging home from work one night through Stalin Square, a vast, cobblestoned area in the center of Minsk, when she noticed with mild surprise that a space the size of a city block had been roped off around the gigantic statue of the dead dictator that towered over the square. Later that night, houses trembled and shook to the heavy tread of tanks and trucks as they rolled through the city streets and took up positions around the statue. By morning a high fence had gone up to conceal the tanks.

Of course there was talk at the pharmacy. "They'll never get it down with chains and tanks," one of Marina's co-workers said. "It's too big. They'll have to use dynamite."

The next night Marina was wakened out of a sound sleep by a series of loud explosions. She sat bolt upright in bed. "Do you hear?" she nudged Alik. "Is it war?"

"No," came a sleepy mumble. "They're just blowing up Stalin."

In Minsk, it appeared, Stalin still had sympathizers who would be offended by the removal of his monument. And so it was being done under cover of night.

The demolition crew was plainly in a hurry and under orders to complete the work before the November 7 parade. But Stalin was too strong for them. The foundations were deep and the monument powerfully wrought. Not even with chains, tanks, and dynamite could the statue be brought down. The head and upper part of the torso had to be dismantled first and the rest demolished piece-meal. It took longer than anyone anticipated, and the work of demolition was still going on when the marchers paraded through Stalin Square (later renamed Lenin Square) on November 7.[7]

Leaving work one icy day in December, Marina fell on the pharmacy steps and hurt her back. Alik was cross with her at first on the baby's account, then anxious, then tender. He had worries of his own. He was losing his hair. Marina consulted her friends and they concocted various remedies at the pharmacy. Each night she came home and massaged his scalp with something new. Nothing helped, and soon Alik dreaded brushing his hair because it seemed to be coming out in clumps. "Don't touch it, don't touch it," he would say to Marina. The more he fretted, the more his hairline receded. Finally, he stopped worrying about it —and his hair stopped falling out.

Once or twice he had nightmares. He mumbled in his sleep both in English and in Russian, and Marina did not know what he was saying. Ill with a fever one night he screamed out in Russian, "I'm going to die, I'm going to die!" She woke him and tried to calm him. "It's all right," she said. "You're going to be all right. The hospital is just down the street. There are doctors there. Medical care is free!"

All through the fall Alik kept a weather eye on the de-Stalinization campaign in both the Soviet press and the back issues of *Time* that his mother continued to send. And his letters to his brother Robert make clear that he rested his hopes of obtaining exit visas for himself and Marina, above all Marina, on the scope and success of that campaign. Moreover, the relaxation of cold war tensions between America and Russia may have reinforced his decision to go home by making him feel that family, friends, and future employers might not, after all, be so very critical of a young man who had chosen to spend a few years in Russia.

On the whole, however, it was the mechanics of getting to America that claimed most of Alik's attention. He was increasingly impatient for a decision from the Soviet authorities. But where he was inclined to push, complain, and go "to the top" when he could, Marina's attitude was, What will be, will be. It was either in the hands of fate, or in those of a temporal power higher than any she could summon.

Alik scolded her about it more than once. He told her not to be so timid. She was *his* wife, under *his* protection, and ought to have more confidence. He had the right to leave the country any time he wanted, and she had the right to come too. He wrote and was forever making her write letters up and down the Soviet bureaucracy; but even when she complied he was never satisfied: "You always *ask* when you ought to *demand*," he said. "A polite letter like *that* and they'll never answer in a year." And so Marina would rewrite the letter, part imperious to please him, part deferential, even supplicating, to please herself and the officials of her country. Who was she, after all, to give fate a shove either way?

What the Oswalds needed was a pipeline into the bureaucracy. And as it happened, they had one, right into the office of Colonel Nikolai Axyonov, head of OVIR, the MVD's Office of Visas and Registration. Lyalya Petrusevich, Marina's best friend, had a new boyfriend. His name was Anatoly, nicknamed Tolka. During his youth, Tolka's father had served with Colonel Axyonov in the army or the MVD and, because of their friendship, Tolka now resided in the Axyonov apartment.

Tolka was a mine of information. During the colonel's endless hours at the office, his wife received guests in the apartment whom she was anxious that her husband not know about. To ensure Tolka's silence, she gleaned bits and pieces of information about his friends the Oswalds. By this roundabout yet reliable route, the Oswalds learned sometime between Tuesday, December 12, and Friday, December 15, that permission for their exit visas had been granted.

Not content with the good news, Alik wanted to know exactly *when* the official word would be coming through. Just after the middle of December, he went to the MVD building and tried to see Colonel Axyonov. He was intercepted by an assistant who promised to pass along his request. Frustrated, he demanded that Marina go to see Axyonov.

"Why should I?" Marina said. "He won't see me any sooner than he'd see you. Why bother anyone? Why not wait? They'll let us know."

Alik did not agree. "If you don't give people a shove, they'll never do anything at all. You'll still be waiting in thirty years."

Eventually Marina gave in, and the following morning, a Monday, on her way to work she stopped at the MVD building and went straight to the headquarters of OVIR. In the anteroom the colonel's male secretary asked her business. Marina explained and she was shown directly into Axyonov's sparsely furnished office.

The colonel was not at his desk. Marina sat quietly by herself for half an hour or so, anxiously expecting a person in the shape of a dark, angry cloud to materialize. Instead, a rather small man came in, his attire civilian, his appearance indeterminate, his hair mouse-colored and fine. It was Colonel Axyonov and he seemed to be slightly rattled. The moment he started speaking Marina felt that he was kind—too kind for the work he was doing.

She stood as he came in. "Sit down, sit down," he said hurriedly. "Please make yourself at home." A uniformed aide entered and laid a stack of papers on the desk. Colonel Axyonov glanced through them and signed half a dozen or so. Then he turned to Marina. "Let's see," he asked absent-mindedly. "What is it you came to see me about?"

Marina explained that she wanted to find out about their exit visas. Would she and her husband be allowed to leave the country? She was very nervous. But she remembered Alik's admonitions: she must be firm and insist on her rights.

Colonel Axyonov asked why she wanted to leave Russia. It was not a matter of loyalty, Marina answered firmly. She had nothing against the U.S.S.R., nor did she care what country she was going to. America was no better or worse than any other. She merely wanted to go where her husband went. After a series of other questions and answers which Marina does not recall, she told Colonel Axyonov that she had come to see him because her husband was anxious.

"Tell your husband not to worry," he said soothingly. "I believe your request will be granted."

Marina asked whether they would hear before the baby came. Axyonov suggested that they wait in any case for the child to be born in the U.S.S.R. He concluded: "I don't know how long it will be before you hear. It isn't up to me." The word would be coming from Moscow. He would let her know as soon as he had any news.

The encounter between Marina and Colonel Axyonov later gave rise to many questions. Why did Axyonov see her? Why was she allowed to leave the U.S.S.R.? And did not her relationship to Ilya Prusakov and the ease with which she was permitted to leave the country signify that she was a Soviet agent?

Axyonov undoubtedly received Marina because he knew who she was. From his lodger, Tolka, or from her own applications for a passport and a visa, he knew her to be the niece of Ilya Prusakov. Both men were full colonels, both worked in the same building, and Axyonov received Marina not in a reception room, as he would a total stranger, but in his private office. Ilya had the highest reputation for discretion, and this may well have played a part, not only in Axyonov's receiving Marina, but in the recommendations that must have been made the previous summer as to whether she should be granted a visa to go abroad. But Ilya was also famous for his utter correctness and his hands-off attitude. He worked for the MVD, not the KGB, and it was not in his character to intervene in the affairs of another ministry, especially one so sensitive as the KGB or even in the work of another section of the ministry he himself was in, the MVD. Nor would it have availed him in the slightest if he had. Besides, Ilya was desperately opposed to Marina's decision to leave Russia, viewing it as a threat to himself and the entire family.

As for Colonel Axyonov, he had made his recommendation in Marina's case months before their interview, and the interview had nothing to do with the outcome. The case had already been decided, and as a matter of politeness to a colleague's relative, he agreed to see Marina. Whatever recommendation Axyonov had made, it may have carried some weight or it may not have. For the decisions in such cases are not made locally but in Moscow, sometimes by the KGB, and sometimes by a special section of the Party Central Committee that deals with travel abroad. Axyonov himself may not have known what agency was handling the case, and at what level. For each case is treated individually, in accordance with its own special features.

The same week that the Oswalds heard informally that Marina would be getting a visa, an identical decision was handed down in another case. But the two cases together were not harbingers of a new policy, for they were not identical —no two cases ever are—and there is not, even today, a predictable Soviet policy on emigration. So great is the role of chance that it is possible that the same case, considered on two successive days, might well be decided differently. For the bodies that make these decisions are isolated and arbitrary, they operate by rules of their own that are known to no one on the outside, and they are strangely impervious to influence from other government agencies and sometimes even from above.

There were, however, several major factors that may have been in Marina's favor. She was not related to a high-ranking officer of the armed services or the KGB, she did not have a university education, had never held a sensitive job, and was not in a position to possess information derogatory to the U.S.S.R. Had she fallen into any of these categories, she would not have been allowed to leave Russia. Moreover, Marina had always stayed as far away from politics as she could. This was probably an advantage, since it meant that she had no political record. Evidently the officials considering her case, probably KGB officials in Moscow and Minsk, concluded that, should she be permitted to go abroad, she was unlikely to do anything to bring the Soviet Union into disrepute, either by her conduct or her political remarks.[8] And there was a good reason for allowing her to go: she was the wife of Lee Harvey Oswald.

From the beginning the KGB had not wanted him in Russia. He had offered radar secrets in return for an opportunity to remain, and it had been decided that he did not have secrets worth knowing. From the reports of Intourist and KGB personnel working at the hotels where he stayed on his arrival in 1959, the KGB had formed a low opinion of his intelligence and emotional stability. He was not a potential recruit for the KGB. Nor did he possess any skill that might be useful to the economy. Worse than that, he had shown himself to be a troublemaker. On being told that he would not be allowed to remain in the U.S.S.R., he had slashed his wrist, in what was reported to the KGB as a genuine suicide attempt that nearly succeeded. Oswald's Diary makes it sound like a mere suicidal gesture. A week later, he had even threatened to repeat the deed. What the KGB learned about Oswald in October of 1959 was that he was a desperate character, one who was willing to do anything, including the use of violence against his own person, in order to get what he wanted. Its conclusion was probably strengthened by his scene at the American Embassy and by his willingness to go public by talking to American reporters.

All these episodes embarrassed the Soviet government into allowing Oswald to remain, and he was helped by the political atmosphere. Khrushchev had just launched the "Spirit of Camp David" and wanted nothing to impede better relations with the United States. The effects of the policy had trickled down and helped even a small fish like Oswald. The "Spirit of Camp David" was later shattered briefly in 1960 by Francis Gary Powers and the U-2 episode, but relations between Russia and the United States were now again on the mend. Oswald was announcing that he wanted to leave Russia, and that he would not leave without his Russian wife. Who was to say that if he were allowed to leave and she, as very often happened in such cases, was refused permission altogether or was delayed by five or six months, Oswald would not again embarrass the Soviet Union by some desperate and very public act, such as another suicide attempt, this time, say, in front of the Soviet Embassy in Washington?

There are experts on Soviet affairs who believe that nothing happens in Russia quite by chance and that the authorities were so anxious, or at least willing, to have Oswald leave that they actually encouraged his friendships with Ziger and with Pavel Golovachev in the knowledge that they would counsel him to go. Oswald saw them daily at the factory and they were also his best personal friends. Ziger is known to have advised him to keep his American citizenship. From everyone he knew, Oswald doubtless heard facts about Soviet life that led him to decide to leave the country sooner than he might otherwise have done. Both may have given him advice on how to return home, on visa tactics, and Ziger and Pavel, in particular, probably told him that if he wanted to leave Russia, and especially if he wanted to take Marina—that was the hard part—he should move while Khrushchev was riding high, since in Russia things could revert at any moment to the way they had been in Stalin's time. Indeed, as it happened, Khrushchev's policy of de-Stalinization reached its high point with the Party Congress of October 1962, so that Oswald may once again, just as his and Marina's exit visas were under consideration, have been the beneficiary of a temporary easing of Soviet policy.

But apart from a brief snippet in Oswald's Diary there is no evidence, from Marina or from anybody else, that Ziger and Pavel did, in fact, coach Oswald on how to leave the country. Their friendships with him appear to have been genuine and spontaneous, and the two men, one perhaps a father figure, the other an older brother, were very likely the best and the truest friends he ever had.

The Russians could have kept Oswald if they had wanted to, by granting him citizenship, by denying his request for an exit visa, or by simply ignoring his request. He was in their country, a police state. But he was an "unsatisfactory" and uncooperative worker of below-average skill, he was occupying an apartment that would otherwise have gone to a factory official, and until a few months before he had been receiving a financial subsidy.[9] He was a drain on the country—and he brought no reward. If allowing Marina—who did not fall into any of the proscribed categories—to go was the price of getting rid of Oswald, why not?

On Christmas Day, Monday, December 25, one week to the day after her interview with Colonel Axyonov, Marina was summoned to OVIR. She stopped by on her way home from work and was informed that both she and her husband had been granted exit visas.

11

Birth of June

MARINA AND ALIK were in splendid spirits when they went to the Zigers' on New Year's Eve. They found Mrs. Ziger alone in the kitchen and told her the good news. She kissed them and confessed that she had prayed for this every night. "Maybe, next year," she added softly, "we will have news, too. Maybe, after all, we shall see one another again." If life was hard in America, if they suffered disappointments there, go to Argentina, she said. "And if you don't like it there, go somewhere else. Go anywhere in the world. But never, ever come back here."

That night the Oswalds told none of the other guests of their good fortune. They were Russians, after all, and it might be an affront to their sensibilities. So they were silent. They ate Spanish rice and Mrs. Ziger's Polish nut cookies, and Alik danced with no one but Marina. He was in as triumphantly happy a mood as she had ever seen him. He even got a little tipsy.

Pavel Golovachev was the only other friend with whom they shared their good news. He let out a low whistle. "Hm," he said, "I never thought they'd let Marina out." To him it meant that things were easing up, and that life might soon be better, not only for those who were allowed to go but for those who were left behind.

Once their visas had been granted, Alik began a flurry of correspondence with the American Embassy. The problem now was Marina. The embassy needed several documents to back up her application for an immigrant's visa to enter the United States, among them an affidavit of support or some other proof that she would not become a public charge. Alik had no job waiting for him, and no proof that he could support a wife. Twice in the first half of January, the embassy suggested to Oswald, who was touchy enough at the best of times and very sensitive on this point, that he precede his wife to the United States.[1] There, he could find a job and obtain the documents he needed. Alik was outraged—"I certainly will not consider going to the U.S. alone for any reason."[2]

Although this had been his position from the start, the embassy letters gave rise to an angry scene with Marina. She was furious and hurt. She thought that the embassy did not want her in the United States and she was not going to be allowed in. She stomped into the kitchen, stood on a chair, plucked her husband's suitcase off its shelf, and proceeded to pack it for him. "There," she pointed in fury. "What are you still doing here? There's your suitcase. There are your things. Take it and go to your America!"

Alik turned the suitcase upside down, dumped the contents on the sofa and the floor, put it back on the shelf in the kitchen, and placed an arm around his wife. "Look," he said, "I know you don't love me. But I love you, and I'm not going to leave without you."

It all ended rather nicely, so both found occasion to repeat the scene. Alik sometimes taunted her: "If it hadn't been for you, I could have gone to America long ago." Marina was ready with a reply: "The only reason you're waiting for me is—you're afraid they'll arrest you if you're alone."

"No," he said. "The reason I'm going to wait is, if I go first you'll never come. Your Aunt Polina and Aunt Valya and Uncle Ilya will keep you here and never let you go. We'll all go together. And if you don't get your visa, I'll stay here."

"Thanks for being so big-hearted," she said. "But feel free to go any time."

Marina believes that he had another reason for refusing to go without her. It was a matter of principle with him that he had a right to do anything he pleased. Moreover, he wanted to show the Russians he could get the better of them. He would leave their country and take a Soviet citizen with him. "As if," she laughs, "the Soviet state would suffer if it had one Marina less."

The Soviet government, however, had complied with his request. The Oswalds were free to leave Russia. It was the American government that was causing the delay; and besides being unusually frequent—between December 27 and January 23 there are four of them—Oswald's letters to the American Embassy during this period were peremptory and, as always, impatient. On January 23 he added a new reason for his haste: "I would much rather have my child born in the United States, than here, for obvious reasons."[3] Oswald had troubled, or dared, to tell the embassy only two weeks earlier, on January 5, that he and his wife were expecting a baby. But to the embassy, Oswald's reasons may not have been "obvious" at all. They might have seemed ludicrously far-fetched. Oswald was expecting a boy, of course. He wanted his son born at home, and not in Russia, so that he could be President of the United States.

"My David will be President," he said a number of times as he lay on his back, stared at the ceiling, and dreamed of the future. But when the visa business dragged on and it became apparent that the child would be born in Russia, he remarked matter-of-factly one day: "Too bad. If it's a boy, he can't be President." Later, when the child was born and was a girl, he said: "That's all right. My son will be born in America. *He* can be President."

It was Marina who suggested a name for the baby if it was a girl. Alik wanted an English, not a Russian, name, and remembering one of her favorite English novels, *The Forsyte Saga,* Marina proposed Fleur and Irene, and then, finally, June.

Alik's arm shot exultantly into the air. "That's it! That's the name for our daughter. Only I'm sure she won't be a girl." He counted back and pointed out that the child had been conceived in June. "Let's name her June Marina. If we stay here, we'll call her Marina. And if we go to America, she shall be June." And that was the way they left it.

Politics scarcely intruded on their lives that winter, so taken up were they with waiting for the baby and with thoughts of leaving Russia. But in January an event occurred which, even though it was a carefully guarded secret, rocked the whole of Russia. An attempt was made on the life of Nikita Khrushchev, and it took place in Minsk.

It was the sort of thing that was unheard of in the modern U.S.S.R. In czarist Russia terrorism and assassination had been a way of life, a familiar form of political struggle. But because Lenin taught that individual terror was not acceptable, and because Stalin deported or slaughtered thousands for nonexistent plots against his life, the assassination of political leaders had faded out. Ordinary men and women were murdered, but if leaders disappeared from the face of the earth it was done at the hands of other leaders and not of the led. Perhaps no one believed any longer that by taking violent action he could alter the course of history. Or perhaps individual Russians felt that they were so small, and the state so large, there was nothing anyone could do. Besides, if one leader died, there was always another, just as oppressive, to step into his shoes.

Then, in January of 1962, Nikita Khrushchev came to Minsk to do some shooting in the Belovezhskoye Pushche, one of his favored hunting preserves. He was accompanied by Wladyslaw Gomulka, leader of the Polish Communist Party, and there was the usual retinue of Soviet and Polish officials. He was staying in a government dacha outside Minsk and hunting in the winter forests when the unthinkable occurred.

Rumors of the assassination attempt swept the length and breadth of Russia, but to this day no one knows exactly what happened. Some said that Khrushchev's entire bodyguard turned against him, others that a row of young men formed a roadblock and, as Khrushchev walked toward them, fired a single, dramatic volley into the air. But the account that seems least fanciful was that a young man from Khrushchev's bodyguard tried to shoot him.[4]

The Oswalds heard about the incident in frightened colorful undertones from Marina's Aunt Lyuba Axyonova, who was not a witness but had been present at the dacha in her capacity as bookkeeper of the Council of Ministers dining room. According to Lyuba, only one member of Khrushchev's bodyguard was responsible. He missed and Khrushchev escaped uninjured. No one knew what happened to the would-be assassin.

Lyuba was afraid to speak of the shooting in detail in front of Alik, a foreigner, since the incident was not made public and, for spreading "anti-Soviet propaganda," or information the government does not want known, a citizen could receive seven to fifteen years. The would-be murderer had been a member of Khrushchev's entourage, and Lyuba was also afraid that in a single, Stalin-esque stroke all other employees who had been anywhere nearby would be sum-marily dismissed. She feared for herself and her job.

It was in this atmosphere of subdued hysteria that Alik first heard of the assassination attempt. He doubtless heard a great deal more talk about it from the men at the factory. Because such a thing was unprecedented at that time, and because it had happened right there, it must have created a tremendous stir in Minsk. And the incident may have been imprinted even more indelibly on Alik's mind because Lyuba's account was whispered and because she was so obviously terrified.

Marina had left her job at the pharmacy on maternity leave just after the first of the year. The last month of her pregnancy was a privileged time, and she enjoyed it to the full. Her legs and thighs ached. Alik rubbed and kissed them and said: "My poor, poor girl. You're hurting yourself just to give life to our baby." He curled up into a tiny ball in one corner of the bed so that she could have the rest for herself. Soon she got used to sleeping with her feet on his back for warmth, as well as for the relief it gave her aching legs. He came to like this and would ask, "Are your feet cold?" Even when the answer was No, he would tell her to "put your feet up there anyway."

Alik had misconceptions about the birth of a child. He thought that an expectant mother produces milk from the beginning of pregnancy. Marina en-lightened him as to the facts. Later, after the baby was born, Marina had too much milk and ran a fever. Alik offered to suck the milk. Marina was shocked, but he assured her that it was "quite natural." She was more surprised still when instead of spitting it out as she expected, he swallowed it. Why not? he asked. It was good milk, sweet and fat. If it was good enough for his baby, it was good enough for him. And he went right on drinking it.

By then, they ate their meals at home, and made use of a communal trash can in the courtyard. One night Alik saw some stray dogs and cats bolting food from the trash can. After that, he put out a special meal for the strays each time he emptied the garbage. "My animals ate up everything I left them," he would report happily to Marina.

They bought a second-hand crib for the baby and Alik lovingly gave it three coats of white paint. Their friends came, as always, in the evenings, only now they brought sheets, which they had sewn for the baby, diapers, which they had also sewn, and toys. Alik's friend Erich was corresponding with a pen pal in England And so, from England, they got a copy of Dr. Spock's *Baby and Child Care.* Well before the baby was due, Alik had the book nearly memorized.

On February 14, Marina woke in the middle of the night and told him the water had burst. Alik jumped out of bed, consulted Dr. Spock and told her, incorrectly, that they had 14 hours to go. Marina went back to sleep, but Alik was too nervous. Finally, at seven in the morning, wild with anxiety, he insisted that they start for the hospital.

Outside it was cold and gray. Everyone was hurrying to work, and there was an early morning crowd at the taxi stand. Pale as a ghost, Alik tried to get to the head of the line by shouting that he was rushing his wife to the hospital. "Your wife's no more pregnant than I am," one man shouted back. "And *I* have to get to work."

They took a bus and Marina was in labor as they walked the last block or so to the hospital. Alik wanted to carry her, but she insisted that she could make it on her own. Each time she felt a thrust of pain, however, it was as if it were stabbing him, too.

It was over, by natural childbirth, in an hour. "Our day for foreign babies," said the doctors. "We've had a Jewish one, a gypsy, a Belorussian—and now an American!"

The mother was disappointed. "A girl, when I wanted a boy," she thought, and did not even want to see it. But when she did see it, she felt a spasm of pity and love. "Poor, helpless little thing. No one on earth to love you. How can I not love you and take care of you?" A new feeling was born in Marina.

Alik, meanwhile, had gone to work since he was not allowed in the maternity section of the hospital. "Congratulations, Papa!" the men shouted when he arrived at the factory. Someone had telephoned from the hospital and left word that his wife had given birth to a baby girl.

Alik had never told the men at the factory that he was expecting a child. But somehow they had found out about it, and the next day at lunch, they held a special ceremony for the new father. They presented him with a big box. Inside were a blanket, a tiny sweater, overalls, little shirts, a yellow bonnet, swaddling cloth—everything a newborn baby would need.

Alik hesitated. He did not know what to do.

"Take it, Papa. What's the shilly-shallying about?" the men said.

Alik took it. He was very touched, but he was so reticent that he did not know how to thank them.

Because of hospital regulations, Alik did not see the baby until it was eight days old, when he arrived to take mother and daughter home. He was, he confessed later, shocked by the sight of the child; like any new father, he expected her to be partly grown and already quite good-looking.

He made their homecoming memorable. In Marina's absence, he had washed the floors, cleaned the apartment from stem to stern, and washed and ironed all the laundry. Ushering the two of them in, his wife and child, he was filled with happiness. He kissed Marina and said simply: "Thank you." Then, quietly, "What a pity we have to wait," meaning for sex. Marina herself felt that if they could have made love on that day, it would have been a kind of completion. It was, anyway, the happiest day of her life. She felt that her husband truly loved her and that, for the first time, he was aware of it.

That evening two of Marina's friends came by to teach her to swaddle and feed the baby. They left, and Marina was alone. Alik had gone to Ilya and Valya's to celebrate Valya's name day. At one o'clock he came home, his cap falling off the back of his head, smiling and tipsy (the fourth and last time Marina was to see him so). "Where's my baby?" he said. "I want to look at her."

The baby was asleep, and Marina objected when he said he wanted to pick her up. So he stood over the crib and gazed at her. That night, and every night thereafter, he dragged the crib over to the bed and insisted on sleeping on the side closest to it.

The young couple were more or less on their own when it came to tending the baby. Aunt Musya came to show Marina how to bathe her, but Alik objected to the casual way she handled the baby, as matter-of-factly as if she were a doll. Aunt Valya, too, dropped by whenever she dared, but she quickly learned to come during her nephew's working hours. His face grew so menacing and pale each time she picked up the baby, and Valya loved holding his "little jewel" so much, that it seemed best to come when the anxious father was out.

Husband and wife differed on how to care for the baby. Alik was faithful to Dr. Spock and loyal to American ways. Marina, of course, preferred Russian ways, and when Alik objected to swaddling the baby, she pointed out that they had no choice, since there were no diapers, no rubber pants, no little shirts or baby pins to be bought in the whole of Minsk. "All right, then, I can swaddle her as well as you," Alik boasted. But his first attempt ended in hopeless confusion, and Marina had to teach him how to do it. He, on the other hand, using Dr. Spock as a guide, taught her how to burp the baby.

In one sense, husband and wife were conspirators. Alik had wanted the baby called June Marina and, as was not unusual for him, he got into a hassle at ZAGS, the registry office, because it was the Russian custom for a child to bear a form of its father's first name as its middle name, or patronymic. The registry officials ("those burerecrats," he called them in his Diary) won out and the baby was named June Lee. But as far as the father was concerned, she was June Marina. When they were alone or with friends, all of whom were thrilled at having in their midst a baby with a foreign name, Alik called her Junka (Junie) or Marinka. But Marina, who shuddered each time she heard the baby called by her own name, called her June or Junka.

To the older generation, however, it would have been a scandal for the child to bear any but a Russian name. When they were with Marina's uncles and aunts, therefore, everyone, even her parents, called the baby Marina. But sometimes Alik forgot and got a warning look or a punch from Marina or one of her friends so that he would not, in the presence of her relatives, give the baby's true name away.

The birth of June brought with it a sudden diminution of Alik's desire to go home. He wrote only one letter to the American Embassy in February and one in March. Perhaps, as with the lull following his marriage the year before, it was the change of focus, the increase of private happiness, that was responsible. But at the same time his anxieties about returning to America were never wholly quiescent. In letters written before and after his daughter's birth, he was still anxious about what might happen to him when he set foot on American soil. In a letter to the American Embassy on January 16, he wrote that he believed his passport might be confiscated on his arrival home.[5]

Then, at the end of the month, a real blow fell. From his mother, Alik heard that his "honorable" discharge from active Marine Corps duty had been changed to "dishonorable." In fact, it was only changed to "undesirable," and it had all happened years before when Alik defected to Russia. But this was the first he knew of it.

Alik lost little time in mailing a new batch of letters. On January 30 he wrote the governor of Texas, John Connally. Under the impression that he was still Secretary of the Navy, he asked Connally to look into the matter. "I shall employ all means to right this gross mistake or injustice," he wrote. He claimed that he was a "boni-fied" American citizen, and had "allways had the full sanction" of the U.S. Embassy and government. He went so far as to compare his sojourn in Russia with that of Ernest Hemingway in Paris during the 1920s.[6] Again Alik had gone to the top. It was the first round of a prolonged, and ultimately futile, battle with the Department of the Navy to change the status of his discharge.

On the same day he wrote Connally, Alik also wrote his brother Robert who, like Connally, was a resident of Fort Worth, asking him to get in touch with Connally about the discharge. He also requested Robert to "ask around again" to see if the government might have charges against him. "Now that the government knows I'm coming," he added archly, maybe "they'll have something waiting."[7]

On February 10, another event sharpened Alik's anxieties. Francis Gary Powers was released from a Russian prison and returned to the United States. In a letter to his brother written the same day his baby was born, and in another letter soon after, he expressed anxiety about Powers's return, as if his treatment was a harbinger of how he himself would be treated on his return to the United States. "I hope they aren't going to try him or anything," he wrote Robert.[8]

Oswald's interest in Powers is striking, for the two men appeared to have nothing in common. Shot down on a high-altitude reconnaissance flight over Russia, Powers was captured, branded a "spy," convicted in a show trial in Moscow in 1960, and spent nearly two years in a Soviet prison. An Eisenhower-Khrushchev summit conference was canceled because of the incident, and Powers became an international celebrity. Oswald was an enlisted man in the Marine Corps whose defection had barely caused a ripple in either the United States or the U.S.S.R.

But the career of Oswald and Powers did have one thing in common—the U-2 high-altitude reconnaissance plane. Oswald, as a Marine, had been stationed at three bases—Atsugi, Japan; Cubi Point (Subic Bay) in the Philippines; and El Toro, California—where U-2 aircraft were kept. Everything about the plane was supposed to be secret: its name, its mission, and above all, the incredible altitude to which it could climb. At each base the planes were kept in a classified, tightly guarded area which no one could enter without a very high security clearance. Oswald had only a low security clearance, but it is likely that he saw the U-2 and heard a good deal of gossip about its mission.[9] And if he glimpsed the plane, it is unlikely that he ever forgot the breathtaking sight. With its fragile fusilage and its slender, incredibly elongated wings, the U-2 looked like a giant bird of beauty and menace.

When a U-2 was shot down over Sverdlovsk six months after his arrival in Russia, and then became the cause of an international scandal, Oswald may have felt that he had had, for the first time, a brush with history. And in Powers he may have seen a little of himself. Powers was much bigger than he was, but both men had dark hair and slightly receding hairlines. Both had high-pitched voices and spoke with slight Southern accents. Powers was a highly skilled "spy in the sky," a man at the center of world attention who had had to defend himself in a klieg-lit trial. Oswald would have liked to be a spy, and he might have enjoyed the spotlight as well.[10]

Oswald may have thought he was like Powers in another way. Nearly all Russians—including Pavel Golovachev, the son of a Soviet air ace, and other men that Oswald knew at the factory—considered Powers a "disgrace." No Russian would have allowed himself or his super-secret aircraft to fall into unfriendly hands. Powers had "betrayed" the United States. That was the core of Oswald's concern. He believed that he, too, had betrayed his country by defecting and denouncing it. And if America sought revenge against Francis Gary Powers, might it not do the same to Lee Harvey Oswald?[11]

The snags in the way of the Oswalds' return had been cleared away on the Russian side; both had been granted permission for their exit visas and Marina now had permission to receive a passport to go abroad. But the delays continued on the American side. First of all, there was the question of money. In addition to his other demands, Alik had informed the embassy that he could not afford the fare to the United States. He could contribute $200, and he expected the embassy to give, not loan, him the rest, preferably $800 or $900, enough to travel by air. The Department of State attempted, unsuccessfully, to raise the money from private relief agencies and asked Marguerite Oswald to help. When Alik learned of it he was outraged. He had written his mother that he did not want her to contribute, and now he told her to ignore the State Department. To the embassy, he wrote: "I request that solicitations toward my relatives be stopped."[12] The embassy, however, had found another solution. It was authorized by the State Department to loan Oswald the amount necessary to cover the costs of the least expensive means of travel back to the United States. As they did for many others whom they considered trapped in Russia, the embassy and the State Department bent over backward to help Oswald.

In Marina's case, they did the same. Her problem was her entrance visa. For proof that she would not become a public charge, embassy officials, surprisingly, accepted an affidavit of support from Oswald himself. They did so on the grounds that he had a place to live, with his mother, and that in the Marine Corps he had been trained in a trade, radar technician, that made him readily employable. The embassy was taken off the hook, however, when Marguerite Oswald's employer later filed an affidavit of support for Marina.

As the wife of an American citizen, Marina was entitled to an entrance visa, if other conditions had been met. But her husband was not just any American. He was a defector. The State Department had no objections to the Oswalds' reentry. But the Immigration and Naturalization Service of the Justice Department did. Its field officer in San Antonio, Texas, after investigating Oswald's history, recommended that Marina be denied a visa because there was doubt as to Oswald's loyalty to the United States.

The State Department intervened. In the opinion of the Office of Soviet Union Affairs, "We're better off with subject in U.S. than in Russia."[13] Its ruling was based on a policy which held that it was potentially less embarrassing for the United States to have its unpredictables and malcontents at home than drifting about in foreign parts. In short, the State Department was not acting solely for humanitarian reasons. If Soviet authorities had granted Marina an exit visa partly to be rid of Oswald, American authorities were prepared to give her an entrance visa partly to get him back and out of harm's way.

The State Department made its position clear by its handling of the one legal technicality that remained. Under the Immigration and Nationality Act, United States consuls abroad are forbidden to issue immigrants' visas inside any country which resists the return of nationals whom the United States wants to deport. The U.S.S.R. was considered such a country. It was a technicality that was easily surmounted, for Marina could obtain a visa from the American consular office in another country, and the embassy in Moscow had already made arrangements with the embassy in Brussels. Once again the State Department intervened. It requested a waiver for Marina. Oswald was considered an "unstable character, whose actions are entirely unpredictable."[14] Like the Soviet authorities, the American authorities were afraid that he might do something politically embarrassing.

By mid-March of 1962, Alik was informed that Marina had been granted a visa to enter the United States, and it was now only a matter of weeks before he and his family would be able to leave Russia. But as late as April, neither he nor Marina had said a word to Ilya or Valya, who were still convinced that the young couple had not received permission to leave from the Soviet side—and would never receive it. The deception was the more remarkable since Marina had quit her job at the pharmacy and now spent part of each day with the baby at Ilya and Valya's apartment.

One day Valya casually asked whether Marina had news of her exit visa, and Marina answered falsely that she had not. Valya had often pointed out that Marina's going might mean trouble for Ilya. "He has so little time left until his pension. He's done so much for you. What a blow if he loses it because of you!" Now she added something new, a letter from Marina's Aunt Polina in Kharkov which she had been withholding lest it upset Marina during her pregnancy.

Valya read a fragment aloud. "I've never been inside a church in my life," the passage began. "But the day Marina goes to America I'll go to church. I'll light a great big candle and pray that her soul may rest in peace. I'll say a prayer for the dead. Then she'll be dead to *me*. I'll forget that I ever had a niece. As for her, she can forget that I was ever her aunt."

Marina knew that Polina's letter reflected cowardice over her husband's job and position. Still, she was profoundly upset. She went home and told Alik about the letter. Marina, like her mother, was superstitious. To her, it was as if her aunt's prayer for the dead, her wish that she were dead, truly had the power to kill her. After brooding a while, she announced: "Alka, I'm not going with you to America. My relatives have done so much for me. I just cannot do it to them."

"Okay," he said. "If that's how you feel, if you care more for them than for me, you can stay."

Bitterly hurt, Marina picked up the baby, grabbed some swaddling cloth, and ran out the door. Alik did nothing to stop her. He sat on the bed and watched her go.

She went to Ilya and Valya's in tears, announced that she had had a fight with Alka and had left him. She did not say what the fight had been about. Valya was sympathetic. Ilya was not; he told Marina she could spend the night, but she was not to come to *him* any more when she and her husband had a fight. He was not going to help.

That night Marina lay awake thinking for a long time. She had had three blows that day: Polina's letter, the fight with Alka, and now it seemed that Ilya did not love her either. She decided that she would not go to America. "Alka doesn't love me," she thought, "and what if something happened to Ilya and Valya on our account after we go?" But in the morning she changed her mind, for she felt that underneath her other emotions, she did love Alka after all. Encouraged by Valya, she set off toward home. She met Alik coming down the street in the other direction.

They returned to Valya's to decide what to do, and there they found Marina's Aunt Musya. She had been angry at Alik for months. Now she had a chance to vent her wrath. She scolded him for being cruel to Marina and trying to take her to America. Alik grew very pale. Finally, he asked Marina to come home with him. When she refused, he said, "Okay, stay if you want. But at least let me take the baby."

Musya grabbed the baby. "You've no right to take a child from its mother," she cried.

Alik went into the next room and stood there, crying quietly by the window. Valya ran back and forth trying to make peace. Alik's tears softened her heart, and she urged Marina to go back to him. "Look what you've done," she said. "He's as pale as a ghost by the window. The tears are streaming down his face. I even heard him say, 'What have I to live for? What am I to do now?' "

At last Marina agreed. She had wanted Alik to suffer and she wanted proof that he loved her. His tears seemed to be the proof she needed. And she had no more right to take the baby away from him than to hurt her relatives.

The tears were still streaming down his cheeks as Valya led him into the room. "You don't love me," Marina said. "I won't go with you."

"I do love you," he said, and, oblivious of Musya, Valya, and his own tears, he kissed Marina and the baby.

That was that. It was the end of Marina's wavering over America. They returned home together, and when they reached the apartment, Alik unswaddled the baby. "Bad Mama," he said, kissing her hands and feet. "She wanted Papa never to see his good girl again."

12

Departure for America

IT WAS as well that Marina's doubts were at an end, for events were picking up momentum. On April 12, Oswald wrote his brother that he expected to be able to leave Russia within a month or two. But then he added a sentence that betrayed both ambivalence and apprehension about his return: "Now that winter has gone, I really don't want to leave until the beginning of fall, since the spring and summer here are so nice."[1]

Oswald hated the cold weather in Minsk. It was one of the reasons, he said, for his decision to leave Russia. But that spring he still complained in his letters home that the American Embassy was as slow with its formalities as the Russians had been with theirs. He made several telephone calls to the embassy, and a secretary in the consular office who spoke with him when the consular officers were out grew to dislike him indelibly. Oswald was very impatient about the delays, and complained, in particular, about travel arrangements. He had been authorized a loan only large enough to cover the cost of the least expensive means of transportation back to the United States—train and ship—but he behaved as if it was his birthright to be wafted home by jet aircraft, or, as a veteran, albeit an "undesirably discharged" one, to be flown home on a government transport.

Throughout the long bureaucratic process of his return, Oswald corresponded regularly with both his mother and his brother, and his letters to the two members of his family who were closest to him are revealing in their contrast. To Robert, Oswald was friendly, open, frank. He shared a few of his problems, his small adventures in Minsk, even his political ideas. There was no sharing in his letters to Marguerite.

The striking thing about Oswald's letters to his mother is that, although they are empty of concern or affection, they are filled with requests. Of the seventeen letters he wrote to Marguerite between the resumption of their correspondence in June 1961 and his departure from the Soviet Union nearly a year later, fourteen contained a request or a reminder of some earlier request. At first, the favors he asked were simple enough: *Time* magazine and books for himself, fashion magazines for Marina, pennies for friends who collected American souvenirs. But it was not long before the errands he asked of his mother, an older woman with a job, were substantial.

It fell to Marguerite to do some of the paperwork for her son's return, including obtaining an affidavit of support for Marina from her own employer. Marguerite even suggested that she raise money for his return through a public appeal. Oswald vetoed the idea; at that moment the very last thing he wanted was publicity. But he instructed her to try to get money from the Red Cross or the International Rescue Committee. Any gifts—not loans—would be welcome. But above all, she was not to send her own money. And concerned about both his military status and the reception he was likely to receive in America, Oswald also asked his mother for his Marine Corps discharge and old newspaper clippings about his defection to Russia.

Oswald asked Robert for favors, too, but they were direct requests, as his criticisms of some of Robert's actions were also direct. With Marguerite he was indirect. He praised, he cajoled, he condescended to let her help him; and he made it plain that it was not for her to offer him advice. Oswald respected his brother, but he seemed to fear his mother and the prospect of any closeness between them. He manipulated Marguerite, always with the twin purposes of exploiting her, yet at the same time keeping her at a distance.

Marguerite's reward was meager. In one letter, Oswald told her that there was no need for her to meet him in New York on his return to America. In a later letter, however, he hinted that he and Marina might come to her: "I cannot say exactly where we shall go at first probably directly to Vernon."[2] Marguerite was living in Vernon, a small Texas town 30 miles northwest of Fort Worth. But having dangled that prize in front of his mother, Oswald quickly snatched it away. In a letter written the very next day, he said that he would visit both her and Robert, but "In any event I'll want to be living on my own and probably will finally live in Fort Worth or New Orleans."[3]

Oswald was playing emotional hide-and-seek with his mother: Now you've got me, now you don't. He used her, he depended on her, and then he pushed her away. Not surprisingly, his correspondence with the American Embassy reflected this same attitude. He had walked out on his country, just as he had walked out on his mother. Now he expected the embassy, like an indulgent mother, to forgive, forget, and go to extraordinary lengths to bring him back, without any thought of a return.

On May 10, an official of the embassy wrote Alik to inform him that it was ready to issue Marina's visa in Moscow. The final impediment had been removed, and the Oswalds could come to the embassy as soon as they got their affairs in Minsk in order. It was the word Alik had been waiting for, but by this time it was as if he no longer cared. He had, after all, proved his point. He had a right to leave Russia if he chose, and to take a Soviet citizen with him. It was now the bureaucratic momentum on both sides that carried him forward, rather than any very positive desire to go home.

Alik and Marina started to get ready for their journey. Knowing, or suspecting, that they would soon be leaving, one or another of their friends came by for a visit every night. With the thrill of vicarious adventure, they rejoiced over Marina's miraculous good fortune. Every one of them longed to see America, to travel freely back and forth across frontiers. Not many, however, would have done what Marina was doing: leave family and country forever, without hope of ever seeing them again.

One day Marina had a memorable encounter. In a shop down the street from the apartment, she ran into Anatoly Shpanko. He had heard the news by the grapevine.

"Take me with you," he said in jest. Then, more seriously: "Write. Let me know where I can find you. One day I'll get to America, too. You'll have money over there. You'll come back for a visit. Some day we'll see one another again."

Marina was uneasy. "I've got to go. I have to get home to feed the baby."

"Baby?" Anatoly was astonished. "Where on earth did you get a baby?"

"I really do have one," Marina said.

"But I saw you three months ago and I saw no sign of it then."

"You didn't see right," said Marina, who had in truth, three months before, wrapped her coat carefully around her so that Anatoly would not see that she was pregnant.

Such was Marina's farewell to the man who had wanted her to be his wife.

As for Alik, he had told almost no one that he was going, only Alexander Ziger and Pavel Golovachev. He also seems to have told another friend at the factory, who exclaimed, "Attaboy! I wish you could take me, too. There's nothing to stick around for here."

Alik gave the factory two days' notice. On May 16 he handed in a statement to the director of the Minsk Radio Plant. His wording was formal and laconic: "I ask to be released from work as of May 18, 1962. I expect to be leaving."[4]

It was a happy time for Alik. He had conquered two great bureaucracies and, as with so many of his other achievements, he accomplished it alone. While it was the victory over the Soviet bureaucracy that yielded the sweeter satisfaction, he was carried forward on the momentum of his double triumph. His old misgivings receded. He showed no sign of second thoughts and tried to encourage Marina. If she was unhappy over there, he said, she could always come back. Marina was doubtful. She would be ashamed to return after struggling so hard to get out.

"I used to think that, too," Alik said. "I threw my passport down and told them I didn't want to be a citizen any more. When, after all that, I didn't like it, I was so ashamed. I said to myself, I'd rather die than ask to go back to America. But time changes the way you look at things. There's nothing wrong with making a mistake and thinking better of it later. People do."

The hardest part was telling Ilya and Valya, an ordeal Marina put off until a week or so before they were to leave Minsk for Moscow. It was painful to be with them after that, painful to speak of parting, yet impossible to speak of anything else.

Ilya had found occasion earlier that spring to say to Marina what he chose not to say to her husband: "Forget America. You never know how it will go. He'll have a better life here. They'll give him a bigger apartment. He can study to be an engineer. He'll never have any worries. So long as Alik stays in this country, he'll always be met halfway."

Another time Ilya spoke out again. "He flits from side to side," he said of Alik, "and is unhappy everywhere. Maybe he'll go back and not like it there and then he'll want to come back here. But he'll never be allowed to come back. People are tired of nursing him over here."

Ilya's last utterance about his nephew-in-law, delivered shortly before the Oswalds' departure, had the tone of prophecy. "He is," Ilya said to Marina, "a man who has lost his way."

Valya did not voice any judgment, only a touching request. She begged Marina to leave baby "Marinka" behind. "You don't know what will happen," she implored. "There's unemployment in America. Alka may have trouble because of having lived over here. You can have other children. I never will. She'll be happy with us. I'll take good care of her. I'll love her more than if she were my own."

Marina knew that Alik would not allow it, but trying to make amends for leaving, she promised to ask.

"Are you crazy?" Alik said. "Have you gone out of your mind? Do you think I'd give up my baby? Never!"

Marina had another painful farewell. Carrying the baby with her, she stopped by the laboratory where Aunt Musya worked. Musya cradled the baby in her arms. Marina saw tears in her aunt's eyes.

"She's a good baby," Musya said. "But the spitting image of Alka." Then, hopefully, "You haven't changed your mind?"

"No," Marina answered. Then, fearful lest she burst into tears too, she took the baby and quickly left.

They had a great deal to do. Anticipating their departure, they had tried to hand over their apartment to Tolka, the friend who lived with Colonel Axyonov, and his bride-to-be, Lyalya Petrusevich. But much to Alik's annoyance, they had been rebuffed by the officials of the Minsk Radio Plant, who were in charge of assigning apartments in their building. Nevertheless, they did succeed in registering the apartment in Tolka's name and he would move in when the Oswalds left. He managed to stay only one week. The factory threw him out and awarded the apartment to someone else. Tolka did not marry Lyalya.

Alik and Marina sold their furniture, including the baby's crib. Before leaving their apartment, they had another piece of unfinished business. Throughout their married life they had had the company of an unbidden presence: a tiny meter, or *schyotchik,* ticking away on the wall, even at night when the other electrical devices were switched off. The Oswalds assumed that it was a bugging device, and had long promised themselves that before they left the apartment for good, *if* they ever left for good, they would set aside an hour or so for absolute forthrightness. They would tell the "schyotchik" exactly what they thought of everyone they knew, who was an informer and who was not, to deny the KGB the satisfaction, as Marina puts it, of "thinking it had us fooled." And so, before they left, they told the faintly ticking, scarcely visible companion of their married life their true opinions about everyone they knew.

On the day before their departure, Alik went to call on Erich Titovyets. He meant to tell Erich—for the first time—that he was leaving. Erich was not at home. He did not learn of his friend's departure until after the Oswalds had actually left.[5]

One of Alik's final duties was to visit OVIR, the Office of Visas and Registration, to have the exit visa stamped in his passport. He showed the visa to Marina and remarked, "I wish I could give it to Ziger."

The Oswalds spent their last night in Minsk at Pavel's. The next day, May 22 or 23, they boarded the train for Moscow. Russian-fashion, their closest friends, including Pavel and all the Zigers, came to the station to see them off. But even there they noticed that they were being watched by a man who was standing, half-hidden, behind a pillar.

"Listen in if you like," Eleonora Ziger practically spat in his face. "We have no secrets here."

Her sister, Anita, added: "I simply loathe people who eavesdrop."

Marina kept glancing anxiously around the station looking for Ilya and Valya. Finally she saw them standing way off, by themselves in a corner. Their faces were forlorn and they looked as if they were fearful of being seen by the KGB.

Marina hurried over to them. "Why didn't you join us?"

"We didn't want to be in the way," Valya said. She turned to Alik: "Take care of Marina. She has nobody now but you." She was on the edge of tears.

"Be sure to write," Ilya broke in, his stoical front intact. Then to Alik: "You heard what Valya said?"

"I promise," Alik replied.

"It's time to go," said Valya, no longer trying to hold back her tears. She kissed the three of them goodbye, lingering longest over the baby. Ilya, too, kissed Alik. Then, for the last time, he kissed Marina.

Mrs. Ziger, for her part, was uninhibited. "We've seen so many off," she lamented. "When will it be our turn?" She spoke to Marina: "No matter how hard it is there, never, ever, come back here. But remember the birch trees, the people, our Russian countryside. Think well of your homeland always."

Marina and Alik boarded the train. They stood at the window as, very slowly, the train started up. Marina's friends Olga and Inessa threw flowers. They were narcissi, the flowers Marina had carried at her wedding.

"Come back if you are not happy there," Pavel called after them. The Zigers shouted at them to write.

Marina heard someone cry, "We'll see one another some day." Then she saw Ilya and Valya. They were huddled together, desolate, looking as if their world had fallen apart.

The last sight Marina saw was their friends Olga, Inessa, and Pavel running along the platform, reaching out to touch the train. They ran a very long way.

For a few minutes, in the compartment, both Alik and Marina were silent. She started to cry. He stroked her as if she were a kitten. "I hope these really are better times," he said. "I hope Uncle Ilya won't lose his job or his pension."

When they reached Moscow, they felt like a pair of carefree children. For three days they stayed at the Hotel Ostankino, on the outskirts of town; then they moved to the Hotel Berlin in the center of Moscow. They went to the American Embassy several times, and Alik showed no fear of being arrested. They felt so relieved that just for the fun of it they smuggled a girlfriend of Marina's, now living in Moscow, into the embassy, past a pair of bewildered militiamen. She sat delightedly inside, in the very citadel of capitalism, poring over the shiny magazines while the Oswalds went about their tasks.

Alik had his passport renewed, and the baby had her photograph taken and attached to her father's passport. Marina was given her American visa, and the embassy made reservations for them on the *Maasdam,* a Dutch passenger ship sailing from Rotterdam for New York on June 4. The embassy loaned Oswald the entire cost of the tickets, $418, and arranged for him to pick them up in Rotterdam. Officials of the embassy also suggested a cheap hotel, or "pension," where they could spend a clean and comfortable night in Rotterdam; and either Oswald or the embassy made the reservation. The embassy helped Oswald pay the railway fare from Moscow to Rotterdam. He contributed 90 rubles ($90), and it contributed $17.71.

Oswald had paid for the train trip from Minsk to Moscow, and he was paying for their hotel room, about 8 rubles a day, and meals in Moscow. He would also buy food during the railway journey to Holland and pay $7 or $8 for the pension in Rotterdam. So his out-of-pocket expenses for the journey home would come to between $200 and $300. Oswald left the Soviet Union owing the United States government $435.71.[6]

Marina was given a medical examination by the embassy doctor, Alexis Davison, a slender, pink-faced young naval officer who spoke impeccable Russian. The son of a Russian woman and a distinguished physician from Atlanta, Georgia—his parents met when his father was on an aid mission in Russia during the 1920s—Davison had a style that was humorous and irreverent, as breezy and American as his strawberry blond crewcut. Marina liked him immediately. He treated her with exactly the right combination of seriousness and levity, reassuring her that life in America was far better than in Russia. He urged Marina to look up his mother in America—Natasha Davison, now a widow, a grande dame in the Russian manner and one of the reigning spirits of Atlanta.

Alik liked Davison, too. He enjoyed the navy doctor's jokes and was grateful to him for cheering up Marina at a moment when his own hands were full and his wife's anxieties substantial. Later the Oswalds came across Davison's name again. In the summer of 1963, the Soviet government accused him of being the go-between for Colonel Oleg Penkovsky, a highly placed Soviet official who was tried and shot as a spy for the United States. For his alleged espionage, Davison was expelled from the U.S.S.R.

The Oswalds had other errands to run. They went to OVIR and to Gosbank, the State Bank, where Alik changed most of the rubles he had saved into dollars. Since they were to cross Europe by train, they had also to pay visits to the embassies of Poland, East Germany, West Germany, and the Netherlands to obtain transit visas. The errands required much sitting and waiting in anterooms, and Marina sometimes stayed behind at the hotel. Alik was happy as a lark. Late one afternoon he burst into their hotel room exhausted but elated. "My, I'm tired!" he exclaimed. "But I wouldn't mind doing this for a year. It's better than working in a factory!"

Their last evening in Moscow was a memorable one. They spent it at the apartment of Yury and Galka Belyankin, who had been a friend of Marina's in Minsk, and the party ended with many farewell toasts. When the Oswalds pulled out of Moscow's green-tiled Belorussian Station late the following afternoon, June 1, it was Galka Belyankina who saw them off. She was the last friend they were to see in Russia.

Their route lay through Minsk, where they were due to arrive early the next morning. Marina had wired Valya, begging her to come to the station, and she was in high excitement as the train pulled in, hoping for another glimpse of her aunt. She and Alik bounded onto the familiar platform, raced up and down, and searched everywhere. But Valya was nowhere in sight. Feeling crushed and trying not to show it, Marina said, "We're breathing Minsk air for the last time." She was in tears when they returned to their compartment. "Don't worry. Don't cry." Alik held her tightly around the shoulders. "Everything will be all right."

Next morning they were due at the border town of Brest. Alik had been puzzling over a problem: what to do with his Diary and the other things he had written in Russia. He had no intention of giving up his precious papers to a customs officer. An hour or so out of Brest, he hit upon a solution. He strapped the sheets of paper around his waist under his clothing. He did not seem specially nervous as he did it, but he told Marina to watch out for one of the conductors, a woman, whom he (and Marina, too) suspected of working for the KGB. The woman was too well educated to be a conductor, he said.

The pair presented a homely tableau as their train drew puffing into Brest. They were sitting in their *myaqky* ("soft" or first-class) compartment, the husband—composed but bulging a little around the waist—filling out customs declarations, the wife and baby surrounded by swaddling cloths which she had rinsed out and hung up to dry. Both were sipping tea in the Russian style from glasses.

Marina, who had expected to be questioned and perhaps searched, was astonished at how simple it turned out to be. A pair of nice-looking officers came into the compartment. One of them opened a suitcase and snapped it shut again without even looking inside.

"Have you any gold or other valuables or foreign currency?" he asked politely.

"Yes," Marina answered, pointing to the baby.

At this the officer broke into a broad grin, saluted, and wished them a happy journey.

The Oswalds hugged each other as the train carried them over the bridge into Poland.

"I can't believe we're on foreign soil," Alik said.

Marina looked back. "It's only a bridge," she thought sadly, "but it cuts you off from your country." She stole a look at Alik. His face was so happy that she did not tell him what she was thinking.

That day they crossed the Vistula River into Warsaw. There they got out, changed a few dollars into zlotys, and bought beer. At each stop Alik clambered out and took photographs. The Polish countryside was flat, like Belorussia, and the people, too, looked poor, except for a stylish lilt to the way the women wore their cotton dresses. Poland was a good deal like what Marina was used to. But that night, waking briefly in Germany, she noticed that there were two Berlins, the "democratic" one, which was dark, and the other, which was brightly lit. Then the next morning, in Holland, she could not believe her eyes. It seemed to her that she was in a fairy tale tableau. They rattled through village after village, each one prettier than the last and so clean that they looked as if they must be inhabited by dolls. It was Sunday. Entire families were walking to church. And, between villages, the meadows were dotted with grazing cows.

When they arrived in Rotterdam, they went straight to the pension the embassy had recommended. The landlady gave them lunch, and then the Oswalds went walking. Never had Marina seen such shops. She floated from window to window, thinking she must be in a dream.

"Alka!" she exclaimed. "When your mother sent us those magazines, I never dreamed you could actually buy those things in stores!"

He was watching her, grinning.

"And look," she said. "Everything's so cheap!"

"It's a whole lot cheaper in America," Alik said. He bought her a Coca-Cola, her first. It was a touch of home he had been pining for. "See," he boasted again, "in Holland you drink American Coca-Cola." It was the only thing he bought her, for it was Sunday and all the shops were closed.

In the pension that night, the sheets were so clean that Marina was afraid to lie down.

They had only that one day in Holland.[7] The next morning, June 4, 1962, they boarded the *Maasdam* bound from Rotterdam to New York.

The voyage marked the beginning of a change in Alik's behavior, and in his relationship with his wife. It was not a change for the better.

On the first day out, the two of them went on deck, struck up a conversation with a Rumanian girl, laughed, and had a fine time. But after that, Alik hardly took Marina out on deck at all. He got seasick there, and she did not. It did not occur to her to go alone.

She spent most of the voyage in their cabin with the baby. Taking several sheets of writing paper with him, Alik would vanish upstairs to the library and remain there for hours. Marina supposed he was writing letters. Often, at night, he went alone to the movies, leaving Marina and the baby behind.

He came to fetch her for meals, and it seemed to Marina that the other passengers were staring and laughing at her. She became self-conscious about her appearance and her clothes, unaware that it was the baby, swaddled from her waist to her toes, that was the object of so much attention. They had never seen swaddling before.

They had a charming waiter, a handsome young man whose name was Pieter. Half Russian and half Dutch, he knew a few words of Russian and wanted to know all about Marina. But Alik was suspicious of him. "Don't tell him anything you don't have to," he warned Marina. "It's no accident that they gave us a Russian-speaking waiter."

Marina ignored his warning. To the extent their languages would allow, she chatted away openly with Pieter, and she discovered that his last name was "Didenko," or something close to it. "Where," Marina asked herself, "have I heard that name before?" Then, with a thud of recognition, she remembered. It was the name of her own, natural father—at least the name her stepfather had shouted at her once in a terrible moment of wrath.

Marina did not know what to make of the change in Alik. Whenever he took her anywhere, it was plain from his expression that he was doing it only out of duty. It was not that he was making other friends. Marina saw no sign of that. She concluded that he was ashamed of her because, as she put it to herself, she looked like "a little Russian fool." Alone much of the time in the cabin, she sank into low spirits. Everything she knew and loved lay behind her; ahead, everything was unknown. Clearly, Alka neither loved her nor cared for her. Why on earth was she going to America?

Finally, she said to her husband, "Alka, are you ashamed of me?"

He did not reply.

"There's a beauty shop on the boat. The girls come out looking like princesses."

"Oh, is there?" That was all he said.

Marina grew angry. She had given Alik 180 rubles in Minsk, payment for her maternity leave and money from the sale of their furniture. He had changed all of it into dollars and she knew that he still had it. Yet he had refused to buy her anything when some boatmen rowed up to the *Maasdam* off the Irish coast with heavy wool sweaters to sell. There were shops on the ship, but he did not buy her anything there either. Nor did he pick up her hint that she should get her hair done. Marina was too proud to ask him for any money. The one thing she asked for was thread. Sitting by herself in the cabin, she sewed the heels of her wedding shoes.

"Don't bother," Alik said, when he saw what she was doing. "I'll buy you shoes in New York."

"I'll sew these until you do," came his wife's laconic reply.

Marina's unhappiness boiled over at a party they attended their last evening at sea. In spite of her attire—the red brocade she had worn the night she met Alik —she felt morose, and looked it.

"Wipe that expression off your face," Alik said. "People are staring at you."

"I can't look any other way," Marina said.

"Why?"

"Because you've changed toward me. Because you don't love me and I feel hurt."

"If you don't care for me the way I am," Alik said, "go away."

"Where am I to go?" Marina said. "There's only one way to go. And that's the ocean."

"Okay. Go."

Marina ran from the table in tears. It was rainy and cold on deck, and below, the water was gray and forbidding. She did not know what to do. She walked around the deck, and finally, she thought of the baby, who was lying asleep in the cabin. "Junie needs me, even if Alka doesn't."

Alik found her in the cabin when he came in an hour later.

"You're here, are you?" he said.

"Only because of the baby."

He quickly went out again. But he returned and they made up. He escorted her to the bar, bought her a liqueur and himself a Coca-Cola. He even allowed her to smoke.

The voyage to America was not a happy one for Marina. She thought that she was somehow responsible for Alik's strange behavior. She did not know the real reason for his abstraction and indifference to her: as the *Maasdam* steamed toward New York, he was once again deeply concerned about what might happen to him when he reached America.

Oswald thought that he would be met at the dock by newspaper reporters. He expected to be asked a series of questions designed to incriminate him with the FBI; and trying to prepare himself, he covered page after page of Holland-America Line stationery with a list of questions and answers. Then, dissatisfied, he wrote out a second draft, one which was more politic, less candid, and apparently, to his mind, more successful, since he ended it with the newspapermen exclaiming, with one voice: "Thank you, sir, you are a *real* patriot!!"[8]

The questions Oswald allotted to the newspapermen reveal his central concern. He was still afraid that by one or more of his acts he had broken laws of the United States. And he was fearful that his answers might incriminate him. Indeed, the questions he sketched out are accusatory, the answers defensive. He was even prepared to deny that he was a Communist. In response to the question: "Are you a Communist?" he drafted two replies. (In the excerpts that follow, errors of spelling and punctuation have been corrected.)

First draft: Yes, basically. Although I hate the U.S.S.R. and (the) socialist system, I still think marxism can work under different circumstances.[9]

Second draft: No, of course not. I have never even known a communist outside of the ones in the U.S.S.R. but you can't help that.[10]

Besides the two sets of questions and answers, which were really scripts for the anticipated press conference, Oswald wrote two long pages, again on Holland-America Line stationery, explaining why he had taken money from a source he believed to be the Soviet secret police. It was the question he dreaded most:

. . . I accepted the money because I was hungry and there were several inches of snow on the ground. . . . But what it really was was *payment* for my denunciation of the U.S. in Moscow. . . . I didn't realize all this, of course, for almost two years . . . I have never mentioned the fact of these monthly payments to anyone. I do so in order to state that I shall never sell myself intentionally or unintentionally to anyone again.[11]

There is no way of knowing how many sheets of Holland-America Line paper Oswald covered with handwriting, only to toss them into a wastebasket on the *Maasdam*. But it is clear from what has survived that he spent part of the voyage working up this imaginary colloquy with the press, and an even longer time drafting a statement of his political beliefs.[12] Again, he apparently thought that he would be questioned on these matters.

I have often wondered why it is that the communist, capitalist, and even the fascist and anarchist elements in America always profess patriotism toward the land and the people, if not the government, although their movements must surely lead to the bitter destruction of all and everything.

I am quite sure these people must hate not only the government but the culture, heritage and very people itself. . . .

I wonder what would happen if somebody was to stand up and say he was utterly opposed not only to the governments, but to the people, to the entire land and complete foundations of his society? . . .

Where can I turn? To factional mutants of both systems [communism and capitalism], to oddball Hegelian revisionists out of touch with reality, [to] religious groups, to revisionists or to absurd anarchism? No!

To a person knowing both systems . . . there can be no mediation. . . .

He must be opposed to their basic foundations. . . .

And yet it is immature to take the sort of attitude which says "a curse on both your houses."

There are two great representatives of power in the world . . . the left and right. . . .

Any practical attempt at one alternative must have as its nucleus the traditional ideological best of both systems, and yet be utterly opposed to both. . . .

For no system can be entirely new. That is where most revolutions . . . go astray. And yet the new system must be opposed unequivocally to the old. That is also where revolutions go astray.

Oswald then launched into criticisms of capitalism: "runaway robot" automation, "a general decay of classes into shapeless societies without real cultural foundations," the "regimentation" of "ideals," and, finally, war.

The biggest and key fault . . . of our era is of course the fight for markets between the imperialist powers . . . which lead to the wars, crises and oppressive friction which you have all come to regard as part of your lives. And it is this prominent factor of the capitalist system which will undoubtedly eventually lead to the common destruction of all the imperialistic powers. . . .

Oswald next considered what he called the "mistakes" of Engels and Marx,[13] chiefly the notion that the abolition of classes would lead to a withering away of the state. He cited with bitterness his own visa experience to illustrate that even with Khrushchev's decentralization, the state did not wither away. To counter the argument that the state had to become strong and highly centralized before it could wither away, he called for "social democracy at a local or community level." Oswald believed that "true democracy can be practiced only at the local level."

Four other long sheets of Holland-America Line stationery have survived, covered with Oswald's scrawl, mutilated and nearly illegible because of scratched-out phrases and words. They are a vaguely programmatic document,[14] apocalyptic in that Oswald apparently expected an armed confrontation between the two camps at any moment, and suggested that afterward he hoped to set up a peace organization that would break with the traditions of both Communist and capitalist systems, which "have now at this moment led the world into unsurpassed danger . . . into a dark generation of tension and fear."

How many of you have tried to find out the truth behind the cold war clichés?
I have lived under both systems. I have *sought* the answers and, although it would be very easy to dupe myself into believing one system is better than the other, I know they are not.

For an American who was only twenty-two, Oswald's experience was unique. He had, as he had written, lived in each of the opposing world camps, more or less as an ordinary citizen. Now, suspended between the two on the voyage home, he was looking at both, weighing both, trying to puzzle out a system that would combine the merits of each. And, as he had done so often in his life before, he was doing it, once again, alone. He had not been to college, nor had he been part of any political or intellectual milieu in the United States. In Russia, he had been cut off completely from such currents as might be stirring young people back home. Yet the political solution he reached, from his own experience, from reading, and from talking to his friends in Minsk, was similar to the solution proposed by a generation of American activists in the later 1960s: participatory democracy at a community level. Oswald was a pioneer, if you will, or a lonely American anti-hero a few years ahead of his time.

The trouble lay not with his ideas but with the emotions underneath. Oswald had been disappointed by Russia, which he had thought to be a Marxist society where each person's needs were met. It was not the thing Oswald expected and found, a system of authority, that drove him from the U.S.S.R. It was what he came seeking and failed to find.

His disappointment, and above all the anxiety he felt on returning to the country of his birth, are evident in the confused style and erratic spelling of his shipboard writings. But his was not a new wound. It had been inflicted long before he went to Russia, and it stemmed from his relationship with his mother. For somehow Marguerite had failed her son. His need for his mother's love had not been met when he was young. Not only was his need unmet, he had been unable to extricate himself from it. He remained enmeshed with his mother, needing her, yet resenting her and hating himself for his dependence. For his need was an enormous threat to him and, once in a while, in order to convince himself that he was free and a man, he had to pull himself together and act. And the action he took very often was one of rejection.

He had rejected Marguerite first when he joined the Marines. But his dependence remained so great that he was able to transform even that institution into a kind of mother. The Marine Corps—the "mother of men"—failed him, too; and in rejecting the Marines, he was, symbolically, rejecting his mother again. Then he defected to Russia, contriving in a single exquisite gesture to reject his real mother, the Marine Corps, and his mother country all at once. So doing, he transformed an unresolved personal conflict into a political act.

Now he had rejected Russia, once more reenacting the central drama of his life. Mother Russia had failed him not because it was authoritarian or because it lacked Marxian "equality." It failed him because it did not meet all his needs. No country, no mother, could—his needs were bottomless. But this rejection was the most portentous one so far, for while rejecting his mother symbolically yet again, he was returning to her physically for the first time. He was returning to the real mother who was the cause of it all.

Marina had no idea of the danger her husband was running in going home. She was hurt and depressed by his shipboard behavior to her. But she had no way back. She was committed to Alik and June, and to the decision she had made in leaving Russia. And she was looking forward with the eagerness of a child to the great adventure that lay ahead. Besides, she was young and forgiving, fully capable of laying aside Alik's cruelty and the warning signals he had given her. She saw in Alik's suddenly altered behavior only his fear of being punished in America. She was right. But she failed to perceive the depths of his turmoil. As he approached the emotional orbit of his mother, he started to behave like a compass approaching its magnetic pole. The needle of his emotions began to swing, wildly and more wildly still, until eventually he was to forfeit his control.

Interlude

During the summer of 1964, I was in the Irving, Texas, home of Ruth Paine, a woman who befriended Lee and Marina Oswald in 1963 and with whom Marina was staying at the time President Kennedy was shot. Ruth and I were talking about Lee Oswald and about the last evening he spent with Marina at the Paines' house, the evening before the assassination.

Suddenly, Ruth broke into our conversation with a warning that an uninvited visitor was walking up the drive. The visitor entered—a small, plump woman, immaculately groomed, with her hair upswept in a bun and a white blouse neatly tucked inside her skirt. I recognized her right away. She was Marguerite Oswald.

She and Ruth started talking and I was surprised at how sensible Mrs. Oswald seemed to be. I had read that she was a mixed-up, contentious woman, who believed the world was against her and was very much concerned with money. Now I thought that what I had read must be wrong. Mrs. Oswald's conversation appeared to be just as well put together as her costume.

She was wearing a flash camera around her neck, and she announced that she had come to take photographs: one of the bedroom in Ruth's house "where *they* slept"; one of the living room sofa, "where I slept that sorrowful night" (Mrs. Oswald spent the night of November 22, 1963, at the Paines' house); and one of what she called the "famous" garage where Lee kept his rifle. Mrs. Oswald explained that she wanted the photographs to add to a scrapbook for Lee's children. "Who would keep it if I didn't?" she asked. Apparently she was compiling a photographic record of Lee's life, for she mentioned that she wanted Marina to give Lee's baby book back to her. "Marina didn't know him that long," she said.

Mrs. Oswald did all the talking, oblivious to Ruth and me, and she was obviously preoccupied with two topics—money and Lee's innocence. She was suing one national magazine, she said, for a false statement about the amount of money she had received "for one lousy speech" about her son. She had allowed another to publish Lee's letters to her because they showed "what a good boy he was," but added mysteriously that she had so far refrained from publishing another twenty-five letters "for security reasons." Proudly she told us that she frequently went to her son's grave to tidy up, and that 90,000 visitors had been to see it already. "Who would get down on their knees and sweep up the mess and plant plastic flowers if I didn't?"

"Wait a minute," I said to myself. "This lady is claiming that her son is innocent and at the same time she is making money off the deed he is supposed to have committed." Mrs. Oswald was falling apart in front of my eyes, just as surely as if her blouse had come untucked and her tidy bun come tumbling to her waist. "Who am I?" I thought. "Where can I turn to touch something real?" I looked at my watch and saw that Marguerite Oswald had been in the house seven and a half minutes.

She was born Marguerite Claverie in 1907 in New Orleans, the fifth of six children of a streetcar conductor. Her mother died when she was four years old, and Marguerite was raised by her father, her older brothers and sisters and, she says, by housekeepers. She was a pretty child and she grew up an attractive young woman. She quit school after the ninth grade, falsified her school documents, and got a job.

At the age of twenty-two, she married Edward John Pic, Jr., a shipping company clerk. They separated a year or so later, when Marguerite was three months pregnant. She claimed that Pic did not want the child and refused to support her. The child was a boy, John Edward Pic, and his father contributed to his support until he reached the age of eighteen. But Marguerite told the boy that his father contributed nothing to his support and that his birth had been the cause of her divorce.[1]

Marguerite met Robert Edward Lee Oswald during her separation from Pic. Like her, he came from a Catholic family of French and German descent. And, like her, he was married and separated. In 1933, both obtained divorces and were married. Marguerite objected when Oswald wanted to adopt John; it might mean the end of support payments from John's father. Their first son, Robert, Jr., was born in 1934. The second,

Lee Harvey, was born on October 18, 1939, two months after his father's sudden death of a heart attack. The accounts of his death vary. Marguerite's sister, Lillian Murret, who also lived in New Orleans, says that he was mowing the lawn when he felt a pain in his arm. He told his wife to rub his arm and give him aspirin, which she did, but while she was telephoning the doctor, he keeled over dead.[2] Years later, however, Marguerite told a social worker in New York that her husband died at 6:00 A.M. and, in order to spare herself and the child she was carrying, she had him buried the same day, an act which so horrified his relatives by its "coldness" that they had avoided her ever since.[3]

But Marguerite's feelings for her husband had not been cold. According to one member of her family, Oswald gave her what she wanted—a car, a house, financial security. To this day when she speaks of him, she says, "There goes the only happy part of my life."[4] At the time of his death, the couple had been hoping for a baby girl.

Now Marguerite was on her own, with three small sons to provide for. She was not destitute. She had her support payments from John's father and, according to a friend, a $10,000 insurance policy from Oswald. In addition, the house she lived in was at least partly paid for. But money was on Marguerite's mind. She rented the house and moved to a cheaper place. And, so that she could go to work, she put the older boys, first in a strict Catholic boarding school, and then in the Bethlehem Children's Home, a New Orleans orphanage, despite the fact that neither was an orphan and John had two parents living.

She kept Lee. He had a shifting babyhood, both in terms of where he lived and who took care of him. He stayed part of the time with Marguerite's easygoing sister Lillian, who was married to Charles Murret and had five children of her own. Mrs. Murret remembers Lee as beautiful, friendly, and affectionate, and she kept him on and off for two years. But the arrangement was occasionally interrupted either by one of Marguerite's squabbles with her sister or by little Lee himself. For, as soon as he was big enough, Lee acquired the habit of running away in his night clothes and slipping through the Murrets' iron gates, only to surface a while later, clad in pajamas, sitting cheerfully in some neighbor's kitchen.

And so Marguerite took him back and had a succession of babysitters—neighbors, and even the milkman, Bud, and his wife. Once she hired a live-in couple for $15 a month, but after two months she noticed that two-year-old Lee had big red welts on his legs. The couple said he was a "bad, unmanageable child." He had thrown a toy gun at the wife and they were whipping him to keep him in line.[5]

At that, Marguerite quit her job briefly to take care of him.

Marguerite tried to put Lee in the Bethlehem Home with his brothers when he was two, but she was turned down because, as she knew very well, the minimum age was three. Marguerite says, "I waited patiently for age three."[6] She returned to work and moved close to the Murrets, leaving Lee with Lillian by day and taking him home with her at night. Finally, on December 26, 1942, the day after Christmas, Lee, aged three years and two months, joined his brothers at the orphanage.

Lee seemed happy there, but he still did not have a steady environment because his mother would take him out for two or three weeks at a time, and either keep him herself or farm him out to the Murrets. He had been at the orphanage just over a year when Marguerite moved to Dallas, taking Lee, but not his brothers, with her. She was engaged in an on-again, off-again courtship with an older man, a "Yankee" named Edwin A. Ekdahl, and was planning, on balance, to marry him. She hesitated, however, and married Ekdahl only a year later, in May of 1945. Meanwhile, five-year-old Lee saw a good deal of Ekdahl and became attached to him. Tall, white-haired, and "very nice," with a history of heart trouble, Ekdahl was an electrical engineer earning $1,000 a month. Relatives thought that money was a motive on Marguerite's side.

After the marriage, the older boys were sent to the Chamberlain-Hunt Military Academy in Port Gibson, Mississippi, while Lee went by car with his mother and stepfather to exotic places like Boston and the Arizona desert. They settled in Benbrook, Texas, outside Fort Worth, in a big stone house with plenty of trees around it. Ekdahl treated the boys "real swell . . . like his own children," John says.[7] One Christmas he showered them with candies and Cokes while their mother voiced loud opposition. Robert says, "We was on Mr. Ekdahl's side,"[8] adding that, "All of us liked Mr. Ekdahl, but I think Lee loved him most of all."[9] John thinks, "Lee found in him the father he never had."[10]

But the marriage was as rocky as it could be, and Lee, the only child at home, got the worst of it. His spirits rose and fell with the ups and downs of his mother's marriage, and his life was unsteady, too. He entered the first grade in Benbrook, but Marguerite left Ekdahl for a few months, settled in Covington, Louisiana, and then returned with Ekdahl to Fort Worth. As a result, Lee touched down in three schools and took two years to finish first grade, although his grades were all A's and B's. Robert remembers "loud arguments" between his mother and stepfather, and it seemed to John that they had "a fight about every other day." One summer evening John brought home the good news that they had made up after one of their fights. He recalls that the news "seemed to really elate Lee."[11] Like the older boys, Lee wanted nothing better than for the marriage to work out.

But it did not. The couple was divorced in June of 1948, and Marguerite resumed the name of Oswald. John was forced to testify against his stepfather, but Lee got out of it on the grounds that he was under age, being only eight and a half years old, and would not know "right from wrong and truth from falsehood."[12]

Once again, money was thought to be the cause of the break-up, for Marguerite, who was better off financially than she had ever been, nonetheless complained that Ekdahl was not nearly as generous with her financially as she had hoped.[13] One couple who knew the Ekdahls saw it differently. They thought it was Marguerite's preference for her youngest child, Lee, that precipitated the divorce. She refused to discipline Lee or allow Ekdahl to do so. The wife says that after Lee's father died, Marguerite "dumped all her love on Lee. She loved him to death and she spoiled him to death. She was too close to Lee." It got so he "demanded so much of his mother's attention" that she and Ekdahl "never could be alone."[14] Even Ekdahl, a sweet-tempered, patient man, complained.

The divorce was a disaster for all the boys. The first thing Marguerite did was drive to Port Gibson, Mississippi, and drag John and Robert out of the Chamberlain-Hunt Military Academy. They were heartbroken; they had been happy there, and might have stayed on scholarships. But Marguerite wanted them home so they could help support *her*. It was downhill all the way after that—a succession of grubby houses in Fort Worth. "We were back down in the lower class again," John recalls.[15] As for Lee, so cramped was the family for space that he shared a double bed with his mother from the age of eight to ten and a half, literally moving into Ekdahl's place.

Lee was apparently Marguerite's favorite. In any dispute among the boys, she always sided with Lee. One night a neighbor was paying a call when Lee came hurtling through the kitchen door, chasing John and brandishing a long butcher knife. He hurled the knife at his brother; it missed and hit the living room wall. "They have these little scuffles all the time," Marguerite said calmly.[16] Not only did she excuse Lee and overlook the injury he might have done to John, but she sanctioned violent behavior by Lee when he was only eight years old.

By the autumn of 1948, all except Lee were working. Marguerite was a saleslady in a department store; Robert, aged fourteen and in the ninth grade, worked in a grocery store on Saturdays and on weekdays after school; and Marguerite demanded that John, who was sixteen and about to enter the eleventh grade, give up school and go to work full time. Burning with resentment, John complied and got a job as a stock boy in a department store.[17]

It was at this moment of rebellion and sacrifice that John began to turn against his mother. He saw that part of the family's joyless struggle against poverty had its existence only in his mother's head. She was a tough and tenacious businesswoman, and John observed that no matter how poor she claimed to be, she always had enough "to buy and sell a house."[18] Each time she did so, she made a profit, and she had by now bought and sold a good many houses. Still, the struggle against poverty went on. Trying to create a family life for themselves at home, the boys would be having a "friendly time" when their mother came in late from work. Then, says John, "we all got into that depression rut again."[19]

Nor did Marguerite provide for the sons who were helping provide for her. She skimped on food; John, who weighed 130 to 140 pounds when he came back from military school, dropped to 118 pounds and regained his normal weight only after he had left home for good. When it came to clothing, Marguerite dressed her boys so shabbily that they were taunted by the neighborhood children. A neighbor who was a witness of their life is harsh in his judgment of Marguerite. He says that she was "selfish," did not care if her boys "were embarrassed about their dress," and plainly considered them a "burden."[20]

John and Robert felt like strangers to Marguerite, as if she did not know them very well and as if they, too, were unaccustomed to her. They missed Captain Herbert D. Farrell, the head of their military school, whom they looked up to and whose discipline they had readily accepted. But their alienation went deeper. They had left home at the ages of six and eight and, apart from one interruption, they had been away for eight years. Exposed to values vastly different from hers, they had adopted them and acquired a detachment that was to protect them from her and her claims. By the time they came home, they were lost to Marguerite forever.

Robert had noticed from an early age that "our family was not like other families." When the parents of other children came to visit at his boarding school, Robert saw that they enjoyed their children. But his mother did not enjoy *him*. "We learned, very early, that we were a burden. By the time we were teenagers, she felt that we should take over some of her burden." The idea even crossed Robert's mind that his mother might want to put him and John up for adoption; anything to be rid of her burden. "Mother felt the world owed her a living," Robert says.

"She felt that her life was harder than the lives of most people. All of us could feel that she wanted to be free of the responsibility—wanted to let someone else face it."[21]

John speaks even more sharply about his mother's obsession with money. "Money was her God," he says, adding that her one thought was to "get as much out of me and as much out of Robert as she could."[22] He saw that his mother's obsession, her placing money where other values ought to have been, had turned their family life upside down. No decision had ever been made on the basis of the children's well-being, but only on the basis of what was cheapest and best for Marguerite. Instead of the more common sight of a mother making sacrifices to feed and clothe her children and give them an education, he and Robert were sacrificed to give their mother the feeling of financial security she would not have had if they had all been millionaires. Thus Marguerite's exploitiveness caused her to lose the one thing that might have given her a better life—her children's love. She embittered them and turned them against her.

Nor was she content to pocket their money and treat her older sons as men. She tried to control their lives to the last detail. She forbade them friends, once locked Robert out for going to a movie, and shrieked at him that he was "on dope" when she found cigarettes in his pocket. And, when he was at an age to feel it most poignantly, she destoyed a romance of Robert's because the girl was Italian and crippled.

Somehow Robert and John survived. They shrugged off their mother's tirades. And they took similar paths. Both quit high school for a year to help support her. Both insisted, over her objections, on returning to school. Battling her every inch of the way, John graduated, and both left home early to enter the service. John at eighteen joined the Coast Guard, and Robert at eighteen the Marine Corps. Both genuinely felt that by leaving home, they would be relieving their mother of a burden. But the real reason Robert and John left was that Marguerite had given them no choice. If they were to salvage anything of themselves, they simply had to get away.

Lee's reaction to Marguerite was different. His mother's ire did not fall on him often, but when it did, he was unable to shrug her off as her brothers had. Instead, he would "sulk or pout," "get upset," brood, or go off by himself to watch television or play with the dog. The one thing he did not do was talk back. He was under his mother's thumb. Robert's departure for the service in July of 1952 left Lee face to face with his mother. He now had no brothers to intercede for him. Twelve-year-old Lee was on his own.

Robert had been gone about a month when Marguerite piled Lee and their possessions into her car and drove to New York. John was living there now. He was still in the Coast Guard, he had an eighteen-year-old bride and a baby, and Marguerite moved right in. On the first day they were there, Marguerite came out of her room crying because Lee had slapped her, and John immediately saw that Lee was no longer the docile child he had known. All of a sudden he was boss.[23]

One day John's wife, Marge, spoke to Lee about his rudeness to Marguerite. He gave her a sharp reply and, after that, treated her as rudely as he treated his mother. A few days later, he was watching television and Marge asked him to turn down the volume. He took out a knife, opened the blade, and moved menacingly toward her. Marguerite entered the room and told him to put the knife away. Lee hit her.

When John came home that night, he listened to both sides of the story. Marguerite, as she had done before, played the episode down. Lee had been whittling, she said, and Marge, seeing the knife in his hand, thought he was threatening her. It was just a misunderstanding. John asked Lee his side of the story, and Lee refused to speak to him. "I was never able to get to the kid again," John recalls.[24] It was true. Lee did not speak another word to John for ten years.

Marguerite and Lee moved up to the Bronx after that. Marguerite went to work and Lee went to junior high school. But he did not find it easy. His classmates made fun of him for his blue jeans and his Texas drawl. Lee was intelligent, but, without knowing it, he suffered from the reading disability (dyslexia) that must have caused him to feel frustrated from his earliest days in school, as if something impalpable, something he could at most only sense, was holding him back and keeping him from doing as well as others less intelligent than he.[25] By the time he was thirteen and in the Bronx, Lee had largely compensated for the disability, but his years of undiagnosed struggle had, typically, left him with a legacy of low self-esteem and disruptive behavior that might have plagued him even had his home life been a happy one.

By January of 1953, when he had been in school less than four months, Lee had played truant two days out of three. With his mother working full time and coming home late, he spent some days at the Bronx Zoo, which he loved, and other days riding the subway as far as he could on a single fare. He got to know the city well, especially the area around Times Square. At home he sat glued to the television set watching dramas of mystery and violence. One of his favorites was "I Led Three Lives," the story of Herbert Philbrick, an FBI agent who posed as a Communist spy.

Truant officers caught up with him and, in the spring of 1953, Lee was remanded to Youth House, a detention home on the lower East Side, where he was sent for psychiatric observation. He was found to be "seriously withdrawn, detached, and very hard to reach," the troubled relationship with his mother apparently the core of his problems.[26] A social worker named Evelyn Strickman, later Mrs. Siegel, interviewed Lee and Marguerite. Miss Strickman found that Lee did have some ability to relate to others, an ability she found surprising in view of his solitary existence and his emotional starvation at home. Lee said his mother never punished him. She told him to go to school but she did not make him do so, and he wished she would. "He just felt his mother 'never gave a damn' for him. He always felt like a burden she had to tolerate." Lee added that he had to "be my own father," and that he and his mother were "very much" alike, since neither of them talked very much. He admitted to having fantasies of being powerful and killing people, but declined to talk about them. Miss Strickman concluded that Lee had "suffered serious personality damage," which might be partially repaired if he could get help soon.[27]

Marguerite was exceedingly reluctant to talk to a social worker at all. She complained to Miss Strickman that the truant officers were making "a criminal out of" Lee. She could manage him if they left him to her. She saw nothing wrong in his seclusiveness, saying she was not gregarious herself and had never felt the need to make friends. She was more interested in Lee's physical than his psychiatric examination. She was dissatisfied with an examination of his genitalia, but on being told that they appeared normal, "she looked at once relieved and disappointed." Miss Strickman concluded that "She didn't seem to see him as a person at all, but as an extension of herself."[28]

These reports were forwarded to the chief psychiatrist at Youth House, Dr. Renatus Hartogs, who interviewed Lee and wrote that he had a "vivid fantasy life, turning around the topics of omnipotence and power." Lee told the psychiatrist that he was "very poor" in school, a remark that impressed Hartogs, since Lee's performance, despite his truancy, was not poor. To Hartogs, the contrast between Lee's actual grades and his evaluation of them showed the "low degree of . . . self-esteem at which this boy has arrived, mainly due to feelings of general inadequacy and emotional discouragement."[29]

Concluding that Lee was not psychotic, Hartogs recommended that he be released from Youth House and placed on probation by the Juvenile Court on condition that he be treated by a male psychiatrist and Marguerite urged to seek psychotherapy. But Marguerite refused help for either of them. Instead, she condoned Lee's truancy, claiming that she saw nothing wrong with it and that in Texas children stay out of school for months at a time. On this as on other occasions she was to prove that she preferred Lee intact, preferred to keep him as he was rather than afford him a chance either to grow or to change. Again and again, faced by a choice between what was unhealthy and what was healthy for her son emotionally, Marguerite reached for the unhealthy. Time was to show that Lee did not have a single antisocial impulse to which she did not, in one way or another, lend her sanction and support.

Lee was scheduled to report at intervals to the Juvenile Court, but Marguerite repeatedly telephoned his probation officer that she and Lee could not be there. In school the following fall Lee was disruptive and belligerent, and his probation officer, having concluded that he had nothing whatsoever going for him in his home environment, tried unsuccessfully to place him in a children's home. Finally the judge referred Lee's case to a social agency called the Big Brothers. On January 4, 1954, a representative of the Big Brothers called on the Oswalds. Marguerite informed him that her boy did not need counseling and, besides, they were going to New Orleans. The visitor reminded her that she was not free to leave the city without permission of the court because Lee was still on probation. Less than a week later, on January 10, 1954, mother and son arrived in New Orleans.

Marguerite rented an apartment from Myrtle and Julian Evans, whom she had known while she was married to Ekdahl. The Evanses observed that fourteen-year-old Lee was even more "spoiled," more "arrogant," and more difficult to control than he had been as a little boy. Mrs. Evans recalls Lee's behavior when he came home from school. "Margie would be downstairs talking to me and he would come to the head of the stairs. He would just stand up there and yell, 'Maw, how about fixing something for me to eat?' and she would jump up right away and go running upstairs to get something for him." Mrs. Evans added that Lee used to "holler" and "scream like a bull." Marguerite never objected. "Her whole life was wrapped up in that boy and she spoiled him to death."[30]

In New Orleans Lee gave up his truant ways and attended school regularly. He began to visit the public library and read. With most people, he was quiet and aloof. Only with his mother was he demanding and loud. Like his mother, and unlike his brothers, Lee left school after the ninth grade. But, like John and Robert, he could not wait to leave home. With his mother's connivance, he tried to enlist in the Marine Corps at sixteen. The attempt failed and, for a year after that, he held jobs as an office boy or messenger boy. The following fall mother and son were in

Fort Worth. There, Lee briefly attended the tenth grade, but dropped out to enlist in the Marines on October 24, 1956, six days after his seventeenth birthday.

Lee's decision to enter the Marine Corps was a dress rehearsal for every other major turning point in his life, and it contained the same elements—rejection of Marguerite and those aspects of her character which he perceived to exist within himself. Throughout his childhood Lee had been exposed to one person unremittingly: Marguerite. The impact of her rigid and unyielding personality upon his emerging one had been undiluted. He had no one else, and especially no man, on whom he could pattern himself. And so he did the only thing he could. He conquered his mother. He took over her personality and he became very like her.

He sensed it—and he loathed it. By joining the Marine Corps, he would not only get away from her but would find a sheltering substitute that would also make up for his lack of a father. But the Marine Corps, too, failed him as a parent, and Lee defected to Russia.

Marina once commented with insight that Lee must have been rejected as a child or he would not have become a Marxist. It is true. In Russia, in what he conceived to be a perfect Marxist society, Lee was again looking for an impersonal mother, a society that would give to him "according to his needs," without subjecting him to the angry vagaries of his real mother. Russia was, moreover, a society that was supposed to have ended "exploitation," such as he and Robert and John had known at the hands of Marguerite. But once again the substitute failed. Lee rejected Russia, and came back to his mother country and the real mother who was at the heart of it all.

By then each of Lee's decisions, including his suicidal gestures, was in part a reenactment of his original attempt to reject his mother and that aspect of himself which was like her. Each time, of course, a new layer of experience had been added, the attempt was a compound of the old and the new, the emotional fallout was heavier, and the debris more difficult to decipher. But underneath it was the same decision, and there is a sense in which, after he was seventeen, Lee never did anything new. For the truth is that he had lost his chance. Marguerite's upbringing, the combination of neglect, resentment, exploitation, the surfeit of some things and starvation of others that is known as spoiling, a spoliation of the emotions—all this had done its work.

John Pic once said that from the moment Lee was born, he had the feeling that "some great tragedy" was going to strike him.[31] And of course he was right. Lee's tragedy lay in the double conquest of the mother he despised. He had conquered her first by becoming like her. And he had conquered her again by winning the battle for her affections. She loved him better than Ekdahl, better than his brothers. She made him feel that he was special. Yet his chances of achieving maturity rested on his perceiving that it was one thing to be special to Marguerite, quite another to be special in the world outside. The fact that he had unlimited prerogatives with his mother did not mean he had unlimited prerogatives with everybody else. If Lee was ever to grow up, he had to relinquish the feeling that he was special, that he was at the center of the universe, and trade it for another and better incentive system. But far from giving up that feeling, he was to spend the rest of his life proving that he meant it.

Lee's conquest of his mother made it hard for him to grow away from her in another way as well. Was he not the sun of her universe? As long as he was the light of her eyes, he had a stake in her view of things. Her view of things was to become his. And here lay a fresh side of Lee's tragedy, for his mother's view was monstrously misshapen. Somehow, as she grew up, half an orphan, in New Orleans, Marguerite too had acquired the notion that she was special. She felt entitled to what she wanted and to a better life than she had. And this feeling alone made her life a hardship, since life could not meet her expectations. Everyday vicissitudes, burdens others manage to accept, were to her a gratuitous imposition. Marguerite became convinced that life was unfair to her and that she was not getting a "square deal." She felt, and felt strongly, that she had a right to do anything she could to even up the score and bring a little perverse justice into the world. She acquired a bias against society and she transmitted that bias to Lee.

Marguerite's feeling that she and Lee were both special, and that Lee was, in fact, the physical and spiritual extension of herself, was to emerge later when she testified before the Warren Commission. Marguerite acknowledged that she had certain "gifts," a gift for singing and a gift for sewing. "So those are gifted things I can't explain," she said. "Lee had certain gifted ways about him also."[32]

The profound resemblance between mother and son came out in many ways. They were alike in a linguistic overreaching, a use, and misuse, of words that were too big for them. The ambitiousness they shared crept even into their language.

The two also shared an uncanny constellation of emotions which had its outcropping in an extraordinary congruity of behavior. Feeling, as they did, that "the world owed them a living," they both carried around with them a prickliness, a miraculous capacity for ingratitude. Marguerite's relatives, the Murrets, saw her only occasionally, between marriages, when she showed up needing help. They always answered her call. They gave and gave, but Marguerite never gave in return. She was even able to accept what they gave in such a way as to deny that they had given her anything at all. They were only giving her her due. Her son Lee was the same. He, too, bristled with an independent aura—"I don't need anything from anybody." But he, too, was forever accepting favors, and failing either to reciprocate or to thank anyone. As he saw it, it was not favors or help he was getting—it was his due. Lee, like his mother, was obsessed by his rights. And every now and then he gave the game away by standing on his hind legs and roaring for them.

Since both felt that they were at the center of the universe, they assumed that others were thinking about them, and even plotting against them. Both were attuned to a whole world of hidden motives. Both loved mystery and intrigue, both suspected others of carrying on secret activities. Lee adored spy novels and spy films. And, as for Marguerite, Robert Oswald says she "still sees a spy behind every door and tree."[33] Mother and son were like twin antennae vibrating to the possibility of conspiracy.

Other things followed from this. Neither Lee nor his mother could open up or allow themselves to be vulnerable to anyone. They had to keep others from glimpsing what was inside their minds. And, since they were holding together a view of the world that was not in accord with reality, they spent a great deal of energy tuning out signals that did not fit. By the age of four, Robert knew that his mother was deaf to anything she did not want to hear. His brother Lee was the same.

As a result, neither knew what reality was. Since the truth was weightless and elusive, they felt entitled to play fast and loose with it. Both of them lied. But in this they differed from one another, for Marguerite apparently had enough contact with reality to control her abuse of it. This was not true of Lee. His sense of reality appears to have been so badly impaired that the line between truth and falsehood was wavy, and falsehood was often truer than truth. He lied pointlessly, to no purpose and all the time, even when he had nothing to hide. Marina says Lee told three kinds of lies. One was *vranyo,* a wild, Russian, cock-and-bull lying that has a certain imaginative joy to it; another was lying out of secretiveness; and still another was lying out of calculation, because he had something to hide. Lying claimed much of Lee's energy and complicated his life a great deal. But he had no choice. He had to keep his reality *in* and the reality of other people *out.* Somehow he realized that the two were not the same, and some desperate, animal-like sixth sense told him that he had at all costs to keep outside reality from breaking in and shattering his precarious inner equilibrium.

Since mother and son both assumed that other people were thinking about them, publicity was essential to them. It did not matter if the publicity was negative, as it had been after Lee's defection, for it confirmed what they had known all along, that the world was against them. Publicity held their world together. It proved that they were the center of the universe.

Mother and son were, indeed, in a state of symbiotic nourishment and support. During Lee's time in Russia, his mother decided that he must be a spy, very likely an American one. Lee had the same idea. He, too, loved to imagine that he was a spy, and on balance an American one. Each had the same fantasy, yet not as a result of any communication that had actually passed between them. It was a case of two minds with but a single thought, and that thought the totally congruous product of two very similar personalities.

Lee would willingly have gone further, would have become a spy and acted out his mother's fantasy for her. It was not his fault that nobody asked him to be one. The same was true of his notorious acts, those that put his mother in the limelight, beginning with his defection to Russia. Marguerite never knew what Lee had done, exactly, since he did not tell her, but she always knew within seconds of the first call from a reporter how to make the most of it. Lee was not only acting out his own fantasies only, and imaginings, he was acting out hers as well.

In the end he was to act on a really grand scale, a scale Marguerite had not dreamed of. But she adjusted right away and took credit for what her son had done. She told the writer Jean Stafford that if it was from her Lee had learned the "truths" that American society was not perfect, then, "I make no apology."[34] Lee's brother John, too, was to say that his mother's feelings against society had given Lee "a little extra push" toward what was to be the climax of his life.[35]

Marguerite had not known what was coming, but she reacted as if to the manner born. It was for this she had been waiting all her life.

PART THREE

❧

Texas, 1962–1963

13

Family Reunion

ON WEDNESDAY, June 13, 1962, the *Maasdam* slid into its pier in Hoboken, New Jersey. The Oswalds were packed and waiting below. Tense and nervous throughout the voyage, Lee literally jumped when they heard a knock at the door of their cabin. He stepped back, whirled around, and stood confronting the door. It was their waiter, Pieter. He had come to say goodbye. Shyly, he showed Marina a photograph of the French girl he was meeting in New York. When he left and the door had closed behind him, Marina sensed the tension seeping out of her husband's body. He had been expecting the police.

With the baby cradled in Marina's arms, the Oswalds made their way up to the deck. Lee's tension returned and he peered anxiously from side to side, looking for policemen. Someone was looking for him, but it was not the police. It was Spas T. Raikin, Russian-born representative of the Travelers' Aid Society, which had been alerted by the Department of State. By the time Mr. Raikin got on board, he found that the Oswalds had cleared Immigration. He had Lee Oswald paged by loudspeaker several times, but no one answered. As Raikin phrased it a few days later in his report: "I had the impression that he was trying to escape meeting anybody."[1]

The Oswalds, meanwhile, engulfed in the chaos of the pier, were waiting to go through customs. Marina did not like the way the customs officers tore open the luggage of rich and poor alike, exposing possessions—and poverty—to view. Otherwise, she was luxuriating in the adventure of arrival. She was pleased that it was raining. Rain meant good luck for her. Likewise the fact that it was June 13: thirteen was her lucky number. As for her husband, Marina noticed he was no longer nervous, only a bit depressed. In Russia he had boasted that reporters would meet them when they arrived in America. Now he declared emphatically: "Thank God there are no reporters!" He also said that he hoped his mother would not be there.

It was on the crowded dock that Raikin found them. He guided them through customs and out to a Travelers' Aid limousine, asking questions all the way. Even in this short span of time, Lee managed to tell quite a few lies, among them that he had been a Marine stationed at the U.S. Embassy in Moscow when he met and married Marina, that he had renounced his American citizenship, and that he had paid the family's entire transportation to New York. He added that he had $63 in his pocket and was headed for his brother's home in Texas. His brother would be unable to help him with the fare. Lee accepted the Travelers' Aid offer of help, Raikin noted, "with confidence and appreciation."[2]

From Hoboken the Oswalds were taken to the Port Authority Bus Terminal at 41st Street and thence, by cab, to the Special Services office of the New York City Department of Welfare, on Franklin Street. They were greeted by a Polish-speaking woman, who gave them coffee and apologized to Marina that the worker who spoke Russian was not in that day. Marina was surprised, to put it mildly, that in an hour or two in New York she had already met a Russian, Mr. Raikin, and now a Pole who was apologizing that there was no one there to speak to her in her native tongue.

The Special Services office was the scene of a confrontation between Lee and members of the Department of Welfare. Told that the Oswalds had no funds, an official of the department, in routine fashion, called Lee's next of kin, Robert, to ask him to furnish $200 for air fare for Lee and Marina from New York to Dallas-Fort Worth. Vada Oswald, Robert's wife, answered the phone. She promised to contact her husband and have the money sent immediately. When Lee was informed, he was "quite angered, really very upset." He "stomped around" and refused to accept his brother's money.[3] It was up to the Department of Welfare to pay the fare, he said. The members of the department stood firm; by law the department was required to ask friends or relatives to meet such expenses if they could. Finally, Lee accepted their decision.

Marina had absented herself in order to breastfeed the baby. Unable to understand English, she missed most of the scene, but she surmised that Lee was misleading the department about how much money he had. To her, the mere fact that he claimed to have only $63 was prima facie evidence that he had more, since "how could he live without lying?" She knew that he had had nearly $200 when he left Moscow and had spent hardly any of it since. Moreover, he had warned her on shipboard not to answer any questions about how much money they had. He wanted *them,* he said, to pay for everything, although he did not say who "they" were.

The Oswalds were taken to the Times Square Hotel, a large, dingy building located at Eighth Avenue and 43rd Street. Lee actually volunteered to pay the bill. He deposited Marina and the baby in their room and quickly vanished, promising to bring them something to eat.

The first thing Marina noticed was how dirty the room was. "Ten dollars a day and such filth," she said to herself. She switched on the radio and decided to take a bath. But the letters on the faucets, "H" and "C," were unfamiliar to her, and she decided to wait for her husband after all. She longed to look out the window. But between her and the view there were Venetian blinds, which she had never seen before, and they were black with soot. She snatched a washcloth and started to scrub them. She was still at it when her husband returned.

He brought hamburgers and French fries, another new experience for Marina. Nervous yet elated, he placed a call to Robert and Vada in Fort Worth. Marina was fascinated to hear him speak English on the telephone. He handed her the phone and told her to say something to Vada.

"Hi, Vada," said Marina, blushing and incredulous to be speaking "English" for the first time.

Afterwards Lee explained about the faucets, and "hot" and "cold" became Marina's first words of English.

She took a bath and washed the baby's swaddling cloths. Then the three of them set off for Times Square. It was ten o'clock at night, the city was just waking up, and Marina was enraptured. With its air of nocturnal excitement, New York reminded her of her beloved Leningrad. And yet it was unlike Leningrad, too. The stores were brilliantly lit and Marina had never seen so much to buy. She was riveted by the window displays and stopped to "oh" and "ah" in front of every one. To purchase these things, she supposed, you had to know somebody, had to have special connections. Oh, no, Lee assured her, you didn't need any connections. The only thing you had to have was money. Grinning at her enjoyment, he steered her into a Japanese shop and bought her a pair of sandals. Then they spotted a flock of Russian tourists, as round-eyed and incredulous as Marina. At the sight and sound of them, certain that she had seen her last Russian for all time, Marina was more incredulous still. They went to a food counter to eat, and then back to the hotel, tired and happy.

The next morning, June 14, Lee returned to the Franklin Street office of the Department of Welfare, and accompanied by a department representative, went to a nearby Western Union office to collect the $200 sent by Robert. At the West Side Air Terminal, on Tenth Avenue and 42nd Street, he bought two tickets for Delta Flight 821. The cost was $183.04. Lee, Marina, and the baby flew to Texas from Idlewild Airport.

Marina was delighted by the smooth flight, even by the uniforms the stewardesses wore. But again she was troubled by the stares of her fellow passengers, who were intrigued by the sight of a swaddled baby. Marina had no idea that swaddling was strange to anyone. She was aware only that the people around her were better dressed than she and that they were staring. She shrank inwardly. She and the baby must look like beggars, she thought again.

Robert and Vada, their four-year-old daughter Cathy and their baby son Robert Lee, met them when their plane touched down at Love Field. The two brothers had last seen each other not quite three years before.

"What? No photographers or anything?" Lee greeted Robert as he swung jauntily through the gate. He asked again as soon as they were settled in Robert's car: Had Robert had any calls from reporters?

Yes, Robert answered. On June 8, nearly a week before, the Fort Worth *Star-Telegram* had published a front-page photo of Lee and a story headed:

"Ex-Marine Reported on Way Back from Russia," based on information given to American reporters by the U.S. Embassy in Moscow. Robert had two or three calls from reporters after that, he said, but following Lee's firm instructions from Minsk, he had told them nothing. Robert had the impression that his brother was "disappointed" by the absence of the press.[4]

Marina, meanwhile, was preoccupied by something quite different. Vada and Robert and their children were all so perfectly dressed. Would they, too, think she was a beggar? Would they notice how clumsily her shoes were sewn together? Her embarrassment deepened on the drive from Love Field to Fort Worth when Vada, with Lee translating, offered to fix Marina's hair. "I must look really dreadful," Marina thought. She did not realize that Vada, a beautician, was simply offering the best she had to give.

"My brother is a worker," Lee told her as soon as they set foot in Robert's house. "Yet look at this. He's got a car and a house of his own!" And to Marina, indeed, Robert's small, one-story house looked like paradise on earth. She had never in all her life supposed that one man, his wife, and children could fill up a whole house by themselves.

She took an immediate liking to Robert and Vada, and she liked the cleanliness of the house. It was frustrating to be unable to speak to them directly without asking Lee to translate. But despite the language barrier, she soon learned why she had attracted so much attention on the plane.

"Why do you wrap up that baby?" Vada asked.

"Because swaddling is better for her," Lee said, defending the Russian way.

Nothing daunted, Vada showed them how to diaper the child. But before they put the baby to bed, Lee told Marina to swaddle her again—"She'll sleep better the way she's used to." After that the baby wore diapers by day and swaddling by night, when Vada did not see her.

Robert Oswald, a salesman for the Acme Brick Company of Fort Worth and, at twenty-eight, five years older than Lee, thought that his brother had changed. His skin was ruddier now and not so fair, he had lost a few pounds and he seemed, at least until he relaxed a bit after the first few days, "tense and anxious." But the biggest change was his hair. It was kinky now, in contrast to the natural curl it had had before, and it had thinned out badly on top. Thinking it over long afterward and reflecting that men in his family all had a full head of hair, Robert wondered if Lee had been subjected to shock treatments in Russia that changed his thinking as well as his hair. The only other change he noticed was that Lee seemed more "outgoing" than he had been before.

The day after their arrival, on Friday, June 15, another member of the family materialized, the boys' mother, Marguerite Oswald. She was working as a practical nurse in nearby Crowell, Texas, and she came to spend the weekend. Marguerite was a small woman, short-legged and a little top-heavy looking. She had a large, square head, gray hair, and spectacles. Her clothes gave the impression of being carefully selected and put together, the choice of a coherent personality. Marina liked her, especially her soft gray hair.

Marguerite was overjoyed to see Lee. He was not quite as happy to see her.

"She's gotten fat," he apologized. "She's changed a lot. She didn't use to be that fat."

"What do you expect?" Marina asked. "She's not a girl of fifteen."

Marguerite and Lee were arguing before the weekend was over. "She thinks that she did it all," Lee grumbled. "She thinks *she's* the one who got us out."

Marguerite told Lee that she was planning to write a book about his defection. She had been working on it for some time. The year before, she had been to Washington and had asked to see President Kennedy as part of the background. "Mother," Lee said emphatically, "you are not going to write a book."

"Lee, don't tell me what to do," Marguerite replied. "I cannot write the book now because, honey, you are alive and back. It has nothing to do with you and Marina. It is my life, because of your defection."

"Mother," Lee said again, "I tell you, you are not to write the book. They could kill [Marina] and her family."[5]

But on another matter mother and son agreed. Both criticized the U.S. Department of State for the "red tape" that had delayed Lee's return. Spontaneously, both made the same complaints, both used identical expressions, and both made the same errors of fact. Robert took no part in the airing of complaints by his mother and Lee and did not seem to look at things the same way.

While old relationships were being renewed, Vada Oswald and her sister, Gloria Jean, were busy transforming Marina, tailoring her to the brilliant Texas sun. They produced a pair of shorts and urged her to try them on. Marina did —and was horrified at the sight of her own legs. Then Vada cut her hair and gave her a permanent wave. Marina emerged into the back yard wearing shorts for the first time in her life, and with short, wavy hair. Robert and Lee rose to their feet. "You're a real American now," Lee said. "You won't stick out any more."

Robert was more gallant. He paid Marina many compliments, so many that it finally dawned on her that to Robert at least she was not just a "little Russian fool." Emboldened, she asked Lee to inquire whether Robert was sorry that his brother had married a Russian.

"Oh, no," Robert answered. "I was afraid he would marry a Japanese."[6]

Lee, meanwhile, had already abandoned the baby's Russian name, Marina, and was calling her "Junka" or "June." And he told Marina to please call him "Lee," not "Alka," or Robert would think she did not know his name. She eventually came to use both names; later, looking back on their life together, she realized that "Alka" was the name she used when she was thinking of their happier, Russian days. "Lee," his American name, was the name she used when she was angry, the name he wrung from her when he was spiteful. Those mean, spiteful moods, when it seemed as if there was no wound he was incapable of inflicting, came upon him at Robert's. They began, it seemed to Marina later, when he started looking for a job. They got worse as time went on, and as being in his old environment again simply got Lee down.

But at first there was gaiety and laughter. Marina loved to laugh. She loved looking at things in a humorous way and was not above clowning now and then. Although Lee often laughed at Marina, he did not always laugh with her. He seemed edgy in the presence of her laughter, wary that it might be directed at him and might belittle him somehow.

Other strains in their relationship began to show almost immediately. Lee was irritated at constantly having to translate for her. He scolded Marina because she had not studied English. "But, Alka," she said, "you didn't let me." He answered that she should have studied English anyway, and would have if she really cared.

After a long weekend talking and getting reacquainted with Robert and Vada, Lee was out on the streets of Fort Worth. The first thing he did was check the Yellow Pages for a public stenographer, and on the morning of Monday, June 18, Miss Pauline Virginia Bates glanced up from her typewriter to see a young man walk in clad in dark trousers and a dark blazer with only a T-shirt underneath.[7]

Lee asked her to do some typing. Out of a large manila folder he took a sheaf of notes and explained that they had been smuggled out of Russia under his clothes. "Some are typed on a little portable, some of 'em are handwritten in ink, some in pencil. I'll have to sit right here and help you with 'em because some are in Russian and some are in English."

They spent a total of eight hours together on three successive days. Miss Bates typed and Lee sat next to her, deciphering his own handwriting, translating Russian phrases here and there, answering her questions about Russia. Not that Miss Bates found him talky. "If you asked him a question, no matter how simple it was, if he didn't want to answer it, he'd just shut up. If you got ten words out of him at a time, you were doing good." She noticed, too, that "he had the deadest eyes I ever saw."

She found his notes "fascinating" but "bitter." His comments about Russia were just as bitter. And each afternoon, when he left, he grabbed up everything and took it with him, even the carbon paper. Finally, on Wednesday, June 20, Miss Bates noticed that he was "nervous." Instead of sitting by her desk he paced up and down, peered over her shoulder, and kept asking how far she had gotten. The moment she finished the tenth page, a third of the manuscript by her reckoning, he stopped her. She had done $10 worth of work and that was all he had to give her.

Miss Bates offered to finish up for free.

"No," Lee said. "I don't work that way." And he took a $10 bill from his pocket, handed it to her, and walked out. That was the last she ever saw of him.

On their second afternoon of work together, Lee told Miss Bates that he had met a Russian-speaking engineer in Fort Worth. He flourished a piece of stationery with the man's letterhead on it. This man, he said, had read all the notes and offered to help get them published. None of this was true, except for the central fact that Lee had met a Russian-born engineer.

On Monday, June 18, the day he discovered Miss Bates, Lee had also visited the office of the Texas Employment Commission in Fort Worth. There, he scouted job opportunities and asked whether there was anyone in town who spoke Russian. He was given two names.

Thus, on the morning of June 19, the telephone rang in the office of Peter Paul Gregory, a consulting petroleum engineer in Fort Worth.[8] Gregory, then approaching the age of sixty, had been born in Chita, Siberia, fled Russia in 1919, and lived for a while in Japan. Eventually he made his way to Berkeley, California, where he received a degree in petroleum engineering, and thence to Texas.

The voice on the other end of Gregory's line was that of a young man who was looking for a job as a Russian-English translator and wanted a letter attesting that he was qualified. Falsely and for no apparent reason, the young man added that he had been given Gregory's name at the Fort Worth Public Library, where Gregory taught a class, rather than by the employment commission.

Gregory had never met the young man and, since they were both speaking English, had no idea of his language qualifications. He suggested, therefore, that the caller come by the office to be tested. At eleven that morning the young man appeared at Gregory's office in downtown Fort Worth, wearing clothes that looked ridiculous in the Texas heat: a flannel suit and "atrocious" Russian shoes. The young man's name was Lee Oswald.

Gregory, a graying man with spectacles and mustache, had a grave and courteous air. Without saying a word or asking a question, he simply reached for the bookshelf and pulled down a standard Soviet secondary school history text. He selected a passage at random and asked the visitor to read aloud in Russian. He did, and very well, too. Gregory asked the young man to translate. He did, also very well. With that, Gregory wrote out a letter and gave it to the young man, addressed: "To Whom It May Concern," and stating that Lee Harvey Oswald was qualified to be a translator or interpreter in the Russian and English languages.

Gregory was curious about Oswald. Noting to himself that he appeared to speak Russian with an accent, Gregory asked if he was of Polish descent? No, Lee answered. He had grown up in Fort Worth, but he had lived in Russia nearly three years and brought back a wife and a baby. Feeling more sympathetic every moment, the kindly Gregory told Lee that he knew of no job openings but would like an address where he might reach him. Then he took Lee to lunch.

Like every Russian who lives in exile, Gregory was intensely curious about conditions in his homeland. Over lunch he asked Lee about wages and prices, about the job he had held, and how people in the Soviet Union were getting on. As for the question of how he happened to go to Russia in the first place, Lee simply answered: "I went there on my own." Gregory delicately shrank from asking more, sensing the question to be a touchy one. But he reflected that it was extraordinary that the young man had managed to get his wife out, for he had heard of countless cases in which exit visas had been refused.

When Lee showed up at Miss Bates's that afternoon, it was Gregory's "To Whom It May Concern" letter that he waved before her; and Gregory who, he told her falsely, had read his manuscript and wanted to get it published. Lee would, in fact, on a later visit to Gregory's office, show him typewritten sheets and say that he was writing memoirs of his life in the U.S.S.R. But Gregory did not read the sheets and Lee never asked him to. Gregory did notice, however, that there were photographs attached to some of them.

Lee was elated by his first meeting with Gregory. "Mama, Mama," he told Marina triumphantly that evening, "I've found you some Russians in Fort Worth. Now you won't be lonely any more." But again, lying to her for no apparent reason, he said that he had been given Gregory's name at the public library and not at the employment commission.

When Gregory told his family that he had met a young American who had just arrived in Fort Worth with a Soviet wife, his youngest son, Paul, was especially interested. He was a student at the University of Oklahoma about to enter his junior year and engaged in the study of Russian. He told his father that he would like to meet the Oswalds, especially Marina, and perhaps arrange to take language lessons from her. Her Russian would be fresh and up to date, whereas that of his father, who had been forty years in exile, might no longer encompass the idiom of young people in Russia. Less than a week after their first meeting, therefore, the Gregorys, father and son, paid a call at the house of Robert Oswald.

Lee was proud as he introduced his wife to the Russian he had found for her. Marina at first was not so sure. She did not quite take to the elder Gregory, a Russian of the pre-Revolutionary generation, who seemed uncertain how to converse with a Soviet girl. Her reservations passed, however, and the four of them visited for an hour, with the Gregorys directing most of their questions to Marina. By the time they left, it was arranged that Paul, after a short visit to San Francisco, would take Russian lessons from Marina.

Lee, meanwhile, had already telephoned the other Russian whose name he was given at the employment commission. Her name was "Gali" Clark, the wife of Max Clark, a Fort Worth attorney. Lee told Mrs. Clark that he had just arrived with a Soviet wife and was looking for a woman for her to talk Russian to. Unlike Peter Gregory, however, Mrs. Clark already knew of Oswald. She had read about him in the Fort Worth paper and her impression had not been favorable. She considered him a turncoat. She put him off by saying that her husband was not at home; she would consult him, and they would call back.

A few days later, on Sunday, June 24, Mrs. Clark telephoned Lee and invited him to drive over that afternoon with his wife and child. But Lee, offended that he had not been welcomed on the first call, was churlish to Mrs. Clark and told her that he could not make it.[9]

That evening at the dinner table with Robert and Vada, he told Marina about the call. She berated him for being rude, and angry words passed between them. They were speaking in Russian, of course, when suddenly, in a shift of mood, he told her to smile, be nice, and not let on to Robert that they were having a fight. Marina refused to pretend. He called her a dirty word, and she quickly got up and left the table. Lee followed her into the bedroom. He was pale with anger and there was a cold, pitiless look in his eyes which Marina had not seen before. Quietly, very quietly, so that Robert would not hear, he cuffed her several times, hard, across the face. He told her to say nothing to Robert or he would kill her.

Marina slipped out of the house in a state of shock. For two hours she walked alone around the neighborhood, trying to make sense of her situation. Now she knew what it was to be completely helpless. She did not speak a word of English. She knew no one. There was no one who could understand her even if she did try to explain her plight. Alka was all she had, her only friend and her support. And he was changing toward her. She was stunned by his capacity for hypocrisy: his ability to be nice to outsiders and at the same time cruel to her, behind their backs. She felt that she would never be able to count on him again.

As Marina walked alone that night, she glanced into the windows of people's houses, saw them watching TV, saw them leading normal lives. Why on earth had she ever left Aunt Valya? She was unhappy about staying with Robert and Vada. It was wrong to live off other people and not know how to help them, how they cooked and cleaned house. She believed that Vada did not like her, and Robert had witnessed the angry scene at the dinner table without saying a word to defend her. But the main thing was Alka. She was beginning to be afraid of him.

She had no choice but to endure. She had the baby. The baby depended on her, and neither had anybody else. With a heavy, automatic feeling, Marina went back—back to Alka and the baby. He was awake in bed, but he did not speak to her.

The next day, things were smoothed over with Alka, somehow, and that day she met Peter Gregory. She did not think of it at the time, but it was her first encounter with someone who could rescue her, someone to whom she could, if she chose, explain her plight in her native tongue.

14

Summer in Fort Worth

LEE'S ARRIVAL in Fort Worth did not go unnoticed. He had several calls from newspapermen, with whom he declined to talk. And he had a call from the FBI, which he could not so easily put off. He agreed to an interview at 1:00 P.M. on Tuesday, June 26, at the FBI office in downtown Fort Worth.

Lee arrived ten minutes early, but Special Agent John W. Fain and his assistant, B. Tom Carter, sat him down and started pelting him with questions.[1] From the outset they found him "tense, kind of drawn up, and rigid. A wiry little fellow, kind of waspy." The question to which they returned again and again was why Oswald had gone to Russia. Finally, in what they took to be a "show of temper," Lee said that he did not "care to relive the past." He would say only what he had told the Russians when they asked him the same question: "I came because I wanted to."

The agents' real purpose that day was to try to find out whether Oswald had been recruited by Soviet Intelligence, possibly as the price for bringing out Marina. Again and again Lee denied it, stressing how hard it had been to get Marina out, how long it had taken and how much paper work it had required. He sketched Marina's life for them, but refused to give names or addresses of any of her relatives, lest it get them in trouble.

The interview lasted about two hours, and in the course of it, Lee repeated familiar untruths, among them that he never sought Soviet citizenship and never offered radar information to the Russians. He stated that because his wife held a Soviet passport, he would be getting in touch with the Soviet Embassy in Washington within a few days to give them her address. But he said that he held "no brief for the Russians or the Russian system," and promised to get in touch with the FBI if Soviet Intelligence made any effort to contact him.

When he filed his report a week or so later, Agent Fain described Oswald as "impatient and arrogant during most of the interview." He felt that Oswald had been "evasive" and recommended that he be interviewed again. Later, looking back at a distance of two years, it occurred to Fain that behind the "arrogance" and the "coldness," Oswald might have been "just scared."

That night, Robert asked Lee how the FBI men had treated him. "Just fine," Lee answered. He then told Robert the most staggering untruth he had perpetrated in quite a while. The FBI, he said, wanted to know whether he was an agent of the *United States* government. "Don't *you* know?" Lee said he had asked them. And he laughed as he told Robert how he had turned the tables on the FBI.[2]

As for Marina, he told her nothing at all, not even that the interview had taken place. She thought he was putting all his energies into job-hunting, and asked every night how it was going. But after a few days she stopped, for she could see that he was getting nowhere. Marina was not surprised. She had heard all her life that unemployment was a problem of crisis dimensions in the United States, and Lee did nothing to disabuse her of the idea. He stressed it, in fact, since it gave him a built-in excuse. Marina did not hound him; she accepted his explanations and gave him her sympathy and support.

But Lee had liabilities in the job market. He had no high-school diploma. He had an undesirable discharge. And he had spent three years in the Soviet Union, a fact he probably did not confide to would-be employers, which left him with an abbreviated job history. The skills he had—radar training, the ability to speak Russian—were not in demand in Fort Worth. He did not want blue-collar work of the kind he had had in Minsk, yet he lacked the education for the white-collar work he would accept, to say nothing of the intellectual work he really wanted. Nor is it clear how hard he was looking for a job. Vada noticed that he spent a good deal of time at home, working for "hours at a stretch going over his notes and adding to them."[3]

Lee and Marina had been living with Robert and Vada for four or five weeks when Marguerite Oswald once again appeared on the scene. She gave up her job in Crowell and took an apartment in Fort Worth so that she, her Prodigal Son, and her Russian daughter-in-law could be united under one roof. According to Robert, Lee was "not overjoyed." He told his mother that he would soon be working, and he and Marina would then want to live on their own.[4] But Marguerite got her way, not so much by arguing the point as by acting as if it were already settled. So it was that Marina, Lee, and the baby moved to the Rotary Apartments at 1501 West Seventh Street in Fort Worth, and settled in the two-room apartment Marguerite had found for them. Lee did not leave a forwarding address at the post office. It was a sign that he did not expect the new arrangement to last.

Marguerite paid the rent. She slept in the living room, while Lee, Marina, and the baby had the bedroom to themselves. Marina found her mother-in-law a superb housekeeper, meticulously neat, and one who used up every scrap of food. Moreover, it was she and she alone who held the key to Lee's appetite. With everyone else, his wife included, he was a finicky eater. But he demolished everything Marguerite cooked for him. Had the way to Lee's heart lain through his stomach, relations between mother and son would have been peaceful indeed.

Marguerite had a car, and the first few mornings she drove Lee around, tracking down leads he got from newspaper ads and the state employment commission. Marguerite would later claim that her son "met obstacles all the way."[5] But on July 17, only a few days after moving in with his mother, Lee started work as a sheet metal helper for the Leslie Welding Company, manufacturers of louvers and ventilators in Fort Worth. He stated falsely on his application that he had had sheet metal experience in the Marine Corps. Lee did well in the job. The manager of the Louv-R-Pak Division of the company for which Lee worked later recalled that he was "one of the best employees" he ever had.[6] Lee's foreman, however, remembers him as a laconic fellow: "He didn't talk to nobody about nothing, so nobody ever messed with him." But he came to work on time and might have become "a pretty good sheet metal man" if he'd stayed in it.[7]

Lee loathed the job which, like his work in Russia, was hard manual labor. But he earned $1.25 an hour, worked up to nine hours a day, and took home $45 to $55 a week. He told Marina again and again that he must pay off his debts to Robert and the Department of State as quickly as he could. Living rent-free with his mother helped, a major reason why he did it, and he started paying back Robert right away.

With Lee gone all day, Marina stayed at home with Marguerite. Although they could hardly speak to one another, the two got along well at first. Marina was overjoyed to have a home and someone she could look to as a mother. She noted with appreciation that Marguerite was good to the baby, although not as lavishly fond of her as her Russian relatives had been. Above all, Marina was pleased by the sudden lift in her husband's spirits. Since finding work, he was no longer so irritable and depressed. Marina almost forgot his behavior on the boat, and his hitting her at Robert's.

Marina washed dishes and tended the baby. But she was unfamiliar with the ways of an American household and was not on easy terms with domesticity anyhow. The lion's share of chores fell on Marguerite, who did all the cooking, the cleaning, and claims to have helped with the baby.[8] She got out of the apartment only rarely, to see a movie or a friend, and seems to have felt stirrings of resentment. Of these Marina was at first blissfully unaware. But when Marguerite discovered that her daughter-in-law recognized Gregory Peck on television and could sing a few words of "Santa Lucia," she began to suspect that Marina, and even Lee, might be spies. Lee made no effort to include his mother in his conversations with Marina. He huddled over books with her and sat with her at the dining room table by the hour, playing a sort of Russian tic-tac-toe. In the late afternoon or early evening, husband and wife went out walking, leaving Marguerite at home as babysitter. Before long, Marguerite complained.

To Marina's surprise, Lee paid little attention to her complaints. He was cool to his mother and had very few words for her. Marina began to fear that Marguerite might blame her for alienating Lee's affections. And she was right. After a fortnight or so, Marguerite started scolding her daughter-in-law when they were at home alone. Marina could not understand her words. She thought Marguerite resented having to cook for her, or that somehow she had displeased her mother-in-law. But one day there was a scene with much weeping and screaming and slamming of doors, and Marina was afraid her mother-in-law was going to hit her. This time she caught the words and she repeated them that evening to Lee —"You took my son away from me!" Mother and son had it out the same night, once again with screaming and slamming of doors. Afterward Lee told Marina to forget it; they would be leaving soon, anyhow.

Marina knew nothing of the relationship between Lee and his mother. She did not know that Marguerite had also fought with her other two sons over *their* wives. She knew only that Marguerite had three sons, and not one of them wanted to live with her. To Marina, Marguerite's jealousy was natural; it was Lee whose feelings seemed unnatural. Furthermore, she still regretted the way she had treated her own mother and she did not want Lee to behave as she had done. Toward Marguerite she continued to show deference and a readiness for affection. She felt sorry for her and urged Lee to show more warmth toward his mother. "How will you feel," she asked, "if Junie won't speak to you when she grows up?"

"Don't meddle," he growled. "You know nothing about it."

On Saturday, August 10, less than a month after they had moved in with Marguerite, Marina and Lee moved out. Lee had found an apartment. Accustomed as he was to the family ways, Robert was astonished to hear loud sounds of discord when he drove up that morning to help them move. Marguerite was screaming, her hair mussed and her eyes red from crying. Lee was calm, but Marina looked bewildered.[9] There was very little luggage, a few boxes and a couple of old suitcases, and Lee and Robert quickly carried them to the car. They confronted their mother's outcries with silence, creating a vacuum into which she poured even louder protestations. When the young people clambered into the car and drove off, Marguerite ran a short way after them.

Pity suddenly broke through the numbness Marina felt. "It's cruel to leave her that way. She'll have a heart attack and die."

Lee was as cool as could be. "She'll be all right," he said. "It's not the first time."

And that was the beginning of their life on their own in Texas.

The apartment Lee had found was a furnished "duplex," one-half of a shabby, single-story clapboard bungalow. It was located among other one- and two-family frame houses at 2703 Mercedes Street, Fort Worth, across the street from a Montgomery Ward retail store and down a dusty road from Lee's job. He had paid a month's rent in advance of $59.50.

Friends who visited the place later described it as "horrible," a "slum," "a shack," "very poorly furnished" and "decrepit." But Marina did not feel that way. There was a bedroom, a living room with a dining area, a kitchen and bath, plus a yard and some grass outside. In Russia, they could have worked a lifetime and not had so much space. The furniture was cheap, but the place was clean, and that meant a lot to Marina. As content as she had been to live with her mother-in-law, Marina was happier still to be alone with her husband.

They slipped into a new routine. Lee went to work in the morning, and in the afternoon, Marina might leave their supper simmering on the stove, take the baby in her arms, and walk down the road to meet him on his way home. He would spot them a long way off and wave. When he caught up with them, he would take June in one arm, put his other arm around Marina and they would slowly saunter home. Other afternoons she might sit on the front steps and wait for him there. The moment he caught sight of her, he would wave and break into a run.

Sometimes, Lee found her inside the house, fixing supper. "Why didn't you meet me today?" he would ask. Then with a glint of amusement: "I know. You were in Montgomery Ward."

Marina had, indeed, found a fount of riches, a cornucopia of daydreams, across the street. With June in her arms, she spent hours wandering through Montgomery Ward, a fairyland of treasures that could not be bought in all of Russia no matter how much money you had. Ties, trousers, notions, dresses— Marina did not want to buy them. It made her happy just to look. When they went to the store together, she would visit the toy and dress departments while Lee, with the most obvious enjoyment, made his way to the gun department. For the first week or so, he gave Marina $2 a week spending money, but except for cigarettes she never spent it. Then he stopped giving her any money at all. "I never cared about money," she remembers. "I don't know why."

Marina believed that the best political system was the one that does most for the people. That was the sum total of her political theories. As she saw it, you went into a store in Russia and there was nothing to buy, you went into a store in America and there was a lot. It followed that the United States cared more about its people and was a better country. Marina liked America, preferred it, right away. At night she would occasionally dream that she was at home again, telling her Russian friends what a paradise America is. "Alka, do anything," she started saying to her husband, "but don't ever, ever make me go back."

She loved grocery shopping. Lee would steer her to a delicatessen and say: "Look, Mama. No need to be homesick. You can get the same things as in Russia." He bought her the foods she liked especially—sour cream, sauerkraut, pickles, kidneys, herring. "Mama, would you like some caviar?" He would lift a jar of the red variety off the shelf. And, for all it cost him, he stuffed it in the shopping basket and took out something he had chosen for himself. When they got home, he sat at the dining table and looked on with a rapturous air while Marina ate the caviar. It was one of the few Russian foods he liked. But he refused to touch it, not even when she tried to feed him with a spoon; he did not want to deprive her.

A few days after their move, a ripple crossed the surface of their tranquility —a visit from the FBI. It was a hot night, Thursday, August 16, and Marina was about to serve dinner. The front door was open, the screen door on the latch. Lee was sitting on the sofa, reading *The Worker* in English. She was setting the table. All of a sudden they heard a knock at the screen door. Lee got up, glanced at the door, then quickly stuffed his newspaper under the sofa cushion. He opened the screen door and invited the caller to come in. A man entered, showed his documents to Lee and, apologizing to Marina for delaying supper, asked him to come out to a waiting car.[10]

Marina peered out and saw Lee in a car with two men. He was gone a long time, at least an hour, and she had to heat up their dinner, she says, "ten times." She was furious by the time he came back. Who were those men, anyway?

Lee was gloomy and dispirited. "They were the FBI."

"And who are *they?*"

"They're the security organs. In Russia it's the KGB. Here it's the FBI."

Marina was angry about dinner, angrier still to hear the dread initials KGB.

"They asked about Russia," Lee said. "They wanted to know if Soviet agents had been here and asked me to work for them. I said No. They said, if anybody comes, please let the FBI know. I told them: 'I will not be an informer for you. Go ahead and do it if that's your job, but don't ask me to do it for you.'"

He ate very little and talked very little and his eyes had a troubled look. "Now it's begun," he said. "Because I've been over there, they'll never let me live in peace. They think anyone who's been there is a Russian spy. Let them think it. It'll just give them more work." He was upset, and the bad mood lingered for several days. He did not tell Marina that he had seen the FBI once before, at the downtown office in Fort Worth.

Agent John W. Fain reported on this second interview with Oswald in detail.[11] He told Oswald that he had not gone to see him at work because he did not wish to embarrass him with his employer; and he chose to interview him in the car, not the house, because he did not want to upset Marina. Oswald pounced on this remark, stored it up, and later on used it again and again.

Fain was impressed by the change in Oswald, who showed no reluctance to see him and even invited him into the house. "He had gotten a job, and he wasn't as tense." Fain thought he talked "more freely" and not so evasively as during their previous interview. But he still refused to answer, to their satisfaction, the question why he went to the U.S.S.R. It was "nobody's business," he said. "It was something that I did. I went, and I came back."

Oswald repeated most of his old lies, and added a new one: that he had moved to Mercedes Street in mid-July, and not just the week before. This time he confided his fears of prosecution on returning to the United States, and admitted that he had been interviewed by officials of the MVD, the Soviet interior ministry, twice: on his arrival in the U.S.S.R., and again before his departure. But noting that he was not employed in a sensitive industry and that the company he was working for had no government contracts, Oswald played down any importance he might have to the Russians. Contrary to what he told Marina afterward, he did, in fact, promise for the second time to inform the FBI should there be any undercover Soviet effort to contact him.

The interview, plus a report which he received from two confidential informants the next day to the effect that neither Lee nor Marina Oswald had anything to do with Communist Party activities in Fort Worth, led Fain to recommend that the FBI close its case on Lee Harvey Oswald.[12] This the FBI did—not long after the moment when Oswald, speaking of FBI persecution, made the gloomy prediction: "Now it's begun."

Oswald made one pregnant remark during the interview. He said that "he might have to return to the Soviet Union in about five years to take his wife back home to see her relatives."[13] And in a letter to the Soviet Embassy in Washington, written within a day or two of his meeting with the FBI, Oswald tossed out another hint. He asked the embassy to send "periodicals or bulletins which you may put out for the benefit of your citizens living *for a time* in the U.S.A."[14]

Oswald said nothing to Marina about any plan to return to the Soviet Union, and it is not clear why, less than a week after moving into his first home in the United States, he suggested twice in as many days that Marina and their child, or all three of them together, might go back to Russia. It is clear, however, that his return to the United States had had a contingent character in his mind from the outset, and that already he was contemplating a way out. Up to now he had always had help in caring for his family, help from the Soviet government and Marina's relatives, help from Robert and his mother. Now he was on his own. He profoundly wanted to be, but perhaps the responsibility made him anxious. Possibly he anticipated trouble of some kind. The probable truth, that the Soviet government would never allow him, a malcontent and an ex-defector, inside its borders again, does not seem to have entered his head.

Marina's pleas to him—"Do anything, Alka, but don't ever make me go back"—suggest that perhaps she guessed what was in his mind. And her unconscious awareness and anxiety must have made the adjustment to her new life much harder. Thus, in involuntary ways, Oswald was ruffling the surface of his married life and rendering his existence more turbulent. The conflicts that had sent him to Russia in the first place had been resolved neither by his defection, nor by his decision to come home. Emotionally he was in the same place he had always been.

The chief source of those conflicts, his mother, soon reappeared, wholly unchastened, on the steps of his house on Mercedes Street. No one quite knew how she got there, since both Lee and Robert had been at pains to conceal the address.

Marina remembers her visit with merriment. About three days after their move, she heard a knock at the door. She looked out and there, to her astonishment, stood "Mamochka," looking just as blithe and unconcerned as if the hysterical scene of parting had never occurred. Marguerite brought a high chair for the baby and silverware, dishes, and utensils for Marina and Lee. Marina welcomed her in, Marguerite played with the baby, and then left.

Lee was upset when he came home that night and heard that his mother had been there. He instructed Marina not to let her in next time. Marina objected. "She's your *mother*, Alka. How can I not let her in?"

"You know nothing about her," he said. "You're not to let her in again."

The next day Marguerite came again, with a live green and yellow parakeet inside a cage. Lee had given the cage and the very same parakeet to his mother nearly seven years before, in November 1955, when he was sixteen years old, with money earned from his first real job as office boy at Tujague's shipping company in New Orleans. Again, Marina welcomed her mother-in-law. She was sorry for her, sorry she had to live alone, and she still thought Alka was to blame.

Marguerite had a camera with her, and she was snapping a picture of the baby when Lee walked in. He started to scold her immediately. Marina thinks he told Marguerite not to come again, but she stood her ground and said she had a right to see her grandchild.

Marguerite would recall a different version of the argument. She said that Lee merely told her not to bring presents any more. She realized, she said, that he was "perfectly right. I should save my money and take care of myself."[15]

The moment Marguerite was gone, Lee turned on his wife. "Why didn't you obey? I told you not to open the door."

"But she's your *mother*," Marina said. "I've no right to shut the door in her face."

"You know nothing about it. She brings these things and is nice to you now. Next, she'll move in. You'll never be able to get rid of her. You'll be sorry then."

"You ought to be ashamed. You've no right to behave as if your mama didn't exist."

Lee was shouting now. "I have a right to tell you what to do! I told you not to open the door!"

"I will not obey."

"You will not open the door!"

"I will, too."

He hit her four or five times across the face.

One day, about a month later, Marina came home to find the parakeet gone. Lee had taken it outdoors and let it fly out of the cage.

Despite her son's hostility, Marguerite came to the apartment fairly often. On one visit she found Marina in the bedroom, nursing the baby with her head down. Eventually she looked up, and Marguerite saw that she had a black eye.

"Mama—Lee," was all Marina was able to say.

Marguerite strode out to the living room, where her son lay reading. "Lee, what do you mean by striking Marina?"

"Mother, that is our affair," he answered.

Marguerite, on balance, agreed. "There may be times," she remarked later, "that a woman needs a black eye."[16] Just as Lee had hit *her* when he was growing up, now he was hitting his wife. And Marguerite Oswald, as she had done then, condoned it.

In fact, from the moment of Marguerite's first visit to Mercedes Street the beatings had become routine—once or twice a week. Typically, after Lee had beaten her, Marina would say: "Alka, I am not your maid. I am good enough not to have you hit me." He, after an hour or two, would repent and beg Marina to forgive him. And the next day he would buy her caviar or a trinket for the baby.

At the smallest sign that he valued her and the baby, Marina forgave him. She forgave and forgot, until the next time. Their sexual relationship also began to deteriorate. Worn out by heavy physical work in hot weather, Lee did not want sex more than once a week or so, and Marina, dispirited at the turn things were taking, did not want sex much, either.

Still, there were happy moments. Marina was grateful for the good times, fatalistic about the bad. Her stepfather, after all, had beaten her, and he had done it exactly as Lee did, with the flat of his hand, across her face. He, too, had had an icy, inhuman anger in his eyes. But he had hit her once and then stopped; Lee hit her again and again. Marina decided that it was God's judgment on her for having been cruel to her mother.

The beatings were a humiliation. They devalued Marina in her own eyes, and she feared that they would devalue her in the eyes of anyone who knew of them. Thus she tried to make light of them. She told herself, and later told others as well, that she had a fair skin that bruised easily and exaggerated the effect of every blow. If they suggested that she had brought the beatings on herself by talking too sharply to Lee when he was under strain, she agreed. In a way, Marina believed that she deserved to be beaten.

She took the very Russian view that beatings are a private affair between man and wife, as private as sex. Still, she hoped that Robert might intervene, just as members of Russian families often did. But in this, Robert disappointed her. He had dropped by to see them one day and Marina, who had a black eye, lingered unobtrusively in the kitchen. But she thinks Robert saw her black eye. If he did, he chose to do, and say, nothing. Robert had suffered from Lee's anger in the past, and whether he was loath to invoke his brother's wrath again or was simply the non-intervening sort, he stayed out of Lee's marital affairs. Any thoughts he may have had about his brother's harshness to Marina, Robert kept to himself.

But by this time Marina was no longer bereft. All her life she had been charming people, attracting them to her and making them want to look out for her. Her charm had given her nine lives already: it was about to give her a tenth.

15

The Émigrés

AROUND THE MIDDLE of August, young Paul Gregory returned from his summer trip to San Francisco. Eager to improve his Russian, he started showing up twice a week in the late afternoons or evenings for Russian lessons with Marina. His visits quickly became a pleasure and a resource to both the Oswalds.

At twenty-one, Paul Gregory was a year and a half younger than Lee and a full-time college student.[1] Lee may have envied him, for he was out on the evening Paul arrived for his first lesson and returned home brandishing a catalogue of night courses he said he hoped to attend at Texas Christian University. Other evenings, too, Lee used to come home late, laden with books from the public library. He said he wanted to go to college, to Texas Christian or Arlington State, and get a degree in history, philosophy, or economics. Both Lee and Paul had attended the same high school, Arlington Heights in Fort Worth. Lee implied that he had graduated, when, in fact, he had been there only a few weeks in the tenth grade. The barrier to a college education for him, Lee suggested, was the need to support his family. But both in the United States and in Russia, where Lee also had to work, he appears to have lacked motivation to study at night to obtain first a high school and then a college degree.

When Lee was out, Paul's "lessons" consisted largely of Russian conversations with Marina, during which she told him all about how she met Lee and their courtship in Minsk. Paul got the impression that she had been a rebel and a nonconformist, and that this was one of the main reasons for her early interest in Lee. Marina also corrected Paul's grammar in an essay he was writing on a play called *Man with a Gun,* by Nikolai Pogodin. She and Paul huddled together over the dining room table while Lee sat reading Lenin on the sofa. When all three of them spoke Russian together, Paul noticed that Lee's Russian, while fluent, was "very ungrammatical" and that he spoke with "a very strong accent." When Marina corrected his errors, "he would get peeved at her. He would wave his hand and say, 'Don't bother me.' " But, according to Paul, he was able to "express any idea he wanted to in Russian."

Inevitably, they talked about politics, and as far as Paul could tell, Lee thought the world's troubles were caused not by "the people," but by leaders. When it came to specific leaders, however, he did not seem to harbor grudges. He expressed no hostility toward any of them. He was enthusiastic about Castro, and, remarkably, continued to respect Paul in spite of their differences over Cuba. As for Khrushchev, Lee described him as "simply brilliant." He was "rough" and "crude," but "you cannot read a speech of his without liking the man." He also liked John F. Kennedy. On their living room table the Oswalds kept, more or less permanently, a copy of *Life* magazine with a cover photo of the President. Marina pointed at it once and said, "He looks like a nice young man." Lee added that Kennedy was "a good leader."

One evening as they were all leaving the house together, Paul got a glimpse of how Lee often treated Marina. She fell off the steps, and she and the baby sprawled on the ground. The baby began to cry and Paul thought Marina had hurt her back. But Lee did not even notice her. He rushed over and picked up the baby, furious at Marina for allowing *his* baby to fall. Marina thought he was going to kill her. It was "a real hot moment," Paul recalls, but husband and wife ran indoors, consulted a Russian book on baby care, and together applied a Band-Aid to Junie's head.

In sum, Paul considered Lee "hot tempered, not very smart, and slightly mixed up." He was "a small person" who was "always ready to flare up." In his normal conversations with Marina, he "would always shout." Paul thought that Lee had an "inability to grasp things." And yet he could not say that he "disliked" Lee. "I enjoyed being with him," although "I enjoyed Marina more. She was a very pleasant person, very pleasant to be with, interesting."

On Friday nights, Paul used to take them shopping in his car. They would go to Leonard's department store, noted for its low prices, to buy groceries. Paul was amazed at how little the Oswalds bought. Lee always haggled over the meat, to be sure they got "the cheapest possible cut." They were, in fact, getting by on very little. They did without milk because Marina was nursing the baby, and they had fashioned a crib by putting two chairs together between their bed and the wall. True, the baby once fell into the crack between the chairs, but Lee wanted to save money more than he wanted to buy a crib. Marina says that he treated his financial obligations to Robert and the Department of State, which he was not under pressure to repay quickly, as "a holy debt." During the month of August, for example, when he netted about $200, Lee spent two-thirds on living expenses and nearly one-third in partial payment of his debts.

It never entered Marina's head that her husband was penurious. From her excursions to Montgomery Ward, she knew that all kinds of things such as nice dresses, cribs, and playpens existed. But it did not occur to her to want them. And when Paul Gregory, shortly before leaving for college, handed her a check for $35, she was overwhelmed. She had never in all her life had so much money. She felt that she did not deserve it. She suspected that the Gregorys, father and son, simply wanted to help her and, rather than offend by giving her money, had devised the pretext of the lessons. Marina knew what she wanted to do with it. She went across the street to Montgomery Ward and bought a pair of shoes for herself ($3.98), and for Alka green work pants, two flannel shirts, and another pair of shoes ($11).

Marina was right; the Gregorys did want to help. Peter Gregory, Paul's father, had been in the Oswalds' apartment and the sight of it evoked his sympathy. He found the living room "practically bare . . . and the rest of the house was the same way."[2] During his visit, Gregory suggested that Marina start to study English. Lee would have none of it. He did not want Marina to learn English, he said, lest he lose his own fluency in Russian. To Gregory, Oswald's answer signified that he cared nothing for his wife, only for himself. But Gregory was a fair man, and slow to judge.

Meanwhile, news of the Oswalds' arrival had spread like a prairie fire among the twenty-five or thirty Russian émigré families in Dallas and Fort Worth. Into that landscape of freeways and flat red earth, of liveoak trees and wide Texas sky had come, a decade earlier, fifty or sixty refugees from various parts of Eastern Europe. Some were Russians, a handful were Poles or Rumanians, the rest were from the fringes of the Soviet Union: Latvians, Lithuanians, Estonians, Ukrainians, Georgians, Armenians. Displaced or uprooted during World War II, every one of them had preferred anything, any fate at all, over a return to the countries or territories dominated by communism. Eventually, after years of hardship and uncertainty, they had made their way to the United States. A few of the women had married American soldiers in West Germany; the rest came by other routes. But the point was that they had arrived, they were on American soil, and the Russians would never lay hands on them again.

Some of the men were lucky. They had geology or engineering in their backgrounds and were able to find jobs in what was then the major industry of the Dallas-Fort Worth area—oil. The others, many of them men and women of some education who would have had fine professional careers back home, had to settle for such jobs as they could find. But before they could do even this, they had a major obstacle to overcome. Most of them had arrived in the United States unable to speak a word of English.

It was at this point that George Bouhe stepped into the lives of many of the émigrés. Bouhe, who had grown up in St. Petersburg as a member of the educated middle class of czarist Russia, had been living in the United States since 1924, and in Dallas since 1939. A lively, inquiring man of fifty-eight, he had become the trusted personal accountant of one of the most powerful men in Dallas, Lewis W. MacNaughton, chairman of the board of the huge and immensely wealthy geological and engineering firm of DeGolyer and MacNaughton.

Bouhe knew very well that it was impossible to get by in America without speaking English. He had personally taken several of the émigrés "by the hand" and led them to Crozier Technical High School, where they learned the rudiments of the language. He had helped them in other ways, too, and over the years he had become the patriarch of the Russian émigré community.

In spite of the hardships that lay behind them, the émigrés had made a remarkable adjustment to Texas life and to what must, to them, have been a totally incongruous world of suburbs, supermarkets, and air-conditioned ranch houses. They were tearfully grateful to the United States, the country which gave them life when they had lost it. But in one sense, the political sense, the section of the country to which they had gravitated was not incongruous at all. It could hardly have been more congenial. For this was deep anti-Communist country and the émigrés, with an exception or two, were virulent anti-Communists. For them it had not been a case of arriving in the Southwest and then adapting to its extreme political conservatism. They were conservatives when they came and would have remained so anywhere on earth. The political climate of Texas may actually have helped them adjust to American life. It was certainly a feature of the country that they liked.

It was an extraordinary community. Nearly all its members were generous, outgoing, and warm. Because they had suffered so much themselves, they could not see another person suffer without doing what they could to help. While they embraced wholeheartedly the American ethos of individualism and hard work, they had also kept the values they brought over from Eastern Europe: the spirit of community, of sharing, of the responsibility of each for all. And they were curious about the country they had left behind. When word got around of the Oswalds' arrival, many of the émigrés were curious to meet them, especially Marina, a member of the younger Soviet generation, with whom none of them had had any contact.

The Gregorys decided to introduce the Oswalds to two members of the émigré community. Marina and Lee were invited to a dinner party on Saturday, August 25, at the Gregorys' home in Fort Worth. There they met Anna Meller, forty-five years old, a large and dramatically handsome blonde from Belgorod, southern Russia, who had been living in the United States since 1952. She had driven over from her home in Dallas with the Gregorys' other guest, George Bouhe.

Bouhe was a bachelor, or a grass widower, with time and sympathy to spare. But he was also cautious. He looked and listened before he leaped. He was eager to attend the dinner party and hear about conditions in his homeland, but he all but burned up the telephone wires between Dallas and Fort Worth before accepting the Gregorys' invitation. Was it prudent to meet Oswald? Was there a danger that this defector, who had accomplished the supposedly impossible feat of leaving the Soviet Union and bringing a Russian wife with him, might turn out to be a Soviet spy?

The man to whom he directed these questions was Max Clark, the Fort Worth lawyer whose wife had had a brief and abrasive contact with Oswald shortly after he arrived in Texas. By virtue of the respect in which he was held in Fort Worth and his marriage to a member of the princely Shcherbatov family (the family which Leo Tolstoy rechristened "Shcherbatsky" and used as models of the Moscow nobility in *Anna Karenina*), Clark was like a highly placed in-law to all the Russians. He and his wife Gali stood at the very apex of the émigré community, maybe a touch above it, and were often called upon as arbiters of its frequent clashes of politics and personalities. Moreover, Clark, as a lawyer for General Dynamics, was thought to have dealings with the FBI. Did the FBI have anything against Oswald? That was what Bouhe wanted to know. If so, Bouhe, who was as anti-Soviet as was humanly possible, and a super-patriot for Texas besides, wanted nothing to do with him.

Clark spoke from common sense and experience only. He did not work for the FBI, nor had he talked with anyone in the FBI about Oswald. But he could see no risk in meeting the man. Doubtless, Oswald was under FBI surveillance and would not be back in this country if he were thought to present any danger. Thus assured, Bouhe accepted the Gregorys' invitation.

From a social standpoint it was the Oswalds' finest hour. No one who was there that evening has forgotten the picture they presented as they came in: Lee, immaculate in jacket, tie, and a white shirt with French cuffs, and Marina, his pretty, frail-looking wife, holding their baby daughter in her arms. Everyone was aware that Lee was a poor man, and they were impressed at his being so meticulously dressed. They were impressed, too, by his quiet manner and his grave, courteous air. They were prepared to respect him as a man who had taken the Soviet Union seriously enough to go and see it, yet was sensible enough to come back. And they were impressed by his affection for his baby, whom he held all evening on his lap.

But Marina was the real sensation. Not only did she appear a childlike, innocent waif, but her use of Russian—and Russians tend to judge other Russians by the way they speak the mother tongue—was very cultivated. Bouhe immediately surmised that Marina had been well brought up, that she had "received good care from some person of the Old Regime," someone "religious, well-mannered and such."[3] His good impression was in no way diminished when Marina told him that she had indeed been taught to speak Russian by her grandmother, who had also taught her to be religious.

The Russians were surprised. They expected Marina, as a member of a generation that grew up long after they left the country, to be what they thought of as "Soviet": sturdy and purposeful, literal, direct, and not very well educated, self-consciously "proletarian," with scorn for good manners and good speech. In every one of their expectations they were confounded. Marina was tiny and thin. She chain-smoked and drank a little wine. She was well mannered and, above all, she spoke that pure Leningrad Russian, innocent of jargon or slang, that to them bespoke intelligence and education. She was like a fragile fossil, a relic of their old and much-loved homeland, that had suddenly been dug out of the Russian earth.

Marina was equally intrigued. To her, meeting these people was like seeing the characters in the plays of Chekhov and the novels of Turgenev and Tolstoy come to life. If they were sizing her up, she was doing the same. "At first," she said to herself of one of the women, "you'd think she was from a good background —but only at first. Peter Gregory does not speak a very pure Russian. He must have come 'up' from somewhere. Bouhe—he's from the Old Intelligentsia." In manner and speech Bouhe reminded Marina of her beloved aunt, Maria Yakovlevna, and she liked him right away. She liked him even better when he told her, in a way that probed and divined her thoughts, that he did not work for any intelligence service and she could therefore speak to him frankly.

Bouhe had brought with him a huge album with maps of St. Petersburg from 1710 to 1914. This he spread out on the floor and, inviting Marina to join him there, peppered her with questions about whether this or that old school, church, or outdoor market was still standing. Marina felt that she was being examined, and not only for her intelligence. She was from a district in which members of the working class and the new Soviet intelligentsia lived, whereas Bouhe was asking about the heart of Old St. Petersburg, where the aristocracy used to live, and where descendants of the Old Intelligentsia, of people like Bouhe himself, were still living. Marina thought he was an aristocrat, and because she was not, she felt anxious and self-conscious. She wondered what these people would think of her when they found out where she really came from.

If it was a test, Marina passed it, for Bouhe liked her very much. He felt stirrings of protectiveness toward her, the beginnings of what was to become a father-daughter relationship.[4] As for Lee, everyone tiptoed around the question in all their minds: Why, having defected to Russia, did he decide to come back? They guessed that his decision signified failure, if only the failure of having to admit that he had been wrong, and they leaned over backwards not to embarrass him. The venturesome Bouhe teetered up to it, indeed, by praising people with the courage and good sense to change their minds. At this, he felt Lee bristle and draw away.

Politics was touchy for them all, for no one was certain whether or not Oswald had renounced his Communist proclivities. The émigrés asked many questions about living conditions, prices, wages, about the smaller freedoms and how life had changed in little ways. And in Lee's answers they took soundings as to where he really stood. Some of those present considered him a trifle quick to protest the virtues of the U.S.S.R. They sensed in him a trace of the "*nashi luchshe*" mentality, a special Soviet attitude that "ours is better," that anything Soviet—a head of cabbage, a pair of shoes, life in general—is better than its counterpart anywhere else simply because it is Soviet. It was only a feeling, of course. But there was no doubt in the mind of anybody there that, of the two, Marina was far more critical of Russia. They agreed with her and they liked her for it.

By the end of the evening, the verdict on her was favorable. As for him, they found him well mannered, but cold. He was, in any case, much better than the émigrés expected of a man who had once been fool enough to defect to Soviet Russia.

Lee had his own feelings about the party. Marina sensed in him that grudging edge of ungraciousness that told her he was doing it for her, so she could meet her countrymen—it was not an evening he would go through for himself alone. In fact, a failure of sympathy between Lee and the émigrés appears to have had its origins that night. In Russia, Lee had grown accustomed to being asked about conditions in America, and he expected to be asked similar questions here. But in his heart of hearts he was scornful of people who appeared to be interested mostly in money and material things. In his scheme of things, they were "bourgeois." Besides, he wanted to talk about bigger things, about political differences between Russia and America, about Castro, Khrushchev, and de-Stalinization. But the émigrés had politely avoided such discussion.

In Minsk, Lee had been able to condescend. He was no better educated than his listeners, but he had spent his life outside Russia, and they were eager to hear anything he had to say. Here it was the reverse. The émigrés were better educated, more widely traveled, and more experienced than he was. Apart from information about wages and prices, he did not have much to tell them—that they wanted to hear, anyway. They sized him up as a half-educated American boy, and they would have considered his Marxist views gauche—if he still held them. To them, such opinions were painfully naïve. Besides, the émigrés were encrusted with good manners. Evenings such as this were a time for polite feeling out, not open confrontation. They wanted no offense to anyone's feelings—his or theirs.

The evening was a turning point for Lee and Marina. It might be supposed that Lee would have a rough go in Texas. There he was, a former defector to Russia, in an anti-Communist corner of the United States, encumbered by a Soviet wife and an undesirable discharge from the U.S. Marines. Surely he would meet hostility everywhere, have trouble finding work, and suffer one rejection after another until he became hopeless and embittered. The reality was altogether different. Because of his meeting with the Russians, especially George Bouhe, Lee's homecoming was warmer and more welcoming than anyone might have supposed. The Russians were to be extraordinarily kind to him. They would surround him and his wife with concern. They would place at his service a flourishing grapevine and see to it that he found a job he liked. They helped Lee as much, and as long, as he would allow—and as they could stand.

In Russia Lee Oswald had been a guest, the Russian people his hosts, and he was given the full measure of that country's magnificent hospitality. Incredibly, the same thing was now to happen again—and in his own corner of his native Texas. For no other reason than the breadth and generosity of the Russian soul, Oswald was once again to be treated, in his own country, as if he were the guest and this handful of émigrés, some of them hardly any better off than he, the hosts. Far from encountering hostility and rejection because of his past, he was accepted more readily than if he had never been to Russia at all.

The evening was a turning point for the Oswalds in another way as well. Their marriage had been undergoing a sea change from the moment they stepped aboard the *Maasdam*. The encounter with the émigrés helped crystallize that change, and the relationship between Lee and Marina was never to be the same again.

16

Ingratitude

AFTER THE DINNER PARTY at the Gregorys', George Bouhe and Anna Meller drove to Fort Worth nearly every weekend to see the Oswalds. They noticed immediately that the refrigerator was bare, that Marina and the baby looked ill-fed and ill-clothed, and that the baby was sleeping in a bureau drawer. They appealed to all their friends for hand-me-downs and gave them to the Oswalds. They noticed, too, that Marina's front teeth were rotting, and they drove all the Oswalds to see Mrs. Elena ("Lyolya") Hall, a Russian émigré who lived in Fort Worth and worked as a dental technician. Mrs. Hall told them where they could obtain low-cost dental care, and she also started soliciting her friends and her employer's wife for money and clothes for the Oswalds. One day, during her lunch hour, she took Marina shopping and bought her a couple of dresses. Bouhe and Mrs. Meller, meanwhile, decided that Marina needed training as an American housewife and they took her to a supermarket to show her the way around.

On Sunday, September 9, using $5 given them by George Bouhe, the three Oswalds took a bus to Dallas. Bouhe met them and drove them to the apartment of Anna Meller and her husband, Teofil, where they had lunch and spent the afternoon. They were joined by Declan and Katya Ford, an American geologist and his Russian wife, and by their baby, Gregory. The Oswalds had brought photographs of themselves and their friends in Minsk, and there was talk about how people lived there.

Lee liked Katya Ford, a dark-complexioned, down-to-earth woman in her early thirties. At first, she was impressed by him, too, especially when with utmost politeness he insisted at the end of the afternoon on carrying her baby's paraphernalia to the car. As for her husband, Declan Ford, he felt "like a piece of air whom Oswald was looking around."[1] The Fords were struck, as people often were, by Lee's eyes. He looked at you with a steady, wide-open stare. He never seemed to blink, but from time to time it was as if clouds moved across his eyes and the expression in them changed.

The afternoon contained an eye-opener for George Bouhe. As tactfully as he could, he asked Lee whether the bus fare he had given him had been sufficient. "Oh, yes," Lee answered. But he offered no thanks and no change.

Bouhe and Mrs. Meller continued to visit the Oswalds' Mercedes Street apartment, and on one occasion Lee's ingratitude became even more apparent. Bouhe brought him a pair of old shirts, and Lee looked at them appraisingly, measuring and remeasuring them. Bouhe suggested that he wear them a few times to work, then throw them away. Lee folded the shirts and handed them back to Bouhe. "I don't need them," he said.

One day Lee came in while Bouhe and Mrs. Meller were at the apartment, peered into the refrigerator, noted that it was full, and asked where the groceries came from. When Marina said they were from Bouhe, Lee was openly displeased. Indeed, he looked displeased so much of the time, and maintained such an air of disapproving quiet, that Bouhe and Mrs. Meller rather quickly learned to come at three in the afternoon on Saturdays, their free day, and stay only an hour or so in hopes of missing Lee, who returned home from work about five.

Bouhe soon realized that Lee resented being helped. It was Marina, of course, who bore the brunt of his resentment. After every visit he pointed to some item that Bouhe or Mrs. Meller had brought and warned her: "They'll want payment for that."

When Marina asked what sort of payment, he replied: "You watch. They'll make you dependent on them."

Lee could not conceive that anyone might be generous and kind-hearted without any ulterior aim. In his view, Bouhe and Mrs. Meller were helping Marina in order to humiliate him. "It's not that I don't want to buy you things," he told her in one angry session, "but I can't. I haven't any money to spare."

"Okay," she agreed. "You can't right now. So what's wrong with accepting their help? They only do it to be kind."

"I can't let them buy my wife. Besides, they're spoiling you."

"Since you can't spoil me," Marina said, "why shouldn't they?"

He hit her, hard, across the cheek. "Don't ever say that again."

"What did I say wrong?"

"I'll be the one to spoil you—when I can. I don't want you depending on other people any more. You chase after anyone who'll spoil you."

The beatings, which began on a regular basis when Marina opened the door to Lee's mother, now continued because of her friendship with the Russians. He reproached her constantly, accused her of "never supporting" him, complained that her friendship with other people was itself a "betrayal." Yet, curiously, he did not forbid her to see them. Nor did he tell them to stop bringing gifts.

Marina was in a quandary. Just as she had been as a child with her mother and stepfather, she felt again that she was "between two fires," too torn to steer a tactful middle course. But she would not give up her new friends any more than she would give up Lee. She was grateful for their kindness. She felt lucky to have found in George Bouhe an older man who was good to her, whom she trusted, and with whom she could be utterly frank.

During one visit, Bouhe noticed that Marina had a black eye. "Did you run into the bathroom door?" he inquired sympathetically. That was what she had told Anna Meller.

"Oh, no," Marina answered matter-of-factly. "Lee hit me."

Bouhe was shocked. "Can it be," he asked himself, "that a civilized man in this day and age would hit his wife?"

Bit by bit the Russians woke up to the reality of Lee's treatment of Marina. They were indignant. And the more they saw of it, the more indignant they became. They sensed Lee's contempt for them, his feeling that they were people of petty, material interests, whereas *he* cared for higher things. They saw, too, that he had by no means given up his romance with the Soviet Union and with Communist ideas. They spotted volumes by Lenin and Marx on the Oswalds' coffee table, and current Soviet magazines that they knew he could ill afford. There was something in Lee's attitude, moreover, which led them to believe that he hated anyone in a position of authority simply because he wanted to be there himself. They joked in their Russian idiom—to them it was a joke—that he wanted to be "at the top" and "a big wheel." He was not really *for* anything. He was, Mrs. Meller later said, "all anti, anti- the Soviet Union, anti- the United States, anti- society in general and anti- us."[2]

They went on helping, nevertheless, but it was Marina and the baby they tried to help, not Lee. Bouhe saw storm signals in the marriage and he gave Marina some advice: "If you are a brave girl, if I were you, I would prepare to stand on my own feet before long. But before you start anything, you have to speak English."[3] He asked if Lee would object if he tried to teach her. "Let's try," Marina said, and they did. Bouhe gave her a first-rate dictionary compiled by Russian émigrés in the United States during World War II as a guide for American officers. He wrote out a few sentences in Russian; under each sentence she was to write a translation and mail the result to him in Dallas. Each week Marina mailed Bouhe a lesson and he mailed it back, corrected and with a new lesson. This went on for five or six weeks until Marina gave up, largely because she felt that Lee did not approve.

Other men besides Lee might have resented the Russians' help. It was said that Bouhe, who had been an accountant all his life, had a way of making some people feel accountable for his acts of kindness. He was free with his advice, exhorting Lee to get an education and lift himself up by his bootstraps. As Bouhe said later, "I think he began to hate me very early."[4]

Lee felt the Russians were bending his priorities. They thought that he ought to take better care of his wife and child, that he ought to feed them and clothe them better. Lee, on the other hand, wanted to spend as little on his family as he could and save the rest to pay off his debts. What the Russians took to be necessities, he considered luxuries, and he resented having to thank them for presents which he did not want and which he thought his family did not need. Thus, when the Russians brought a crib and mattress for June, he accepted it. But when Bouhe and Mrs. Meller drove up a week later with a playpen, he was furious. "I don't need it," he said, and condescended only with reluctance and an air of affront to help unload it from the car.

In reality, Lee was accepting the Russians' help, and in his own backhanded, ungracious manner, he even encouraged it. On September 22, at Lee's request, Robert Oswald co-signed an application by Lee for a charge account at Montgomery Ward. His first purchase was a surprise—a television set. He told Marina that he had bought it to keep her from being lonely, and that weekend they had an orgy of television-watching. But on Monday, Lee took the set back to the store. The Russians, he said, would be critical: they would think the Oswalds were "playing poor to get help, yet all the time they could afford a TV."

Lee had decided to continue "playing poor." Evidently, he did feel accountable to the Russians. Moreover, he was always especially kind to Marina just before any visit from them so she would not tell them he beat her. Yet he did have a choice. He could have refused to see the Russians, or he could have consented to see them but refused to take any more help. Instead, he sank back into his familiar dependent stance: that of accepting help and even feeling entitled to it, but at the same time disguising the fact that he was taking help by acting churlish toward those who gave it. What the Russians saw was his erect posture, the swagger of independence, the stiff arm that kept everybody at a distance and seemed to be saying, "Don't help me—I don't need it." What they did not see at first, and what some never noticed at all, was the position of the other arm. The elbow was bent, the hand slightly outstretched, and with it Lee Oswald was taking all the help that came his way. Had he been halfway gracious, he could have had a great deal more.

The hectic Sunday of October 7 tells the story. The first to arrive that day was Marguerite Oswald who, while still unwelcome at her son's house, nevertheless dropped in from time to time. Next were Gary and Alexandra Taylor, a young couple who arrived from Dallas about four in afternoon, bringing their baby son. Alexandra Taylor was the daughter of George de Mohrenschildt, an émigré in Dallas who had met the Oswalds about three weeks before. Apparently Alexandra, too, had met Marina, but it was her husband's first encounter with the Oswalds. The Taylors put their eight-month-old son in the playpen with Junie, who was five days younger than he. There, with varying degrees of inattention and apprehension, their mothers kept an eye on them for the rest of the afternoon.

Gary Taylor later observed that Lee's mother was "a plump woman, out of place in the crowd that was there that afternoon,"[5] who did not seem very interested in what was going on, and who left about 4:30. She was not to see her son again for more than a year.

The "crowd" that had gathered included George Bouhe and Anna Meller, and Lyolya Hall and her estranged husband John, who was also meeting the Oswalds for the first time. As usual, there was no food or drink; the Oswalds' was simply a meeting place. But there was a lot of talk and most of it was in Russian.

At some point that afternoon, Lee announced that he had lost his job. Saturday had been his last day at work. It was "seasonal" work, he said, and he had been laid off. He had no other job in view, and his rent was overdue. In spite of their feelings about Lee, the Russians were ready to help. Since Dallas was bigger than Fort Worth, they thought Lee would have a better chance of finding work there, and John Hall, together with George Bouhe and Gary Taylor, worked out a plan to help Lee move and look for a job. It was decided that Marina, who had a dental appointment the next day in Dallas, would leave that night with the Taylors, stay there two or three days, then return to Fort Worth and stay with Lyolya Hall until Lee had a job in Dallas.

Lee did not object, and that evening, after most of the visitors had left, Marina and the baby drove with the Taylors to Dallas. The next evening, Robert Oswald joined his brother at Mercedes Street and helped him pack his bigger belongings. John and Lyolya Hall then arrived, loaded the Oswalds' possessions into a pick-up truck belonging to the Patterson Porcelain Laboratory, where Mrs. Hall worked, and stored them in the Halls' garage. On the night of Monday, October 8, Lee took the bus to Dallas.

So far, so good, except for one pivotal fact: Lee had not lost his job. His work was not "seasonal," as he told the Russians, and the Leslie Welding Company had no thought of firing him. In fact, on Monday, October 8, the day after the gathering at his house, Lee turned up for work as usual, spent all day on the job, and simply walked off that afternoon without telling anyone he was quitting. Company officials were surprised when he failed to show up the next day, and more surprised still to receive a note from him a few days later asking that his last two paychecks be sent to a post office box in Dallas.

It is probable that the Russians would have helped the Oswalds whether Lee had been fired or had simply quit. But Lee was not taking any chances; he did not quit until after he was sure of the Russians' willingness to help him out. Earlier, he had put himself in a posture to get help, "playing poor" and using Marina and the baby as bait, perhaps without even realizing it himself. But this time, it was a matter of cool calculation and conscious manipulation, the timing determined, apparently, by the fact that he had just paid off one of his debts, the $170 due to Robert for the air fare the previous June.

In spite of his grumblings about the Russians and his warnings to Marina about becoming dependent, it was Lee who had made himself dependent. His move to Dallas was predicated on their offers of help in finding a job and on the certainty that they would care for his wife and child until he got on his feet. He could not have made the move without them.

Marina and June spent three nights with the Taylors in Dallas, and Lee came to see them several times. On Monday and Wednesday of that week, Marina was driven to the Baylor University dental clinic by Jeanne de Mohrenschildt, Alexandra's stepmother, who noticed that Marina brightened at the sight of the dental assistants in their white uniforms and showed signs of wishing to return to pharmacy work herself. Marina had six teeth extracted and new ones put in. The fee of $70 was paid by George Bouhe.

After her last dental appointment, Marina and June took the bus to Fort Worth and settled in with Lyolya Hall. There, except for October 15, when Marina had a final dental appointment in Dallas and spent the night with George and Jeanne de Mohrenschildt, she and June stayed for nearly a month. Throughout this time their grocery and other expenses were paid by the Taylors, by Mrs. Hall and others in the émigré community. Lee never asked who was paying, did not offer to contribute, and did not tender any thanks.

On Tuesday, October 9, Lee started looking for a job in Dallas. His first act was to call Anna Meller. She appealed to her husband, Teofil, who had once worked with a Mrs. Helen Cunningham, now at the Texas Employment Commission in Dallas. Reluctantly, Teo Meller telephoned Mrs. Cunningham and asked her to find work for Oswald, whom he described as a Fort Worth boy who had lived in Russia, married a Russian girl, and had a child. Mr. Meller said that the need was urgent. Mrs. Cunningham was probably aware that Oswald had been a defector to Russia. But she was a kind woman, she liked and respected Mr. Meller, and she wanted to do him a favor. She said she would give Oswald the standard forms. If a prospective employer wanted to know more, he could ask.[6]

Through Mrs. Cunningham, Lee was referred to a graphic arts firm called Jaggars-Chiles-Stovall. He made a good impression on John Graef, head of the photographic department, who thought he was "serious," "determined," and "likeable," with a "slight edge" over one or two competitors for the job.[7] On Thursday, Graef told Oswald he was hired. Lee was overjoyed. Friday, October 12, was his first day at work.

George Bouhe had tried to help Lee in Dallas. Lee was staying at the YMCA, and Bouhe stopped by to inquire how he was getting along. He may also have given him a little money to tide him over until he found work. Once Lee had a job, Bouhe encouraged him to go to Crozier Tech night school to add to his qualifications, and asked him to stay in touch.

Lee's response baffled Bouhe. The first few evenings after he started work, he called Bouhe from a pay telephone. Each time he said simply, "I'm doing fine." With these words, and these only, he hung up. No small talk, no thanks, not a single detail about the job. When he moved out of the "Y," he told Bouhe he was staying at the Carlton Boarding House, in the Oak Cliff section of Dallas. Later, it turned out that he had never been there at all. Bouhe could see no reason for Lee to conceal his whereabouts. It was part, he says, of what he calls Lee's "incessant mystery making."[8] Lee probably wanted to drop Bouhe. He had by this time gained everything he wanted from him—a new job in a new town, and temporary surcease from the responsibility of caring for Marina and the baby.

Both Bouhe and the Mellers were puzzled by his behavior. They did not know of his lies; nor did they know that without their permission he was using their names as references, going so far as to list Bouhe at a false address. But, indomitably generous as he was, Bouhe made a decision "not to go all out" for Lee. He was tired of being used and of Lee's ingratitude. "He always got what he wanted," Bouhe remarked later.[9] Anna Meller phrased it in a way that reflected her European experience. "He would trample over you in hobnail boots," she said, "in order to get what he wanted."[10]

As far as they were concerned, Lee simply violated every rule of human intercourse. He so outraged their notions of what decent conduct ought to be that he stunned them into giving him what he wanted. At first they had no way of dealing with him. But after a while they regrouped, pulled together the bits and pieces of his behavior and made sense of it, and managed to resurrect their defenses. They continued to help Marina after that. But they never helped Lee again.

There were, however, others who would. For one of the curious facts about Lee Oswald is that he always had help when he needed it without giving anything in return. As a result, he has left behind two impressions: one, that of a poor, lost soul who had no style for his relationships except to exploit people, and who did not do that very well; the other, that of a cool manipulator who was pulling strings and keeping every situation more or less under his control. It is scarcely any wonder that a thread that runs through the recollections of nearly all the men and women whom Oswald met following his return from Russia was a sense of having been ill-used. Ultimately, not one of them could think of him without pain, outrage, and a feeling of personal betrayal.

17

Dallas

LEE STARTED to visit Alexandra and Gary Taylor during the few days that Marina and the baby were staying with them in Dallas. He used to come on foot or take the bus from downtown. The Taylors thought the atmosphere between Lee and Marina was one of estrangement, and that they did not like, let alone love, one another, because they never made any attempt to be alone together. Lee seemed to care nothing for Marina or for her feelings. Instead, he spent all his time with the baby, playing and gurgling to her in Russian. But he seemed to have been lonely after Marina and June went back to Fort Worth, for "he popped in and out" of the Taylors' often for the next few weeks.

Alix has said that Lee "could be very polite if he wished. He could be very sarcastic, very blunt if he wished. He could be a very friendly person if he wished, and he could be very quiet if he wished. It just depended who the people were."[1] She adds, however, that he could also be "very, very rude. He appreciated absolutely nothing you did for him. He never thanked you for anything. He seemed to expect it of you." She did not understand why her father's Russian friends tried to help him. He did not deserve it, they did not owe it to him, and yet she got the feeling that he thought they did.

Gary Taylor was a little younger than Lee. He had many irons in the fire, and one of them was politics. He was an ardent Democrat, with a distaste for the John Birch Society, which was then very active in Dallas. Like his father-in-law, George de Mohrenschildt, Gary was a vociferous anti-Bircher and, if he disagreed with someone politically, was likely to dismiss him with, "Oh, he's a Bircher." Gary was probably the first person Lee actually met who felt strongly about the John Birch Society.

Lee enjoyed talking politics with Gary. "He was easy, not too hard to get along with," Alix says. "We argued with him but it was always friendly."[2] And, according to Alix, Lee could be very persuasive. "He could make almost anybody believe what he was saying." He was forever telling the Taylors that they were "stupid," but because they were his age, more or less, and perhaps because he thought they were "stupid" and presented no threat to him, Lee opened up with Gary and Alix. With them he did not feel the same chip-on-the-shoulder need as he did with Bouhe and Mrs. Meller to defend the U.S.S.R., and he gave the Taylors the impression that he had been very, very unhappy in Russia and did not want to go back.

"He disliked Russia just like he disliked the United States," Alix said later, in an analysis of Lee's character and political beliefs that was far from "stupid."

He disliked Russia very much. He didn't agree with communism and he didn't agree with capitalism. He believed in the perfect government, free of want and need, and free of taxation, free of discrimination, free of any police force, the right to be able to do exactly as he pleased, exactly when he pleased, just total and complete freedom in everything. He believed in no government whatsoever, just a perfect place where people lived happily all together and no religion, nothing of any sort, no ties and no holds to anything except himself. I really don't know if he planned to work or not. I don't know what Lee wanted to do in life. I think he wanted to be a very important person without putting anything into it at all. He expected to be the highest paid immediately, the best liked, the highest skilled. He resented any people in high places, any people of any authority in government. My husband told him you can't be something for nothing, can't expect to get high pay and receive a good position with no education and no ambition. No particular goal, no anything. He just expected a lot for nothing. I don't think he knew what he wanted, and I don't think he was too interested in working toward anything. He expected things to be just given to him on a silver platter. But in his ideas, he was extremely devoted. You couldn't change his mind no matter what you said to him.[3]

Alix asked Lee if he had written anything about Russia and he brought her his manuscript one evening. She read it and told him he ought to publish it. His answer was No, it was not for people to read.

Lee himself was reading a good deal, Hitler's *Mein Kampf,* and William L. Shirer's *Rise and Fall of the Third Reich.* He also reread George Orwell's anti-Communist classics *1984* and *Animal Farm,* both of which were loaned to him by Alix's father, George de Mohrenschildt.

The Taylors did not know where Lee was living. They thought he was at the YMCA at 605 North Ervay Street in downtown Dallas. Once, after an evening at their house, they dropped him off on the curb outside. Another time Gary picked him up inside. But Lee was actually at the "Y" only one work week, from Monday, October 15, until Friday morning, October 19. No one knows where he was living from October 8 to 13, or from October 21 to November 2. The Taylors helped him look for a room to rent and once spent an hour hunting for Lee at a North Beckley Street address given them by Alix's stepmother. "We went up and down and up and down and never found the place," Alix says.[4] Lee endorsed two checks that month, on October 16 and 22, his final paychecks from Leslie Welding. Both times he wrote not his own, but the Taylors', address on the back with his signature. Even Marina had no idea where he was staying, and their Russian friends joked that her husband was sleeping on a park bench. He probably had a room in Oak Cliff, very likely on North Beckley Street. Why he bothered to keep the address secret is anybody's guess.

Lee was happy in his job. Jaggars-Chiles-Stovall was an advertising photography firm that made billboards, posters, and advertisements for newspapers and magazines. For the first few days Lee, an apprentice cameraman, followed his supervisor, John Graef, around to find out how things were done.[5] Graef noticed that the new man did not seem to mind taking orders. Lee learned the intrinsic quality of various types of paper and film, and then he learned various photographic and developing techniques, including distortion photography. He was paid between $1.35 and $1.50 an hour, a forty-hour week. He had never had a job he liked so well.

Marina, meanwhile, was outrageously happy in Fort Worth with Lyolya Hall. With no Lee, no one "beating on her nerves," she says, she slept until two every day—the baby being trained, more or less, to do the same—and spent her afternoons in delicious solitude. Mrs. Hall returned late from work and the two had down-to-earth conversations in Russian. Mrs. Hall offered to take Marina to her doctor for contraceptives. According to Mrs. Hall, Marina replied that her married life was so strange, Lee was so cold to her, and they had sexual relations so seldom that she doubted she was in danger of conceiving a child.[6]

Marina's version is a little different. She says that she took Mrs. Hall into her confidence as an older woman and asked her advice. Lee was not strong "as a man," Marina explained, and came to a sexual climax very quickly. Was she to blame? What could she do to help? Were there any home remedies? Should one or both of them see a doctor?

When she had been at Mrs. Hall's a few days, an episode occurred that was pure Marina. She wanted to baptize the baby, although she knew Lee was opposed to it. Mrs. Hall called Father Dmitry Royster, the American-born priest of St. Stephen's Eastern Orthodox church in Dallas, to arrange it. And on the evening of October 17 the two women drove to Dallas, where Father Royster baptized June Lee Oswald, with Elena Hall as godmother.

But that was not the end of the conspiracy. The next day was Lee's twenty-third birthday. Marina had saved up some money and bought him socks, a shirt, and a sweater. On the night of October 17, Alexandra Taylor heard a knock at her front door, and there on the steps she found Mrs. Hall and Marina with June in her arms. They explained that they had just had the baby baptized on the sly, and since they did not dare go to the "Y," they asked Alix to give Lee his presents and invent a story to conceal the fact that they had been in Dallas.

Marina did not leave it at that. When she got back to Fort Worth, she telephoned Lee and told him to stop by the Taylors'. He did as he was told, and so did Alix. She made up a story about the presents, but Lee put two and two together. After that, Marina quickly broke down and admitted over the telephone what she had been only half-trying to conceal: that she and Lyolya had been in Dallas and had the baby baptized.

"Silly girl," he said. "Why didn't you tell me?"

"I thought you'd forbid it."

"It's your right to do as you please," he said to Marina's astonishment.

On the night following the baptism, Lyolya Hall was injured in an automobile crash and was in the hospital more than a week. But Marina was not left all alone. Gali Clark (Mrs. Max Clark) came by nearly every day and drove her to the grocery store, where she not only paid for the groceries but also bought Marina a carton of cigarettes. A chain smoker, starved for cigarettes by her disapproving husband, Marina was grateful. But she was intimidated by Gali Clark. Gali was a "society" person, from the "old aristocracy," Marina commented later. Manners meant a lot to Gali and at times Marina could not tell what she was thinking. Complicated as Marina might be herself, she preferred a proletarian directness in other people. She wanted to know where she stood with them.

Alex Kleinlerer, a friend of Lyolya Hall's, also came every day during his lunch hour to check up on Marina. At 1:30 in the afternoon he would wake her up by banging on the front door and ringing the bell. Inside he found chaos—dirty dishes in the sink and baby clothing everywhere. He did the cleaning and sometimes came back at suppertime. He and Marina took turns cooking; he would cook a Polish supper one night, she a Russian supper the next. Once or twice he took her and the baby out to eat.

Lee came by bus to Fort Worth for all or part of every weekend to see Marina and the baby. They missed each other and their weekend interludes were comparatively idyllic. But Lee's attitude toward Mrs. Hall's hospitality was paradoxical in view of his own Spartan style of living. "This is your house. I give it to you —all!" he would announce to Marina, sweeping his arm grandly about the entrance hall upon his arrival on a Friday. "Isn't this a fine house I bought you?"

Marina remembers that he was "always running to the icebox," a thing he never did at home when he was paying for the groceries himself, to fix a Coke or a sandwich. "A full icebox!" he would exclaim delightedly before he pounced. He was fascinated by the kitchen gadgets, like the electric can opener, the sort of thing that Mrs. Hall and the other Russians thought he scorned. And at night, he made love to Marina while watching another "gadget," the bedroom television set, a distraction which helped slightly his problem of premature ejaculation. Afterwards, the two of them slept in separate bedrooms, a luxury which Lee said made him feel "like an aristocrat."

Lee took an acute dislike to Alex Kleinlerer, a short, dark man of about forty who sported a black mustache, spoke with an accent, and dressed with European flair. The facts of Kleinlerer's relationship to Marina were innocent, but it was no secret that he dropped by Mrs. Hall's on weekdays when Lee was not there. Kleinlerer's feelings for Marina were intensely, and obviously, protective. Lee was furiously jealous.

On Friday, October 26, Mrs. Hall returned from the hospital, and on Sunday, Alix and Gary Taylor picked Lee up outside the Dallas "Y" and drove over for the evening in Fort Worth. The major topic of conversation was Cuba. President Kennedy had learned of the build-up of Soviet missiles on the island and demanded their withdrawal. The previous Monday, the President had declared a naval blockade of Cuba, and for nearly a week the world had been teetering on the brink of thermo-nuclear disaster. Lee observed that in Dallas people were hoarding food in anticipation of war. Marina was certain that *her* country would never go to war over a tiny nation like Cuba, and Lee agreed. He had been to Russia, he said to Mrs. Hall, to Kleinlerer, and the Taylors, and he was sure the Soviet government would not start a war. When the missile crisis was over, Marina was greatly relieved, for throughout that ten-day period she had felt torn between her own country, which she continued to love, and the kind Americans with their nice-looking President, Mr. Kennedy.

If Lee and Marina agreed about Russia, it seemed as if they disagreed about everything else. Mrs. Hall later said that Marina "was stubborn, and he was just cruel to her, and they would argue" over "nothing, just nothing and he would beat her all the time."[7] Kleinlerer for his part thought that Lee "treated Marina very poorly. He belittled her and was boorish to her in our presence. He ordered her around just as though she were a mere chattel. He was never polite or tender to her. I feel very strongly that she was frightened of him." Kleinlerer was also critical of the way Lee had dumped his wife and child on Mrs. Hall and failed to contribute to their support. Lee "did not express any thanks or evidence the slightest appreciation," Kleinlerer said. "He evidenced displeasure and contempt. He acted as if the world owed him a living."[8]

On Friday night, November 2, the telephone rang in Kleinlerer's apartment. It was Marina, announcing that Lee had found them an apartment and she was moving to Dallas that weekend. Lee came abruptly on the phone. He "directed" Kleinlerer, in Kleinlerer's words, to come to the Halls' the next day to discuss the move, since the Oswalds' possessions were in the garage and Mrs. Hall was away in New York.[9]

On Saturday, soon after Kleinlerer arrived, he witnessed a memorable scene. "Oswald observed that the zipper on Marina's skirt was not completely closed," Kleinlerer later recalled.[10]

He called to her in a very angry and commanding tone of voice just like an officer commanding a soldier. His exact words were "Come here!" in Russian, and he uttered them the way you would call a dog with which you were displeased in order to inflict punishment. He was standing in the doorway. When she reached the doorway he rudely reprimanded her in a flat imperious voice about being careless in her dress and slapped her hard in the face twice. Marina had the baby in her arms. Her face was red and tears came to her eyes. I was very much embarrassed and also angry but I had long been afraid of Oswald and I did not say anything.

By what appears to have been a bit of foresight on Mrs. Hall's part, only Kleinlerer had a key to the garage. His presence during the removal of the Oswalds' goods the following day was therefore a necessity. The Taylors drove over from Dallas to help, and Lee and Gary went off and rented a U-Haul trailer. But there was trouble when Lee started to load it, for Kleinlerer recalled that there were "several instances in which I had to intervene when Oswald picked up some of Mrs. Hall's things to place in the trailer. I could not say whether this was deliberate or inadvertent, except that there were several instances."[11] Lyolya Hall's wariness had not been misplaced.

The apartment Lee had found for them was at 604 Elsbeth Street, in the Oak Cliff section of Dallas. Marina had not yet seen it, and when they arrived that afternoon, she and Alix Taylor reacted identically. "It was terrible," Alix says, "very dirty, very badly kept, really quite a slum." Outside, the place was "overrun with weeds and garbage and people."[12]

Marina did not want to move in. She said the place was "filthy dirty—a pigsty." Lee thought they could fix it up. They were still arguing when Gary and Alix left to return the trailer. It was their second drive to Fort Worth in behalf of the Oswalds in a single day, a round trip each time of nearly three hours. As they were leaving, Lee thanked them for helping him with the move. "It was a very brief thank you, and that was that," said Alix.[13] It was the only time she ever heard him say it.

On the first night in their new apartment, November 4, Marina stayed up till five in the morning, scrubbing everything in sight. Lee helped for a while. He cleaned the icebox, then left about ten in the evening. He had paid for a room at the "Y," he said, and he might as well use it. But since the YMCA has no record that he stayed there after October 19, it is likely he spent a final night in whatever rooming house he had been living in for the last two weeks.

Their reunion was not a happy one. Within a day or two, they were fighting again. Lee told Marina that she had been spoiled by the Russians. He said that George Bouhe was trying to "buy" her. "I understand, he doesn't want you as a woman. But he wants to have you in his power." He went on to accuse Marina of "whoring" after the Russians because they gave her money and possessions—"If you like them so much, go live with them!"

Marina was angrier than she had ever been. Perhaps, after her month away from Lee, she had forgotten his brutality and how hard he could be to live with. Or perhaps, having been treated with kindness, she had grown to think better of herself, and what she had considered her due only a few weeks before seemed intolerable to her now. Besides, Lee had used the Russian *blyad,* a very strong word for "whore," which was simply so insulting and profane that it seemed to give her no choice. Trembling, she ran out the door.

"Go. I don't care," Lee shouted after her. "I don't need you."

She forgot the baby. And she did not have a dime. But a garage attendant listened carefully to the name she kept repeating to him and dialed the telephone of Teofil Meller. Anna Meller answered the phone. After a brief pause during which she convinced her recalcitrant husband, Mrs. Meller told Marina to come by cab right away. They would pay for it when she got there.

Marina went back to the apartment, grabbed the baby and a couple of diapers, and went out again. Lee was stretched out on the bed.

She went into a doughnut shop and somehow conveyed to the waitress that she needed a cab. By eleven o'clock that night she was at the Mellers'. They found her shaking and upset, but she did not cry much and did not say what she and Lee had been fighting about. Mrs. Meller noted that the baby had nothing but diapers, a shirt, and an empty bottle, and that Marina was wearing a light summer blouse and skirt (in early November). "She had no coat, no money, nothing."[14]

The next day the Russians had a council of war, as usual led by George Bouhe. "I don't want to advise or interfere," he told Marina. "But if you want my opinion, I don't like Lee. I don't think you can have a good life with him. I can't come between a husband and wife. If you leave him, of course we'll help. But if you say one thing now and then go back, next time no one will help."

"I'll never go back to that hell," Marina promised herself.

18

George de Mohrenschildt

A NEW VOICE had joined the chorus of Russians in Dallas—Alix Taylor's father, George de Mohrenschildt, who met the Oswalds while they were in Fort Worth in September. It was a fateful meeting.

An unlikelier pair of candidates for a friendship than Lee Harvey Oswald and George de Mohrenschildt can hardly be imagined. On one side was Oswald, twenty-three years old, 5 feet 8 or 9 inches in height, pale, balding, slender with sloping shoulders, Puritanical, friendless, more or less lacking in humor, a lower-middle-class American with a ninth-grade education and a head full of self-taught Marxist theories.

On the other was De Mohrenschildt, fifty-one years old, 6 feet 1 or 2 inches tall, handsome, dark, broad-shouldered, a man of arresting physique who frequently wore bathing trunks on the street the better to display it, loud, hearty, humorous, a man who was forever dancing, joking, and telling off-color stories, and who could drink all night and never show it, lover of innumerable women, a European aristocrat so secure of his lineage that there was no one whose friendship could demean him, holder of higher degrees from universities as far apart as Antwerp and Dallas, and a refugee from Communist Russia who would proclaim, as if the subject were closed: "Marxism, the sound of that word is boring to me. When it comes to dialectical materialism, I do not want to hear that word again."[1]

The contrast between two men could not have been more complete. Yet in what was at most fifteen or twenty encounters during the fall and winter of 1962–1963, George de Mohrenschildt became by far the most important of the new people that Lee Oswald met following his return to the United States.

So unlikely a pair were they that some who knew them denied they were really friends at all. De Mohrenschildt, these people claimed, was a patron, not a friend, of Oswald's. He was just one of the many "stray dogs" (some pedigreed

214

and aristocratic, others not) whom George de Mohrenschildt and his wife Jeanne took in out of generosity. Others said that De Mohrenschildt, having alienated nearly everyone else in Dallas, had no one but people like the Oswalds to fall back on, and that his friendship with Lee and Marina, which itself pushed other friends away, was a measure of how far he had fallen. Still others likened the relationship of the two men to that of Trigorin, the aging writer, and Nina, the young girl, in Chekhov's play, *The Seagull:* "A man came along, saw the seagull and, having nothing better to do, destroyed it." Such people felt that De Mohrenschildt knew very well what sort of man Lee Oswald was and played him like a violin. Consciously or unconsciously, De Mohrenschildt, they said, understood Lee's capacity for violence and used him to act out his own violent fantasies.

Different as they were on the outside, the older and the younger man actually had a good deal in common, starting with the connection they both had with Minsk. It was near there that George de Mohrenschildt was born, in Mozyr, Belorussia, in 1911.[2] As he was later fond of pointing out, he was a one-man melting pot, a mixture of Russian, Polish, Swedish, German, and Hungarian blood. But the family name was Swedish (Mohrensköldt) and the Mohrenschildts traced their ancestry back to the Baltic nobility at the time of Sweden's Queen Christina—the proudest nobility in all Russia. The men of the family had a right to be called "Baron," but such were their liberal opinions that neither George's father, Sergei von Mohrenschildt, nor his Uncle Ferdinand (first secretary of the czarist embassy in Washington, who married the daughter of William Gibbs McAdoo, Woodrow Wilson's son-in-law and Secretary of the Treasury), nor George himself, nor his older brother Dmitry, ever made use of the title.

Before the Russian Revolution of 1917, Sergei von Mohrenschildt had been a minor official of the czar. He was Marshal of Nobility in Minsk Province, the landowners' elected representative in the local government. But although he was an aristocrat, Mohrenschildt was a classic liberal in the Russian mold, and deeply critical of the oppressions of the czar. He wanted a constitution that would guarantee the rights of the individual, freedom of speech, and freedom of worship. And he strongly opposed anti-Semitism, a touchstone in Belorussia, where there was a large Jewish population and where pogroms—"Beat the Jews and save Russia"—had been a scourge of the Jews for generations. He did all he could to help persecuted Jews whose troubles came to his attention.

The elder Mohrenschildt eventually resigned as Marshal of Nobility and, through his connections, obtained a job as director of the extensive interests of the Nobels, a wealthy Swedish family, in Russia. For a while the Mohrenschildts lived in Baku, where Sergei supervised the Nobels' enormous holdings in the oil fields. They also lived from time to time in Moscow and St. Petersburg, and they were in one of those cities when the Revolution struck in February and again in October 1917. Later, when the anarchy and violence that accompanied the Bolsheviks to power was compounded by famine, the family fled to their old home in Minsk, which was then under German occupation. But soon the Bolsheviks took over and Sergei von Mohrenschildt was thrown in jail for openly opposing them. A Jew whom he had helped in the old days and who now held a position of power with the Bolsheviks (so many members of the formerly oppressed minority had joined their ranks that both the Bolsheviks and their opponents the Mensheviks were thought of by some as "Jewish" parties) heard about his plight and obtained his release.

When the Bolsheviks finally secured a permanent hold on Minsk in 1920, Sergei von Mohrenschildt could have fled to Poland, where he and his wife had an estate; but he elected to stay. For his loyalty and his liberal views, and because he could still be of use to them, the Bolsheviks rewarded him with an appointment to the Belorussian Commissariat of Agriculture. For several months "we lived more or less happily," George de Mohrenschildt remembers, although like everyone else the family was afflicted by famine.

But Sergei von Mohrenschildt's outspokenness soon got him into trouble again. He opposed the anti-religious policy of the Bolsheviks, and was arrested, tried, and sentenced to live out his life in Siberia with his wife and younger son, George. Dmitry, the older son, was already under sentence to be shot. While the mother went about the country looking for influential friends who could help them, ten-year-old George was left to run wild. "I remained on the street making my own living somehow."

In jail in Minsk, Sergei von Mohrenschildt fell ill. Miraculously, he was once again saved by Jews he had helped—this time, the prison doctors. They told him to eat very little and appear as sick as possible. They then advised the government that he might die and suggested that he be allowed to go home until such time as he recovered his health and could survive the journey to Siberia. The government agreed, and Sergei von Mohrenschildt, his wife, and George made their escape to Poland in a hay wagon. (Dmitry was released in a prisoner exchange with Poland.) But the three wayfarers contracted typhoid on the difficult journey, and the mother died. It was 1922; George was eleven years old.

Father and son struggled to their feet in the town of Wilno, Poland, just across the border from Russia. The family estate of 6,000 heavily wooded acres in Polesie, near Wilno, had been taken over by the peasants. But Sergei von Mohrenschildt regained ownership and sold the land back piecemeal to the peasants, so that he and his son were not, as many Russians in Wilno were, penniless refugees. And he became head of the Russian-language gymnasium, or high school, in Wilno, which was run for the children of refugees.

George de Mohrenschildt grew up close to his father, lived with him until the age of eighteen, emulated and adored him. While his older brother, Dmitry, left for the United States, earned degrees at Columbia and Yale, and became a professor at Dartmouth College, George graduated from the gymnasium at Wilno, attended the Polish cavalry academy, and left for Belgium at the age of twenty to attend the Institute of Higher Commercial Studies in Antwerp. He spent five years there, was awarded a master's degree, then earned a doctor of sciences degree in International Commerce from the University of Liège. Throughout his seven years in Belgium, he made frequent trips to Poland to see his father. With a girlfriend, he became part-owner of a successful ski clothing boutique. But in 1938 De Mohrenschildt, aged twenty-seven, broke with the girlfriend, dissolved their partnership, and left for America.

He carried with him to the New World certain assumptions, certain ways of looking at things, which he had acquired during his storm-tossed early years in Russia. He had, first of all, the aristocratic assumption of privilege; and, second, a sunny resilience and an optimistic conviction that even in the worst of circumstances, he would always know someone "at the top" who would come to his rescue. But he had also learned that life is like a yo-yo, that one can plummet from top to bottom in no time and must, accordingly, learn to live by one's wits and make the accidents of fortune work *for* one. George de Mohrenschildt, a man of devastating charm, was to do just that in America.

And yet he had other qualities that were to stand in the way of his success. His was an outlook predicated on privilege, on the possession of sprawling, poorly tended estates which yielded just enough income to send the owner off on long, leisurely visits in Moscow and St. Petersburg now and then before returning to carry on some enlightened but ill-fated experiment with the peasants. The Mohrenschildts were landowners no longer, yet George still had habits that were rooted in possession. He was not a riotous spender, but a certain ease of living became him. It suited him not to think about money. Something in his upbringing, his aristocratic forebears perhaps, had endowed him with an enduring lack of interest in making money, and nothing, not all the burgher institutes of Belgium, could imbue him with a motive that was not really there. He needed to be able to take an income for granted. Lacking one, it was more congenial for him to marry than to make one.

Along with his aristocratic way of looking at things, his easy way of mingling, as one friend put it, with the rich, the highly placed, the "top men in any form of government," George de Mohrenschildt had a liberal set of opinions and was often extraordinarily outspoken in expressing them.[3] Thus he had a strong feeling for the freedom of the individual and a hatred for anything that interfered with it. He loathed oppressive government; he loathed restrictions of any kind. Some felt that he hated all authority, that he was a perpetual rebel, a sort of one-man revolution, all in himself. He was high-spirited and irrepressible, so much so that one could say of him what was said of the famous Russian anarchist Bakunin: that for his courage and his qualities of leadership he would be invaluable on the first day of the Revolution, but on the second he would have to be shot.

Many of George de Mohrenschildt's opinions, and certainly his forthrightness in expressing them, could be traced to his father. But there was a crucial difference. Sergei von Mohrenschildt had, after all, been living through his country's greatest crisis. It was a requirement of history that he speak out. He was a Don Quixote, in a sense, and amid the chaos of Revolutionary Russia his actions had been as efficacious as a puff of smoke. But he had his existence in a genuine historical setting, and he did what a constitutional liberal of his time and place had to do. His son was not to be so lucky. Where the father had been pitted against society—a rotten czarist society first and a ruthless Bolshevik society afterwards —the son came to be pitted merely against "society," the moneyed families of

New York and Long Island, of Philadelphia, Denver, and Dallas. These were the people who, in the New World, were to clasp him to their bosoms time and again for his charm, only to throw him out for his unconventional political opinions —and his outrageous behavior. Again and again he was on the "inside," again and again he was tossed out.

The son had, it seemed, mastered his father's experience all too well. Time and again his father had been on the inside, first of the czarist, then the Bolshevik, government, and time and again he had been driven out, until ultimately he was driven from the country altogether. Four times when he was between the ages of five and ten, George looked on as his father plummeted from a position of influence, down into danger and disgrace. The sight seems to have impressed him very much for it was to become the central dynamic of his own life. But George's "exiles" were only parodies, mindless reenactments of his father's early, unforgettable odysseys into disgrace. The historical setting had been lost, the model was gone (Sergei von Mohrenschildt died in an air raid in Germany in 1945), and George's friends, to say nothing of his wives, were at a loss to understand why he had to shock people so.

And so, much as they had loved one another, there was to be in the end a vast difference between the experience of father and son. Where Sergei had been cloaked in the dignity of history, George de Mohrenschildt was merely trying to "épater les bourgeois." He was a wound-up, toy Don Quixote, truly tilting at windmills. And he had lost his latest battle. Where he had recently been "inside" Dallas society, George de Mohrenschildt, by the time he met Lee Oswald, was finally, irrevocably out—and longing to be back in.

As a young man in 1938, De Mohrenschildt spent his first summer in the United States with his brother and his American sister-in-law at Bellport, near East Hampton, on the eastern, ocean tip of Long Island. White Russian noblemen were then very much the thing in the watering places of the very rich, sought after for their charm, their princely titles, their picturesque stories of woe. The bearers of some of the proudest names in all Russia could be found on weekends sunning themselves on the beaches of Newport and Long Island's North Shore, frequently men and women of infinite breeding and cultivation who had to drag themselves gamely back at the weekend's close to New York City and such incongruous jobs as salesmen at Brooks and Bonwit Teller.

In this world De Mohrenschildt quickly made friends, among them a blond, soft-spoken young woman by the name of Janet Lee Bouvier, her handsome, dark, estranged husband John, known as "Black Jack" Bouvier, a scapegrace of New York society, and the Bouvier father and sisters. "We were very close friends," De Mohrenschildt says of himself and the Bouvier clan. "We saw each other every day." De Mohrenschildt is said to have liked Janet Bouvier very much and during his frequent visits to the family, he saw a good deal of Janet's and Jack's nine-year-old daughter Jacqueline and five-year-old Caroline Lee.

For the next few years, De Mohrenschildt commuted between two lives: that of fashionable Park Avenue on one hand, and that of the penniless émigré trying, as he put it, "to make a buck" on the other. His Belgian degrees safely tucked into his past, useless in late-Depression America for a Russian still wrestling with the English tongue, he did brief, disheartening stints as a salesman for a series of perfume and wine and fabric concerns in New York. For all his ebullience and bonhomie, De Mohrenschildt's early years in this country were poignant ones, "just tough going," he admitted later, adding that had it not been for his brother and his friends he might have starved.

The story was an incongruous one—the European aristocrat, product of generations of breeding, accustomed to a life of privilege but not really interested in money, trying to make it in the land where money is king. But George de Mohrenschildt always had friends. Among them was Margaret Clark Williams, member of a family with vast oil holdings in Louisiana. Armed with letters of introduction from her, De Mohrenschildt landed a job with the Humble Oil Company and ended up as roustabout on an oil rig in Terebonne Parish, Louisiana. It was hard physical labor, and he excelled at it until he had an accident on the rig, was badly hurt, and contracted amoebic dysentery. He then tried and failed to get a job as polo instructor at a boys' boarding school in Arizona, had little better luck as an insurance salesman in New York, was called up by the Polish army but just missed the last boat back to Europe in 1939, and had a fling making a documentary movie about the Polish resistance.

For De Mohrenschildt these were years of high adventure; they were also years of failure and bruises to the ego. It has been said that during the late 1930s, he did odd jobs for the Polish Intelligence service in the United States, and before America entered World War II, he worked under cover for French Intelligence in the United States as well, buying up American oil for France to keep it out of Axis hands. He also fell in love with a Mexican, Lilia Larin, the widow of a Mexican chocolate king, whom he described as the "love of my life." Buoyed by a $5,000 legacy from his friend in New York, Mrs. Williams, he spent nearly a year in Mexico City, painting and "going out" with Lilia, until a Mexican general fell in love with her and had De Mohrenschildt expelled from the country. Even then, he managed to snatch something out of the jaws of defeat: in New York he had a one-man showing of water colors he had painted in Mexico. It was like so many other things he did in those days. The critics said the paintings were original, but they did not sell.

On that memorable foray into Mexico, De Mohrenschildt had what proved to be the first of many brushes with agents of the United States government. Driving along the deserted coast between Corpus Christi and the Mexican border, he and Lilia stopped at a wild spot called Aransas Pass to swim and do some sketching. What they were sketching proved to be the site of a Coast Guard station, and suddenly five toughs erupted from the bushes, ransacked the car, and accused De Mohrenschildt of being a German spy. As he protested indignantly later on, he was spying for no one at the time, not even France. He was the recipient of intermittent attention from the FBI after that, and, if Lilia was the love of his life, the FBI became his great hate.

In the course of things, De Mohrenschildt was married several times. His first wife was Dorothy Pierson, a very young, well-connected American girl in

Palm Beach, by whom, on Christmas Day, 1943, he had a daughter, Alexandra. At times during the marriage De Mohrenschildt was utterly charming, while at others he flew into violent rages. She left him after seven months of marriage, charging her husband with physical cruelty and infidelity. Her parents were under the impression that their son-in-law had been pro-Nazi in his sympathies; others who knew him at this time considered that he was, if anything, pro-Communist.[4]

After the divorce, De Mohrenschildt decided to go into the oil business, and went to the University of Texas to obtain a master's degree in petroleum geology, at which he was said to be "brilliant." But from this period, too, there were well-concealed rumors of destructiveness. De Mohrenschildt's roommate, Tito Harper, was a handsome and highly intelligent young man from a ranching family at Eagle Pass, Texas. The family was deeply religious, it stood at the very apex of the social aristocracy of the border, and Tito was thought to have a splendid future. Instead, he suffered a complete change of personality. He renounced his American citizenship and moved to Mexico, where he turned to drink and drugs, and later died mysteriously, possibly a suicide, in Mexico City. To the end, his family blamed their son's disintegration on the atheistic and antisocial influence of George de Mohrenschildt.[5]

Once he had his degree, De Mohrenschildt went to Venezuela prospecting for oil. In the late 1940s, he turned up in Rangely, Colorado, one of the great boomtowns of the country, on a project compiling statistics and engineering data for the oil companies that were drilling there. He spent three years in Rangely and was married a second time, to Phyllis Washington, the daughter of an American diplomat. Afterwards he characterized her proudly as an "international beauty, with bikinis, walking around the oil fields," a "wonderful, beautiful girl," who "created a terrible confusion in Colorado." The job eventually petered out, as did the marriage. Once again there were rumors of violence, but De Mohrenschildt was later to claim that he remained on the most amiable terms with Phyllis Washington and her family.

Next, De Mohrenschildt went into oil partnership with a young man named Eddie Hooker, his nephew by marriage. By this time, De Mohrenschildt had a reputation as a very good man to do business with—one who played the game with zest but was straight and honest and never pursued his purposes in any ulterior fashion. He had affairs with the wives of countless oil tycoons, for example, but it was said of him with respect that he never used any of them to promote his own business fortunes. His easygoing attitude affected his partnership with Hooker, however, for Hooker wanted to make a killing, while all De Mohrenschildt wanted, to hear him tell it, was "a reasonable living." "We made money, we lost money," he says of the partnership, "but it was a pleasant relationship. We are still very good friends." Friendships, mingling with the right people, the wrong people, any people, meant more to George de Mohrenschildt than vast sums of money ever did.

In 1951 De Mohrenschildt, aged forty, was an exciting man to look at. He was intellectually exhilarating—and he had money besides. It was then that he met and married Wynne ("Didi") Sharples, a practicing physician from a wealthy

Philadelphia Quaker family. They moved to Dallas where, sparked by Didi's aspirations, they cut a wide social swath: charity balls, country club outings, the works. But Didi seems to have lacked humor, a requisite of marriage to De Mohrenschildt. And difficulty deepened into tragedy when two children were born in rapid succession suffering from cystic fibrosis. It was the De Mohrenschildts who started the National Foundation for Cystic Fibrosis. (Several years later Jacqueline Kennedy, whom De Mohrenschildt had known as nine-year-old Jacqueline Bouvier, became its honorary chairman.)

After he and Didi were divorced in 1956, De Mohrenschildt, afflicted for the first time with physical infirmities and an inability to concentrate, decided not to stay in oil promotion. Instead, basing himself in Dallas, he took on a series of oil and natural gas consulting jobs abroad, mostly in Africa and Latin America, and went on a U.S. government junket to Yugoslavia. After his trips to Yugoslavia and Ghana, he is known to have been debriefed extensively by the CIA. Those who knew him best, however, believe that he was never employed by the agency and there are CIA documents that appear to support this.

It was in Dallas, after the journey to Yugoslavia, that De Mohrenschildt made his fourth and most enduring marriage, to Jeanne LeGon. Jeanne (pronounced "Zhan") had been born and raised in Harbin, China, as Evgenia Fomenko, like De Mohrenschildt a White Russian.[6] Her father, also like De Mohrenschildt's, was a prominent man, the director of the Chinese Far Eastern Railway, who was eventually killed by the Communists—Russian, Japanese, or Chinese, Jeanne never knew which. She and her first husband Robert LeGon (born Valentin Bogoyavlensky), had been a successful dance team in Tientsin and Shanghai before coming to the United States in the late 1930s. They were about to sign into the Rainbow Room in New York City when Jeanne became pregnant; after her daughter was born, and she was unable to dance any longer, she took a job as a model.

It was a lucky choice, for on Seventh Avenue Jeanne blossomed. She became a successful fashion designer, living in New York and California, and traveling all over the country, with frequent side trips to Europe. She was said to be so aggressive in business that if you pushed her out the window, she came back through the door. Some years Jeanne earned over $20,000, plus clothing and travel expenses, although, prodigal Russian that she was, she never saved a cent. Her husband, Robert LeGon, showed none of her resilience. He grew depressed, dwelled more and more on his family's loss of fortune in China, and, unable to adjust to a new life in the United States, eventually became a mental patient in California.

After Jeanne started seeing George de Mohrenschildt, Robert LeGon came twice to Dallas. He is said to have gone after his wife's admirer with a revolver, then hired a private detective. But, like so many others before him, he succumbed to the De Mohrenschildt charm. He declared that he would grant his wife a divorce on one condition—that De Mohrenschildt promise to marry her. De Mohrenschildt pronounced his rival "a charming fellow" and proceeded to do exactly as he had been asked.

A year or so later, shattered by the death of his son (by Didi) from cystic fibrosis, George gathered up Jeanne and their dogs and set off on a year's walking trip through Mexico and Central America. It was his way of forgetting the tragedy. But it was a rugged trip, much rougher than they had imagined, and by the summer of 1962, nine months after their return to Dallas, they had barely recovered from their exertions. Moreover, their savings were gone, furrowed into the wilds of Mexico. George was writing a report of their Mexican adventure, hoping to publish it as a book. He had even written a letter to President Kennedy, asking him to contribute the preface. And Jeanne, to support them, had taken a job in the millinery department of the Sanger-Harris department store. Financially, they were in one of their valleys.

Socially, things were not much better. Where once De Mohrenschildt had been a habitué of the higher reaches of Dallas society, knowing, or claiming to know, such people as H. L. Hunt, the wealthy Murchison family, the banker Serge Semenenko, and even the Shah of Iran, he was now persona non grata. It was not that people did not like him. On the contrary, nearly all of them were enchanted, very often against their better judgment. Summer and winter, in blazing heat and freezing cold, he would dash about Dallas in his open Cadillac convertible, impervious to the ravages of weather. There was the magnificent build, the splendid chest. De Mohrenschildt was never unaware of his body—or the effect it was having on others. Women had always toppled into bed with him, while men envied him his swashbuckling charm. One friend, Max Clark, says that "he should have lived three or four hundred years ago and been an explorer or pirate or something."[7] Bouhe thought that "George never missed a chance to be grandiose,"[8] while to the admiring Samuel B. Ballen, George de Mohrenschildt, for all his faults, "was like Hemingway and Lawrence of Arabia rolled into one."[9] Morris I. Jaffe, the attorney who represented him in the 1960s, was less favorable in his opinion. He says George felt "the world owed him a living and he will not use his tremendous abilities and intelligence to any constructive end."[10]

His attractions were enormous, but so was his capacity to outrage. Although De Mohrenschildt proclaimed himself a "fighting atheist," he liked nothing better than to show up at one of the two Russian Orthodox churches in Dallas on a Sunday morning, clad in his shorts, not to worship but because he loved to sing in the choir, and found it "amusing" to consort with the Russian folk afterwards. On such an occasion he might say: "The Communists don't believe in God and neither do I. We will all be fertilizer after we die." A close friend, Igor Voshinin, has said he was "absolutely unpredictable."[11] He might appear at a dinner or cocktail party bare-chested. Then the next time in a shirt but no tie. On still another occasion, he might drop in on a formal party bare-footed. Again, he might be perfectly clad. You never knew what to expect.[12]

As for his fourth wife, Jeanne, she was even more extreme. Middle-aged and spreading a bit, she had platinum blond hair and went around in tight pants and a very tight top, "like a teenager," one of the Russians sniffed. Jeanne insisted on playing tennis clad only in the briefest of bikinis, years before the bikini was "in." In Jeanne, in fact, George had at last found a helpmeet so wildly unconventional as to make him seem staid by comparison. Her conduct was often more outrageous and antagonistic then his. Like her husband, she thought religion a "fraud" and lost no opportunity of saying so. But the worst thing was her passion for her dogs. Jeanne had two little Manchester terriers with whom it was not too much to say that she had fallen in love. She would go nowhere without them, and friends who asked the De Mohrenschildts to dine found that they had asked the dogs too. She dressed them in diapers and fondled them ostentatiously the entire time. People were driven away in droves.

The De Mohrenschildts delighted in shocking even those friends who had remained loyal to them. At a celebrated gathering of the Bohemian Club in Dallas at which close Jewish friends of George's were present, he scandalized and hurt his friends by declaring in a speech that Heinrich Himmler had not been so bad.[13] He knew that his friends the Voshinins hated Hitler particularly, and so he rarely met them without the greeting: "Heil Hitler!" "He would love to do just exactly what people would object to," Mrs. Voshinin explained. Whatever you favored politically, he would tell you that he held the opposite view. And if he could not get at you through politics, he would tell you that he favored free love. Whatever you were for on any subject, George took the opposite side. And he was "for the underdog, always." She would not exactly call George a liar, Mrs. Voshinin added, but "he is certainly loose with the truth." Igor Voshinin later called George and Jeanne "the most unconventional people I have ever seen," both emotionally and politically, "and they seemed to enjoy it." Voshinin allowed for George's elaborate exaggerations, "taking, of course, thirty or forty percent off of what he says."[14] With Jeanne, the figure was said to be 90 percent.

Another close friend has conceded that social occasions with the De Mohrenschildts "did have a way of ending up in tension. The discussion would get personal, heated, intimate. Normal inhibitions were not present."[15] And although the De Mohrenschildts' only "race prejudice" was said to be against white Anglo-Saxon Protestants, their feelings ran high against their fellow Russians, too. When they were at a party together, emotions often grew so intense that the party simply broke up in anger. "You are all one-sided reactionaries," Jeanne would explode at her compatriots. People would walk out and not speak to one another again for months.

That was how matters stood in the summer and fall of 1962, when the De Mohrenschildts found that doors formerly open now were closed to them. Yet George was a compulsively gregarious man, who hated to spend an evening by himself and whose energies were by no means fully absorbed by his effort to write a book. And Jeanne was a generous but indiscriminate collector of "stray dogs" —human ones, that is.

One day in the middle of September, De Mohrenschildt was in Fort Worth with an American friend of Russian descent, Colonel Lawrence Orlov. They decided to pay a call on the couple who had newly arrived from Russia, and went to the Oswalds' Mercedes Street apartment. They were appalled at the "horrible surroundings," the "slum" in which at first they found only Marina and her baby. To De Mohrenschildt, Marina looked "a lost soul," and the child unwell. But he quickly established a bantering tone by telling her that little June, with her big, bald head, resembled nothing so much as a miniature Khrushchev. Marina sat her visitors down and gave them sherry. Colonel Orlov found her "very nice."

Soon Lee came home from work and, after a few words in English, switched to Russian (confounding Orlov who, his surname to the contrary, did not speak the language). Right away George spotted Lee as a "semi-educated hillbilly," a Texan "of the very low category." But, like many an aristocrat, De Mohren-schildt had a perfect democracy of manner. Besides, it struck him that there was "something charming" about the fellow. He drew Lee into conversation and found him "very sympathetic." Then and there he conceived a liking for him.

Jeanne for her part had been hearing about the Oswalds from George Bouhe for weeks, but she had not done anything to help them and she felt ashamed. When Marina came to Dallas for her appointments at the Baylor Dental Clinic, she stayed with George's daughter and son-in-law, Alix and Gary Taylor, and Jeanne drove her to the clinic. On October 15, when Marina again arrived in Dallas from Fort Worth for a final appointment at the clinic, she and the baby stayed overnight at the De Mohrenschildts'.

Late that evening, after George had gone to bed, Jeanne sat her guest down with a little wine and a lot of cigarettes and encouraged her to talk. Talk Marina did, about her life and that of other young people in Russia. Anxious to entertain and if possible to shock, she told stories of sexual orgies in Leningrad, leaving it unclear whether she had engaged in them or not.

Jeanne was taken aback. "Somehow she was not at all what I would picture as a Soviet girl." To Jeanne, Marina seemed totally lacking in a sense of purpose; she was like a piece of flotsam, rising and falling on the surface of life without any goal whatsoever. It was the reverse of what Jeanne expected. She concluded that Marina represented a "degeneration," a falling off in the quality of Soviet youth.

On the other hand, Jeanne had to admit that her visitor had charm. "She impressed me as an honest girl, and not malicious." Jeanne gave Marina a nightgown with a housecoat to match. Marina was speechless—she sat there simply stroking her gifts with joy. Jeanne was touched by that. She decided that Marina was "a very, very pleasant girl," a girl who "loved life" and "loved the United States absolutely." As a matter of fact, Marina's response to America, one of childish surprise, reminded Jeanne of her own feelings when she first came to this country.[16]

But she considered Marina a terrible mother. She could not get over the way Marina snatched the baby's pacifier off the floor, popped it into her own mouth, which was filled with rotting, infected teeth, and then into the baby's mouth. How the child survived Jeanne did not know. Nor did she understand how Marina, who had grown up in a country where there was supposed to be a high level of medical knowledge and who had been trained as a pharmacist besides, could do such a thing to a child. She also considered Marina "lazy," noting the late hour at which she rose the next morning.[17]

In spite of her mixed feelings for Marina, Jeanne was enthusiastic about continuing to help. George, meanwhile, was doing what he could for Lee. When he appeared in Dallas looking for a job, George urgently recommended him to his friend Samuel B. Ballen, a former New York businessman who was on the boards of several Dallas corporations. De Mohrenschildt told Ballen that Oswald was unusual in that he had "absolutely no hatred" of Russia. He was "very critical, knowingly critical" of both Soviet Russia and the United States, yet he was "outside the cold war on either side." A compassionate and liberal-minded man, Ballen was intrigued. But after two hours with Oswald, Ballen concluded that rather than having "no hatred" for either side, he had, to the contrary, "a little disdain for both." He seemed "a little too aloof," as if he knew "all things a little too affirmatively, too dogmatically," and would too often close off discussion with an uncaring shrug. Ballen was drawn to a stubborn, self-educating, self-improving quality he detected in his visitor, but reluctantly came to the conclusion that Oswald "wouldn't fit in." He was "too much of a rugged individualist, too hard-headed, too independent, a man who would upset any team operation." Ballen thought that Oswald was "a humanitarian" and "a truth-seeking decent individual with a bit of Schweitzerian self-sacrifice in him—so much so that I didn't want him working for me." Ballen decided he was "too hot to handle." [18]

Despite their disaffection from Lee, the Russians stood ready to help when he did find a job and was able to bring Marina and the baby to Dallas. Both Jeanne de Mohrenschildt and George Bouhe hoped they would settle nearby, and Jeanne even looked for an apartment for them in the University Park section where she and George were living. But Lee disappointed them once again by finding the apartment in Oak Cliff, a neighborhood on the opposite side of town from where all of them lived. Then, suddenly, there was Marina, with her baby in her arms, standing on the Mellers' doorstep. And when she announced that she had left Lee, the Russians, including George and Jeanne de Mohrenschildt, once again came to her rescue.

19

Reconciliation

ANNA MELLER was a large, handsome woman with faded blond hair. Her husband, Teo, was small and dark, with an expression at once winsome and observant. On his arm he had a tattoo acquired in a Nazi concentration camp. A professor of philosophy back in Poland, he was employed at the Sanger-Harris department store. His wife had a full-time job, too, as draftswoman for the Dallas Power and Light Company. Both were gone all day, and they invited Marina to stay in their apartment until she decided what she would do next. Marina was grateful to be alone and to rest. But the apartment was small, she and the baby were sleeping on makeshift beds in the living room, and once again she felt "in the way."

The Mellers were anxious about her health. Marina was "skinny and undernourished and had pains all over her body." Bouhe and Mrs. Meller took her to a gynecologist, Dr. Paul Wolff, who confirmed what they wanted to know, that she was not pregnant, but he added that she was "very undernourished" and needed to gain weight right away.[1]

It was soon decided among the Russians, probably after a request from Lee to George de Mohrenschildt, that Lee and Marina should meet and decide for themselves whether their separation would be permanent. Bouhe had given up on Lee. He sensed such "inner resistance" in him that it seemed useless to go on helping. He excoriated his treatment of Marina, considering it "crude and cruel," and was eager to pry her away from him. But he did not want to be present at the meeting, did not want to confront Lee face to face. "He's such a wild man," Bouhe explained to Marina, "that I don't want to listen to his threats. If he sticks his fists in my ears it will suit neither my age nor my health." He was frankly afraid of Lee. He and the Mellers spoke of him among themselves as "megalomanic," "unbalanced," a "psychopath."[2]

"I am scared of this man," he said to De Mohrenschildt. "He is a lunatic."[3]

De Mohrenschildt, possessor of a universally admired physique, replied: "Don't be scared. He is just as small as you are."[4]

Everyone knew that Lee stood in awe of the "size and weight and muscles" —Bouhe's words—of George de Mohrenschildt. The meeting of husband and wife was accordingly set for Sunday morning, November 11, at the De Mohrenschildts' apartment. "Don't worry," Bouhe reassured Marina as he drove her to the rendezvous. "George will be a good shield for you. He is big and strong. I'm not. He'll protect you like a wall." Bouhe escorted Marina inside, conferred a moment with De Mohrenschildt, and quickly left.

When Lee arrived, he was nervous, pale, and obviously embarrassed to be having such a scene in front of the De Mohrenschildts. George immediately started to lecture him. "Look," he said, "do you think it's heroic to beat a woman who is weaker than you? I've beaten women myself. I can see it once or twice, for something serious, but not all the time." Lee was discomfited and did not answer.

Jeanne, who adored her husband, joined him in all his enthusiasms and backed him in everything. Now she was feeling parental. "You have to grow up," she told Lee and Marina. "You cannot live like that. This is not a country that permits such things to happen. If you love each other, behave. If you cannot live with each other peacefully, without all this awful behavior, maybe you should separate, and see. Maybe you really don't love each other after all."[5] She was speaking Russian, although, Marina says, she had lived so many lives and knew so many languages that she now used all of them badly, speaking each as if it were English.

"You *seem* to love one another," George added. "What I can't figure out, God damn it all, is why you can't find a common language?" Both the De Mohrenschildts used profanity a good deal, but they used it so naturally, it was so much the coin of their personalities (especially Jeanne's), that it came out sounding like a caress.

Marina entered the conversation. "I'm tired of his brutality, George," she said. "I can't take it any more."

"I'm not always in the wrong," Lee spoke up at last. "Marina has such a long tongue, sometimes I can't hold myself back."

"The two of you talk," De Mohrenschildt told them. "I don't want to interfere." He and Jeanne left them alone.

Lee was subdued and ready to make up. "I have nobody now," he said. "I don't know what I'll do if you leave me. I don't want to go on living."

"No," said Marina. "I don't want to live with you. I want a divorce." On one hand she was afraid Lee would believe her. On the other she wanted him to, wanted to hurt him for the hurt he had done her.

He pleaded with her to come back to him.

"No," she answered a second time.

When the De Mohrenschildts returned, she told them that she was not going back and she wanted to take her clothing from the apartment. The De Mohrenschildts agreed that separation for a few months might be best until they could decide whether they really loved each other. As Jeanne said, it was "absolutely useless to continue the way they were."

The four of them then drove to the Oswalds' apartment on Elsbeth Street in George's big gray convertible. Marina smoked cigarette after cigarette, nervous but triumphant, knowing Lee was powerless to stop her smoking now that she was under George's protection. Nobody said a word. Lee made a perceptible effort to control himself. But he was unable to contain himself once they reached the apartment. He showed "real nastiness" and became "a little violent," according to Jeanne, "a little bit uppity," according to George. They later said that he swore he would "get even" and grew so ugly that De Mohrenschildt threatened to call the police.[6] He said, again according to the De Mohrenschildts, he would smash the baby's toys and tear up all Marina's dresses if they took her away.

"And where would that get you?" Jeanne inquired. "Then you lose her forever." Lee was quiet, but Jeanne later said that he "boiled, and boiled."[7]

Suddenly, to their surprise, he caved in and promised that he would do nothing violent. As George says, "He completely changed his mind." He trotted obediently after George, who was loading the car, and helped carry out Marina's and the baby's belongings. "Lee did not interfere with me," George said. "He was small, you know, a rather puny individual."[8]

Marina denies that Lee grew violent and made threats. But as they packed up her belongings, his voice quavered and he was holding back tears. Marina was sorry for him, but she was afraid to show it.

Lee drew her into the kitchen. "I'm asking you one last time to stay."

"No," she answered a third time, feeling such pity that she longed to stay. "I was good to you," she thought. "Now you can come after *me.*"

"Go this minute," he said in a loud, angry voice. "I don't want to see you another second."

The De Mohrenschildts delivered Marina and her possessions to the Mellers', and that same day George Bouhe drove her, the baby, and their most needed belongings to the house of Declan and Katya Ford. The Fords had a young baby and a big house. Mr. Ford would be away that week at a geology convention. It would be easier for Katya to have them for a few days than for the Mellers.

Katya Ford had grown up in Rostov-on-Don and escaped Russia during the war. She married an American G.I. and came to the United States. Eventually she was divorced and then married a second time, to Declan Ford, a consulting geologist. Scrupulous and realistic in her relationships, Katya had a devastating eye for character. She had been favorably impressed by Lee at their first meeting, but her impression had quickly changed.

Marina had been at the Fords' for two days when Lee went to George de Mohrenschildt and found out where she was staying. Lee then telephoned, and when Katya answered, asked to speak to Marina. Or, rather, he refused to hang up until he had spoken to Marina. Marina did not want to talk to him. "You'd better tell him yourself," said Katya.

Marina was very curt with Lee. She told him it was no use calling any more, she was not going to come back.

Lee persisted. He started to call once or twice an evening after that. Marina was abrupt for a night or two, but the third night she allowed herself to be drawn in. Lee had something on his mind: his brother Robert had invited them to spend Thanksgiving in Fort Worth. "Go by yourself," Marina told him. It was a prospect that humiliated him and she knew it. She felt herself weaken, wondered how he would manage without her, wondered what Robert would think of her for running away. She asked Katya whether she ought to go back.

Katya considered Lee a brute. She felt that there was something strange, something not quite right about him. In her view, hitting Marina was like hitting a frail, skinny kitten, and Katya could not forgive him. But she felt that Marina, too, was to blame. If Lee was unstable, Marina was immature. With a husband as highstrung, as ready to erupt as Lee, Katya thought it foolhardy and provocative to talk back as sharply as Marina did. A wife, the one person who is privy to all a man's weaknesses, simply has to have tact, Katya believed, and Marina did not have an ounce of it.

Besides, Katya was practical. Marina was no good at housework. It seemed out of the question for her to find a job and a home as a live-in domestic helper, her best hope until she learned English. Until Marina could stand on her own feet, Katya thought, she had no choice but to go back to Lee. She advised Marina to start studying English right away and equip herself to hold a job. She could break away when the baby was old enough for nursery school.[9]

Marina was of two minds. She felt that she could not go on living off other people forever, but she did not see, although her friends were doing their best to make her see, that she actually had a choice and could live alone. She missed Lee and she missed home. Of their quarrelsome, nearly hungry, existence she thought: "It's a poor home, but it's home all the same." But she would not go back right away. She would hold out a while and teach Lee to value her more.

George Bouhe had Marina's promise that she would not go back to Lee. The week of November 12, while she was at Katya's, he took her to lunch with Mrs. Frank (Valentina, known as "Anna") Ray. Mrs. Ray was a Russian married to an American and they had three small children. Immediately, she invited Marina to stay at her house. Mrs. Ray would teach Marina English and put her in night school. Marina would live with the Rays until she could manage on her own. To George Bouhe, it was the answer to a prayer. It was Marina's chance to break away and she accepted.

That weekend Declan Ford delivered Marina and the baby to the Rays'. Marina had told Lee where she was going. Within minutes of her arrival, he telephoned and begged her to see him. "I'm lonely," he said. "I want to see Junie and talk to you about Thanksgiving."

Marina caved in. "All right," she said, "come over."

Declan Ford and Frank Ray picked him up at the bus stop.

"I think you know Mr. Ford," Ray said, starting to introduce them.

"I believe I do," Lee answered.

Ford disliked him for that remark and for the cold way in which it was spoken, when they had, in fact, spent an afternoon at the Mellers' in September. He made a mental note about Lee: This guy is looking for someone to support him and it sure as hell isn't going to be me. Twice, Frank Ray asked Lee where he was working, and twice Lee changed the subject and avoided an answer.[10]

Marina's heart jumped when she saw her husband. They went into a room by themselves.

"Forgive me," he said. "I'm sorry. Why do you torture me so? I come home and there's nobody there. No you, no Junie."

"*I* didn't chase *you* out," Marina said. "*You* wanted it. You gave me no choice."

He loved her, he said. It wasn't much, he knew, but he loved her the best he knew how. He begged her to come back to him. Robert, he added, had invited them for Thanksgiving and it would be terrible to show up without her.

Marina realized that Lee needed her. He had no friends, no one to count on but her. Harsh as his treatment was, she knew he loved her. But she brushed him away when he tried to kiss her. He went down on his knees and kissed her ankles and feet. His eyes were filled with tears and he begged her forgiveness again. He would try to change, he said. He had a "terrible character" and he could not change overnight. But change he would, bit by bit. He could not go on living without her. And the baby needed a father.

"Why are you playing Romeo?" Marina said, embarrassed at his being at her feet. "Get up or someone will come in the door." Her voice was severe, but she felt herself melting inside.

He got up, protesting as he did so that he refused to get up until she forgave him. Both of them were in tears.

"My little fool," she said.

"You're my fool, too," he said.

Suddenly Lee was all smiles. He covered the baby with kisses and said to her: "We're all three going to live together again. Mama's not going to take Junie away from Papa any more."

After supper Frank Ray drove the three of them back to Elsbeth Street.

Greatly relieved, Lee wrote his brother that very night: they would be happy to come for Thanksgiving.[11] He had engineered the reconciliation in the nick of time—Thanksgiving was only four days away.

The Russians were furious. Even Katya Ford said to Marina: "You mean you took advantage of all your friends just to teach Lee a lesson?" Still, they had qualms about consigning her completely to the tender mercies of her husband, and among themselves they discussed what they ought to do next. But one thing was clear: Bouhe had had it. "George," he said to De Mohrenschildt, "I cannot go on. This guy is nuts and we are going to have trouble."

"Oh, come on," George said. "You're too critical. You're a snob. Just because he didn't come from St. Petersburg, you drop them like a hot cake. They are nice young people."

"All right, George," said Bouhe. "You carry the ball."[12]

Which is precisely what happened. After that the Russians, with the exception of the De Mohrenschildts, saw very little of the Oswalds. Nevertheless, there were bulletins from the battlefront. "They're off, they're on, he's beating her, they've broken up"—so it went.[13] One day the De Mohrenschildts seemed to favor separation, while the next they favored reconciliation. Rumors about the Oswalds flew all the way to Fort Worth, where Max Clark heard that De Mohrenschildt "got hold of Oswald and threatened him—picked him up by his shirt and shook him like a dog and told him he would really work him over if he ever laid another hand" on Marina.[14]

A still more colorful story concerned the scene of reconciliation at the Rays'. No sooner had the couple made up, the story went, than Lee plucked the cigarette from his wife's lips and snuffed it out on her shoulder. The Russians recalled that in the early days of the Bolshevik régime, officers of the Cheka, as the secret police were called, used to extinguish a cigarette on human flesh when they were trying to break a prisoner. Marina denies that her husband did any such thing to her ever. But the Russians believed that he did—stunning testimony as to how they felt about Oswald.

Distracted by the sounds of battle and utterly repelled by Lee's violence, the Russians, with the exception of Katya Ford, misunderstood the heart of the relationship between Marina and Lee, which was founded on a mutual willingness, indeed a mutual need, to inflict and accept pain. They were deeply and reciprocally dependent. The Russians were puzzled and angered by Marina's decision to return to her husband because they misunderstood her motive for marrying him in the first place. They thought she had married him to come to the United States, and far from considering such a motive reprehensible, they approved and respected it. Several of the women among the émigré group had done the same. Having come to the United States, they had tried their best to make their marriages work; if they had divorced, it was only because the marriage was impossible. But not one of them would have stayed five minutes in Marina's marriage. They underestimated the strength of the tie that bound her to Lee.

Marina had married Lee not to come to America, but because he was an American. His choice of her had bolstered her self-esteem and confirmed her feeling that she was special. Marriage to an American gave her a way of expressing her rebelliousness and her lack of conformity to Russian ways. Once she was in the marriage, however, Marina's motives for staying in it were deep indeed. Language, the question of whether or not Marina would learn English, tells a good deal of the story. It is virtually a paradigm of their marriage. Marina was quick. She could easily have learned English if she had wanted to. And yet after only a few weeks she gave up her lessons with Bouhe. The De Mohrenschildts gave her a small Victrola with some language records, and she never used them. She abandoned any effort to learn English because Lee did not want her to, and she was afraid of him. Moreover, she sensed that he wanted her to be dependent on him and she was content to leave it that way. Dependence and low self-esteem had carried her into the marriage and, together with a willingness to suffer, they were enough to make her stay.

As for Lee, he wanted Marina dependent on him because it enhanced his control over her. He even wanted control over every penny she spent. He did not allow her to buy groceries and he no longer took her to the grocery store with him. Instead, he had her make out a shopping list and bought everything himself.

Lee wanted control not only over their money but absolutely over Marina herself. For him there was no in between: either he controlled everything or he controlled nothing at all.

Lee was right in one thing. His control over Marina was precarious. She had entertained telephone calls from her old boyfriends most of the time they had lived in Minsk. Even in the United States she had only to meet a handful of her compatriots and they were willing to rush to her rescue. As Lee looked at it, if Marina mastered English, her life might become one long escape hatch from him. She would have neighbors to appeal to; she would have friends; she might even meet other men. His control over her would be jeopardized and he might easily lose her. Indeed, he had nearly lost her to her Russian friends already.

Lee had other reasons for keeping Marina from learning English. He truly did want to keep his command of Russian. Even in Minsk before coming to the United States, he had in the back of his mind the idea that he might return to live in Russia, and he wanted to keep his Russian for that. Moreover, knowing Russian gave him a reputation for being intelligent, and that helped make up for the profound feeling, stemming from his reading disability, that his intelligence did not receive its due.

Finally, apart from his desire to control all the circumstances of his existence, including his wife, he needed to keep Marina ludicrously, outlandishly dependent on him in order to mask the fact that he was deeply and humiliatingly dependent on her. Indeed, in the view of those who knew them best, Marina, not Lee, was the fulcrum of their marriage. Dependent as they both were emotionally, he seems to have been even more dependent on her than she was on him. He was exasperated by the fact that for the second time in his life he found himself dependent on a woman. And at times it made him so angry that he was driven to strip Marina not only of autonomy in the matter of language but, by his beatings, of any sense that she was a human being at all. The beatings, in turn, depressed her and made her even less capable of breaking away from him than she had been before.

Dependence was, indeed, the glue of the Oswalds' marriage and it held them together to the very end. But in the meantime Marina had temporized and had lost her advantage. She had lingered with her Russians to gain leverage and make her life more bearable with Lee. But typically, she had lost more than she had gained, for she had now relinquished their support. Even the De Mohrenschildts, who were the most sympathetic to the marriage, were "disgusted" when she failed to make a real separation of it and stay away two or three months. "We wasted the whole day," Jeanne says. "So much aggravation, and then she dropped the whole thing. So why bother, you know?"[15] As for her truest friends, Bouhe, Mrs. Meller, and the others who had been willing to open their homes to her, they were no longer standing by for the rescue. They had offered her a way out, they had given her her chance—and she lost it. Lee had her in his power once again.

At first, after their reconciliation, Marina and Lee were like children together and, like children, they had a good time. Grinning, holding aloft a cup of cocoa in one hand and a doughnut in the other, Lee did the Twist in the kitchen a night or so after her return. "Come dance with me," he said. "I can do it without spilling." Marina declined out of fear of looking ridiculous.

Every night he took her walking and bought her doughnuts and coffee. He escorted her to a bowling alley down the street and suggested that he teach her to bowl. Again she declined, this time because the balls were too heavy. He played "Moscow Evenings" on the jukebox while they watched others bowl and he crooned the words to her in Russian. "No one but us here speaks Russian," he said, well pleased with himself.

For a few days he approved nearly everything she did. Fired by a new spirit of independence, Marina refused to draw his bath. It was three days before he objected. "Do you think you're a prince?" she told him. "You always complain, anyway. First I make it too hot, then I make it too cold. Jeanne doesn't draw George's bath."

And that was that. Except for a few occasions when she felt like "spoiling" him, Marina never drew his bath again.

Thanksgiving fell on Thursday, November 22. They went to the bus station that morning. They had to wait, so the three of them squeezed into a booth and had themselves photographed.

"In real life you're not bad to look at," he said, examining the result, "but you take a terrible picture. You've no idea how to pose."

Marina responded with a criticism of his hair. He had had it cut short in back and long on top in imitation of his brother Robert.

"You don't like my haircut?" he asked.

"On Robert it's fine," she said, "but on you it's no good at all. You look like a squashed frog."

He laughed.

Still staring at the picture, she added: "Anyone can see you ran away from Russia. You look frightened to death."

Again he laughed, and then he played the title song from the movie *Exodus* four or five times on the jukebox.

Robert Oswald and John Pic met them at the Greyhound Station in Fort Worth. John was now an air force sergeant stationed in San Antonio, Texas, and he, his wife, and children were staying with Robert for the holidays. It was the first meeting of the three brothers since Lee's childhood and the only time they would all be together with their wives and children. Marguerite Oswald, mother of all three boys, their opposing object and unifying force, was not present that day. None of them wanted her.

All of Lee's life, John had expected "some great tragedy to strike" his youngest brother. Now that Lee had defected to Russia and come back, John supposed that he had had his tragedy and was curious to see how he had come out of it. John found his brother thinner and balder than he expected, with eyes somewhat sunk in his head. John was slightly bemused. He had not really talked to him since that day ten years before in New York City when Lee, who was then only twelve years old, had threatened John's wife, Marge, with a knife. Lee and

John had seen each other once or twice, and could have met other times, but Lee, still steaming over the family quarrel, had refused to speak to his elder brother. John wondered if Lee still remembered.[16]

Lee at first gave no sign. The brothers greeted each other warmly and chatted amicably in the car. They were welcomed at Robert's by the two wives, Marge Pic and Vada Oswald, and the four children, John's two and Robert's two. All afternoon the children played together. Lee seemed happy to see his brothers and especially to tell John about his experiences in Russia and the Marine Corps. Marina noticed that her husband did not have that "What am I here for?" attitude he displayed on most social occasions. But Marge Pic picked up a different signal. Lee was friendly enough when he greeted her. But in a way that was quite unmistakable he omitted to address another word to her all day.[17]

Marina was bored. She longed for someone she could talk to without Lee's having to interpret. She telephoned her old pupil, Paul Gregory, who was home in Fort Worth for the holiday, and at six in the evening he came over.

It was at this moment that Lee's hostility came into the open. As Paul Gregory appeared in the doorway, Lee introduced John as his "half brother," a designation the three boys had been at pains all their lives to avoid. They had always stood together as full brothers and fellow sufferers at the hands of Marguerite. Suddenly, John was aware that Lee was still smoldering with the old antagonism. He was not one to forget.[18]

Marina and Lee said goodbye to the family. They spent the evening at the Gregorys', where they spoke Russian and ate turkey sandwiches. Then they took a late bus back to Dallas, arriving at one in the morning. It would be a year and a day before Lee saw any of his family again—on November 23, 1963, when Robert visited him in a jail cell in Dallas.

20

Lee and George

WITH MARINA'S RETURN to the Elsbeth Street apartment, the Oswalds began their new life together in Dallas. It was a lonely life for Marina, with Lee at work all day and only infrequent contacts with her Russian friends. One day shortly after Thanksgiving, Gary Taylor dropped by to return a copy of Lee's essay "The Collective." He intended to stay only a few minutes, but so warm was his welcome —Marina ran down the street and bought doughnuts for the three of them—that he stayed for an hour or two. The Oswalds hardly ever had callers, and Marina was overjoyed to see a face from outside. Gary thought husband and wife were getting along well.[1]

Another visitor after Thanksgiving got a very different impression. She was Lydia Dymitruk, a friend of Anna Meller's and a fellow émigré. Marina had called Mrs. Meller, upset because the baby was ill and Lee would not take her to a doctor because he was afraid he could not pay the bill. Mrs. Meller did not have a car, but Mrs. Dymitruk did, and she could provide transportation.[2]

Marina was distraught when Mrs. Dymitruk arrived. The baby was burning with a fever of 103 degrees, and they drove immediately to the emergency room of Parkland Hospital where the nurses gave the baby medicine for her fever and announced that a pediatrician would be in at five in the afternoon. They would do nothing more. Lydia, who had never had a child of her own, was frightened because the baby seemed to be having trouble breathing, and embarrassed because Marina kept telling her the undoubted truth—that in *her* country such callousness toward a sick child would be unthinkable. They drove on to a clinic, where they were dismayed to find forty sick children ahead of them. Lydia begged the nurses to take little June right away. She had a fever; her case was an emergency. She would have to take her turn, the nurses said, and that might not be for three or four hours. Lydia told them that she would hold them legally responsible if anything happened to the baby. Still they refused to give treatment.

Lydia left Marina and the baby at the Elsbeth Street apartment, promising to return. Lee was not yet home from work when she reappeared about five in the afternoon; and, afraid to go off without him, Marina asked her to wait. Lee came in, calmly ate dinner, and announced that he refused to take the baby to the hospital. "She'll be all right, she doesn't need it," he said. "Besides, I can't afford it. I can't pay." His attitude was the more extraordinary because he doted on "his" baby and generally trembled with fear if she so much as hiccupped or coughed.

He and Marina went into the kitchen to discuss it and Lydia heard the sounds of a verbal battle royal. Marina won. Husband and wife soon emerged and announced that they were going to the hospital.

At Parkland, a doctor took a blood test and X-rayed the baby's lungs. When he had finished treating her, he signed some forms and told Lee to take them to the service desk. There, the nurse asked his address. Lee gave a false reply. She asked his job. He answered that he was unemployed. Did he receive unemployment compensation? "No," he replied.

"How on earth do you live?" she asked, astonished.

"Friends help," Lee shrugged.

Lydia did not hear the questions and answers. But she heard Marina, standing behind Lee in line, hissing at him in Russian, "You liar! What on earth are you saying *that* for?"

The nurse gave Lee a slip requiring a token payment to the cashier. Lee merely stuffed the paper inside his pocket and muttered, "Let's get out of here." They clambered into the back of Lydia's car and immediately fell to fighting over which one would hold the baby. Marina berated Lee all the way home. The baby was sick, had been seriously sick for three days, and Lee was lying again. Would it ever end?

Up front, Lydia heard only Marina's shrewish, schoolteacherish tone, not the substance of the battle. She was sorry for Lee. Lydia sensed that he was angry and tense, sitting with fists clenched, trying to hold himself in until he came to his front door. The one thing he did say was that he ought not to have to pay at all, that in Russia doctors and medicines were free, and they ought to be free here, too.

Lydia was disgusted with both of them by the time she dropped them off, but much more disgusted with Marina. "No wonder he's so mean to you," she said to her later on. "In his place I'd be the same. I'm sorry for Lee. I don't see how he stands it. You have a dreadful disposition. I couldn't live with you a single second. You simply ate him alive."

Self-critical as ever, Marina agreed. She thought she did, indeed, have a dreadful disposition and maybe a dreadful character as well. She actually liked Lydia for criticizing her to her face. But mentally she remarked: "Just you try living with Lee, and then see how you behave."

Marina had caught her husband in another lie that afternoon, and that, in addition to the lies he told at Parkland, had been responsible for her vehement outburst. Sometime earlier Lydia had asked her to send back a pair of dictionaries loaned to her by Bouhe and Anna Meller. Marina answered, in all truthfulness as far as she knew, that Lee had already returned them. But when he came home from work, she found out that he had not returned them at all, as he had told her he had. In fact, he had even hidden them so that she would not find out.

Marina was furious. All through their marriage it was Lee's lying and Marina's telling him frankly what she thought of it that caused the worst fights between them. His lies were bad enough, but what made her even angrier was that he often placed her in a position where, knowingly or unknowingly, she ended up telling a lie, too. Marina hated lying; it was alien to her nature. Yet she found herself caught between two fires: either she told the truth and was a disloyal wife, by her lights, or she was compelled to lie to cover up for her husband. It was the sorest point of their life together as far as she was concerned.

When the Russians heard of Lee's behavior at Parkland and Marina's tongue-lashing, they were confirmed in their hands-off policy toward the Oswalds. What was the point of helping people who were hell-bent on hurting themselves? George Bouhe was incredulous. "Just think!" he said. "Lee took help from the doctors. He was rude and contemptuous to the nurses, he told innumerable lies to get out of paying—two dollars!" Lee did indeed get a bill from Parkland in the mail for exactly $2. He paid it without a murmur and even mentioned how little it was.

Bouhe understood by now that Lee's energies were so drained by inner turmoil that he had nothing left for anybody else. But his sympathies, as always, were with Marina. De Mohrenschildt said that Bouhe was still worrying about her as if she were his daughter. If Marina had behaved badly at the hospital, Bouhe said to himself, it could only have been because Lee had goaded her beyond bearing. Bouhe thought and he thought, and he came up with the direst of prophecies. "Just you wait," he announced to the other Russians. "He'll get her pregnant again."

Alone among the Russians, the De Mohrenschildts did not give up on the Oswalds. George dropped by every other week or so, and he generally brought Jeanne. The couples presented quite a contrast: the hearty, high-spirited George and the flamboyant, energetic Jeanne, side by side with the grave and humorless Lee and the drab, dispirited Marina. "Ho, ho, ho, how are you getting along these days?" George would greet them as he came in the door. Then, to Marina, "And are you planning to leave Lee again?" No, not right away, she would say. Jeanne would remark that Marina's return to Lee had all but killed George Bouhe, and this brought another roar of laughter from De Mohrenschildt. His high spirits had a way of rubbing off on those around him, and he always left the Oswalds in a far more cheerful mood than he found them. But Marina noticed that his visits left her with very little else—a few anecdotes and dirty stories but no residue, nothing of substance at all. Yet she was always looking forward to the next encounter.

It pleased George to get along with someone the other Russians had written off. It gave him a chance to tell them they were stuffy and narrow-minded. He particularly liked to show up George Bouhe on this score. Maybe it was a class thing—De Mohrenschildt was an aristocrat; Bouhe was not—but he felt distaste for Bouhe's bourgeois, bookkeeping approach. One of the reasons he liked Lee was that he was "not a beggar, a sponger," and he had bridled at taking help from Bouhe.[3] If De Mohrenschildt gave you help, he promptly forgot all about it. There were no strings attached; it never occurred to him to ask afterwards what you had done with it.

George was delighted to discover in Lee a pearl, where the other Russians had found only a prickly oyster. Besides, George thought that in Lee, he had found an original. The émigrés were disgusted because Oswald, having seen Soviet reality, still had not given it up, still was reading Marx and praising Khrushchev. George, on the other hand, was enchanted when he asked Lee why he had left Russia and he answered simply, "Because I did not find what I was looking for." "I knew what he was looking for," George was to say later. "Utopia, and that does not exist any place."[4] But he was overjoyed to have found a fellow seeker.

Both George and Jeanne, however, also found him an enigma. "He switched allegiance from one country to another," George remarked, "and then back again, disappointed in this, disappointed in that. He did it without the enjoyment of adventure. For him it was a gruesome deal."[5] Lee did not have any fun. His lack of gaiety, indeed, what might be called the deadness of his spirit, was a puzzle to the De Mohrenschildts, who had suffered and enjoyed so much. What to them would have been a glorious adventure, to Lee was just another drink from life's long, cold bucket of disappointment. But they resolved to back him up. When Katya Ford gave it as her view that Lee was "all mixed up and not very bright," the two of them sprang to his defense. "No, no," George objected. "He's all right. The boy is thinking."

Marina got the impression that as the De Mohrenschildts saw him, Lee was an unbourgeois, uncalculating spirit who had dared go to Russia without giving a damn for the consequences—in short, a young man who was as unconventional as they were. Whatever it was they saw in him, both the De Mohrenschildts, and George in particular, gave Lee a warmth, an approval, and an emotional support that, after his return to America, he got from nobody else. And unlike the other Russians, they seemed, after the separation at least, to prefer Lee and look down on Marina. Part of the reason, of course, was George's rebelliousness against his fellow émigrés. But there was another aspect to their relationship. George said of Lee: "He could be my son in age, you see."[6] George's only son had died and he had not recovered from the loss. That fall he was losing one son-in-law by divorce, Gary Taylor, with whom he was on good terms politically, and, for political reasons, he was on deteriorating terms with Jeanne's son-in-law, Ragnar Bogoyavlensky-Kearton. Jeanne, too, was underfulfilled as a mother. She had no son of her own and, other things being equal, she liked men better than women. But the great thing both De Mohrenschildts shared was a passion for underdogs. As Jeanne was to put it later, Lee could be "disagreeable, very very disagreeable. The personality he had would make anybody miserable to live with." But they also saw him as "a puppy dog everybody kicked."[7] For the two of them, that was enough.

If George considered Lee one of those rare Americans who cared nothing for money or possessions, he viewed Marina, by contrast, as a real American in spirit, a more or less "normal" person, a "happy-go-lucky" bourgeois mouse who was bewitched by the gadgetry of American life and wanted more of it. They saw her as Ulysses saw his son, Telemachus: as a more or less "blameless" being, "centered in the sphere of common duty." She seemed simply buried in problems: a baby, diapers, beatings, no money, no friends. Even Jeanne, a woman so generous that one friend said she had "an overdeveloped mother tendency,"[8] appears to have been irritated by the bottomless pit of need that Marina represented. Moreover, the De Mohrenschildts felt that Marina always had her hand outstretched, that she would take anything you gave her. Not Lee—Lee had pride.

As for the Oswalds, both of them were charmed by George. And Marina liked Jeanne right away, although Lee complained after their first meeting that she was too fat and lavished too much affection on her dogs. But he soon changed. He saw that Jeanne was a good cook, a splendid companion, and a loyal, devoted wife. He admired her for helping George financially. In fact, it was not long before he was holding her up as an example Marina ought to follow.

George was a tonic for Lee, and shook him out of his depressed spirits. More than anyone else he met after his return to the United States, Lee was drawn to George, opened up with him, paid attention to his opinions, even sought his advice. They probably saw one another fifteen or twenty times in all, but people with resources far greater than the Oswalds' still found any encounter with George unforgettable. And their score of meetings had all the more impact on Lee because they occurred in a vacuum. Outside the men he saw at work, he knew nobody else. Moreover, his usual way of dealing with people simply vanished when he was with this older, more experienced man. Lee used people to get what he wanted and then drove them away if they tried to get too close to him, if their usefulness was over, or if they expected something in return for their kindness. But when he saw that George expected nothing and did not intrude upon him, he left off maneuvering. He even lied less to George than he did to anybody else.

Curiously, De Mohrenschildt, too, who loved nothing better than to bruise the sensibilities of his bourgeois friends, was exquisitely tactful with Lee. Where nearly everyone else considered Lee arrogant, De Mohrenschildt found him "very humble. If somebody expressed an interest in him, he blossomed, absolutely blossomed. If you asked him some questions about himself, he was just out of this world. That was more or less the reason that I think he liked me very much."[9]

De Mohrenschildt later insisted, however, that once the novelty wore off, once he and Jeanne had learned all they thought Lee had to tell them about Russia, they kept up with the Oswalds mostly out of sympathy. After that, George said, the relationship was "purely to give a gift": take the Oswalds to a party, introduce them to people, feed them a much-needed meal. George's epitaph of Lee might have been the epitaph of one of his dogs: "He was responsive to kindness."[10]

Lee was indeed responsive. Sometimes, after they had talked over some political event and Lee heard what George had to say, he would alter his opinion. "George is right," he would announce. It was Lee's supreme accolade. With

George alone among the émigrés, he did not feel that he had to defend the U.S.S.R. With George alone his discussions of Soviet affairs did not degenerate into argument and were not laced with hostility. Not feeling that he had to defend Russia, Lee spoke knowingly and from the inside, and far more critically with George than with anybody else. He received several Soviet newspapers, and George used to ask what was in them. Very often the two of them would compare the Soviet version of some event with the stories in the American press. Both assumed the American version to be the true one, and they had many a good laugh over the discrepancies between the two. "Those poor Russians," Lee used to say. "They don't know *what's* going on."

Both men admired Khrushchev, his de-Stalinization and his policy of peaceful co-existence. Besides, Khrushchev's high spirits, his cheerful, slightly manic way of exuding aggressiveness, were not altogether unlike George's own. But even George roared with laughter when Lee told him how Stalin's statue had been dynamited in Minsk and carried away under cover of night. "So they're still doing things the same old way," George said. "Things haven't changed over there."

Lee paid George another tribute. He asked him to read his manuscript, "The Collective," which he had shown previously only to the typist Pauline Bates, his brother Robert Oswald, and to Gary and Alexandra Taylor. It was George's opinion he cared about the most.

Lee must have been disappointed. George gave the manuscript only the most cursory glance. What he said of it to Lee is not known, but what he thought of it is. "He showed me his little memoirs," George said afterwards. "I did not take him seriously. That is all. All his opinions were crude." George characterized Lee as a man of "exceedingly poor background who read rather advanced books and did not understand even the words in them. He read complicated economical treatises and just picked up difficult words out of what he had read and loved to display them. He loved to use the words to impress me. He did not understand the words—he just used them. So how can you take seriously a person like that? You just laugh at him. But there was always an element of pity I had, and my wife had, for him. We realized that he was a forlorn individual, groping."[11]

Like the other Russians, George considered the possibility that Lee might be a Soviet spy. He discounted the idea; Lee was "too outspoken in his ideas and attitudes." He later said: "I would never believe that any government would be stupid enough to trust Lee with anything important. An unstable individual, mixed-up individual, uneducated individual, without background. What government would give him any confidential work? No government would. Even the government of Ghana would not give him any job of any type." During one of their conversations, George recalled, "I asked him point blank, 'Are you a member of the Communist Party?' And he said no. He said, 'I am a Marxist.' Kept on repeating it." George did not discuss it any further because, "knowing what kind of brains he had, and what kind of education, I was not interested in listening to him, because it was nothing; it was zero."[12]

Whatever his private opinion, Lee *felt* that George respected him, perhaps because George, with his perfect democracy of manner, treated him exactly as he treated everyone, and Lee took a lot more teasing and criticism from George than he would from anybody else. Marina put her finger on it when she said: "The word 'respect' just doesn't fit George. George has a respect for nature. But he does not respect human beings. He probably respects his dog or a good bottle of wine more than he respects any person." Still, she thought that George liked her husband and treated him as an equal.

To both Oswalds, the De Mohrenschildts were figures of authority. Jeanne also treated Lee with warmth and respect, but she was frank with him, too. She scolded him for his strictness with Marina, whom he forbade to drink, smoke, or wear makeup. "Why do you forbid her to smoke?" Jeanne would ask. "She only does it because you disapprove. Let her smoke. I'm sure she'll stop if you do."

It was the same when it came to the English language. Both George and Jeanne told Lee emphatically that he must allow Marina, must encourage her, to study English. Lee refused with the usual excuse that he would forget his own Russian if he did not practice with Marina. "That is a very egotistical attitude on your part," George said. Lee did not reply.

Jeanne was frank with Marina, too. Knitting away on a tiny jacket for one of her dogs, she advised Marina to give in to Lee more often. "You ought not to fight over trifles," she said. But when Marina, encouraged, felt invited into the older woman's confidence and sought some advice about sex, Jeanne was repelled. Sexually, Marina confided, Lee was "not strong." He came to a climax very quickly. Was it her fault? Were there pills he could take that might help? Ought they to go see a doctor?[13]

Jeanne later claimed that Marina's confidences were made in front of Lee, in front of all of them, and that she ran him down sexually to his face. Marina denies this vigorously, and her denial has the ring of truth. For one thing, her only other sexual confidences to friends were made in private. For another, she knew that Lee would beat her terribly if she dared say any such thing.

Like his wife, George avoided personal confidences. He had already interfered in Lee's private life by encouraging Marina to leave him when they first moved to Dallas. He had seen Lee's capacity for violence, he knew that Lee had beaten Marina, and he may have been fearful for her safety. But he respected the private lives of others and he was not going to interfere again. Besides, George had a certain delicacy. He was discreet about his own sexual exploits and evidently did not readily lend an ear to those of others. What was more, he approved of Marina's return to Lee. Maybe she had gone back too soon, as Jeanne and the other Russians thought, but she had made the right decision. George considered Lee a good fellow, and he hoped the marriage would stick.

The subject that George really liked to talk about with Lee was politics. He was later to claim that once they had exhausted the topic of Russia, he and Lee had little to say to each other.[14] That, apparently, was not true. The two talked politics all the time. Sam Ballen and Declan and Katya Ford thought this was the real bond between them, and Marina remembers their talking politics every time they met. They spoke in English and Marina missed most of what they said.

Anyway, it was her job to keep the baby out of the way so that Lee could make the most of his moments with George. But when it came to his political ideas, she feels certain that her husband had no secrets from George. In this sphere alone, and with this one man, Lee was comparatively frank. Except for Alexander Ziger and Pavel Golovachev, Lee's friends in Minsk, Marina thinks George knew her husband's political views better than anybody else—and that he read Lee like an open book.

Domestically, the subject closest to them both was civil rights. Lee told George that "it was hurting him, the fact that colored people did not have the same rights as white ones." They agreed that President Kennedy was doing a good job, doing more for the black man than any President had before him. "Yes, yes," Lee would say, "I think he is an excellent President—young, full of energy, full of good ideas."

The Cuban missile crisis may have tempered Lee's opinion of Kennedy, although in spite of himself he may well have admired Kennedy's bravura display. Lee did not say much about the crisis, but when he did talk about it, it was to George—perhaps in the week of the crisis, and certainly many times thereafter. Those who saw George at the time recall that on this occasion, and this occasion only, he was critical of Kennedy and that he was, as always, highly sympathetic to Castro. George sided with the underdog on principle, while Lee had long admired and even hero-worshipped the Cuban dictator, so the two were in strong agreement about Castro.

Another topic they discussed was the integration of Ole Miss, the University of Mississippi at Oxford. Four times that fall, in September and early October, federal marshals and officials of the U.S. Department of Justice had tried to enroll James Meredith, a black man, in the university; and four times they desisted because of opposition from Governor Ross Barnett, and because an angry crowd, egged on by retired U.S. Army Major General Edwin A. Walker, threatened to erupt into ugly violence. Finally, President Kennedy called out the National Guard, sent U.S. army troops to nearby Memphis, and Meredith was allowed to register, but at the cost of a riot in which two men lost their lives.

Ironically, the same General Walker who exhorted the segregationists at Ole Miss had been ordered by President Eisenhower in 1957 to lead 1,000 paratroopers into Little Rock, Arkansas, in the battle to integrate Central High School. He was then sent to Germany, where he used his post to disseminate extreme right-wing propaganda to the troops. Because of congressional objections, he was removed from his command. He retired from the army to live in Dallas, and soon became a leading figure in the John Birch Society. For his provocative role in the demonstrations at Ole Miss, Walker was arrested on charges of insurrection and seditious conspiracy, sent to the U.S. prison and medical center at Springfield, Missouri, for psychiatric observation, and later released on $50,000 bond.

The John Birch Society, based in Massachusetts, had risen to national prominence while Lee was out of the country. But he had read about it, and about Walker, in the news magazines his mother had sent to Minsk. He talked frequently about the "Birchers" and the "Minutemen" with Gary and Alexandra

Taylor when he first moved to Dallas. And the fact that Walker, who seemed to carry about in his very person the threat of "fascism" in the United States, actually lived close at hand in Dallas seems to have stirred Lee a good deal. He and George had endless discussions about the Birchers, Walker, and the danger of fascism. George was well aware from their conversations that Lee "disliked," even "hated," General Walker and, by his own remarks, George may not only have helped fuel Lee's hatred, but, in an odd way, may have given it his approval.

The fundamental bond between Lee and George, then, was politics; and despite the differences between them as human beings, their political views were strikingly alike. Both were rebellious and contumacious toward authority. Both were seekers. Unknown to either of them, however, what they were seeking was not a better world that lay ahead but a better world that lay behind, buried in the past of each. For each had lost his birthright, had lost something he considered rightly his. George had at one stroke lost his country, his mother, and his place in a secure social order. And the effect on him was magnified by the fact that the father he loved was suffering the very same losses. In later life George was to wander from country to country and never really feel at home in his adopted land, the United States. Yet his loss had at least been palpable, measurable, while Lee's was infinite. For Lee had never known his father. He even attributed his character to this one fact, and had written that his father's early death had occasioned in him "a far mean streak of independence brought on by neglect." What George and Lee had in common, then, was not just their politics but something deeper that they shared—a lifelong drama of dispossession. It was this that gave depth to their relationship, this that gave consonance and resonance to everything that passed between them.

Politically each was a sounding board for the other, but any account of the echoes which bounced back and forth is incomplete without reckoning in the wives, each of whom was likewise a sufferer in the drama of dispossession. Jeanne's father had been killed by Communists and, in exile from her homeland, China, she had taken first a French, and then an American identity. Marina was illegitimate, had never been at home in any of her Russian "homes," and, like the other three, had left the country of her birth. All four were rebels. Thus the influence which George had on Lee may have been amplified by the women and especially by Jeanne, who was far out and vociferous in her opinions and was the only woman whose political views Lee respected.

But the differences were crucial, too. George, for example, had innumerable avenues through which he was able to express the central drama of his life, that of yearning to be "in," yet having to be thrown out. He and Jeanne had countless harmless ways in which they could shock and outrage. As for Marina, she abhorred "politics." It was Lee who was different. Unlike the De Morenschildts, Lee had no hobbies, no eccentricities, no minor ways of expressing himself. His only outlets were major ones. He had already expressed his political ideas on a grand scale twice, by abandoning first America, and then Russia, all before he had reached the age of twenty-three.

One pair of onlookers spotted the critical difference between George and Lee, and that was Declan and Katya Ford. Their perspicacity was curious, for they liked George and disliked Lee. But it was Lee they respected. Lee was a "serious seeker," an "idealist," while George only wanted to be "a commissar," wanted to be "on top" himself.[15] George was a talker. What the Fords saw about Lee was that he was capable of acting on his beliefs.

Everyone who knew them agrees that Lee looked to George as a father. Marina says that her husband was slightly afraid of George and that for George alone, he might even go so far as to amend his political opinions. Gary Taylor thought that Lee would do anything George told him to do. He would even take his advice on such matters as what time to go to bed, where to stay, and whether to get a new job. Whatever George's suggestions, Gary says, "Lee grabbed them and took them."[16] George himself has said that "He was clinging to me. He would call me. He would try to be next to me."[17]

It did not occur to George what effect his political talk might have on Lee. Marina sensed that her husband was merely "the latest exhibit in George's collection of friends," and that George thought, "It would be interesting to see how he turned out." George himself said that "He is just a kid for me, with whom I played around. Sometimes I was curious to see what went on in his head. But I certainly would not call myself a friend of his."[18]

Such condescension, no matter how artfully concealed, must have been maddening to Lee. It was seldom that he looked up to anyone. And now he, who set the distances of all his relationships and kept nearly everyone at arm's length, was himself being kept at arm's length by the one man he longed to be close to, the one man whose esteem he coveted.

As the winter of 1963 began, the idea seems to have taken shape in Lee's mind that by a single, dramatic act whose political thrust George would approve, he might compel George's respect.

Marina Alexandrovna Medvedeva, not quite four, in Murmansk, wearing a dress brought by her Aunt Taisya from America.
(MARINA OSWALD PORTER)

Lee Harvey Oswald (*front row, third from left*) in grade school in Texas. (NATIONAL ARCHIVES)

Marina (*bottom left*) at the age of twelve, with classmates in Leningrad. (NATIONAL ARCHIVES)

Mr. and Mrs. Edwin A. Ekdahl (Marguerite Oswald), Lee's mother and stepfather, after their marriage in 1945. (NATIONAL ARCHIVES)

Marina, at the age of fourteen and about to enter pharmacy school, in the woods outside Leningrad. (NATIONAL ARCHIVES)

Lee, at the Hotel Berlin in Moscow, at the time of his defection in 1959. (NATIONAL ARCHIVES)

Lee's inscription in his Russian-English dictionary: "Moscow, November 22, 1959, Lee Harvey Oswald." (MARINA OSWALD PORTER)

Lee in a photograph taken at the Minsk Radio Plant in mid-January, 1960.
(NATIONAL ARCHIVES)

Lee in the summer of 1960 relaxes in the courtyard of the Minsk Radio Plant with some of the men who taught him Russian. (NATIONAL ARCHIVES)

Lee engaged in a favorite hobby in Minsk, summer of 1960, with his friends Mrs. Ziger and her daughters Anita (*front*) and Eleonora.
-   (NATIONAL ARCHIVES)

Lee on a picnic in Minsk with Eleonora Ziger and a friend in the summer of 1960. (NATIONAL ARCHIVES)

Lee's birthday, October 18, 1960, with his best friend, Pavel Golovachev, and Ella Germann (*upper right*), the girl who refused to marry him.
(NATIONAL ARCHIVES)

Marina in the spring of 1961, at about the time she met Lee.
(NATIONAL ARCHIVES)

Lee just before his marriage. (NATIONAL ARCHIVES)

Marina and Lee on the balcony of their Minsk apartment in the summer of 1961.
(NATIONAL ARCHIVES)

The Oswalds' apartment house in Minsk. Marina identified the location of their
apartment with an arrow. (MARINA OSWALD PORTER)

Marina on the balcony.
(NATIONAL ARCHIVES)

Lee's handwriting identified by Marina shows this view from their balcony in Minsk.
(MARINA OSWALD PORTER)

opera house left
ministry right
View from balcony
Lee's hand writing.

Lee in the summer of 1961. (NATIONAL ARCHIVES)

Marina and Lee with her Aunt Lyuba Axyonova on a picnic in Minsk in the early autumn of 1961. (NATIONAL ARCHIVES)

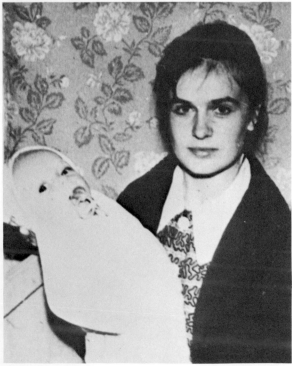

Marina and June Oswald in the spring of 1962. (NATIONAL ARCHIVES)

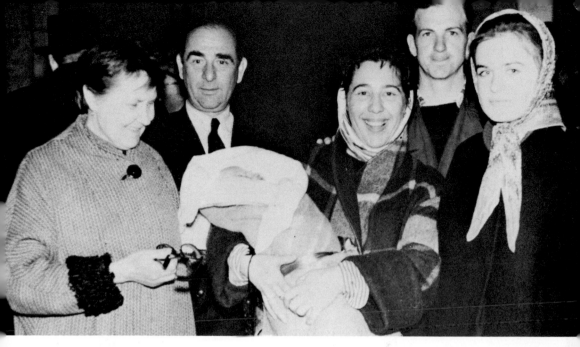

The Zigers see the Oswalds off at the Minsk railway station in May 1962. (NATIONAL ARCHIVES)

Lee and Marina say goodbye to Minsk on the first step of their journey to America. (NATIONAL ARCHIVES)

Lee, Marina, and June on a park bench in Moscow on May 29, 1962, just before their departure from Russia. (MARINA OSWALD PORTER)

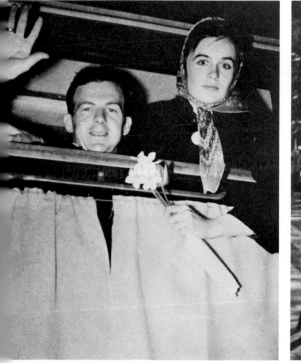

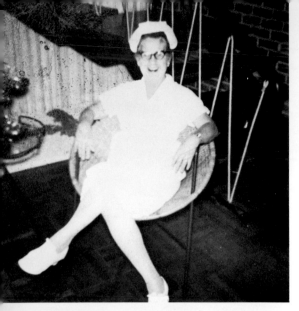

Marguerite Oswald (*left*), in her uniform as a practical nurse, in a photograph she sent to Lee and Marina in Russia.
(NATIONAL ARCHIVES)

Marina, Lee, and June (*above*) squeezed into a photo booth at the Greyhound Bus Station in Dallas, enroute to Robert Oswald's home in Fort Worth, Thanksgiving Day, November 22, 1962.
(NATIONAL ARCHIVES)

Lee, posing with his rifle and pistol, holding copies of *The Militant* and *The Worker,* in a photograph taken by Marina in the backyard of their apartment on Neely Street in Dallas, March 31, 1963.
(WIDE WORLD PHOTOS)

Lee in a photograph taken in September 1963, probably in New Orleans.
(NATIONAL ARCHIVES)

George and Jeanne de Mohrenschildt holding a photograph of President and Mrs. Kennedy.
(WIDE WORLD PHOTOS)

Marina (*right*) and the author in Santa Fe, New Mexico, October 1964.
(Courtesy of DAVID C. DAVENPORT)

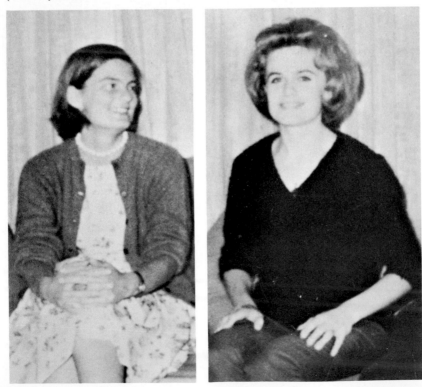

21

The Revolver

ON DECEMBER 28, Lee and Marina climbed into the back seat of George's big gray convertible and drove to the Sanger-Harris department store to pick up Jeanne. "Her former husband is in a mental hospital," George said, and he told them of Jeanne's success designing clothing in New York. She had so much drive that she always got what she wanted. Plainly George was proud of the woman he had married. When they reached the department store, he fairly leaped out of the car to fetch her.

Lee and Marina talked it over. "He's probably lying about his Jeanne and how much money she makes," Lee remarked. "She probably makes a lot but not as much as he says." In fact, Lee liked Jeanne for being able and willing to support her husband.

They were on their way to a combination Christmas and New Year's party at Declan and Katya Ford's. It was Jeanne who had arranged the evening.[1] She was worried about the Oswalds' being alone over the holidays and had telephoned Katya to ask if she might bring them to the party. Katya, who hoped she had seen the last of the Oswalds, gulped a little and said Yes. Jeanne also arranged for a neighbor to babysit. It was the first time the Oswalds had been anywhere without June.

The Fords' sprawling modern house on Brookcrest Drive was brightly lit for the occasion. A fire was blazing in the huge stone fireplace in the living room. The guests, many of them Russian, were astonished to see the Oswalds. Like Katya, they thought they had seen the last of them.

The first person Marina saw was George Bouhe. She kissed him on the cheek and greeted him with embarrassed affection. Lee's reaction was typical. "Why are you sucking up to him?" he said to her the first chance he got.

Lee spent most of the evening with Yaeko Okui, a young Japanese girl who had come with Lev Aronson, an émigré from Latvia and a well-known cellist with the Dallas Symphony Orchestra. They sat on stone steps at one end of the room, deep in conversation. No one had seen him so attentive to a woman before.

Relieved to be rid of Lee, Marina moved happily from friend to friend, ate heartily, and ended up with a group singing Russian songs at the piano. She was enjoying herself. As the Russian at the party most recently arrived in the United States, she was the cynosure of attention.[2] She felt, moreover, that everyone was genuinely happy to see everyone else. She sensed a welcome absence of hypocrisy, of fake party manners, in the air. Watching her, however, George Bouhe and Anna Meller thought she was not looking well. Mrs. Meller wondered if she had enough to eat at home.[3]

Lee, too, was something of a sensation. He was obviously enjoying the company of Miss Okui. He had liked Japan and appreciated Japanese women. They talked about Japanese and American customs, and about Ikebana, the Japanese art of flower arrangement, which Miss Okui was certified to teach. But Marina noticed that she spoke Russian and was drinking only Coca-Cola, nothing stronger. It occurred to her that Miss Okui might work for American Intelligence. During an interval in the kitchen, she cautioned Lee against talking politics and especially against praising Khrushchev. "Watch out," she said. "That girl is pretty and very charming. Only, she may be a spy. Don't be too frank with her." Never before, and never again, was she to feel prompted to warn her secretive husband to keep his mouth shut.

One other person reacted to Miss Okui exactly as she did—George de Mohrenschildt. To all appearances he was busy chasing a couple of girls, but his antennae were out and he remarked to Marina: "That Japanese girl—I don't trust her. I think she works for some government or other, but which one, I don't know." Others at the party noticed that Miss Okui's escort, Lev Aronson, was more than a little jealous of Lee. "My God," they claim to have heard him say, "what an idiot that is!" Lee also made a strong impression on Katya Ford's teen-age daughter Linda. Toward the end of the party, Declan Ford played a record called "The First Family" in which the comedian Vaughn Meader gave a hilarious imitation of President Kennedy. While the others laughed, Lee stared at Linda with his large, solemn eyes wide open and never once cracked a smile. Linda felt so uncomfortable under that unblinking stare that afterwards she could remember nothing else about the party. The Oswalds left about midnight with the De Mohrenschildts. They were not invited to the other Christmas parties given by the Russians in the next few days.

It was Marina's first Christmas in America and she longed for a tree. She begged Lee to buy her one as they walked home from the grocery store one night. "No," he said. "It's too expensive, because you have to buy toys and decorations. It's nothing but a commercial holiday, anyway."

Later that evening Marina slipped out on the street, found an evergreen branch, propped it up on their bureau in front of the mirror, and spread cotton around it for snow. The next day she gathered up 19 cents which Lee had left lying about and made for the five-and-ten-cent store, where she bought colored paper and miniature decorations. She shredded the colored paper into tinsel; the decorations went on the branch. Lee was proud and surprised. "I never thought you could make a Christmas tree for only nineteen cents," he said.

Lee's reactions were often inexplicable. Around this time, Marina lost a purse containing $10 he had given her for groceries and she expected to be scolded or even beaten. When he hardly responded at all, Marina broke into tears. Lee tried to cheer her up by talking baby talk and then talking like a Japanese. He played games on the way to the grocery store, where he bought her red caviar, smoked herring, and other treats.

On New Year's Eve, the biggest holiday of the Russian year, Lee, oblivious, or uncaring, went to bed about ten. When midnight struck, Marina was alone in the bathtub thinking of her friends in Russia and wondering how they were celebrating. She pretended that the bathtub was filled with champagne. In her imagination she could see corks flying into the air and her friends back in Minsk singing and drinking New Year's toasts. By the time she emerged, tears of homesickness were pouring down her face. She was furious at Lee for going to sleep. She felt that he did not love her, that her marriage and her life with him in America were a fraud.

In that mood she sat down at the kitchen table and wrote a letter to Anatoly Shpanko, the medical student whose offers of marriage she had refused both before and after meeting Lee. Now that she was safely at a distance, thousands of miles away, her feelings for her rejected suitor came pouring out. She realized that she had cared for him deeply, more than she knew at the time, and she believed that, had it not been for Lee, she would have married Anatoly. With him she would have been happier.

This was Marina's letter, as she remembers it.

Anatoly dear,
Very late, I am writing the letter you asked me for.
Late, I want to wish you a Happy New Year.
It is not for this I am writing, however, but because I feel very much alone. My husband does not love me and our relationship here in America is not what it was in Russia. I am sad that there is an ocean between us and that I have no way back. . . .
Alik does not treat me as I should like, and I fear that I shall never be happy with him. It is all my fault, I think, and there is no way of setting it right. How I wish that you and I could be together again.
I regret that I did not appreciate the happy times we had together and your goodness to me. Why did you hold yourself back that time? You did it for me, I know, and now I regret that, too. Everything might have turned out differently. But maybe, after the way I hurt you, you would not have me back.
I am writing because you asked me to write you the truth about my life here and because I hope we are still friends.
I kiss you as we kissed before.

Marina
P.S. I remember the snow, the frost, the opera building—and your kisses. Isn't it funny how we never even felt the cold?

Marina was weeping as she finished.

She kept the letter three or four days, just as she always did. Then she took 25 cents' worth of stamps from the drawer, stuck them on the envelope, and mailed it. A day or so later, on Monday, January 7, Lee came home from work waving an envelope.

"A letter for you," he said. "Who were you expecting to hear from?"

"Aunt Valya?"

No, he said, and she suggested two or three others.

"Who did you write this to?" He shoved the letter to Anatoly in front of her, then quickly snatched it away.

She wanted to tear it out of his hands, but he hid the letter behind his back. "You've no right to read my letter," she cried.

"You'll read it aloud," he said.

She jumped up and tried to run out of the room, but he caught her and forced her to sit down. He sat facing her and began to read the letter. Halfway through, he stumbled over her handwriting and asked her what the rest contained. She would not tell him and he slapped her twice across the face.

"It's enough, what I read already." He disappeared into the kitchen.

Marina snatched the letter and hid it in the drawer where their bed linens were kept.

"Is it true what you wrote?" Lee asked when he returned to the living room.

"Yes," she said.

He slumped onto the sofa and sat there, his head in his hands, for a long time. Finally he straightened up. "Not a word of it is true," he said. "You did it on purpose. You knew they changed the postage and that the letter would come back to me. You were trying to make me jealous. I know your woman's tricks. I won't give you any more stamps. And I'm going to read all your letters. I'll send them myself from now on. I'll never, ever trust you again." He made her get the letter and tear it up under his eyes.

Marina says that there were times when she tried to make Lee jealous, but this was not one of them. The postal rates had not changed; Marina's mistake seems to have been that the letter was overweight.

Again, Lee's response was a good deal milder than she might have expected. After all, he frequently beat her for nothing. But this time he merely slapped her, and he did not have the mean, murderous look he generally had when he hit her. Marina even had the impression that he slapped her only because he felt he had to: "It was like a heroic gesture in the movies." She considered it a "just re-proach." But she was baffled by the inappropriateness of his reaction. He practically ignored it when she did something dreadful, yet for a mouthful of sharp words or a bit of mulish behavior he would beat her up.

She did not write to Anatoly again. She repented her foolishness and was relieved that he had not received her letter. But from now on, nearly everything she wrote went through Lee. She handed each of her letters to him in an unsealed envelope. Then, no matter to whom it was written, but especially if it was to a girlfriend who knew Anatoly, he would scan it for a hidden or separate message inside. Marina accepted his censorship like a child. Once in a while she did slip a letter past Lee to one of her girlfriends in Minsk requesting news of Anatoly, exactly as Lee feared. But aside from these breaches of discipline, she lapsed into helplessness. Stamps were expensive, and she depended on Lee for them, except for such change as she could scrounge from his bureau.

There were ten apartments in the building at Nos. 602 and 604 Elsbeth Street, and Lee avoided his neighbors whenever he could. He hated to run into any of them, hated being seen coming or going, refused to exchange pleasantries in the hallway, and invariably used the back door of the building, although there was a perfectly good entrance in front.

Marina was more gregarious. One day she stopped by to visit Mrs. Mahlon Tobias, the wife of the elderly, white-haired manager of the building. She did not speak English, of course, but when Mrs. Tobias remarked that "your husband says that you're Czech," Marina understood enough to shake her head vigorously —"No, no, I'm Russian."[4] Again, she had caught Lee in a lie and she demanded an explanation. He told her that he was afraid he would be fired or that the landlord would throw them out if Marina was known to be Russian. In fact, the owner of the building at Nos. 602 and 604 Elsbeth Street, William Martin Jurek, was of Czech origin and Lee, who could be clever about such things, probably knew it. If so, he may have thought that Mr. Jurek would prefer a Czech to a Russian tenant.

When Lee was at home on the weekends, the Tobiases noticed that he seldom let Marina out of his sight. He even came with her to fetch the vacuum cleaner, use of which was shared by all the tenants.[5] What they and the other neighbors did not know was that it was Lee who vacuumed the apartment, carried out the garbage, did most of the dishes, and turned down the bed every night. He rarely refused a household chore. He was not only a dutiful but an affectionate husband, and there were periods when he would follow Marina around all day. At such times, she says, he literally "wore me out with his kisses." He allowed her, besides, two indulgences. One was deciding whether and when they would have children. The other was letting her sleep in the morning. He got up by himself very early, made his breakfast, and left coffee on the stove for Marina. On weekends he very often served her breakfast in bed. On Sundays, and Saturdays if he did not go to work, it was Lee who made up their bed.

He played with the baby daily and, most evenings, it was he who gave the baby her bath. He did not trust Marina and was afraid she would drown the child. He drew the water and tested its temperature with great care before he lowered the baby into the bathtub. Then, to Marina's horror, he would step in himself, utterly naked, with the exception of a washcloth over his private parts. Then he would splash June and play with her as if he longed to be a little child himself.

"Mama," he would shout to Marina, "we got water on the floor." Marina would tell him to mop it up himself. "I can't," he would shout back to her. "I'm in the bathtub with Junie."

"Mama," he would call out again, "bring us our toys." And she would bring them.

"Mama," came the call a third time, "you forgot our rubber ball." And, to the baby's delight, he would splash the rubber ball in the water.

"Mama," he would call out one last time, "bring us a towel, quick. We have water on our ear." Junie could not have cared less, but Lee was squeamish about *his* ears (he had had a mastoid operation as a child) and tenderly wiped the water off the baby's ear, as if she were squeamish, too.

The first weeks of the New Year were fairly peaceful for Marina. Lee was happy in his work and able to control himself at home. He continued to hit Marina, but their battles were within limits both could bear. Toward the middle of January, however, things somehow, subtly, began to change. Marina's letter to Anatoly may by itself have been the cause. But a series of other events occurred at about this time that may have led to what was to be a dramatic shift in his behavior.

One morning at the beginning of January, George de Mohrenschildt came by the Elsbeth Street apartment for a brief visit. Lee was at work, George was in Oak Cliff on business and he felt like gossiping. He and Marina chatted about the Fords' party, and as he was leaving, George asked her how she found Lee sexually?

"Oh, nothing special," she answered cheerily.

"How about I show you sometime?" George said.

It was a parting remark, the only one of its kind ever to pass between them. As George's suggestions to women went it was nothing, a mere way of getting out the door. But Marina remembered it long afterwards.

Lee was fiercely jealous of his wife. Marina never told him of George's remark, but since he suspected everyone, Lee may have suspected that George, too, was attracted to Marina. Whenever they were going to the De Mohrenschildts' and Marina put on a dress, Lee told her to take it off, a sweater and slacks were enough. It was the same when they went anywhere, to the park or even the grocery store; Lee was taking no chances. So jealousy may have been still another of the emotions he felt for George de Mohrenschildt.

On January 10, Marina suddenly was afraid that she was pregnant. She sat in the kitchen and sobbed, while Lee tried to comfort her. "It's nothing to cry about," he said. "I'll be glad if we have another." In fact, he told her, he would be glad to have a child every year, "enough for a whole football team." The scare came to nothing, however.

A few days later, on January 14, Lee signed up for a night-time typing course at Crozier Technical High School, which was to start at the end of the month. But he did not commit himself; he did not pay the enrollment fee.

Then one night after the middle of January, Lee and Marina had an extraordinary conversation, another in the chain of events that may have harmed Lee's peace of mind. They were lying in bed together, the light out, in a companionable mood. It was one of those times when it seemed as if there was an alliance between the two of them against the rest of the world. Speaking Russian, they were using the lingo of children and Lee was describing his old girlfriends. Marina asked him to tell her in advance if ever he was planning to be unfaithful. "If I were planning it, I wouldn't tell *you,*" he said, teasing. Suddenly he scrunched up his eyes. "Have you been with any other man since we got married?"

"Yes," she said.

"When?"

"When you were in Moscow."

"Tell me how it happened."

"You took the plane to Moscow. Leonid phoned the same day. We made a date for the evening. We had a wonderful dinner. He had bought wine at the French exhibition, and we had a very good time."

"Then what?"

"Then it was a very sad story. He wasn't able to do a thing. He was impotent."

"Why?" Lee asked.

Marina noticed that he was smiling and appeared uncertain whether to believe her or not. He was straining to catch every word.

"Because he was a virgin. And I wasn't about to be his teacher. I never wanted to see him again."

"And you didn't?"

"I ran into him once or twice on the street."

"And nothing happened?"

Marina, laughing: "You were home. Where on earth could we go?"

"You're making the whole thing up."

"No, I'm not," Marina said, adding that there had been nothing good in the experience. It had been a lesson to her for the whole of her life and had killed her desire for anyone but Lee.

Lee switched on the light and leaned over her. He had a skeptical, untrusting expression. "Look at me," he said. "Do you give me your word of honor that it really happened?" They had a game that whenever either of them said "word of honor," the other had to tell the truth.

"Word of honor," she answered.

"Enough of your lies," Lee said. "I want to sleep."

The next morning, as he was dressing for work, he brought up the subject again. "Is it true what you told me last night?" he asked.

"Yes."

"I don't believe it. You women are all alike. You want to make a man jealous." Then, suddenly: "If ever I see you with another man, I'll kill him right off."

"And what will you do to *me?*" Marina was amused.

"We'll see about *that.*"

Marina made her confession out of a desire to bid up her own value, a wish to make a clean breast of things, and a momentary lapse into the old trust and frankness that cropped up from time to time between them, especially on her side. Lee, for his part, refused to believe a word she had told him. He decided that her letter to Anatoly had been a ruse and her infidelity with Leonid a lie, and that both had been concocted by Marina to make him jealous. As usual he denied the plain truth, and thought up other "truths" instead.

Lee loved working at Jaggars-Chiles-Stovall. He signed in promptly every morning by 8:00 or 8:15, and stayed until 5:00 or 5:30 in the afternoon, often later.[6] He begged for overtime because it meant extra pay, and he came to work eagerly every Saturday whenever he was asked. He never missed a single day's work. Marina for the life of her could not understand what he did there, although he explained it in detail.

He would point to an ad in a Dallas paper. "See that!" he would exclaim. "I did that! Isn't Papa wonderful?"

"Why boast?" she would ask. "Why not leave it to others to praise you? Nice people don't praise themselves."

About mid-January, however, Lee began having trouble at work—trouble with the job itself and trouble with the other men. Everything had been going smoothly up until then. For his first three months there, he had been a trainee, and as promising as any other. But in January, his status became about the same as that of any other employee. He was expected to take more responsibility for the company's clients and see each piece of work through from start to finish. According to his supervisor, John G. Graef, who had hired him and had a stake in keeping him, Lee started to make mistakes—"too many mistakes." "It wasn't that he lacked industry or didn't try," Graef recalls; "he somehow couldn't manage to handle work that was that exact." Moreover, in the extremely tight confines of the darkroom, Graef concedes, Lee's "personality began to come out."[7]

Dennis Hyman Ofstein, who was a year younger than Lee and the closest thing he had to a friend at the plant, described Lee's behavior in more detail: "Well, we work in a rather tight area. There is little room to move around in the darkroom, just about enough room for a man to stand by the developing trays and allow one person to squeeze behind him and get by, and he would make it a habit of just bursting through there head-on with no regard to who was in the room . . . I think he thought he had the right of way in any case—either that or he was just in a hurry to get through, and through his hurrying he made no regard for anyone else's well-being or anyone else's jobs."[8]

At home, too, Lee began to make more trouble than usual. His quarrels with Marina now occurred over trifles. He was often cruel and capricious, and treated her harshly without any pretext. Sometimes he got so angry that he would stalk out cursing her in English. "That's lovely, Alka," Marina laughed. "Go right ahead. You can swear at me that way all night and all day and I won't understand a word."

Marina was more and more puzzled. One day Alka was the perfect husband, affectionate with her and the baby, while the next day he hit her for no reason. "I don't see how you can kiss me one day and beat me the next," she complained.

"We're young," Lee said. "We haven't yet learned to give in to each other yet. All couples quarrel over something."

"I know," she answered, commonsensically. "But not all husbands beat their wives."

They had their moments of tenderness. Lee worked on Saturday, January

26, from 8:00 in the morning until 5:30 in the afternoon. They went to bed early that evening, and about three the following morning Marina woke him, feeling sexual desire.

"What do you want?" he mumbled.

"I want a son," she said.

"But only last time you were crying. I thought you didn't want a baby."

"I want you to have a son."

"I want a son very much."

Marina did not want another child. But she felt lazy. She did not want to get out of bed and they made love without taking precautions. It was a "wonderful night" for Marina. She felt closer to Lee and closer to being satisfied by him sexually than ever before. But the next day she regretted what she had done. Nor did Lee show any happiness over the night before, or elation over the possibility of another child.[9] He had his mind elsewhere.

Lee had managed to save $600 to pay back his loans from Robert and the U.S. Department of State. Robert had been repaid by October 7. On January 25, in the form of two postal money orders totaling $106, he paid the final installment of the State Department loan. And on Sunday, January 27, free of debt for the first time since his return from Russia, Lee filled out a form and sent it to Seaport Traders, Inc., a mail order firm in Los Angeles. He enclosed $10 in cash and ordered the first of two weapons he was to acquire that year, a .38 special caliber Smith and Wesson revolver, whose barrel, originally 5 inches long, had been shortened to 2¼ inches. The balance of the cost of the revolver, $19.95 plus shipping charges, was to be paid on delivery.[10]

Lee did not order the gun in his own name. The form was signed "A. J. Hidell." The order had to be witnessed by someone who could attest that the signer was an American citizen and had not been convicted of a felony. The "witness" was "D. F. Drittal." Experts later testified that the signatures of "Drittal" and "Hidell," as well as the form itself, were in Oswald's handwriting.[11] The form contained one other lie: "Hidell" said he was twenty-eight years old. Oswald was twenty-three. The address to which the revolver was to be sent was Post Office Box 2915 at the Dallas General Post Office. From October 9, 1962, to May 14, 1963, this was the mailing address of Lee Harvey Oswald, at which he had also authorized "A. J. Hidell" and Marina Oswald to pick up mail.

The day after he ordered the revolver, on Monday, January 28, Lee committed himself to the typing course for which he had signed up tentatively two weeks earlier. He put down his $9 enrollment fee in cash and started to attend typing classes at Crozier Technical High School, which was only a few blocks from where he worked. George Bouhe had advised him to take the course. Typing, in combination with the photographic skills he was acquiring at Jaggars-Chiles-Stovall, would enable him to get a better job. They might even qualify him for a newspaper job and, as a matter of fact, Lee had already put out feelers for part-time work as a stringer in photography.

Soon after going to work at Jaggars-Chiles-Stovall, Lee had persuaded his colleague, Dennis Hyman Ofstein, to teach him techniques he did not know, using the company's lab and materials after hours, a practice the company tried to discourage. First, Lee made sample calling cards for himself and for George de Mohrenschildt.[12] Then he made other samples of his work, which he sent to two left-wing newspapers in New York: *The Militant,* newspaper of the Socialist Workers Party, the Trotskyite party in the United States; and *The Worker,* the newspaper of the Communist Party. Lee had begun corresponding with both organizations soon after his return from Russia, and he subscribed to both newspapers. Now he offered his services in printing and photographic work. In reply, *The Worker* thanked him for his "poster-like blow-ups" and said that "from time to time we shall call on you."[13]

The typing class, his photographic skills, and his effort to obtain free-lance work on a left-wing newspaper fitted well with the peaceful expression of Lee's political ideas. But the night typing course fitted in with something else as well. It gave Lee a cover, so that he would not have to account for his evenings to anyone.

The typing class met three nights a week, on Mondays, Tuesdays, and Thursdays, from 6:15 to 7:15, but when he started the course it seemed to Marina that Lee was never home any week night before seven, and he often came in even later. Marina also noticed that her husband spent a great deal of time by himself in the kitchen. He did not have a typewriter to practice on, but he had a large textbook with a printed keyboard. He sat bent over the textbook and seemed to be writing out lessons. But he had a bus schedule, too, and two or three maps of Dallas. He was studying a layout of the city and Marina, of course, asked why. He answered that he was trying to figure out the quickest way from work to night school, and he told her not to make any noise. Marina never looked closely at the maps, never realized that Jaggars-Chiles-Stovall and Crozier Tech were only a few blocks apart, and never stopped to ask herself—he had trained her that way —why it seemed to be taking him so long, hunched over the kitchen table, to puzzle out so straightforward a question. In fact, Lee now had three, not two, ports of call in downtown Dallas: his job, night school, and the main post office at Bryan and Ervay Streets, where he had his post office box. All three were within easy walking distance. The bus schedules and maps had almost certainly nothing to do with his work or night school.

It was also at about this time, toward the end of January, that Lee began to hint to Marina that he was thinking of sending her and the baby back to Russia. He complained that it was hard supporting a family in America. Alone, he would not have to worry so much about holding onto his job. He could live in a rooming house, learn how to drive, and buy a car. Then, if he lost one job, he could pick up and move to another town.

His hints made Marina feel even more miserable, guilty, and "in the way." "Alka doesn't love me," she thought. She felt that she was the sole cause of his increasing irritability and that marrying her had ruined some far-reaching scheme he had for his life. "You needn't have brought me to America," she said. "You could have left me behind."

Although his hints were more than enough to poison her frame of mind, she did not really believe them. "He has started speaking Russian so badly, he no longer knows what he is saying," she said to herself. "Besides, he gets pleasure out of tormenting me." But the fact is, Lee knew very well what he was saying, and he did indeed have a far-reaching scheme. It is a scheme he may already have had in mind when he took the Elsbeth Street apartment in early November. Alexandra Taylor noticed that on the day he moved in, he inspected all the doors and windows with care, perhaps to check whether the neighbors could witness his comings and goings.

22

The Sanction

FOR MARINA, the month of February 1963 was far and away the worst in all her married life. Lee had been hitting her ever since they arrived in America; in February there was a dramatic change in the style and ferocity with which he did it. No longer did he strike her once across the face with the flat of his hand. Now he hit her five or six times—and with his fists. The second he got angry, he turned pale and pressed his lips tightly together. His eyes were filled with hate. His voice dropped to a murmur and she could not understand what he was saying. When he started to strike her, his face became red and his voice grew angry and loud. He wore a look of concentration, as if Marina were the author of every slight he had ever suffered and he was bent on wiping her out, obliterating her completely. To Marina it seemed that it was not even a human being he saw in front of him. Most horrifying of all was the gleam of pleasure in his eyes.

Their fights occurred over nothing, with Lee's anger ballooning up quickly, out of all proportion to the occasion. He became even stingier than usual, and if by accident Marina left some item off the grocery list she gave him, or if she went to a store herself and bought some item, no matter how cheap, that they did not absolutely require, it might be the cause of another beating.

Marina could defend herself only with words. "Your beating me shows your upbringing," she said on one occasion.

"Leave my mother out of this!" Lee cried, and struck her harder than before.

He stored up every grievance, and at the tiniest pinprick from her, they all came pouring out. "I'm not hitting you just for *this,*" he would say, naming the pretext of the fight, "but because I'll never forgive you for running off to your Russians. Oh, what humiliation you made me suffer. Always you go against me! You never, ever do what I want!" Or, if they were fighting over one thing, he would ask, "Do you think I've forgotten *that?*" and bring up something entirely different. "I'll never, ever forget."

Marina yearned for some sign of affection. But whenever she tried to wheedle it out of him, he would say, "I know what you want," meaning sex, and Marina's feelings were so hurt that she would run from the room. His sexual demands were violent. Late on a Saturday or Sunday afternoon he might bark at her: "Stop washing the dishes. Lee's hot!" and try to force himself upon her. He insisted on having sex any time he felt like it, whether Marina wanted it or not. He would pin her down by the arms and legs and take her by force while the tears came pouring down her cheeks.

Marina thought that it was only the violence, the struggle, that made him want her at all. Once she told him he was "crazy."

"What's that you said?"

"You're crazy."

He grabbed her by the throat and threatened to kill her if ever she said that again.

But the complaint that came up like a refrain was her disloyalty in "running off" to "her Russians." When she asked why he had begged her to come back, he said it was only because of the baby.

"It wasn't me you needed at all?"

"No—not at all."

"There's nothing for me here, then," Marina said, crushed.

On another occasion he told her he had asked her back to prove that he had power over her, more power than Bouhe and the other Russians, and that "I could get you back if I felt like it."

"What on earth do you want from me, Alka? What is it you need?"

"You're my property," he said, "and I'll do with you as I please. So long as I want you, you'll stay. If not—then off with you. Don't you forget as long as you live that you belong to me any time I want."

In Minsk, Lee had urged Marina more than once, in matters outside their home, to stand up for herself, "be her own person" and express her individuality. But now he behaved like a slaveowner, smiling triumphantly when he had forced her to beg his forgiveness. Wistfully Marina recalled a halcyon time, the Stone Age, she thought it was, when she read that there had been matriarchy before patriarchy reared its ugly head. She wished she were in a matriarchy now. Looking back on it with wry humor, Marina describes their life together as "a period of slave ownership with a number of slave revolts in between." She adds with regret, however, that the "slave revolts" were quickly put down by force.

At work, Lee's behavior was also growing more erratic. One day in the darkroom, Lee and another man, each hurrying as usual to meet a deadline, were trying to develop film in the same pan. The man asked Lee to move over a little, and Lee refused, saying he had gotten there first. In the midst of narrow aisles and delicate equipment, they were on the edge of fisticuffs when John Graef spotted trouble on the far side of the darkroom and moved in to break it up. It was this incident that awakened Graef to the fact that of the eighteen or twenty men in the photographic department, not one liked Lee. Graef was slowly reaching the conclusion that "everybody couldn't be wrong."[1]

Lee was also growing more and more secretive. When he starting typing school, he began to sign out of work half to three-quarters of an hour later than he had before. On Wednesdays, when he did not have a class, he regularly, and from the outset, signed out even later. It is possible that during this time, when most of the other employees had gone home, Lee rifled the files of Jaggars-Chiles-Stovall and reproduced its tax returns, an item he later appended to a curriculum vitae as an example of his photographic proficiency.[2] And it is possible that it was at this time that he produced the forged documents later found in his possession: a Selective Service notice of classification and a Marine Corps certificate of service, both in the name of Alik James Hidell—the name he had used to order the revolver. It is also likely that on his way from work to typing class, he regularly stopped by the post office to see if the gun had arrived, which would account for the fact that he often "slipped into" class late and out of breath.[3]

Lee's increasing inability to control himself both at home and at work suggests that emotionally he was in turmoil. What cannot be known is whether his deterioration was the result of a cumulative process that had been taking place for months, or whether in January he suffered some sort of precipitous "break-down," triggered perhaps by Marina's letter to Anatoly on January 7, her brief pregnancy scare on the 10th with its hint of added responsibility, and her subsequent confession of infidelity. The previous fall, in his correspondence with the Socialist Workers Party and the Communist Party, Lee had made tentative moves toward the peaceful expression of his political views. Signing up for night school on January 14 fitted in with that plan; but it may also have been an indication that he had conceived another plan—a violent, destructive expression of his political views that would require a cover. Ordering a revolver on January 27 under a false name, and his hints to Marina starting the same day that he was thinking of sending her back to Russia without him, both suggest that he was leaning further toward violence. And during the first week of February, he twice misdated his time sheets at Jaggars-Chiles-Stovall. It was the sort of error he made when he was under stress and in conflict. Gradually, with what appears to have been pain, he was reaching a decision to use the gun.

On Wednesday, February 13, Lee and Marina went to a dinner party at the De Mohrenschildts'. The party had been organized around a showing of the De Mohrenschildts' film about their adventures in Mexico. Lee had seen the movie before, so he simply ignored it. The other guests, and there were six or eight of them, remember Lee and another young man standing in the center of the room all evening locked in conversation. Each of them stood out: Lee for the informality of his attire (he was wearing slacks and an open-collared shirt while the rest of the men were in business suits), the other for his blond, unmistakably German good looks. He was Volkmar Schmidt, twenty-seven or twenty-eight years old, a bachelor, and a geologist for Dallas's Magnolia Laboratory of Standard Oil of New York. Schmidt had arrived only recently from Germany and was going back there in a week or two on holiday.

Presumably Lee was interested in Germany, and Schmidt in Lee's account of his experiences in Russia. But George de Mohrenschildt must have been astonished by the rapport between these two young men whose politics, he knew, ought rightly to have set them at war. Lee was a liberal. Schmidt was not. George happened to like Schmidt, but he teased him for being a rabid reactionary, and it was one of his many jokes to call him "Messer Schmidt," after the Nazi fighter plane of World War II.[4]

It is not known what Lee and Schmidt discussed, although Schmidt did say later their conversation lasted "several hours" and had been about politics. Schmidt remarked that Lee was "very frank" and "very articulate in his descriptions of U.S. and Russian societies." He felt that he had a "burning dedication to political truth." He also felt that the young American had enormous ambition but was resigned, because of his limited education, to being unable ever to fulfill it. Summing up his impression of Lee, Schmidt said: "Oswald did not express any views which would indicate violent future action but appeared to be a violent person."[5]

George drove Lee and Marina home after the party, and the talk at first was of nothing but Volkmar Schmidt. George was at the wheel of his convertible, with Lee and Marina in the back seat. Marina remembers Lee's intense concentration on every word George said, and the use by both of them, for the first time in her hearing, of the word "Fascist," which is the same in both Russian and English.

"Just imagine." George leaned back toward Lee and spoke in Russian. "Such a young man! Yet a Fascist from his brains to his bones!"

"Oh, I liked him," Marina said. "Fancy meeting a real, live Fascist! Are there really any in America?"

"A whole organization," George explained, in Russian again, and he described the John Birch Society. Schmidt's ideas, he added, were much like those of the Birchers. "He has such frightful ideas it would make your hair stand on end."

Then they began to speak in English, a sign that George and Lee were talking politics. Marina could not follow what they were saying, but she has always felt that this evening was a turning point in Lee's life. She believes that Lee pounced on some remark George made, a remark that affected his later actions. She suspects that George said something that inadvertently, in her words, "influenced Lee's sick fantasy," and that Lee, having seized the idea, squirreled it away out of sight so that neither she nor George would guess where it came from.

Not only did George hate the John Birch Society, he was also convinced that a group of Birchers and FBI men had together broken into his apartment while he was in Mexico and rifled his papers. He and Lee had often discussed the John Birch Society and its most visible spokesman, General Edwin A. Walker. Just what it was that George may have said or implied about them on this occasion, or in some earlier discussion, is a matter for speculation. Samuel Ballen, who was George's closest friend at that time, says that in conversation with Lee as with everybody else, "unconventional, shocking, humorous and irreverent ideas would have been coming out of George all the time." Asked whether he might have said something like this to Lee about Walker—"Anybody who bumps that bastard off will be doing this country a favor"—Ballen answers, "Exactly."[6] Marina and the

Fords agree that these words, or words very like them, were probably spoken by George to Lee on the night of February 13 and possibly on other occasions as well.

What George did not know was that Lee already was thinking of killing Walker. He had ordered his weapon and had been studying maps for two weeks. But he was not yet wholly committed to the deed. Had he been, and had his pistol arrived, he could have shot at Walker that very day, for he had given a well-publicized speech that afternoon on the campus of Southern Methodist University, not far from where De Mohrenschildt lived. Lee was still hesitating.

The evening of February 13 may have been the catalyst Lee required. First there was his talk with Schmidt, who was rumored to be the son of an S.S. officer and who may have reminded Lee of the attempt on Hitler's life by officers of his own staff in 1944 which, had it been successful, might have ended the war early and saved the lives of many Germans. Then there was his talk with George, who may again have equated the John Birch Society and General Walker with the "Fascist threat" in the United States. Lee was later to say that "If someone had killed Hitler in time, many lives would have been saved." He was not original in the way he phrased things, and in this case even his words may have come from Schmidt or De Mohrenschildt. It hardly matters. With or without them to say it for him, it is clear that Lee looked on Walker as the "Hitler" of tomorrow.

So did George, and in this consonance of views with a man whom he admired and whom he very much wanted to impress, Lee may have found the sanction —the permission—he needed to go ahead with his plan. He would at one stroke win George's respect and even awe, save the United States from fascism, and prove to the world that Lee Harvey Oswald was a dedicated idealist willing to make any sacrifice for the sake of his political beliefs.

As it happened, on the next day the Dallas *Morning News* announced that Walker would join the well-known right-wing evangelist Billy James Hargis in a cross-country speaking tour to warn against the dangers of communism. The tour, to be called "Operation Midnight Ride," was to begin February 27 in Miami and end in Los Angeles on April 3. Dallas was not on the itinerary.

On the night of the De Mohrenschildts' party, February 13, or the night after the announcement of the Walker tour, February 14, Marina is not sure which, she heard Lee talking in his sleep. He spoke very loudly and enunciated each word so clearly that Marina sat upright in bed, thinking he was talking to her. But he was speaking in English, not Russian, and was repeating the same words again and again. Marina did not understand what he was saying, but it was the first time he had talked in his sleep since they were in Minsk, when Lee was making up his mind to return to the United States and was afraid that he would be arrested by American officials.

The next morning Marina repeated Lee's words to him.

"Where did you find *that* out?" Lee looked stunned.

"You told me in your sleep."

"Wake me up next time."

"And what were you saying?" Marina as always was afraid he was talking about an old girlfriend.

"Nothing at all." He smiled one of his enigmatic smiles. "Better for you not to know."

"I'll know *all* your secrets soon."

Again, he said nothing. But he was anxious after that and once or twice in the weeks that followed asked whether he had talked in his sleep the night before.

Right after the initial announcement, there were more stories about Walker's anti-Communist, anti-Castro crusade. They made Walker seem very real, very human, and very close. Indeed, he was close; he lived in Dallas just across the river from Lee. The stories must have been electrifying to Lee, yet filled him with anxiety at the same time. Either he must kill Walker right away, or he would have to wait for six weeks, until Walker returned from his tour. Meanwhile the revolver had not arrived, a choice of weapon which indicated that Lee meant to kill Walker at close range and at the risk of his life. There seemed to be no question of obtaining another weapon. Lee was not the man, at any time, to show his face in a gun shop and buy a weapon openly.

Lee was apparently very anxious for his gun to arrive. His colleagues John Graef and Dennis Ofstein remember that he was always headed for the post office when he left work, and yet whenever they offered him a ride he invariably declined. He was checking for his gun. He could pick up a package at the post office only between 8:00 and 5:30 on weekdays, hours when he was normally at work, or between 8:00 and 12 noon on Saturdays. On Friday, February 15, the day after the Walker trip was announced, Lee signed out of work at 5:15 P.M., early enough to pick up a package at the post office. The next morning, Saturday, for the only time in all his months at Jaggars-Chiles-Stovall, he signed in at 9:00 A.M., a full hour later than usual, an indication that he may again have stopped by the post office hoping to pick up the revolver. It was not there.

That same day Lee received another piece of news that must have confounded his plans and emotions—until he found a way to fit them together. Marina told him on his return from work that she was pregnant. This time she was sure of it. Lee was pleased. Marina was not. What do you expect, he asked, when you don't even bother to take precautions? June had had her first birthday only the day before, and Lee said: "Very good. Junie is one year old and Mama is cooking up a present. A baby brother. What better present could there be?" He crowed and exclaimed for a day or two and then, uncharacteristically, he seemed to forget all about it. He did not take Marina to a doctor.

On Sunday, February 17, the Dallas *Morning News* carried a long feature story on Walker's "crusade." It was the story that made Walker seem the closest and most human of any, and it stressed the anti-Castro side of his trip. On that very day Lee made good his earlier threats. He forced Marina, a Soviet citizen, to sit down and write to Nikolai Reznichenko, chief of the consular section of the Soviet Embassy in Washington, asking officially that she and June be allowed to return to the U.S.S.R. alone, without Lee. In a message that was dictated by Lee, Marina asked the embassy to give her "material aid" for the journey. Having moved heaven and earth to get his wife and child out of Russia, Lee, less than a year later, was asking the Soviet government to pay for their return.[7]

Marina's handwriting, which is usually neat, was sloppy and the message brief and casual, almost to the point of disrespect. She must have been distraught and seems also to have been seeking to sabotage her husband's purpose. She adored America and had constantly pleaded with Lee: "Do anything. But don't ever, ever make me go back!" She had no idea of her husband's motive, nor did he say a word to enlighten her. And so she simply supposed that he no longer loved her and that she had become to him what she had been to nearly everyone else all her life, unloved and "in the way." She would be going back to relatives who did not want her and with the stigma of her husband's rejection. All this, plus her pregnancy, was very nearly more than she could bear.

Marina was waking up to how calculating Lee could be—and how far ahead he laid his plans. But she merely suspected that he wanted her out of the way in time for expenses of the new baby's birth to be paid by the U.S.S.R., and, in part, she was probably right.

Yet Lee usually had several objectives at once. For one thing, he seldom slammed a door. He always left it open a crack just in case he decided to pass through again. When he defected to Russia, he failed to take the oath renouncing his American citizenship, a simple act that would have irrevocably prevented his return. And when he did return, he hinted to officers of the FBI, the Soviet Embassy—and Marina herself—that he might want to go back to Russia. That was a major reason why he refused to allow Marina to learn English or become too attached to American life. His restlessness can perhaps be traced to an incapacity to accept responsibility, for Marina, his children—or himself. He had expected the Soviet government to take care of him while he was in Russia and he had expected the American government to pay for his journey home. In Texas, he had maneuvered the Russian émigrés into helping him, and now it was once again the Soviet government's turn. His actions had a thread of consistency. Only days after he learned of Marina's first pregnancy in Minsk, he had set in motion the machinery for their return to America. The day after he learned of her second pregnancy, in Dallas, he began to prepare for her return to Russia.

This time, however, it was different. A pregnant Marina, and June, were to go back to Russia alone. It fitted with Lee's plan to kill Walker. On the day he ordered his revolver, January 27, he first hinted to Marina that he was thinking of sending her back to Russia—to get her used to the idea. And the week he seems to have decided that he would actually carry out the scheme, he took the initial steps for her return.

At first, Lee had probably assumed that a close-up assault on Walker would immediately result in his own death. Then it seems to have occurred to him that he might be captured alive. Killing Walker would be perceived by everyone as a political statement against "fascism" and the American right. From his prison cell, or in a trial, he could enunciate that statement, and the Soviet government would approve. He would ask for asylum in Russia. With Marina and his child already there, the American government might agree to expatriate him, and the Soviet government might agree to accept him. By sending Marina and June to Russia, then, he would be creating his own asylum in advance.

The plan was unrealistic—but it was Lee.

The week after Lee forced Marina to write to the Soviet Embassy was the most violent in all their married life. As his anxiety mounted, she was increasingly the object of his rages. He showed no concern for her pregnancy and treated her in a manner that reached the point of ferocity. One day he hit Marina so hard across the face that her nose started bleeding. The moment Lee saw blood, his arms fell motionless to his sides. "Oh my God. I didn't mean *that.* I didn't mean *that.*" He made Marina lie down. But his anger was not spent. He slammed the door and went out. He found the front and back doors locked when he came home. Quietly, he smashed a pane of glass in the kitchen door, then coolly reached in and unlocked it. He scooped up the pieces of glass and piled them neatly on top of the kitchen trash. He strode into the bedroom and, without a word to Marina, lay down on the bed with his back to her.

As baffling as his anger were his repentances, for sometimes his fury departed quickly. Then he would burst into tears and beg Marina's forgiveness. At the sight of his tears she, too, would burst into tears, and the two of them would cling to one another and cry. Marina, of course, saw that Lee was in terrible inner turmoil. She had no idea what was causing it, and told herself that perhaps he struck out at *her* because he had to hold himself in at work and she was the only person he could get angry at. She also told herself that she was to blame, that she brought on many of their quarrels, and that her punishments were the least she deserved. She continued to beg for affection—he had none to spare.

Marina, too, was at the breaking point and her tongue lost none of its acerbity. Lee warned her to watch out, begged her not to egg him on. "You know my terrible character," he pleaded with her after one of their fights. "When you see I'm in a bad mood, try not to make me mad. You know I can't hold myself in very long now." But Marina continued to lash out at him. Her sharp words probably brought on a few beatings, but they also helped keep her intact, helped her feel that she was still a human being in spite of humiliations that imperiled her fragile self-respect.

"You weak, cowardly American," she would say to him, bitter at the choice she had made. "What a fool I was! I was afraid to marry a Russian because Russian men beat their wives. You! You're not worth the soles of their feet. How I wish I had woken up sooner!"

Lee, of course, hit her. "I'll *make* you shut up," he said.

"Of course you can shut me up by force. But you'll never change my mind. It's better to be a drunkard than what you are. When a drunken man beats you, it's one thing. When a sober one does it, it's something else."

Marina survived Lee's beatings, she struggled to survive them, but what did not survive was her respect for Lee. She went on loving him, in a way. But she was beginning to see him as a sick man who needed help.

The crisis came on February 23, General Walker's last Saturday in Dallas. Lee did not go to work. He was gone the whole day; his whereabouts and activities are unknown. He may have been spying on Walker but he was not stalking him —the revolver had not arrived.

Before going out that morning, Lee had asked Marina to fix him something special for dinner, a Southern dish called red beans and rice. Marina had never heard of it. But Hungarian dishes have a good deal of rice, so she took her Hungarian cookbook off the shelf and pored over it. She found nothing helpful there and fell back as usual on Mother Russia. She put everything in a skillet and cooked it with onions.

Lee started scolding her the second he got home. He told her that she ought to fix the rice separately and then pour the beans over it.

"What on earth difference does it make?" she asked. "You mix the whole thing into a mess on your plate anyway."

"I work," Lee complained. "I come home and I find you can't even do a simple thing like this for me."

"And of course I sit home all day with nothing to do but spit on the ceiling." Marina threw down her cooking spoon, told Lee to fix it himself, and stomped out of the kitchen.

Lee came after her and ordered her to fix his dinner.

"I won't."

"You will."

"I won't."

"I'll force you to."

Marina stomped back into the kitchen and threw the whole dinner out.

The next thing she knew she was in the bedroom and he was about to hit her. "You have no right," she said. "If you lay a finger on me, I'll throw this at you." She was holding a pretty wooden box, a present from a friend in Minsk. It was heavy with jewelry: Lee's cufflinks and watch and all Marina's beads and pins.

He hit her hard across the face, then whirled and started to leave the room. Marina hurled the box as hard as she could and it grazed Lee's shoulder. He spun around and came at her white with rage. His lips were pressed together and he had an inhuman look of hate on his face. He hurled her onto the bed and grabbed her throat. "I won't let you out of this alive."

Just at that second the baby cried.

Lee suddenly came to his senses. "Go get her," he ordered.

"Go get her yourself." Another second, Marina thinks, and he would have strangled her. She had never seen him in such fury.

Lee went to the baby and sat alone with her in the next room for a long time while Marina lay on the bed and sobbed. She was shocked and ashamed. Why go on living if Lee would not spare her even while she was carrying their child? And why bear children to be witnesses of such a life? Lee did not treat her like a human being. For five minutes he was kind to her—then cruel. Why on earth had he brought her to America if he only meant to send her back? A hundred thoughts went through her head, and then turned to apathy. The baby cried and she scarcely heard. She went into the bathroom, glanced into the mirror, and saw bruises all over her face.

"Who on earth needs me?" she wondered. "The one person I came to America for doesn't need me, so why go on living?"

She picked up the rope she used for hanging the baby's diapers, tied it around her neck, and climbed onto the toilet seat.

Lee came in from the living room. A glance at Marina and his face became horribly twisted. Even at that moment he could not control his rage. He hit her across the face.

"Don't ever, ever do that again," he said. "Only the most terrible fools try *that.*"

"I can't go on this way, Alka. I don't want to go on living."

Lee lifted her off the toilet seat and carried her gently to bed. He went back to the baby in the living room, with the door open so he could watch Marina. Then he sat beside her on the bed and tenderly stroked her hair.

"Forgive me," he said. "I didn't mean to do what I did. It's *your* fault. You saw what a mood I was in. Why did you make me so mad?"

"I only tried to do to myself what *you* tried to do to me. I'm sick of it, Alka. Every day we fight, and for no reason. We fight over things so tiny, normal people wouldn't speak of them at all."

Lee lay down and took her in his arms. "I never thought you'd take it so hard. Pay no attention to me now. You know I can't hold myself back."

They both began to cry like babies. "Try to understand," he begged. "You're wrong sometimes, too. Try to be quiet when you can." He started kissing her as though he were in a frenzy. "For God's sake, forgive me. I'll never, ever do it again. I'll try and change if you'll only help me."

"But why, Alka, why do you do it?"

"Because I love you. I can't stand it when you make me mad."

They made love the whole night long, and Lee told Marina again and again that she was "the best woman" for him, sexually and in every other way. For Marina, it was one of their best nights sexually. And for the next few days, Lee seemed calmer, as if his attempt to strangle Marina had been a substitute for killing Walker. In conflict over his plan, frustrated by the failure of the gun to arrive as the day approached when Walker would be leaving Dallas, Lee had taken out his rage on Marina.

For weeks the Oswalds' neighbors had been troubled by the sounds of discord from their apartment. As far back as December, a comparatively peaceful time, the noise already was ominous enough so that one neighbor went to Mahlon Tobias, the building manager, and complained, "I think he's *really* hurt her this time." Mrs. Tobias cooked up a pretext and dropped by to see if Marina was all right.[8]

When the noise grew even louder, and the frightened baby began to wake up, wailing, in the middle of the night, another neighbor complained to Tobias: "I think that man over there is going to kill that girl."[9]

Tobias went to Mr. and Mrs. William Martin Jurek, the owners of the building, who in turn paid a call on Lee, warning him that he and his wife would have to stop fighting or move. Lee tried to shrug it off, but the visit told him what he was uncomfortably aware of already. He had too many neighbors on Elsbeth Street, too many eyes and ears upon him. His movements were being observed.

People knew he was beating his wife. What might they notice next?

Lee kept the Jureks' visit secret from Marina. But he made up his mind to move. As usual, he scouted "For Rent" signs in the neighborhood, not newspaper ads, and before the week was out he announced to a startled Marina that he had found them a new place to live. If she liked it as well as he did, they would move.

It was on the second floor of a building at 214 West Neely Street, only about a block from the Elsbeth Street apartment. It was cleaner than the place they had and the rent was less, $60 a month instead of $68. But the big attraction was a balcony. "Just like our balcony in Minsk," Lee said. "You can plant flowers on it. And it's healthier for Junie. She can crawl out there and you needn't watch her all the time." He also pointed out one of the apartment's other advantages. There were fewer neighbors there, fewer witnesses to their comings and goings. He would like that, he said.

The greatest attraction, however, as far as Lee was concerned, was a tiny room, not much bigger than a double coat closet, which he could use as a study. And this "study" had a strikingly unusual feature: two entrances, one from the stairs outside the apartment and one from the living room. Lee could lock both doors, and enter and leave the apartment without Marina's knowledge.

Marina was content on Elsbeth Street. She had fixed up the place so it suited her perfectly. Even more important, she hated to hurt the Tobiases' feelings. They had been good to her. She knew nothing of the warning Lee had received, and it embarrassed her to leave for no reason people who had befriended her. But she gave in, as usual. "After all," she said to herself, "it doesn't really matter to me. And I like the balcony, too."

So, on Saturday, March 2, they piled their belongings—Lee's books, the baby's things, a few dishes—on top of the baby's stroller. With that, the clothing in their arms, and the baby herself, they walked away from Elsbeth Street, owing a couple of days' rent.

Tobias and his wife looked on. They were sad to see Marina go. A few days later, Mrs. Tobias told the FBI that the Oswalds had moved. A report by Agent James P. Hosty, Jr., of the Dallas office of the FBI, dated September 10, 1963, contained this item:

On March 11, 1963, Mrs. M. F. Tobias, apartment manager, 602 Elsbeth, Dallas, Texas, advised [that] on March 3, 1963, Lee Harvey Oswald and his wife Marina moved from that apartment building to 214 West Neely Street in Dallas, Texas. Mrs. Tobias advised they had considerable difficulty with Mr. Oswald who apparently drank to excess and beat his wife on numerous occasions. They had numerous complaints from the other tenants due to Oswald's drinking and beating his wife.

Lee's suspicion that he was being watched was not altogether ill-founded.

23

"Ready for Anything"

GENERAL WALKER left Dallas on February 28, two days before the Oswalds moved to West Neely Street.[1] Lee's plan had to be postponed, and the move itself may have been a welcome sidetrack. Now he had time. Walker would be gone for five or six weeks. During that breathing space, Lee could reconsider his plan; he would compose his mind as he had not been able to do before; and, above everything, he could write the justification for history that appears to have been nearly as important to him as the deed itself. Now that he had decided to go ahead, but in his own way and in his own time, Lee's behavior changed dramatically. His violence toward Marina almost stopped and he hit her rarely, if at all. From having been absorbed by turmoil within, he now shifted to the world outside, and in that world he moved with speed and efficiency.

Marina supposed his new calm to be a product of their move, experience having taught her that any move to a new apartment bought her a few days of peace. Sure enough, Lee devoted his first two evenings on Neely Street to fixing up the apartment. He was handy at carpentry, building window boxes for the balcony and painting them green. He also built shelves for his special room and moved in a chair and a table, creating his own tiny office. Marina realized that it was this "office," and not the balcony he had used as bait for her, that was the reason he had moved them to Neely Street.

"Look," he said to her. "This is my little nook. I've never had my own room before. I'll do all my work here, make a lab and do my photography. I'll keep my things in here. But you're not to come in and clean. If ever I come in and find that one single thing has been touched, I'll beat you."

Marina, who had been warned often enough not to pry into her husband's affairs, of course complied.

They again had something of a life together as man and wife. Once or twice Lee asked her if she loved him.

267

"I do," she said.

"Why?"

"For your beautiful legs and your bottom and your ugly disposition."

He removed his trousers and stared at himself in the mirror. The sight seemed to please him. "Do I really have beautiful legs?" he asked.

"You do."

Trousers off, he would sit with legs extended on the coffee table, or he would drape a leg and a thigh over one arm of the sofa, his way of asking for a kiss or, if they had had an argument, of asking to make up.

When he took a bath, he would ask her to wash him. First he stretched one leg in the air. When she had finished and was ready to do the other leg, he would say No, the right one wasn't clean yet. He made her wash one leg four or five times before he would consent to raise the other. "Now I feel like a king," he would say, beatifically. But he cautioned her to be more gentle. "I have sensitive skin, while you have rough, Russian ways."

Next, he would refuse to get out of the tub, his complaint being that the floor was cold, and he told her to put a towel down for him. When she had done as he asked, she would say, "Okay, prince, you can get out now."

At her urging, Lee at last read *All Quiet on the Western Front* by Erich Maria Remarque, a great favorite in Russia. He was not impressed. He closed the book with a disgusted air, went to the public library, and took out a biography of Leon Trotsky. That was more to his liking.

One evening, in a romantic mood, he asked her to put on the red brocade dress she had worn on the evening they met. Marina was amused, reflecting that she was not a Cinderella at a ball any more, but a wife who was pregnant with her second child.

He even remembered that she was pregnant. Whenever Marina saw Lee on the bed, his arms folded under his head, gazing up at the ceiling, she knew he was thinking about the new baby. Once or twice he asked her to lie down beside him. Which side ached most, he wanted to know, and what were her other symptoms? He was heartened to hear that her symptoms were different from those while she was carrying June.

"This time it's sure to be a boy. Our David is going to be President!"

Marina, too, wanted a boy, but to please Lee, not because she wanted any son of hers to be President. She thought politics was sick, and that anyone engaged in politics had to be sick as well. "Don't make me laugh," she said. "You can hardly support a family, much less give our son the education he needs to be President. A President has to go to college."

"Not all Presidents have been to college," Lee said.

Marina's feelings about having the child were still mixed. She was reluctant and ashamed, anxious to conceal from the other Russians that Bouhe's prophecy had been fulfilled. Since it *had* happened, however, she told herself that there was merit in having two children close together. They would both be in school that much sooner. Then she would go back to work and support Lee so he could go to college.

Lee was not thinking about college. Sitting in the kitchen that first week of March, he asked Marina to fetch him his Sears, Roebuck catalogue. Marina was overjoyed. He was going to buy a present for her and June. She brought him the catalogue, then crept behind his chair to see what he was going to buy. Abruptly, he snapped the catalogue shut. Next time she got a better look. It was not dresses or toys he was looking at. He was reading the section on rifles.

Lee's life appears to have been fairly normal that first week of March. He signed in and out of work at regular hours and seems to have attended typing class as usual. Mrs. Gladys A. Yoakum, his teacher, has described him as a young man who liked to "slip in, unobserved," while her "back was turned." Instead of sitting up front by the keyboard chart with the other beginners, where she could help him, Lee "gravitated" from the outset to the back-row seat beside the window. Thus Mrs. Yoakum never had occasion to give him individual attention. Nor did she see what he was typing. She noticed, however, that each night he brought his textbook wrapped in brown paper or a brown paper bag, unwrapped it, propped it up in front of him, and typed from it, or from something he placed inside it, throughout class. Mrs. Yoakum says that he could easily have been typing something of his own without her noticing it. She recalls that she "never once saw him talk to anyone else, or come in or leave with anyone else." She also noticed that he sometimes left a little early. She assumed that Lee, like some of her other students, was taking the course to escape an unhappy marriage.[2]

It is not known what he was typing in class, but it may have been drafts of a letter to *The Militant* which Lee almost certainly wrote, and which appeared in the March 11 issue under the heading: "News and Views from Dallas," signed with the initials "L.H."[3] The author of the letter praised the paper as "the most informative radical publication in America," but criticized it for failing to publish more about reform movements inside the Democratic Party, especially in California and New York, and about an Independent campaign for the U.S. Senate in Massachusetts. The writer then described the case of a Mrs. Marie Ortiz, of Dallas, who had been left ill and unable to work with six children, and who had also suffered a fire. "Would it not be better to fundamentally reform the social conditions which are presently the cause of unemployment . . . than to rely on the sympathy of a few of the rich at Christmas . . . ?"

The letter has several features that help trace it to Lee. Among the most telling are the caustic reference to Christmas, and the sarcastic remark that "some kind person" had suggested to Mrs. Ortiz that "she turn her children over to an orphanage," but "she replied that she did not wish to live without her children." The remark appears to reflect Lee's own bitterness over having been sent to an orphanage and his desire that his mother, like Mrs. Ortiz, had refused "to live without her children."[4]

Sunday, March 10, marked the first known deviation from Lee's routine that month. He rode a bus to the vicinity of No. 4011 Turtle Creek Boulevard, the home of General Walker, and took photographs.[5] Five survive: one shows the alley behind Walker's house; two show the rear of the house itself; and two a set of railway tracks running through woods about half a mile from the house.[6] Lee probably took more than five photographs, for Marina recalls that he later told her that "he wanted to leave a complete record so that all the details would be in it. He told me that the entries [in a notebook he kept] consisted of the description of the house of General Walker, the distances, the location, and the distribution of windows in it."[7] These entries were almost certainly accompanied by the photographs.

Lee probably developed the photographs at work the following evening, March 11, and something—his study of Walker's house or the photographs—convinced him that a different crime was possible from the close-up, virtually suicidal act he had had in mind in January when he ordered his revolver. *This* crime could be committed at a distance. From it he had a chance of escape.

Thus, on March 12, using not the Sears catalogue but a coupon clipped from the February issue of *American Rifleman* magazine, Lee went to the main post office and ordered a high-powered Italian carbine, called a Mannlicher-Carcano, from Klein's Sporting Goods Company, a mail order house in Chicago. He sent the coupon air mail with a postal money order for $21.45 ($12.78 for the rifle, $7.17 for the scope, to be mounted by a gunsmith employed by Klein's, and $1.50 for postage and handling). The rifle was to be delivered to "A. Hidell, Post Office Box 2915, Dallas, Texas."[8]

About the same day Lee ordered the rifle, he received a letter from his brother Robert, whom he had last seen four months before. Robert wrote that his company had promoted him and transferred him to Malvern, Arkansas. He asked Lee and Marina to visit, adding that occasionally he came to Dallas and would like Lee's home address so he could stop in and see the family or, if Lee was not at home, at least visit June and Marina.[9]

Lee's reply is revealing.[10] It hints at the affection he felt for his brother, and yet he refused to give Robert his home address. Instead, he sent only his post office box number, on the grounds that "I shall always have it." Lee had rented the Neely Street apartment for a purpose, and he did not think he would be there long.

The intensity with which Lee was thinking about his plan is underlined by the extraordinary hours he put in on the day he mailed his answer to Robert. It was Saturday, March 16, a day for which he would receive overtime pay, and he contrived to work for ten hours. He was eager for every penny he could earn.

Marina, meanwhile, had received an answer to her letter of February 17 to the Soviet Embassy. With utmost politeness the embassy explained that in order to return to the U.S.S.R. she would have to furnish a long list of documents and photographs, all in triplicate, plus letters from her relatives in Russia. The embassy said that the process would take five or six months.[11] Marina was elated. Faced by the mountain of red tape that she had lived with all her life, she knew it would take the bureaucracy of her country not five or six months to clasp her to its bosom once again, but more like five or six years. So, on Sunday, March 17, when Lee forced her to sit down a second time and fill out the embassy's forms, she was not as catastrophically affected as she had been the month before.[12]

During the week of March 18, Lee resumed his vigil at the post office. His time sheets at Jaggars-Chiles-Stovall reveal that he signed out early enough nearly every day that week to pick up a package if it arrived.[13] But a real coincidence was in the making. The revolver that Lee had ordered in January from Los Angeles and the rifle he had ordered from Chicago in March were both shipped on the same day, March 20. Lee probably received notice of their arrival early in the morning on Monday, March 25, and he signed out early enough that day, and only on that day of that week, to pick up his rifle at the post office.[14] The revolver, meanwhile, had arrived by REA Express, and to pick it up Lee had to ride a bus two miles from downtown Dallas to an office close to Love Field. No one remembers today what hours REA kept in Dallas in 1963, but Lee probably picked it up on Monday or Friday evening of that week.[15] Marina recalls, however, that she first saw the rifle toward the end of the week. It was propped up in Lee's office and he had camouflaged it, more or less, by draping his raincoat over it.

Thursday of that week was the last time Lee attended typing class. Mrs. Yoakum later described his arrival that evening:

The last time I clearly recall seeing him, he walked past my desk and stood momentarily scanning the crowded room for a seat, and as usual he took the back row. . . . He seemed to be as straight and thin as a figure "1" in profile. Later, on TV I hardly recognized him because . . . he appeared filled out. . . . I've asked myself why he usually "seemed" to try to slip in when my back was turned; yet the last time I recall seeing him he seemed to "want" me to observe him before he located his seat. . . .[16]

But that night, Lee wanted Mrs. Yoakum to notice him. And he had, in fact, lost weight. During February, he had been so upset that he nearly stopped eating and Marina was afraid he was "starving himself." In March, he was too busy to eat. There were evenings when he came home from work and slipped into the apartment so quietly that Marina did not hear him. The first she knew he was racing down the stairs, going out again. "Back soon," he would shout up to her. She would run to the balcony and trace his silhouette as it disappeared down the street. She does not know where he went or what he was doing.

He would return for supper and then retire to his "little closet," as Marina calls it. There he worked out his plan of attack. Months before, George Bouhe had given him a blue looseleaf folder, and Lee now filled it with a description and photographs of Walker's house, a description of the route he planned to use to escape after he shot Walker, and more photographs and a description of the place where he was going to bury his rifle. He may also have included a brief autobiography with photographs of himself in Russia and the Pacific. It was all part of the record he intended to leave for history.

In addition, Lee wrote on lined paper a fairly long historical rationale, which was both a justification for what he was about to do and a political program for the future. The first document, the historical rationale, is apocalyptic in tone and is hand-printed, not written, as if he had attempted several drafts, then printed it carefully.[17] Even so, he made mistakes and had to cross out a good many words, a sign that he was excited, hurried, or disturbed when he wrote it. Lee predicted that a "total crisis" of some kind would soon destroy the capitalist system and the government of the United States. "We have no interest in violently opposing the U.S. government," he said, or "in directly assuming the head of government." But in order to prevent foreign intervention and set up a "separate, democratic, pure communist society," he proposed the formation of a small party made up of disenchanted radicals, socialists, even remnants of the Republican Party, to defend "the right of private personal property, religious tolerance and freedom of travel (which have all been violated under Russian 'Communist' rule)." Lee concluded:

No rational man can take the attitude of "a curse on both your house's." There *are* two world systems, one twisted beyond recognition . . . the other decadent and dying.

A truly democratic system would combine the better qualities of the two upon an American foundation, opposed to both . . . as they are now.

The other document was handwritten, not printed, and set out Lee's political program in detail.[18] For example, no individual would be allowed to own the means of production; free speech, racial and religious freedom would be guaranteed; there would be heavy taxes against surplus profits but none on individuals; medical care would be free; and there would be general disarmament and "abolition of all armies except civil police force armed with small arms." Under the category "sale of arms," Lee wrote: "Pistols should not be sold in any case, rifes [rifles] only with police permission, shotguns free." Lee Oswald was for gun control.

Lee drafted and redrafted these documents until midnight or 1:00 A.M. many nights during March, reported to his job regularly and, for the sake of the time-and-a-half pay, worked long hours every Saturday that month except March 2. Still he made time for family life on Sundays. Each week he took June and Marina to a nearby lake to have a picnic. He loved to swing Junie on the swings. Then he would treat "his two girls" to ice cream. He did some fishing which, next to hunting, was his favorite sport, and he had luck catching goldfish. One night they lugged his catch home and Marina made fish soup for dinner. Lee could not bear to go into the kitchen while the cooking was going on, for the fish were swimming and thrashing in the pail right up to the moment Marina thrust them into the pot of boiling water.

He did not hit Marina now, a blessing she attributes to his "little closet" and the fact that he had "nobody beating on his nerves." But he was often cold to her, sometimes snappish and cross, and frequently the very sight of her seemed to annoy him. The baby was his only real joy. Often he came home at night, sat on the balcony with June on his knee, sipped a bottle of Dr. Pepper, and gazed down at the street below. But if Marina joined them, he would stare at her in displeasure. "What did you come out here for?" he would say, or, "Haven't you any housework to do?" Sometimes he stood up and left.

Marina was upset when she discovered the rifle. She hated guns and was annoyed that Lee was spending money on what she called "this dangerous toy" at a time when they were scrimping and saving even on food.

"Why did you buy a gun?" she asked. "Why don't you think of your family first?"

Lee shrugged. "Maybe I'll go hunting sometime."

Marina reflected that it was his money; he earned it, and he had a right to spend it as he liked. She liked dresses, he liked guns.

Sunday afternoon, March 31, Marina got a huge surprise when Lee came up to her in the backyard and asked her to take his picture. The sun was out, their ground-floor neighbors were away, and the Oswalds had the fenced-in yard to themselves. Marina was hanging up diapers.

"Why me?" She was startled. "I've never taken a picture in my life."

He promised to show her how.

Her surprise was transformed into astonishment when she glanced up from the clothesline a few minutes later to see her husband descending slowly, triumphantly, down the outdoor staircase dressed, as she had never seen him before, all in black—a black shirt and slacks. At his waist he was wearing his revolver. In one hand he carried his rifle, in the other he had a camera and a couple of newspapers. On his face was an expression of sublime contentment. Marina's eyes grew large and round. The diapers fell from her hand. She broke into peals of laughter.

"Why are you rigged out like that? And where on earth did you get those guns? From Intourist?" One of the chief aims of Intourist, the Soviet travel agency, is to impress foreigners. Marina thought that her husband was trying to impress *her*.

"Take my picture," Lee said. He was serious.

Marina stopped laughing. "Are you crazy? I've never taken a picture in my life. I'm busy and I don't know how. Take it yourself."

Lee had two cameras, one a Soviet Smena-2, the other a duo-lens American Imperial Reflex. The Smena-2 could be set automatically, so you could be in the picture and take it, too. But Marina remembers that Lee could not buy film for it in the United States. So he had to recruit her to snap the shutter of his Imperial Reflex.[19]

He showed her how to do it. Marina thinks it was about 4:00 P.M. for she recalls that Lee was worried about the shadows. She also thinks that she held the camera incorrectly, at eye rather than waist level. She snapped the shutter, he reset it, and she snapped it again. It was over in a minute. Not until months afterward did she realize, on being shown a pair of photographs, that she had snapped the shutter not once, as she first remembered, but twice.

Marina was puzzled by Lee's performance. "If that's his idea of a good time," she said to herself, "then I hope he enjoys it. Just so he leaves me alone." But before going back inside, she asked him why he had to have his picture taken with guns, of all stupid things? He explained that he was going to send the picture to *The Militant* to show that he was "ready for anything."

Marina did not know it, of course, but Lee had a special reason for sending his picture to *The Militant*. In the photograph he was holding two newspapers, *The Worker* of March 24, the one that had most recently arrived, and, thrust forward a little more prominently, *The Militant* of March 11, the issue containing a letter from Dallas that was signed "L.H." Hoping to go down in history, Lee wanted *The Militant* to know exactly whom it had had the honor of publishing, and that the author had meant every word when he said that he "questioned" the system. He was, indeed, "ready for anything."

"What a weird one you are!" Marina exclaimed. "Who on earth needs a photograph like that?"

Lee probably developed the photographs at work the following day, April 1. He handed one of them to Marina and told her to keep it for the baby. On it he had written: "For Junie from Papa."

"Good God!" Marina was appalled. "Why would Junie want a picture with guns?"

"To remember Papa by sometime."

24

Walker

THINGS AT LAST came to a head at Jaggars-Chiles-Stovall. One day during a slack moment John Graef had noticed that Lee was reading the Russian humor magazine, *Krokodil.* "I wouldn't bring anything like that down here again," Graef warned him quietly, "because some people might not take kindly to your reading anything like that."[1] Graef had also noticed that Lee's appearance was going downhill markedly. He used to dress well for work, but now he was wearing nothing but a white T-shirt with his slacks. Nor had the quality of his work improved. Lee worked fast, everyone agreed upon that, and he tried almost desperately to work well. But in the course of a normal day, many more of his jobs than average had to be done over because they failed to meet company standards. Graef hated to fire any trainee, but, he said, "I reached the opinion that he would never be the kind of employee I was looking for, giving him every chance."[2]

Graef did not have his own office, so he spoke to Lee in the most deserted spot he could find, a place in the darkroom where he could lower his voice and break the news without embarrassing Lee. He told him that business was pretty slow, " 'but the point is that you haven't been turning the work out like you should. There has been friction with other people and so on ' . . . I told him, 'I think you tried to do the work, but I just don't think you have the qualities for doing the work that we need.' "

Graef recalled that Lee made no outburst, no protest. "He took this the whole time looking at the floor, I believe, and after I was through he said, 'Well, thank you.' And he turned around and walked off."[3]

The date of this conversation must have been Monday, April 1, for on the top of his time sheet that day Lee wrote: "Please note new mailing add. P.O. Box 2915."[4] Until almost the very end, the company had had no address for Lee but that of Gary Taylor, the one he had been using when he found the job six months before.

Lee worked at Jaggars-Chiles-Stovall the rest of that week, through April 6. He did not tell Marina he had been fired. He kept to himself his disappointment at losing the only job he had ever really liked. His failure had almost certainly been caused by the emotional troubles that became apparent in mid-January. Those troubles must have made it exceedingly taxing for him to do precise work requiring concentration. And they destroyed his capacity to get along with the other men. For example, he had become unable to tolerate the presence of anybody near him in the close confines of the dark room. It was a vicious circle, for Lee's frustration and sense of failure on the job, which are vividly described by everyone who worked with him, must have made his emotional trouble worse. Next there was his indecision in February about whether and when to kill Walker, and the accompanying torment that nearly erupted in murderous violence at home. Then in March, with his mind made up and his energies released, he took on a crushing schedule—long hours at work, constant checking at the post office, typing classes, and late hours at night while he painstakingly prepared his documents and his plan of attack. Graef said later that Lee took the news more quietly than most men would have; the subdued response was typical of him.

Lee's timing was uncanny. Somehow he managed to be fired between the date when he received notice that his weapons had arrived and the date when Walker was expected back.[5] This coincidence, together with Lee's own behavior, gives rise to doubt as to what it was he wanted most. In March he had written confidently to his brother Robert that he had become "adept" in his work and was expecting a raise. Yet he flaunted a Russian newspaper, which contributed greatly to his being fired. And when, after he was fired, his colleague Dennis Ofstein gave him the names of other printing plants where he might look for work, Lee merely laughed his wry laugh and said that if he failed to find anything else, he could always go back to Russia.[6]

The truth appears to be that Lee, even now, needed a final push to go through with his plan to shoot Walker. The arrival of his guns was a portent, but, by itself, it was not enough. By maneuvering matters, or helping maneuver them, in such a way that he was fired, Lee handed himself a part of the "trigger" he required. All his life he had responded to being hurt, or rejected, by whirling around and hurting someone else. The firing was a catalyst—it would help galvanize him into making his characteristic response. And the rest of the push he needed would be supplied by the return of the Evil Man himself.

Marina, meanwhile, had found a friend, her first since she had given up her Russians. She was an American named Ruth Hyde Paine.

They had met at a party on February 22 given by Everett Glover, a chemist at Socony Mobil Oil in Dallas and a tennis-playing friend of the De Mohrenschildts.[7] Glover knew that Marina was badly treated by her husband and was in need of a friend with whom she could speak Russian. He invited six or eight guests to the party, among them Ruth and Michael Paine, who were in a madrigal-singing group with him. Michael was unable to come, but Ruth attended the party. Most of the evening she chatted with Marina in her halting Russian while Lee held forth on his experiences in the Soviet Union. Ruth was studying Russian and hoped to teach it. If Marina needed a friend who spoke Russian, Ruth did, too.

Ruth drove to Neely Street to visit Marina twice during the first half of March and the two women took their children to the park. June Oswald was one year old and Ruth's two children were two and three years old. The two mothers talked while their children played together. Ruth's spoken Russian was hesitant and Marina's English was almost nonexistent. Still, Marina, frank as always, managed to convey the worst of her troubles: she was pregnant again and ashamed to let the Russians, who were her only friends in Dallas, know it; her husband wanted to send her back to Russia, a sort of divorce without a divorce, and Marina did not want to go. Ruth, who at thirty-one was ten years Marina's senior, felt that this girl did indeed need a friend. On her third visit, toward the end of March, she picked up June and Marina and drove them to her house in Irving, Texas, a suburb on the other side of town. Marina enjoyed the outing hugely.

Ruth and Michael Paine invited the Oswalds to supper at their home on Tuesday, April 2, and undertook to arrange transportation. Michael Paine was a research engineer at Bell Helicopter Corporation, on the road between Dallas and Fort Worth. He left work sometime after five that afternoon and drove to Oak Cliff. He found the apartment on Neely Street and arrived just before seven o'clock.[8]

Marina was not yet ready. She had not packed the baby's diapers, bottles, and toys, and could not decide what to take. Michael welcomed the delay. He had heard about Lee's experiences in the Soviet Union and was glad of a chance to talk to him before the evening got under way. He was curious to find out what made Lee "tick." But from the outset Michael was upset by the scene before him: Lee Oswald ordering his frail-looking wife around (in Russian) like a drill instructor, telling her in a loud, harsh voice what to pack but doing nothing to help. He sat on the sofa talking to Michael, interrupting himself only to bark out a new order. "Here is a little fellow who certainly insists on wearing the pants," Michael thought. And he considered Lee's treatment of Marina "outrageous."

Nevertheless, Michael said later that their conversation was "the most fruitful half-hour" he and Lee ever spent.[9] Lee was as frank as he had it in him to be. Why, Michael asked, had he gone to Russia? Lee said he hated exploitation, adding with an edge in his voice that the company that employed him—a printing and engraving plant—earned a lot more from his labor than it ever paid back to him. He did not mention that he had just been fired.

Michael noted that Lee's voice was laced with scorn for both Russia and America. In Russia, he said, you could not choose your job or where you were going to live; why, you could not even own a rifle unless you belonged to a club that was really a paramilitary organization. Lee clearly adored rifles.

Marina had now packed, the car was bursting with baby things, and they were off to Irving. On the way, Marina recalls, Lee was shy and Michael did most of the talking. Once they were at dinner, however, the feeling crept over Michael once again that Lee's treatment of his wife was "medieval torture." Marina caught snatches of the conversation and Lee had to translate the rest, which he did with an air of supreme annoyance, as if it were an imposition. So perfunctory were his interpolations that Michael did not trust them and wished that Ruth were translating instead. She might not be as fluent as Lee, but she would be at pains to give a full account. Michael was appalled that Marina had no way of communicating with anyone except through Lee, and was dependent on him for everything she knew. "Take *that* away," Michael thought a trifle grimly, "and he will lose his power over her."

Lee was scrupulously polite to Ruth. He asked where she had learned Russian and whether she had found it hard, adding that he was delighted that Marina now had a friend with whom she could speak her own language.

After supper, Ruth and Marina washed dishes and spoke Russian in the kitchen, while the men sat in the living room and picked up their conversation where they had left off. They discussed Russian and American politics, and when the name of General Walker came up, Michael later remembered, Lee smiled an "inscrutable" smile.[10]

When the women rejoined them, Michael tried to include Marina in the conversation. But once again, Michael recalls, Lee kept "slapping her down" and "calling her a fool." The whole evening left Michael "shocked" and "offended." He thought that Lee's behavior toward Marina, his treating her like a vassal and enjoying it, was in cruel contrast with the affection he showed toward his child. Then and there Michael conceived the idea of helping Marina "escape," of freeing her from "her bondage and servitude to this man." The idea was uncharacteristic, for Michael Paine was a man who respected privacy above everything. He would not for the world intervene in someone else's affairs unless goaded by outrage and an inner, irresistible prompting. But so appalling was Lee's treatment of Marina, so offensive to his notion of human dignity, that a reservoir of charity opened up in him which he would have denied he possessed at all. Still, Michael kept his calm politeness. On the way home in the car, Marina remembers that the two men talked again about politics.

Lee's feelings about the evening contrasted sharply with Michael's. He was elated when he got home. "Look," he said, "I've found you a friend to talk Russian to. You will help her with her Russian and she will help you learn English." Lee was also pleased that Ruth was the mother of small children. That way neither of the women would have time for "foolish" things. "She will be good for you," he told Marina. "She's a fine, upright person and she'll have a good influence on you. She'll show you how to be an American mother."

"Am I a bad mother, then?" Marina asked.

"No. I didn't mean that. But she can tell you better than I can how things are done over here."

Lee also liked Michael, who had listened, or so it seemed to him, to his political ideas with respect. As for Marina, she was grateful to her husband for sanctioning this new friendship, for she had nobody else. It was one of the very few times Lee ever mentioned that she might learn English, and that pleased her, too. It did not occur to her that Lee may have been looking forward to a moment, in the not too distant future, when she would *need* an American friend who spoke

Russian. Ruth and Michael Paine fitted very neatly into his plans.[11]

Lee had not yet tried out his new weapons. As nearly as can be determined, it was on Wednesday, April 3, the day after the dinner at the Paines', that he used his rifle for the first time.[12] He signed out of work at five, rode the bus home, slipped upstairs to fetch his rifle, and slipped out again without Marina's hearing him. Moving as rapidly as he could, he walked a half-dozen blocks to the corner of Sixth Street and Beckley Avenue and boarded an inbound bus. He rode a mile and a half, a five- to seven-minute ride, to the intersection of West Commerce Street and Beckley Avenue. He got off the bus and strode quickly down the levee to an uninhabited area 35 feet below called the Trinity River bottom.[13] There he practiced with his second-hand Mannlicher-Carcano C2766 and his four-power telescopic sight. He did not have much time, for the sun set at about 6:45 P.M.

The tasks Lee had to accomplish were these. He had to get the feel of the trigger action of this particular rifle, which was new to him and more powerful than any he had used before; and he had to learn to work the bolt smoothly so as not to disturb the alignment of the barrel. He also had to adjust the sight so that all his shots landed within a fairly small radius. It was the first time he had owned a four-power sight and he had to get used to it. According to experts, learning to use a telescopic sight is easy (General Walker calls it "very easy") and a skill that vastly enhances accuracy. It has been estimated that a man of Oswald's training and experience would be able to adjust to the new rifle and scope, "would be capable of sighting that rifle in well, firing it," with only ten rounds of practice.[14]

Oswald was apparently confident in his ability to handle firearms. Small-game hunting with his brothers in his early years seems to have given him an ease and familiarity with guns. His training in marksmanship in the Marine Corps, at Camp Pendleton, California, was intensive, and he learned to sight, aim, and fire from a variety of positions at targets up to 500 yards away.

In December 1956, at the end of his training, Oswald was tested and scored 212—2 points above the minimum for "sharpshooter" on a scale of expertise ranging in ascending order from "marksman" to "sharpshooter" to "expert." By civilian standards, he was an excellent shot. Two and a half years later, in May 1959, on another range where the details of weather, light, quality of rifle, and ammunition are not known, Oswald scored 191, only 1 point over the minimum for "marksman." But those test results would establish him, by civilian standards, "as a good to excellent shot." Moreover, he now had a four-power telescopic sight, which would more than compensate for a lack of recent practice.

On Friday, April 5, two days after his first practice session with his new rifle, Lee signed out of work at 5:05 and arrived home just as Marina was about to take the baby for a walk. Out of breath, Lee announced that he would like to join them; go on ahead, he said, and he would catch up with them. Marina pushed the baby slowly in her stroller and Lee caught up with them before they had walked two blocks. He was moving even more rapidly than usual and Marina could not help noticing that he was carrying his rifle, clumsily wrapped in his green Marine Corps raincoat.

"Where are you going?" she asked.

"Target practice," he replied, and asked her to walk him to the bus stop.

Marina was angry and disappointed. As often happened between them, he had promised her something and then yanked it away, in this case the pleasure of a walk. When they came within sight of the bus stop, she burst into open reproach.

"Instead of coming with us, you go someplace to shoot."

"It's none of your business. I'm going anyway!" He caught a glimpse of the bus over his shoulder and started sprinting.

"Don't bother to come home at all," she shouted after him. "I won't be waiting for you. I hope the police catch you there."

As the bus flashed by, she saw a sign in front: "Love Field." But by the time she got to the bus stop, Lee had leaped aboard and was gone.

Lee was too secretive to show his face on a rifle range, and there is no evidence that he did so at any time following his return from Russia. So anomalous was he, however, that he was perfectly capable of climbing onto a crowded bus carrying a rifle poorly concealed in his raincoat. It was about nine o'clock when Lee returned home. He said he had been practicing, and Marina told him to watch out for the police. He said that where he had been, there was no one around to hear him practice.[15]

Marina has said that she watched Lee clean the rifle three to five times that week. The first time was March 31, the day she took his photograph, when he cleaned the rifle "on the sofa" although he did not fire it that day. Thus it is possible that the evenings of Wednesday, April 3, and Friday, April 5, are the only occasions Lee ever practiced firing the Mannlicher-Carcano. However, Saturday was his last day at work, and he may have practiced on Sunday, April 7. Marina could not have seen him clean the rifle after that—Lee did not have it at home.

Marina detested the rifle. She dreaded it and found its presence in the apartment distasteful. Terrified lest it go off, she never went near it, never touched it or moved it no matter where it might be. Compulsive housekeeper though she was, she did her cleaning in a careful circle all around it. Yet she did not ask any questions. Lee had said he was going hunting, and it made sense to her that he might go target-shooting first.

Sometime that first week of April, on Thursday or Friday, the 4th or 5th, Jeanne de Mohrenschildt came to call. George was away in New York and Jeanne, anticipating that they would soon be leaving Dallas for good, had already quit her job. She had free time during the day and the use of George's convertible, and she paid her first visit to Marina on Neely Street. Somehow as she was showing Jeanne around, Marina was drawn, not to Lee's "office" but to a clothes closet where he was keeping his rifle.

"Look at that!" Marina said. "We have barely enough to eat and my crazy husband goes and buys a rifle." She told Jeanne that Lee had been practicing with it.

Jeanne's father had been a gun collector and she knew her way around rifles. Instantly, she spotted something that meant nothing at all to Marina: Lee's gun had a telescopic sight. She said nothing to Marina, but she filed the fact away in her mind; when George got back from New York, she seems to have told him that poor as the Oswalds were, Lee had bought a rifle with a scope and had been practicing.[16]

Marina's worst worry that week had nothing to do with the rifle or with her husband's target practice. She was upset because he was talking in his sleep again—the first time in six weeks. She did as he had told her and woke him each time he started talking. But during those last days of March and early in April, she sometimes had to wake him twice a night. She was beginning to be afraid that he was ill.

Saturday, April 6, was Lee's last day at Jaggars-Chiles-Stovall. He worked from 8:00 A.M. to 5:30 P.M. and then returned home. He still had not told Marina that he had been fired. On Sunday, April 7, he vanished. He left the apartment with his rifle and stayed out all day. When he came home for supper at six that night, he no longer had the rifle. He left the apartment again after supper, and Marina does not remember at what hour he came home.

Lee's activities that Sunday will never be known. But General Walker was due back in Dallas early the following week, and it is almost certain that Lee was keeping watch on his house at No. 4011 Turtle Creek Boulevard. He was ready to put his plan into action, and he later explained to Marina that he buried his rifle near Walker's house that Sunday, in a wooded spot beside some railroad tracks that he had picked out and photographed exactly one month before. Lee's hiding place, rendered better hidden still by large stacks of underbrush nearby, was in a park running northeast to southwest of Walker's house, 25 to 30 feet above street level next to a footpath 90 feet from the curb line of Turtle Creek Boulevard. By the most direct auto route, it was not quite half a mile from the point where the footpath met the curb line to the Walker house. On foot, however, the spot could be reached by walking east or southeast from the rear of the house, and the distance was somewhat less.[17]

Monday, April 8, was Lee's first day out of work. He deceived Marina by rising early as usual, putting on a T-shirt, and leaving the apartment as if he were going to work. Again he was out all day and only one of his activities is known. He visited the Texas Employment Commission and told the sympathetic ladies there that he was out of a job. This time they did not come up with any leads. Once again he may also have been watching Walker's house. If so, he surely noticed increased activities there. Walker came back, he himself recalls, "in the late afternoon or break of evening" that day.[18]

Lee had his supper at six. Then he went out again, and Marina, who had no idea that he had quit typing school, assumed that he had gone to Crozier Tech. She noticed that he returned earlier than usual after typing class, but it did not occur to her to ask why.

It was several days before she learned where he had been. After supper he bought a newspaper and boarded a bus, not the bus he took to Crozier Tech but one of several buses that would carry him close to the spot where he had buried his rifle. He was on his way to shoot General Walker.

On the bus, Lee was to claim later to Marina, he glanced at the church announcements in the paper. They were more numerous and more prominent than usual because it was Holy Week, the week between Palm Sunday and Easter. Reading the paper, he noticed that the Church of Latter Day Saints, the Mormon church at 4027 Turtle Creek Boulevard just behind General Walker's house, was having a service Wednesday night that would get out at about nine o'clock. "Good," Lee thought. "There'll be people and cars around there on Wednesday and I'll have a better chance of getting away." He climbed off the bus, came home, and postponed his attack.[19]

The next day, Tuesday, April 9, Lee no longer pretended to go to work. He told Marina that it was a holiday and he was going to collect his paycheck. For the third time since his final Saturday at Jaggars-Chiles-Stovall, he was gone the whole day. He came home at six and after supper walked down the street as he often did to buy a newspaper and a bottle of Dr. Pepper. When he returned, he sat out on the balcony where, after two months of being irritable—not, Marina says, on an ascending curve of irritability but merely irritable all the time, with an occasional outcropping of good humor—he unexpectedly turned tender toward her. "Come sit with me," he coaxed her onto the balcony. He asked in the friendliest way whether she had heard from her girlfriends in Russia? Had she seen anything special in *Soviet Belorussia* or *Krokodil?* He drank a sip or two of his Dr. Pepper, then handed the bottle to her and grandly urged her to drink it all.

On the morning of Wednesday, April 10, Marina thought Lee looked pensive and rather sad. With tears in his eyes, he confessed at last that he had lost his job. "I don't know why," he said. "I tried. I liked that work so much. But probably the FBI came and asked about me, and the boss just didn't want to keep someone the FBI was interested in. When *will* they leave me alone?"

Marina ached with sympathy. She had no idea how to comfort him; and when he went out for the day she supposed he was looking for work. He was dressed in his good gray suit and a clean white shirt.[20]

As nearly as Marina can recall, Lee did not come home for supper that night. She waited until seven, an hour past their usual suppertime, then absent-mindedly cooked something for herself. Between eight and nine she was busy putting June to bed. Then she began to grow uneasy. Lee had taught her not to pry, not even to ask *herself* what he might be up to. He had accustomed her to his absences at hours when most workingmen and above all, most family men, are at home with their wives. But Marina knew her husband well. For months he had been tense, preoccupied, ready, like his rifle, to "go off." Nor, despite efforts to censor her curiosity, could she suppress an awareness that his comings and goings had been out of the ordinary. Now it turned out that he had been fired. Marina sensed, too clearly for her own peace of mind, that this element on top of the rest made up a recipe for danger, although what kind of danger she could not have said.

While she was waiting for Lee, she thought back to the last time he had been so late. It was their last week on Elsbeth Street, late in February.[21] Frantic with worry, she had gone to the Tobiases next door and asked if she might use the phone. With Mrs. Tobias doing the dialing, she called George de Mohrenschildt, told him Lee had not come home, and asked him to find out what he could. George called the printing plant and then called back to report that Lee had left hours before. When he came home that night, Lee was angry at what Marina had done. He said his boss disapproved when the men got phone calls at work. He told her never to do it again.

Now Marina's resources were more meager still. She no longer had a neighbor with a phone, and Lee no longer had a job where, in a pinch, she could try to reach him. There was nothing she could do but wait. She paced anxiously from room to room, doing her best not to think. On an impulse, about ten o'clock, she opened the door to her husband's study. There on the desk she saw a key with a sheet of paper lying under it. At the sight of the key, Marina felt a thud inside: Lee was never coming back.

She picked up the paper and read the note he had left her in Russian.[22]

1. Here is the key to the post office box which is located in the main post office downtown on Ervay Street, the street where there is a drugstore where you always used to stand. The post office is four blocks from the drugstore on the same street. There you will find our mailbox. I paid for the mailbox last month so you needn't worry about it.
2. Send information about what has happened to me to the Embassy [the Soviet Embassy in Washington] and also send newspaper clippings (if there's anything about me in the papers). I think the Embassy will come quickly to your aid once they know everything.
3. I paid our rent on the second so don't worry about it.
4. I have also paid for the water and gas.
5. There may be some money from work. They will send it to our post office box. Go to the bank and they will cash it.
6. You can either throw out my clothing or give it away. *Do not keep it.* As for my personal papers (both military papers and papers from the factory), I prefer that you keep them.
7. Certain of my papers are in the small blue suitcase.
8. My address book is on the table in my study if you need it.
9. We have *friends* here and the *Red Cross* will also help you.
10. I left you as much money as I could, $60 on the second of the month, and you and Junie can live for two months on $10 a week.
11. If I am alive and taken prisoner, the city jail is at the end of the bridge we always used to cross when we went to town (the very beginning of town after the bridge).

Marina's eyes took in what Lee had written but her brain did not. She had no idea what his message was supposed to convey. Only two words meant anything to her. They were "prisoner" and "jail." She saw them and started shaking all over.

At 11:30 Lee walked in, white, covered with sweat, his eyes glittering.

"What's happened?" Marina asked.

"I shot Walker." He was out of breath and could barely get out the words.

"Did you kill him?"

"I don't know."

"My God. The police will be here any minute. What did you do with the rifle?"

"Buried it."

Marina's teeth started to chatter. She was certain that police dogs would track down the rifle and be at the house any second.

"Don't ask any questions." Lee switched on the radio. There was no news. "And for God's sake don't bother me." He peeled off his clothing and hurled himself on the bed. There he lay, spreadeagled, on his stomach. He fell asleep right away and slept soundly the whole night through.

Marina could not go to sleep. She lay awake for hours listening for the barking of police dogs and the footsteps of policemen on the staircase. She glanced over at Lee, who was lying like a dead man beside her, and she felt sorry for him. She felt a pity almost physical in its closeness, and fear of what the police would do to him. "There will be time," she thought, "to scold him and punish him later. But not now. Not while he is in danger."

An idea flickered across her mind. She would go to the police and tell them, in sign language or some other way, what her husband had done. She put the thought aside. The truth is that she had no one to lean on but Lee and was deathly afraid of losing him. "I'll be alone without a husband," she said to herself, "and what good will that do anyone?" Nor, with her lack of English, did she know *how* to tell her story, much less make anyone believe her. The police would only send her home, and Lee would give her a beating.

So great was Marina's dependence upon Lee that she did not consider other alternatives. She was forever picking up loose change from Lee's bureau and buying the cigarettes he forbade her. She could have picked up a dime, called the De Mohrenschildts from a public phone, and asked them to drive her to the police station and interpret for her. Failing the De Mohrenschildts, she could, in sign language or in some other way, have asked her former neighbors, the Tobiases, to help, and they lived just around the corner. Nor did it occur to her that the police might be able to find a Russian interpreter.

Even if Marina had considered any of these alternatives, there was another factor that would have held her back: her Russianness.

She had grown up in a world where police spies are everywhere and it is your duty by law to inform on anyone, even the person closest to you, if you know he has committed a crime. Failure to do so makes you criminally as liable as he. In such an environment the only honor, the only way of keeping faith, is never, ever, to inform. The law says you must; Marina's private morality says that you must not. And so it would be one thing to scold Lee harshly, to his face, and try to change him, or even to appeal to friends to try to change him, but quite another to go to the police or involve the state in any way. To do *that* would breach a relationship beyond repair.

Marina would have been incapable of going to court even in self-defense when her stepfather tried to frame her as a prostitute. As she saw it, *her* going to court against him, even though it was *he* who brought the charges, would have destroyed their relationship. Now it was the same with Lee. A wife would have to hate her husband to inform on him. How on earth could they live with one another, much less trust one another, after that? She did not know that in this matter Soviet and American law are directly opposite. Here, in most states, it was *not* her duty to go to the police; and she would not in any state have been allowed to testify against Lee in court. But since she assumed that her legal duty in the United States was exactly what it would have been in Russia, her failure to act made her in *her* eyes—and perhaps in Lee's—his accomplice.[23]

So Marina did not go to the police, or consider it for more than a moment or two. Although she told herself that it was her legal duty to inform on Lee, her personal morality stressed loyalty to her husband above everything. And this loyalty was to expose her to a crushing sense of guilt when many people told her that if only she had gone to the police "after Walker," a later, lethal event would not have happened. But even after that event, Marina's feelings of guilt continued to cluster incongruously around the dim, but intact, figure of General Walker. Her guilt over her failure to inform on Lee "after Walker" was to save her, until she could better bear it, from facing the huge, intangible and infinitely more complex question of what responsibility, if any, she bore in a much greater tragedy.

25

Legacies

MARINA WOKE UP the next morning exhausted and with a headache. Lee was in the living room, leaning over the radio. He turned to her, crestfallen. "I missed. They don't say much. Just that somebody unidentified took a shot at General Walker."

Marina was hugely relieved, but she was still too nervous to touch her morning cup of coffee. Lee went out to buy a paper. When he came home he was angry. "Oh, hell!" he said. "Walker moved his head at the last minute. That's the only thing that saved him. My aim was perfect. It was only accident that I missed."

Marina now asked the question she had been wondering about all along. Who was Walker? She had heard the name before but she had no idea what he had done that might make Lee want to kill him.

Lee did not go into details. He merely said that Walker was a "Fascist" and a former general, a madman and the leader of a Fascist organization.

Marina objected that no matter who he was, Lee had no right to kill him. Maybe he had a wife and children.

"He lives alone," Lee answered abruptly. "If someone had killed Hitler in time, many lives would have been saved."

That stopped Marina. All her life she had heard about Hitler's atrocities and she could not think how to respond. She asked Lee how he had escaped and where he had left his rifle.

General Walker, he told her, had been sitting at the back of his house near a window, working at his desk. Lee aimed and fired only one shot. He did not wait to see whether he had hit his mark. The church meeting next door was breaking up. Plenty of people, plenty of noise. Lee ran. By the time he heard the wail of police sirens, he was far, far away.

It is not clear from Marina's account whether Lee rode one bus home that night or two. It is logical that he would have run straight through the woods to his hiding place, buried the rifle, then hurried to a bus stop and ridden home. But it is not certain he did it that way. Marina, for some reason, was haunted by the idea of police dogs. They would pick up Lee's scent and trace the rifle to its hiding place. "Don't you worry about the dogs," Lee reassured her. "Lots of people go by that house. So they trace it as far as the bus. That's where they lose the scent. I buried it a long way off." From that remark it could be inferred that Lee boarded a bus near Walker's house actually carrying his rifle, hopped off close to his site in the woods, buried the rifle, and then took another bus home. He did tell Marina that the bus he took was not the one he generally rode when he went to General Walker's.[1]

The Dallas papers of Thursday, April 11, ran front-page stories about the attempt on Walker's life. Lee left the apartment to buy both morning and after-noon editions, and lay on the sofa listening to news bulletins on the radio. It was reported that the police had identified the bullet as a 30.06. It was also reported that an aide to the general had noticed two men in a "late-model, unlicensed car" in the alley behind Walker's house on the night of his return. After the shooting, a fourteen-year-old boy, Kirk Newman, who was a neighbor of Walker's, claimed that he had seen two cars, one with one man in it, the other with several, speed away from the scene.

Reading that, Lee roared with laughter. "Americans are so spoiled!" he said, proud of his escape. "It never occurs to them that you might use your own two legs. They always think you have a car. They chased a *car.* And here *I* am sitting *here!*" Once again he said that before any car left the scene, "my legs had carried me a long way."[2]

Lee also laughed at the police identification of the badly smashed bullet.[3] "They got the bullet—found it in the chimney," he said. "They say I had a .30 caliber bullet when I didn't at all. They've got the bullet and the rifle all wrong. Can't even figure *that* out. What fools!"

Low as his opinion of the police was, Lee was angry at himself and disappointed. "It was such an easy shot," he said again and again. "How on earth did I miss? A single second saved him. I fired and he moved. A perfect shot if only he hadn't moved!"[4]

That Thursday morning, only a few hours after his attempt on Walker's life, Marina saw Lee thumbing through the blue looseleaf notebook in which he kept his typing lessons. She noticed that he stopped now and then to read a page.

"And what is that?" she asked.

"My plan."

"And those pictures?"

"Walker's house."

He was sitting on the sofa with the notebook in his lap. Marina stood facing him across the coffee table. "May I see?"

He handed it to her. She saw photographs of a house from various angles and the book was filled with lined sheets covered with handwriting. There were pages of typing, too, and Marina guessed—correctly—that some of the handwriting, all of which was in English, was the political justification for Lee's act.

"I had it so well figured out," he boasted. "I couldn't make a mistake. It was only accident that I missed."

Marina realized that he was proud of himself. "And what do you mean to do with this book?" she asked.

"Save it as a keepsake. I'll hide it somewhere."

"Some keepsake! It's *evidence!* For God's sake, Alka, destroy it."[5]

She left the room so that he could make up his mind by himself.

The next thing she knew he was standing by the toilet with some sheets of paper in his hand and a box of matches. Slowly he tore the sheets in half, crumpled them into balls, and one by one touched a match to them. As each ball of paper caught the flames, he dropped it into the toilet. He did this thoughtfully, with great reluctance, as if it were the funeral pyre of his ideas. But apparently he destroyed only the details of his plan. He did not burn the handwritten pages which contained his political philosophy and program.

Afterwards, they ate their lunch in silence. Lee was so sorry to part with his papers, and Marina so relieved, that neither could think of anything to say. Lee seemed withdrawn, and fearful for the first time that he might be caught. Marina had seen how reluctant he had been to burn his papers. "I wonder if he burned them," she asked herself, "because he does not trust *me?*"

That night, twenty-four hours after his attempt on Walker's life, Lee suffered anxiety attacks in his sleep. He shook all over from head to toe four times at intervals of a half hour or so, but without waking up.

The following day, Friday, he was still frightened, yet not too frightened to go downtown and file a claim for unemployment compensation. His claim was refused a few days later on grounds that his earnings at Jaggars-Chiles-Stovall were too low for him to qualify, a ruling that was later reversed. That night he again suffered convulsive anxiety attacks in his sleep.

Marina, meanwhile, was grateful that she had chores to do, anything to keep her from thinking. She now knew that Lee took his politics far more seriously than she had ever, in her wildest dreams, supposed. She knew, for the first time, that he was capable of killing in cold blood, merely for the sake of his ideas. But her fears for the future started and ended with General Walker. She saw that Lee was bitterly disappointed by his failure to kill Walker, that he still was keyed up and tense, and that his desire to do the deed had by no means burned itself out. She was afraid, terrified, that he would take another shot at Walker. It never occurred to her, then or at any time thereafter, that he would try to shoot anybody else.

With her ear still cocked for the yelping of police dogs, Marina immediately began to beg Lee, and try to force him to promise, that he would never do such a thing again. She told him that when Walker moved his head at the last minute it had been a sign from fate. "If God saved him this time, He will save him again. It is not fated for this man to die. Promise me you'll never, ever do it again."

"I promise."

His promise was not enough. "Look," Marina said, "a rifle—that's no way to prove your ideas. If someone doesn't like what you think, does that mean he has a right to shoot *you?* Once people start doing that, no one will dare go out of doors. In Russia you used to say that there was freedom of speech in America, that everyone can say what he pleases. Okay, go to meetings. Say what you want to say *there.* Or are you afraid you have so little brains you can't make anybody listen?"

She scolded Lee on personal grounds as well. "Even if you didn't think of me," she said, "you ought to have thought about Junie."

"I did," he said coldly. "I left you enough money for a while." And he added, with a touch of malice in his tone, "The Russians here like you. They'd have helped."

Somehow Marina and Lee got through Thursday and Friday, but they still had one more ordeal. It occurred on Saturday, the eve of Easter, which happened to fall on the same day that year in both Western and Orthodox churches. They were not expecting callers and were getting ready for bed when they heard a sudden commotion at the door—the very thing they had been dreading. But instead of police dogs barking, it was George de Mohrenschildt, booming out a loud hello. Hugely relieved, Marina and Lee went downstairs to let the De Mohrenschildts in.

Jeanne came in first, dressed to the nines and clutching a pink plush rabbit for June. Handsome and hearty, George shouldered his way in behind her. The first words out of his mouth struck the Oswalds with the impact of a bomb.

"Hey, Lee," he roared out in Russian. "How come you missed?"

Lee and Marina, standing at the foot of the stairs as their guests went up with their backs to them, stared at one another in horror. Which of them had told George about Walker? Each one supposed the other had.

Lee was the first to recover. "Shhh," he said as they reached the top of the landing. "Junie's sleeping."

"You always forget the baby," Jeanne reproved her boisterous husband. "Let's go out on the balcony."

Luckily for Marina and Lee, it was dark out of doors and hard for the De Mohrenschildts to see their faces, or so they hoped. George and Jeanne had just come from a party. They were euphoric, on top of the world, and Marina reflected gratefully that they both seemed a little bit high. Maybe they would not notice her discomfort. Lee, for his part, rushed back and forth carrying chairs for all of them to sit on.

George seemed at first to have only one thing on his mind: the attempt on General Walker. He had read every morsel in the Dallas papers and was eager to discuss it with Lee. He knew so many of the details that Marina concluded that Lee, uncharacteristically, had taken George into his confidence.

Lee scarcely uttered a word. He continued to jump up and down and kept running in and out with cups of coffee. "Oh, yes," he at last remarked with apparent detachment, "wouldn't it be fascinating to know who did it and why and how?"

Marina thought that Lee's behavior was fairly composed under the circumstances. George said later that even in the dark Lee "shriveled," was "tense" and wore a "peculiar" look.⁶ But it is not clear how much George really noticed. Even by his soaring standards he was unusually ebullient and the conversation soon shifted to another topic. George had just returned from a trip to New York, where he had clinched a new job in Haiti, prospecting for oil and other resources for "Papa Doc" Duvalier in return for the right to live in the government compound in highest luxury and operate a sisal plantation for such profit as he could reap from it. He and Jeanne would be leaving within the month for Port-au-Prince. After being down for so long, the De Mohrenschildts were on their way up again.

Sitting in the dark, still numb with shock, Marina was scarcely able to follow the conversation. Even years later, remembering how close George had come with his opening remark, she shook all over with fear. Finally, at about ten o'clock, the De Mohrenschildts got ready to leave and Marina went into the back yard, picked an armful of roses, and handed them to Jeanne.

The instant they were out the door, Lee turned to her. "Did you telephone them and tell them it was me?"

"Of course not," Marina said. "I thought *you* did."

"You're out of your mind," he said. "But isn't it amazing how he guessed? It's a lucky thing he couldn't see my face. I was hardly able to speak. Maybe he was only kidding, but he sure hit the nail on the head."

Lee believed Marina's disclaimer, she believed his, and they were both right. No one had told George that it was Lee who shot at General Walker. He had simply guessed.

George later denied any responsibility for influencing Lee's actions and explained why he had made his remark. "I didn't want him to shoot Walker," he said. "I didn't want him to shoot anybody. But if somebody has a gun with a telescopic lens, you see, and knowing that he hates the man, it is a logical assumption, you see."⁷

That evening was the last time Lee Oswald ever saw George de Mohrenschildt. On April 19 the De Mohrenschildts left Dallas, made their round of farewells in New York, Washington, and Philadelphia, and returned to Dallas at the end of May. There they commenced packing; they were taking some of their belongings with them to Haiti, and the rest were going into storage in Dallas. They wanted to see the Oswalds one more time, but heard that they had already left town. Jeanne was to remember, however, that before their departure in early June, they received something in the mail from Lee, and that it bore a New Orleans address.⁸

The De Mohrenschildts did not return to Dallas for more than three years. They came back in 1966, and when they got around to retrieving their possessions from storage, in early 1967, they had an enormous surprise. There, among all the boxes and bundles, they found one which they could not recall having received at all. It was wrapped in brown paper and contained a stack of records that they had loaned to Marina in an effort to help her learn English. They were unable subsequently to remember whether the bundle bore a postmark or not.

But the greatest surprise was still to come. It was not the bundle of records itself, but something that had been laid neatly and purposefully on top—a photograph of Lee with his guns and dressed in black, one of the two Marina had taken.[9] The back of the photograph bore two inscriptions. Across the top, in Russian, were the words: "Hunter for the Fascists—ha-ha-ha!!!" Under the inscription, which was bold and clear, was a small sketch of a terrier, of the kind the De Mohrenschildts owned. Marina today, fourteen years later, has no recollection of having written it. But the writing and the sketch both appear to be hers. And in the lower left-hand corner, catty-corner and in English, was another message in handwriting that appears to be Lee's. It read: "For my friend George from Lee Oswald." Beneath the inscription was the date written, as Lee might have done it, in a combination of Latin and Arabic script: "5/IV/63." The date was probably supposed to be May 4, 1963, and Lee had, as nearly as can be guessed, mailed the records—and the photograph—from New Orleans.[10]

What happened, apparently, is that after George's lucky guess on April 13, Marina, half idly, and half as a warning to Lee that he must not go around shooting people or he would be found out, simply took one of the photographs and wrote on it, mocking Lee, "Hunter for the Fascists," a word she had heard both Lee and George use, and "ha-ha-ha," an expression that was characteristic both of her and of George. The sketch of a little dog links her inscription to George's remarkable guess. She must have done it, characteristically, to warn Lee and simultaneously to mock him, to laugh him out of further dangerous adventures.

Lee's choosing a copy of the photograph that had this inscription on it to send to George was itself a message that contained a whole world of meaning. George, and George alone, had made a guess that it was Lee who tried to kill General Walker. Those who knew them both, notably Samuel Ballen, had observed "a mutuality," "an emotional complicity," between Lee and George, and of course Ballen was right.[11] Each of them, Lee and George, during that winter of 1962–1963, knew perfectly what the other was thinking politically. And Lee wanted to seal their understanding. As the days following the Walker episode passed without discovery and Lee realized that there was going to be no evidence, not even a clue, to link him to the attempted killing, he decided to let George know that his uncanny guess had been on the mark. It was to George that Lee made his confession.

Why should it have been the loudmouthed George to whom Lee chose, above all other men, to confess? The answer is simple. Lee had done the deed for George. George was the one friend he had, the one person whose respect, admiration, even affection, he coveted—and it was George whom he had wanted to impress. George had been Lee's "constituent" in the sense that Lee believed he had been acting as George himself might have wanted to do, and in a manner that would win George's approval.

In his attempt on General Walker, Lee had other constituents as well. He told Marina that he was sending a copy of his photograph to *The Militant,* to show that he was "ready for anything." In the picture, he was holding the issue of *The Militant* that contained the letter from him, signed "L.H." He had expected that by the time the editors received the photograph, Walker would be dead and the initials "L.H." would be famous. They would then see how right they had been to print his letter; they would see that their intrepid Dallas correspondent had indeed been "ready for anything."

De Mohrenschildt and *The Militant,* then, were Lee's two chief constituents when he fired at General Walker, with De Mohrenschildt, the flesh-and-blood friend whose approval he desired, far and away the more important. But Lee appears to have had still other inner, or emotional, constituents: the American Communist Party, whose newspaper, *The Worker,* he was also holding in the picture; and possibly the Soviet Embassy in Washington, whose help he desired for himself and Marina.

In the photograph, Lee was dressed in black, the color of death, and he was bristling with guns. If there was in the picture a message to George of boastfulness, love, and pride, there was a message of a very different sort as well: a message of hate. George had allowed himself to become a father to Lee. Yet without a scruple of remorse, without a twinge of regret, indeed, with insulting jubilation, he was leaving Dallas, leaving Lee. Like his father and like Edwin A. Ekdahl, the stepfather Lee genuinely cared about, George was abandoning him. And now Lee wanted to avenge himself on everyone who had ever let him down in that way.[12] One means of doing so was to leave town before George did—abandon George, rather than be abandoned by him. Another way was to send the photograph. For the photograph, with its black and its guns, conveyed the message that in addition to the profoundly favorable feelings Lee had for George, he had murderous feelings as well.

Envy is another of the emotions Lee appears to have harbored toward his friend. George had been born to a title, where Lee only *felt* entitled. George, unlike Lee, had known and loved his father and had grown up close to him. And George, the possessor of a powerful physique, had called Lee "puny" and treated him as if he could be trifled with. At the request of George Bouhe and Anna Meller, he had intervened in Lee's private affairs and "liberated" Marina a few months before. The De Mohrenschildts noted at the time that Lee "boiled and boiled" and then meekly gave in. But Lee was not meek and he was not the man to forget. Now he was saying to George what he had forborne to say in November, that, armed with weapons, he was as powerful as any man. Belatedly, he was expressing resentment at George's interference and warning him not to try his physical superiority again—not on him and not on Marina.

Lee was making still another statement. He was saying that in politics as in physical strength, he was as good a man as George, a better one, in fact. "You talk—I act," Lee seems to have been saying. He had even made an attempt to act out George's ideas for him. And now he was declaring that no matter where it might lead, even to death, the plebeian son was prepared to go his aristocratic father one better.

In addition to the many meanings implicit in the photograph, George may have played other roles in Lee's fantasy life. George was the only person Lee knew who had connections "at the top," to President and Mrs. Kennedy. By virtue of his acquaintance with Jacqueline Kennedy and her mother, George had written to the President and asked him to provide a preface for his book about his adventures in Mexico. He supposed that these adventures fitted admirably with the President's physical fitness campaign. Throughout the winter when Lee and George knew one another, George was awaiting a reply. Thus it is possible that George was an emotional lightning rod linking Lee's fantasies about the presidency—clearly, he had such fantasies, since he wanted his "son" to be President and even wanted to be President himself—to the real human being who was President. Anything George said about the Kennedys in Lee's presence, although Marina recalls that it was very little, could have helped bring the President within Lee's emotional range.

Finally, it is conceivable, although mere speculation, that the feelings Lee had for George were an emotional profile, a shadow, a clue, to feelings which he was later to develop for the President. For there were resemblances between the two. Both Kennedy and De Mohrenschildt were dashing and well-born men. Both had fathers who had loved them. Both were masters at keeping others at a distance. As George himself vanished from Lee's life to recede into the jungles of Haiti, Lee may, without being aware of it, have taken the feelings he had for George and displaced some of them onto President Kennedy.

George's stunning and insightful "How come you missed?" was the true end of the Walker affair for Lee because it stripped away the layers of rationalization and hit him full in the face with what it was he had really been after. Lee's bullet had missed General Walker—but it had found its mark. Something George had said on the evening of February 13 caused Lee to feel that George had given him the sanction he required to go ahead and shoot General Walker. Now, on April 13, George had given him the recognition, the token of admiration, Lee desired. By his uncanny remark as he came in the door on that excruciating Easter eve, George had shown that a part of him understood "who did it, and why, and how." That was what Lee had wanted.

And so the next day, Easter Sunday, April 14, just after supper but before dark, Lee returned to his hiding place by the railroad tracks, dug up his rifle, and carried it home. The publicity and the manhunt that followed the attempt had subsided anyhow, with disappointing speed as far as Lee was concerned.

Marina knew her husband well. She saw that he still was keyed up and tense and that, because of the failure of his attempt, he had a reservoir of unexpended inner energy and was casting about for a way to use it. She was afraid that he would take another shot at Walker. When he came home that night, she begged him to sell the rifle. "We need the money for food," she said.

"Money evaporates like water," Lee answered. "I'll keep it."

Marina felt helpless to change his mind and she did not nag him. She was correct in her fear that Lee might be dangerous still, but what she did not understand was that his mind was like a stove: he might have one pot bubbling away on the front burner, taking up nearly all his attention, but he generally had another pot or two simmering away at the back; and when his obsession with the front pot eased or when he met resistance, he was quite capable of moving one of those pots up front. That is what he briefly did now.

Cuba, as always, was in the news, with calls for a new invasion and the overthrow of Castro being sounded by the nest of exiled leaders in Miami and their powerful supporters in Congress and at intermediate levels of the Pentagon. These calls from the right to which Lee was steadily exposed in the two Dallas dailies were mirrored on the left by two of the weeklies he subscribed to, *The Militant* and *The Worker,* which were demanding a "hands-off" policy toward Cuba on the part of the Kennedy administration.

Lee, moving his preoccupation with Cuba from the back of his mind to the front, decided to act. In his little "office" he fashioned a placard: "Hands Off Cuba! Viva Fidel!" He hung it around his neck and went out, quite possibly on the day after digging up his rifle, to stand on a street corner and hand out pro-Castro leaflets. He wrote with pride to the Fair Play for Cuba Committee (F.P.C.C.), a pro-Castro organization based in New York, that he had distributed all his leaflets—some fifteen or so—in forty minutes. "I was cursed as well as praised by some," he reported, and asked to have forty or fifty more pamphlets sent to him at his Dallas address. The committee mailed them at the end of the week, on Friday, April 19.[13]

Thus, only days after his attempt on General Walker, Lee had once again invited the attention of the Dallas police—and in a manner that must have seemed guaranteed to obtain it. Once again he failed. Not a clue came to light that linked him to the Walker affair, and his demonstration on behalf of Castro went unnoticed.

Marina did not know about the picketing. But she heard Lee talk in his sleep again that week and she watched as he scanned every edition of the Dallas papers looking, as she knew, for his name. He longed for publicity and attention. From this, from the reluctance with which he had burned his papers about the Walker attempt, and from his refusal to get rid of the rifle that might incriminate him, she also understood that Lee had wanted to be caught.

Marina was now aware that Dallas was a dangerous place for Lee, dangerous because it was full of temptation, and by "temptation" she meant General Walker. If she had failed in her effort to make Lee get rid of his rifle, she could try to do the next best thing—get him out of town. Just as quickly as she could, she would remove him from proximity to his target. She told him that she longed to move to New Orleans. New Orleans was a port city, she pointed out, and she had been raised in one, too—Archangel. "I'd like to see the city you were born and grew up in," she said, adding that she had heard a lot about his relatives there, especially his "good" Aunt Lillian Murret, and was eager to meet them.

Lee hesitated. He doubted the Murrets would want to see him. They had failed to answer a letter he had written them from Russia and he was afraid they disapproved of him for going there. But he did not turn Marina down. She found him instead curiously receptive, as if he half-welcomed the idea.

From Easter Sunday on, Lee and Marina discussed what they ought to do next. Ostensibly, Lee was looking for a job. But when Lyolya and John Hall drove over from Fort Worth to attend Easter services at one of the Orthodox churches and afterwards went to see the Oswalds, they noticed that Lee was discouraged. He complained about the lack of job security in America and hinted that he was thinking of going back to Russia.[14] Marina tried to cheer him up. She pointed out that in America unemployment compensation is as high as an engineer's salary in Russia. "You'll have a rest," she said, "and we'll all have a paid vacation." When that failed to cheer him up, she volunteered to go to work. She would take in ironing or find a job polishing silver. "No," said Lee. "You're my wife and it's up to me to support you."

Conceivably, it was Lee who subtly suggested the move to New Orleans and allowed the idea to sink in rather than, as Marina supposed, she who suggested it and he who gradually picked it up. Either way, they were talking about it during the evening of Wednesday, April 17, when Lee suddenly agreed to move. "Okay," he said, "I'll show you New Orleans." They did not set any date. But it is significant that Lee now knew that the De Mohrenschildts were soon to leave Dallas. With George gone, it would be easier for Lee to move, too.

Marina was greatly relieved, and on Saturday, April 20, she, Lee, and June went to a lake nearby to have a picnic with Ruth Paine and her children. But the next morning, Sunday, April 21, all her fears were revived. Lee went out early to buy a newspaper and some doughnuts, the two had breakfast together, and afterwards—while Marina was doing the dishes, straightening the apartment, and dressing the baby—Lee sat in the living room and read the newspaper. It was the Dallas *Morning News,* which had a banner headline that day: "Nixon Calls for Decision to Force Reds Out of Cuba." The lead story, accompanied by a front-page photograph of the former Vice President, reported a speech which Richard Nixon had delivered the day before in Washington, accusing President Kennedy of being too soft on Castro and demanding a "command decision" to force the Russians out of Cuba. The speech could have been interpreted as a call for a new invasion.

Marina had no idea what Lee was reading. But she noticed after finishing her chores that he had laid the paper carefully on the coffee table as if he wanted her, or someone, to see it. Then she noticed that the door to his office was open, which was unusual. Suddenly Lee stood before her, dressed in his gray slacks, white shirt, and a tie. He had his pistol at his waist and was about to put on his best jacket. His face was white.

"Where are you going?" she asked.

"Nixon is coming to town. I am going to have a look." He spoke slowly and with deliberation.

"I know what your 'looks' mean."

Marina had no idea who Nixon was and she did not care.[15] She knew his life was in danger and that was enough. Thinking fast, she went into the bathroom and asked Lee to follow her there. Once he was inside, she squeezed herself out and shut the door. It was a door that could only be locked from inside, but Marina held it as hard as she could, bracing her feet against the wall.

"Let me out. Let me out," Lee screamed. "Open the door!"

"I'll do nothing of the kind," Marina said. "How *can* you lie to me after you gave me your word? You promised me you'd never shoot anyone else and here you are starting in all over again. I'm pregnant. I can't take it all the time. I could lose the baby and you wouldn't even care." Marina was hurt, angry, and in tears, with red nervous splotches all over her face, a frowsy little figure in her housecoat.

"Let me out!"

"Over my dead body I will. I have evidence against you. I'll take it to the police."

"Just you try."

Their tug of war lasted three minutes, with the advantage sometimes on her side, sometimes on his. Although she weighed less than 100 pounds, Marina could summon up a wonderful, concentrated energy at moments like this. She had held Lee in the bathroom before at least once in their apartment in Fort Worth, and she was to do so three or four times again, in New Orleans, almost always to avoid a beating.

But her words seemed to unman him this time: "I could lose the baby because of you. You'll have killed your own child."

Lee relented. "Okay, I won't do it. Open up."

"Only if you give me your gun."

"Okay. Only open the door."

She opened it and Lee came out. His face was red from exertion and his eyes had the angry glitter she knew well.

Marina was trembling all over. She eyed him like a watchful bird.

"Give me the gun," she said.

He handed it to her.

"Take off your clothes."

He stripped to his T-shirt and shorts.

Marina went quickly into the bedroom carrying the revolver. She shoved it under the mattress without looking to see if it was loaded.

"If you're going to keep me here all day," he yelled, "at least give me something to read."

She looked around for his book.

"Over there, on the coffee table," he said.

She brought it to him. Then she took away his shoes. For two or three hours Lee sat on the toilet seat, reading with the door closed. Marina could not see him but she kept her eyes on the door and her ears alert for any sound.

Finally, at three or four in the afternoon, he came out of the bathroom and sat in the living room, reading in the undershorts which were all Marina would allow him. They did not exchange a word. Toward evening, he carried the baby to her bath and sat with her, naked, in the tub. They played more quietly than usual and he did not use baby talk.

It was only now, when he was naked and in the bathtub, that Marina let him out of her sight. She ran downstairs and bolted all the doors, including the back yard gate. She wanted to make sure that if she was busy later on, cooking or getting the baby to bed, she would hear him if he tried to get out, hear him fiddling with the locks.

Marina ate her supper first, eyeing Lee warily the whole time. Then, with a contemptuous air, as if she were keeping a prisoner, she allowed him to come to the table—"You may eat if you wish."

He brought his book to the table and neither of them spoke for the rest of the evening.

As they were getting ready to go to bed, he asked if he might have his pistol back.

"No."

He rummaged through all the drawers. "Where did you hide it?" he asked.

"You can have it—but only if you promise you'll never do that again."

"I promise."

"I wouldn't be surprised if our baby is born insane. I can't stand it any more. Either the baby will be crazy or I will."

"Okay, give me my gun and I'll put it back where it belongs."

Marina did not want to touch it; she was afraid that it might go off. She merely motioned to the mattress. Lee drew the pistol out and put it where he usually kept it, on the top shelf in his office. But, curiously, he left her in possession of the "evidence" against him which she had mentioned to him that day. It was the note he had left her, in Russian, on the night he went to shoot General Walker. Marina allowed Lee to have his pistol back. But she kept the note, moving it from place to place, until it finally came to rest among her cookbooks.

With the "Nixon" drama over, Marina sensed a falling off, an easing of her husband's tension. Since his attempt on Walker, he had been hanging over an emotional precipice. He had geared himself up to kill, to be captured, and face trial and punishment. The failure of anything to happen had been a fearful anticlimax. And so Lee poured his energy on the nearest person, the safest person —and it worked. He could easily have won the battle of the bathroom if he had wished. Instead, he spent himself in the struggle and emerged harmless. With Marina as his tool, he disarmed himself emotionally.

Exactly what he had in mind when he said he was going to "look" at Nixon will never be known. From the painstaking way he had laid the paper face up, on the coffee table, perhaps he hoped to be caught at something and make a show of his concern for Cuba. But Nixon was not in Dallas. The very next day, Monday, Governor John Connally of Texas, with whom Lee had corresponded in a fruitless effort to alter his "undesirable" discharge, was due in Dallas to speak at the Marriott Hotel. And the day after that, Vice President Johnson would be at the same place. He might have tried to shoot either of them, but Lee had lost his keenness to kill.

Marina later observed that their little charade had been aimed not at "Nixon" but at her. She sensed that it had been Lee's purpose to wound her or test her in some way. She was right. Lee was testing her to see whether, when he reached a certain frame of mind, he could count on her to stop him. She passed that test with flying colors. But she failed his other test. Lee mentioned Nixon, the one American politician whose name he knew she might recognize because Nixon had been to Russia, in order to warn her that he might kill somebody else, not just Walker. Lee sent that message—but Marina did not understand. It was too terrible. She continued to cling to the idea that General Walker was the only political figure who might be in danger from Lee.

But Marina had learned a lot about Lee, knowledge she would rather not have had. She now knew the full extent of his interest in politics, which she had not measured before. Not only that, she saw that he was willing to act on his ideas. She had also learned how calculating he could be. Isolated phenomena which she had been trying for months not to notice suddenly fell into place—Lee's maps, his guns, his bus schedules, even the photograph for June. Lee had been planning his attempt on General Walker for at least two months, had planned and foreseen every detail, and had lied unblushingly to her. And she had learned that he wanted to be caught. She began to see that her husband was, in his own eyes, a great man who was unjustly ignored by the world and would do anything to wrest its attention.

Yet Marina's worst discovery by far was her awareness that Lee would kill abstractly, for the sake of his ideas. He had tried to strangle *her*, of course, and for months she had been afraid of him. But to kill your wife in a fit of rage was nothing new. To kill someone you did not know, had never met, a man who had done you no harm, all for the sake of politics—to her that *was* unbelievable. It was sick. To learn that Lee was capable of that, Marina says, was "a terrible shock and discovery, like all the shocks in the world put together, a volcano." It took a while to sink in, and she never got over it.

Marina was not a coward. Even Lee's beatings had done nothing to temper the audacity of her tongue. "You'd be the greatest wife in the world," he often said, "if only you couldn't talk." Yet her outspokenness had saved her. Lee could beat up her body but he could not beat up her spirit, nor alter in the slightest what she thought. Thus far Marina had survived. But now it was another matter. Now she knew that *she* was in danger. It was a cataclysmic revelation. "I tried not to think about it much and I didn't change quickly. But I began, really, to be afraid."

What was she to do? Something in Marina, something commonsensical, resisted getting inside Lee's head and "making her brain spin the way his did." Already she had learned more about him than she could handle, and she saw that if she thought deeply about the Walker affair and all it told her about Lee, she would go out of her mind. It was with relief that she turned to the baby, the cooking, the cleaning. They saved her from dwelling too long on the new knowledge of which she was now the uneasy possessor.

And yet she had to do something. Should she leave Lee? Take the baby and live alone? Or stay with Lee and try to change him? Just as her decision not to go to the police after the Walker shooting bore the stamp of her Soviet upbringing, so did the decision she came to now. In true Russian fashion, she decided that she was, indeed, her husband's keeper; he was her responsibility, and it was up to her to straighten him out. In a phrase that could have come directly from a Soviet tract on family morality, she told herself that "I must apply all my strength to help correct my husband and put him on the right path." She saw that she would have to use as her tools sympathy, affection, and understanding, and not so many of the harsh words that flooded all too readily from her tongue. They only made Lee pull away from her. Now it would be her task to draw him out. She must enter into his world and help him see where he was wrong.

After the Nixon episode they decided to move to New Orleans right away. Lee would go on ahead and look for work while Marina stayed on Neely Street until he sent for her. She was heartened by his willingness to move. Walker and Dallas appeared synonymous to her, and the two together spelled violence. Lee's agreeing to leave Dallas must mean that he was giving up violence and choosing a peaceful life instead. Moreover, Marina hoped for succor from his family in New Orleans. They would help Lee find a job and would serve as a moral influence and a restraint. Their influence, on top of hers, would deter him. Marina was sure that he would be ashamed to shoot anybody in a city where he had a right-thinking family looking on. Things would be better in New Orleans and, once they were settled in their new home, she would figure out how to go about remaking him. "There, on the spot," Marina said to herself, "I'll see better how to do it."

Marina could not have known it, but with the Walker attempt over, the cruelest and most poignant days of her marriage were over, too. That attempt, and the Nixon episode which followed, sealed a curious compact between husband and wife. Marina had not gone to the police after Walker and, in her significant motion at the mattress on the night of April 21, she had allowed Lee to have his pistol back. He for his part never asked her for the note he had left behind on the night he attempted to shoot General Walker. It was an odd sort of trust—she trusting him with his weapon, he trusting her with evidence she could use to stop him in the future. Yet with that compact, if that is what it was, things did change a little between them.

Slowly, very slowly, Lee began to admit Marina to the more daring and private of his two worlds. Where before he had kept her confined to the mundane, family side of his life only, now he would occasionally permit her a glimpse of the world that meant most to him, what Marina calls the "high-flying world of his ideas." She says that she was still "an obstacle in his way, but he no longer showed it as openly as he had before. I was someone with whom he could take off his mask," and whom, for a moment now and then, he could trust.

If Marina had learned a good deal about Lee from his attempt on General Walker, he, too, had drawn lessons—portentous ones. First, he had learned that if ever he was to win attention for himself and his ideas, he would have to do it on a very grand scale. He had shot at the most famous man in Dallas, he had missed him by less than an inch, and the only newspaper coverage had been a single, front-page story in each of the two Dallas papers and another tiny story inside one of them. Three stories—and not a single one mentioned his name. Next time, if it was an act of violence that was to make him famous, he would have to go after someone "at the very top."

Second, Lee was astonished at how easily he got off and at the ineptness of the police. They had the bullet, yet they identified it wrongly and wrongly identified the type of rifle from which it was fired. Moreover, they had apparently been thrown off by rumors about cars and co-conspirators, rumors Lee knew to be false. Lee concluded, as he said to Marina, that you can do anything and get away with it if only you think it out ahead. He had tried something cataclysmic —and he had not been caught. He had not even been touched.

Thus by far the greatest legacy Lee carried out of the Walker attempt was the conviction that he was invulnerable, that he stood at the center of a magic circle swathed in a cloak of immunity. It was a feeling which fitted dangerously with the feeling he already had that he was special, that he had particular prerogatives. He and he alone was entitled to that which was forbidden to everybody else.

Interlude

Why, after the failure of his attempt on General Walker, did Lee choose to go to New Orleans? It was the one place where he had resources—relatives who might shelter him and help him pick up the threads of his life. For Lee, going to New Orleans was not like going some place new. It was the city where he was born and in which he had spent seven of his twenty-three years, more than in any other place. He had memories there.

Lee had lived in New Orleans until he was four, staying by turns with his mother, with his good-natured Aunt Lillian Murret and her family, and in a children's home with his brothers. At fourteen he had come to live there again, after an unhappy year and a half in New York during which he had barely escaped being sent to a home for delinquent children. New Orleans had been a refuge to him then, and it was to be a refuge to him now.

The two and a half years Lee had spent there as a teenager—January 1954 to June 1956—when he was fourteen to sixteen years old, were filled with portents for his future. It was there he became interested in a cause, Marxism; there he began to visit the public library and read *Das Kapital* and other Communist books; and there he spoke for the first and only time about shooting a President of the United States. Indeed, during the summer that lay ahead of him, the summer of 1963, it was as if everything that happened to Lee had already happened before. He was a little like an actor on a stage, walking through a part he had already played.

But of course it was not the same. Lee was a man now, not a boy of sixteen. His cause this time was to be Cuba, not a vague, impersonal Marxism. And if he thought about killing anybody now, it would be as a volunteer for Fidel Castro, shooting up the American invader. The summer of 1963 was to be Lee's time of peaceful political action, the time in which he came closer than ever in his life before to creating a serious, nonviolent, political identity for himself. By picketing, handing out leaflets, debating on the radio, Lee tried everything he could think of to change American policy toward Cuba. To him it was part of something bigger. He wanted to make a dent in the complacent American society he saw around him and change it peacefully from below.

Still, one gets the feeling of repetition. Shortly before his seventeenth birthday, from Fort Worth, Lee had written the Young People's Socialist League in New York to ask if there was a local Y.P.S.L. chapter he could join. Now, during the summer of 1963, he was to engage in correspondence with three left-wing political organizations in New York and try to found his own chapter of the Fair Play for Cuba Committee. Even when he left New Orleans for the last time, it was like a repetition of something he had done before: on September 19, 1959, he had embarked from New Orleans for the U.S.S.R. Almost exactly four years later, on September 25, 1963, he was to leave New Orleans again, this time trying to reach Cuba via Mexico City.

Lee's memories of his adolescent years in New Orleans contained both good and bad. There had been the Friday night seafood suppers at his Aunt Lillian's—evenings he had loved and looked forward to. But there had also been fights: a fight with some white boys for riding in the black part of a segregated bus, and a couple of fights with the boys at Beauregard Junior High where Lee attended eighth and ninth grades. The boys at the school were a rough lot, and Lee got into fights because "he didn't make friends," and "he wasn't going to take anything from anybody."[1]

But Lee did make a friend or two in New Orleans. One was Edward Voebel, who patched him up in the rest room after his second fight at Beauregard. Voebel, a gentle boy who loved his piano lessons, occasionally dropped by the apartment Lee and his mother shared at 126 Exchange Place. Lee and Voebel would go downstairs to the pool hall just below the apartment, shoot a few games of pool, and spend some time throwing darts. Afterwards they would walk along the riverfront.

It was to his friend Voebel that Lee, the proud but dissatisfied possessor of a plastic .45, confided his plan to break into a store on Rampart Street, using a glasscutter he had, and steal a real pistol that he had spotted in the window. Voebel accompanied Lee to the store, went inside to case it with him, then quietly talked him out of his scheme on the ground that the glasscutter would set off the burglar alarm. Voebel found Lee easy to dissuade.[2]

Another friend, Palmer McBride, with whom Lee worked as a messenger in a dental lab after quitting high school, remembered a threat that he made. They were listening to classical music when Lee announced that "he would like to kill President Eisenhower because he was exploiting the working class." McBride recalled afterwards that Lee did not seem to be speaking "in jest."[3] Lee also suggested to McBride that they join the Communist Party together to take advantage of its "social functions."[4]

And a boy called William Wulf, then president of the New Orleans Amateur Astronomy Association, was engaged in only his second conversation with Lee when Lee came right out and said "he was looking for a Communist cell in town to join but he couldn't find any . . . he couldn't find any that would show interest in him as a Communist." The two boys got to arguing, with Lee "hollering" about communism in a "loudmouthed" and "boisterous" way.[5] Wulf's father, a refugee from Germany who was touchy in political matters, overheard them. He took Lee by the arm and politely ordered him out of the house.

"We were sixteen," Wulf remembered later, and Lee "was quite violent for communism." Then Wulf gave the epitaph, not only for Lee at sixteen, but for Lee during the summer of 1963 and indeed throughout his life. "He seemed to me a boy that was looking for something to belong to." But, Wulf concluded, "I don't think anybody was looking for him to belong to them."[6]

Boy or man, it can at least be said that Lee was looking for truth. There is something touching in the fact that this man, for whom it was a struggle, because of his reading disability and his limited education, even to write at all, should have spent scores of hours in lonely written dialogue with himself over what a good society ought to be.

It may be, as Marina once said, that it was nothing but fame Lee was after. It may be that when he looked up from his books, it was not human beings he saw around him, but only an abstract vision of humanity. It may be that, struggling with the devils inside and pasting them onto politics, it was not others he was trying to help, only himself. And it may be that it was not truth he was seeking, only personal salvation. It may be that Lee was only an egotist after all.

But his ideals say something in his favor. He had lived in two great opposing social systems and tried to make sense of them. He believed that the perfect society would combine the best features of both. He thought that government ought to take care of people, give them medicine and education, guarantee their civil liberties and put an end to racial discrimination. And he believed in disarmament among nations.

It says something for Lee that the ideals he cherished were good ones, and that, had they been carried into practice, they would have meant a better life for others. Unlike the Nazis', Lee's was not an ideology of power. He opposed the supremacy of any racial or ethnic group over any other. He favored the weak over the strong. It was a better world he was after, and he had a generous vision.

And if at the end he failed, if the undertow of his old, angry, tumultuous self overwhelmed him one last time and swept him under, who is to deny that he made at least *this* attempt to carry his vision peacefully into practice?

New Orleans, in the summer of 1963, was the place where he made his last try.

PART FOUR

New Orleans, Mexico City,
Dallas, 1963

26

Brief Separation

ON THE MORNING of Wednesday, April 24, Ruth Paine drove from Irving to
Dallas and arrived on Neely Street with her two children, ready for another
outing with the Oswalds, something like their picnic a few days before.[1] She was
surprised to find the three of them, Lee, Marina, and little June, perched on a
mountain of luggage.

The Oswalds explained that they had decided to move to New Orleans. Lee
was going ahead to look for work, while Marina and the baby would stay on Neely
Street, keeping only a minimum of possessions and waiting until Lee could send
for them.

Lee asked Ruth to take him to the bus terminal. She agreed, and all six of
them, children and grown-ups, crowded into Ruth's station wagon around Lee's
gear. They drove to the Continental Trailways terminal, where Lee went inside
to check his bags and buy two tickets, one for him to use that night and one for
Marina when she came to join him.

Ruth sat in the station wagon gathering her thoughts. It would be hard for
Marina on Neely Street without a telephone, knowing only a few words of English
and with no easy way of reaching Lee. And the bus trip to New Orleans would
be an ordeal. It was twelve or thirteen hours long, and Marina was pregnant. She
would have a small child in tow, and although Lee was plainly carrying everything he could, she would still have clothing, dishes, a playpen, a stroller, and
a crib to get on board.

Ruth had been worried about Marina almost from the moment they met.[2]
She felt that Marina was lonely, troubled, and in need of a friend. She started
worrying a good deal more after one of their outings in March, when Marina
confided that Lee meant to send her back to Russia and she did not want to go.
Marina had not mentioned it since, and Ruth was mystified as to where the
Oswalds' marriage stood. But both she and Michael felt that it was "cruel" of

Lee not to let Marina learn English. They were appalled that she might have to go back to Russia against her will. It had occurred to them that they might be able to offer her an alternative if the need became acute. As Michael was to put it later: "I thought out of the largesse of this country it should be possible for her to stay here if she wanted to. . . . She struck me as a somewhat apolitical person and yet true, just, and conscientious, so it was agreeable to me to look forward to financing her stay until she could make her own way here."[3]

Ruth had already done more than just think about helping out. Fearful that she might offend and that, with her limited Russian, she might not be able to find the proper words in conversation, she had sat down on April 7, taken out her English-Russian dictionary and, with enormous effort, written a letter to Marina. In it she suggested that if things became too difficult between her and Lee and they were not able to work out their problems, then she and June would be welcome to stay at the Paines' for as long as they needed.[4] Ruth placed one condition on her offer: that she be able to speak to Lee directly about it and that Marina's acceptance be agreeable to him. She had talked to Michael about her offer, but the fact is that Ruth was willing and able to make it because Michael was not living at home, there was an extra room, and she was lonely.

Ruth did not mail the letter. To come between the Oswalds was the last thing she wanted to do. But now, as she sat in the car, it occurred to her that she might be able to help during the days just ahead. Having summoned up language to write the letter, she realized that she had the words at her command to make her invitation in Russian, so that Marina, as well as Lee, would understand.

When Lee returned to the car, Ruth made her suggestion. Instead of going back to Neely Street, why didn't Marina and June stay with her in Irving? As soon as Lee sent for them, she would drive them to New Orleans.

Lee did not hesitate. It is not even clear that he consulted Marina. He accepted, strode back into the terminal, redeemed Marina's ticket, returned to the car, and handed Marina part of her fare to use as spending money. He did not offer to contribute to groceries or other costs of the suddenly expanded Paine household.

As they were driving back to Neely Street to pack up Marina's and the baby's possessions, Lee asked Ruth if she would stop for a moment at the central post office. Ruth noticed as he emerged that he was carrying a stack of magazines.[5] Lee had not closed his post office box; he merely cleared out what was in it. The "magazines" Ruth noticed may have included the fifty leaflets which the Fair Play for Cuba Committee had mailed on April 19 from New York.

When they got back to the apartment, Lee began to load the baby things into Ruth's car—the playpen, the crib, the stroller. He packed up a box of dishes and laid Marina's and the baby's clothing loosely over them. Since the suitcases were going with him, Marina had at most an overnight bag.

The helter-skelter nature of his packing differed sharply from the careful job he had done the night before. Then, he gave everything the most sedulous attention and refused to let Marina help. It wasn't woman's work, he said. He had traveled more and had more practice. The result was that Marina forgot about the rifle. She forgot to ask what he was going to do with it—leave it with her or take it to New Orleans? But Marina was not as worried as she had been. Lee was calmer than she had seen him in months. He was subdued, even downcast, over their separation and the uncertainty ahead. Marina's fears that he might try to shoot someone had subsided. She felt that his agreement to move signified a renunciation of violence—as, in a way, it did.

Ruth, Marina, and the children set off for Irving about four in the afternoon, leaving Lee behind in the apartment. Once again, just as when he moved from Fort Worth to Dallas, he had found someone to take care of Marina and June while he got settled in a new city. Ruth had been expected that day and Lee knew that she would agree to drive him and his baggage to the bus station. Her last-minute offer to take Marina to Irving came as a convenient surprise; but Lee, in confronting Ruth with his helpless wife and child, must at least have been counting on her to watch out for them on Neely Street. He had, as usual, taken her help for granted. He stayed only a few hours in the Neely Street apartment after Marina and Ruth left, then boarded an evening bus for New Orleans.

Early the next morning, April 25, Mrs. Lillian Murret's telephone rang at 757 French Street, New Orleans.

"Hello, Aunt Lillian."

"Who is this?"

"Lee."

"Lee?" She was very much surprised.

"Yes," was the laconic answer.

"When did you get out? When did you get back? What are you doing?" The last Mrs. Murret had heard of her prodigal nephew, he had defected to the U.S.S.R. with considerable publicity, to the great embarrassment of them all. They thought that what he had done was reprehensible, and they supposed that they would never be seeing him again.

"Well, I'm glad you got back," Mrs. Murret said.

Lee asked his aunt if she could put him up for a while, and she agreed. When he arrived at the house, "he was very poorly dressed," Mrs. Murret said later. He had no jacket, just a sport shirt, "and a very poorly pair of pants."

"Lee," she said, "you don't look too presentable. I am going to buy you some clothes." No, no, he protested. He had everything he needed. He had checked his luggage at the bus terminal.[6]

Lee was overjoyed by his reception. He had written the Murrets from Russia but had not had an answer. They were extremely conservative, they disapproved of his going to Russia, and he was afraid they might not welcome him to New Orleans. Anticipating this, Lee had confided to Marina that he suspected the Murrets lived beyond what his uncle's earnings would support. Lillian's husband, Charles Ferdinand, or "Dutz," Murret, as he had been known since his prizefight days, was a steamship clerk, and Lee thought that his uncle might be engaged in some other activity on the side, like bookmaking. There is no evidence that this was so; but that was Lee's way of accounting for their discomfiture at his going to Russia and the possibility that they might not be glad to see him. He thought they did not want to do anything that might bring attention to them. By confiding his suspicions to Marina, Lee had covered in advance his own embarrassment in case they refused to help him.

Lillian Murret had taken care of Lee both as a child and as a teenager, and if her own children had been jealous of him, they had never once shown it. The Murrets were a close-knit Catholic family and the children were raised to be kind. They considered Lee different from other children and felt sorry for him. But Mrs. Murret says that they "loved Lee. . . . They have always loved him."[7]

Only two of the five Murret children were at home now—John, or "Bogie," four years older than Lee, who had attended Loyola and St. Louis universities, had been a professional basketball player, and was working as a salesman for E. R. Squibb and Company; and Marilyn, Lee's favorite cousin. Marilyn was a schoolteacher, tall, thin, and thirty-five, with straight dark hair. Marilyn shared Lee's love of travel. She had spent three and a half years roaming the world on tramp steamers and had taught in places as far away as Australia, New Zealand, and Japan. She liked Lee, Lee liked her, and they were pleased to see each other again.

It was six or seven years since Dutz had seen Lee. "He looked older," he recalled, "but he hadn't changed too much."[8] But in Bogie's view, Lee had changed. He seemed really intelligent. Bogie thought Lee had grown intellectually, especially his vocabulary, although he realized that Lee purposely picked his words to impress people. Still, Bogie says, "he was impressive."[9] As for Marilyn, she had noticed even as a child that Lee would read an encyclopedia where anybody else would read a novel. She conceded that he was not outgoing, that he would be liked by some and "hated" by others, but she had always respected him precisely because he was "different." He was "refined," he loved nature, he liked to "sit in the park and meditate."[10] And so once again, the whole Murret family was ready to help Lee if they could. Lee, as usual, stood on his pride, appeared to ask nothing, acting as if he did not want help and yet, as usual, accepting it.

They talked a little about Russia, but the Murrets noticed that Lee seldom spoke of the country unless they asked. They, for their part, did not pry. The person from whom he would take more frank talk than from anyone else was his sixty-three-year-old Aunt Lillian. She was a small woman, a little plump, with a calm, unruffled look. She saw the faults of others, but did not hold them to account for them. It was to Lillian that Lee owed most of his happy memories, and there was little she could say that would put him off. As soon as he arrived from the bus terminal, it was to her that Lee confided his plans. He wanted to stay with her a few days while he looked for work. When he found a job, he would send for Marina and the baby. Lillian asked what Marina was like. "Just like any American housewife," came the reply. "She wears shorts." Lillian was impressed by Lee's eagerness to bring her to New Orleans.

He began looking for jobs right away. He got dressed, skipped breakfast, scanned all the want ads in the morning paper, and started off about 8:30 in the morning. He was out all day and came home just in time for supper at 5:30 or

6:00 P.M. After supper he sat down with the rest of the family and watched television. He generally went to bed early.

On one of his first evenings with the Murrets, Dutz drove Lee to the Continental Trailways terminal to pick up his bags. When they were home again, Lee refused to allow his uncle to touch anything. He unloaded everything himself and stacked it in the Murrets' garage. The family attributed his insistence on doing it all himself to his being the old Lee they knew so well, the proud, independent Lee who did not need anything from anyone. But Lee may have had another motive. His rifle, and perhaps his pistol, were in the luggage.

On Sunday morning, three days after Lee's arrival, they were talking about relatives. Suddenly, Lee turned to his Aunt Lillian.

"Do you know anything about the Oswalds?"

She did not. "I don't know any of them other than your father, and I saw your uncle one time. I don't know anything about the family."

"Well, you know," Lee said, "I don't know any of my relatives. You are the only one I know."[11] He added that he had been embarrassed when Marina's family in Russia had asked about his relatives and his descent. He had to admit that he did not know. After that, he realized that he missed not being close to his family and not knowing anyone on his father's side.[12]

That very morning he boarded the streetcar that ran past the Murrets' house to the end of the Lakeview line and the cemetery where his father was buried. The cemetery keeper helped him find his father's grave.

Later that same Sunday, the conversation turned again to the Oswalds. Lee sat down with a telephone directory and called every Oswald in the book to ask how he could contact his grandfather, Harvey Oswald.[13] Finally, he reached an elderly lady in Metairie who was able to answer his question. Harvey Oswald was dead, she said, and so were all his four sons: Thomas, Harvey N., William Stout, and Robert E. Lee Oswald, Lee's father. Her name was Hazel, the widow of William Stout Oswald. She had a large, framed photograph of R. E. Lee Oswald which Lee was welcome to have.[14]

That was enough for Lee. Using the street map he carried with him at all times, he figured out how to get to 136 Elmeer Street in Metairie. Hazel Oswald received him graciously. She gave Lee his father's photograph and explained who his relatives were. It turned out that the Oswalds, like Lee's family on his mother's side, the Claveries, were of French and German descent. Although his uncles were dead, Hazel said that his father had three sisters, all alive and in New Orleans. Lee also had six first cousins in New Orleans and at least one first cousin once removed. But the family had drifted away from Lee's father. R. E. Lee Oswald had been separated from his first wife for some time when he met Marguerite, and he got a divorce only when he decided to remarry. As Catholics, most of the family did not like it and saw little of R. E. Lee after that.[15] A few of them continued to see him and his new family, but his funeral in August 1939 had been the end of it. Only Hazel had seen Marguerite since, but she had never met Lee.

Proudly, Lee showed his aunt a photograph of Marina. Hazel, like the rest of the family, had read of Lee's defection in the papers but had been too tactful to bring it up. On seeing Marina's photograph, however, her curiosity involuntarily slipped out. "Is she Russian?" Hazel asked. Lee flinched and said, "Why do you ask that?"[16] When he got back to the Murrets' that night he reported that his aunt had been "very nice," "very, very happy" to see him, and had invited him to come back again.[17]

He never did. Nor did he look up his cousins or his aunts or go back to visit his father's grave. Perhaps he had discovered all he wanted to know; perhaps Hazel's question put him off; perhaps his father's photograph was a disappointment; perhaps his interests simply shifted. But he had made at least an attempt to trace his father's history, to find out where he came from, to whom he belonged. In the city of his birth, he had gone back to the beginning of his life in search of the father he had lost, a loss that was perhaps in the forefront of his mind since he had said goodbye to George de Mohrenschildt only two weeks earlier. He found a grave and a photograph, nothing more. He did not tell Marina that he had visited his father's grave or gone to see Hazel Oswald. He did not show her his father's photograph. The picture did not turn up later among his possessions.

Lee continued his search for a job by answering newspaper ads and through the Louisiana State Employment Office, where characteristically, he lied about his previous job history and claimed, on his unemployment compensation forms, to have applied for jobs he had not applied for at all. His references, too, were works of imagination. He often used his Uncle Dutz Murret's name, although he had not asked his permission. Occasionally he listed "George Hidell," whom he described as a "college student" at "705 Polk Street."[18] The address and occupation were fictitious, while the name "George Hidell" appears to have been made up of his own alias, "Hidell," and the first name of De Mohrenschildt. Lee also fell back for references on William S. Oswald, Jr., Alice Barre, and William S. Oswald III, an uncle, aunt, and cousin, respectively, whom he did not know, did not bother to look up, and whose addresses he sometimes gave incorrectly.

Finally, two weeks to the day after his arrival in New Orleans, Lee found a job as a greaser and maintenance man at the William B. Reily Company, distributor of Luzianne coffee. On his brief application there, he may have set his own record for lies. He said that he had been living at 757 French Street (the Murrets') for three years; that he had graduated from a high school that he had attended for only a few weeks; and he gave as references his cousin John Murret, whose permission he did not ask; Sergeant Robert Hidell (a composite of his brother Robert and his own alias "Hidell"), "on active duty with the U.S. Marine Corps" (a fiction from beginning to end); and "Lieutenant J. Evans, active duty U.S. Marine Corps" (the surname and first initial of a man he was to look up later that day, combined with a fictitious Marine Corps rank and identification).[19]

The job was manual labor, but at $1.50 an hour it paid more than his last job at $1.35. Lee had applied for photography jobs, or so he claimed on his unemployment compensation forms; but when the Louisiana State Employment Office actually arranged a job interview in photography, Lee did not bother to show up. On the morning he got his new job he came back to the Murrets' waving his newspaper in the air, grabbed Aunt Lillian around the neck, kissed her, and triumphantly announced, "I got it, I got it!"

Lillian was not impressed. "You know, Lee," she said, in one of those remarks that only she could get away with, "you are really not qualified to do anything too much. If you don't like this job, why don't you try to go back to school at night and see if you can't learn a trade?"

"No," Lee said. "I don't have to go back to school. I don't have to learn anything. I know everything."[20]

The same day he found the job, Lee also found an apartment. Myrtle and Julian Evans had known Lee and his mother when he was growing up, and Marguerite had once rented an apartment from them. Lee went to their building and Julian Evans, who was seated at breakfast drinking his last cup of coffee, recognized him right away. He had known Lee both as a child and as a teenager, and there was something about him that neither he nor Myrtle liked. Julian finished his coffee, shook hands with the caller, and left for work. His wife Myrtle, a heavy-set woman in her fifties, who wore glasses and had reddish hair in a bun, peered at Lee closely. "I know you, don't I?"

"Sure, I am Lee Oswald. I was just waiting to see when you were going to recognize me."

"Lee Oswald! What are you doing in this country? I thought you were in Russia."[21]

He explained that he was back, that he had a Russian wife and a child, and was looking for an apartment. There was nothing available at the Evanses, but Myrtle volunteered to help him look. It occurred to her that if he was going to work at the Reily coffee company, they might as well try on Magazine Street so Lee could live close to his job. They drove up and down Magazine Street looking for "For Rent" signs. Lee spotted one and they went in.

There were two apartments for rent at 4907 Magazine Street, and the bigger one looked as if it might do. It was on the ground floor. It had a long living room, a screened-in front porch, a yard, and the kind of iron fence children can't crawl through. The rent was $65 a month. Myrtle advised Lee that it was the best value for his money and he'd better take it.

The landlady was Mrs. Jesse Garner, and Lee gave her a month's rent and an application for utilities along with a $5 deposit. But then he told another of his funny, pointless lies. He said he worked for the Leon Israel Company of 300 Magazine Street. The company existed, but it was not the company that had hired him

Myrtle Evans took Lee home with her for lunch. They talked about New Orleans, about Lee's mother and brothers, and about Russia. Mrs. Evans's curiosity was piqued about Marina. She said she would like to meet her.

"Just come any time," said Lee.

That was the last Myrtle Evans ever saw of him.

Lee called Marina that evening to tell her about the job and the apartment. The next day, Friday, May 10, he went to work at the Reily coffee company for the first time and spent the night in his new apartment. On Saturday, he showed up early at the Murrets'. Marina was expected that day, and they decided to move Lee's luggage before she came. Again Lee loaded the car by himself, then he and Dutz sat in front with Marilyn and her mother behind, and the four of them drove to Magazine Street together. Lee was obviously eager for Marina to arrive. And he was delighted with the apartment. The neighborhood was not good, but the apartment had been freshly painted, the icebox was new, and some of the furniture looked new. Lee was not sure that Marina would like it, however. It had high ceilings, and Marina, like many Soviet Russians, did not like high ceilings.

For Marina, the two weeks she stayed at Ruth Paine's were like a vacation. She was tired; she was still trying to absorb the horrifying new facts she had only just learned about her husband. It was a relief to be taken care of and have no responsibility other than looking after June. It was a relief not to have to anticipate Lee's moods every second, and try to guess what new and dreadful surprise might be lurking around the corner.

Marina was very grateful. But Ruth Paine was of all Americans the very last whom Marina's experience could have equipped her to understand. Like the De Mohrenschildts, the Paines were an extremely unlikely couple to have befriended the Oswalds. Even seeing Ruth and Marina together was a study in contrasts.

Ruth was tall, slender, lithe, with a figure like a dancer. She had a thin, longish face with freckles and short, slightly wavy brown hair. The appearance of seriousness she gave was enhanced by a pair of rimless glasses. And she had a tendency to go around singing. Like many people who have been serious even as children, she had a good deal of unexpended child in her. Ruth could be a little bit fey.

Ruth Avery Hyde grew up in the Middle West, the daughter of parents who felt strongly about the value of education and good works. When she was only thirteen, Ruth spent a summer on a truck farm in Ohio as her way of contributing to the effort to win World War II. The next summer she was with a traveling Bible school, teaching in Ohio and Indiana. At nineteen, as a student at Antioch College in Ohio, she became a Quaker, a convinced Quaker, often the most dedicated kind. She wanted to be a teacher, and by the time she graduated she had held an astonishing array of jobs. She had taught in elementary schools in the East and the Middle West and had been a recreation leader at Jewish community centers in Ohio and Indiana, at a club for elderly immigrants in Philadelphia, and at a Friends' work camp in South Dakota. Whatever the job, Ruth was liked and respected, and was always asked to come back.

She was a teacher, aged twenty-five, at the Germantown Friends' School in Philadelphia when she met and married Michael Paine. The marriage was not only suitable, it appeared inevitable, so much did Ruth and Michael share. They met through a common love of madrigal singing and folk dancing; both were children of divorce, and both came from families of exceptional social conscience. But their marriage was in trouble from the start, before the start, really, because Michael was not sure about his capacity for love. They moved to Texas, and in September 1962, they separated. Michael was now living alone in an apartment in Grand Prairie, Texas, and came home two or three times a week. This, the break with Michael, which she was hoping against hope to mend, was the sorrow of Ruth's life. It was the aching place which Marina, slightly and for a while, was to fill.

Ruth had spent her life helping others, but charitable though her every instinct was, she had mixed feelings about Lee. She sensed that Lee was using her. On the morning of April 24, when Lee was on his way to New Orleans, he had simply taken it for granted that she would ferry him to the bus terminal. Lee did not ask, he *expected.* But her awareness of this did not deter Ruth from inviting Lee's wife and child to stay with her. And when he accepted without even offering to help with their expenses, Ruth's concern, characteristically, was for Marina, not herself. Marina was not a sponger. She had pride. Ruth thought that Lee must not love his wife at all if he could place her in so awkward a situation and go to so little trouble to take care of her.

She was right on the mark. Marina genuinely liked Ruth. She liked her company and loved being at her house. But she had qualms of conscience. She hated being a burden, hated being in a position where she had little to give. On April 24, even before the two women left for Irving, Marina seems to have sought reassurance. Lee gave it, telling her that she had nothing to be ashamed of. "Ruth is lonely," he said. "You'll be company for her. And you can teach her Russian."

Still, Marina hardly had a penny, she contributed nothing to the household, and she was ashamed. She helped with the cleaning and washing up. And she helped Ruth with her Russian. Marina tried to tell herself that she was doing more for Ruth than Ruth was doing for her, and Ruth, too, told her the same thing many times. But it would not wash. Marina was deeply in Ruth's debt and she knew it.

The relationship had its other angularities. Ruth was thirty-one, Marina twenty-one, and to Marina the gap was enormous. She was in Ruth's home, dependent on her, and it was natural to place her in the role of mother. Whenever she and June were talking, Marina spoke of Ruth as *Tyotya,* or "Aunt Ruth," an ordinary way of speaking in Russia, where close women friends of the family are called "aunt." But to Ruth, the word had an unwelcome sound. She wanted to be a friend and an equal. Not only that. Ruth guessed that Marina's feelings toward her mother had been very mixed, compounded of hate as well as love. She sensed that any relationship in which she was cast in the role of mother could turn out to be a minefield of complications.

There was also the language barrier between them. Ruth had a splendid education, but in Russian she was only a beginner. There was a huge, frustrating gap between what this thoughtful, sensitive woman might be thinking and what she could say in Russian. Ruth later recalled that her lack of Russian was "a terrible impediment to talking and to friendship" with Marina; it was "a terrible embarrassment" and an ironic one as well.[22] Here she was in her own house, commanding the telephone, recruiting lawn mowers and babysitters, making arrangements with marvelous efficiency, yet linguistically she was on Marina's turf. Ruth felt as helpless as a child.

Marina for her part kept enormous reticences. But they were reticences of loyalty, not of language. She chattered freely about her life in Russia, her girl-friends, her aunts, her boyfriends. But she said no more about Lee's plan to send her back to Russia. She never mentioned that Lee beat her. She did not know that Ruth was a pacifist, nor even what a pacifist is, but she had the wit not to mention that Lee had a rifle and had attempted to kill General Walker. Nor did she say that she had persuaded Lee to move to New Orleans out of fear of his using it again. Ruth has said that knowledge of the Walker attempt would have altered all her actions toward the Oswalds. She would have gone to the police and found a psychiatrist for Lee, or done both, as soon as she learned of it.

With such portentous silences on Marina's side, it is scarcely a wonder that Ruth eventually concluded that Marina was a bit of "an enigma," that they were "different sorts of people."[23] But her awareness was a long time coming, and meanwhile the two of them trotted along, like a pair of tired ponies, in easy harness. It was a friendship of shared exhaustion. Doubt as to whether their husbands loved them and would ever want to live with them again—this was the rock on which their companionship was built. Both of them, after the ordeal of their marriages, required a rest. Ruth was later to say that she and Marina gave each other "great moral support" at a difficult time for both.[24] As for the differences between them—lack of language, their fundamental incongruousness as friends—even these made for a restful distance, a feeling of live and let live, and respect for each other's privacy.

As she got to know Marina, Ruth's reservations about Lee grew to active dislike. It looked to her as if Lee "just wanted to get rid of his wife."[25] He had not even taken her to a doctor although she was three months pregnant. Ruth had made almost a life's work out of finding the best in people, but she had yet to find anything good in Lee.

Talking with Marina, Ruth came away with the impression that although she was troubled about Lee, she was committed to their marriage and would give her all for its survival. But Ruth had no inkling of how frightening Marina's worries were. To Marina, the Walker affair and its "Nixon" sequel meant that Lee loved "politics" more than he loved her and June. She feared that he could not wait to ship them both off to Russia in order to resume the political activities they had unwittingly interrupted. Life, or Lee, she limply supposed, would carry her as far as New Orleans. After that, Russia loomed like an iceberg.

As for Ruth's feelings about Michael, Marina had the evidence of her own eyes. On the days when Michael was expected, Ruth hummed with happiness. She went skipping, almost airborne, about the house, singing madrigals in antici-pation. And at suppertime—Michael generally came on Tuesday and Friday evenings—she set the table with great care and served dinner by candlelight. Ruth was in love with Michael. She would do anything to patch up their marriage.

It was Michael whom Marina could not figure out. She was familiar enough with the ways of anger, but coldness she could not understand. To her it appeared that Michael had no feelings for anyone, not for Ruth, not even for his own children. What Marina could not have known was that Michael blamed himself bitterly. He yearned to be in love with his wife. He, too, would mend the marriage if he could. And what Marina could never have guessed was that underneath Michael's reserve, his icily intellectual New England exterior, lay considerable compassion for herself.

Marina and Lee were in touch. She had a happy note from him, written the day after his arrival in New Orleans, announcing that his Aunt Lillian had taken him in warmly, that he was looking for work and would write to her as soon as he found it.[26] Marina was pleased that he signed the letter with the Russian *Tseluyu*—"I kiss you" or "Love"—a greeting he did not use even with his own mother. Maybe in spite of all that had happened he really did love her after all.

Once she called him on the telephone. And another time she wrote him a letter in which she mentioned that Ruth was driving east on her vacation and had offered to take her along. Marina wondered if she ought to go, ought to scout job possibilities in Washington, New York, and Philadelphia where there were Russian-speaking communities and where her language might be a help, not a hindrance, in finding work. Ruth has said that Marina was "quite excited" by the idea.[27] Her enthusiasm was in contrast with the passivity she had shown a few months earlier when George Bouhe and Katya Ford had tried to show her that she was not bound to Lee, that she could find a job and free herself. Now, for the first time, she seemed open to the idea.

The fact that she was at a distance from Lee and living in the household of a woman who was preparing to be self-supporting probably had something to do with the change. But Marina may also have been suggesting, as she had before, that she could try to find work and help support them if Lee was unable to get a job. Or she may have been offering him an "out." If he really did not love her and did not want to live with her again—or if he had any more horrors in store—then here was a chance to get rid of her without forcing her to go back to Russia.

And yet, for Marina, writing to Lee about finding a job was also the sort of ploy she used when she was trying to win somebody's love. By hinting that she, too, had choices, that other people thought she could find a job, she was bidding up her own value to win back Lee's love. She knew that it would make him jealous, and that for his jealousy she would have to pay. But it was utterly like her to get him to love her now—and pay later.[28]

Then came another cheerful letter from Lee in which he said that he still had not found a job, but his uncle had offered him a loan of $200.[29] Finally, on May 9, he called with triumph in his voice to announce that he had found a job and an apartment, and to ask them to come to New Orleans right away. Lee's voice told Marina what she had been longing to hear: he loved her, he missed her, he wanted to pick up their family life again. Once more she began to have hope.

Overcome with joy, she cried out: "Papa loves us! Papa loves us!" to little June as if she did not believe it herself.

By noon the next day Marina, Ruth, and the three children were off in Ruth's station wagon on the 500-mile journey to New Orleans.

27

Magazine Street

MARINA HATED the new apartment. She took one look at the high ceilings and the cockroaches and could barely hide her disappointment. Lee tried to show her how nice it was—the screened-in porch and the yard with wild strawberries growing in it. He had mopped the floor and cleaned the place, hoping she would like it. Marina knew it, knew his desire to please, but her feelings showed through. Seeing them together, it occurred to Ruth that Lee might or might not care about Marina, but he certainly cared about her opinion.

Marina and Ruth had arrived earlier that afternoon at the Murrets'. The five of them—two tired women and three small children—tumbled out of the station wagon and created chaos. Lee was beside himself with pride as he introduced Marina and the baby. He carried June on his shoulders and was ecstatic to see her walking for the first time.

Marina, too, was pleased, thinking that this house was to be her home. It was clean, cozy, neat—everything she had ever wanted. Then the truth reached her; she was going to have to live somewhere else. The Murrets were very kind to her, but Marina was miserably self-conscious. She thought she looked ugly and pregnant.

After an hour at the Murrets', they drove to Magazine Street, and once Marina recovered from her initial shock, the five of them settled in fairly quickly. Ruth and the three children slept in the living room and a small extra room beside it, while Lee and Marina used the bedroom in back.

They were happy to be together again—"I've missed you so," Lee said again and again—and they made love three times that night and the next morning. It was the first time they had made love since March 29 or 30, the weekend when Marina had taken Lee's photograph with the rifle. In the morning Ruth, on her way to the bathroom, passed by as they were making love.

"Do you think she saw?" Marina asked anxiously.

"Of course," said Lee.

They were both embarrassed. Lee hardly dared face Ruth in the kitchen, and Marina felt the same way.

As for Ruth, she noticed that, pleased as Lee and Marina had been to see one another at first, irritation and even anger flared up quickly between them, very often over nothing at all. She and Marina had bought blackberries as they drove across Louisiana, and on Sunday Lee tried to make blackberry wine. Marina was sharp with him—"What are you doing, wasting all those good berries?" Lee kept on with it, but he was disheartened by Marina's anger and, when she was not looking, he threw the whole mess out, berries, wine, and all. Shrewish as Marina was, Lee was even worse. He was in a bad temper the entire time. "Shut up," he would say whenever Marina opened her mouth, and Ruth thought he was "rude" and "discourteous" to Marina throughout her visit.[1] So ferocious was their bickering that Ruth decided the presence of three extra people must be adding to the strain. She and her children left on Tuesday, a day or so ahead of schedule.

But the bickering went on, for it was the currency of their relationship. Marina says that even on quiet days the marriage was a succession of "tears and caresses, arguments and reconciliations." Lee did not beat her, but their fights were amplified in Russian, an unfamiliar tongue, and their neighbors in New Orleans were soon in nearly the same condition of shock as their neighbors in Dallas. The state of the marriage, the state of mind of the principals, had to be measured by something other than the decibel count. With the Oswalds, ordinary conversation sounded like argument, and a real argument like a fight to the finish. What counted was the mood of the marriage, and in New Orleans, the first couple of months were hard. Marina was depressed and Lee preoccupied. They fought constantly, with little humor in their battles.

They fought about everything. A week or so after Marina's arrival, Lee bought some crabs, brought them home, and left them simmering on the stove. Not knowing that he meant to cook them his own way, Marina added spices, the ones she knew from Russia. Lee was furious.

They fought about cockroaches, too. Marina sometimes got up at night and went to the kitchen for something cold to drink. The place would be swarming with cockroaches.

"Come in and admire your handiwork," she would call out toward the bedroom—it was "his" handiwork because Lee did not allow her to use the spray.

He would run in naked from the bedroom, brandishing a can of roach spray and squirting it everywhere. Marina laughed, because he was too stingy to buy decent spray, too stingy to use enough of it, and because he put it in the wrong places.

"You woke me up, and now you're laughing at me." He was hurt.

Every day while he was at work, Marina scrubbed the floor and the furniture. But the apartment was old and dark and, no matter how hard she tried to clean it, the place still got her down. But she loved to go walking at night with Lee, letting him show her New Orleans, even though she sometimes felt that he did it because he thought it was his duty and not because he wanted to. Strolling through one neighborhood or another, Lee would sometimes wave at a building and crow, "I went to that school." It happened often enough that Marina began to wonder just how many schools he had been to.

What she enjoyed most were their walks along Bourbon Street. She adored the lights and the music and the glimpses of strippers dancing. She begged Lee to take her inside. He refused, said Bourbon Street was "a dirty place," and put on a show of inattentiveness as they walked past the famous swinging doors. Marina thought that he liked Bourbon Street just the same.

Marina made no secret of her interest in sex. At the newsstands, where they fairly often found themselves at night, she would pick out the most unwholesome-looking magazines she could find and pore over the photographs of nude men and women. Lee affected to be above it all. He read the news magazines. But more than once she spied him flicking through a girlie magazine.

Aside from June, whom they both adored, sex was again the brightest feature of their marriage. For all his Puritanism, Lee enjoyed making love. After intercourse, he would go into the bathroom to wash off, emerge singing one of his arias, and lie down with his back to Marina.

"Don't touch me," he would say. "And don't say a word. I'm in paradise now. I don't want my good mood spoiled."

There was a mirror at the foot of their bed, and Lee would pile up pillows at the head of the bed so he could watch them making love. Marina did not like it. She pulled the pillows down or turned her head away. She was hurt that the mirror seemed to excite Lee more than she did.

Sometimes when she was sitting in front of the mirror brushing her hair, he would bend down to kiss her, looking into the mirror, and call her "Mama" or "my little girl."

"Who are you kissing me for—me or the mirror?"

"You mean you don't like it?"

"Of course not," she would answer, and give him a little rap on the rear end.

Although Marina insists that their sexual life was improving right up to the end and that, well over a year after Lee's death, she still would have chosen him over any other man, the fact is that the balance had shifted. In Russia it was Lee who wanted sex more; now it was Marina. Sometimes when Lee came home hot and tired from work, he would beg off making love on the ground that he would be unable to keep it up long enough to satisfy Marina. But even when her pregnancy made intercourse uncomfortable for her, Marina was glad to give him satisfaction even if she did not receive it in return.

For she was no longer sure that Lee loved her, and she wanted to be needed and reassured. Every day she expected to hear that he still meant to send her back to Russia. Waiting for the ax to fall, her fears abated only when they were walking along Bourbon Street at night. Then the lights and the music and the sight of people enjoying themselves lifted her spirits a little.

On May 12, the day after Marina arrived in New Orleans, Lee made out a change-of-address card, closing his post office box in Dallas and giving his new home address. The change became effective May 14, and Lee once again began to receive the magazines and newspapers to which he subscribed, among them *Soviet Belorussia,* a daily subsidized by the Soviet government, and *The Militant.* News of Fidel Castro, then on a month-long tour of the Soviet Union, was featured in both papers, and *The Militant* in particular was critical of recent speeches by President Kennedy and his brother, the Attorney General, hinting that the United States government was working for Castro's overthrow.[2]

Lee had not forgotten Fidel Castro. The move to New Orleans, and the search for a new job and a new apartment, had distracted him from politics only briefly. Now he was to become more deeply involved in the Cuban cause than he had ever been, and was to identify himself more strongly than ever with this particular revolution and its heroes. On May 22 he paid his first visit to the New Orleans Public Library, applied for a borrower's card, and took out his first book. It was *Portrait of a Revolutionary: Mao Tse-tung,* by the biographer Robert Payne. Marina says that Lee compared himself to the great men he read about in books and genuinely believed that he was one of them.[3]

At this moment, however, Lee was thinking more about changing the society he was in than about building a new one, as Mao and Castro had done. And what he hoped to change first was United States policy toward Cuba. On May 26, therefore, he wrote again to the Fair Play for Cuba Committee at its national headquarters, 799 Broadway, New York, announcing that he wanted to form a New Orleans chapter. He requested a charter for his chapter, formal membership for himself, said he was thinking of renting an office for $30 a month, and asked how he might acquire membership blanks and bulk literature. For the office he was hoping to set up, he added that "a picture of Fidel, suitable for framing, would be a welcome touch."[4]

Without waiting for a reply, Lee then set about printing his own literature. On May 29, after he had apparently scouted several similar establishments, he walked into the Jones Printing Company of 422 Girod Street and handed the secretary an 8 by 10 looseleaf sheet on which he had sketched a handbill:[5]

HANDS
OFF
CUBA!

Join the Fair Play for

Cuba Committee

New Orleans Charter
Member Branch

Free Literature, Lectures

Location:

Everyone welcome!

He said his name was Lee Osborne, and two days later he returned to put down $4 cash on the order. On June 4, he paid the remaining $5.89 in cash and picked up 1,000 copies of the handbill. He also ordered, from the Mailers' Service

Company on Magazine Street, 500 copies of a yellow, 4 by 9 membership application for his New Orleans "chapter" of the Fair Play for Cuba Committee, once again under the name of Lee Osborne. He picked up that order, paying $9.34 in cash, on June 5. Finally, about the same time, he ordered 300 copies of a 2½-by 3½-inch membership card in the same New Orleans "chapter." John Anderson, who took the order at Mailers' Service, recalled that "Osborne" at first was not satisfied because he wanted heavy, "card-type" paper for his membership cards rather than the "thick paper" the company had used. However, he accepted the order, paid $3.50 in cash, and went off with the cards.[6]

Vincent T. Lee, national director of the Fair Play for Cuba Committee, replied to Lee's letter on May 29. It was the longest, warmest letter he had ever received from the head of any organization. It offered him, for the first time in his life, a real chance to work with a political group. And it offered advice.

Vincent Lee counseled Lee against opening an office and suggested that he work out of a private home instead, using a post office box as his address. He also suggested that Lee use only first-class mail on committee business and never put a full name on the return address on the envelope. He sent Lee a membership card in the F.P.C.C., a copy of its constitution and by-laws, and he closed his letter: "Naturally I would like to communicate with you a great deal more concerning yourself so that we can get to know you and possibly be of some assistance. . . . We hope to hear from you very soon and are looking forward to a good working relationship for the future. . . . Fraternally, V. T. Lee."[7]

Lee, of course, did not tell Marina about the letter right away—she as yet had no idea what he was up to—but he was elated by it. In one regard, however, the letter must have been a disappointment. Vincent Lee wrote that he had gone through the committee's files and could scarcely conceive of a chapter "with as few members as seem to exist in the New Orleans area," but he would gladly issue a charter if Lee could come up with enough members. Nor did he send the application forms and membership cards that Lee had requested. It was probably just after he received the letter that Lee decided to print up his own forms and cards.

Marina might have guessed that he was again becoming involved in "politics," for the blow she was dreading had fallen. Less than two weeks after her arrival in New Orleans, and even before he wrote to the F.P.C.C., Lee told her that he did not love her. She was "in his way," he said, and he still meant to send her back to Russia.

"I'll go to Cuba, then China, and you will wait for me in Russia," he told her in his coldest tone. "I love to travel and with you I can't."

But his behavior was inconsistent. Sometimes he went a whole day without speaking, then spent the next day making up to her. He would take her and Junie to the park, do the laundry, mop the floor. He would even hang up the wash, while Marina leaned out the window and shouted directions, and Junie waved at her "Papa." He often told Marina how much he had missed her. And he was proud of her when he took her to the Murrets. They thought that Marina and Lee were a "cute," "family-conscious" and "devoted" couple.[8] But Marina was anxious.

She was afraid that Lee was nice to her only because he would soon be getting rid of her.

She was not entirely helpless, however—she did have a friend. Two weeks after her arrival in New Orleans, Marina wrote to Ruth Paine: "As soon as you left, all 'love' stopped. I feel very hurt because Lee's attitude toward me is such that every minute I feel as if I am tying him down. He insists that I leave America, and this I don't want at all. I like America very much and I think that even without Lee I would not be lost here. What do you think?"[9]

Ruth had invited Marina to stay with her in October, when the new baby came. So far she had said nothing about a more permanent haven. But Marina was intuitive. Ruth was her hope of salvation.

The strain on her began to take its toll. On Saturday morning, June 1, Lee took Marina and June to the Napoleon Branch of the public library, the branch nearest their apartment, to look for books in Russian for Marina. All they found were some novels in English translation. But Lee took out two books for himself: *The Berlin Wall* by Dean and David Heller, and *The Huey Long Murder Case* by Hermann Bacher Deutsch. They walked along for a bit, with June in her stroller; then Marina and the baby waited outside while Lee ducked into a store and had his photograph taken—evidently for a passport.[10] The three walked along farther and crossed the street.

"Don't go so fast," Marina said. "I don't feel well." Lee kept on walking, thinking it was only a joke. She leaned against a store front. "Wait a minute, Lee," she called out. Next thing she knew she was lying on the sidewalk and Lee had his arms around her. He carried her inside the store, and some strangers brought her to with ammonia.

"You'll be okay, you'll be okay," Lee encouraged her. "Can you walk?"

Marina nodded, and they went home. He put her to bed, brought her some juice, and tiptoed around the rest of the day, taking care of June. "Shhh, Junie, Mama's sleeping," Marina heard him say.

Later that same week, on June 4, Marina received a letter from the consular section of the Soviet Embassy in Washington. It asked that she come to Washington if possible and, otherwise, that she write the embassy her reasons for wishing to return to the U.S.S.R.[11]

Marina turned the letter over and stared at it a long time. What puzzled her was the address. It had been mailed directly to her at 4907 Magazine Street, New Orleans. When Lee came home that night, she asked how the embassy knew her now address. He told her that he had sent it. Marina thought she heard her death knell toll again.

Later that same night, she at last discovered what Lee was up to.

"Come here. I want you to sign something," he said.

"What is it?"

"My card for this organization about Cuba."

"What organization? The one with only one member?"

"It'll help me to have this card. People will believe in me more. They'll think I have a real organization."

He wanted Marina to sign a membership card in the New Orleans "chapter" of the Fair Play for Cuba Committee, not in her own name but with the alias he had been using for several months.

"I won't do it," she said.

"You've got to." He grabbed her and held her hard by both hands.

"Sign it yourself. I won't," she answered. "I'm not going to get mixed up in your affairs."

He pleaded with her. "There have got to be two handwritings. You're my wife. You never help. You never support me. And I ask so little of you. You'll be sorry if you don't."

Marina remembered the letter that had arrived from the Soviet Embassy that day. "What will you do to me if I don't sign? Will you beat me?" she asked.

"Maybe. We'll see."

His eyes had begun to glitter and Marina thought she had better sign. She told herself that it was nothing but child's play anyway, and it was better for him to be playing with bits of paper than with a gun. But she had no idea what she was signing. "It could have been my own death sentence," she said later.

As long as she was going to sign, however, she wanted her writing to look pretty.[12] Several times, on a piece of scratch paper, she practiced writing the name Lee wanted her to sign. He thrust the card in front of her, and with some care, she wrote "A. J. Hidell." He was "President" of the New Orleans "chapter" of the F.P.C.C.

"What's that?" she asked, commenting on the name. "An altered Fidel?"

"Shut up." He was blushing. "Don't meddle in what you don't understand."

"So America has its Fidel," she said sarcastically. "Don't you think you're taking a bit too much on yourself?"

He was ashamed at being caught and admitted there was no such person as "Hidell." But he wanted people to think he had a big organization.

"Do you mean that you have two names?" she asked in wonder.

"Yes," he said.

Two days later, he put his alias to another use. He took a standard yellow international vaccination certificate, wrote his name at the top, stamped it "Dr. A. J. Hideel" (sic) and, in his own handwriting this time, forged the name "A. J. Hidell" above the stamp. In addition to being president of the New Orleans "chapter" of the F.P.C.C., "Hidell" was also his doctor.[13] Three days after that, Lee listed "A. J. Hidell" and Marina Oswald as persons entitled to receive mail at the post office box he had opened on June 3.[14]

All of these things together—the handbills, his remarks to Marina about going to Cuba or China, the passport photos, the vaccination certificate, his intention to send Marina back to Russia—suggest that a multiple scenario was beginning to take shape in Lee's head.

A third important letter arrived during the first week in June, this one from Ruth Paine. Much of the letter was written in English for Lee. Ruth repeated her offer for Marina to come to Texas to have her baby at a clinic in Grand Prairie. She explained how much it would cost, said that Marina would have to bring her medical records from New Orleans, and expressed hope that she would go to a doctor soon to anticipate any complications in her pregnancy.

Coming so soon after Marina's fainting spell of June 1, the letter seems to have had an effect on Lee. On Saturday, June 8, he took Marina for a medical examination at the New Orleans Charity Hospital, a large institution near their home. Unfortunately it was a state hospital, permitted to treat only Louisiana residents or emergency cases. Marina had not lived long enough in Louisiana to qualify as a resident, nor was hers an emergency. Although Lee spent a full hour pleading to have a doctor examine her, the Oswalds were turned away.[15]

The impact could hardly have been more dramatic. "Everything is money in this country," Lee said, his face contorted with anger, awash with apology and shame. "Even the doctors are businessmen. You can't even have a baby without money." The tears were rolling down his cheeks.

"It's okay. I understand. Everything will be all right," Marina said to comfort him. Lee always had an extra $10 in his pocket, and Marina later realized that he could have taken her to a doctor. But she was too sorry for him to think of it at the time. She wanted to see a doctor, but she put the idea aside and was not examined until she was in her ninth month.

The week that began two days later, on Monday, June 10, was a memorable one in the presidency of John F. Kennedy and a memorable, as well as tragic, one for the civil rights movement. On June 10, President Kennedy gave the famous "American University" speech in which he hailed the Russian people for their achievements and asked for a world "safe for diversity." On the evening of the speech, Lee sat down and wrote a letter to *The Worker,* the newspaper of the U.S. Communist Party in New York City. He announced that he had formed a Fair Play for Cuba "chapter" in New Orleans, asked for Communist Party literature for his "office," and sent honorary membership cards in his "chapter" to Gus Hall and Benjamin Davis, leaders of the Party in the United States.

The following day, June 11, was a landmark in the civil rights struggle that had been raging that spring with its focus in Birmingham, Alabama. In January a governor named George Wallace had been inaugurated in Alabama with a speech promising that he "would stand in the schoolhouse door, if necessary," to resist court-ordered desegregation. On June 11, Wallace fulfilled his promise by standing in the doorway of the registration building of the University of Alabama at Tuscaloosa. Twice Wallace held out his hand in a "stop" signal, and twice James Hood and Vivian Malone, two black students who were accompanied by the Deputy Attorney General of the United States, Nicholas Katzenbach, had to retreat. As the day wore on, President Kennedy, in Washington, signed an order federalizing part of the National Guard in Alabama. As guardsmen walked on the campus, Governor Wallace walked off, and the two students were allowed to register.

That evening President Kennedy went on the air from the White House to call for a sweeping new civil rights law. But it was a night that ended in tragedy. Only a few hours after Kennedy finished speaking, Medgar Evers, field secretary of the NAACP in Mississippi, was shot and killed by a sniper who had been lying in wait outside his home in Jackson, only 200 miles from New Orleans.[16]

Lee had often spoken of the necessity for greater understanding between the United States and the Soviet Union. He claimed that racial discrimination in America was the chief reason he had become a Marxist. But if he recognized that President Kennedy had that week taken major steps toward better relations with Russia abroad, and toward better relations between the races at home, he did not give the slightest sign of it. His mind appeared to be fixed on Cuba.

On the afternoon of Sunday, June 16, the day Evers's tumultuous funeral was reported in every newspaper in the land, Lee went, without a word to anyone, to the Dumaine Street Wharf, where the U.S.S. *Wasp* was berthed. There he passed out his white "Hands Off Cuba" leaflets, F.P.C.C. literature which he had received from New York, and yellow application forms for his Fair Play for Cuba "chapter" to such sailors and civilians as happened to come off the boat. Approached by Harbor Patrolman Girod Ray and asked whether he had a permit, Lee replied that he did not and he had no need of one. He was within his rights distributing leaflets anywhere he liked. Patrolman Ray informed him that he was on property of the New Orleans Port Authority and that a permit was, indeed, required. Either he must show a permit or be arrested.

Lee Harvey Oswald left.[17]

28

Castro and Kennedy

LEE OSWALD'S INTEREST in Castro was not new. As early as the fall of 1958, when he was barely nineteen and was stationed in the Marine Corps at El Toro, California, after his tour of duty in the Far East, he was already cheering Castro on. Castro was not yet in power at the time. He was leading a guerrilla band in the Sierra Maestre, fighting to overthrow the Cuban dictatorship.

Oswald had a friend in the Marine Corps named Nelson Delgado, a New Yorker of Hispanic extraction. Over Christmas of 1958, Delgado went on leave. When he returned, just after January 1, 1959, Castro was the ruler of Cuba. "Well," Oswald greeted him, "you took a leave and went there and helped them, and they all took over."[1]

Castro was hailed when he visited America four months after he came to power. He was received by the Secretary of State and acclaimed as a hero in a huge rally at Harvard University. Castro had not yet embraced communism. As for Oswald, he told Delgado that he mistrusted both the Communist and the American forms of government. He thought that Castro was the pioneer who would show the way. He was what a revolutionary hero ought to be.

That spring Oswald and Delgado talked about going to Cuba. They and the other men in the barracks had heard of an army enlisted man named Morgan who became a legend because he quit the U.S. Army with a dishonorable discharge, fought under Castro in the Escambres, and came out a Cuban Army major. Oswald and Delgado thought they would have a head start. They would have honorable discharges, and between Delgado's knowledge of Spanish and Oswald's ideas about government, which seemed to fit with those of Castro, things might go well for them in Cuba. The idea of becoming an officer had great appeal for them both.

"We could go over there and become officers and lead an expedition to some of these other islands and free them, too," Delgado explained long afterward.[2]

One of the ideas they had was to "do away with Trujillo" and free the Dominican people.

But Delgado was only talking—Oswald meant what he said. Very soon he was "making plans." He peppered Delgado with questions about how they could get to Cuba and become part of the revolutionary movement. On Delgado's advice, Oswald bought a Spanish-English dictionary and started studying Spanish. Delgado also suggested that Oswald contact the Cuban Embassy; he assured him there was nothing subversive about it because the United States was on friendly terms with Cuba. And there is evidence that Oswald actually did contact the Cuban consulate in Los Angeles in hopes of getting into Cuba.[3] But when the men in the barracks discussed where they would seek refuge if ever they were in trouble at home, Oswald never hesitated: Russia would be his place of refuge.[4]

As the months went by and Castro started arresting political opponents, Delgado cooled off on Cuba. Not Oswald. He held stubbornly to his faith, claiming that Castro was getting a bad press and that "in all new governments, some errors have to occur." Delgado had the impression that the rumors of arrests and executions were, if anything, making Oswald "more reverent" toward Castro.[5]

Oswald did not go to Cuba, but to the Soviet Union instead. Once he was disappointed there, Cuba seemed all the more like a truly revolutionary country, like Russia before it went wrong, before bureaucratic ossification set in. In his eyes, Castro was still what a revolutionary hero ought to be. Besides, Cuba was small, beleaguered, an underdog. With all these things Oswald was in sympathy.

Once again he had come full circle. Four years earlier, he had thought about gaining Castro's trust and joining his revolution. Now, in the summer of 1963, he was thinking about the same thing. His effort to establish a chapter of the Fair Play for Cuba Committee in New Orleans appears to have been two-pronged, both an attempt to change American policy toward Cuba by peaceful political action at the grass-roots level, and an attempt to win the trust of the Castro government.

Lee Oswald needed a social system to idealize, and that for the moment was Cuba. He also needed a hero with whom he could identify; that hero was Fidel Castro.

The pseudonym a man uses, his alias, tells a good deal about him and who he would like to be. Lee Oswald's alias, the only one he ever used consistently, was Alik James Hidell. "Alik" was, of course, the name Oswald's fellow workers had given him in Minsk. "Alik" was Oswald himself at a period in his life when he liked himself better than usual.

There is no "James" who is known to have meant anything to Oswald in real life. But the name may have been taken from James Bond, the fictional hero created by Ian Fleming, whose novels Oswald read with enjoyment. Bond is a spy, as Oswald often said he would like to be, and he had the altogether miraculous quality of extricating himself from every danger. James Bond was, indeed, at the center of a magic circle of invulnerability, just as Lee supposed himself to be, especially after his attempt on General Walker and his own miraculous escape.

"Hidell" is, however, the most suggestive part of the alias. As often happens, the idea for the name probably came to Oswald from several sources. In Atsugi, Japan, he had known a fellow Marine who hailed, as he did, from New Orleans, and whose name was John Rene Heindell, nicknamed "Hidell."[6] But his reasons for choosing the name lie much deeper. Since the purpose of an alias is to hide one's identity, the name "Hidell," pronounced with a long "i," has an exquisite economy, defining its use, "hide," to perfection. But if the "i" is pronounced as a long "e," the name becomes "Heedell," a simple rhyme of Fidel. It was Marina who first spotted the similarity, for in Russian the letter "i" is pronounced as a long "e," and in the Russian alphabet the consonant "kh" or "h," as in "Hidell," comes immediately after "ph" or "f," as in "Fidel."

The beauty of "Alik James Hidell," then, is that it held within it Oswald's Russian name, "Alik," linked it with the magical properties of James Bond, and made Oswald one with his hero, Fidel.

Lee used both his own name and his alias on his leaflets and handbills. He bought two boxes of metal letters and put them together to form stamps. When Marina first saw him making the stamps, she scornfully called it his "jewelry work." On some of the leaflets he stamped: "L. H. Oswald, 4907 Magazine Street," and on others: "A. J. Hidell, P. O. Box 30016."[7] At first he was reluctant to let Marina see what he was doing, but one day, the second or third week in June, he proposed a trip to the zoo, backed out of it, and Marina went alone with the baby. Returning sooner than he expected, they found him in the living room with handbills—Marina calls them "papers"—spread out all over the coffee table. Taken by surprise, Lee hesitated guiltily and then started to put his "papers" away. Marina asked why he was hiding them.

Lee put on a special, wheedling voice, a mixture of pleading and baby talk. "Do you like Cuba?" he asked.

"Yes."

"Do you like Uncle Fidel?"

"Yes."

"Well, these papers will help make people be on the side of Cuba. Do you want them attacking little Cuba?"

"No," Marina said, "and you don't have to hide them from me, either. Sit there and play your childish games."

He put his handbills away and spent the rest of the day playing with June, doing housework, and making up to his wife in every way he could.

They spent a lot of evenings after that with Marina sitting in the rocking chair and Lee, seated at the coffee table, stamping leaflets. Marina was not happy to see him busy with "politics" again, but she told herself that as long as it had to do with papers and not a gun, she need not worry too much. It got so she hardly noticed.

Besides, Marina was preoccupied by troubles of her own, especially her fear that Lee would force her to go back to Russia. Night after night she sat rocking June to sleep with tears cascading down her cheeks.

Sometimes Lee pretended not to notice. Sometimes the sight of her tears actually put him in good spirits and he would break out singing or whistling. "Why are you crying?" he would ask.

"How can you be so cruel?"

"I'm not cruel. I've thought it out. It'll be better for you there."

"Why did you bring me here if you were only going to send me back with two children? You know what a disgrace it is to go back without a husband."

"You have a husband," he said icily. "I'll send you money. I thought it would be a disgrace to come back here. But it wasn't."

He kept her under unremitting pressure to write the Soviet Embassy and ask for her visa to be speeded up, and she unremittingly refused. He tried to force her to write the embassy whenever she did or said anything that displeased him, and nearly every night when he got home from work he asked whether she had written yet. Every night she answered that she had not. One night he twisted her wrist to try and make her give in.

But what hurt Marina most was something she only suspected: that Lee's coldness was only a mask, and that it took all his cruelty and self-command to keep it from slipping off. She believed it was his family, June and herself, whom he loved in his heart, but that in accordance with his lofty ideas about himself, he disguised his real feelings and forced himself to put politics above everything. It seemed to her that Lee was not being true to himself. Marina longed to cry out to him: "Why do you torture us so? You know you don't believe half what you are saying." For some reason she stifled her own cry.

Marina could understand someone's giving *her* up. But she did not see how, for the sake of his "foolish politics," Lee could give up June, whom he loved above everyone, and a new baby he had never even seen.

"Oh, I'll see it sometime," he said airily.

"Do you think you are such a great man?" Marina asked. "Do you think you are the only one who can do anything for 'little Cuba'?"

Indeed, Lee did give Marina grounds for suspecting that, icy and indifferent as he tried to appear, underneath his feelings were not so cold. He obviously loved June, and every so often, on an impulse, he would put his arms around Marina and kiss her, too. Marina was glad of his kisses. She says she was like a "blind kitten" who, for the sake of one caress, keeps coming back to the person who hits it.

But it was not long before the poor blind kitten put her tail up. Sometimes Lee's cruelty so repelled Marina that she could not bear to be in the same room with him. She would pick the baby up and go to another room to cry.

Suddenly one night she piped up: "Okay, I'll go back to Russia so long as you give me a divorce."

"And whom would you be planning to marry?" Lee asked with a little leer. "Anatoly?"

"I don't know. Maybe."

"There'll be no divorce," Lee said in a hard voice. "I may want to come to you sometime. I won't give you a divorce." He put down the book he was reading.

"You're my wife and you'll stay my wife. The children are mine. You'll wait for me just as long as I want. There will be no divorce. That's it. The conversation is over."

Sometimes Marina had moods in which she thought she might go back to Russia if it would please Lee. But she did not want to go. She wanted to keep Lee and stay in America. She counted on time, Soviet red tape, and a change in their relationship to save her. But now she had hit upon another device. She saw that Lee, for some reason she could not comprehend, would not allow her to go back to Russia without legal ties to him. And it worked. Each time she mentioned the word "divorce," Lee balked. If she continued to insist on a divorce, perhaps he would change his mind entirely.

Meantime an explosive new element had been introduced into their arguments: the name of Anatoly and, with it, jealousy. Once the name was out of the bag, it came up again and again, and it was Lee who kept bringing it up. He reminded Marina of the letter she had written to Anatoly the previous winter and told her he would never forget. He mentioned Anatoly every time they had a fight. If Marina reminisced about some escapade she had had in Minsk, he assumed that she had been with Anatoly. "Stop it," he would say. "I can't stand it." And if she herself spoke of Anatoly, he would say: "Shut up. I don't want to hear about your boyfriends."

Once Marina went too far and remarked that Anatoly used to kiss so well it had made her head spin. Lee literally clapped his hand over her mouth to hush her up. "You're my wife," he said. "You're not to speak of any other man ever again."

But another time, when she again had the temerity to mention Anatoly's kissing, Lee asked her to teach him how. At that moment Marina felt the full sweetness of revenge. Anatoly, she replied, half in humor, kissed so well that if Lee spent his whole life trying, he would never learn to kiss that way.

Marina's talk of Anatoly was not just a ruse to make Lee jealous. Her life with Lee had been so hard that anyone who had ever been good to her now seemed like an angel. Anatoly had been good to her, and she had been "crazy" about him. After Lee intercepted her letter to him and read it aloud, she had resolved to forget him. But Marina was not in full control of her thoughts. Anatoly started cropping up at night, in her dreams. If she did go back to Russia, he was the man she would marry—if he would have her.

Marina gave up trying to forget Anatoly. In fact, she bought a photograph of President Kennedy to remind her of him. An attentive observer of physical characteristics, a girl who was constantly drawing comparisons between the features of this person and that, Marina saw a resemblance between the two men: the ruffled, unruly hair, the heavy, slightly hooded eyelids, the nose, the lips, the lower half of the face—except for the generous Kennedy allotment of teeth. Nor was Kennedy the only man whose features reminded her of Anatoly's. The film actor Mel Ferrer, who played Prince Andrei in the film version of Tolstoy's *War and Peace,* reminded her of Anatoly, too.

As far as Marina is aware, Lee never knew that in her eyes the President's features were a prized reminder of the love she had lost. She did not tell him of the resemblance. Yet knowing her capacity to arouse jealousy, and Lee's proclivity to be jealous, it could very well be that she somehow telegraphed her feeling that Kennedy resembled Anatoly and that her message got through to Lee. In any case, Lee had seen Anatoly on the night he first met Marina, and if a resemblance truly existed and was marked, he may have observed it for himself. He was, justifiably, jealous of Anatoly. And he was jealous of Kennedy, whether he had seen a resemblance or not. Once Marina said casually: "He is very attractive—I can't say what he is as President, but, I mean, as a man." Lee's response was as usual: "You mustn't like any other man but me."

In the summer of 1963 both Lee and Marina, like so many others in America, had special feelings about the Kennedys. The names of the President and his wife were a staple item of their household conversation. Lee appears to have had a small, special feeling for Mrs. Kennedy. He admired her, he said, for accompanying her husband on his travels (a reproach to Marina) and, from reading *Time* and the newspapers, he seemed to have about as detailed a knowledge of her obstetrical history as he had of Marina's. He told Marina that, in addition to Caroline, John, Jr., and the child she was due to have that autumn, Mrs. Kennedy had lost two children, one a miscarriage and one a stillbirth. Marina was very, very sorry.[8]

As for the President, Lee said that he was Roman Catholic, one of a large family of brothers and sisters, a Democrat, and that his father was a millionaire who made money in the whiskey business. "His papa bought him the presidency," Lee remarked, and to Marina's surprise she failed to detect resentment in the way he said it. "Money paves the way to everything here," Lee added, and she thought she did hear resentment in that remark—not against the President but against capitalism. Lastly, he told her that in spite of his father's help, Kennedy was equipped to be President and deserved it.

Marina admired Kennedy in his own right—not only as a reminder of Anatoly. The more she saw of him the better she liked him, and it got so that she would flip through the pages of every magazine she could lay her hands on asking: "Where's Kennedy? Where's Kennedy?" With a patience that was utterly unlike him, Lee translated everything for her, every article and every caption— about the President, his wife, their children, and the Robert F. Kennedy family. He did not balk, as he did when she asked him to read about movie stars, nor did he scold her for being unable to read it herself. He seemed nearly as interested in the Kennedys as she was and, if the article was favorable, he seemed to agree with it. About three times that summer they heard Kennedy give a speech over the radio (they still did not have a TV). Lee listened intently and said "Shh" once when Marina asked him to translate while the President was still speaking. After one speech, probably the one of July 26 when Kennedy announced the signing of a nuclear test-ban treaty in Moscow, Lee told her that the speech had been an appeal for disarmament. But generally he refused to tell Marina what the speeches were about. He went quietly back to his book without a comment.

Marina got the impression that her husband liked and approved of the

President and believed that for the United States in 1963, John F. Kennedy was the best President the country could hope to have. His only reservation seemed to be that socialism was a better system. Lee did say that some critics blamed Kennedy for "losing" Cuba. He added, however, that Kennedy would like to pursue a better, more gentle policy toward Cuba but was not free to do as he wished. A President, he explained, had to reckon with the opinions of others.

As for Marina, her reactions were entirely personal. If anything, she thought more about Mrs. Kennedy than about the President because Mrs. Kennedy, like herself, was a wife and mother, and both of them were pregnant. To Marina, Jacqueline Kennedy was a latter-day goddess. She might conceivably have passionate feelings underneath but Marina supposed that, being Catholic and upper class, she must have been taught to restrain them. Indeed, Marina wondered whether the First Lady, unlike herself, was not a bit of a "cold fish." But she was aware of "Jackie" as a human being, too. She was interested in what she wore and how she fixed her hair, and she was concerned about her pregnancy.

Marina's feelings for the President were once again utterly personal. She loved photographs of Kennedy that showed him with his face wide open in a smile. Most of all she loved the pictures of him walking along a beach or on the golf course, his hands thrust into his pockets and wearing an old sweater and a pair of khaki pants, just like anybody else.[9] She was astonished that in this country such photographs of the President were allowed to appear. It seemed odd to her that the President's picture could be taken "in such an informal pose."

"They take his picture in all poses," Lee said.

In her admiration for Kennedy, Marina had only one reservation: he was in "politics." When she thought of Lee or of other men she had known, it was clear to her that anyone who cared about politics, especially any man who was even slightly tempted to place politics over his own family, must be sick or trying to escape personal unhappiness. To her, President Kennedy's interest in politics meant that something was missing in his life.

Marina speculated—to herself, not to Lee—about the President as man and lover. Since he looked like Anatoly, she wondered if he kissed like Anatoly. The resemblance suggested that he did. Marina did her best to convince herself that because he had a bad back, he probably wasn't much of a lover. Even so, the words Marina now uses to sum up her feelings toward the President are identical to the words she uses of only two other men in her life until then, Anatoly and Lee. The words are: "I was in love with him."

Marina had her photograph of President Kennedy and Lee had his of Fidel Castro, which he clipped out of the Soviet magazine *Ogonyok* and pinned to the living room wall. Marina did not know what he planned to do with all his leaflets; she did not know that on the afternoon of June 16 he had passed some of them out at the Dumaine Street Wharf. But she did notice that Lee's habits were beginning to change. He was getting very sloppy. By late May and early June, he had become alarmingly indifferent to the way he looked, and went around wearing only sandals, work pants, and a dirty T-shirt. Marina would beg him, when they were going out, please to put on a fresh shirt. He refused—and she would cry. She was ashamed to be seen on the street with him.

When he went to work he looked even worse. "My work isn't worth getting dressed for," he told Marina.

"Do it for yourself, then," she said. "Or if you won't do it for yourself, do it for me."

"I simply don't care," he replied.

He stopped shaving on weekends and by mid-July shaved only every other day. Where formerly he had brushed his teeth three times a day, now he brushed them only at night. He stopped washing his face in the morning. And, when he took a bath, he even stopped using soap. He just sat listlessly in the bathtub until he could stir himself to get out. "I'm not dirty," he would say.

He refused to let Marina darn his socks, preferring to go around in old, holey ones instead. She had to steal his socks if she was to mend them at all. He would burp at meals without excusing himself, and he got his hair cut at the nape of the neck so he had hair only on the top of his head. "I'll wear it any way I like," he said.

Marina told him that her Russian relatives had thought he was from a good family because he was clean and good-looking. "If you'd looked this way when I met you, I never would have married you at all."

His breath got bad and Marina used to beg him to brush his teeth, especially if he was going to kiss her. "You're my wife. You're supposed to love me any way I am," and he would come at her, his mouth open, breathing as hard as he could. He would try to kiss her, yet his eyes were so full of hate she thought he was going to kill her instead.

It got so he was dirty, unshaven, and unwashed nearly all the time. He knew it made Marina angry. "Ah-ha," he would say. "You can't stand me this way. I won't wash and I won't clean up just because you want me to." But Marina saw that it had nothing to do with her. He had simply lost all desire to take care of himself.

Lee's behavior was also unpredictable. Often he would look up from his book to propose an outing. Marina would get dressed and would dress the baby, too. Then, at the last minute, Lee would change his mind and tell them to go without him. Sometimes it was a ploy to get rid of them so he could work on his writings alone. Yet he hated their being away for long and was distraught if they were as little as half an hour late getting home.

By far the worst change, however, was the return for a few weeks in June of Lee's feeling that Marina was his property, or slave, and he her owner. This meant he had the right to take her, sexually, by force any time he liked, and now and then he tried.

Marina was outraged. "You advanced revolutionary," she shouted at Lee as he was stamping his pro-Castro leaflets. "You have a moral code no better than that of ancient Egypt." She now realized that Lee existed in two worlds: a fantasy, political world, of which he gave her barely a glimpse, and an everyday, down-to-earth world in which June was the one human being he truly loved. Marina, too, was part of this world, and it was her role to rear and protect his "treasure," June.

But there was another world she knew nothing about: the real political world. Lee existed in that world, too, and from time to time it seems to have intruded upon his fantasies. Thus on June 23, a Sunday, when he had more time than usual to read the newspaper, the New Orleans *Times-Picayune* carried a front-page story to the effect that President Kennedy had left Washington by air for a major journey to Western Europe.

On the next day, Monday, June 24, Lee took the first step toward putting travel plans of his own into effect. Exactly one year after his old passport had expired, he went downtown and applied for a new one. He said on the application form that he expected to be traveling three months to a year as a tourist in England, France, Germany, Holland, the Soviet Union, Finland, Italy, and Poland. He expected to leave New Orleans between October and December 1963 on the Lykes Steamship Line, the same one he took in 1959 when he defected to the Soviet Union. And he gave Lillian Murret, not Marina, as the person to notify in case of his death. Presumably he did not know where Marina might be at such a time. He received his passport the next day.

Marina knew nothing of his application. All she knew was that Lee was having trouble in his sleep again —the first time since February. One night he cried, yet when he woke up he could not remember what his dream had been about. He started having nosebleeds, once or twice he talked in his sleep, and one night toward the very end of June he had four anxiety attacks during which he shook from head to toe at intervals of half an hour and never once woke up. Just as in the period when he was making up his mind to shoot General Walker, these attacks appear to have presaged a decision that was causing him pain.

Marina, too, was sleeping badly because of her fear of being sent back to Russia. She looked tired and unhappy all the time. "What's wrong with you?" Lee would ask. "Don't you like it here? Your face is making me nervous." Sometimes he went a whole day without speaking to her or, if he did, he would say, "Hey you," do this or that, without ever calling her by name.

But one night, Marina was sitting in her rocker holding back her tears when she noticed that Lee looked unhappy, too. He stole a glance in her direction and she saw a look of sadness in his eyes. He put his book down and went into the kitchen by himself. Marina waited a few minutes. Then she put the baby down and followed him. Lee was sitting in the dark with his arms and legs wrapped around the back of a chair and his head resting on top. He was staring down at the floor. Marina put her arms around him, stroked his head, and could feel him shaking with sobs.

"Why are you crying?" she asked. Then, "Cry away. It'll be better that way." Finally she said: "Everything is going to be all right. I understand."

Marina held him for about a quarter of an hour and he told her between sobs that he was lost. He didn't know what he ought to do. At last he stood up and returned to the living room.

She followed him, and he was quiet at first. Then he said suddenly, "Would you like me to come to Russia, too?"

"You're kidding."

"No," he said.

"You mean it? You're not just joking?"

"I do."

Marina danced around the room for joy and then curled up in his lap.

"I'll go with my girls," he said. "We'll be together, you and me and Junie and the baby. There is nothing to hold me here. I'd rather have less, but not have to worry about the future. Besides, how would I manage without my girls?"

A while later they were in the kitchen together. Lee held her by the shoulders and told her to write the Soviet Embassy that he would be coming too. He would add his visa request to her letter.

In bed that night they spent hours talking about where they were going to live. Marina was for Leningrad; she wanted to show him her city. But he preferred Moscow, and she gave in. She was afraid he wouldn't come at all if she insisted.

That weekend, the 29th or 30th of June, Marina wrote her longest, warmest, and so far her only uncoerced letter to Nikolai Reznichenko, head of the consular section of the Soviet Embassy in Washington. She joyfully announced that her husband wished to accompany her to the U.S.S.R. and begged him to hurry up their visas. She added that they were too poor to visit the embassy in Washington (as the embassy requested) and could not even pay their medical bills. They would need financial help from the embassy to get back to the U.S.S.R.

Lee told Marina what to write—"more tears and fewer facts," he ordered. But fairly certain that he would not bother to read her letter when she had finished, Marina added a sentence or two of her own. She made a formal request that they be allowed to live in Leningrad on the grounds that she would have a better chance of finding a job as a pharmacist there.

"Make us happy again," she closed the letter. "Help us win back what we by our foolishness lost."[10]

If Marina played a trick on Lee by asking to live in Leningrad, he tricked her as well. Before he mailed her letter to the embassy, he appended one in English of his own:[11]

Dear Sirs:

Please *rush* the entrance visa for the return of Soviet citizen Marina N. Oswald.

She is going to have a baby in *October,* therefore you must grant the entrance visa and make the transportation arrangements before then.

As for my return entrance visa please consider it *separatably.*

Thank you
Lee H. Oswald
(husband of Marina Nicholeyev)

The letter was startlingly similar in tone and content to Lee's correspondence with the American Embassy in Moscow years before. Once again he was asking a government, this time a foreign government which was under no obligation whatsoever to him, to make his travel arrangements and pay his bills. Again he sought to place the responsibility for his wife and child on somebody else. Confronted with problems in his life, he repeatedly sought the same old solutions. His peremptory demands had worked in the past. He still expected, still felt, that he deserved special treatment.

Lee asked the Soviet Embassy to consider his application separately from Marina's because he knew that Marina, as a Soviet citizen who had requested a visa nearly five months before, might receive it much sooner than he, and he did not want to delay her return. But he was not deceiving her entirely. He does appear to have been considering a return to Russia himself, or at least holding it open as a place to fall back on. He had told Marina that he wanted to go to Cuba or China, but as yet he did not have any definite plans. With Marina and the baby in Russia, he might travel anywhere he liked, and return to them when it suited his convenience.

The Oswalds had maintained a lively correspondence with relatives and friends in the U.S.S.R. ever since their arrival in America, and apparently they both took their plan to return to Russia seriously enough to write friends in Leningrad and Minsk that they had applied to come back. Their friends seemed surprised—and shocked. In their replies, they welcomed the Oswalds on one hand and warned them on the other. One couched his warning in the strongest terms. He urged Lee to think it over, advising that this next Atlantic crossing, *if* he made it, was certain to be his last. For the friend to have written so explicit a warning, aware that it would be read by authorities on both sides, was a testament to the very great loyalty be bore the Oswalds. The risk he was running was a real one.[12]

On Monday, July 1, the same day he wrote the embassy, Lee paid another visit to the Napoleon Branch of the New Orleans Public Library. He had recently been reading a spy novel, space fiction, a few volumes on communism and on Russia. Today he borrowed only one book. It was William Manchester's *Portrait of a President,* a biography of John F. Kennedy.

29

Arrest

MARINA'S SPIRITS lifted the moment Lee said he would go back with her to Russia. In her euphoria, it made no difference to her what country they lived in, just so the two of them could be together, and with the children. Marina had told Lee that she could not go on living if he left her, and she meant it. Now he had, by his actions, reassured her, had shown that he needed her and was not going to throw her away. She realized that he loved her as best he knew how.

No longer as afraid as she had been that he was going to send her to Russia alone, or that he might, without warning, kill someone, Marina was able to be more understanding. She saw that Lee was torn and confused and did not know what to do. She felt sorry for him. She decided to try to be more kind and affectionate so that he would confide in her and express his feelings more openly. She knew that she, too, was responsible for their fights, and she resolved to turn over a new leaf and not be so quick to take offense.

Lee also changed. Up to now, he had been keeping his feelings out of sight as only he knew how to do. But the tears he had shed in the kitchen seemed to release him a little, and he became less edgy and tense. Nor did he try quite so hard to hide what he was feeling from Marina. As a result, they became closer. Their marriage acquired a softer tone, a milder temperature.

Neither was an angel, of course, and they had no revolution in their home. Lee still wanted exactly the right shirt at the moment he wanted it, still paced back and forth in front of the ironing board muttering to Marina, "Faster, faster, you do everything too slowly." Like Marina's stepfather, he still had the irritating habit of leaning back in a chair with his dirty shoes all over the kitchen table, so that Marina was forever having to wash and rewash the table. He continued to complain about her cooking, and she about his wanting to make love without brushing his teeth and about the outrageous way he spoiled the baby. They still had fights, but there was humor in their battles now, and an hour or two afterwards both of them forgot what they had been fighting about.

There were times when Lee refused to touch the last piece of meat on his plate at supper. He was saving it for Marina because she was pregnant. She put it in the refrigerator, but later in the evening she would take it out and try to get him to eat it. He would refuse and insist on saving it for her. In this and in other ways, Marina says, "We gave each other everything we had." She realizes that perhaps it was not enough, perhaps what each had to give was not what the other needed most. Still, they leaned on one another and gave each other what they could.

Lee remained reluctant, however, to share very much of himself. He still kept secrets from Marina, such as the type of work he did. He had told her he had a job in photography, but when he came home night after night smelling of coffee and covered with grease and coffee dust, she knew he had lied to her again. She was certain that his job had to do with coffee when he started bringing home packages of coffee and coupons. They used the coupons to buy a coffee pot and a huge saucepan for cooking crabs. Marina was pleased that Lee was doing something for their home, but she begged him to stop bringing the coupons home. She knew that he had stolen them, and she said that his job meant more to them than coupons.

In fact, Lee hated his job and felt degraded by it. He was one of four maintenance men at the Reily coffee company responsible for keeping the processing machines clean and oiling them after they had been in use. The man who broke him in said later that Lee from the very first day did not seem to care whether he caught on or not.[1] He would squirt his can of oil here and there and more or less hope the oil landed in the right spot. He scarcely spoke to the other employees, and later it would be discovered that he was lying in his greasing log, claiming to have lubricated machines that he had not touched. Lee had been there only a few weeks when the personnel manager who hired him had already come close to firing him more than once. He refrained only because there was a shortage of men in the maintenance department.[2]

Lee did not fraternize at all. He ate his lunch alone at Martin's Restaurant down the street and sometimes, during a break, while the other men were sitting in the driveway smoking and shooting the breeze, Lee sat on a bench by himself. He stared straight into space, and if anyone happened to speak to him, he looked right at the person and did not reply.[3] Lee had another curious form of greeting. When he met Charles LeBlanc, one of the men on the maintenance crew, he would cup his fist, stick out his index finger as if it were a gun, and say, "Pow!" without even cracking a smile. "Boy, what a crackpot this guy is," LeBlanc thought, guessing that he must have family troubles or not be quite right in the head.

One day while LeBlanc was greasing one of the machines, Lee offered to help. Suddenly Lee asked, "You like it here?"

"Well, I ought to," LeBlanc replied, "I've been here eight and a half years."

"Hell, I don't mean this place," Lee said. "I mean this damn country."[4]

The men had a couple of breaks a day that were supposed to be fifteen minutes each. Gradually, Lee's breaks got longer. Twenty minutes, half an hour, three quarters of an hour—and no one knew where to find him. He was next door at the Crescent City Garage, where he would get a Coke out of a machine and lose track of time.

Lee talked with Adrian Alba, the owner of the garage (by coincidence, it was the garage the Secret Service used in New Orleans) about guns.[5] He was very nearly in love with a Japanese rifle Alba owned; and when Alba told him that, as a member of the National Rifle Association, he had been able to buy a carbine for $35 that was easily worth $75 or $100, Lee begged him to sell it to him or buy another. Alba explained that he did not want to sell and under N.R.A. rules he was entitled to purchase only one. But Lee acted as if he had not heard, and hinted that he would make Alba an offer for his rifle that he could not refuse. Apparently it never crossed his mind that at the cost of only $5 he, too, could join the N.R.A. and buy a carbine himself.

Lee had no interest in handguns, only rifles, and he and Alba held earnest conversations about the killing power of small-caliber versus large-caliber bullets when used against a human target. Both agreed that the small-caliber bullet was deadlier, that being hit by it was like being hit by a 2- or 3-inch icepick compared with a 10-inch bread knife because there would be more internal bleeding.

Alba had 100 or more issues of various gun magazines—*American Rifleman, Field and Stream, Argosy, Guns and Hunting*—lying around his office. Lee read them there, or borrowed one or two at a time and kept them between three days and a week. Before borrowing any new ones, he always made a great point of showing Alba that he had brought back the ones he had.

Marina was to be twenty-two on July 17, and Lee had promised her something special, a dress or a new pair of shoes. He went to work that day and returned home as usual, oblivious of the date. Over supper Marina looked morose and he asked her why. "Today was my birthday," she said.

A few minutes later, Lee said, "Come on. Let's go out."

"The stores are closed now anyway," she answered without enthusiasm.

He took her to the drugstore across the street and bought her face powder and a Coca-Cola.

The next day he gave her his news: "Tomorrow is my last day at work." He had been fired by the Reily coffee company.

Marina took it well, as usual attributing his loss of work to widespread unemployment in the United States and not to any failings in her husband. "Don't worry," she said. "You'll have a little vacation, and then you'll find another job."

The loss of his job, no matter how he felt about the work, must have been a great blow to Lee, much greater than for most people, because his picture of himself was further out of line with reality. Certain that he was a great man who had been unjustly denied recognition, he now had been told that he could not even grease a coffee machine adequately. Lee could tell himself what he pleased, but with each new hurt or disappointment of this kind it was characteristic of him to draw deeper into a world of his own imagining and to retreat further from the world of reality.

About the time he was fired from Reily, and at the same time that he had just finished reading Manchester's *Portrait of a President,* Lee began to talk about himself and his future in exalted terms. It began with talk about the new baby. "I am sure this time it will be a boy," he said. "I'll make a President out of my son." He had spoken this way before the birth of his first child, and again early in Marina's second pregnancy, before he tried to shoot General Walker. But now, he went a step further. He said that in twenty years' time, *he* would be President or prime minister. It did not seem to matter that America has no prime minister.

Marina poked fun at him. "Okay," she laughed. "Papa will be prime minister. Son will be President. And what will I be—chief janitor in the White House? Will I be allowed to clean your room, or will you tell me I'm not to touch your papers even then?"

"We'll have to see what kind of girl you turn out to be." He was in earnest.

One night as she stepped out of the bathtub, Marina held up her underclothes to show him the worn-out elastic. "Papa," she asked, "when you are President, will you buy me a new pair of panties?"

"Shut up."

Marina was laughing at her own joke. "When you're prime minister, you can buy me something fancy, but right now I'd like something for thirty-nine cents."

"Shut up," he groaned.

Marina, too, had her dreams, much closer to reality than Lee's. She was ashamed of Lee because he lacked a college education, and in five years or so, when the children were in school, it was her intention to go to work and support him so that he could study philosophy and economics. Those were his choices, and she approved of them, because she thought they might straighten out his thinking and help him see his mistakes.

"Don't you want to be the wife of a prime minister?" he would ask.

"No, please."

"Why not?"

"Because I don't want to be fairy godmother in your castle of air."

His idea seemed so unreal, so unconnected with life, that she was ashamed of him for even daydreaming about it. She begged him to come out of the clouds, come down to earth and be like other mortals.

"Look, Junie," she said, pointing to Lee. "Look at our future prime minister."

Lee postured and struck a pose. "You laugh at me now. But I'll watch you laugh in twenty years when your husband is prime minister."

"By that time," Marina said to him, "you'll be on Wife Number Ten. I won't live twenty years with the life you're giving me now. I don't want to be the wife of a prime minister."

If Marina asked him to play dominoes, it was in these words that he chose to refuse: "In twenty years you can have plenty of amusements. Not now."

"In twenty years, when you're prime minister, I'll be dead."

Marina asked how on earth he meant to be President when he had no training for it and had not even been to college. "I'll teach myself," he said.

"That's the kind of thing you learn better from practice than from reading books."

She told him the world was changing. Maybe it had once been that way, but these days a President had to have been to college.

"Be quiet. You don't understand. It's none of your business," he said.

Marina recalls that Lee was reading a particular book when he began to talk about becoming President: Manchester's biography of Kennedy. Ordinarily, Lee read books rapidly. He took his time over this one, and when he returned *Portrait of a President* to the Napoleon Branch of the public library, he took out two other books. In his biography Manchester mentioned, in passing, that Kennedy had recently read Alan Moorehead's *The White Nile.* Lee borrowed Moorehead's *The Blue Nile.* He also took out Kennedy's own Pulitzer Prize-winning volume, *Profiles in Courage.*

That summer Lee read more about and by Kennedy than any other political figure. And from his boast to Marina that he would become President in twenty years—when he would be forty-three, Kennedy's age when he was elected to the presidency—it appears that Lee wanted to be like Kennedy and perhaps follow in his footsteps as closely as he could. Reading Manchester's book may have reminded him that in some ways he was like Kennedy already. Both loved to read books, both loved foreign travel, both had served with the armed forces in the Pacific, both had poor handwriting and were poor spellers, both had very young children, and both had a brother named Robert. But there was an unbridgeable gulf between them and of this, too, Lee must have been poignantly aware. For Kennedy not only read books, he wrote them, and had received a Pulitzer Prize for his writing. Kennedy had not merely served in the Pacific, as Lee did; he had seen action and become a hero of World War II. Of the two, Kennedy was, of course, the taller and better looking and was, as far as Lee knew, a more impressive physical specimen. (Marina says that her husband did not know that the President had Addison's disease.) Finally, Kennedy had a wealthy, affectionate father, who would do anything on earth for him and had, as Lee mentioned to Marina, "bought him the presidency."

Although he cultivated the appearance of impermeability, of having made up his mind about everything, Lee was also suggestible, and there was a thread running through the Manchester biography that may have fascinated him—the theme of death. Lee had tried to commit suicide at least once, and had attempted a political murder that might have resulted in his own death. Thus he may have been particularly spellbound by Manchester's many references to Kennedy's close brushes with death. During the PT-boat episode of World War II, Manchester wrote, Kennedy's superiors assumed that he had been killed in action. Throughout the book Manchester emphasized the President's fatalism, his conviction that he was "fighting the clock." He even cited a remark by Kennedy to the historian Arthur Schlesinger who, when he came to writing a book about Kennedy's presidency, Kennedy said, would have to call it *The Only Years,* because he was going to have only a single term. Even when he was speaking solely of politics, the words Manchester used were suggestive. He called Kennedy, in the purely political sense, "the biggest target in the land."

Manchester was captivated by the President and mystified that he was not yet preeminent in the affections of his countrymen. Kennedy, he conceded, was not so lovable as Lincoln had been. "He has a weaker grip on the nation's heartstrings," Manchester wrote, "and the reason isn't that he hasn't been shot." How might Lee Oswald read a passage like that?[6]

Immediately after finishing Manchester's biography, Lee read a book by the President himself, *Profiles in Courage*. In it, Kennedy tells about eight U.S. senators who, when called upon in a crisis to choose between the politically popular course and the course they believed to be right, had chosen the right course even at the cost of their careers. Kennedy called upon every citizen of the United States to bear on his shoulders all the burdens of the politician. Every man must do as his conscience required, do the great, the lonely, the unpopular thing, the thing that would in the long run be best for the people. He might be reviled, he might even lose his life, but history would vindicate and understand. With such words it is possible that President Kennedy handed his assassin the very weapon he needed most, not the gun or the bullet, but the argument.

If Lee, at this time, did start to consider another act of violence that would awaken the American people to the danger they were in, then he very quickly shoved the idea onto a back burner of his mind, where it might well have simmered forever. Cuba remained on the front burner, and he resumed his peaceful political activity in behalf of the Fair Play for Cuba Committee. Near the end of July, he wrote an extraordinary letter to Vincent T. Lee, the organization's national director in New York, in answer to Vincent Lee's friendly and encouraging letter of almost two months before.

In his undated reply, Lee Oswald answered that he had made some "inovations" in his activities on behalf of Cuba, and "I hope you won't be too disapproving."[7] One innovation was that "against your advice I have decided to take an office from the very beginning." This was a lie, for Lee never rented an office. He enclosed one of his handbills, in which he claimed to have a "charter chapter," another lie. He also enclosed the membership application he had had printed and gave Mr. Lee a lecture on the system of dues he had set up, assuring him that it would not cheat the national office out of any money.

Vincent Lee was disgusted. He had hopes of what a discreet and energetic new member might be able to achieve even in territory so inhospitable as Louisiana. But this man was obviously a nut. He had gone off and "violated all the rules." Even the few steps he had taken made clear that Oswald was the kind who would be "isolated" no matter what community he was in.[8] What was worse, he was claiming to speak for the F.P.C.C. when in fact he was exposing it to reprisals that could be a public embarrassment. By being associated with such a freebooter, the F.P.C.C., which was in a precarious situation anyhow, had much to lose and nothing to gain.[9] Vincent Lee decided to sever communications. He did not answer the letter. Oswald did not perceive for some time, if ever, that the F.P.C.C. had cut him off. He kept on writing Vincent Lee, sending clippings, trying to impress him. Vincent Lee did not reply.

Lee was diligent at first about looking for a new job. He scoured the Help Wanted ads in the newspaper, and applied for a variety of them, jobs in photography, clerk-typist jobs, even a job as yard man at a marble and granite company. He filed a claim for unemployment compensation based on his employment in Texas and was granted maximum benefits payable at $33 a week for thirteen weeks. But in order to qualify for the payments, he had to visit the Louisiana Employment Commission every Tuesday and list the names of the concerns where he had applied for work. Again, Lee embroidered reality; the number of enterprises at which he falsely claimed to have sought employment was in the scores.[10] From the end of July, he looked for work only desultorily, and after the middle of August, he stopped looking altogether. He had started to receive unemployment compensation, and on these payments, plus what he had saved while he was working, he managed to live until October.

Meanwhile, although unemployed and unable even to hold down a job as a manual laborer, Lee was oddly enough capable of a public life of a kind. His cousin Eugene Murret, who was training to be a Jesuit priest, wrote from Mobile, Alabama, inviting Lee to speak at his seminary about Russia. Overcoming his anti-religious scruples, Lee accepted, and on a Saturday at the end of July Lillian and Dutz Murret drove him and Marina to Mobile. Lee was to speak that night.

Aunt Lillian, not realizing that in his own eyes Lee was a public man already, urged him to make notes so that he would not be nervous. She was surprised at his airy reply: "Oh, don't worry about me. I give talks all the time."[11]

Lee spoke for half an hour about his everyday experiences in Russia, then answered questions. What he liked best about Russia, he said, was that the state takes care of everyone. If a man gets sick, no matter how poor he is, the government will provide for him. What he liked best about America was the material prosperity. He said that he was a Marxist and favored a brand of socialism that would combine the best of capitalism and communism. Two of the priests who were present said later that Lee had handled himself well. Both had the impression that he was at least a college graduate.[12]

Now that he had time on his hands, Lee became more and more active on behalf of Castro. He was turned away from a printing shop where he tried to order 3,000 more "Hands Off Cuba" leaflets, and Vincent Lee had failed to answer his most recent letter. But he did find encouragement from another quarter. Early in August Arnold Johnson, director of the Information and Lecture Bureau of the U.S. Communist Party, wrote answering a letter that Lee had written *The Worker* two months before.

Johnson's reply, dated July 31, was terse and routine: "It is good to know that movements in support of Fair Play for Cuba has [sic] developed in New Orleans. . . . We do not have any organizational ties with the Committee, and yet there is much material that we issue from time to time. . . . Under separate cover we are sending you some literature. . . ."[13]

Such a letter could have been a source of aggrandizement only to a man like Lee. Thus, at about this time, he wrote another letter to Vincent Lee that was even more extraordinary than the one that had preceded it:

. . . I rented an office as I planned and was promply closed three days later for some obsure reasons by the renters, they said something about remodeling, ect., I'm sure you understand. After that I worked out of a post office box and by useing street demonstrations and some circular work have substained a great deal of interest but no new members.

Through the efforts of some Cuban-exial "gusanos" [a word for the anti-Castro exiles often used in *The Militant*] a street demonstration was attacked and we were officialy cautioned by police. This incident robbed me of what support I had leaving me alone.

Nevertheless thousands of circulars were distrubed and many, many pamphlets which your office supplied.

We also managed to picket the fleet when it came in and I was surprised in the number of officers who were interested. . . .

I continue to recive through my post office box inquires and questions which I shall endeavor to keep answering to the best of my ability.[14]

The letter was dated August 1 and postmarked August 4, and it contains not a single true fact apart from the reference to picketing the fleet, which had occurred a month and a half before.

The uncanny thing about the letter is that on Monday, August 5, the day after he mailed it, Lee started to bring about the events he had just described. He visited a clothing store run by Carlos Bringuier, New Orleans representative of the Cuban Student Directorate, an organization of anti-Castro exiles.[15] Bringuier was having a conversation with a couple of teen-aged boys. Lee listened awhile, then joined in. He told Bringuier that he, too, opposed Castro and communism. He said that he had been in the Marine Corps, had been trained in guerrilla warfare, and would gladly train Cubans to fight Castro. He wanted to join the fight himself. The teenagers who were present were intrigued when Lee explained to them how to make a homemade gun, how to make gunpowder, and how to derail a train. He told them in detail how to blow up the Huey Long Bridge, as if learning this delicate art had been the part of his training he relished most.

Before leaving, Lee put his hand in his pocket and offered to contribute to Bringuier's cause. Bringuier was skeptical because he had been warned that the FBI might try to infiltrate his organization and he was not sure what breed of cat Oswald was, whether he was from the FBI or whether he might, on the other hand, be pro-Castro. He refused Oswald's money. Undaunted, Lee returned to the store the next day and left his *Guidebook for Marines.*

A few days later, on Friday, August 9, Bringuier received word that a young man was demonstrating on Canal Street, wearing a homemade placard that said "Viva Fidel!" and passing out handbills. Bringuier and two friends went in search of the man and found themselves face to face with Lee Oswald. Lee looked surprised, then smiled and held out his hand to Bringuier. Bringuier exploded. He explained to the crowd that this man had presented himself a few days earlier as an anti-Castro volunteer; now it turned out that he was a Castro agent and a Communist. Bringuier's Latin anger had its appeal and the crowd began shouting at Oswald: "Traitor! Communist! Go to Cuba!" and, to each other, "Kill him!"

A policeman told Bringuier to keep moving and let Oswald hand out his literature. But one of Bringuier's companions grabbed a handful of Oswald's leaflets, tore them up, and hurled them in the air. Bringuier removed his eyeglasses and went up to Oswald as if to hit him. Lee crossed his arms in front of his face and said quietly: "Okay, Carlos, if you want to hit me, hit me."

Just then two patrol cars arrived and took all four of them, Oswald and the three exiles, to the police station. Bringuier noticed at the station that Oswald appeared confident, cool, very much in command of himself. Bringuier and his friends each put up $25 bond and were told to show up in court on Monday. Oswald did not put up bond and stayed overnight in jail.

On arriving for work the next morning, Francis Martello, a lieutenant in the Intelligence Division of the police department, decided to have a talk with Oswald.[16] Lee was flattered that Martello listened seriously to his views about Russia and Marxism. He claimed that the New Orleans "chapter" of the Fair Play for Cuba Committee was comprised of thirty-five members and met monthly at various addresses, which he declined to divulge, with about five in attendance each time. Martello's later account suggests that Lee was in a grandiloquent frame of mind, but his response to one question was strikingly succinct. Asked his opinions of Kennedy and Khrushchev, Lee said tersely: "They seem to get along very well together." Martello was impressed by Lee's calm, his almost professorial demeanor, his lack of aggressiveness or emotional outbursts, and the fact that Bringuier, for all his efforts, had been unable to taunt him into physical combat. Martello later called Oswald "a very passive type."

On the telephone, Lee was his old, demanding self. He called the Murrets several times and ordered them to bail him out. Dutz was away on a religious retreat and Lillian was in the hospital, recovering from an ear operation. The only member of the family on the spot was the older daughter, Joyce Murret O'Brien, who was on a visit from Beaumont, Texas. She came to the jail, but when she learned that her cousin's trouble had to do with politics, with helping Castro in some way, she became frightened and did not want to bail him out. Martello assured her that the offense was mild. Joyce conferred with her mother and they decided that the best course was to call Emile Bruneau, a politician of their acquaintance, and ask his help. Apparently it was Bruneau who sprung Lee.

Lee, meanwhile, had made an unusual request. He told Lieutenant Martello that he wished to speak with someone from the FBI. It was Saturday morning, and the agent who came to the police station, John Quigley, had never seen Oswald's file, did not recognize the name, nor realize that another FBI agent, Milton Kaack, was already engaged in a mild investigation of this very man. Kaack had visited Oswald's landlady and the Reily coffee company only a few days before, on August 5.

In an hour and a half interview with Quigley, Lee told a number of lies that was unprecedented even for him.[17] But why, given his fear and hatred of the organization, did Lee ask to see someone from the FBI? No one from the agency had been to see him in a year, and there is every reason to suppose that Lee would stay as far away from the FBI as he possibly could.

Perhaps, as Lee's brother Robert has suggested, it was part of Lee's continuing effort to create mystery and drama around himself. Perhaps he wanted to impress the officers at the police station, encourage them to think that he had been acting as an FBI provocateur and thereby secure an early release. Or perhaps, finding himself in jail for the first time, Lee needed to feel singular and important, and summoning the FBI gave him that feeling. It is even possible that the FBI's lack of overt attention over the past year, relief though it was, had created a feeling of suspense in him and had strained his sense of self-importance.

Lee may also have anticipated that local FBI officers would read about his street scene in the newspapers. By being the first one to tell them about it, and in his own terms, he may have felt that he could control the situation. Lee knew, moreover, that the FBI would have been most interested in his recent attempt on General Walker. Now that he was in a police station, obviously up to no good, he may, without quite knowing it, have hoped to catch the eye of someone who would stop him before he did anything worse. Finally, after the anticlimax of the Walker affair, Lee still wanted, in a way, to be punished. By deliberately inviting the FBI into his life again, perhaps he thought he could control even his own punishment.

The lies he told Agent Quigley did help revive the FBI's interest in him. But for the moment, what Lee carried away from his incarceration was a brief but exhilarating memory. He had been locked up just long enough so that he could later claim to have paid a price for the pro-Castro cause. He had turned the tables on the FBI, summoning an officer at *his* pleasure rather than being summoned at theirs. And by far his happiest recollections were his talks with Lieutenant Martello. From them he learned that prison need not be all bad. Prison can provide a forum for your ideas. People pay attention and listen to you there.

Lee arrived home in scapegrace good spirits, dirty, rumpled, unshaven, with a glint of humor in his eye and an air of gaiety about him. "I've been to the police station."

"I thought so," said Marina. "So that's the way it turned out."

She wanted to know where he slept. He explained that the beds had no mattresses, so he had taken off all his clothes and made a mattress of them.

"You slept without any pants on?"

"It was hot. And it was just men, anyway. If they didn't like it, they could have let me out sooner."

He added that in the morning he had been taken to see a police officer, a good man and "a kindly uncle," to whom he explained his theories. "He listened to my ideas and let me out."

Marina had been worried when Lee failed to come home the night before. She knew that he was out with his leaflets and guessed that he was in trouble with the police. At least he was not with another woman. She had memories of the Walker evening, however, and so she had checked Lee's closet. The rifle, thank God, was in its place. Even so, Marina had not been able to get to sleep until three o'clock in the morning.

Now that her prodigal had come home, she fed him and he took a nap. A little sheepishly, he confessed on awakening that there was supposed to be a trial. "If I pay ten dollars there will be no trial."

Marina was terrified of trials. "Pay, of course," she said. "We don't need any trials. But do you see where your little jokes lead?"

That evening, Dutz Murret, home from the retreat, went immediately to the Oswalds'. He noticed with horror Castro's photograph pinned to the wall, and asked Lee straight out if he was part of any "Commie" group. Lee answered that he was not. Dutz told him in no uncertain terms to show up in court the next day and, after that, go out, get a job, and support his family.

Lee appeared in court on schedule, sat squarely in the middle of the black section of the segregated courtroom, pleaded guilty to the charge of "disturbing the peace by creating a scene," paid his $10 fine, and left.

30

"You Understand Me"

ONE NIGHT just before he was arrested, Lee was shaving in the bathroom. June asked him for a piece of soap from the cabinet and he absent-mindedly gave her Marina's makeup mirror instead. She banged it on the toilet seat, the mirror slid out of its frame and shattered against the toilet pipes. Marina cried. To her superstitious mind the shattered mirror meant bad luck. She was afraid that something was going to happen to herself or the baby she was expecting in October.

President and Mrs. Kennedy were expecting their child just a few weeks before that. The Oswalds had been discussing Mrs. Kennedy's pregnancy ever since it had been announced. Lee hoped it would be a girl; Marina wanted them to have a boy. She expected a son and wanted Jackie to have the same. One day in August—the 7th—Lee came home looking cheerful.

"Guess what, Mama? Jackie's had her baby, and it's a boy."

He asked Marina, not for the first time, what sex *their* child would be, and again she predicted a son. "I can believe you this time," he said, "especially since you were right about theirs."

Gently, because he knew Marina was worried about their own baby, he went on to break the news that all was not well with the Kennedys'. The doctors were afraid for his life and had rushed him to a special hospital. The doctors, Lee added, would be the best and the baby would probably survive.

The next day, Lee listened to bulletins on the radio about the baby. Each time she heard the name "Kennedy," Marina asked the news. "Still the same," he would say, but Marina noticed that he was anxious and more and more reluctant to tell her anything. As evening came on, he admitted that Patrick Kennedy was very sick and the doctors did not have much hope.

Coming on top of the broken mirror, the news signified to Marina that things would go badly for their baby, too. "For heaven's sake," she said to Lee, "if it's a choice between me and the baby, keep the baby."

"Other babies we can have," he said. "Junie has to have a mother."

Marina had not yet even seen a doctor, and she thinks that both she and Lee were anxious about the same thing: if the President's baby could not be saved—the President, for whom everything could be done—then what about their baby?

"If anything happened to our baby, who would care?" Marina asked.

"No, no, you're not to worry," Lee tried to reassure her. "You'll be taken care of. Once you're in the hospital, the doctors don't care whose baby it is. They do the same for everyone. I'll borrow money. I promise you, you'll never be thrown out of the hospital."

When the news came over the radio early on August 9 that Patrick Kennedy had died during the night, Marina wept. Lee tried to comfort her. Maybe it was better for the baby to die rather than be sick all its life.

Jackie was frail, he said. She had lost other babies. He thought he had even read somewhere that she got sick on planes.

"We'll have an easier time," he said. "We haven't any money and maybe we can't get good doctors. But you're strong. We've got a baby already. Ours will be healthy. Everything will be all right."

Friday, August 9, the day Patrick Kennedy died, was the same day Lee was arrested. And as soon as he was released, he started stamping leaflets again. He and Marina sat many nights after that, she sewing and he pausing now and then to listen as she tried to talk him out of it. Sometimes he stole the leaflets from the closet when she was not looking and tried to stamp them on the sly. She told him to do it openly. "Up to your old games again, are you, big boy?" she said.

"For God's sake shut up," he said. "Why did God send me a wife with such a long tongue? I've been a good boy all day. Why can't you leave me be at night?"

Marina was trying to drag him back to reality and make him see himself as others saw him. She told him he was no genius, "not like a tall pine tree on a flat plain," towering above everybody else. Even if he were clever and everyone else stupid, he still had to understand how others looked on things before he could win them over. How could you convince anyone, living in the clouds and taking into account nobody's views but your own?

"Be content to be an ordinary mortal, as you are," Marina said. "You're nobody special. Cuba has lived without you and it can continue to get along without you now. One Lee Oswald can't do anything. Do you think you're such a great man that you're the only one who can help?"

Cuba was "a tiny country surrounded by enemies," Lee explained. "If only everyone would do a little, the way I do, then we could help Uncle Fidel. With these leaflets I can wake up the American people."

Marina said sarcastically that she had never seen leaflets passed out except in old movies of the Russian Revolution. It surely would be fascinating to see it happen in real life. "Look at our neighbors," she said, "the people living all around us. They don't care about leaflets. They are peace-loving people, busy with their families. They don't want a revolution. No one does, here. If it's a revolution you're waiting for, I tell you, this country isn't ready for it yet."

"You're right," Lee sighed. "I ought to have been born in some other era, much sooner or much later than I was." "I know, but you were born now," Marina said. "Better forget the whole thing." Lee added that he had no desire to be like their neighbors. "They're petty bourgeois. I'm not interested in the stupid things they care about."

Marina did not mention the obvious—that he ought to be out looking for work rather than spending the little money they had on guns and leaflets and fines. But she did say, "Poor great man sits here all by himself. He's part of a great cause, and yet he has nothing to eat. Nobody sees that he's a genius."

"You laugh now," Lee said to her. "But in twenty years, when I'm prime minister, we'll see how you laugh then."

Their conversations went on like this for weeks, and it seemed there was nothing Marina could say to convince her husband that he was only an ordinary person. Her efforts were further subverted by the letter Lee received in early August from Arnold Johnson of the Information and Lecture Bureau of the Communist Party. Perfunctory as it was, this letter, together with Vincent Lee's letter of May 29, contributed, Marina thinks, to Lee's feeling that he was a great man—a man of loftier concerns than the common herd.

"Okay," she said to him, as he was stamping leaflets one night. "So you take two hundred of these things. You go out on the street and give them to people. They toss them away. Has one person come to you as a result of them? People don't care about that here."

Lee's eyes filled with tears. He threw down his leaflets and read Johnson's letter aloud. "See this?" he said, waving it in front of her. "There are people who understand me and think I'm doing useful work. If *he* respects what I'm doing, then it's important. He's the Lenin of our country."

Lee had already told Marina that American Communists were not like Russian ones.[1] The Communists in Russia are careerists, he said. They join for a job or an apartment. Here it's like Russia in the old days. The members are people of principle. They work underground, in conditions of persecution. Knowing Lee's respect for the American Communists, Marina was routed. "Okay," she said. "Go ahead and stamp your papers if it makes you happy."

On Friday, August 16, wholly unchastened by his arrest just a week before, Lee waited with unaccustomed patience for Marina to iron his favorite shirt. He had already called the local TV stations to tell them that there would be a Fair Play for Cuba demonstration that day in front of the Trade Mart building in downtown New Orleans.[2]

Lee hired two recruits, a nineteen-year-old boy named Charles Hall Steele, Jr., and another young man who has never been identified, to help him hand out his leaflets. The fifteen- or twenty-minute demonstration went off without trouble, and pictures of Lee were shown on the television news that night.

Marina refused to go to the Murrets' to watch the broadcast. "I see you every day at home in all forms. I don't want to see you on TV. Besides, how come you're not ashamed to telephone the stations yourself?" Marina was appalled that her husband had sought publicity. To her it was very poor form. But it was just what Lee wanted, and there was more to come.

At 8:00 A.M. the next day, Saturday, August 17, William K. Stuckey, a young reporter with a weekly radio show on station WDSU, drove up to the Oswalds' in search of Lee, whose name and address he had obtained from Carlos Bringuier. New Orleans was a hotbed of right-wing political activity, and now that a bona fide left-wing organization had appeared, Stuckey wanted to cover it on his program, "Latin Listening Post." He expected to find a "folk-singer type," a fellow in sandals and beard, and was startled when a cleancut young man appeared, clad only in Marine Corps fatigues—no shirt—and invited him onto the porch. He would like to ask Stuckey in for coffee, Lee said, but his wife and child were still asleep.

Stuckey explained who he was and invited Lee to record a five-minute interview for his show that night. If Lee would come to the station about 5:00 P.M., well before the 7:30 broadcast, they could have a long interview and Stuckey could cut it to the required few minutes. Lee accepted.

He showed up punctually and recorded an interview of nearly forty minutes. Then, in Lee's presence, Stuckey cut the tape to four and a half minutes. Lee was pleased as he heard the tape being played back.[3] He felt he had "scored a coup." He had not allowed himself to be lured out of his depth or led into talking about subjects he did not wish to pursue. Nor was anything said about his years in Russia, since Stuckey knew nothing about them.

Stuckey, too, was pleased, and he used the edited tape on his program that evening. He found Oswald highly "articulate," a man who seemed "deliberate" about every word he spoke and every gesture he made, the sort who would inspire confidence because of his self-control.[4] He was more than a little amused that such a man should have materialized as a pro-Castro organizer in kooky, anti-Communist New Orleans. Hoping to persuade the news director of his station to let him run the entire thirty-seven-minute tape, he asked Lee to call him on Monday.

The news director would have none of it. Indeed, he said, there had been an angry public reaction already. Rather than run the uncut tape, he urged Stuckey to schedule a radio debate with some local anti-Communists to refute Oswald.[5]

With his usual imperturbable punctuality, Lee telephoned Stuckey on Monday and was asked to take part in a debate on Wednesday, August 21. The other participants were to be Carlos Bringuier—"to add a Cuban flavor," Stuckey said —and Edward Scannell Butler, director of the Information Council of the Americas, a propaganda organization that taped interviews with Cuban refugees and refugees from Iron Curtain countries and distributed them to radio stations south of the border. Lee agreed to the debate.

Meanwhile, Stuckey had decided to do some checking on Oswald. That same Monday, he made the entire thirty-seven-minute tape available to the local FBI office, where the stenographer pool made a transcript, then returned the tape to Stuckey along with a copy of the transcript.[6] While he was talking to an FBI source over the telephone that day, Stuckey, as he remembers it, was put through to the chief or deputy chief of the New Orleans bureau, and this man read aloud to him over the phone portions of Oswald's FBI file, including the facts that he had been to Russia, tried to renounce his U.S. citizenship, stayed there nearly three years, and married a Russian woman. Stuckey went to the FBI office and was permitted to examine the file, as well as newspaper clippings from Moscow at the time of Oswald's defection.[7]

While Stuckey was at the FBI office, Edward Butler received a visit from Carlos Bringuier and a fellow Cuban exile, Carlos Quiroga, who had done some investigating of their own. On the evening of the demonstration in front of the Trade Mart, Quiroga, posing as a Castro sympathizer, had paid Oswald a call to see what he could find out. Oswald, who suspected that Quiroga was an agent either from Bringuier or from the FBI, told him nothing. But while the two men were talking on the porch, June came running out and spoke to her father in Russian. Bringuier and Quiroga reported the incident to Butler, and told him they had information that Oswald had been to Russia and had a Russian wife. Butler tried to reach someone in Washington by telephone.[8] Later in the day he informed Stuckey that he, too, had learned of Oswald's Russian background—from someone at the "House Un-American Activities Committee."[9]

Stuckey and Butler agreed over the telephone that they would bring Oswald's Russian past to light on the program, expose him as a Communist sympathizer, and destroy his organization.

On Wednesday, Lee arrived at the station first, wearing a heavy flannel suit that was totally wrong for the New Orleans heat, and looking nervous because he knew that this time he faced opposition. He had been practicing at home all day. He wrote down what he wanted to say on scraps of paper, then he strode around the living room delivering his remarks with what he thought were appropriate gestures.

When Stuckey arrived, Lee joshed him a bit about inviting people "to gang up on me." Bringuier was the next to appear; Lee went up to shake hands, and Bringuier remarked humorously that if ever Lee wanted to join his side, the anti-Castro side, he would have nothing against him personally. Lee answered good-naturedly that he believed he was right and was doing his best.

The debate was taped for broadcast that evening, and it was a disaster for Lee. Stuckey started off by announcing that Oswald had a Russian past, had tried to renounce his U.S. citizenship, and had concealed it on their interview only a few days before. The rest of the "debate" amounted to a verbal pummeling: did not Oswald's self-proclaimed Marxist faith and his residence in the U.S.S.R. signify that the F.P.C.C. "chapter" of which he was "secretary" had to be Communist? Lee had been sandbagged, and there was little he could do but keep his temper, which he did.

Afterwards he looked "dejected," and Stuckey invited him to have a drink. They went to Comeaux's, a bar down the street from the station, where Lee slowly nursed a beer. When Stuckey pointed out that he was not doing well with his beer, Lee answered that actually he was accustomed to vodka—his father-in-law, a colonel in the Red army, had taught him to drink it straight.[10]

Lee told other lies, as well as one or two truths, to impress Stuckey. And, in general, Stuckey was impressed. He thought Lee was open, friendly, relaxed, and perhaps even relieved that his Russian past at last was out in the open. But Stuckey also got the impression that Lee, without being arrogant exactly, felt he was living in a world of clods, of men and women who were his intellectual inferiors.[11]

In fact, Lee was far from relieved. "Damn it," he said to Marina when he returned home, "I didn't realize they knew I'd been to Russia. You ought to have heard what they asked me! I wasn't prepared and I didn't know what to say."

Still, he was anxious to hear what he had said. He called the Murrets to let them know about the program. They were not amused. An irate Dutz said later that they had not heard the whole of the program, "but enough."[12]

Long before the program was to go on the air, Lee switched on the radio and sat in the kitchen waiting. "Come quickly," he called out to Marina. "I'm about to speak now."

Marina did not understand who was saying what, but she could tell who was on what side and that Lee was claiming to be secretary of an organization. She also could tell from his voice when he was lying.

Afterwards she asked, "Are they such fools there at the station that they actually believe you have an organization? One man is chairman, secretary, and sole member!"

"Maybe the debate will help and others will join," Lee said.

"I doubt it," Marina replied. Her reaction was not one of pride at hearing her husband speak, but of amusement at the way he sat, "proud as a rooster," listening to his own voice.

"Twenty minutes!" he said, when the program was over. "And I spoke longer than any of them. Every minute costs a lot on radio. And I talked by far the most."

Whatever euphoria he may have felt at the moment, after thinking it over, Lee seems to have realized that his position as a political organizer in New Orleans had been drastically changed as a result of his exposure as an ex-defector. All through August he had continued to write Vincent Lee of the F.P.C.C. and Arnold Johnson of the Communist Party. He had sent both a small clipping from the New Orleans *Times-Picayune* of August 13 about his arraignment for "disturbing the peace," and had also written Vincent Lee about the August 16 demonstration and his original appearance on Stuckey's program. But he had had no response.

Now he was baffled. Having been exposed as Marxist and possibly pro-Soviet, was it any use to go on trying to organize an F.P.C.C. chapter, or had he been totally discredited? He made a strange decision. He would seek advice; but instead of appealing to the F.P.C.C., the organization which he feared he had compromised, he would write to the Communist Party. Since he was going to write the Party, it would have been logical to write Arnold Johnson. Instead he decided, typically, that he would go straight to the top, to the Central Committee —the Party's highest governing body. It was a breach of protocol, for he was not a Party member. But it shows how seriously he took himself and his dilemma. It also reveals that, as usual, he felt entitled to special consideration, even when he might have done wrong.

The letter itself was presumptuous. It opens with the greeting, "Comrades," and closes: "With Freternel [sic] Greeting," both Party salutations which Lee was not entitled to use since he was not a member. The letter is likewise remarkable for its execrable spelling, a sign that Lee was upset, and for its totally uncharacteristic tone of humility. Lee wrote that he had lived in the Soviet Union and, on his return, had organized a branch of the F.P.C.C. in New Orleans, "a position which, frankly, I have used to foster communist ideals." But now that his previous history had been made public in a radio program, he wondered whether he could continue to wage the struggle against "anti-progressive forces above ground," or whether he would have to go underground. The letter closes: "I feel I may have compromised the F.P.C.C., so you see that I need the advice of trusted, long-time fighters for progress. Please advise."[13]

As so often happened with Lee, his letter did go to the top. It reached Elizabeth Gurley Flynn, secretary of the Communist Party, and she asked Arnold Johnson to reply. Lee received an answer three weeks later. It was soothing in tone, suggested that the F.P.C.C. was broad enough in character so that Oswald might be able to work in the "background" without going "underground," and added, in response to still another letter which had been received from him, that the Communist Party might find a way to get in touch with him later.[14]

Throughout August, Lee must have been considering his next move. And after the radio debate of August 21, he was ready to face the situation. He had passed out nearly 1,000 handbills and membership applications, had engaged in public demonstrations, and had spoken twice over the radio. And he had not yet attracted a single follower. Nor had he had a single word of encouragement from the F.P.C.C. He had to face the fact that for him, in New Orleans, the F.P.C.C. was a lost cause. And so once again he fell back on an old plan that had been at the back of his mind for years. He would go to Cuba to fight for Castro.

The obstacles were formidable. Lee had saved a little money, but possibly not enough to get to Cuba. Moreover, the State Department had banned travel to Cuba by American citizens, and all that summer *The Militant* had been filled with stories about Americans who faced imprisonment and fines on their return. That was only a minor deterrent, however, for Lee did not intend to return. He hoped to stay in Cuba. Or, if he did not like it there, he would go to China, or else seek readmission to Russia, where he would rejoin Marina. But the problem was how to get to Cuba in the first place.

Finally, Lee came up with a solution. About the third week in August, possibly just after his exposure in the radio debate, he announced to Marina that he had decided to go to Cuba. Since there was no legal way to get there, he was going to hijack an airplane.

"I'll be needing your help," he added.

"Of course I won't help," came the wifely response.

Lee immediately started exercising to strengthen his muscles—deep knee bends and arm exercises. Each evening he tore through the apartment in his undershorts for half an hour, making practice leaps as he went. June, who thought he was getting ready to play with her, jumped up in bed, followed him everywhere with her eyes, and burst out laughing.

Marina could not help laughing, too. "Junie," she said, "our papa is out of his mind."

Lee pretended not to hear.

"With shoulders like yours, exercises couldn't hurt," Marina commented helpfully.

Lee came up to her and flexed his muscles. "You think I'm not strong? Just feel those arms. You think I'm weak and not a man?"

"Of course. You're just a foolish boy."

"And whose is that?" he asked, pointing to June. "I made her."

"That didn't take much time," Marina answered tartly. "I spent nine months of my time and health on her. I made her."

Lee kept up his exercises for a couple of weeks, causing much merriment in the household. Afterward he rubbed himself all over with strong-smelling liniment, took a cold shower, and came out of the bathroom as red as a lobster.

Meanwhile, he had brought home airline schedules and a large map of the world which he tacked up inside the porch. He started measuring distances on the map with a ruler, and Marina heard him mention "Key West."[15] Next, he told her that the problem was to find a plane with fuel enough to fly as far as Cuba. A Miami-bound flight would not do; they would have to find something bigger, a plane headed for Philadelphia or New York that had plenty of fuel.

Marina listened with disbelief as Lee explained how he planned to hijack the plane. He would be sitting in the front row, he said. No one would notice when he got up and quietly moved into the pilot's cabin. There he would pull his pistol and force the pilot to turn around.

"And how about the passengers?" Marina asked.

"I have strong muscles now. I'll deal with them."

His eyes shining, he told Marina what she would have to do. First, they would buy tickets under different names so no one would know they were man and wife. She was to sit in the rear of the plane. Once Lee had subdued the pilot, she was to rise, holding June by the hand, and speak to the passengers, urging them to be calm.

Marina reminded him that she did not speak English.

"Right," Lee said. "That script won't do. I'll have to think up something new." He sat her down on the bed, went out of the room, then burst through the bedroom door pointing his pistol straight at her: "Hands up and don't make any noise!"

Shaking all over with laughter, Marina reminded him that she could not speak those words either. But Lee refused to give up. If only she would play her part, he promised to buy her a small, woman-sized gun. He said he had been shopping for one already.

Marina could restrain herself no longer. "Do you really think anybody will be fooled?" she said. "A pregnant woman, her stomach sticking way out, a tiny girl in one hand and a pistol in the other? I've never held a pistol in my life, much less shot anyone."

"I'll show you how."

"No thanks. I can't stand shooting. I'd go out of my mind."

He implored her just to hold the pistol even if she did not mean to use it.

"No," she answered again. "If you want to break your neck, do it alone."

He ran through the script again. "I'll be up in the front row. No one will think twice when I go into the cabin. I'll whip out my gun and order the pilot to turn around. Then I'll open the door and stand where both the pilot and the passengers can see me."

"And you don't think the passengers would try to rescue him?" Marina asked.

"Ugh, they're cowardly Americans," Lee said. "They won't even dare to move. They'll just sit there like cows."

"Do what you like," Marina said. "But don't count on me. It's not my nature to go around killing people and I don't advise you to do it, either. The whole thing is so funny, it even makes the baby laugh."

Lee assured her he had thought of everything. Nothing could go wrong. Marina told him lots of things could go wrong; there was plenty he hadn't thought of. It wouldn't turn out the way he thought.

Lee went to the airport and obtained more schedules, this time of flights not from New Orleans but from a smaller city nearby so he would have fewer passengers to subdue. For two days he was carried away by that. After he had tried about four times to talk Marina into joining him in his scheme, and had failed, he told her he had been looking for someone who would help him, someone who might want to go to Cuba. But he had given up. The reason he gave could not have been more significant: "Your accomplice is your enemy for life"— meaning that an accomplice can be a witness against you as long as you live.

At this stage of their marriage, Lee was confiding in Marina, making her his touchstone, his lightning rod to reality. And Marina understood what he was asking of her. Even though she wondered, as he unfolded his hijacking scheme, whether or not he was crazy, she drew funny word pictures for him to show how his plan looked in the clear light of day. Ever since the night, at the end of June, when he had broken down and cried in the kitchen, she perceived that Lee needed her. With what appears to be an inborn sympathy for anyone who is lost or in trouble, or on the outs with the world, she reached out and responded to his need. "Do you know why I loved Lee?" she once said. "I loved him because I felt he was in search of himself. I was in search of myself, too. I couldn't show him the way, but I wanted to help him and give him support while he was searching."

Indeed, by August of 1963 their relationship had become an extraordinary feat of empathy on Marina's part, one which few people could have achieved, much less a girl of twenty-two. No doubt it was this quality that had enabled her to get through to Lee and win from him such trust as he was capable of giving. Yet his "trust" was a crushing burden for her too.

As the one person whom Lee trusted, and feeling responsible for his actions, as she did, Marina was painfully at odds with herself and her surroundings. She, too, had been a rebel. In part, it was this that had drawn her to Lee, and this that still helped her to understand him. But now she was about to be the mother of a second child and, carrying the full weight of the family, she badly needed an anchor. Everything in her strained toward staying in one place, settling in America, building a nest. Lee's responsibilities had changed but he had not. He was still a rebel, and he kept repeating the same actions again and again. He yanked Marina away from the stability she coveted, placed her squarely outside American life, and prevented her from building her nest.

Even that was not the worst—for husband and wife were also at odds over right and wrong. Marina tried, not always successfully, to resist complicity in Lee's deceptions. She refused to approve such of his schemes as she knew about. But she now insists that he had a stronger character than she, "because he brought me low and made me cover up his 'black deeds,' when it was against my morality to do so. I felt too much pity for him. If only I had been a stronger person, maybe it would have helped."

Marina's words are an apology for her failure to make a different man of Lee and alter the outcome of his life. They are an admission of the guilt she felt for the way that their life together worked out. But the truth is that there is no such thing as being married to a man like Lee Oswald and not becoming his emotional accomplice.

Meanwhile, she went on trying to help Lee find his way without letting him get dangerously off course. "Look," she said to him about the hijacking scheme, "it's not a good omen that the mirror broke. It means you've got to be careful. Go to Cuba if you must. But try to find a legal way. Don't do anything dangerous when you get there. And don't do anything illegal. If it doesn't go right, come back home right away."

She reminded him that they had one child and would soon have another. "If you want my support, I'll give it to you. I'll save money and do what I can for you here. Of course," she added, lowering her voice, "it would be better to save for the new baby. But I'll sacrifice and try to save on that if it will help you to do what you want."

Her words found their mark. A day or two later, Lee burst into the apartment. "Guess what, Mama? I've found a legal way. There's a Cuban Embassy in Mexico. I'll go there. I'll show them my clippings, show them how much I've done for Cuba, and explain how hard it is to help in America. And how above all I want to help Cuba. Will you come to me if I send for you there?"

"Hmm," Marina said, "we'll see." She accepted his going to Cuba, so long as he did it in a legal way, for she knew that he would have to see the country with his own eyes before he could give up his dream. But she was skeptical. It was her guess that no country would satisfy him and that he would be home in three months to a year. And she could not resist teasing him. "If you do go," she said, "for heaven's sake take some American soap. It will be dirty there."

"Okay," he replied. "You can send me packages if you're still here." Then he begged her again to come with him.

"Not to Cuba," she said, "but Havana—a lovely city."

Lee promised that she could study free of charge and get a job. Since he was American and the Cubans would be flattered to have an American defector, they would give him privileges—a job and a nice little house.

Marina hated that about her own country: Russians felt that foreigners were somehow better than they were and gave them every privilege. She could not believe the same might be true of Castro, of whom she had heard nothing but good.

"No, no," she said. "They have real communism there. You earn according to your work. You'll have to work for ten years before they'll give you any privileges. The place is full of poor people already. Besides," she added, dropping her voice again in mild reproof, "it's not *who* you are but *what* you are that will make all the difference to them."

Marina had no thought of joining Lee in Cuba. Cuba, China, there was no telling where he might want to go next. Of course she would have to join him if she had no way of living in America. But the wisest course was to wait and see. It was her hope that he would become disillusioned in Cuba as he had in Russia, and that this time he might learn something from it. He would come home, settle down, and live a normal life with his family.

That was her dream. His was that she would join him wherever he pleased —"I go to China, you'll go to China." Or, more ominous and more likely—"I'll send you back to Russia. And if I don't like Cuba, I will join you over there." He added that while he was in Mexico City, he would go to the Soviet Embassy and try to speed up her visa.

Marina did not realize that Lee could not go to Cuba and simply come home when he had had enough. Instead, this time, he would face a *real* danger of imprisonment. Nor was it easy for an American to gain admission to Cuba, even from Mexico City. He would first have to go to the Soviet Embassy and apply for a visa for Russia. Then he could go to the Cuban Embassy with his Russian visa, and apply for a visa to visit Cuba "in transit" to Russia. That was where Marina came in. She was his pretext and his fallback plan. He was going to Russia to join his wife and children. Lee had not changed at all. Russia was still a place of refuge in his mind, the place he would go if he got in trouble or if he ran out of choices elsewhere. Even though he had now experienced life in the Soviet Union for himself, Russia continued to hold the same place in his thoughts that it had five years earlier, during his talks with his Marine Corps comrades.

Once he was in Cuba, of course, Lee counted on the old magic to work. He would do in Havana exactly what he had done in Moscow in 1959: persuade the Cubans to let him stay. He would show them his clippings, his F.P.C.C. leaflets, his correspondence with the F.P.C.C. and the Communist Party, all his bona fides as a Castro enthusiast, and convince them that he was a believer and not a spy. Maybe they would allow him to join the army and train recruits in guerrilla warfare. Maybe Castro would send him out to help liberate neighboring islands. Or maybe he would stand by to help if there was an invasion from the United States. All he asked was to be allowed to fight for Castro.

Later, if he got tired of Cuba, he might go to China or take his American passport and visit various countries in Western Europe at a leisurely pace on his way to join Marina in Russia. Money, of course, was a problem, but maybe he would have earned some as a mercenary or as a Castro volunteer. Maybe he counted on Cuba to give him a subsidy as Russia had. Or maybe he did not think about money at all.

Lee's plan bore a haunting similarity to his defection from America to Russia only four years before. Once again he would forsake his homeland and count on a foreign government to take care of him. The plan made no sense, of course. Even if Marina was permitted to return to Russia, it was extremely unlikely that he would be readmitted. There were no guarantees that he would be allowed to visit Cuba in transit, much less to remain there. And if he did succeed in visiting Cuba and was then denied readmission to Russia, he would face prosecution and imprisonment if he tried to return to America.

Real or unreal as the plan might be, Lee before the end of August was studying Spanish again, as he had done in 1958. At the close of each lesson he asked Marina to give him a little test, especially a pronunciation test, since he had trouble with the Spanish "r."

Lee appreciated Marina's acquiescence, or her awareness, anyhow, that it was no use telling him what to do, and that the only way for him to learn whether he liked Cuba was to go there and experience it for himself. After she had given him her consent to go peacefully, via Mexico, he gave her his highest accolade —"You understand me."

Despite the harmony that presently prevailed between them, there was an occasional sign that it was not a case of two minds with but a single thought. They had always agreed that their next child, a boy, was to be named "David Lee." But for some time Lee had been turning another name over in his mind and he cautiously broached it to Marina. He told her, stealing up a little on the subject, that he thought it might be a nice touch to call their new baby "Fidel."

Marina had been trying to give in, trying to understand and accept Lee, and do nothing to jangle his nerves. But this was too much. Was she, or was she not, about to be the mother of this child? To think that politics, the cause of all her woes and the thing she hated most in life, was to be insinuated into her family, into her very belly, was more than Marina could abide.

She reasserted herself in all her old magnificent asperity. "There is no Fidel and there will be no Fidel in our family."

31

Parting

THE OSWALDS' neighbors are astonishingly unanimous about Lee's movements after he lost his job. One of them was out of work too, and it seems he enjoyed nothing better than noticing Lee's comings and goings. All the neighbors agree that Lee was "in and out" of his apartment during the day but invariably home at night.[1] After reading at home all morning, during the afternoon he would sometimes catch a bus on the corner headed toward the business section, or walk that way. But he was never out for long. Once in a while he walked to a confectionery store on the corner of Magazine and Dufosset Streets, bought some ice cream, and carried it back to the apartment.[2] The Oswalds did their grocery shopping at the Winn-Dixie on Prytania Street.

The Garners, managers of the building, recall that Lee was never on time with the rent. Mrs. Garner vividly remembers Lee, clad only in a pair of out-grown, gold high-school basketball shorts—no shirt—going up and down the street at night stuffing his garbage into everybody's cans, including hers, because he could not or would not spend money to buy a garbage can for himself.[3]

Lee spent most of the day and the early evening, until the light began to fade, reading on the screened-in side porch of his apartment. As summer lengthened and dusk came on earlier, he carried a lamp onto the porch so he could read a little later. But the seriousness and even the quantity of his reading had fallen off. During the first part of the summer, he had read political books, biographies, and books about Russia and communism, from one of which he confronted Marina one night with the surmise that she must be illegitimate. She blushed deeply and denied it. But after the beginning of August, most of his reading consisted of a lighter diet of spy novels and science fiction. Marina had no idea what he was reading, but from indoors she could see that sometimes Lee was not reading at all. He was just sitting on the porch looking out on the street. "He's been inside all day and wants to see the people out walking," she said to herself.

One evening during the last week of August, she and June went for a stroll. Arriving home about twilight, they found Lee on the porch perched on one knee, pointing his rifle toward the street. It was the first time she had seen him with his rifle in months—and she was horrified.

"What are you doing?" she asked.

"Get the heck out of here," he said. "Don't talk to me. Get on about your own affairs."

A few evenings later, she again found him on the porch with his rifle.

"Playing with your gun again, are you?" she said, sarcastically.

"Fidel Castro needs defenders," Lee said. "I'm going to join his army of volunteers. I'm going to be a revolutionary."

After that, busy indoors, Marina frequently heard a clicking sound out on the porch while Lee was sitting there at dusk. She heard it three times a week, maybe more often, until the middle of September. Often she saw him clean the rifle, but this did not worry her because she knew that he had not taken it out of the house to practice. "So it's Cuba this time. If he's got to use his gun," she thought to herself, "let him take it to his Cuba. They're always shooting down there anyway. Just so he doesn't use it here." But just in case, she exacted a promise from him that he would not use his rifle against anybody in the United States. *"Ya ne budu"*—"I won't"—he promised her in a quiet voice. Marina felt reassured.[4]

In the early days of September, Lee increasingly concentrated on one thing —Cuba. He was anxious to be on his way. When he was able to leave for Mexico, however, would depend on the one person whom both the Oswalds now looked on as their "savior"—Ruth Paine. "When is Ruth coming?" he kept asking. Or, "How many days before Ruth is due to arrive?"

Ruth and Marina had been exchanging letters all summer. Ruth was sedulous about Lee's feelings. She always asked how he was, and whenever there were decisions to be made, she addressed sections of her letters, in English, to him. Ruth was not certain that she liked Lee, but she thought he was a vulnerable man and she respected his feelings. So long as the Oswalds stayed together, Lee was very much a part of her friendship for Marina. She went out of her way not to hurt him.

About the middle of July, more than a month after two letters had arrived from Marina announcing that things were not going well between her and Lee, Ruth wrote renewing her invitation to Marina to stay with her in Irving before and after the new baby's birth. But now, for the first time, she extended an indefinite invitation: Marina could stay as long as she needed if it would save her from going back to Russia against her will. Ruth told Marina that she was welcome to stay "for two months or two years."[5]

Before issuing the invitation Ruth talked it over with her husband, Michael. He tended to favor it since Marina's earlier visit had worked out well and had contributed to Ruth's happiness, but he decided to consult Frank Krystinik, his best friend at work, about whether Lee might turn out to be a "violent person," capable of taking out on Ruth such displeasure as he might feel at Marina's being there. Michael and Krystinik concluded that if Lee were handled in a "gentle and considerate" manner, so that his feelings were not offended, he would not be a danger.[6] They decided that Lee was not "going to stab Ruth or Marina." Only after they had considered the possibility that Lee might be violent and rejected it did Ruth go ahead and invite Marina for the longer stay.

At this point, about mid-July, Marina wrote that her marriage was going better, she no longer felt the need of rescue, but would like to hold the invitation in reserve in case "Lee gets rough with me again." Despite a false assurance from Marina that she had been to see a doctor, and despite a postscript from Lee about the cost of maternity care in New Orleans, Ruth somehow divined that she was going to be needed even before the new baby arrived. Accordingly, she wrote Marina that, after a roundabout tour of relatives in the East and the Midwest, she would stop in New Orleans about September 18. Marina could make up her mind then whether she wanted stay in New Orleans, drive back to Dallas with Ruth to await the baby, or come later on her own closer to the due date.

But during the first ten days of August, Lee's thoughts must have turned decisively toward adventure—or at least toward divesting himself of responsibility for his wife and children—for he told Marina to write Ruth that he had lost his job and they were out of money. She was not to speak of Cuba in the letter or say that he had agreed to go with her to Russia. Marina was not to mention him at all if she could help it.

Marina did as she was told, and her letter (postmarked August 11, the day after Lee's release from the police station) contains a ring of embarrassment or evasion.[7] This time, unlike the previous spring when she omitted to tell Ruth anything about the Walker affair, Marina was not, on her own initiative, withholding information out of loyalty to Lee. Instead, she consciously allowed Lee to use her as an instrument to get what he wanted out of Ruth. Marina was embarrassed because Lee was so obviously appealing to Ruth to take her off his hands. But what was she to do? The baby was due before long, Lee wanted to be rid of her, and she had nowhere else to turn. Ruth was her one hope of staying in America.

On August 25, Ruth mailed a letter from Paoli, Pennsylvania, promising to be in New Orleans on September 20 exactly, and during the daylight hours if she could make it. Coming from Ruth, the promise might have been written on granite. From the day it arrived, about August 27 or 28, Lee knew that he would be free to leave for Mexico within a few days of September 20 and he started making his plans. He was already, that last week of August, dry-firing his rifle on the porch. But as if to underscore the connection between his plans and Ruth, he stopped dry-firing the gun, Marina says, "a few days before Ruth arrived." It was as if Ruth Paine was his conscience.

While he waited for Ruth's arrival, Lee wrote three remarkable letters. In one, dated August 31 and addressed to Mr. E. Bert, managing editor of *The Worker* in New York City, he applied for a job as a photographer and announced that he and his family would be "relocating" into the area "in a few weeks."[8] The letter was accompanied by a sample of Lee's work and was incorrectly addressed.

Also on August 31, Lee wrote a letter (misdated September 1) to the Socialist Workers Party in New York, announcing that he and his family were moving to the Baltimore-Washington area in October and asking how to get in touch with party representatives there.[9] And on September 1, he wrote a letter to the Communist Party asking how to "contact the Party in the Baltimore-Washington area, to which I shall relocate in October."[10]

Although Lee was obsessed by his desire to go to Cuba and had no intention of returning to the United States, where this time he would surely face prosecution, these letters apparently represented an alternative in case he never got there at all. In that event, perhaps he thought he might move to the Northeast and try to establish himself as a left-wing activist. Why did he choose New York, Baltimore, or Washington? They were, first of all, the cities with Russian-speaking communities that Ruth had mentioned where Marina might be able to find a job. Lee had scolded Marina for even considering a visit to those cities with Ruth, but now, characteristically, he picked up the very same idea. If there was not much prejudice against people who knew Russian and had been to Russia, then perhaps he, instead of Marina, could find work there.

Lee may still have hoped to get a job with *The Militant* or *The Worker,* and probably expected that he could form a more active link with either the Communist Party or the Socialist Workers Party in the Northeast than in Texas or Louisiana. And because the civil rights activities that were most heavily covered in the press, including *The Militant,* that summer—such as the highly publicized March on Washington in August and the unremitting racial turmoil in Cambridge, Maryland—had occurred in the Baltimore-Washington area, Lee may also have decided that it was in the Northeast that he would have the best chance of putting together a politically oriented life.

Lee acquired the *Bulletin* of the New York School for Marxist Study for the fall term of 1963. And he spent time composing a detailed résumé of his life, including his various activities: "Radio Speaker and Lecturer," "Street Agitation," "Organizer," "Photographer," "Marxist," "Defector," and "Resident of U.S.S.R."[11] It was handwritten on looseleaf paper and he evidently took it with him to Mexico. In one of the appendices included with the section called "Photographer" were the photographs he had taken of tax returns of Jaggars-Chiles-Stovall, perhaps to prove to some intended recipient that his Marxist convictions were so strong he was not above rifling even the most private files of his capitalist employer.

It is fruitless to try to make the fragments of Lee Oswald's mind fit together as neatly as a jigsaw puzzle. It is better to leave the puzzle loose, with fragments scattered here and there. But it is noteworthy that since his return from Russia, Lee had exchanged somewhere between fifty and seventy items of correspondence with the Soviet Embassy in Washington (a necessity, since Marina was a Soviet citizen), with the left-wing bookstore in Washington through which he subscribed to Soviet periodicals, and with left-wing newspapers and organizations in New York.[12] Much of the correspondence was routine—change-of-address cards, requests for speeches by Trotsky or for the words of the Communist hymn, "The Internationale." But the volume of his correspondence was significant and certain of his letters very revealing. In October 1962, only five months after his return from Russia, Lee requested membership in the Socialist Workers Party, clearly his first choice. The party turned him down because it had no branch in Texas. He next applied for free-lance photographic work in the Southwest for both *The Militant* and *The Worker*. Both responded politely, but nothing came of it. The F.P.C.C., after one encouraging letter, proceeded to ignore him.

Obviously, these affiliations mattered to Lee. He had shot at General Walker partly to establish himself as a hero of the American left. And he was still trying to attach himself to left-wing causes. He needed a cause to belong to, something outside himself that was bigger than he was and could be reflected back into his inflated self-image to help sustain it. Yet the very same quality that required him to seek recognition also made any sort of real belonging wholly impossible. His self-image was so far out of line with reality that he was unable to see himself as others saw him or to deal with them on a real footing—as either an equal or a subordinate.

Lee had another difficulty and it, too, arose out of his estrangement from reality. There was a flaw in his signal system, his antennae, his equipment for receiving messages. Lee picked up countless signals from newspapers and people and books, but somehow they were distorted in transmission. He was unable to understand what others were trying to say to him. Instead, he heard only what he wanted to hear. He lacked that capacity for communication that is at the heart of working with other people. The most he was capable of was a sort of pseudo-belonging to something very far away that existed only in his mind.

Yet here he was, on the eve of his departure for Cuba, trying, as he had been since boyhood, to belong to something—the Communist Party, the Socialist Workers Party, one of their newspapers. And they scarcely knew who he was. Their letters were distant, polite, the sort of letter an organization writes to someone it is not actually rebuffing but with whom it has no relationship. To the American left, Lee Oswald did not exist. Yet this was the community he yearned to belong to and whose hero he hoped to become.

On Labor Day Lee called the Murrets and asked if he and his family could come for a visit. There, for the first time in two months, he saw his favorite cousin Marilyn. She had just returned from a two-month bus trip through Mexico, Central America, and Panama, and Lee soaked up everything she said.[13] He told no one that he intended to go to Mexico, let alone Cuba. The fact that three of the people he liked best, Marilyn and George and Jeanne de Mohrenschildt, had all been to Mexico, must have made an impression on Lee, but he gave no hint of that either.

The Murrets once again challenged Lee for discouraging Marina from learning English. His answer was as usual—he wanted to keep up his own Russian. His Aunt Lillian wanted to know why. "Do you intend to go back to Russia?" she asked.[14] Luckily for Lee, somebody broke into their conversation and he was spared from having to meet his aunt's perspicacity head on.

John Murret took Lee and Marina home that night. On the way he drove them past the church in which he was soon to be married and the large house in which his fiancée lived. Lee did not say anything, but Marina could tell that his fists were clenched in anger. Lee, she says, did not hate the owners of these houses, but he did hate the system that made it possible for anyone to be so wealthy. Stingy as he was, and forever saving up in little ways, Lee did not want a lot of money for himself. That was not where his ambition lay. Like virtually everyone who knew him, Marina, too, believes that her husband could not have been "bought." What she sensed in him that night—an impression so strong that it was almost palpable—was his hatred of American capitalism.

It was less than three weeks before Marina would be leaving for Dallas and Lee for Mexico City. They might be parted for a short time, or forever, and those last weeks together in New Orleans contained episodes that were funny, touching, sad.

It was fearfully sultry and hot, and their only air conditioning was an old kitchen fan. Lee went naked around the apartment a good deal of the time and sometimes spent the whole day lying on the sofa on his stomach, without a stitch on, reading a book. Marina warned him that it was bad for Junie to see him nude.

"Oh, she's too young," he said. "It doesn't matter."

"By the time she's that old, it will be too late."

He played with Junie continually, took baths with her, and spent a good hour and a half putting her to bed every night. These were boisterous sessions, with Lee getting so much into the spirit that he sometimes leaped into Junie's bed himself, as if the two of them were babies going to sleep together.

He behaved like a baby with Marina, too, competing with Junie for her attention. He might be lying on the sofa wearing a shirt. "Come here, girl," he would summon Marina, and hold out one arm, then the other, to allow her to pull it off. It was the same way when he dressed. He would stick out one leg, then the other, and let Marina put on his underpants.

He was at his most babyish when he and Junie emerged from the tub. "Wipe my back first," he would say to Marina in baby talk. Or, "Quick, quick, there are drops of water on my leg!" If Marina did not dry him off quickly enough or refused to mop up the puddles he and the baby made on the floor, he threatened to stay in the bathtub all day. "Stop it, Alka," Marina pleaded. "I haven't got time to play."

"Our mama isn't good to us," he said to Junie. "She doesn't like looking after little children."

If Marina was busy with something else and was not able to dry him off, he strode naked through the apartment, splattering water everywhere. He knew that Marina hated that; she was afraid to have the neighbors see him naked. "If you won't dry me off," Lee said, "then they'll have the pleasure of seeing me."

Once in a while the baby was naughty and Marina gave her a little slap on the behind. "Come to Papa," Lee would say. "Papa will take pity on you. Mama doesn't love our Junie. Otherwise she'd be ashamed to hurt such a tiny girl's feelings. Let's go and find Mama." Then he would go to Marina and give *her* a little slap on the behind.

Marina told him to stop; it undermined her authority. "I'll never get her to obey." Lee said the baby was too little to understand. "She understands more than you know," Marina replied.

Junie was the joy of Lee's life, his tie to reality, the one person, Marina thinks, with whom he came down from the clouds and behaved like a human being. He was often cruel to Marina, but never to June. "His general mood was one thing," says Marina. "How he was with babies was another." She frankly admits that she was jealous.

The three of them seldom went out together.

But there was one expedition they all enjoyed. Although they were living on very little money and spent almost nothing on recreation, Lee loved taking Marina and June to the amusement park at Lake Pontchartrain. There was a horse race game at the park at which he always got lucky. He considered everything he won there pure profit, and nothing made him happier than to spend all his winnings on hamburgers for his "two girls."

He spent almost nothing else, and tried to save every penny. He even starved himself to save money. During the last several weeks in New Orleans, he ate very little and became so thin that his ribs and collarbone stuck out. His face and legs were bony, too. Marina thinks he was starving himself not only to save money but also because he was in a wave of emotional tension. He had lost weight other times—just before he went to the American Embassy in Moscow in July 1961, and again the month before his attempt on General Walker—but his last month in New Orleans was the worst.

Marina scolded him for being stingy. And he, in turn, scolded her for the way she spent even the small amount of money that he did give her. Lee, of course, was saving for his trip to Mexico, although neither of them spoke about it much. Marina said nothing when Lee failed to pay the $65 rent due September 9 for the following month, even though she was so ashamed that she did not dare leave the apartment during the day for fear of running into Mr. or Mrs. Garner. But finally she could contain her feelings no longer.

Just before Ruth was due to arrive, they were playing a game of poker. Lee promised Marina he would lend her money to play with, and when she won she started jumping around the room for joy.

"No, no, you didn't win," Lee protested. "I loaned you the money to begin with. If you win the next game, you can have the money. If you lose, then you'll owe me again."

Furious, Marina threw down the money and the cards and said: "Play by yourself, you greedy pig!"

"Why are you so angry?" He followed her as she stormed out of the room. "It's only a game."

"I'm sorry, Alka. I see this game in real life every day. Even in games, even in little things, you're always greedy for money. You know I don't have a cent. Supposing I do owe you money, where will I get it? Steal it from you? You know I can't steal."

"Then you didn't have to play by those principles."

"I'm tired of your principles," she said. "Even in games I see your petty spirit. I see it in the grocery store. We go in and you give me thirty cents. Afterwards you want to know what I spent it on. I earned thirty dollars teaching Russian and spent all but four of it on you. I wasn't sorry I spent it on you—I was glad. Lyolya Hall gave me twenty dollars and I spent every penny of it on you."

All Marina's grievances came pouring out. It was as if she had been storing them up like firecrackers in her mouth and Lee had touched a match to them. She exploded.

"On your principles I breastfed Junie until she was ten months old just to save you money. I'm sick of your principles. Even in a simple game you can't change them. I spare nothing to help you. Just what do you think you look like —like a skeleton, that's what. That's your principles, too. It's greed, not principles at all. You save on everything. What for? To buy a dress for your wife? Food or a toy for your child? No. You have money for a gun. You have money for your Mexico. But for your own baby, no! What joy is your Cuba, your Mexico, your Castro, to me? You never even think about our new baby. I have to ask Ruth to help because Papa has got something more important on his mind. I'm tired of your 'important' things. When will you start to think the way normal people do? You imagine that you're a great man. Nobody thought that up but you."

Marina was so angry, and her words poured out so rapidly, that Lee was silent. Then she started to pack all her clothes in a suitcase. She was going to the Murrets' until Ruth came.

He pushed her gently onto the bed. "My God," Lee said. "Out of such tiny things she makes such a fight. That's women for you!"

"Ah, women again," said Marina. "There's not a woman who would stay with you more than one day. Any other woman would have run away the day after she married you."

Lee took Marina's clothes out of the suitcase and hung them back in the closet. She took them out and packed them again. "I'm the only one who's fool enough to do it," she went on. "I try to put up with you. And the whole time you're giving me hell and saying I never 'support' you. What on earth do you mean by that? That I ought to carry you in my arms? With a normal man it would be the other way around. He would carry his wife in his arms."

"I can carry you in my arms," Lee said, and started to lift her.

She pulled away from him and kept on packing, while Lee tried to soothe her and begged her not to leave.

"Alka," she said, "what is it, what more do you want from me? Never again say to me that I 'never support you.' I can't even bear to hear those words. I do more for you than I should and more than I can."

Lee tried to calm her. He apologized. He had not meant to make her angry, he said. He offered to give back the money she had won at cards, but Marina refused to touch it.

"Go choke on your lousy money."

After she had packed and been unpacked twice, Lee kissed her and she finally quieted down. She went to bed and Lee disappeared into the bathroom to read.

Later, he stole into the bedroom and asked if he might lie down.

"Unhappily, I have no choice," she said.

He crept cautiously into bed, afraid to take up an extra inch. Then he got bolder and asked if he might move over a little.

"No," she said. "Go sleep on the floor." But after a few minutes she weakened and moved over.

Marina's outburst had been caused in part by her sorrow and anxiety about the parting that lay ahead. Realizing that she might never see Lee again, she begged him to take her with him. "Where on earth can I take you?" he said. "You're in the last stages of pregnancy." He promised to bring her to Cuba or else rejoin her in Russia. Marina hated both choices, but she knew it was useless to protest. In the meantime, she was not to tell Ruth where Lee was, nor would he write to her at Ruth's. But if she had not heard from him in two weeks (his Mexican tourist visa was good for two weeks), then she would know he was in Cuba.

On Friday afternoon, September 20, Marina went out to buy a few last-minute groceries. By the time she got back, Ruth and her children had arrived and Lee was greeting them on the porch. He was overjoyed to see Ruth and she, for her part, was impressed by the change in him. He seemed to be in good spirits, "very outgoing and warm and friendly."[15] She had never seen him in such a good mood before.

Ruth and her children stayed the weekend and they all had a pleasant time. Lee appeared genuinely concerned about Marina's welfare and where she would have her baby. He was grateful to Ruth for taking over the arrangements. He gave her a duplicate tax form from Jaggars-Chiles-Stovall, his Dallas employer from October 1962 to April 1963, to present to Parkland Hospital in Dallas as proof that Marina was a one-year Texas resident, hence entitled to care based on her ability to pay. In case the hospital authorities asked, he was anxious that Ruth avoid any suggestion that he had "abandoned" his wife. He, of course, made no mention of his plans to go abroad. He told Ruth that he was going to Houston or Philadelphia to look for work; as soon as he found it, he would be back to fetch Marina. Thus Ruth assumed that Marina was coming to stay with her for only a few weeks.

Contrary to his usual contempt for anyone who helped him, Lee had a grudging admiration for Ruth. She was "too tall" and "a fool"—Lee called everyone "a fool"—but he was sympathetic to her marital troubles. In a reversal of his customary moralistic stance, Lee, prompted by Marina, declared that Ruth would be "a fool" *not* to take a lover. It would help her forget Michael. So, when Ruth wrote them a postcard from New York announcing ruefully that she had not yet succeeded in her mission, Lee was tickled a good deal. He laughed and said that Ruth was "really something."

That weekend Marina wanted to take Ruth on a tour of the nightclubs on Bourbon Street. They urged Lee to come with them but he refused. He hated nightclubs and had never, in all the time Marina knew him and in spite of much cajoling on her part, been inside one. So Marina and Ruth made the tour, "a tall

Quaker lady," as Marina describes it, holding a small boy and girl by either hand, and a small, very pregnant woman, holding her tiny daughter by the hand. They did not go into any of the clubs. They just peeked through the swinging doors, while the children tried to dance to the striptease music.

When they got back, they found Lee in a marvelous mood. He had washed the dishes, straightened up the apartment—and started packing. Ruth was impressed by Lee's insistence on doing every bit of packing himself. She had never seen him such a gentleman before. What she did not know was that among the items he was loading with such care in her car was, almost certainly, his rifle, dismantled, wrapped in brown paper and a blanket, and tied up in heavy string. Somehow he led the Paines to understand that it was "camping equipment."[16]

The parting on Monday morning, September 23, was hard for both Lee and Marina. Lee tried to conceal his distress by doing chores. When he had finished loading the car—again, all by himself—he assured Marina that he knew he did not have to worry about her so long as she was with Ruth. "She is good and she will help you." But when he kissed Marina goodbye, his lips were trembling and it was all he could do to keep from crying. Marina thought that he might be wondering, for the first time, whether he had a right to act in a way that could hurt his wife and baby. Marina remembers that he looked at her "as a dog looks at its master." And in that pathetic look she thought she could see that he loved her.

Marina, too, was close to tears and tried to conceal from Ruth how much the parting was costing her—the pain of perhaps leaving Lee forever. She was ashamed at being dumped on Ruth, ashamed most of all that she could not tell the truth even to the friend who had come to her rescue.

No sooner had they said their goodbyes and driven off than Ruth noticed a rumbling in one of her tires. She pulled up at a gas station one block from the apartment to have it changed. Lee, in his sandals, followed them there. Marina took him to one side and they parted all over again. She was tender to him, telling him to be careful and eat properly.

"Stop," he said. "I can't stand it. Do you want me to cry in front of Ruth?"

For him, too, the hardest thing was to conceal from Ruth that the parting might be forever. And so, while the two of them fought back their tears, Lee held Junie in front of the Coke machine to help them regain their composure. "Come on, Junie," he said. "Show me with your fingers what you want." Then, when he had a grip on himself, he warned Marina that, above all, she was not to tell Ruth he was going to Cuba.

32

A New Disappointment

A HOST of controversies has arisen about the months that Lee Harvey Oswald spent in New Orleans, in particular the time from July 19 onwards, when he was unemployed, and the two days between Marina's departure for Texas on September 23 and Lee's own departure for Mexico City on September 25. Clandestine meetings and conspiratorial relationships have been attributed to Oswald during this period. But the available evidence suggests that both were unlikely, if not impossible. Taking Marina's recollections of her husband's activities, the testimony of the Oswalds' neighbors, the minimum number of visits Lee paid to the public library—occasions when he actually checked out a book (twenty)—his visits to the Louisiana Employment Office (sixteen), the times he went looking for jobs between July 22 and the middle of August (an unknown but considerable number), occasions when he was out picketing or at the radio station (five), his forays to printing establishments (perhaps a dozen), his visits to Winn-Dixie and his post office box, his trips with Marina and June to the Murrets' (four or five times), to Lake Pontchartrain, the zoo, the botanical garden, or just exploring the French Quarter, to say nothing of times when he spent the entire day reading in the public library or when Marina sent him to the movies so she could catch up on housework or have a little time to herself—all of these added together account for most of Oswald's time in New Orleans while he was not actually at work. Only one, and possibly two, people whom he may have known slightly during these months remain unidentified: one of the two young men to whom he paid $2 on August 16 to help him pass out handbills; and a "Negro" at Reily with whom he told Marina he used to go drinking, a man whom she never saw and who may have been a creature of Lee's imagination, since Marina reports that Lee never came home late and never drank anything stronger than Coke, iced tea, or Dr. Pepper.

Lee was, of course, highly secretive. He had wanted to be a spy and he was, in fact, a nearly successful assassin. Since it is difficult, if not impossible, to prove a negative, it cannot be established that conspirators did not ever contact him, or he them. But for anyone who was contemplating something serious, Oswald would appear to have been too conspicuous, especially in the Southwest, for he was an ex-defector to Russia who flaunted his Russian and had a Russian wife, he was an almost inevitable magnet for the FBI's attentions, and he was a young man who blatantly sought publicity instead of avoiding it. And if his outer characteristics rendered him an unlikely recruit, his personality rendered him unlikelier still, for he was so incapable of cooperating with anyone that he had been unable even to establish the loosest of relationships with the F.P.C.C., fifteen hundred miles away. Apart from the rare occasions when their living arrangements forced him to admit to Marina what he was doing, or when a momentary breach in the armor of his mistrust allowed him to confide in her, he trusted no one with his secrets. He had proven that he was capable of taking drastic actions and dangerous risks—but always alone.

As to whether or not he was susceptible to influence, a few months before in Dallas, eager for George de Mohrenschildt's approval, he does appear, without his or De Mohrenschildt's being aware of it consciously, to have been influenced to shoot at General Walker. But after April he had no George de Mohrenschildt. With the possible exception of Marina, there was no one in his environment whose love and approval he craved. Even if there was an attempt to influence him by someone who might have known him casually—and there appears to have been no such person in his life—the metaphor of the pool hall seems appropriate. Someone desiring to influence Lee might shoot a ball, an idea, at him, but there was no way to predict how it might come caroming off.

Judging by the eagerness he had shown to be off for Mexico, one might expect that Lee would have left on Monday, the 23rd, the same day that Ruth and Marina left New Orleans. He did not leave until Wednesday, the 25th, and his movements over the next two days have given rise to conflicting testimony, even among eyewitnesses, as well as to much controversy.[1]

On Sunday, while Lee was loading Ruth's station wagon, Jesse Garner, spotting nearly all the Oswalds' belongings in the car, asked him if he was leaving.[2] Lee, who owed two weeks' rent, said No. His wife was going to Texas to have her baby and would return. He was staying there. He did stay in New Orleans for two more days, but his movements were so furtive that neighbors could not agree on when they saw him actually leave the apartment. Two of them reported later that they saw Lee racing to catch a bus on the corner, carrying a piece of luggage in each hand, at five or six in the evening. But one of them thought it was Monday, the other that it was Tuesday, evening. On Wednesday, Jesse Garner entered the Oswalds' apartment and found it empty. Lee was gone.

Whether or not he stayed in the apartment Monday or Tuesday night, Lee was obviously trying to cheat the Garners out of the rent. That appears to have been the only secret activity in which he was engaged during those two days. Moreover, money was also the reason he waited until Wednesday to leave for Mexico City. He had only about $150 for his trip, and by staying in New Orleans on Tuesday, he was able to visit the Louisiana Employment Commission and file claim for the next to last of the thirteen unemployment compensation checks to which he was entitled from the State of Texas. He filed the claim and the check was forwarded to him the following week in care of Michael Paine in Irving.

By waiting until Wednesday morning, Lee was also able to go to his post office box at the Lafayette Square substation and pick up the $33 unemployment compensation check for which he had filed a claim the week before. While there, he popped a change-of-address card in the mailbox and it was stamped at the main post office at 11:00 A.M. According to postal officials, this meant that Lee had picked up his check at the Lafayette Square post office station no later than 10:20 that morning. He then went to the Winn-Dixie store on Magazine Street (on his street, but not the branch store he generally patronized) and cashed the check sometime before noon. He had, in all probability, already deposited his baggage at the bus terminal, which gave him freedom to complete all his business on Wednesday morning without risking a return to the apartment and a confrontation with Mr. Garner. And by cashing his $33 check at a store where he was not known, he also hoped to avoid being seen or recognized by his neighbors. He owed Mr. Garner for fifteen or sixteen days, one-half of his monthly rental of $65. He therefore saved almost exactly $33, the same amount as his unemployment check.

Lee's departure from New Orleans resembled his departure nearly five months earlier from Dallas. Both times Ruth and Marina left ahead of him, and both times he stayed at the apartment and checked his luggage at the bus terminal prior to his departure. Lee probably left New Orleans at 12:20 P.M. on Wednesday by Continental Trailways Bus No. 5121, bound for Houston. There were no eyewitnesses to his arrival there, but after that he blazed a fairly conspicuous trail.

That night in Houston, a woman named Estelle Twiford, the wife of a merchant seaman named Horace Elroy Twiford, received a telephone call at her home from a man who identified himself as Lee Harvey Oswald. He said that he was on his way "by air" to Mexico, would be in town a few hours, and would like "to discuss ideas" with her husband. Mrs. Twiford told him that her husband was out of town. Lee left his name and said that he was with the Fair Play for Cuba Committee. Mrs. Twiford relayed the message to her husband the next time he was home.

Twiford was a member of the Socialist Labor Party. Earlier in the summer, in response to a request for literature from Oswald, the Socialist Labor Party in New York had passed on Oswald's name to Twiford. He then mailed Oswald at least one issue of a small paper he put out called the *Weekly People*. That was the only knowledge the Twifords had of Oswald, and his telephone call was their only contact.[3]

Lee left Houston about 2:35 on Thursday morning, September 26, aboard Continental Trailways Bus No. 5133, transferred to Mexican Red Arrow Bus No. 516 at Nuevo Laredo, Mexico, and arrived in Mexico City about 10:00 A.M. on Friday, September 27. He made no secret of his identity or the reason for his trip. He told Dr. and Mrs. John B. McFarland, an English couple who were fellow passengers, that he was secretary of the Fair Play for Cuba Committee in New Orleans. He was going to Mexico to evade the American ban on travel to Cuba, he said, and was on his way to Cuba to see Castro if he could.[4]

Lee also got into conversation with two Australian girls on the bus. He asked if they had been to Russia, took out his old U.S. passport to show them his Soviet visa, and said he had lived there two years. While he acted very much the world traveler, the girls noticed that he was at a loss with the Spanish menus. Thus, every two hours, when the passengers disembarked for a food and rest stop, Lee was unable to pick and choose—he just pointed at something on the menu and had to eat a full meal. He told the girls he loved Mexican food. Their nickname for him was "Texas." Although "Texas" ate every meal alone, he did make an exception for the McFarlands, with whom he had breakfast as they were approaching Mexico City on Friday morning.[5]

Less than an hour after his arrival, Lee was installed in Room 18 of the Hotel del Comercio, four blocks from the bus terminal. The room cost $1.28 a day, and the maid was impressed not only by the paucity of his personal effects but by the fact that he did his own laundry, leaving a few items to dry in the bathroom each time he went out.[6]

He lost no time getting about his business, and spent most of Friday and Saturday bouncing back and forth between the Soviet and Cuban embassies, which were located at some distance from his hotel but within a few blocks of one another.[7] At the Soviet Embassy he told the consular official with whom he spoke, probably Valery Vladimirovich Kostikov, that his wife, a Soviet citizen, had applied several months earlier to return to the U.S.S.R. with their child. He said that he had been in touch with the Soviet Embassy in Washington about a reentry visa for himself, and he displayed various pieces of evidence of his prior residence in the U.S.S.R. and his membership in a pro-Castro organization in the United States.

At the Cuban Embassy, Lee fell into the sympathetic hands of Sylvia Duran, a twenty-six-year-old Mexican woman who was a Cuban consular official. He displayed a sheaf of documents, including his new and his expired passports, which showed that he had lived in the U.S.S.R.; the labor card he had had in Minsk, showing that he had worked there; his marriage certificate; his correspondence with the U.S. Communist Party and the Soviet Embassy in Washington, some of which was in Russian; his two Fair Play for Cuba cards, one signed by "A. J. Hidell," the other by Vincent T. Lee; and his "résumé," the several looseleaf, handwritten sheets on which he had summarized his life as an "Organizer," "Marxist," "Defector," and so on.

Mrs. Duran was impressed by all this, especially the fact that Oswald was the leader of an organization calling for "Fair Treatment for Cuba." "Admittedly exceeding her responsibilities," as she put it later, she "semi-officially" telephoned someone at the Soviet consulate to see if she could facilitate issuance of a Soviet visa to Oswald, but was told that it would take at least four months. When she informed Lee that a Cuban visa could not be issued until he had a Soviet visa, he became annoyed and said he had a right to go to Cuba in view of his background and loyalty and his activities in behalf of the Cuban movement. Mrs. Duran told him that she could do nothing more.

On Saturday morning, Lee returned to the Cuban Embassy and Mrs. Duran put him into direct contact with one or two persons at the Soviet Embassy, probably by telephone. The story was still the same, and Lee became so excited and angry that Mrs. Duran begged the Cuban consul, Señor Eusebio Asque, to come out of his office and talk to Oswald himself. Asque likewise called the Soviet consulate and confirmed that there would be a waiting period of four to six months. He suggested to Oswald that he leave Mexico and return when he had a Soviet visa, at which point he would be given a Cuban transit visa.

At that, Lee again became furious and demanded his rights in a scene which may have resembled his behavior at the American Embassy in Moscow in 1959. Exasperated, Asque finally told him that if it were up to him he would not give him a visa at all, and that "a person of his type was harming the Cuban Revolution rather than helping it." But Mrs. Duran apparently took pity on Lee. She handed him a slip of paper with her name and telephone number on it, and she went ahead and processed his visa application. Fifteen to thirty days later, a routine reply arrived from Havana approving Oswald's visa application on condition that the Soviet visa be obtained first.

There was nothing more Lee could do. On Sunday he apparently visited museums and did some sightseeing in Mexico City.[8] On Monday he went to a travel agency and purchased bus tickets from Mexico City to Laredo and thence to Dallas. And on Tuesday, October 1, he attempted a final assault on the fortress of Soviet bureaucracy. He somehow contacted the Soviet military attaché and asked whether a reply had been received to a telegram which the Soviet consul had promised to send the embassy in Washington. The military attaché referred him to the consulate. A guard outside the consulate went inside and returned with the message that the telegram had been sent but no reply had been received.[9]

His visit a failure, Lee left Mexico City by bus on Wednesday, October 2. Even his departure was troubled. In the middle of the night he was pulled off the bus at the border by Mexican officials because of a supposed irregularity in his tourist papers, and was heard to grumble as he climbed back on, "My papers were in order before and I don't know why they bother me now." At the U.S. customs station in Laredo at 1:30 in the morning of October 3, he was seen "gulping down" a banana. A customs official reassured him that he would be allowed to take it into the United States and did not have to eat so fast.[10]

By 2:30 on the afternoon of October 3, Lee was in Dallas, only one week and one day after leaving New Orleans. He had spent perhaps $100 on the trip, but its cost to him could not be measured only in money. The real cost was the destruction of his hope. He had yearned to belong, to join a cause, to become a revolutionary, a volunteer for "Uncle Fidel." He had wanted to deploy his shooting skills in behalf of a tiny, embattled country that surely needed him. Instead, he was told by no less a figure than the Cuban consul that people like him were harmful to the cause of revolution. He must have suffered a grave new wound to his self-esteem.

Lee was left with nowhere to go. If he ever had real thoughts of moving to the Northeast and becoming a political activist, those thoughts evaporated now. He lacked emotional energy to strike out for any place new. It was the most he could do to crawl back to the old places and attempt to do what he had done before: get a job, save money, support Marina and his children.

He did not even call Marina when he arrived in Dallas. He went straight to the offices of the Texas Employment Commission, filed a claim for the last of his unemployment compensation checks, and announced that he was once again looking for a job.[11] He then went to the YMCA—the same "Y" where he had stayed one year before—registered as a serviceman so he would not have to pay a membership fee, and spent the night there.[12]

Next morning he went to Padgett Printing Corporation in response to a newspaper advertisement and applied for a job as a typesetter in the composing room. Theodore Gangl, the plant superintendent who interviewed him, said he was "well dressed and neat" and "made a favorable impression" on the foreman. Gangl was inclined to hire him, especially since he already had experience at Jaggars-Chiles-Stovall. But after he spoke to Robert Stovall on the telephone later in the day, he made the following notation at the bottom of Oswald's job application: "Bob Stovall does not recommend this man. He was released because of his record as a troublemaker. Has communistic tendencies."[13] Lee did not get the job.

He called Marina only after his interview. She was very happy to hear his voice and relieved beyond measure that he had not gone to Cuba. He asked to have Ruth drive to town to pick him up. Marina explained that Ruth had just given blood at Parkland Hospital in case it was needed during the baby's birth, and was not up to the long drive to Dallas. And so Lee hitchhiked and got a ride all the way to the Paines' house with a black man. He was there before lunch.

Marina stood in the bedroom and stared at the prodigal who had come home to her. He kissed her and asked if she had missed him? Then he started right in: "Ah, they're such terrible bureaucrats that nothing came of it after all." He described his shuttling from embassy to embassy, how each one told him he had to wait and wait, and see what the other one did, and how the whole time he had been worried about running out of money. He was especially vociferous about the Cubans—"the same kind of bureaucrats as in Russia. No point going *there.*" Marina was so delighted that she could scarcely believe her ears. Indeed, Lee's disenchantment with Castro and Cuba was complete. He never again talked about "Uncle Fidel," nor sang the song "Viva Fidel," as he used to do, nor used the alias "Hidell."

In spite of his disappointment, Marina thought he seemed happy, his spirits vastly improved over what they had been before he went to Mexico. He followed her like a puppydog around the house, kissed her again and again, and kept saying, "I've missed you so."

Lee spent the weekend at the Paines'. Ruth left them alone as much as she could, and even tried to keep June out of their way. Carefree as children, they sat on the swings in the back yard.

"Is Ruth good to you?" Lee asked.

"Oh, yes," said Marina, adding that Ruth had taken her to a doctor and arranged for the baby to be delivered free.

Lee told Marina a little about his adventures in Mexico City, and she got the impression that, apart from his one great disappointment, he had enjoyed his stay. All weekend he showed the greatest solicitude toward her, trying to get her to eat more, especially bananas and apples, to drink juices and milk, things that would strengthen her before the baby came. But Marina saw that he was distracted—worried about finding a job. As Ruth drove him to the bus station at noon on Monday, Lee asked if Marina could stay until he found work. Ruth answered that Marina was welcome to stay as long as she liked.

Lee had some job interviews that week but failed to turn up anything. He rented a room from a Mrs. Mary Bledsoe and paid her $7 for the week. Against her wishes he kept milk in her refrigerator, and ate sardines, peanut butter, and bananas in his room, another thing she did not like. He used her telephone to fuss and scold at someone (his ordinary tone when he was talking to Marina) in a foreign language. Mrs. Bledsoe commented to a friend: "I don't like anybody talking in a foreign language." Most bothersome of all, he was in and out during the daytime and at home all day on Friday, disrupting her nap.

On Saturday morning, before leaving for Irving, Lee told Mrs. Bledsoe that he wanted his room cleaned and clean sheets put on his bed. She announced that she refused to rent to him any more. Without pausing to ask why, he demanded $2 of his $7 back. Mrs. Bledsoe refused.[14] Evidently, Lee concluded that the FBI had been asking for him. He had used his real name at Mrs. Bledsoe's, and the next week, when he rented a room, he took it under the alias "O. H. Lee."

Lee was again a good husband and houseguest that weekend. The baby was due any day now, and Lee told Marina not to worry. He insisted that he was not discouraged; he had only just started looking for a job. He again asked Marina if Ruth was good to her. "Does she make you do extra housework because I don't have a job and don't help with the expenses?" he asked. Ruth gave Lee his first driving lesson; and when she asked him to plane down a door for her, he removed it from its hinges and took real pleasure in doing a good job for her.[15] He played with her little boy, Chris, watched football on TV and, as Ruth wrote happily to her mother afterwards, "added a needed masculine flavor" to the household.[16]

For the second weekend in a row not a single harsh word passed between Lee and Marina.

Everybody noticed the change. Ruth thought Lee had improved greatly. He showed affection for Marina and June, and seemed to want to find a job and provide for them.[17] When Michael Paine visited the house that weekend, he found Lee "quite a reasonable person." He was "nice" to Ruth and the children, and above all nice to Marina. "It looked to me," Michael said afterwards, "as if the strain was off the family relationship. They were not quarreling. They billed and cooed. She sat on his lap and he said sweet nothings in her ear."[18]

Even Marina thought her "prodigal" might be getting ready to settle down. She was encouraged by his concern for her and the new baby, and she felt that the weight of his interests had shifted away from politics toward family life, a sign that he might be growing up. For Marina looked on her husband as a mere boy, who had married too soon and had a series of childhood diseases to go through before he arrived at maturity. Lately, he had had two especially horrid ones—Walker and Cuba. Now, perhaps, he had been through them all and the two of them could start making plans for a peaceful life together.

Ruth and Michael shared Marina's hope. But each of them sensed Lee's terrible fragility, and each, in a different way, drew back from probing too far. Ruth stepped all around Lee's prickly places and points of special vulnerability. Out of loyalty to Marina and her marriage, and out of her own great quality of charity, she tried not to see Lee's darker side. Michael, it is true, did try to draw him out and soften his bitterness. But Lee would have none of it. Encountering a solid wall of rejection, Michael gave up, and later blamed himself for having done so too soon. But Lee could not have tolerated a real relationship with Michael or with anyone, and so overwhelming was Michael's respect for the privacy of others that he honored Lee's right to turn him away even in his own house.

As for Marina, she had trained herself to accept a great deal in Lee and had a huge stake in blindness to the rest. She must have been considerably taken up with the new life to which she was about to give birth. And she continued to be concerned most of all with the eternal question of whether Lee loved her. Preoccupied with that, she failed, as Ruth later pointed out, to realize her "own great power over" Lee.[19] The power that might have counted was that of observation.

What Marina, like everyone else, failed to observe was that far from being better after his trip to Mexico, Lee was worse. All his life he had been close to an invisible border that separated reality from fantasy in his mind, and now he was closer than ever to slipping over into a world made up entirely of fantasy. More than ever he inhabited a world of delusions held together by the frailest baling wire. Animal-like, he knew that he must keep his delusions hidden or, like an animal, he would be caught. Living alone five days a week with no one to talk to, he was not exposed to the scrutiny of those who knew him, and the strain was off him of keeping his inner world out of sight. And on weekends, in a world of women who were exhausted by the rituals of child rearing, he escaped for hours on end in front of the television set. His hosts, the Paines, were creatures of exquisite sensibility who shrank from touching his weak spots. Thus, all through October it was as if the little household in Irving was perfectly geared, indeed, existed for no other purpose, but to help Lee keep his inner world whole.

Lee got a job his second week in Dallas. A neighbor of the Paines, Linnie Mae Randle, mentioned that her brother, Wesley Frazier, worked at the Texas School Book Depository and there might be a job opening there. At Marina's urging, Ruth called Roy Truly, superintendent of the depository, and asked him to consider Lee. Mr. Truly suggested that Lee apply in person.

Lee appeared the following day and made a good impression. He was "quiet and well mannered," called Mr. Truly "sir," and said he had come straight from the Marines. Mr. Truly liked that because it very often happened that a young man came to him right out of the service, got on his feet working at the depository, and then went on to better things. Lee looked like a "nice young fellow" with every chance of doing well. Mr. Truly told him that while he did not have a permanent opening, he could offer him a temporary job at $1.25 an hour. Lee accepted gratefully and said he needed the job badly to support his family because he was expecting a second child any day. Mr. Truly told him to report for work the next day, October 16, at eight o'clock.[20]

When Lee called Marina that night, it was with a boast in his voice, as if to say that they only had to take one look at him at the depository and they could not turn him away—"they just hired me," he said. Next day he called again and said he liked the job. He told Marina that it was "good to be working with books," and that the work was "interesting and clean," not dirty or greasy as many of his jobs had been. He said it did not tire him so much. He liked Mr. Truly a great deal and the other men were nice to him, too.

Lee's birthday fell on Friday, the 18th, his third day on the new job, and Marina and Ruth prepared a surprise birthday party. Michael was there, and Ruth had bought wine, put decorations on the table, and baked a cake. Lee was overcome. When they carried in the cake and sang "Happy Birthday," he was so "nervous and touched and self-conscious," Marina remembers, that he could not hold back the tears. It was his twenty-fourth birthday, but when Lee counted, there were less than twenty-four candles on the cake. Even so, he could not blow them all out at once.

They drank more wine, joked a little, and then Lee said that he would like a special present. "I'd like the baby to be born today, my birthday. I don't like late birthday presents. I don't accept them."

"You won't keep your baby?" Marina asked.

"We'll see."

The rest of the evening he trailed Marina everywhere, asking if she felt any pains. He was upset that there were no signs. But he was tender, too. The veins had burst in Marina's ankles and her legs and ankles ached. He rubbed them and kissed them and cried. He told Marina that he was sorry to put her through such an ordeal and he would never do it again.

Next day he was up bright and early scanning the second-hand ads in the newspaper. He was looking for automobiles and washing machines. "I'll stay here awhile," Marina said. "We'll save money. And you'll have to have a car."

Lee said that a cheap car cost a lot in gas and repairs. "I don't have to have a car. I can keep using the bus. We'll buy you a washing machine."

Marina was very happy. Contrary to later reports, she had not asked him for a washing machine. Lee thought of it himself. To her it was another sign that he valued her and might really be willing to settle down and put his family life first.

The whole day was a happy one. In the evening, after supper, Lee asked Marina to sit with him and watch TV. They ate a banana together and later she curled up on the floor with her head in his lap and dozed. Marina was tired of being pregnant. "I do so want to go to the hospital," she said. Lee rubbed her stomach and said, "Don't worry, it won't be long, it will be any day now." Every now and then after that she felt him sit up straight and strain toward the television set, greatly excited. She had very little idea what he was watching.

Lee saw two movies that night, both of them saturated in violence. One was *Suddenly* (1954), starring Frank Sinatra, which is about a plot to kill the President of the United States. In the film Sinatra, a mentally unbalanced ex-serviceman who has been hired to do the job, drives into a small Western town where the President is due to arrive by train, debark, and get into a car that will drive him into the High Sierras for some mountain fishing. Sinatra finds a house overlooking the railroad station and seizes it, subduing its occupants. He leans out of a window and gets the railroad tracks into the cross hairs of his rifle sight. He waits and waits; finally, the train comes into view. But it chugs through town without stopping, and in the end Sinatra is killed.

Marina dozed through the first movie, and the one that followed—*We Were Strangers* (1949). This, too, was about assassination. Based on the actual overthrow of the Machado dictatorship in Cuba in 1933, the movie stars John Garfield as an American who has come to help the cause of revolution. He and a tiny band of cohorts plot to blow up the whole cabinet, including the president, at a single stroke. The plot fails and Garfield dies, but the people rise up in small groups all over Cuba and overthrow the dictatorship.

Marina remembers the movie's end—people were dancing in the streets, screaming with happiness because the president had been overthrown. Lee said it was exactly the way it had once happened in Cuba. It was the only time he showed any interest in Cuba after his return from Mexico.

Later, as they lay in bed talking, Marina remarked: "You know what, Alka? I never *think* of Anatoly any more but last night I *dreamt* about him."

"And what did you dream?"

"We kissed, as we always did. Anatoly kissed so well it made me dizzy. No one ever kissed me like that."

"I wish I did."

"It would take you your whole life to learn."

Without a trace of the jealousy he always showed when Marina spoke about her boyfriends, he put his hand over her mouth and said to her with surprising gentleness: "Please don't tell me about the others. I don't want to hear."

He kissed her, they made love, and Marina was exceedingly happy. It was the last time they had full intercourse.

Ruth made a Chinese supper on Sunday and Marina started feeling sick the moment she saw it.

"Eat," she said, as she got up from the table. "I'll get ready to go."

"Oh," Lee said, his eyes large and frightened, "maybe it'll be today. Where are the pains?"

"I haven't any."

"Oh, maybe it won't be today, after all." He was very disappointed.

But Marina did have labor pains later in the evening and she got ready to drive with Ruth to Parkland Hospital.

"I have to stay home and babysit," Lee said, "and I do want to go with you."

"There's nothing you could do anyhow."

Thus it was Ruth who sat with Marina until she was ready for the labor room. Then she drove home and found that Lee had put the children to bed and had gone to bed, too. Although his light was on and Ruth thought he was not yet asleep, he did not come out of his room to ask for news. Again, it was Ruth who sat by the telephone, called the hospital, and, shortly after eleven, was told that Marina had been delivered of a baby girl. Lee's light was out by then, and Ruth, taking her cue from him, did not wake him with the news. She told him in the morning before he left for work.[21]

He returned to Irving that afternoon with Wesley Frazier, but for some reason seemed reluctant to visit the hospital. Puzzled, Ruth guessed that he was afraid to go lest someone at the hospital find out that he had a job and charge him with expenses of the birth. And so Ruth told him that the hospital already knew he had a job; she had been asked the night before at the admissions office and had told the truth. But it did not make any difference. The delivery and maternity care still were free. After learning that, Lee agreed to go.[22]

Marina never knew of his reluctance. "Oh, Mama, you're wonderful," he said, as he sat down on her bed. "Only two hours. You have them so easily." He had tears in his eyes.

"But it's a girl again," she apologized.

"Two girls are wonderful," he said. "We'll keep trying. The next one will be a boy."

"No, Alka, there'll be no next one. I can't go through ten babies just to get a boy."

"You're right," he said. "Whatever you say. Besides, a girl doesn't cost so much. She gets married. You've got to educate a boy."

He asked Marina if she had had any stitches or anesthetic and praised God she had not needed either. He treated her like a heroine.

They had already talked about a name. If it was a boy, he was to be David Lee (no more "Fidel"), and Lee had promised that in the choice of a girl's name he wouldn't interfere. But he now asked Marina what name she had put down on the baby's certificate. She had chosen "Audrey Rachel," "Audrey" for Audrey Hepburn and "Rachel" because Ruth had a niece called Rachel and Marina liked the name very much.[23]

Lee took exception to Rachel. "It sounds too Jewish," he said. "Please call her Marina. Do it for me. I want our little girl to have your name."

The next day Marina simply added "Marina" to the certificate—"Audrey Marina Rachel Oswald." But from the outset the baby was called Rachel, and Rachel she is to this day.

33

Lee and Michael

AFTER THE BABY was born, to save money, Marina and Lee continued to live apart. Marina and the children stayed with Ruth, while Lee, using the alias "O. H. Lee," was already installed in a rooming house at 1026 North Beckley Street, in the Oak Cliff section of Dallas where he and Marina had lived before.

If the owners, Mr. and Mrs. Arthur Carl Johnson, the housekeeper, Mrs. Earlene Roberts, or the other roomers noticed "Mr. Lee" at all, it was for his extreme apartness. "That man never talked. That was the only peculiarity about him. He would never speak," Mrs. Johnson said later. Not every evening, but once in a while, he joined the other roomers and watched television. He might sit there as long as thirty or forty minutes and not speak to anyone.

Mrs. Johnson remembers that he came home at the same hour every night, 5:30, and made a phone call in a foreign language (to Marina). He switched to English if anyone happened to be nearby but no one was fooled. Marina was annoyed by these digressions into English. She did not understand what he was saying, and she thought his effort to cover up the Russian was foolish.

During the week, Lee was alone in his room all evening, every evening, and he never, in the five or six weeks he was there, had a visitor. Mrs. Johnson, the landlady, estimates that he spent 95 percent of his evenings alone in his room and the other 5 percent watching television.

He was allowed to keep food in the refrigerator. That is how Mrs. Johnson came to notice that this particular roomer drank half a gallon of "sweet milk" a day. He kept peanut butter, sweet preserves, and lunch meat there, too. Sometimes he had supper in his room and, occasionally, "if there was no one in the kitchen, he would sit in the kitchen, but if there was anyone there, he would take it in his room." Mrs. Johnson describes him as "spotless. He never kept anything cluttered."[1]

Once in a while Lee had breakfast ("eggs over, light") at the Dobbs House restaurant across the street, and once or twice he told Marina that he had supper there, too, for about $1.25. Except for weekends, that was the only change in his lonely and austere routine.

Lee was an order-filler for the School Book Depository, mostly for Scott-Foresman textbooks, which were located on the first and sixth floors of the building. He wrote several orders on his clipboard, found the books, and then brought them to a first-floor room where the orders were processed. It was a job that did not require teamwork. He made an occasional mistake in his orders, but Mr. Truly calls Lee "a bit above-average employee," who "kept moving" and "did a good day's work." He paid attention to the job, did not spend time talking to the other men, and did his work by himself. "I thought it was a pretty good trait at the time," Truly said later.

Truly saw him every day. "Good morning, Lee," he would say.

"Good morning, sir."

Mr. Truly would ask how his new baby was, and Lee's face just broke wide open into a smile.[2]

The depository was an easygoing, live-and-let-live sort of place. The men mostly gathered in a small, first-floor recreation room they called the "domino room." There they ate sandwiches at noon, made coffee, and played dominoes. Lee sometimes ate a sandwich there alone and then went outside. But two or three times he came in with raisins or a bunch of grapes and ate with the other men. And occasionally Mr. Truly glanced up and saw him swing across Dealey Plaza, the park in front of the Book Depository Building, about noon and come back a few minutes later with a newspaper or a sack of potato chips in his hand. Most days Lee made a point of getting to work early and reading newspapers that had been left in the domino room the day before. One of the men, Bonnie Ray Williams, noticed that Lee did not read about sports, as the others did. "One morning I noticed he was reading something about politics and he acted like it was funny to him. He would read a paragraph or two, smile or laugh, then throw the paper down and get up and walk out."[3]

Several influences Lee was not aware of himself could have affected the way he was looking at things, could even have affected what it was that caught his attention in the newspaper and made him smile or laugh in that derisory way of his. One of these influences was place. He was back in Dallas. Exactly one year before, in October of 1962, Lee had been living in a rooming house that has never been identified but was probably on Beckley or North Beckley Street, the very same area in which he was living now. Then as now he had been living alone to save money—Marina was at Lyolya Hall's in Fort Worth—and then as now he had no family with him to ground his fantasies in reality. It was during that earlier period in Dallas that he may first have thought of killing General Walker. And Lee had a way of repeating things.

Another influence could have been the time of year—what psychiatrists call "anniversary reaction." Many, if not most, of the critical events in Lee's life had taken place about this time: his birthday (October 18), his enlistment in the Marine Corps (October 24), his self-inflicted gunshot wound in Japan (October

27), his arrival in Russia (October 16), and his attempt at suicide in Moscow (October 21). He had last seen his mother on October 7 of 1962; Marina had left him, ostensibly never to return, on November 11–17 of the same year; and Lee had last seen his favorite brother Robert on November 22 the year before. Because so many important events in Lee's life, mostly sad ones or events that signified failure, were clustered in October and November, the autumn may have been a troubled time for him.[4]

And now there was something else, the birth of Rachel, which not only added to Lee's burdens but placed him in a position that was curiously similar to the position his own father would have been in had he been alive when Lee was born. For Rachel was a second child, as Lee had been. She was a girl following a girl, while Lee had been a boy following a boy, but in each case a child of the opposite sex had been desired. And what Lee's father had done to him by dying before his birth, Lee was to do to Rachel shortly after hers.

Whatever the subtle influences on Lee's thoughts may have been, it is clear that now that he was settled, with a job, a place to live, and the baby's birth out of the way, he had time for politics again. On Wednesday, October 23, only two nights after his first glimpse of Rachel in the hospital, he went to a right-wing meeting at which General Walker addressed 1,300 people.

Two nights later, at the Paines', Marina remembers that Michael attempted to draw Lee out on the subject of politics. Michael was there each Friday when Lee came to Irving. He sensed that Lee needed an older brother or a friend, and he tried to reach out to him. Michael knew that Lee called himself a "Marxist," and yet he had turned his back on Russia. Why, Michael wondered? How had Lee's values changed; what were his ideals and his vision of a better society? Lee refused to say. He refused to talk about the better world that might lie ahead, but only about what was wrong with the world today. Michael kept asking how the changes Lee wanted were to come about—and Lee never answered. Michael inferred that Lee had given up on changing things peacefully, since he never mentioned any sort of peaceful, evolutionary change he might favor. He did not consider it worthwhile "fussing around" trying to change anything.

Michael was certain that Lee's opinions, and his way of clinging to them, were founded in his emotions, but he had no success in probing those emotional roots. In fact, something in Michael resisted understanding Lee emotionally, and he finally gave up exploring this side of his nature. For Michael sensed that, except for June, "people were like cardboard" to Lee, and this repelled him.[5]

The two men could not have been more unlike: they were as different as earth is from air. Michael was a brilliant man, with a quality of sunlight about him. He was tall, slender, sensitive, with gray, sad eyes that seemed to light up only when the talk turned to aerodynamics. Even Michael's mind appeared to be airborne; he had been curious about everything all his life. It was Michael's gift to think originally, to look at things in a way no one had thought of before. He was an inventor, and he especially loved to invent things that expressed the beauty, the harmony, the wholeness of life. As a boy of ten, hearing that there might one day be an energy crisis, he tried to invent a car that would run on a minimum of oil. Next, it was gliders, and by the time he was a teenager, he was building a hydrofoil boat.

At the time he and Lee met, Michael was working on new concepts in helicopter design. But it was his dream to quit his job, live in an old barn, and design an airplane so cheap, so functional, so exquisitely economical, that people could own it the way they own cars. A visionary as well as a scientist, Michael hoped that with so many people flying over national frontiers, borders might be wiped out entirely.[6]

Michael came from a family of visionaries and eccentrics with roots reaching deep into the New England past. The families that produced him, the Paines and Forbeses, had fortunes derived from the China trade, railroads, and the telephone company—and consciences hammered out of guilt. Some of them, the best, perhaps, shuddered at the word "aristocrat," but they were aristocrats and they knew it, and most arrived at an acceptance of it by embracing the thought of their common ancestor, Ralph Waldo Emerson, that one's place in life, one's privileges even, can be redeemed by good works. Michael's grandfather, George Lyman Paine, was a renowned clergyman, a low church Episcopalian, who had run for state office in Massachusetts as a socialist. Michael calls him "a fierce stone." Michael's father, Lyman Paine, was an architect who was also a political activist. During the thirties, he had been a member of the Trotskyite wing of the American Communist Party and it is said—Michael himself is uncertain as to the truth of it—that he was one of a group of American leftists who went to see Trotsky in Norway.

Michael, like his wife Ruth, was a child of divorce. He had seen his father only half a dozen times before he reached the age of twenty, and yet he loved him devotedly. Indeed, he felt as if the two were "like one person trying to live in two bodies." All three men, the grandfather who was a socialist and a clergyman, the father who was a Trotskyite and an artist, and now Michael, who was a scientist and a liberal, had come to an identical belief: that man's material needs must be met, but that his deepest hunger is a hunger of the spirit. Each in these three generations of Paine men had in his own way come back to the Emersonian conviction that it is a necessity for every individual to do as his conscience requires.

It is one of many ironies of the situation that Lee, a steady visitor at the Paine household and a beneficiary of its generosity, never even inquired who Michael might be or knew that his father had been a member of the very same Trotskyite wing of the American Communist Party which Lee had tried to join in its later form, the Socialist Workers Party. And it is characteristic of Michael that he never told him. Nor did Lee stop to consider that Michael, a physicist at Bell Helicopter, might have a security clearance—he did, and he was continually being turned down for higher clearances because his father had been a Trotskyite—and that Lee, by receiving *The Militant, The Worker,* and all his Russian newspapers at Michael's house, might be jeopardizing Michael's job. Again, it was characteristic of Michael that he, too, did not consider it and, indeed, would have scorned to do so.

As an intellectual, Michael was accustomed to thinking in abstractions, but as an inventor he was also at home with facts. His mind was open and questioning. And he never lumped things into categories, for no sooner had he thought of a category than his mind blazed with exceptions and defiances. Lee, he discovered, was the opposite. His mind was closed and dogmatic. He was at home with nothing but categories, and into them he stuffed every fact or observation that came his way. The category he clung to hardest, and insisted on throughout their discussions, was the "exploitation of the worker" under capitalism. Lee admitted that exploitation existed everywhere, but he insisted that in the Soviet Union at least the state reaps a profit, whereas in a capitalist society only the employer gains. Under capitalism, he said, all institutions, churches, schools, everything exists to exploit the working class. Each is a part of an interlocking structure that is interested only in maintaining itself in power.[7]

Michael tried to argue with Lee by pointing out that there are other values besides material ones. There is science, there is art, and there are spiritual values. These, too, and not just politics and economics, affect the way men look at things and the way they organize their lives. Lee would not listen. None of it made any difference. Capitalism must be destroyed. In one of their more animated discussions, Michael got the impression that Lee was dreaming of "revolution in the United States—crowds storming the Winter Palace."[8]

On Friday night, October 25, the conversation turned from politics to religion, with the Paines, who belonged to a Unitarian congregation, describing how their church worked and trying to explain to Lee that it, at least, had no interest in keeping any one political group in power. But Lee again refused to listen. He insisted that the Church, all churches, are merely an arm of the state, and their function is to keep people blind.[9] Marina did not understand what they were saying, but she detected a nastiness and anger in Lee's tone that she had not heard from him in months. She did not see how the Paines could be so nice to him. They were so polite that she thought, with some surprise, that they must really like Lee.

The Paines were polite; but that night, and other nights, too, they got angry at Lee's dogmatic way of arguing. Ruth was the more offended. Talking to Lee, she thought, was like talking to a stone wall. He refused to listen to logic, refused to listen to facts, and when he was up against a fact that appeared to refute what he believed, he repeated the same old arguments as if that was all there was to it. Michael tried to check himself, and felt, with some shame, that he showed his anger more openly than Lee did. He could tell, of course, that Lee was very angry too, saw that his hands were even trembling, but it looked to him as if Lee was a fellow who had had a good deal of practice at keeping his feelings under control.[10]

After that evening in late October, Ruth gave up trying to talk to Lee about religion or politics, but Michael did not. When Lee mentioned over supper that two nights ago he had been to hear a speech by General Walker, Michael remarked that that was odd: he had attended a meeting of the John Birch Society that same evening. Michael, a liberal, wanted to understand the workings of the right-wing mind. He was interested in better communication between "right" and "left," what little "left" he could find in Dallas. He told Lee that he went to meetings, too, first one group and then the other.

As a matter of fact, Michael was going to one that very night. It was a meeting of the American Civil Liberties Union (A.C.L.U.), a liberal organization to which he and Ruth belonged. It was to be held on the campus of Southern Methodist University, and he invited Lee to come along. Lee accepted. He whispered to Marina as they were leaving: "If only Michael knew what I wanted to do to Walker! Wouldn't he be scared!"[11]

Michael asked Lee to the meeting because he sensed his bitterness. He wanted to "make him a little happier," and help him see that the gulf between what he desired and what might actually be achieved was not so unbridgeable as he supposed.[12] He also wanted to give Lee a sense of participation, a feeling that he, too, could be effective in bringing about change in quiet ways. And he wanted to encourage in Lee a more generous attitude toward those whom he conceived to be his "enemies." In Michael's view, the world was complex. He hoped that Lee, too, would some day see it that way and accept the fact that "his enemies, the employers, were not so fully in control of the situation as he made out."[13]

One of the speakers at the meeting happened to say that the mere fact of a man's being a Bircher did not necessarily mean he was an anti-Semite. Lee rose. "I disagree with that," he said, adding that he had been to a right-wing meeting two nights before at which spokesmen for the John Birch Society had made anti-Semitic and anti-Catholic statements. Michael said later that Lee spoke "loud and clear and coherently," out of keeping with the mood of the meeting, but intelligibly nonetheless.[14]

After the meeting, Lee talked with two of the men who had been there. One was a fellow worker of Michael's, the other an older man. They talked about Cuba and civil rights. The President's name came up and Lee said, with what Michael's friend subsequently considered to be a certain, special emphasis, that President Kennedy was doing a "real fine job" in civil rights.[15]

On the way home, Michael and Lee talked about the people they had met. As the son of a Trotskyite who had tried to shield him from knowledge that could hurt him later, Michael had learned not to pry, not to ask another man outright what his opinions might be. And this is how he was with Lee. He was curious as to whether Lee might be a Communist, but he preferred to guess for himself from such signals as Lee chose to send out rather than ask him directly. A week or so earlier, Lee had hinted that he was a Communist. He showed Michael a copy of *The Worker* and said you could tell what "they" wanted you to do if only you read between the lines. Now Lee asked Michael whether, in his opinion, one of the men at the meeting was a Party member. Michael did not think so. "I think he is," Lee said, on the grounds that the man was pro-Castro. "If that's the way Lee is meeting his Communists," Michael said to himself, "then he hasn't found the real group here in Dallas—supposing there is one."[16] Michael concluded that Lee could not be a Communist after all, for his "communications," his way of meeting like-minded people, were too tenuous.[17] Neither Lee's judgment nor his way of going about things seemed to be those of a Communist.

During the same drive home, Michael explained what the A.C.L.U. was all about. He told Lee that its sole purpose was to defend civil liberties—free speech and other rights of the individual. Lee was amazed that any organization could exist merely to defend a *value,* as Michael put it later, and not to fight for a political objective. Lee remarked firmly that he could never join an organization like that—it wasn't political enough.[18]

Another time Lee confessed to Michael, exasperated, that he could not fit him into a category. He wasn't a Communist or a capitalist or a socialist or a Bircher or anything Lee could lay his hands on.[19] Soon, however, he did find a cubbyhole—Michael was religious. "He has religion, but he has no philosophy," Lee confided to Marina with a superior air, which meant that he was now able to dismiss Michael.

As for Michael, he considered Lee's style in relating himself to communism "Dick Tracyish."[20] But, being perceptive, Michael, out of three or four long conversations, subsequently put together a picture of Lee's ideas that almost paraphrases the program and philosophy Lee himself had spelled out several months earlier, evidently as a historical justification of his attempt on General Walker. To this day Michael has never seen what Lee wrote, but he guessed from what Lee said to him that he did not believe in the goodness or dignity of man. Lee felt, to the contrary, that the majority of men are evil, conniving, and stupid. They are blind to their lot and prefer to remain that way. Their condition needs changing, yet they are fooled by the powers that be. Thus change, if it is to occur, will have to be imposed on them. Their system, the capitalist system, is rotten and yet, paradoxically, strong because everything—the Church, the power structure, the educational system—is all bound together to maintain things exactly as they are. Because of capitalism's impermeable strength, peaceful change is impossible. Nothing but revolution will do. There would, Michael explains, in his paraphrase of Lee's beliefs, "have to be an overthrow of the whole thing."[21]

What Michael did not know was that Lee had already tried to change the system, both peacefully, in attempting to organize a Fair Play for Cuba chapter in New Orleans, and violently in attempting to shoot General Walker. And he had tried to become a revolutionary by going to fight for Castro.

Not knowing any of this, Michael was unable to piece together the whole of Lee's "logic" at the time, but he was able to do so later on. And the rest of his reconstruction is this. Revolution was unlikely because the "power structure" was too strong. Thus the most the individual, acting alone, could do was to commit an act that would help destroy society not because of any sense it contained but because of its symbolic meaning.[22]

Lee had not yet followed his logic to its conclusion either, and he had no inkling that history was on the point of giving him an opportunity to act on it. But his logic, his experience since the Walker attempt, and his entire life, all were pointing him in the same direction, toward a decision to strike another violent blow, this one aimed at neither the right nor the left, but simply at the top—to decapitate the political process. Lee approved and admired the man who happened to stand at the apex of American political life. But the better that man was, the more effective at making capitalism workable and attractive, then the more devastating the blow to capitalist society would be.[23]

Michael came to this fuller interpretation later on. What he did see in Lee that autumn was a quality that people had been noticing about him since his high-school days and even now were noticing about him at work—his stoicism. During their discussions of October 1963, there were moments when Lee reminded Michael of nothing so much as Lawrence of Arabia holding his finger to a match. Lawrence said it was nothing—all you had to do was stand the pain. That was how Lee seemed to Michael, gritting his teeth and bearing pain.[24]

So, placed in what Michael calls "a duck-blind situation" in which he was unforeseeably granted a chance to alter the course of history, Lee, having despaired of peaceful change, would be able to act in only one way. But he would have to summon up all his stoicism to do it. He must not allow such kindly, personal feelings as he might harbor for the victim to stand in his way.[25]

Michael realized that Lee's beliefs implied an advocacy of violence. He saw this clearly one day when he mentioned to Lee that the qualities he believed in most profoundly were diminished by violence. Lee did not answer, and Michael interpreted his silence as disagreement.[26] What he did not perceive was that Lee himself was capable of acting violently.

It is natural that it was the intellectual side of Lee that Michael, an intellectual himself, was best equipped to grasp, and that Michael, a man of reason, failed to perceive that Lee's "reasons" were mainly on the surface. What mattered most with Lee were the tumultuous emotions underneath. But some inexplicable inner principle in Michael resisted probing any deeper. Lee was ungracious, intractable, dogmatic; so much Michael could see. He did not take the step that followed and see that Lee was irrational as well.

In this regard it was Ruth who understood Lee better. She realized that he was "primarily an emotional person," and saw that while he talked of ideology and philosophy, he acted, and reacted, emotionally. Ruth thought he was vulnerable, "tender," and "unusually sensitive to hurt." But she, like her husband, was not only charitable in her judgments but a devoted pacifist. Apart from a fleeting moment the summer before, when she had confided to a friend that she thought Lee might be capable of a crime of passion if he thought someone was trying to take Marina away, Ruth considered it unlikely that Lee would spill over from "mild maladjustment to active, violent hostility."[27]

If Ruth inhibited her insight, cultivated the quality of opacity with respect to Lee, and kept herself from fully apprehending in him what a part of her suspected, Michael also operated under comparable restraint. During the summer he, too, had discussed with a friend whether Lee might be capable of violence. Now, the Oswalds' belongings were stored in the Paines' garage, and Michael was constantly moving Lee's "camping equipment" from place to place because it was in the way of the drill press and other shop tools he came home specially to work with on Sundays. The "camping equipment" was tied up in what Michael calls a "greenish rustic blanket," and despite himself, he realized that the bundle was too heavy, and the shape not quite right, to be camping equipment of the type manufactured at that time. It was, of course, Lee's rifle, dismantled, with its telescopic sight. Michael wondered about the bundle, suspecting nothing definite but simply that the bundle was not what it was said to be; and he was tempted to peek inside. But he never did. He had too much respect for Lee's privacy. Michael himself was a pacifist, opposed to owning firearms. But whatever it was that Lee had in that mysterious bundle, he had a right to keep it in Michael's garage.[28]

Lee was on his good behavior at the Paines', and he treated Marina better there than at any time since the two of them left Russia. Yet his demands were still incredible. He brought his dirty laundry to the house each weekend for Marina to wash and iron, and he often refused to wear a shirt she had just ironed on the grounds that she had failed to do it exactly right. No sooner would they sit down at the dinner table than he would snap at Marina: "Why didn't you fix me iced tea? You knew I was coming out." Or he would put on a baby face and complain in baby talk that he couldn't eat because Marina had forgotten to give him a fork and a spoon. He never once got up to fetch for himself or help a wife in the final stages of pregnancy, nor when she had just had a child and was nursing it.

Sometimes Lee finished eating ahead of the others and simply got up, left the table, and went into the living room to watch television. Sometimes he refused to eat what Ruth had cooked for them and demanded immediately afterwards that Marina fix his favorite Russian dish, pan-fried onions and potatoes. Marina was ashamed and embarrassed. "Stop being so capricious," she said. "You can't carry on like that here. It's not as if you're in your own home. You are a guest in this house." Sometimes she did, and sometimes she did not, fix him his pan-fried potatoes.

It was the football season and Lee spent more time than ever watching television. He would wolf down his lunch at high speed, hoping Ruth would not notice how much of her food he was eating, and then during the game he would race to the kitchen and ransack the cupboards and refrigerator for apples, bananas, raisins, cookies, and milk. Even though Lee had a job, he still did not contribute to the household expenses.

The Paines gave no sign of resenting his behavior. Ruth admits that Lee was never very gracious, but he did try to stay out of her way. Anything she asked him to do, like gluing together Junie's training chair, he did gladly. Both Paines understood that Lee was saving money so that he could get an apartment for himself and Marina. They had no thought of his contributing to the expenses, and it never so much as occurred to Michael to resent the fact that he was supporting Lee's family. As Michael looked at it, Marina was a companion to Ruth and a help to her with her Russian. That made it an equal exchange, not an act of altruism on his part.

Lee and Marina had no big fights during the weekends they were together at the Paines', nothing that caused them to stop speaking, just spats. Still, there were enough minor irritations for Marina to say to Ruth: "You see that we fight and that Lee doesn't love me at all."

"You fight because you do love each other," Ruth replied. "You wouldn't fight if you didn't care."

Marina made no effort to hide their disagreements. Whether Lee loved her or not was a major topic in her weekday conversations with Ruth, which had now become close and confidential. She wanted Ruth to see Lee in all his guises so that she could get her opinion on this most crucial of questions. Ruth continually reassured Marina that Lee did, in fact, love her.

Lee's attitude toward Ruth, however, had taken a turn for the worse after he came back from Mexico. He started to make fun of her. He said it was ridiculous for "such a long, tall, stringbean" to jump around and dance with her children, as Ruth did. And he made fun of her for working so hard on her Russian. "Better she should finish college than sit and study Russian all these years." (Ruth had finished college years ago.) He thought it "stupid" of Ruth to be religious.

None of this surprised Marina, who knew that her husband considered himself an unrecognized authority on everything and felt that if others did not agree with his ideas, it was merely because they were "stupid." Then, too, Marina knew there were times when Lee hated and despised a woman simply for being a *woman*. He felt that way toward her sometimes, and she could see that he felt the same way toward Ruth. But after her phone call to Truly, Lee's attitude toward Ruth changed. He knew that it was to this call he owed his job. And Ruth never mentioned it, never asked for his gratitude. After that, apparently, it dawned on Lee that Ruth's kindness was genuine—she wanted nothing from him.

Marina helped the change along. "You know, Lee, you mustn't just *use* Ruth," she said to him the last weekend in October.

"Why not?"

"Ruth doesn't *need* me. She doesn't need my company or my Russian. I may even be in the way. She only has me here to help me out."

Marina, who can be reticent with the confidences of others, now told Lee a little more than before about the Paines' marriage. She told him of an occasion when Michael had been there for supper and then left, and Ruth cried. When the Paines were married, Marina said, Michael had not wanted children right away and had left home shortly after their second child was born. Ruth still loved Michael deeply. She did not know whether to give up or keep trying.

Up to now, Lee had liked Michael well enough in spite of his being "religious." But now he grew angry at him. Lee thought it was a man's obligation once married to want his wife and want children. He was indignant at Michael for having married without wanting children. And he condemned Michael for coming home, eating supper, and seeing his children just like a married man, and then leaving.

Besides causing Lee to be more sympathetic toward Ruth and less so toward Michael, Marina's disclosures had other side effects as well. Lee was not ordinarily interested in other people's private affairs. But now he regularly asked Marina, over the telephone and on his arrival for the weekend, how Ruth and Michael were getting along. For the first time, he seemed aware of the Paines as human beings. He even gave signs of awareness that he and his family might be in the way in the modest, one-story ranch house, and that Ruth and Michael might need privacy in which to work out their problems. He was sorry for the Paine children, too, especially the boy Chris, and he actually tried to make up to them for the fact that their father did not live with them. Thus, he started playing more with Chris, who was two and a half, than with June. Marina was jealous for June and asked why he played so much with Chris.

"He'd rather be with a man," Lee said. "He's tired of you women. A boy needs a father to play with."

In spite of small spats, the relationship between Lee and Marina continued, as of the last weekend in October (25–27), to be "unusually good," in Marina's words. Lee was happy with his new baby and his new job. Marina remembers him on the floor in front of the television set with a pillow between his legs and Rachel on the pillow. During the commercials, if she wasn't asleep, he talked to her in Russian.

"See, baby, it's your papa. See Papa?"

"Look," he said to Marina, "she doesn't smile at me."

"To her," Marina answered, "Papa probably looks upside down."

He held the baby to his shoulder and stroked her head. "She's the prettiest, strongest baby in the world," he boasted. "Only a week old and already she can hold up her head. We're strong because Mama gives us milk and not a bottle that's either too hot or too cold. Mama gives us only the very best." He studied her fingers, her "tender little mouth," and her yawn. He was delighted with them all and proclaimed that his baby was getting prettier every day. "She looks just like her mama," he said.

34

Agent Hosty

ON FRIDAY, November 1, Lee went to the post office in Dallas. There he dropped into the mail a membership application which he had picked up at the October 25 meeting of the American Civil Liberties Union, the meeting he had attended with Michael Paine. With the application he sent in a $2 membership fee. The application was processed in New York on November 4, and Lee formally became a member of the organization he had only just told Michael he would never join because it was not political enough.

He also transacted an item of business at the post office. He rented a box for the period of November 1–December 31 for a total fee of $3. The boxes were rented at $1.50 per month, and Lee, who counted every penny, probably would not have rented a box for a two-month period unless he expected to be in Dallas the entire time. The box was not at the main post office, which he had used before, but at the terminal annex station, near his job. He took it in his name and Marina's, a sign that he expected that by the end of the year they would be living in Dallas. He listed as nonprofit organizations entitled to receive mail at his address the Fair Play for Cuba Committee and the American Civil Liberties Union.

And he mailed another letter to the Communist Party. Arnold Johnson, information director, had long ago answered Lee's letter from New Orleans requesting information about how to contact the Party when he moved to the Northeast. He had suggested that Oswald get in touch with the Party in New York when he moved, and the Party would find a way to contact him in Baltimore or wherever he might be.[1]

Lee's new letter, postmarked November 1, was a continuation of the earlier correspondence. He announced that he had not moved north after all but had settled for the time in Dallas. He went on to report that he had been to a right-wing meeting "headed" by General Walker on October 23, and to a meeting of A.C.L.U. on the 25th. "As you see, political friction between 'left' and 'right' is very great here," he wrote. He added that A.C.L.U. was in the hands of liberal, professional people, including a minister and two law professors; "however, some of those present showed marked class awareness and insight." Lee's question was this: "Could you advise me as to the general view that we had on the A.C.L.U. and to what degree, if any, I should attempt to *highten* its progressive tendencies?"[2] It was an unreal and remarkable letter, using "we" as if he were a Party member and seeking advice in the same spirit.

That same day, in Irving, Ruth and Marina had a visitor. A day or two earlier, they had come home from their errands to be told by a neighbor that a strange man had been asking for them. The neighbor, Dorothy Roberts, informed Ruth that the man paid a call on her and asked who was living at the Paines'. Ruth translated for Marina and the two decided that it must be someone from the FBI.

Marina was frightened of the FBI, partly because she equated it with the KGB in Russia, of which she had been afraid all her life, and partly because she knew that Lee desperately feared the FBI. But she noticed that Ruth took the news calmly and that her conscience was clear. Therefore Marina did not worry much about the visit, even though the man had said to Mrs. Roberts that he would be coming by again.

On the afternoon of Friday, November 1, the children were sleeping, Marina was using Ruth's hair drier to beautify herself for Lee's arrival, and Ruth was doing jobs around the house when the visitor reappeared.[3] Ruth was not surprised to find a dark-haired stranger at the door who introduced himself as Agent James P. Hosty of the FBI. She greeted him cordially, asked him in, and the two sat in the living room talking pleasantries. Hosty said that, unlike the House Un-American Activities Committee, the FBI was not a witch-hunting organization.

Gradually, Hosty switched the conversation to Lee. Was he living at Ruth's house? Ruth answered that he was not. Did she know where he was living? Once again the answer was a surprising "No." Ruth did not know where Lee was living, but it was in Dallas somewhere and she thought it might be Oak Cliff. Did Ruth know where he was working? Ruth hesitated. She explained that Lee thought he had been having job trouble on account of the FBI. Hosty assured her that it was not the FBI's way to approach an employer directly. At this Ruth softened, told him where Lee was working, and together they looked up the address of the book depository in the telephone book. Lee worked at 411 Elm Street.

While they were talking, Marina wandered in. She was frightened and a little repelled when Hosty introduced himself and showed her his credentials. He saw that she was alarmed, was aware that she had lately had a child, and tried to calm her. He explained, with Ruth translating, that he was not there to embarrass or harass her. But should Soviet agents try to recruit her by threatening her or her relatives in Russia, she had a right to ask the FBI for help. Marina was delighted. She liked this plumpish, pleasant-looking dark-haired man who was talking to her about her rights and offering to protect her. No one had given her so much attention in a long time, much less offered to protect her rights.

The talk turned to Castro. Hosty remarked that from what he had read in the American papers, he thought Castro was a threat to the interests of the United States. Marina said she doubted that the American press was being fair. Hosty said he knew of Lee's activities passing out pamphlets for the Fair Play for Cuba Committee in New Orleans and asked whether he was doing anything similar in Dallas. Marina thought of the series of childhood diseases her husband had lately been passing through and said cheerily: "Oh, don't worry about *him*. He's just young. He doesn't know what he's doing. He won't do anything like that *here.*"

Before Hosty left, Marina begged him not to interfere with Lee at work. She explained that he had had trouble keeping his jobs and thought he lost them "because the FBI is interested in him." (He had, in fact, blamed the loss of his job at Jaggars-Chiles-Stovall on the FBI, but not the loss of his job in New Orleans.)

"I don't think he has lost any of his jobs on account of the FBI," Hosty said softly.

Ruth and Marina urged the visitor to stay. If he wanted to see Lee, they said, he would be there at 5:30. But Hosty had to get back to the office; and since he did not have a second man present (as is the FBI custom during an interview), and since the New Orleans office had jurisdiction over the case until it was established that Oswald had a residence in Dallas, he was not eager to see Lee. But he asked Ruth to find out where he was living. Ruth thought that would be no problem; she would simply ask Lee.

Hosty had another reason for not being anxious to see Lee. The FBI had learned of his visit to the Soviet Embassy in Mexico City and was now worried about him as an "espionage case." The bureau did not want to give away to him either what it knew of his trip, or the techniques by which it had acquired the knowledge. "We would be telling him more than he would be telling us," Hosty said.[4]

Hosty's visit ended as it began, on a friendly note. Marina was all smiles. She would be glad to have such a pleasant visitor any day. Hosty wrote out his name, office address, and telephone number for Ruth to give to Lee. Since Ruth was sure Lee had nothing to hide, she expected that he would go straight to the FBI himself.

Lee arrived late that afternoon in a fine, outgoing frame of mind. But when Marina told him about Hosty's visit, his face darkened. He wanted to know everything—what Ruth had said, how long the man stayed, and what he had said. Marina explained that she had not understood much and Lee scolded her. Marina was astonished at how nervous he had suddenly become, and at the effort he was making to conceal it.

While they were at supper Ruth, too, told Lee about Hosty's visit. "Oh," said Lee, elaborately casual, "and what did he say?" Ruth described their conversation and handed Lee the slip of paper with Hosty's telephone number and address.

Ruth realized that both Lee and Marina were afraid. She had heard that fear of the FBI was typical of many people coming out of Russia, especially if they *were* Russian. To reassure them and show that she was not afraid, she told them of her experience during World War II, when her brother and many of his friends were Conscientious Objectors. Ruth had been only a high-school student, but she realized that the FBI was visiting the neighbors and asking about her brother and his friends. So far from threatening their rights, she concluded that the FBI had protected them. She told Lee and Marina that the FBI men she had seen were "careful and effective."

Ruth was certain that Lee was not an agent and knew nothing of interest to a foreign power. It seemed clear to her that he was "neither bright enough nor steady enough to have been recruited" by anyone.[5] Since he had nothing to hide, she thought by far the best thing he could do was go to the FBI office, preempting their initiative, and tell them everything they wanted to know. Only in this way would they, too, see that he had nothing to hide.

Marina was watching Lee's reactions. To her eye he was a changed man. He was sad and subdued throughout supper and he scarcely spoke a word all evening long. For the first time since his return from Mexico there was no sex at all between them that weekend, not even the limited sex that had been possible since Rachel's birth. The next day he again asked Ruth about the visit. Marina could tell that he was straining to catch every word, yet at the same time trying not to betray his nervousness.

He put diapers in the washing machine for Marina, hung them on the line, and tried to carry on his family life as usual. No one but Marina understood how distraught he really was. During the afternoon, he watched a football game on television and his spirits seemed to improve. Then he drew Marina aside and instructed her that the next time the FBI came she was to study the car with care, note what color it was, what model, and write down the license number. They might send a different agent, he explained, but the car would still be the same. He even told Marina where to look for it. If the car was not across the way from Ruth's, he said, it would be down the street in front of the neighbors'. Marina was puzzled by his behavior. Again she could see that he was calculating at great speed, trying to think of everything, yet at the same time hide his anxiety. Still, telling her what to do seemed to calm him.

On Sunday, Ruth gave Lee his second driving lesson—parking. He wanted to take June along but Marina forbade it. "If you want to break bones, break your own," she said.

He came back to the house pleased with himself. "I haven't practiced much," he boasted, "and look how well it's going."

His elation was momentary, however, and for the rest of the weekend Lee was withdrawn, taken up with thoughts of his own. Marina tried to leave him in peace, but by now she, too, was annoyed at the FBI. Not at Mr. Hosty—she knew he was only doing his job—but at the astonishing change his visit had wrought in Lee and in their relationship. Everything between them had been wonderful, or nearly wonderful, for a month. Now he would hardly speak to her.

Lee went to work on Monday morning and on Tuesday, November 5, Hosty came again. He was on his way to Fort Worth with another agent and he decided to stop at the Paines' to see if Ruth had Lee's address. He says the interview was brief: "I didn't go in the house. I just went in the front door." Ruth met both men at the doorstep and said that Lee had been there over the weekend but she had not gotten his address. Lee had told her he was a Trotskyite, and Ruth said to Hosty, with a trace of amusement, that she considered him "a very illogical person." Hosty asked Ruth whether in her opinion there might be anything wrong with Lee mentally. She answered, in a fairly light way, that she did not understand the thought processes of anyone who claimed to be a Marxist.

Hosty says he did not see Marina on this visit; Ruth says he did. Marina appeared toward the end of the visit, and both Ruth and Hosty were surprised to see her. Marina, for her part, remembers this visit as being the longer, and more charming, of her conversations with Hosty about her "rights." She was no longer afraid. On the contrary, she was glad to see Hosty because, as she puts it, he had "a nice personality." At the end of their conversation, however, she did appeal to him not to come again because news of his first visit had upset Lee very badly.

Ruth had thought, while she and Hosty were talking, that Marina was in her bedroom taking care of Rachel. So she was, but at some point—it could have been while Hosty and the other agent were at the doorway before they came in the house—she slipped out of the bedroom, into the kitchen and dining area, out of the kitchen door, and around the house.⁶ She had no trouble finding Hosty's car and, without the smallest feeling of being in a hurry—"I am a sneaky girl," she laughs—she walked around and around it, trying to figure out what make it was. This she was unable to do because she could not read English. But she studied the color and memorized the license number. Then she came back inside the house. Once Hosty had gone, she wrote the number on a slip of paper and left it for Lee on their bureau.⁷

Later, she and Ruth discussed whether to tell Lee about the visit. Ruth thought it might be better to wait until the weekend and Marina agreed. Each time he called that week (he called twice a day, during his lunch break and at 5:30 in the afternoon), he started by asking: "Has the FBI been there?" Each time Marina said No.

No sooner had he arrived on Friday than Lee went outside where Marina was hanging diapers and asked: "Have they been here again?"⁸

Marina said Yes.

"Why didn't you tell me before?"

"I had a lot on my mind. I forgot. Besides, it wasn't that important to me."

"How on earth could you forget?"

"Well, it upset you last time and I didn't want to upset you again."

"It upsets me worse if you keep it from me. Why must you hide things all the time? I never can count on you. What did he want to know?"

"Ask Ruth. She remembers better."

"I want to hear from you."

"It was the same nice man as before, darkish and very likable."

"I didn't ask what he was like; I want to know what he said."

Marina said that through Ruth he had explained to her that if anybody from the Soviet Union or the United States harmed her or tried to use against her the fact that she was from Russia, she had a right to ask the FBI for help. "He's such a nice man, Lee. Don't be frightened. All he did was explain my rights and promise to protect them."

"You fool," said Lee, his voice full of anger, as if it were Marina's fault that Hosty had come at all. "Don't you see? He doesn't care about your rights. He comes because it's his job. You have no idea how to talk to the FBI. As usual, you were probably too polite. You can't afford to let them see your weaknesses. What did he say next?"

Again, Marina told him to ask Ruth. By now she was angry at Lee for ruining her good spirits and refusing to believe the favorable things she had to say about Hosty.

Her words had no effect at all. Lee was angry at *her* because she failed to remember every detail and had forgotten to warn Ruth in advance that she was not to say anything to Hosty. His tone went beyond anger: he was accusing Marina.

It is Marina's recollection that Lee then went straight to the kitchen and quizzed Ruth, who was fixing dinner. After that, he found Marina in the bedroom and started pumping her all over again. He treated her as if she were untrustworthy and had no understanding of how important the whole matter was. "You fool," he said again. "You frivolous, simple-minded fool. I trust you didn't give your consent to having him defend your 'rights'?"

"Of course not," said Marina, "but I agreed with him."

"Fool," he said again. "As a result of these 'rights,' they'll ask you ten times as many questions as before. If the Soviet Embassy gets wind of it and you agreed to let this man protect your 'rights,' then you'll really be in for it. You didn't sign anything, did you?"

"Nobody asked me to, Lee. But I promise you I'll never sign anything without your consent."

Suddenly he remembered something. "Did you write down the license number?"

Marina gave a little wave. "It's on the bureau," she said, repeating the number out loud.

"You've got a good memory," he said, "but only for *some* things."

Marina was exhausted. She felt as if he had squeezed her dry.

At supper Lee questioned Ruth again and this time she saw more clearly than the previous weekend just how upset he was. She tried to be reassuring. "You have a right to your views even if they're unpopular," she said.

Lee complained that he felt "inhibited" by the FBI and hated being bothered all the time.

Ruth wondered if he was worried about his job, and he said he was.

Ruth then told him the only other thing there was to tell. Hosty had inquired whether he might have a mental problem. Lee did not even answer. He barely suppressed a "scoffing laugh."[9]

Lee was pensive and withdrawn for the rest of the evening. Seeing how disturbed he was, a part of Marina decided that she must be a fool indeed not to have understood the seriousness of the whole affair. But another part kept telling her that Lee was making a mountain out of a molehill. She was tired of the way he was always blowing things up out of all proportion and trying to make her as suspicious as he was himself.

Early the next day, Saturday, Lee asked Ruth if he might use her typewriter. Ruth assented and, as he began typing, she carried Junie in her high chair over beside him, where he could keep an eye on her. When she came near, Lee quickly covered up the paper written in longhand that he was typing from. His gesture aroused her curiosity.[10]

About eleven that same morning, after Lee had finished typing, all seven of them—Ruth, the Oswalds, and the four children—piled into Ruth's station wagon and drove to the Texas Drivers' License Examining Station in the Oak Cliff section of Dallas. Lee wanted to apply for a learner's permit, get a license and then a car so he would qualify for better jobs. But the station was closed because of the Veterans Day weekend. Finding themselves in a shopping center, all seven then trooped into a dime store, where Ruth bought a few items for her children and Lee bought rubber pants for June and Rachel. "Rachel is so rich," he said with pride. "Junie didn't have so many clothes when she was born and I didn't, either. She's lucky. She was born free of charge, and the neighbors have given her lots of clothes and such a fine bed!"

On the way home in the car, Lee was as cheerful as Ruth had ever seen him. "He sang, he joked, he made puns" and word plays on the Russian language that caused Marina to double up with laughter.[11]

Marina was relieved at the change in him. She understood that whatever he had written that morning had calmed him after his fright of the evening before. He had been similarly calmed after ordering her to obtain the license number, and calmed again after he took the number off their bureau.

Ruth left the house to vote after lunch, and Lee, cutting up a little again and behaving like a naughty child, said: "Hurry up, Marina. Make me some potatoes and onions before Ruth gets back."

"As if Ruth will mind if you eat potatoes."

"I feel funny eating her potatoes every day."

Marina fried some potatoes and onions mixed with flour and eggs, and for once it was a success. "Finally it came out right," Lee said, seating himself on the floor in front of the television set. "I told you again and again how to do it and at last you know. Now I feel like a king!" He proceeded to down it with gusto.

When there was a break in the football game, Lee shepherded the children down the street to buy popsicles. Chris Paine ran on a little ahead and Lee was afraid that he would end up under a car. He caught Chris, smacked him on the bottom, and carried him the rest of the way. When they got home, he still had Chris on his shoulders. "This little brigand got away," he explained, "and I was afraid he'd be hit by a car. So I gave him a little spank on the behind. He's such a big boy that I can hardly carry him on my shoulders."

Marina told Lee that he had no right to spank somebody else's child.

"Thanks," said Lee. "And if anything happened to him it would be my fault."

After the football game he got down on all fours, allowed Chris to ride on his back and played "Horsey" on the living room floor. The two of them enjoyed it greatly, and Marina could see that her husband still was dreaming of having a son.

That night was a special one for them. It started on a playful note, with Marina, in bed, begging Lee to give up any thought of going back to Russia.

Half teasing, half thinking out loud, he said: "We'll go to Russia. I'll get a decent job at last. I'll work, you'll work, the children will go to kindergarten. We'll see Erich and Pavel."

"I don't want to go to Minsk. Let's go to Leningrad."

"I don't want Leningrad. Let's go to Moscow," he said.

"Alik, if you want Moscow, I won't go. Come on, Alka, let's not go to Russia at all."

"Okay," he said.

"Hooray," Marina nearly shouted, pouncing around the bed like a kitten. "Do you swear?"

"I swear."

"Word of honor?"

"How come you need my word of honor?"

"Because sometimes you promise one thing and do another."

"I won't betray you this time."

At that moment he looked just the way Marina liked him best—"no clouds in his head."

Suddenly Lee turned tender and was more frank with her than he had ever been before. Neither of them had said much to the other about the lives they had led before they met, for what each had been seeking in marrying the other was a new life. In fact, it had only been a month or so before, in New Orleans, that Marina finally told Lee that as a teenager in Leningrad she used to go around cold, hungry, and threadbare, delivering telegrams during the New Year's season. She had hardly ever mentioned Petya and Tanya, her brother and sister, or her stepfather Alexander Medvedev.

Lee had told Marina even less, but tonight he wanted to talk about every woman he had ever cared about before he met her. The first had been in Japan while he was stationed there in the Marine Corps. She had been thirty-four years old, nearly twice his age, but she looked much younger than she was. He threw her over, he said, after she had taught him something about sex and he realized that she wanted to marry him. The next one had been thin, but she had had a great many lovers and he was afraid of catching venereal disease. The third had cooked for him and he saw more of her than of anybody else. "But she was fat, I soon got tired of her, and she bored me," Lee said. "I went to see her more for her cooking than for love." He had had five other women in Japan.

In Russia, he had at first gone without a woman for a year. Then there had been a whole parade. "But it's all in the past," he said. "I was only tricking them. Then a girl came along in a red dress—and she tricked me."

The girl in the red dress was Marina, of course, but he did tell her a little about the others, especially Ella Germann, the girl he had asked to marry him.

"Her grandmother scared her away," Lee said. "Being American, she thought that I must be a spy." He added that he was grateful to Marina because she had never thought he was a spy. And he told her that of all the women he had known, she was the only one he ever loved.

"Oh, Alka, you don't love me. Look at the way we fight."

"Everyone does that."

"If you loved me, maybe we wouldn't fight."

"You silly, don't you see that I love you?" He stroked her hair. "Did you grow your hair long especially for me?"

"Who else but you?"

"Mama will have long hair now. See how pretty her hair is. I love Mama's eyes, her little bones, her nose, her ears, her mouth." And he began to kiss her. "Who taught you to kiss?" he asked her, looking into the mirror above her head.

"It's all in the past," she said.

The next morning, Sunday, Ruth was up ahead of everybody else. She went to the living room and there, on her desk, lay the handwritten note Lee had been typing from the day before. The note was folded and Ruth started to read below the fold. The words she saw were these: "The FBI is not now interested in my activities . . ." Ruth was thunderstruck. She had no idea to whom these words were addressed, but she of all people knew they were not true. She was not accustomed to reading other people's letters without permission. But Lee was using her typewriter for his lies and she felt, in a way, that she had the right. So she read the whole thing:

Dear Sirs:

This is to inform you of events since my interview with Comrade Kostine in the Embassy of the Soviet Union, Mexico City, Mexico.

I was unable to remain in Mexico City indefinitey because of my Mexican visa restrictions which was for 15 days only. I could not take a chance on applying for an extension unless I used my real name so I returned to the U.S.

I and Marina Nicholeyeva are now living in Dallas, Texas.

The FBI is not now interested in my activities in the progressive organization FPCC of which I was secretary in New Orleans Louisiana since I no longer live in that State.

the FBI has visited us here in Texas. On Nov. 1st agent of the FBI James P. Hasty warned me that if I attempt to engage in FPCC activities in Texas the FBI will again take an "interest" in me. This agent also "suggested" that my wife could "remain in the U.S. under FBI protection," that is, she could defect from the Soviet Union.

Of course I and my wife strongly protested these tactics by the notorious FBI.

I had not planned to contact the Mexican City Embassy at all so of course they were unprepared for me. Had I been able to reach Havana as planned the Soviet Embassy there would have had time to assist me. but of course the stuip Cuban Consule was at fault here I am glad he has since been replaced by another.[12]

Ruth was suddenly alarmed.[13] She wondered what sort of man she was giving shelter to, and she saw immediately that he was a good deal "queerer" than she had supposed. The letter sounded to her less like that of a spy than of someone who was trying to make an impression on someone else who was a spy. It contained, in any event, statements she knew to be lies, weird language like "the notorious FBI," references to Mexico, and a false name. Ruth wondered whether a single word was true.

The shower was running; Ruth hoped that Lee might be in it, and she hurriedly made a copy of the letter, stuffed it in an envelope, and shoved it deep into a corner of her desk. If anybody from the FBI came that week, she would hand it over right away, for she wanted to be rid of the thing. Ruth was convinced that the FBI must know a lot about Lee, more than Hosty had let on. She therefore expected that the FBI would know what to make of her discovery. Meanwhile, she put the original of the letter back where she had found it, right in full view on the desk, and there it lay all day Sunday as it had lain all day Saturday. Its being there for everyone to see did not seem to bother Lee a bit.

As usual he looked at football that afternoon. Michael was at home and had occasion to step over Lee while he was lying stretched out on the floor. Michael felt a pang of self-reproach. He thought he was being rude, stepping over Lee that way without even trying to make small talk. But he had given up trying to build a bridge to Lee or understand him because Lee seemed to block it somehow. Michael thought it a shame that they should be there, two men in the same house, and be unable to talk to one another. He wished they could communicate better.

Michael had another thought. He did not resent Lee lying on his floor, watching his television, and crowding his house a bit. But he did feel that for a man who professed to be a revolutionary, Lee had an awful lot of time on his hands. To be a revolutionary, Michael thought, is a perfectly good and valid thing. But if Lee wanted to be a revolutionary, he ought to go out and be one. To lie around watching television all day, Michael said to himself, "is one hell of a way for a revolutionary to be spending his time."[14]

Late in the afternoon Ruth gave Lee his third driving lesson—backing, parking, and a right-angle turn. She thought Lee really got the feel of parking that day.

In the evening she decided to rearrange the living room furniture and she asked Lee and Michael to help. Preceding them into the room, she saw Lee's letter still in full view on her desk. She popped it inside the folding front and the three of them moved the furniture around. When they were through, she put the letter gingerly back where it had been before.[15]

At the end of the evening, Ruth was still upset by the letter and knew that it would be a while before she could get to sleep. She sat on the sofa next to Lee, who was watching a spy mystery, hoping to ask him about the letter. She wanted to say, "What is this I found on my desk?" But she did not want him to think that she was watching him and she was fearful. Mostly, the letter made her think that something was wrong with Lee mentally. But supposing he was a spy. Would it not be better in that case just to give the letter to the FBI? Ruth did not know what to do.

Suddenly, Lee turned sweet with her. "I guess you are real upset about going to the lawyer, aren't you?" he asked sympathetically, knowing that Ruth was to see a divorce lawyer in a day or two.

Ruth was disarmed. It had been thoughtful of Lee to ask. She watched the mystery a moment longer, then left him and went to bed.[16]

It was the Veterans Day weekend and Lee did not have to go to work on Monday. Ruth was gone the first part of the day and parked her children with a neighbor, leaving the Oswalds to themselves. Lee was pensive and withdrawn. He sat alone in the back yard on the children's swings. Then he came into the house and went back to work on his letter. He told Marina that he was writing the Soviet Embassy in Washington to complain about the FBI. He even asked her to sign it. She refused. She was sorry he was fussing with the embassy again but somehow she felt that she was never going to have to go back to Russia.

She noticed that Lee was nervous. He typed the letter twice before he got it right and had to do the envelope at least four times.[17] Once he put the return address where the embassy's address ought to be and other times he simply left letters out of the address.

Lee's letter is similar but not identical to the draft version Ruth had seen. In one significant change in the next to last paragraph of the final version, he betrayed his newly made promise to Marina that they would never return to Russia. The paragraph read: "Please inform us of the arrival of our Soviet entrance visa's as soon as they come."[18]

That Monday afternoon, while they were hanging up diapers again, Lee and Marina had another talk about the FBI. After Christmas the two of them expected that they would have saved enough money to find an apartment of their own. Lee insisted that their new address should remain a secret from the FBI. But Marina told him that after all Ruth had done for them, she could and would not turn her back on Ruth and keep their address a secret. How, then, to keep it secret from the FBI?

"I know," said Lee. "Ruth is too honest. If you ask her not to say a certain thing, she won't be able not to. She doesn't know how to lie. She'll tell them where we are living and how. And I don't want the FBI to know anything about me."

Marina repeated that it would be a "swinish" trick not to give Ruth their address. She liked Ruth and wanted to remain her friend.

"I'll think of something," said Lee.

And he did.[19]

The next morning, Tuesday, November 12, he kissed Marina goodbye while she was still in bed. He lifted Rachel's foot and kissed it, too. "She's so warm. And I've got to go to work." Then he either left his letter to the Soviet Embassy for Ruth to mail along with her letters, or he dropped it into a mailbox opposite the house of Wesley Frazier, with whom he was riding into town. The letter bears the postmark: "Irving, Texas, 5:00 P.M., November 12."[20]

Lee reported for work at the book depository, and during the noon hour, taking Ruth's advice, in a way, he went to the main FBI office at 1114 Commerce Street, not far from the depository. He walked up to the receptionist, Nanny Lee Fenner, looking "awfully fidgety," with what she later said was "a wild look in his eye" and an unsealed envelope in his hand. He asked if Agent Hosty was in, and she told him Hosty was out to lunch. "Well, get this to him," he said, and tossed the envelope on her desk. He turned and walked back to the elevator.

Soon afterward Hosty stopped by. "Some nut left this for you," Mrs. Fenner said, and handed Hosty the letter. The envelope, a 10-inch white business envelope, had one word written across it—"Hasty." It contained a single sheet of 8 by 10 bond paper. It had no greeting, no signature, and no return address. There were only two handwritten paragraphs. One stated that Hosty had been interviewing the wife of the author without permission and the author did not like it. If you want to see me, come to me. Don't bother my wife, it said. In the next paragraph, the writer warned that if Hosty did not stop talking to his wife, he would be forced to take action against the FBI. He did not say what that action might be.[21]

Since the note was not signed, Hosty was not certain who had left it. He surmised that it might be Oswald or one other person who had been giving him trouble. Either way the complaint seemed "innocuous," the kind he got a good many of, and it did not appear to require action. He put it in his work box and left it.[22]

Oswald's letter to the Soviet Embassy and his warning note to the FBI are the work of a man who had come a long way in only a few days down the road of his own delusions. It is true that Oswald had suffered an accumulation of disappointments in the year and a half since his return from Russia and had lately suffered a serious blow at the hands of Castro's chief consul in Mexico City. The letter to the Soviet Embassy confirms what Marina had noticed: an ebbing of her husband's enthusiasm for Cuba and a revival of his faith in the U.S.S.R. But what apparently completed his inner undoing, and in little more than a week, were the visits of FBI Agent James P. Hosty to the Paine household on November 1 and 5.

The FBI is, indeed, an organization with an exceptional capacity to magnetize, then crystallize, the fears and longings of many people. And Oswald's feelings toward the FBI did contain an element of longing, did have their favorable side. In a New Orleans jail only a few months earlier, he had asked to see an agent of the FBI, and his request had been granted. The FBI's attention elated him then, for it was proof of his importance. Moreover, his summoning the FBI into his life that summer, two months after he had for the first and only time paid a visit to the grave of his father, suggests that for Oswald as for others, the FBI was a symbolic father whose approval and protection he craved.

Now it was altogether different. Oswald's state of mind was no longer what it had been in August. And this time, unlike the last, it was the FBI which was coming after him. To Oswald, this apparently meant only one thing—he was about to suffer retribution for all his sins, both those he had actually committed and those which existed only in his imagination. It was not simply a loving father who had found him out, but an avenging one. It was this he had been dreading, it was for this he had been waiting, all his life.

There was something else, too. Maybe Marina described Hosty's visits in a teasing, slightly provocative manner, or maybe Oswald merely took her description that way, but the visits evidently caused him to feel that his sexual hold over her was in jeopardy.

Thus the threat which the Hosty visits held for Oswald could scarcely have lain deeper than it did. It was a threat that was both heterosexual and homosexual in nature, for it entailed the threat of being found out and punished for his "sins," on the one hand, and, on the other, the threat and promise of unification, of being joined with and becoming part of the symbolic father whom Oswald dreaded and loved at the same time.

The visits to Ruth and Marina by an obscure agent of the FBI appear to have been linked in Lee's mind with the forthcoming visit by President Kennedy, which was now only ten days away. Since Hosty was an emissary of the government, his arrival was like a herald, or a precursor, of President Kennedy's. And since Hosty's status with the FBI made him a sort of stand-in for a father, his visits were a paradigm, an emotional equivalent, of the President's.

Ironically, the visits to Irving by an agent of the United States Government appear to have been a catalyst and a precipitating element of the events that lay ahead.

35

The President's Visit

RUTH PAINE had a lot on her mind. She was teaching part time and, besides attending to her own children's needs, she was busy ferrying Marina and her children to the dental and medical clinics where they had appointments. Lee's presence throughout the long Veterans Day weekend had been a strain on her. And on top of that had been her discovery of Lee's letter to the Soviet Embassy and her perplexity about what to do.

Ruth now had two copies of Lee's letter: the one she had made and the handwritten original that Lee had left on her desk, either out of carelessness or because he wanted her to see it. She decided to consult Michael. The next time he came to the house, probably on Tuesday, November 12, she handed him Lee's letter. "I never knew he was such a liar," she said, and she asked Michael to take a look.

Michael was sitting by the picture window in the living room, gazing outside and reading *Time*. He was daydreaming, he later said, of another job and another wife—"another fate and another mate." The harder Ruth tried to claim his attention, the harder he resisted.[1] Finally, he glanced at the letter, but he read the opening not as "Dear Sirs" but as "Dear Lisa." What on earth was Ruth doing, he thought, reading Lee's mail? He resented her being so nosy. He read on, however, and saw that Lee was writing about an encounter with the FBI. Michael imagined that he was boasting of his fictional exploits to some friend.

"Yes, it is shocking that he'll make up stories like that," Michael said, handing the letter nonchalantly back to Ruth. He, too, thought the letter was an example of Lee's "colossal lying."

Ruth asked whether he thought they ought to do something about it.

"Let's have another look," Michael said.

"Oh, never mind." Ruth was annoyed. "If you didn't get it the first time, forget it."

406

Michael's lack of interest deflated Ruth. Had he responded, she might have taken the initiative and gone to the FBI herself. As it was, she did nothing, although if Hosty had come by again that week, she would probably have given him the letter.

Would it have made any difference? Between them the Paines knew a lot about Lee. He was not just an angry misfit; they both suspected there was more to it than that. Suppose they had been on better terms with each other and had pooled everything that between them they now knew or guessed about Lee. Suppose they had decided to give Lee's letter to the FBI. Would it have changed anything?

The answer appears to be No. The FBI had opened its file on Lee Harvey Oswald in October 1959, at the time of his defection to the Soviet Union; when he returned to the United States in 1962, FBI agents interviewed him twice in Fort Worth. It was decided that he was not a security risk, and in August 1962, his case was closed. The FBI continued to gather such information about him as came its way, but there were no further investigations. As a Soviet citizen, however, Marina remained of interest to the FBI, and she, as a "pending, inactive case," was assigned to Agent Hosty of the Dallas office. In checking on her whereabouts in March 1963, Hosty learned of her troubled marriage. When he reviewed Oswald's file and found that he was subscribing to *The Worker,* a Communist publication, he recommended that his case be reopened.

From that time on, the FBI kept a check on Oswald, but it was consistently six weeks to three months behind his movements. He was traced to New Orleans, for example, but jurisdiction over his case was transferred to the New Orleans office only in September, as Oswald was getting ready to leave for Mexico. After the bureau learned through the CIA in October that he had been in touch with the Soviet Embassy in Mexico City, it intensified its search for his whereabouts; but it was not until the end of that month that Marina was traced to the Paines'. When Hosty visited Ruth and Marina in the first week of November, he learned where Oswald worked in Dallas, but he still did not know where he lived, and jurisdiction over the case had not yet been transferred from New Orleans back to the Dallas office.

When jurisdiction had been transferred, and when he had learned Oswald's home address, Hosty, who was usually assigned to watch right-wing activists and members of the Ku Klux Klan, meant to follow up on Oswald. But as far as he was concerned, Oswald was a small fish, about one of forty or no cases that he was carrying in November.[2] Moreover, the FBI's primary interest was in subversion. As a malcontent who had defected to the Soviet Union and returned with a Russian wife, there was always the chance that Oswald had been recruited as a spy and posed a threat to the political security of the United States. Hosty had accumulated enough evidence to warrant watching him for security reasons, yet there was nothing to suggest that he might pose a threat to the life of the President. It never crossed Hosty's mind to cite Oswald to the Secret Service, the agency specifically charged with protecting the safety of the President.

Even if Ruth and Michael had given the FBI Oswald's letter to the Soviet

Embassy, the most they might have accomplished was to cause the FBI to step up its surveillance of Oswald as a possible security threat. Hosty had, in fact, received a note which he suspected was from Oswald, but it did not alarm him or attract his particular attention. For the all-important missing ingredient was violence. Oswald was not known ever to have uttered a threat against the President or Vice President. He was not known ever to have shot at anyone. That secret —the secret of Oswald's attempt on General Walker—was locked up inside two people, Oswald himself and Marina.

There was one last irony. During the week following Hosty's visit to the Paine household, the Secret Service and the FBI were busy with President Kennedy's forthcoming visit. The visit had been announced on September 13, nearly two months before, but final confirmation that the President was to be in Dallas on November 22 was published only on November 8. On November 12, the Protective Research Section of the Secret Service arrived in Dallas, and, working with the FBI and the local police, began to investigate possible threats to the President's safety, which were, of course, believed to come from the right. Final details of the President's visit were made known only on November 19. Hosty was not aware until the night of November 21 that the President was to have a motorcade through Dallas the next day. And not until the afternoon of November 22 did he realize that the motorcade had passed beneath the windows of the Texas School Book Depository, the place where he had discovered that Lee Harvey Oswald worked.

Marina thought that living at Ruth's house was "wonderful." It made her realize how hard her life was with Lee—she never had any good times with him, really. Marina enjoyed little things, like sitting and having coffee with the neighbors, visiting, doing favors, treating other people with decency. She had discovered that there was such a thing as suburban, middle-class American life, and she liked it. She knew she would have to give it up when Lee, with his angry and mistrustful nature, took her to live with him in Dallas.

And there was Ruth herself. Marina did not want to lose her. They had a good time together; they confided the details of their marriages to one another and gave each other much-needed moral support. And yet they were not so close that it was a strain for either of them to be with the other all the time. Marina found that Ruth had a way of respecting distances and leaving the other person alone. Her house was an oasis of serenity.

In short, Marina was in no hurry to go back to Lee. She missed him during the week when they were apart, but minutes after he appeared on the weekends there was friction again. Marina knew all too well what living with him was going to mean. He would try to cut her off from everyone. She hoped to prolong her stay at Ruth's until after the holidays, and in the meantime build up her bargaining power with Lee. Maybe if she stayed away long enough, he would make concessions and not force her to give up her other friends. Marina could not bear to let that happen, to lose touch with what was decent and sane in her life.

And it was a matter of principle. Marina simply would not do to Ruth what

Lee had forced her to do to her émigré friends the year before—cut her off. She was not going to have that on her conscience. After all that she had done for her, Marina was not going to turn her back on Ruth Paine.

Marina expressed the worry that was nibbling at her in a way that was disconcerting to Ruth. When she moved to Dallas, Marina of course meant to give Ruth her address. But one evening as they were standing at the sink doing dishes, Marina said suddenly: "When we have our apartment, please, Ruth, our address is private. Don't give it to anyone."[3]

Ruth failed to connect the remark to Hosty or the FBI. Not knowing Marina's train of thought, she was surprised by the remark. She was surprised, too, at the hint of asperity in Marina's tone.

Lee called on Friday, November 15, at lunchtime, to ask if he could come out that day. Marina hesitated. She sensed that he had overstayed the weekend before. "I don't know, Lee," she said. "I think it's inconvenient for Ruth to have you come every time." Marina added that it was the birthday of Lynn, the Paines' little girl, and they were going to have a party the next day.

"Will Michael be there?" Lee asked.

Marina said that he would.

"Well, it's a family celebration. I don't want to be in the way."

Marina does not know whether Lee acceded as readily as he did because he no longer liked Michael; whether, to the contrary, he respected the Paines' privacy and thought they ought to have a chance to be alone; or whether he had other things to do. He simply said: "Fine. There's plenty for me to do here. I'll read and I'll watch TV. Don't worry about me."

Marina says that Lee did not get angry or withdrawn, as he did when his feelings were hurt. Lee liked to be alone, and Marina recalls that on an earlier weekend either he had stayed in Dallas until Saturday, giving as a reason, or pretext, that he was looking for a job in photography, or he had mentioned to her that one of these weekends he would be staying in alone on Friday night. This weekend, in any case, he gave none of his familiar signs of feeling rebuffed. He even called again that night.

It was Ruth who spoke to him first. She apologized for being unable to take him to get his learner's permit the next day. But she told him that he could go back to the Driver's Station in Oak Cliff and take his test without a car. Lee was surprised that he did not need a car.[4] Then Marina talked to him. She urged him not to stay alone in his room the whole weekend but to get out and take a walk in the park. Their conversation was friendly and warm.

Lee called again the next day, Saturday, November 16, in fine humor. He claimed that he had been to the Driver's Station but there was a long line ahead of him and he was informed that his turn would not come before closing time. Lee did not wait. He told Marina that he had taken her advice instead and sat in the park. "Do you remember?" he asked. It was the park they had been to in the spring.

"Only, Papa, be sure and eat better," Marina begged, worried that if he was alone he would starve himself as usual.

Lee called that night again, this time to ask if the children were enjoying the party. Marina said Yes. Was "his" Junie having a good time? She was.

"I ate very well," he assured Marina. "I found a good place where you can get a fine meal, steak, French fries, salad and dessert, for only $1.25. Don't be worried about me."

Marina missed him. She wanted to ask what he was going to do the next day, but she refrained.

Lee's landlady said later that he never left his room for more than a few minutes all weekend except to carry his laundry to the Washeteria across the street.[5] Someone else saw him there reading a magazine.

Lee's reading that weekend is a matter of enduring curiosity, but he almost certainly read a good deal about President Kennedy's visit, which was to take place the following Friday. The Dallas papers were full of it, and Lee had more newspapers around him, and more time to read them, than if he had been at the Paines'. Although the visit had been announced two months before, the atmosphere in Dallas was so hostile to the President that there had been some question as to whether he ought to come. On October 24, Adlai Stevenson, U.S. ambassador to the United Nations, had been in Dallas for a meeting and had been struck and spat upon by a right-wing crowd armed with placards that had been stored in the home of General Walker. The police had lost control of the crowd and there was widespread doubt as to whether they could cope with a visit by President Kennedy. Stevenson himself advised the President not to go. In the wake of the Stevenson affair, the mayor called upon the city to redeem itself. The police were stung by all the criticism, and statements by Police Chief Jesse Curry began to appear, claiming that the local police would be in charge of arrangements to protect the President. Reading about the thoroughness of their preparations, Lee may well have laughed that scoffing laugh of his; for he, too, had had nothing but contempt for the Dallas police ever since they missed him by a long mile following his attempt on General Walker.

On Friday, November 15, at about the hour that Lee was leaving work, the Dallas *Times-Herald* reported that the Dallas Trade Mart might be chosen as the site where the President would have lunch the following Friday. On the next day, Saturday, the *Times-Herald* reported that the presidential party was likely to "loop through the downtown area, probably on Main Street," on its way to the Trade Mart. If Lee saw the story, it would have been his first hint that the motorcade might come close to the building in which he worked.

Sharing the front pages with the Kennedy visit that weekend was another story in which Lee was interested. It concerned Frederick C. Barghoorn, a Yale political science professor who had been arrested for "espionage" during a visit to the U.S.S.R. The story broke on November 12. Two days later, on Thursday, President Kennedy made the Barghoorn case the centerpiece of what was to be his last press conference. The President asserted vigorously that Professor Barghoorn was not a spy, and he broke off the cultural exchange negotiations with the Soviet Union which were then in progress until Barghoorn was released. On Saturday, November 16, one of the Dallas dailies featured on its front page an

A.P. story reporting Barghoorn's release, together with the White House announcement that the presidential motorcade would loop through downtown Dallas.

Lee told Marina about Barghoorn's arrest, apparently over the telephone, shortly after the story broke on November 12, adding that he had read about it in the newspapers and heard about it on the radio as well. He was sorry for Barghoorn. "Poor professor," Lee said. "He's the victim of a Russian provocation. It isn't the first time and it won't be the last."

Nor was it the first time Lee had taken an interest in the plight of Americans caught in the U.S.S.R. He had followed the case of Francis Gary Powers. First Powers and now Barghoorn were accused of being spies, both were imprisoned in Soviet jails, both attracted worldwide publicity, and both touched the politics of the presidency. Lee felt that he, too, had been trapped inside Russia, but he was different from Powers and Barghoorn in that no publicity surrounded his name, and no one had come to his rescue. President Kennedy went all out for Barghoorn. No one cared about the fate of Lee Oswald.[6]

On Sunday, November 17, Lee failed, uncharacteristically, to call Marina. She missed him, and when she saw Junie playing with the telephone dial, saying "Papa, Papa," she decided impulsively, "Let's call Papa."

Marina was helpless with a telephone dial, so it was Ruth who made the call. She dialed the number Lee had given her weeks before while they were awaiting Rachel's birth, and a man answered.

"Is Lee Oswald there?" Ruth asked.

"There is no Lee Oswald living here."

"Is this a rooming house?" Ruth wanted to know.

"Yes."

"Is it WH 3–8993?"

"Yes."

Ruth thanked the man and hung up. "They don't know a Lee Oswald at that number," she said. Marina looked distinctly surprised.[7]

The next day, Monday, November 18, Lee called as usual at lunchtime. "We phoned you last evening," Marina said. "Where were you?"

"I was at home watching TV. Nobody called me to the phone. What name did she ask for me by?"

Marina told him. There was a long silence at the other end. "Oh, damn. I don't live there under my real name."

Why not? Marina asked.

Lee said he did not want his landlady to know he had lived in Russia.

"It's none of her business," Marina retorted.

"You don't understand a thing," Lee said. "I don't want the FBI to know where I live, either." He ordered her not to tell Ruth. "You and your long tongue," he said, "they always get us into trouble."

Marina was frightened and shocked. "Starting your old foolishness again," she scolded. "All these comedies. First one, then another. And now this fictitious name. When will it all end?"

Lee had to get back to work. He would call later, he said.

Marina, of course, told Ruth about the alias. She was tired of it, she said, tired of Lee's fears and suspicions, tired of his attempts to cover up the fact that he had lived in Russia. It wasn't the first time she had felt caught between "two fires," loyalty to Lee and a conviction that what he was doing was wrong.

Ruth could make nothing of the alias, either.

Lee called back that evening while Ruth was fixing supper. It was she who picked up the telephone. Marina did not want to talk to him, but Ruth said she could not tell Lee that his own wife refused to speak to him. Reluctantly, Marina came to the telephone.

Lee started right off by addressing her as *devushka* or "wench," a word that in Russian has such an insulting ring that a man might use it to a servant, perhaps, but not to his wife. When spoken by a husband to a wife, it suggests that everything is over between them. It is a word designed to annihilate intimacy.

"Hey, wench," he said, "you're to take Ruth's address book and cross my name and telephone number out of there."

"I can't," Marina said. "It's not my book and I have no right to touch it."

"Listen here." Lee was angry. "I order you to cross it out. Do you hear?"

"I won't do it."

Lee started to scold Marina in as ferocious a voice as she had ever heard. She hung up the telephone.

Marina told Ruth what Lee had asked her to do. The two of them were puzzled: why had Lee given them a number they weren't supposed to use? And why was he using an alias? Marina said he had mentioned the FBI. "I don't think it's worth living under an assumed name just for that," Ruth said in a mystified tone.

Until their argument on the telephone, Lee and Marina had been on good terms, and the significance of this quarrel, only one of hundreds they had had, seems to have lain in its timing—after Hosty and before Kennedy. Because of his fear of the FBI, Lee had been living under an alias since October 14. Now he had been found out. Hosty was closing in on him and Marina had discovered his alias. With Ruth in on the secret as well, it would be no time before the FBI tracked him to his lair. Most significant of all, after the Hosty visits and their shattering impact on his emotions, any falling out with Marina was bound to have an amplified, and destructive, effect on Lee.

But how was Marina to know? She, too, was furious—furious at her discovery that Lee had an alias and was again living a lie. After the string of surprises Lee had been springing on her ever since their arrival in the United States, Marina had been continually anxious. Despite her hopes of a more peaceful life she had not, since Walker, had an easy moment. It did not now cross her mind that he might be up to his old tricks, to anything like a new Walker attempt—that was too frightening even to think about—but the alias obviously meant no good. It might even mean danger.

Lee did not call Marina the next day, Tuesday, or the day after. "He thinks he's punishing me," she said to Ruth.

Lee went to work as usual on Tuesday, November 19. That day, for the first time, both Dallas papers, the *Morning News* and the afternoon *Times-Herald,* published the route of the presidential motorcade. The President would go from Love Field via various lesser streets to Main Street, then "to Houston, Houston to Elm, and Elm under the Triple Underpass to Stemmons Freeway, and on to the Trade Mart."[8] President and Mrs. Kennedy, along with Governor John Connally and his wife, would pass under the windows of the School Book Depository Building, which lay at the northwest corner of the intersection between Houston and Elm.

Lee learned of the route either on Tuesday, November 19, the day it was published, or Wednesday, November 20, when he might have entered the domino room first thing in the morning and read the announcement in the previous day's paper. Whenever he learned of it, it was the most important day of Lee's life. He now knew, if he had not pieced it together from the weekend's reports, that history, fate, blind accident—call it what you will—had placed him above the very route that John F. Kennedy would take two or three days hence.

It is impossible to exaggerate the impact of this realization on Lee. Seven months earlier, before his attempt to kill a leader of the American right, he had composed a document predicting a "crisis" that would destroy capitalist society forever. Without his having been able to foresee it, an opportunity had now been vouchsafed to *him,* of all men, to deal capitalism that final, mortal blow. And he would strike it not at the right nor at the left, but, quite simply, at the top. It had become his fate to decapitate the American political process. *He* was history's chosen instrument.

The announcement of the President's route was the last in a chain of twelve or fifteen events without any one of which Lee might have approached his decision in a very different frame of mind. The first of these events, curiously, appears to have been the attempt on Nikita Khrushchev's life in Minsk while Lee was living there in January 1962. Another was Lee's failure to receive any sort of punishment on his re-defection to the United States later that year. Still another was Marina's letter of January 1963 to her former suitor, Anatoly Shpanko, who in her eyes and possibly in Lee's as well, bore a resemblance to President Kennedy. There had been the failure of Lee's attempt on General Walker and the heightened sense of immunity which he carried away from that episode. When Lee had moved to New Orleans, there was the murder, in June 1963, of Medgar Evers, in a town nearby, and only a few hours after a speech by Kennedy. Then there was the passage in William Manchester's book, comparing Kennedy to a President who had been assassinated; and the death of the Kennedy baby at a time when the Oswalds, too, expected a baby. There was Lee's brief incarceration in New Orleans, an interlude during which he had two enjoyable conversations with Police Lieutenant Francis Martello and realized that prison could be an excellent forum from which to proclaim his political ideas. And there was the fiasco of Lee's visit to Mexico and his failure to obtain a Cuban visa which, curiously, may have turned Castro into a negative constituent. Far from wanting to fight *for* Castro, Lee may now have wanted to *show* him, as he almost always did after he was dealt a rebuff, what a good fighter he had missed out on.

During that very month of November 1963, several events occurred which were profoundly disturbing to Lee, by far the most shattering being the visits of Agent Hosty to Marina. Only the week before, there had been the Barghoorn affair. And now the bitter quarrel with Marina over the alias. Lee's wildly disproportionate anger at Marina was a symptom that while he was able to cope, just barely, with the demands of his life on the outside, he was on the point of coming apart within. Lee himself was like a rifle that has been loaded and cocked and is ready to go off. Now, suddenly, unforeseeably, he had been placed in a situation in which he had an opportunity to alter the course of history.

On Wednesday, November 20, at about one o'clock, a small but seminal incident took place at the book depository. Warren Caster, a textbook company representative who had an office in the building, went to Roy Truly's office to show off a pair of purchases he had made during the lunch hour. Caster proudly drew from their cartons two rifles, one a Remington .22 which he had bought as a Christmas present for his son, and the other a sporterized .30–06 Mauser, which he had bought to go deer hunting. Truly picked up the Mauser and, without cocking it, lifted it to his shoulder and sighted it. He handed it back to Caster and said it was a handsome thing.[9] A number of men were present in Truly's office. Lee Oswald happened to be among them. Marina thinks that this could have been the decisive moment. Lee now knew the route, and he had seen guns in the building. If anyone should accuse him later of keeping a rifle there, he had a pretext. There were two rifles in the building already, so why should he be under suspicion?[10]

Still, he had not made up his mind. Marina had not noticed in him anything like the "waves" of tension that she had seen three times earlier: before his visit to the American Embassy in Moscow in 1961, when he expected to be arrested; before his attempt on General Walker; and before his visit to Mexico City. Each time he had been nervous and irritable for weeks in advance, each time he had talked in his sleep and suffered convulsive anxiety attacks at night, and each time he had lost weight. This time he showed none of those signs. Lee was even 7 pounds above his lowest New Orleans weight, a certain indication that he had not been worrying or preparing anything momentous. Even now, on Wednesday, he did not do what he could easily have done. He did not telephone Marina, make up with her, and go out to Irving to fetch his rifle at a moment when bringing it into town would be far less conspicuous than it would be later in the week. And it is clear that he made no plan of escape.

Indeed, it appears certain that Lee's decision was an impulsive one, not only because the route had been announced at the last minute, but because the deed was so momentous and Lee's feelings about it apparently so ambiguous that if he had had time to prepare he might very possibly have failed, as he did in the case of General Walker, or he might somehow have slipped and given his plan away.

Lee was still hesitating on the morning of Thursday, November 21. When he dressed that day and left the rooming house, he did not take his pistol with him, as he is likely to have done had he made his mind up and realized that he would need his revolver for self-defense. On the other hand, he broke his routine that morning in a way that suggests he was coming to a decision. Instead of making breakfast in the rooming house, as he generally did, he went across the street to the Dobbs House restaurant and treated himself to a special breakfast. He complained that his eggs were cooked "too hard," but he ate them anyway.[11]

At last, after his arrival at the book depository, Lee took a decisive step. Between eight and ten in the morning, he sought out Wesley Frazier, who lived near the Paines with his sister Linnie Mae Randle, and asked for a ride to Irving that afternoon. He said he was going "to get some curtain rods. You know, put in an apartment."[12] Later that day Lee took time to fashion a bag 26 or 27 inches long, made of the brown paper and tape that were used by the book depository employees.

Marina was in her bedroom with Rachel late in the afternoon when Lee arrived unexpectedly. He had not called her ahead of time, and ostensibly they were still angry at one another because of their fight over Lee's alias. Marina saw Frazier's car stop at the house and Lee get out. She did not go to greet him. She looked sullen as he entered the bedroom. Inwardly she was pleased that he had come.

"You didn't think I was coming?"

"Of course not. How come you came out today?"

"Because I got lonesome for my girls." He took her by the shoulders to give her a kiss.

Marina turned her face away and pointed at a pile of clothes. "There are your clean shirt and socks and pants. Go in and wash up."

Lee did as he was told. "I'm clean now," he said, as he emerged from the bathroom. "Are you angry at me still?"

"Of course," she said, turning aside another kiss.

Marina tried to leave the bedroom, but he blocked the door and would not let her go until she allowed him to kiss her. With utter indifference, like a rag doll, she acceded.

"Enough," Lee said, angry that she was not glad to see him. "You get too much spoiling here. I'm going to find an apartment tomorrow and take all three of you with me."

"I won't go," Marina said.

"If you don't want to come, then I'll take Junie and Rachel. They love their papa and you don't love me."

"That's fine," said Marina. "Just you try nursing Rachel. You know what that's like. It'll be less work for me."

Lee then spoke of the FBI. "I went to see them," he said. "I told them not to bother you any more."

Marina left the bedroom and went outside to bring the children's clothes in off the line. Lee went to the garage for a few minutes, then the two of them came inside and sat on the sofa in the living room folding diapers. "Why won't you come with me?" Lee begged. "I'm tired of living all alone. I'm in there the whole week long and my girls are here. I don't like having to come all the way out here each time I want to see you."

"Alka," Marina said, "I think it's better if I stay here. I'll stay till Christmas and you'll go on living alone. We'll save money that way. I can talk to Ruth and she's a help to me. I'm lonesome by myself with no one to talk to all day."

"Don't worry about the money," Lee said. "We have a little saved up. I'll take an apartment and we'll buy you a washing machine."

"I don't want a washing machine. It'll be better if you buy a car."[13]

"I don't need a car," he said. "I can go on the bus. If you buy a used car, you have to spend money to get it fixed. It's not worth it. I don't want my girl to have to do all the laundry in the bathtub. Two babies are a lot of work." Lee pointed to the pile of clothing. "See what a lot of work it is? With two babies you just can't do it all alone."

"We'll see," Marina said.

Just then Ruth drove up to the house. The car was filled with groceries and Lee, followed by Marina, went out to help. He picked up a load of groceries and went in the house, while Marina lingered outside and apologized to Ruth for his unexpected arrival. The two women guessed that Lee had come to make up.

As Ruth went into the house, she said to Lee: "Our President is coming to town."

"Ah, yes," Lee said, and walked on into the kitchen. He used the expression so often that Ruth paid no attention to his extraordinary casualness.[14]

Marina had also mentioned the President's visit. While they were sitting on the sofa folding diapers, she had said: "Lee, Kennedy is coming tomorrow. I'd like to see him in person. Do you know where and when I could go?"

"No," he said blankly.

Just for a second it crossed Marina's mind that it was odd that Lee, who was so very interested in politics, was unable to tell her anything about the President's visit.

Lee went out on the front lawn and played with the children until dark—the Paine children, the neighbors' children, and June. He hoisted June to his shoulders and the two of them reached out to catch a butterfly in the air. Then Lee tried to catch falling oak wings for June.

Marina stood nearby as Lee and June sat on a red kiddie cart together. Lee spoke with all the children in English, and then turned to Marina and said in Russian, "Good, our Junie will speak both Russian and English. But I still don't like the name Rachel. Let's call her Marina instead."

"Two in one family are too many."

It was while they were outside, Marina thinks, that Lee asked her for the third and last time to move in to Dallas with him. His voice was now very kind, quite different from what it had been in the bedroom. Once again he said that he was tired of living alone and seeing his babies only once a week. "I'll get us an apartment and we'll all live peacefully at home."

Marina, for a third time, refused. "I was like a stubborn little mule," she recalls. "I was maintaining my inaccessibility, trying to show Lee I wasn't that easy to persuade. If he had come again the next day and asked, of course I would have agreed. I just wanted to hold out one day at least."

Marina expected to be with Lee after the New Year. But she enjoyed being in a position where Lee for once had to win *her* over, persuade *her*, prove again that he loved her and that she was not utterly at his mercy. He had given her a horrible scare with his alias and she wanted to teach him a lesson.

The evening was a peaceful one. Lee told Ruth, as he had Marina, that he had been to FBI headquarters, tried to see the agents, and left a note telling them in no uncertain terms what he thought about their visits.[15] Marina did not believe him. She thought that he was "a brave rabbit," and this was just another instance of his bravado.[16] After that, the conversation at supper was so ordinary that no one remembers it; but Ruth had the impression that relations between the Oswalds were "cordial," "friendly," "warm"—"like a couple making up after a small spat."[17]

After supper, Marina stacked the dishes by the sink. Ruth bathed her children, then read to them in their bedroom for an hour. Marina nursed Rachel and Lee put Junie to bed. Then he cradled Rachel in front of the television set and got her to sleep, while Marina put away the toys. Lee went on watching television, a movie about World War II, and Marina went in to do the dishes.

Despite the banality of the evening, there was an undercurrent of tragedy, a ludicrous lack of symmetry between what husband and wife were doing. They were apart. In the kitchen, engaged in her tasks at the sink, Marina was no longer angry at Lee over his use of an alias, although she still could not understand why he bothered with such childish games. She was wondering as always whether Lee loved her. And Lee—what was he thinking? Marina had refused his pleas that she move in to Dallas with him "soon." He would not be looking for an apartment "tomorrow." He now had no need for "curtain rods," but earlier in the evening he had spent time in the garage. Did his requests to Marina have a deeper meaning, a desperation, even, that was masked by his calm acceptance of her refusals? Alone that evening for the first time and staring at the television, what were Lee's thoughts?

Marina was still at the sink when Lee turned off the television set, poked his head in the kitchen, and asked if he could help. Marina thought he looked sad.

"I'm going to bed," he said. "I probably won't be out this weekend."

"Why not?"

"It's too often. I was here today."

"Okay," Marina said.

Ruth was aware of Lee padding back and forth between his bedroom and the bathroom getting ready for bed. It was about ten o'clock, an hour earlier than was usual for him before a workday. Ruth went to the garage and painted blocks for her children for half an hour or so. Someone had been there before her, left the light on, and moved a few things around.[18] She supposed that Lee had gone there to fetch some clothing, for the weather was turning cool and the Oswalds had their warm clothes in the garage. But Ruth did think it careless of Lee to have left the light on.[19] When she returned to the living room, she and Marina sat on the sofa, folded more laundry, talked of nothing in particular, and said good-night.

Marina as usual was the last to bed. She sat in the tub for an hour, "warming her bones" and thinking about nothing in particular, not even Lee's request that she move in to Dallas. Lee was lying on his stomach with his eyes closed when she crept into bed. Marina still had pregnancy privileges; that is, she was allowed to sleep with her feet on whatever part of his anatomy they came to rest. About three in the morning, she thinks, she put a foot on his leg. Lee was not asleep and suddenly, with a sort of wordless vehemence, he lifted his leg, shoved her foot hard, then pulled his leg away.

"My, he's in a mean mood," Marina thought. She realized that he was sleepless, tense, and she believed that he was so angry at her for refusing to move to Dallas right away that it was no use trying to talk to him. She thinks that he fell asleep about five o'clock in the morning.

Lee usually woke up before the alarm rang and shut it off so as not to disturb the children. On the morning of Friday, November 22, the alarm rang and he did not wake up.

Marina was awake, and after about ten minutes she said, "Time to get up, Alka."

"Okay."

He rose, washed, and got dressed. Then he came over to the bed. "Have you bought those shoes you were going to get?"

"No. I haven't had time."

"You must get those shoes, Mama. And, Mama, don't get up. I'll get breakfast myself."

Lee kissed the children, who were sleeping. But he did not kiss Marina, as he always did before he left in the morning. He got as far as the bedroom door, then came back and said, "I've left some money on the bureau. Take it and buy everything you and Junie and Rachel need. Bye-bye." Then Lee went out the door.

"Good God," thought Marina. "What has happened to my husband that he has all of a sudden gotten so kind?" Then she fell back to sleep.

During the days and weeks that followed, Marina realized that there had been several small, out-of-the-way occurrences during Lee's brief visit. He had played much longer than he usually did with Junie out of doors the day before. Could he have been saying goodbye to the creature whom he loved more than anyone on earth? It seemed to Marina, looking back, that there had been a farewell quality to his playing, something valedictory almost, in the way he reached out for the falling oak wings. He had never reached for them before. And his being unable to tell her anything about President Kennedy's visit had been out of character, to say the least.

He had been angry and tense in bed that night and it was nearly morning before he fell asleep. Marina supposed he was just angry at her for refusing to give in to him. Later on she wondered, what *had* he been thinking about?

There was the odd circumstance of his telling her not to get up to fix his breakfast. There was no danger that she would—she had never done so before. Why would he tell her not to? Could it be that he did not want to run the tiniest risk of her seeing him enter the garage—and leave it?

Then there was his telling her with unaccustomed gentleness to buy everything she and the children needed. He had never told her such a thing before. When she got up that morning and looked into the bureau, she found the extraordinary sum of $170. It must have been nearly everything Lee had.

And Marina also remembered that twice after his arrival in the afternoon, he had tried to kiss her and she had turned him away. It was only on the third try, when he had his arm around her, that she relented and allowed him an obligatory kiss. He had tried to be tender with her, and she had been obdurate with him.

Finally, she remembered one more thing, the most earth-shaking of all. Three times he had begged her to move to Dallas with him "soon." Three times she had refused. And he had tried to kiss her three times. Everything had happened in threes. That, for Marina, was the key.

36

November 22, 1963

ABOUT 7:15 on the morning of November 22, Linnie Mae Randle was standing by her kitchen sink when, through the window, she saw Lee coming from the Paines' house carrying a long brown package. She opened her back door a bit to see what he was doing. He walked up to her brother's car, opened the right rear door, and put the package on the back seat. Mrs. Randle went back to the sink, looked up a moment later, and there, staring in at her through the window, was Lee. Startled, she called to her brother, Wesley Frazier, that Lee was waiting for his ride.[1]

The two men climbed in the car and started off. As they were going out the drive, Frazier glanced in the rear and noticed a long brown package extending halfway across the back seat. He asked Lee what it was and Lee mumbled something about curtain rods. "Oh, yes," said Frazier. "You said you were going to get some yesterday."[2]

The two men drove into Dallas and Frazier parked the car in a lot two blocks from the depository building. They usually walked from the lot together, but this morning, Lee got out of the car first, picked up the package, and walked to the building ahead of Frazier.

At 8:00 A.M. Roy Truly, superintendent of the Texas School Book Depository, and William Shelley, Lee's supervisor, arrived at the building. Both noticed that Lee was already at work.[3] Charles Douglas Givens, who waited each morning for Lee to finish reading in the domino room before going in to read the papers himself, noticed that Lee did not go to the domino room that day.[4]

Lee went about his job of filling orders and, sometime between 9:30 and 10:00, he and another order-filler, James ("Junior") Jarman, were on the first floor in a room filled with bins. Lee was at the window, Jarman joined him, and Lee asked what the people were gathering on the corner for. Jarman, who had only just found out himself, said that the President was supposed to pass by. Lee

420

asked Jarman if he knew which way the President was coming?

"I told him, yes. He [would] probably come down Main and turn on Houston and then back again on Elm."

"Oh, I see," Lee said, and went back to filling orders.[5] The turn from Houston into Elm would bring the presidential motorcade directly in front of the southeast corner of the Book Depository Building.

President Kennedy's plane, *Air Force One,* landed at Love Field at 11:40 that morning. Vice President Johnson, whose plane had landed a few moments before, was there with Mrs. Johnson to greet President and Mrs. Kennedy and Governor and Mrs. Connally after their brief flight from Fort Worth. There was a welcoming ceremony before the Kennedys boarded the presidential limousine for the drive through Dallas. The limousine was a specially designed Lincoln convertible equipped with a bubble top. But the weather was clear and the President had asked to have the bubble removed. He sat in the right rear seat with Mrs. Kennedy at his left. Governor and Mrs. Connally rode in jump seats in front of the Kennedys. The presidential party was due at the Trade Mart for lunch at 12:30.

At the book depository, Charles Douglas Givens, Bonnie Ray Williams, and three other men were laying a new plywood floor on the sixth floor of the building. At 11:40 A.M. Williams saw Lee on the east side of the sixth floor but paid no attention to what he was doing.[6] There were Scott-Foresman books on that floor and he could have been filling orders.[7]

At 11:45 or 11:50 the five men who were laying the floor broke for lunch. They headed for the west, or rear, side of the building, got on the freight elevators, and raced each other to the ground floor. On the way down they saw Lee standing by the fifth-floor gate.[8]

Once he was on the ground floor, Givens realized that he had left his jacket, with his cigarettes in it, on the sixth floor. He rode back up and once again saw Lee. He was on the sixth floor now, not the fifth, and instead of being on the northwest side of the building, where Givens had seen him at the elevator gate, he was walking toward the elevators from the southeast corner, the corner overlooking the route the presidential motorcade was scheduled to take. Lee was carrying his clipboard, but he did not have any books in his hand, and he did not appear to be filling orders.[9] The time was 11:55.

The men who were laying the new floor had moved a lot of heavy cartons from the west to the east side of the sixth floor. The southeast corner window, in particular, was totally shielded from view because cartons had been stacked around it in a crescent.[10] Lee appeared to be coming from that window.

"Boy, are you going downstairs? It's near lunchtime," said Givens.

"No, sir," Lee said. "And when you get downstairs, close the elevator gate."[11] The elevator was automatic and would operate only if the gate was closed.

"Okay," said Givens, and rode the elevator down.

There was a good deal of excitement about the motorcade among the men at the book depository. In order to watch, a lot of them took their sandwiches outside and ate in front of the building. Harold Norman and "Junior" Jarman went outside, but then decided that they would get a better view from inside. They went to the rear of the building and took an elevator to the fifth floor. Meanwhile, Bonnie Ray Williams had eaten his lunch—chicken, Fritos, and a bottle of Dr. Pepper—by the third or fourth set of windows on the south side of the sixth floor. He could see nothing to the east of him because the cartons were stacked up so high.[12] But he thought there was nobody there and he wanted someone to watch the motorcade with. He went down a flight of stairs and found Norman and Jarman in the southeast corner windows of the fifth floor. He took a position at a window near theirs. The time was 12:20 P.M.

The presidential motorcade had left Love Field just before noon, and the procession of cars drove rapidly through the thinly populated outskirts of Dallas. The crowds were large and enthusiastic when the motorcade reached the downtown area. The President's limousine traveled along Main Street, turned right on Houston, and headed toward the intersection of Houston and Elm Streets. The limousine slowed to about 11 miles an hour as it made the sharp left turn into Elm, directly in front of the southeast corner of the faded, orange-brick Book Depository Building. It then began to move slowly downhill away from the building. The time was 12:30 P.M.

Just then, from their lookouts at the southeast corner windows of the fifth floor, Bonnie Ray Williams and Harold Norman saw the President raise his right hand as if to salute or brush back his hair.[13] It was a movement they had seen him make on television. But as he did it, they heard a sound like a shot. "Junior" Jarman and Williams thought it was a motorcycle backfire. Then there was another sound and, out on Dealey Plaza, people started dropping to the ground in fright. The President's car lurched forward and there was a third sound right after the second. Two of the three men on the fifth floor saw the President slump, or "lean his head," but they did not see any more.

Bonnie Ray Williams paid no attention to the first shot "because I did not know what was happening." But, he says, "the second shot, it sounded like it was right in the building, the second and third shot. And it sounded—it even shook the building, the side we were on. Cement fell on my head." The floor above was nothing but bare boards with daylight showing between them, and Norman and Jarman saw dust in Williams's hair. "You got something on your head," Norman said. "Yes, man, don't you brush it out," Jarman added.[14]

Because of his location in the southeast corner window of the fifth floor, it was Harold Norman who heard the most. He did not hear anybody move above him, no creaking, no human sound. But what he did hear, with the bare floor only 12 or 14 feet overhead acting as a sounding board, was the bolt action of a rifle clicking three times, and the thump, thump, thump of three expended cartridges dropping to the floor. "Man," he said to the others, "someone is shooting at the President and it's coming from right over us. It even shook the building."[15]

Jarman said, "We'd better get the hell out of here."[16]

All three men knew where the assassin was—he was directly over their heads. None of them was armed. And none of the three wanted to go upstairs for fear of being shot to death. And yet they did a curious thing. They looked out the window and saw everyone, people, policemen, running toward the opposite side of the building where, for some onlookers, the crack of the rifle *appeared* to have come from. Williams said, "We know the shots came from practically over our head. But since everybody was running, you know, to the west side of the building, towards the railroad tracks, we assumed maybe somebody was down there. And so we all ran that way, the way that the people was running, and we was looking out the window."[17]

Lee had stationed himself in the southeast corner window of the sixth floor, barricaded inside the crescent of book cartons. No one had seen him that morning as he carried his brown paper package to the window, removed the rifle, assembled and loaded it. No one saw him toss the empty sack into the corner where it was later found. Nor did anyone see him as he arranged a book carton and two smaller cartons as a gun rest in front of the window.

He sat on another carton and waited until the President's car came into view. He took aim and fired three quick shots. At the moment of the final, farthest shot, President Kennedy was about 88 yards away. Through Lee's four-power telescopic sight, he appeared to be only 22 yards away.[18] After firing his last shot, Lee moved rapidly from the front to the rear of the sixth floor and crammed the rifle, scope up, on the floor between cartons that were stacked up just before the entrance to the stairway.

A Dallas patrolman, Marrion L. Baker, was on his motorcycle at a point in the motorcade several cars behind the President, and was headed straight for the School Book Depository when he heard the first shot. Baker had lately been deer hunting and he was certain that the shot was from a high-powered rifle. He looked up and saw pigeons scattering from their perches atop the building. He raced his motorcycle to the building, dismounted, and pushed his way to the entrance. There he encountered Roy Truly, who identified himself, and the two men ran for the elevators in back. Finding that both were on an upper floor, they started up the stairs. It was less than two minutes since the last shot had been fired.

When Truly and Baker reached the second-floor landing, Baker caught a glimpse of someone in the lunchroom. Revolver in hand, he rushed to the door and saw a man 20 feet away walking to the far end of the room. The man was empty-handed. Baker ordered him to turn and walk toward him. The man obeyed. He seemed normal and not out of breath. Truly was on his way to the third floor, missed the patrolman, and ran back to see what was delaying him. He found Baker face to face with Lee Oswald, his revolver pointed straight at him. Lee did not look excited; startled, perhaps, but not excited.[19]

"Do you know this man? Does he work here?" Baker asked.

"Yes," Truly said.

Baker lowered his revolver and the two men went on with their search.

Mrs. Robert Reid, a clerical supervisor, had watched the motorcade from the front of the building. When she heard the shots she ran back inside, hoping that none of the employees was going to fall under suspicion. She was entering her office on the second floor when Lee entered from the opposite, or lunchroom side, where there was a Coke machine. He was holding a full bottle of Coca-Cola.

"Oh," said Mrs. Reid, "the President has been shot but maybe they didn't hit him."

Lee mumbled something in reply, seemingly "very calm." Both of them kept on walking and that was the end of the encounter.[20]

Lee crossed the second floor, walked down the stairs to the ground floor, and left the building by the main entrance. Outside, a crew-cut young man, who Lee thought was from the Secret Service but who may have been Robert MacNeil, a reporter for NBC, dashed up to ask where he could find a telephone. Very calmly, Lee pointed to the building and told the man that he thought he could find a pay phone inside. About three minutes had elapsed since the last shot had been fired.

Lee walked seven short blocks east on Elm Street and boarded a bus that was headed back toward the School Book Depository en route to Oak Cliff. He was spotted immediately by Mrs. Mary Bledsoe, his reluctant landlady during the week of October 7, as he passed her to take a seat in the middle of the bus. Later she said that he looked "like a maniac." "He looked so bad in his face," his face was "distorted." He was dirty, he had a hole in his right shirtsleeve, and the buttons had been torn off his shirt.[21]

"The President has been shot," the bus driver said, and the passengers started talking about it. "Hope they don't shoot us," someone said. Traffic was in a hopeless snarl and in four minutes the bus had gone only two blocks. Lee slipped out the front, not neglecting, as he went, to pick up a transfer to another bus bound for Oak Cliff.

He had so far tried two means of escape that he had used after the Walker attempt, his own feet and the bus. Now he tried something else. Four blocks from the place where he left the bus, he went up to a cab which was standing near the Greyhound Station. The driver, William Whaley, was about to get out to buy himself a pack of cigarettes. He later remembered that a man dressed in work clothes approached, asked politely, "May I have this cab?" and Russian fashion, climbed into the front seat beside him.

Just then an elderly lady stuck her head in the window past the passenger and asked the driver to call her a cab.

Very politely the passenger started opening the door and said, "I will let you have this one."

"No," said the lady, "the driver can call me one."

The passenger told Whaley he wanted to go to 500 North Beckley. Everything around them was in turmoil, sirens wailing, police cars crisscrossing in all directions. "What the hell," Whaley said. "I wonder what the hell is the uproar?" The passenger did not volunteer anything. "I figured he was one of these people who don't like to talk so I never said any more to him."[22]

The man left the cab at the corner of Beckley and Neely. He handed the driver $1 for a 95 cent fare, got out, and closed the door. Whaley later identified his passenger as Lee Harvey Oswald.

It was about a six-minute walk, or a five-minute trot, to Lee's rooming house at 1026 North Beckley. He was going to get his pistol and a jacket. He arrived at 1:00 P.M. "Oh, you are in a hurry," Mrs. Roberts, the housekeeper, said. She was watching television, and wanted to talk about the shooting. But Lee did not answer her. He went straight to his room and stayed there three or four minutes. He picked up his pistol and a jacket, and was zipping up the jacket as he went out the front door. Just a few moments before, at Parkland Memorial Hospital, President John F. Kennedy had been pronounced dead of a massive injury to the head.

Back at the book depository, Roy Truly and Patrolman Baker had completed their search. They had looked through every floor except the sixth and had inspected the roof, especially the west side, the direction from which Mr. Truly thought the shots had come.

As they walked back down to the seventh floor, Baker said: "Be careful. This man will blow your head off."

"I think we are wasting our time up here," Truly answered. "I don't believe the shots came from this building."[23] But because of the way he had seen the pigeons scatter, Baker thought they did.

When the two men returned to the first floor, Truly saw policemen in clumps taking down the names of men who worked in the building. He glanced from one group to another and noticed that Lee Oswald was missing. He knew nothing about Oswald—neither that he had been to Russia and had a Russian wife nor that he was a "Marxist." Lee had told him that he was straight out of the Marine Corps. But Truly had Oswald on his mind because he had seen him just a few minutes before in the lunchroom, and now he was not with the other men.[24]

Quietly, he turned to Bill Shelley, Oswald's supervisor, and asked if he had seen him. Shelley glanced from group to group and said No. Truly picked up a phone and called the warehouse where the job application forms were kept. He obtained Oswald's full name, an accurate physical description, and his telephone number and address at the Paines'.

Truly walked over to a chief of the Dallas Police Department, who was standing a few feet away. "I don't know if it amounts to anything or not," he said, "but I have a boy missing over here."

"Just a minute," the chief said. "We will tell Captain Fritz."

They took an elevator to the sixth floor, where Captain J. W. Fritz, chief of the homicide bureau of the Dallas Police Department, appeared to be occupied by the stairway. Truly told Fritz that he had a boy missing and handed him the slip of paper on which he had written Oswald's address in Irving, his telephone number, and description.

"Thank you, Mr. Truly. We will take care of it."[25]

Captain Fritz at that moment knew something Mr. Truly did not know. Three empty brass cartridges had been found by the southeast corner window of the sixth floor. And a rifle had been found near the stairway.[26]

Fritz left the building almost as soon as he heard about the missing man. He drove to City Hall to see if the man had a criminal record. And there he got news that a police officer had been shot.

About 1:00 P.M., Dallas Patrolman J. D. Tippit was cruising the Oak Cliff area. Over his police car radio he had heard about the shooting of the President and a description of the suspect, which had been broadcast four times.[27] About 1:15, nine-tenths of a mile from the rooming house at 1026 North Beckley, Tippit spotted a man who bore a resemblance to the description. The man was rapidly walking east. Tippit slowed down and drove parallel and very close to the man. The man kept walking. Finally, when the police car was nearly grazing the curb, the man stopped. He leaned into the car, rested his arms on the open window ledge on the far side from Tippit, and the two men exchanged a few words.

The man stepped back. Meanwhile Tippit opened his door, climbed out slowly, and walked toward the front of the car. He was at the left front wheel when the other man, who was near the windshield on the right, pulled out a revolver and fired. He hit the patrolman four times, and Tippit instantly fell to the ground, dead. His cap skipped a little onto the street. The gunman started away in a trot, ejecting the empty cartridge cases from his pistol and reloading as he went. It was just after 1:16 P.M.

An automobile repairman, Domingo Benavides, was parked in his pickup truck 15 feet away when he heard three shots, watched Tippit fall to the ground, and saw the gunman empty his gun and toss the shells into some bushes as he jogged away. Benavides went to the fallen patrolman and, using Tippit's radio, reported the shooting to police headquarters. Several other bystanders had also seen the shooting and the fleeing gunman and, by 1:29 P.M., the police radio noted a similarity between the descriptions of the man who had shot Tippit and the suspect in the Kennedy shooting.

Police cars began to arrive in the area of the Tippit slaying while, eight blocks away, Johnny Calvin Brewer was in his shoe store listening to the radio. The President had been shot, and news now came over the radio that a policeman had been shot in Oak Cliff. Brewer heard sirens approach and, looking up, saw a man duck into the lobby of his store and stand with his back to the street. A police car came close, made a U-turn, and drove off. As the wail of the sirens faded, the man, who looked "scared," "messed up," and as if "he had been running," peered over his shoulder, made sure the police car had gone, then turned into the street and walked a short way to the Texas Theatre. Brewer followed him there. He asked Julia Postal, the cashier, whether she had sold a ticket to the man who had just entered the theater. "No, by golly," she said. Brewer and the usher checked the exits to make sure that none had been used, and then, in the darkness, scanned the audience. They did not see the man they were looking for. Mrs. Postal called the police.

Shortly after 1:45, fifteen police officers converged on the Texas Theatre, alerted that the suspect in the Tippit shooting might be there. Someone turned up the houselights. Accompanied by several policemen, Brewer stepped on the stage and pointed to the man who had ducked in without paying. He was sitting by himself in the orchestra, near the back, close to the right center aisle. Patrolman M. N. McDonald walked slowly up the aisle. He stopped abruptly when he came to the man and told him to get on his feet. The suspect rose, raised his hands, and said, "Well, it is all over now." He struck McDonald and reached for his own revolver. He was grabbed by two or three officers and, in the scuffle, McDonald wrenched the revolver away. The man cursed as the officers handcuffed him. "I protest this police brutality," he said.

As he was being led from the theater the man stopped, turned, and shouted so that everyone could hear him, "I am not resisting arrest—I am not resisting arrest." He was driven to police headquarters and arrived in the basement about 2:00 P.M. There were reporters milling around in case a suspect in the President's murder should be brought in. He was asked if he would like to cover his face as he was taken inside. "Why should I cover my face?" he replied. "I haven't done anything to be ashamed of."

At 2:15 P.M., Captain Will Fritz of the homicide bureau returned to police headquarters from the City Hall office where he had been checking on Lee Oswald, missing from the book depository. He walked up to two of his officers, handed them an address in Irving, and told them to "pick up a man named Lee Oswald." One of the officers pointed to the man who had just been arrested at the Texas Theatre. "Captain," he said, "we can save you a trip. There he sits."[28]

37

The Wedding Ring

MARINA AWOKE on the morning of November 22 with a strained, unhappy feeling. Something had been wrong the evening before: Lee's asking her to move into Dallas with him so insistently, her refusing, his practically kicking her in bed. There had been something nasty between them.

But she was soon distracted. Knowing Marina's fascination with the President and Mrs. Kennedy, Ruth had left the television on when she went out. Marina did not bother to get dressed. She tended to Rachel, gave cookies and milk to little June, and settled down on the sofa to watch the President. She saw him arrive at Love Field and give a speech. Jackie, dressed in a raspberry-colored suit, looked wonderful. Marina watched a rerun of a breakfast Mr. Kennedy had attended in Fort Worth. Somebody gave him a ten-gallon hat and he seemed to enjoy it.

Marina was glowing by the time Ruth returned home about noon. She said that it was a pity Ruth had missed the President's arrival. What a welcome he had had!

Ruth went into the kitchen to fix lunch and Marina went to her room to get dressed. The television set was on and suddenly Marina heard a lot of noise. Ruth ran into the bedroom, very pale, and said that someone had shot at the President. The two women dashed to the living room and stared at the set. There was no picture now, only a newsman reporting what had happened. Marina kept asking Ruth to translate. Was it very serious? Was Jackie all right? Ruth listened closely, then said the President had been taken to the hospital. There was not much news of him yet, but he had been hit in the head.

They forgot about lunch. Ruth lit some candles and she and her little girl prayed. Marina went to her room and cried. She wondered what Ruth would think of her for crying for a man who was not even her President. She prayed for the President's life, and also for Mrs. Kennedy, who might be left alone with two children.

A little later, Marina was outside hanging up clothes. Ruth came to join her and told her that the reporters were saying the shots that hit the President had come from the Texas School Book Depository. At that, Marina's heart "fell to the bottom."[1]

"Is there really anyone on earth but my lunatic husband crazy enough to have fired that shot?" she asked herself. Unlikely and unexplained occurrences suddenly started to drop into place: Lee's unannounced visit the night before, his shrugging and saying he knew nothing about the President's visit. Marina hid the fear that had seized her; she did not want to reveal it to Ruth.

She need not have worried. Ruth was not thinking that way. It had not occurred to her to connect Lee to the crime. She merely thought they knew someone in the building, close to the event, who would give them a first-hand account.[2]

Neither Ruth nor Marina had realized that the place where Lee worked was on the President's route. Ruth knew that the book depository had two warehouses and she was not certain which of them Lee actually worked in. She had copied Lee's address, 411 Elm Street, three weeks earlier for James Hosty, but she had forgotten it.

Marina was numb. She left Ruth at the clothesline and went to the house. When she was certain Ruth could not see her, she crept into the garage, to the place where Lee kept his rifle wrapped in paper inside the heavy blanket, a green and brown wool blanket of East German make that he had bought in Russia. Looking for parts to June's baby bed three weeks earlier, Marina had rolled back a corner of the blanket and spied the rifle's wooden stock. Now she found the bundle and stared at it. It was lying on the floor, below, and parallel to, a window in the garage. Marina did not touch the blanket, but it looked exactly as it had before. Thank God the rifle was still there, Marina thought, feeling as if a weight had been lifted from her. Yet she wondered if there was really "a second idiot" in Dallas, anyone else crazy enough, besides her husband, even to think of such a deed. And so, in spite of the blanket's reassuring contours, she was unable to compose herself.

She was sitting on the sofa next to Ruth when the announcement came over television that the President was dead. "What a terrible thing for Mrs. Kennedy," Marina said, "and for the children to be left without a father." Ruth was walking around the room crying. Marina was unable to cry. She could not believe the news. She felt as if her blood had "stopped running." A little later an announcement came that someone had been captured in a movie theater. No name.

An hour, or a little less, after the President's death was announced, the doorbell rang. Ruth went to answer. She was greatly surprised to find six men standing on her doorstep. They were from the sheriff's office and the Dallas police, they said, and they showed their credentials. Ruth's jaw dropped.

"We have Lee Oswald in custody," one of the policemen said. "He is charged with shooting an officer."

It was Ruth's first clue that Lee might be linked in any way to the events of the day.

The men wanted to search the house. Ruth asked if they had a warrant. They did not, but said they could get the sheriff in person. Ruth told them to go ahead and search.[3]

The men could not have been more rude. They spread out all over the house, "turned the place upside down," Marina recalls, and took everything they wanted, even records and photographs, belonging to both the Oswalds and the Paines. Marina felt like a sleepwalker, and it was hard for her later to remember what she did, or how she managed to move at all. But she was aware that her hands and her feet were cold, and her face covered with cold sweat. She glanced out the window and saw more men standing outside. They were in civilian clothes and they seemed to be wearing special insignia on the underside of their lapels. Marina was surprised to see so many of them.

"Your husband is under arrest," somebody said to her. "It's probably an accident," Marina thought. "They're picking up everyone who has been in Russia and, besides, Lee is always under suspicion."

Then came a question: "Does your husband have a rifle?" "Yes," Marina said in Russian, and led them straight to the garage, with Ruth following to translate.

Ruth, meanwhile, was telling the officers what she believed to be the truth, that Lee did not have a rifle. Whispering rapidly in Russian, Marina corrected her. She told Ruth that Lee did have a rifle, and it was inside the blanket. Forgetting her Quaker faith, her pacifism, her impeccable truthfulness, Ruth stood on the blanket in an instinctive gesture to protect Marina. At the same time, paradoxically, she faithfully translated to the officers exactly what Marina had said to her—that Lee Oswald did have a rifle, and it was inside the blanket.

The officers ordered her to step off it.

The blanket looked exactly as it always had, as if there were something bulky inside. As always, it was carefully tied in string. Marina shook all over, trying not to show her fright, as an officer stooped down to pick it up. It hung, limp, on either side of his arm.

Ruth looked at Marina. She had gone ashen.[4]

"So it *was* Lee," Marina thought. "*That* is why he came last night." For Marina it was again one of those moments when kaleidoscopic and inexplicable occurrences suddenly clicked into place. She knew now why Lee had told her to buy "everything" she and the children needed, why he had left without kissing her goodbye.

About three o'clock they went back inside the house. At that moment Michael Paine appeared.

In the cafeteria at Bell Helicopter that noon Michael had been talking to a co-op student about the character of assassins.[5] Just then a waitress came over and told them the President had been shot. Michael considered it a bad joke. Then he noticed a group of people clustered around a transistor radio and went to join them. He was unable to hear anything, but he realized that the waitress had not been joking. He returned to his lab and tuned in to the radio there. Before long, the name of the Texas School Book Depository was mentioned. Michael's heart jumped.

"Isn't that where Lee Oswald works?" Michael's fellow worker, Frank Krystinik, asked.

"I think so," said Michael. "He works for that organization."

"You don't think it would be him?" Krystinik ventured.

"No, of course not. It couldn't be him," Michael said.

For the next half hour Krystinik, who had met and talked with Oswald at the A.C.L.U. meeting on October 25, kept telling Michael that he really ought to call the FBI.

Michael resisted. Lee Oswald had been to Russia. He was already a black sheep, Michael thought, and "everybody will be jumping on him." Michael did not want "to join the hysterical mob in his harassment." He was, after all, one of the few people who stood in a position of friendship to Lee.

But Michael was nervous. He was trying to assemble a vibration meter and his fingers trembled so badly that he was unable to put in the screws. And his efforts at concentration were interrupted constantly by Krystinik, who went on urging him to call the FBI.

Michael still refused. He knew something about Lee's beliefs. And he did not, at that moment, see how the act of assassination fitted Lee's philosophy or "how it was going to forward his causes." Lee would have to be irrational to do it, and, Michael says, "I didn't think he was irrational." On the other hand, Michael knew that in principle Lee was not against violence. And so Michael did not consider such a murder automatically out of the question.

While Michael was carrying on this inner dialogue, a report came over the radio that shook him a little more. An eyewitness who had seen the assassin in the book depository window reported that the man fired "coolly," that he took "his jolly good time," and drew his rifle back inside the window "just as unconcerned as could be." To Michael, it sounded like Lee.

News reports came over the radio that the police were chasing suspects all over town. Then, less than an hour and a half after the President's shooting, there was word that a man had been captured in a place called the Texas Theatre, in Oak Cliff, for the shooting in cold blood of a Dallas police officer, J. D. Tippit. The man's name was Lee Harvey Oswald.

Michael knew that Lee had a job at the School Book Depository. And now he had been arrested in a part of town far away from where he worked for the random killing of a police officer. Years later, still trying to put distance between himself and the event, Michael said: "I realized that Lee must be uptight about something—and I'd better be getting on home."[6]

Lee had another friend whose intuition was working that day. George and Jeanne de Mohrenschildt were at a reception at the Syrian Embassy in Port-au-Prince, Haiti, when they heard that President Kennedy had been shot in their home city of Dallas. As they drove away from the reception, they wondered who on earth the assassin might be. Could it be anyone they knew?

They went to the home of a friend who worked for the American Embassy. He greeted them and told them a suspect had been captured. The name was "Lee, Lee, Lee Someone," or else it was "Somebody Lee."

All of a sudden George remembered the rifle with a telescopic sight. "Can it," he cried at the top of his voice, "be that crazy Lee Oswald?"

"Yes," said the host, to the incredulous De Mohrenschildts. "That *is* the name, I guess."[7]

The moment they discovered that Lee's rifle was missing, the police announced to Marina and the Paines that they would all have to go to police headquarters in downtown Dallas. It was plain that every one of them, Marina and the Paines, were under suspicion.

Marina, who was wearing slacks, wanted to change into a dress. "Come along, hurry up, we don't have time to wait for you," the policemen told her, and refused to allow her to change. Ruth protested, but the police not only refused to let Marina change, they also refused to allow her to use the bathroom with the door closed. Marina was angry. "I'm not a criminal," she thought. "I didn't do anything."

Soon she was outside the house, with no idea how she got there, and she was shaking all over with fright. She had her children with her, and the Paines had theirs.

On the way to Dallas in a car, Marina turned to Ruth and asked the question that was uppermost on her mind: "Isn't it true that in Texas the penalty for shooting someone is the electric chair?"

Ruth said that it was true.

Marina turned to her again. This time, with characteristic bluntness, she said: "Your Russian has suddenly become no good at all."[8]

At police headquarters, all of them were interrogated, with Ruth acting as Marina's interpreter. Marina was shown a rifle and was asked if it belonged to Lee. She hated rifles; to her they all looked alike. She knew that Lee's was dark and had a sight on it. Beyond that, she could not say. Glancing through a glass partition as the rifle was being held up in front of Marina, Michael suddenly realized what had become of the "camping equipment" he had held in his arms.

Marina was truthful in her inability to identify the rifle, but she was in a quandary over what she might be asked next, and what she ought to reply. She had no idea that Lee was charged with shooting a police officer; she had never even heard the name Tippit. She was aware only that Lee was suspected of killing President Kennedy, and she had no idea whether or not he was guilty. The facts appeared to be against him, but then, Lee was always in trouble, and Marina thought that his arrest might be a provocation or a misunderstanding. Whatever she did, she did not want to add a scintilla to any evidence the police might have against him. For behind the President, as she alone was aware, lay General Walker. Suppose Lee was cleared of killing Kennedy. They still might find out about Walker. And Marina mistakenly assumed that Lee was as likely to be put in the electric chair for an attempted murder as for murder itself.

Marina asked to see Lee. She was told that he was upstairs being interrogated and she could not see him that day.

Everything was topsy-turvy—Marina could make no sense of it at all. At first she had been offended and angered by the way the police officers had burst into

Ruth's house, ransacked everything, routed them out, and brusquely carried them off as if they were all criminals. But at the police station she felt badly frightened, and she expected to be arrested any second. That was how it would have been in Russia. Even if your husband were innocent, they would arrest you until it was straightened out. Now, inexplicably, the police were much nicer than they had been at Ruth's. One officer offered to get her coffee and another offered help with the baby. They saw her fear and tried to calm her. Even the officer who questioned her was kind. He was not harsh with her and did not try to twist her answers or catch her out in a lie. That was lucky, Marina thought. She did not want to say anything that might hurt Lee.

After the police finished questioning her, Marina saw Marguerite Oswald, Lee's mother. It was the first time Marguerite had seen Rachel—indeed, she had not known that Marina and Lee had been expecting a second child—and she greeted Marina and the children warmly. Marina also caught a glimpse of Lee's brother, Robert. He was sitting alone, very pale, with his head in his hands.

Marina has no idea how long they were at police headquarters, but eventually she, Ruth, Michael, and the four children were allowed to go back to the Paines'. She does not remember whether they ate, or what they ate, or who did the cooking. But the house was in an uproar. It was overrun by reporters who wanted to talk to Marina, Ruth, and Marguerite. Suddenly there were angry words between Ruth and Marguerite. Ruth was defending Marina's right to speak, but Marguerite would not allow it. "I'm his mother," she shrieked. "I'm the one who's going to speak." Then she told Marina that neither of them should talk to the reporters and Marina, without being told, understood her reason—money. For a while they had the television on, and Marina remembers watching Lee being led through a corridor at the police station.

Despite the shocks she had had, Marina had her wits about her. Alone in the bedroom she found June's baby book which, by some miracle of oversight, the policemen had left behind. In it were the two small photographs of Lee dressed in black and wearing his guns. He had given them to her to keep for June. Not looking at them closely, Marina thought they were two copies of the same photograph. These, she realized, were evidence. She took them out of the baby book carefully and, in the privacy of the bedroom, showed them to her mother-in-law. "Mama," she said, pointing to the photographs and explaining as best she could in English, "Walker—this is Lee." "Oh, no," Marguerite moaned, raising her hands to her head. She gesticulated a bit, put her finger to her mouth, pointed toward Ruth's room, and said, "Ruth, no." She shook her head, meaning that Marina was not to show the photographs to Ruth, or tell her anything about them.

Marina later made a terrible discovery. She happened to glance at the bureau and saw that, again by a miracle of oversight, the police had left another of her possessions behind. It was a delicate little demi-tasse cup of pale blue-green with violets and a slender golden rim that had belonged to her grandmother. It was so thin that the light glowed through it as if it were parchment. Marina looked inside. There lay Lee's wedding ring.

"Oh, no," she thought, and her heart sank again. Lee never took his wedding ring off, not even on his grimiest manual jobs. She had seen him wearing it the night before. Marina suddenly realized what it meant. Lee had not just gone out and shot the President spontaneously. He had intended to do it when he left for work that day. Again, things were falling into place. Marina told no one about Lee's ring.

Before they went to bed that night, Ruth and Marina had a talk in the kitchen. Ruth thought Marina was "stunned." Marina said that everything she had ever heard about the Kennedys came from Lee. If he had minded translating articles about them or telling her what he knew about the President, she was sure she would have known it.

Something else hurt Marina and left her bewildered. Only the night before, she told Ruth, Lee had suggested that they get an apartment together in Dallas soon. How could Lee have made such a suggestion, she wondered aloud, when he must already have been planning an act that would destroy their life together?[9]

"Do you think he did it, then?" Ruth asked.

"I don't know," Marina said.[10]

Marina did not sleep that night. All she saw before her was the electric chair. She knew nothing about American law, the long trials and appeals that might take years in the courts. She thought that it would be over in three days and that Lee would be electrocuted.

What should she do if he were tried? She thought she would have to testify and would be committing a crime if she failed to tell everything she knew. She could tell them nothing about the Kennedy shooting. But she did know about Lee's attempt on Walker. If they asked her about that, she would not be able to lie. And yet to say anything about it would be to incriminate Lee, help seal the case against him, and put him in the electric chair. To send your husband to his death—that would be a *real* crime.

Marina did not know if Lee was guilty, although the signs seemed to point that way. And so, of course, she could not know if he would confess. He might, claiming that his actions had been justified. Then again he might not. Either way, Marina thought, he would love being in the spotlight and would use it to proclaim his ideas. In his eyes, his political ideas stood higher even than himself. He would talk about Marxism, communism, and injustice all over the world.

None of this helped Marina as she tried to figure out what to do. Again and again, her thoughts came back to the electric chair. If Lee was guilty, then within three days he would be strapped in that chair and he would be dead. She herself would be in prison. What provision do they have in America, she wondered, for babies whose parents are both gone, one dead, the other in prison?

38

An End and a Beginning

THE FOLLOWING MORNING, Saturday, November 23, evidently with Marguerite's consent, reporters from *Life* magazine whisked Marina, Marguerite, and the children from the Paine house in Irving to the Hotel Adolphus in downtown Dallas. Shortly after they were installed there—with reporters and photographers from *Life*, a woman interpreter, an FBI man named Bardwell Odum, and a clackety teletype machine—Marina and Marguerite were told that they could see Lee. They went to the city jail about 1:00 P.M.

Marina had now convinced herself that Lee was innocent after all, and was under suspicion merely because he had been to Russia. His arrest had been a mistake. It would be straightened out soon.

Such thoughts were cut short the moment she caught sight of Lee. He looked pitiful, his eyes full of trouble. She could not reach out to him or kiss him because a glass partition separated them. They could talk only over a pair of telephones.

"Why did you bring that fool with you?" Lee said, glancing over at Marguerite. "I don't want to talk to her."

"She's your mother," Marina said. "Of course she came. Have they been beating you in prison?"

"Oh, no," Lee said. "They treat me fine. You're not to worry about that. Did you bring Junie and Rachel?"

"They're downstairs. Alik, can we talk about anything we like? Is anybody listening in?" Marina had folded the photographs of Lee dressed in black with his rifle and revolver and tucked them carefully inside her shoe. She had them there that very moment, and she wanted to ask Lee what to do with them.

"Oh, of course," he said. "We can speak about *absolutely* anything at all."

From his tone Marina understood that he was warning her to say nothing.

"Alka," she began again, "they asked me about the gun."

"Oh, that's nothing," he said, "and you're not to worry if there's a trial."

His voice was high and he was speaking rapidly. "It's a mistake," he said. "I'm not guilty. There are people who will help me." He explained that there was a lawyer in New York on whom he was counting for help.

His words were the old Lee, full of bravado, but Marina could tell by the pitch of his voice that he was frightened. She saw fear in his eyes and the tears started rolling down her cheeks.

"Don't cry," he said, and his voice became tender and kind. "Ah, don't cry. There's nothing to cry about. Try not to think about it. Everything is going to be all right. And if they ask you anything, you have a right not to answer. You have a right to refuse. Do you understand?"

"Yes," Marina said.

Lee had tears in his eyes, too, but he did his best to hold them back and he talked for a few minutes with his mother. Then he asked to speak to Marina again.

"You're not to worry," he said. And in words almost identical to the ones he had written her in the "Walker note," he added: "You have friends.[1] They'll help you. If it comes to that, you can ask the Red Cross for help. You mustn't worry about me. Kiss Junie and Rachel for me."

"I will," Marina promised.

The guards stood behind him now, ready to take him away, yet trying to give them an extra minute.

"Alka," Marina said. "Remember that I love you." She was telling him that he could count on her not to say anything that would betray him.

He got up and backed out of the room, edging toward the door so that he could see her until the very last second. He was saying goodbye with his eyes.

Marina was now certain that Lee was guilty. She saw his guilt in his eyes. Moreover, she knew that had he been innocent he would have been screaming to high heaven for his "rights," claiming he had been mistreated and demanding to see officials at the very highest levels, just as he had always done before. For her, the fact that he was so compliant, that he told her he was being treated "all right," was a sign that he was guilty.

Was he sorry for what he had done? Marina's impressions were mixed. Lee seemed to be closing in on himself like a sea creature, a contented mollusk or a clam, trying not to show what was inside. After the Walker affair, when he failed at what he had set out to do, he had remained keyed up and tense until the "Nixon" charade eleven days later somehow relieved him of strain. Now he was altogether different. He had succeeded. The inner tension was gone. Marina sensed in him a glow of satisfaction that she had not seen there before.

She thought that he was glad he had succeeded, and yet at the same time sorry. What he had done so impulsively could not now be undone. In spite of his obvious satisfaction, it seemed to her that he was also carrying a burden of regret heavier than he, or anyone, could bear. He was on the edge of tears all the time they were together and was barely holding them back. He did not want to break down and show himself, or his fear, to the police. And, while much of his anger was spent, Marina saw that Lee's act had failed to lift off him the inner weight he had with him all the time, nor had it made him any happier. He had looked at her, altogether uncharacteristically, with supplication in his eyes. He was pleading with her not to desert him. He was begging for her love, her support and, above all, her silence. He knew that this was the end.

Marina did not see Lee alive again. As she, Marguerite, and the children left the city jail, she was pelted with questions from reporters. "What did he say? What did he say? What did your husband say?" Some of them spoke to her in Russian. Marina did not answer. "Leave me alone," she wanted to say to them. "It is hard for me now."

Marina was tired. She had not had much sleep, and she was not accustomed to having policemen and reporters around her. She felt that everyone must be looking at her with hatred because of what Lee had done. And that was one of the heaviest things to bear, her feeling that the world was against her.

Isolated by language, not seeing television much, busy, in fact, nursing Rachel, Marina had less idea than most people what had happened to her husband since they had said goodbye on Friday morning. She did not know that on leaving the Book Depository Building with only $15.10 in his pocket, he had gone to his rooming house, fetched his pistol, and run in the direction of their old homes on Neely and Elsbeth Streets. She did not know that in the very vicinity where they had lived the previous spring, a patrolman had stopped him, and he had shot the patrolman dead. She had never heard of J. D. Tippit. It was only on Saturday that somebody told her of his murder. Until then, she knew only that her husband was suspected of killing President Kennedy.

In fact, Oswald had been suspected of killing Kennedy from the moment Captain Fritz learned that he was missing from the Book Depository Building. And when Fritz returned to police headquarters to discover that the man he was looking for was already there, he did not waste a moment. He sent a posse to the Paine house. And, in his glassed-in office on the third floor of the Police and Courts Building, he started to question Lee Oswald.

Fritz had been trying for months to obtain a tape recorder for the homicide and robbery bureau. But he had not succeeded. As a result, the only record of Oswald's twelve hours of interrogation that weekend comes from the notes and memoranda of those who happened to be present. There were seven or eight men moving in and out of the room—detectives from the homicide squad, a Secret Service inspector, a pair of FBI agents—but no one was there the entire time. If Fritz was called out to interview a witness or give an order, others picked up the questioning. "We were," Police Chief Jesse Curry said later, "violating every principle of interrogation."[2]

Despite the untranquil atmosphere, Oswald managed to keep his composure. He refused a lie detector test, appeared to anticipate questions that might incriminate him, and declined to answer them. One of the few times his calm failed him was at 3:15 P.M. on Friday, when two FBI men entered and Oswald learned that one of them was James P. Hosty. He became "arrogant and upset" and accused Hosty of twice "accosting" his wife. Fritz asked what he meant. Oswald answered that Hosty had "mistreated" his wife on two occasions when he talked to her and "practically accosted her."[3]

Hosty asked Oswald if he had been to Russia, and Oswald said Yes. Hosty then asked if he had been to Mexico City, and Oswald's composure deserted him again. "He beat his fists on the table and went into a tantrum," Fritz said later.

By 3:00 P.M. on Friday afternoon, it became known that a suspect had been apprehended, and not just Fritz's office but the entire Police and Courts Building was in an uproar. It was a policy of the Dallas police to be accessible to the press, but now, with reporters from Dallas, from all over the country, and even from abroad clamoring to get in, the guards virtually gave up trying to check press credentials. Almost anyone could get to the third floor. And among those who did was a nightclub operator named Jack Ruby who was seen there at 11:30 P.M. on Friday, and again at a midnight press conference in the basement.

The place was a tumult of reporters and cameramen, cables and tripods and television lights. Several times that day Oswald was led from Fritz's office to a basement assembly room for police lineups. He was mobbed each time. Microphones were thrust in his face and questions shouted at him. He told reporters that he demanded a shower and his "civil rights." By curious contrast, he did not complain to the police about the way they were treating him—only the press.

At 7:10 on Friday evening, Lee Harvey Oswald was brought before Justice of the Peace David L. Johnston and arraigned for the murder of Officer J. D. Tippit.

That night Gregory Olds, president of the Dallas chapter of the American Civil Liberties Union, who did not know that Oswald was a member, went to the jail to see if he wanted a lawyer. Three people—two police captains and Justice of the Peace Johnston—assured Olds that Oswald had been informed of his rights and had so far declined counsel. Just before midnight, Oswald was taken to the basement for a press conference and Olds decided to attend. During his brief appearance Oswald did protest that, at his arraignment, "I was not allowed legal representation during that very short and sweet hearing." He requested "someone to come forward and give me legal assistance." But Olds did not hear in the hubbub, and he went home.

Oswald was asked at the press conference whether he had killed the President. He replied: "Nobody has said that to me yet. The first thing I heard about it was when a newspaper reporter in the hall asked me that." It could have been Oswald's way of saying that he had tried to kill the President and this was the first he knew that he had succeeded.

On Saturday, at 1:36 A.M., Lee Harvey Oswald was brought again before Justice of the Peace Johnston and formally arraigned for the murder of John F. Kennedy.

That morning, having apparently decided during the night whom he wanted to represent him, Oswald told Fritz that he wanted a lawyer—John J. Abt of New York City. Fritz wondered why he did not want someone in Dallas. Oswald said he did not know Abt personally, but he had defended "victims" charged under the Smith Act—the 1940 law making it a crime to advocate violent overthrow of the government—and Abt was the man he wanted. Failing that, he would appeal to the A.C.L.U. However, he told Fritz, he lacked money for the long-distance call. Fritz said that he could use the prison phone and call collect. Fritz explained how to place the call and trace Abt even though Oswald lacked a telephone number or address for him.

At 1:40 P.M., just after his visit with Marina, Oswald tried to reach Abt. He succeeded in obtaining Abt's home and office numbers from the New York operator, but he failed to find him at either place. Abt was the lawyer he had told Marina about during their visit, the lawyer he was "counting on." He did not tell Marina, nor did he mention to Fritz, that John Abt was a lawyer for the U.S. Communist Party.

Fritz later asked whether Oswald had succeeded in reaching Abt. He answered that he had not, then courteously thanked Fritz for allowing him to use the prison phone.

At 4:00 P.M. on Saturday the telephone rang at the Paines'. Ruth answered. "This is Lee," said the voice at the other end of the line.

"Well, hi!" Ruth said.

Lee asked Ruth to call John Abt in New York City and request him to be his attorney. He gave her the numbers he had obtained and told her to call after 6:00 P.M., when long-distance rates went down. Ruth agreed and he thanked her.

No sooner had she hung up than the telephone rang again. It was Lee. In a word for word repetition of the call he had just made, he asked her again to call Abt.

Ruth was stunned—stunned by his gall, his assumption that her friendship for him would not have been affected by what had happened, and that she would go right on helping him just as she always had. She thought he seemed utterly "apart" from the situation he was in.[4]

Appalled and angry though she was, Ruth did try to reach Abt and, like Lee, she failed. Abt was at a weekend cabin in Connecticut.

Shortly after 5:00 P.M. on Saturday, H. Louis Nichols, president of the Dallas Bar Association, appeared in the office of Police Chief Jesse Curry. Curry was relieved to see Nichols and led him immediately to Oswald's maximum security cell on the fifth floor. Oswald was at the center of three cells with no one on either side. He was lying on his cot. He stood up to greet Nichols, and the two men talked on a pair of bunks 3 or 4 feet apart. Nichols explained that he had come to see if he wanted an attorney.

Did he, Oswald asked, know a lawyer in New York City named John Abt? Nichols said that he did not.

Well, Oswald said, that was the man he would like to have represent him. Failing that, Oswald said he belonged to the A.C.L.U. and would like someone from that organization to represent him. But if that should fall through, he added, "and I can find a lawyer here [in Dallas] who believes in anything I believe in, and believes as I believe, and believes in my innocence"—here Oswald hesitated —"as much as he can, I might let him represent me."[5]

Apparently, Oswald intended to continue trying to reach Abt himself. But he asked Nichols to return the following week and, if he had failed to find someone of his choosing, he might ask the Dallas Bar Association to find him a lawyer.

Nichols and Curry left the cell area together wondering aloud whether Curry had an obligation to reach Abt, wherever he was, even though Oswald had not asked Nichols, Curry, or Fritz to do it for him.

Oswald's choice of Abt, together with his remarks to Nichols, appear to bear out Marina's belief that her husband had every hope of making his a political trial, a forum for his ideas, at which he would either proclaim his innocence or proclaim that his deed had been justified by history.

Throughout his interrogations, Oswald made many statements about his actions on November 22 that the police already knew to be lies. He lied about his whereabouts at the time of the assassination. He lied about the rifle. And he lied about the manner of his flight from the depository building. But he talked about his political affiliations. Not only had he lived in Russia for three years, he said, but he was in touch with the Soviet Embassy and received Soviet newspapers and magazines. He mentioned repeatedly that he was a member of the F.P.C.C. and had been "secretary" of its New Orleans "chapter." He was also a member of the A.C.L.U. He claimed proudly to be a Marxist. Asked if he belonged to the Communist Party, he replied that "he had never had a card," perhaps a way of saying that his sympathies belonged to the Party, but he was not a member.

Whenever he could, Oswald steered his interrogators toward politics, and he appears to have talked more freely to Hosty than to anybody else. The views he espoused, his choice of Abt, which the policemen failed to understand since they had no idea who Abt was, together with the fact that his last two letters had been written to the Communist Party and the Soviet Embassy in Washington, are a clue to what was in Oswald's mind. Once again, as when he had shot at General Walker, he was trying to establish himself as a hero of the left. Just as at that earlier time, in April, he had in his mind a list of fantasy constituents, people and organizations with which he had been corresponding: *The Worker*, the Communist Party, *The Militant*, the Socialist Workers Party, the Soviet Embassy and government, and the F.P.C.C. and he hoped they would come to his aid.

Only one of the old constituents was missing, or rather, was distinctly less important in November than he had been in April, and that was George de Mohrenschildt. Not that Oswald had forgotten De Mohrenschildt. He had listed his name twice on job applications the previous month, and on one he had written after the name De Mohrenschildt, "best friend." De Mohrenschildt still mattered to Oswald; but he appears no longer to have been what he was before, the person for whose approval, above that of everyone, Oswald had done the deed. He was still a constituent, but a lesser one now.

Not that any of Oswald's "constituents" approved what he had done or would have come to his aid. Indeed, they hardly knew who he was. They were constituents only in Oswald's head, and he knew little more about them than he had conjured up in his imagination.

As willing as he was to expatiate about politics to his interrogators, Oswald denied having killed anyone. He had not shot "any of them," he said, adding that he did not know Governor Connally had been hit, a way of saying, perhaps, that he had not been aiming at Connally—he had been aiming at someone else.

As for the President, while giving hints, in his own way, as to the truth, Oswald outwardly, and steadfastly, denied killing John F. Kennedy. He and his wife, he said, liked the President and his family—"they are interesting people." He had his own ideas about national policy and doubted that American policy toward Cuba, for example, would change as a result of the assassination. Anyway, Oswald said, "In a few days people will forget and there will be another President."

After their visit with Lee on Saturday afternoon, Marina, Marguerite, and the children were moved from the Hotel Adolphus to the Executive Inn Motel, near Love Field. That evening, Marina dealt in her own fashion with the bothersome photographs of Lee. She removed them delicately from her shoe, tore them in two, placed them in an ashtray, and lit a match to them. She was unaware that other copies had been found by the police among their belongings in the Paines' garage. Lee had already been confronted with enlargements at the police station. Adding to his other lies, he said he had never seen the photographs before, admitting that they showed his face but with a different body.

Marina thought of one more thing. She telephoned Ruth that night, explained carefully where Lee had left his wedding ring, and asked Ruth to keep it for her.

Ruth's telephone rang one more time that night. It was 9:30 and, once again, it was Lee. But this time, unlike his two calls in the afternoon, he was speaking Russian. He did not ask Ruth if she had reached Abt. He appeared to have only one thing on his mind. It was, "Marina, please," the same abrupt words in which he had always asked for her.

Ruth explained that Marina was not staying with her. Lee was incensed. He asked Ruth to convey a message to Marina, in strong terms, that he wanted her at Ruth's. As Ruth understood it, he wanted Marina in a predictable place, wanted to know her whereabouts every second, so that she would be available to him at any moment he might try to reach her.

That night at the Dallas Police Department, Chief Jesse Curry decided to move his prisoner to the county jail the next day. His decision was in keeping with the police department's practice of transferring prisoners who have been charged with felonies from the city to the county jail. A Secret Service agent, Forrest Sorrels, asked Curry to make the transfer at an unannounced hour, possibly during the night. Curry, however, wanted to accommodate the press. No definite time was announced for the transfer, but he told waiting reporters that they would not miss anything if they were there by ten in the morning.

On Sunday, November 24, at 11:10 A.M., after another interrogation that lasted longer than expected, Oswald was ready to be transferred. But the shirt he had been wearing when he was arrested had been sent to a crime lab in Washington, and he had on only a T-shirt. Some hangers with his clothing were handed in to Fritz's office, and the officers selected what they considered the best-looking shirt for him to wear. Oswald was adamant. No, he said, and insisted on wearing a black pullover sweater with jagged holes in it. He was now dressed, as he had been in the photographs taken by Marina, all in black—black trousers and a black sweater. Fritz then suggested that he wear a hat to camouflage his looks. Once again, as he had done on entering the jail two days earlier, Oswald refused. He would let the world see who he was.

Accompanied by Captain Fritz and four detectives, Oswald was taken to the basement of the police station where he was to step into a waiting car. The basement and the ramps leading out of the building were crowded with reporters and cameramen, three television cameras, and nearly 100 policemen. Oswald reached the basement at 11:20 A.M., and was promptly led to the exit.

A few minutes earlier, Jack Ruby, carrying $2,000 in cash and a .38 caliber revolver, entered the Western Union office on Main Street, a block from the police department. At 11:17 he sent a money order for $25 to one of his nightclub strippers in Fort Worth, left the Western Union office, and headed for the police department. He walked down the Main Street ramp toward the basement without impediment. Because of his demi-monde life, Ruby was known to some of the officers and he was not even noticed. Everyone was straining to see Oswald.

Someone shouted, "Here he comes!" Along with Captain Fritz and the four detectives, Oswald walked through the door toward the car that was waiting for him. At 11:21 A.M., Jack Ruby stepped out of the crowd and fired a single, point-blank shot into Oswald's abdomen.

At 10:30 that morning, Robert Oswald met two Secret Service agents at a Howard Johnson's motel halfway between Dallas and Fort Worth. The Secret Service had recruited Peter Gregory, Marina and Lee's first Russian-born friend in the United States, to act as interpreter, and the four of them drove to the Executive Inn Motel, where Marina, Marguerite, and the children had spent the night. Marguerite appeared to be unhappy, and Robert decided to move them all to a farm owned by his wife's parents outside Fort Worth. It also occurred to him that they might be safer there.

As he was loading their belongings into his car, one of the Secret Service men came up to him. "Now, don't get excited," he said, "but we've just gotten word that Lee's been shot."

Robert did not tell Marina or his mother what had happened. He asked the Secret Service men to drive them to his in-laws' farm and left immediately for Parkland Hospital.

Marina and Marguerite had been promised a visit with Lee. So, when they and the children left the motel with the Secret Service agents and Peter Gregory, they thought they were going to the county jail. But the agents said that they could not go right away, and drove them around for what seemed to Marina to be hours. Then one of the men told them that Lee had been shot. The normally voluble Marguerite was silent. Marina asked whether Lee's wound was serious. The agents said No. They were listening to the car radio. Finally, they told

Marina that it was serious and that Lee had been taken to the hospital.

They were driven to the house of Jesse Curry to await further news. Marina remembers that the house was beautiful, that everyone was quiet and kind to her, and Mrs. Curry even brought her a glass of water. Marina sensed that it might be a few days before she returned to the Paines', and she telephoned Ruth to ask her to gather together some of her clothing, some of the children's things, Lee's wedding ring, and the money he had left her.

When she was back in the living room, Peter Gregory came up to her, and Marina could tell from his expression what he was going to say. "Marina," he said. "Get hold of yourself. He's dead."

Marina felt her heart turn to stone. So *her* children, too, were orphans, Rachel only four weeks old and June just learning to walk.

Her one thought was to see Lee. Peter Gregory tried to dissuade her. It might be dangerous, he said. There would be an angry crowd outside the hospital and she had no right to risk the children. Marina surmised that it was his own life Gregory feared for. She did not wish to place him in danger, but she and Marguerite were agreed. "We're going," Marguerite said.

The doctors at the hospital were kind, but they did not want Marina to see Lee. "He doesn't look good," one of them said. "It's terrible," said another. "We don't want you to see."

Lee did look terrible. His face was yellow and unshaven, and his nose stuck out. Marina wanted to see the wound that had killed him, she *had* to see it, but he was covered by a sheet. She reached out to lift the sheet away, and someone arrested her arm. So she kissed Lee and touched his hand. It was like ice.

Marina was angry as well as sad. "In Russia," she thought, "it wouldn't have happened. They would have taken better care of him."

From Parkland Hospital, the Secret Service drove all of them, including Robert, to a new hideaway, the Inn of the Six Flags, near Fort Worth. Word had come from the Attorney General, Robert Kennedy, and the new President, Lyndon Johnson, that the Secret Service was to protect the Oswald family. Within an hour the inn was an armed camp, with men patrolling outside armed with carbines. "All we need is to have one more of you killed," one agent said, "and we're in real trouble."

Marina was unable to eat. Although the agents solicitously brought her food, she only smoked and drank coffee. Robert cried, and little June was sick. And, all afternoon and evening, they were not allowed to watch television or see the newspapers. They were wholly cut off from the outside world.

Except for one thing. It had fallen to Robert to arrange Lee's funeral.[6] It was not easy. One cemetery after another refused even to countenance the suggestion that they sell Robert a plot for his brother's body. A funeral director took up the search and finally found a cemetery in Fort Worth.

The same thing happened with ministers. Four of them turned Robert down. The office of the National Council of Churches in Dallas asked two Lutheran ministers to go to the inn and offer help. Only one dared visit Robert in person. The funeral was arranged for four o'clock Monday afternoon, and the minister, with a hesitation that to the grief-stricken Robert was all too apparent, reluctantly agreed to officiate.

On Monday morning, Marina heard that President Kennedy's funeral was being shown on television. She whispered to Robert that she wanted to watch, and Robert switched on the set. A Secret Service man switched it off.

"No," said Marina, "I watch."

And watch she did, right up to the moment when she left to attend Lee's funeral.

The Oswalds arrived at Rose Hill Cemetery in Fort Worth to find it, too, heavily guarded, with policemen stationed all along the fence that surrounded the burial ground. They drove to the chapel, expecting to have a religious ceremony. They found the chapel empty and unprepared. They realized with a shock that all they were to be allowed was a hurried service at the grave.

Robert had forgotten to select pallbearers. Without the family's knowing it, a group of reporters who were covering the funeral volunteered. It was they who, even before the Oswalds arrived, had carried Lee's body down from the chapel to its grave.

Word arrived that the Lutheran minister who had promised to officiate would not be there after all. But a minister named Louis Saunders of the Council of Churches in Fort Worth had driven out on his own to Rose Hill Cemetery to see if he could help the family. It was the Reverend Saunders who pronounced the simple words of Lee's funeral ceremony.

Marina was humiliated. It had been furtive and meager.

That night, the lowest of her life, Marina received a telegram. She could not imagine who had sent it, unless a friend in Russia. It was from a group of American college students. Marina could hardly believe the words Peter Gregory read to her:

We send you our heartfelt sympathy. We understand your sorrow and we share it. We are ashamed that such a thing could happen in our country. We beg you not to think ill of us. You have friends and we are with you.

There was a long list of names at the end.

It was Marina's first hint that in the life ahead of her she did not have to be an outcast.

Epilogue

After Lee's funeral, Marina expected to go on living at Ruth Paine's. But
Robert Oswald was firmly against it. He had taken one look at Ruth and
Michael Paine at the Dallas police station on the afternoon of November
22 and decided that if Lee had indeed killed President Kennedy, then
these tall Eastern stringbeans, whom he had never heard of as being
friends of his brother, must be behind it somehow. The Secret Service
men who were assigned to protect Marina seconded Robert's advice.
Ruth was not under suspicion, they said, but she and Michael were active
in the A.C.L.U., an organization many Americans considered left-wing.
Moreover Michael was under a special cloud, the nature of which was
not made clear, but which seems to have derived from the fact that his
father had once been a Trotskyite. Marina was allowed to understand
that if she wished to remain in the United States, she had better put
distance between herself and the Paines. Thus in one of the first acts of
her widowhood Marina did what she had sworn she would never do—she
turned her back on Ruth Paine.

Marina was incommunicado, living at the Inn of the Six Flags Motel
and cut off from everyone except government agents and members of
the Oswald family when, on November 30, 1963, Ruth took to the Dallas
police station two books in Russian that Marina had often used and

which Ruth thought she might need. One was on baby care, the other a book of household advice on matters such as cooking and sewing. On December 2, two Secret Service agents confronted Ruth with a Russian-language note which had been found inside of one of the books, and accused her of having tried to convey a secret message to Marina. Ruth had never seen the note before. On December 5, Marina herself was confronted with the note, which proved to be the one Lee had left for her on the night he tried to shoot General Walker.

Marina had previously decided not to say anything about the Walker attempt, and she had forgotten the note entirely. She was still distraught by Lee's death and felt that she ought to be all the more on his side since he was dead. Besides, Walker was still alive and the attempt had come to nothing. She freely admits to being "tricky" with the FBI in those days, and Robert Oswald says that from the outset the FBI was "extremely hostile" toward her.[1] In any case, she explains, "Lee had too many murders on his soul already." She would be a witness against him if she had to be, but only where she thought it really mattered.

With the discovery of the note, however, Marina had no choice but to add to the weight of evidence against her husband. She then blamed Ruth for the fact that she had been compelled against her wishes to go into the Walker affair, and she used this as a rationalization for having severed their communications. But it would not wash, and Marina came to feel overpoweringly guilty about two things: her failure to go to the police "after Walker," and turning her back on Ruth. The barrier of guilt became so high that Marina was unable to take steps to mend the breach between them, although it would have eased her conscience to do so.

Ruth for her part felt that Marina had not dealt squarely with her; she ought to have told her, while she was living in her house, about the Walker attempt, the trip to Mexico, and the rifle in her garage. Knowledge of these things, Ruth said afterwards, would have altered her behavior toward the Oswalds. Still, Ruth missed Marina's friendship, and would probably have repaired the breach if she could have.

They were very different people: Marina all intuition, Ruth all conscience and consideration. Marina was on edge with women who were a little older than she, even though she needed them, and she held against Ruth the fact that she had no faults. Marina was not at ease with flawless people and was certain that eventually she would lose their good opinion. But she says that she and Ruth were "close." They confided completely in each other about their marriages, if not about other things, and Marina has said that she herself "suffered" over Ruth's unhappiness with Michael. She also tried to alter Lee's attitude toward Ruth for the better. And she and Ruth were a real source of moral support to each other during the spring and fall of 1963. Despite the very large differences between them as human beings, there was more to their friendship than Marina at first allowed herself later to admit.

It was not only the Walker affair that Marina would have preferred to keep secret. Less than a week after the assassination, she was confronted with copies of the photographs she had taken of Lee with his rifle. Marina was very much aware that she had destroyed the same photographs, not knowing that there were other copies in the Paines' garage, and at first she denied knowing anything about them. She was then assured that nothing she said about the photographs would be held against her, and she also realized that unless she told what she knew, someone else might be unjustly accused of having taken them. She then told the truth.

On November 29, 1963, and again on January 17 and 22, 1964, Marina also denied any knowledge of Lee's trip to Mexico, although soon afterwards she told what she knew about that, too. She explained her reluctance on this score by saying that she continued to hate the FBI for pestering her and, in her bad moods, she could not refrain from showing it. She still felt loyal to Lee and, thinking in a manner that was very like Lee, she said to herself that if the FBI was so clever, "let them find out for themselves." While she realized that it would not be easy to reverse herself on the Mexico trip, Marina also confided that she had been hoping to save up a morsel or two as a special surprise to tell the Warren Commission on her first appearance before it in February.

There was still another matter on which Marina held out—Lee's threat to kill Nixon. At first she forgot all about it, since it had led to nothing, and Robert says that she first mentioned it to him on January 12, 1964. When she spoke of it to James Martin, manager of the Inn of the Six Flags Motel, on whom she had come to rely, he advised her "to try not to think about these things too much." But Marina's feeling that she ought to protect Lee was fading and it was not long before she also told about the Nixon episode.

With no place else to go, Marina considered living with Marguerite. But Robert once more was against it. It will go all right for a week, he said, but after that. . . . Marina took his advice. By default, she moved first to the home of James Martin and his wife and children, and he became for a time her business manager. Marina needed help of this kind, for she received film, magazine, and book contract offers from all over Europe and America and, in addition, kind-hearted Americans simply sent her money in the mail. About $70,000 reached her in this fashion. Late in the winter, however, there was a break between Marina and Martin, and Marina moved briefly to Robert's, then to the Fords', and finally, using the money which had been sent to her and which she had received for interviews, she bought a modest home of her own in the Dallas suburb of Richardson.

Marina's fears that she would be sent to prison—for failing to prevent the assassination, omitting to go to the police after Walker, and burning the photographs of Lee—gradually faded, but for months she remained afraid that she still might be sent back to Russia. Marina did not, of course, want to go. But her feelings were contradictory—and typical. She had always behaved toward the Soviet Embassy in Washington in filial fashion and had even sent the embassy a New Year's card from herself and Lee at the end of 1962. Now that she, a daughter of the Soviet Union, was in trouble, she was puzzled and hurt that no one from the embassy came forward to offer sympathy and ask her how she was bearing up. Marina did not see why her own government would have nothing to do with her.

If she was at a loss to understand the political realities that surrounded her, Marina's understanding of the human factors was clear. She never could bring herself to be angry at Jack Ruby, for example, and, when Ruby went on trial, she wrote a letter to the prosecutor asking, as Lee Oswald's widow, that his life be spared. Marina did not believe in "an eye for an eye." There had been too much killing already, and the taking of one more life would not bring anybody back—not Kennedy, nor Tippit, nor Lee.

Marina hated what Lee had done to President Kennedy and to Officer Tippit, and she worried about their widows and children. Even as she read articles about them and sympathized with them, however, she went to painful lengths not to blame Lee for what he had done to *her,* leaving her, a Russian who was unable to speak English, alone, widow of the President's assassin, in a suspicious if not hostile country, almost untouchable. The most she could bring herself to say was, "Lee had a right not to think about me. Maybe he didn't love me. But he was *obliged* to think about the children."

Marina in the early days was like a person in the eye of a storm, with wreckage around her on every side, but in the poorest position of anyone to assess what had happened. First, the shock was too great, and the event itself, the President's death and her own involvement in it, too immense and too improbable to absorb. Second, she was alone in her bereavement, for the man she was mourning was the nation's Number One enemy, a man whose very name caused embarrassed silence to fall across any room she happened to be in. Apart from her brother-in-law, Robert, who was there to join her in mourning him, or enter into her feelings at all? Finally, she was also grief-stricken over President Kennedy, the nation's Number One martyr, and there was something a little strange and out of kilter in Marina's grieving simultaneously, in an utterly personal way, over both the President and his assassin. But isolated as she was in Texas, Marina was at odd angles to reality, and there was no way of being with her continuously without joining her in the upside-downness of her world.

When I first met her in June of 1964, the air around her was still thick with Texas promoters in their black suits and two-tone Italian silk shirts, proposing deals in which they would exploit Marina and she, her predicament. One offer was that she would be paid to tour the country with Lee's body. Because it fitted so perfectly her own low view of herself, this proposal, and others that were equally outlandish, did not offend Marina nearly as much as they might have. And there were situations, some of which had to do with magazine or television interviews, in which Marina went to the opposite extreme and tried to drive a hard bargain because she knew nothing about "business" and did not want to be taken for "naïve" and a "little Russian fool." Marina trusted no one in those days. Above all, she did not trust herself.

For ten months she spent hundreds of hours being interrogated, first by the Secret Service and then, increasingly, by the FBI. She liked Wallace Heitman, the FBI man who came most frequently to see her and treated her like his own daughter. But Marina never did surmount her fear of the FBI, and any visit from one of its agents, even Mr. Heitman, made her feel sick all day ahead of time in apprehension.

Besides, the endless questions she was asked had mostly to do with "hard" evidence. At what time had Lee come home on a certain night, or, where had he buried his rifle? Such questioning was of no help to Marina in coming to terms with the questions that were peculiarly hers, questions of the emotions, questions of guilt and responsibility. Indeed, the lengthy hours of interrogation tended to submerge the very difficulties that were troubling her the most, and Marina had critics, especially among her former Russian friends, who thought that she did not behave with sufficient dignity, or as if she felt her proper share of responsibility.

Indeed, Marina became a little wild, taking only fitful care of her children and spending as many waking hours as she could on escapades with boyfriends and neighbors, on all-night bowling sprees, and on well-publicized sorties to a Dallas nightclub called the Music Box, where she was soon a favorite. Aware of her self-destructiveness, Marina calls 1964 her "second Leningrad period." Having an abased view of herself already, she was unable to absorb the notion that, as a helpless and pretty Russian widow with two children, there was a reservoir of sympathy for her among the American people. Marina would have been incredulous if she had known this and would have been driven to destroy a good public image if she had suspected that she had one.

As it was, she courted scandal, and apparently wanted to plummet into danger and disgrace and carry everyone she knew down with her. Marina, better than anyone, understood the downward spiral in her behavior, lacking not the insight but the will to arrest it. And, as always, she had boyfriends. They were from various walks of life and some, out of bemusement at her quicksilver ways, or perhaps in a spirit of noblesse oblige, would gladly have lifted her from her outcast state and raised her a few rungs up the ladder of what Marina calls "culture." But she contrived not to marry them. Once again, her opinion of herself was so low that she simply could not risk placing herself in a position in which she would have to sustain the world's regard.

During that year of 1964, Marina had reason to fill her waking hours with activity, for her dreams when she was asleep were harrowing. Sometimes she was looking for Anatoly, but once she found him, he might turn out to have the character of Lee. Most of her dreams, however, appear to have reflected a feeling that she was Lee's "keeper." In one dream she dragged him up a marble staircase and shoved him into an elevator to get him away from a mob that would have killed him. Always there was a mob, and always the two of them were together. Once, when they had been running from a crowd, Lee, with his old nonchalance, seated himself on the grass to drink a cup of tea. Suddenly Marina looked over at him—and he was gone. Lee had vanished into the ground.

For more than a year after he died, perhaps because she was angry at Lee, yet unwilling to blame him for abandoning her, Marina was unable to speak to him in her dreams, or he to her. Finally, when most of the government questioning was over and the interviewing for this book nearly done, she had a dream in which Lee told her in Russian that he loved her and Marina was able to answer. She was happy the whole day after that.

Marina's trouble, of course, was that long after Lee was dead she loved him and wanted him back. Her most prized possession was a miniature straw donkey which he had brought her from Mexico. It had cost him only five cents, but to Marina it was a treasure. Then, in June of 1964, seven months after Lee died, she had a terrible shock. Without her knowing about it in advance, the Dallas *Morning News* published Lee's "Historic Diary." Marina had watched as Lee wrote the Diary in Minsk and had listened to him as, writing, he sang the theme song from *High Noon.* But she had not read the Diary and, even after Lee died, nobody told her the contents. Only now did she learn what Lee had written—that he had married her to get even with another woman. Marina had known about Ella Germann and had even seen her, but she had never had any inkling that Lee's motive in marrying *her* had been to avenge himself on Ella. It was as cruel a blow as any she had suffered, for it caused her to call into question the validity of every one of her private memories—above all, the memory that Lee had loved her the best he knew how.

So great was her hurt and humiliation that for two months after publication of the Diary she did not mention Lee's name if she could help it and she never did speak of him in quite the same way again. Marina learned to hold herself erect for new and cruel revelations. It was as if she was afraid of speaking, even privately, about moments of tenderness between them lest suddenly it be proven in public that Lee had never loved her at all. Marina's view of Lee, and of the two of them, had been altered forever.

Even his bringing her breakfast in bed, his great indulgence and one of which she had been proud, now appeared not to have been proof of Lee's love, but merely insurance against that far-off day when, intending to slip out and kill someone, he would not want her to see him go. As for his plan to send her back to Russia, that, too, fell into place. Marina saw that she had been only a pawn that Lee moved across the chessboard of his life merely to make his travels easier. She was convinced that anyone who could use another so could not, ever, have loved that other person. Her awareness hurt her the more because it fitted so exactly the abased view of herself which she had had all along—that she was nothing.

Luckily for Marina, she did grow outraged at Lee, although she has never, on her own account, been as angry at him as I think she has a right to be. I asked her if Lee had once had a sense of right and wrong, but then lost it. Marina was furious. Lee had no moral sense at all, she said. Only egotism, anger at others on account of his failures, and inability to understand his mistakes. Although she saw that his act in killing the President had in part "a political foundation," she refused to countenance the idea that Lee gave any thought, ever, to the good of anyone but himself. Yet, displaying once again her feeling that she as

Lee's wife was responsible for him, she said, referring to the assassination, that, "If he came back to earth and I could talk to him, I'd give him such a scolding that he would die all over again."

Marina was stuck with her Russian, "brother's keeper" mentality that if your "comrade" commits a crime and you have failed to prevent it, then you are as guilty as he. Clearly, she felt guilty that she had failed to report Lee to the police after Walker, and she felt that guilt so strongly that it obscured such feelings of responsibility as she might have had on any other score. Had she informed on Lee then, he would have had a terrible fright. And had he been convicted of the attempt, he might have been in prison in November and Kennedy would have been saved.

As for November 21, the evening before the assassination, when Lee asked her to move with him to Dallas, Marina did not berate herself for her refusal because she had had no idea what Lee was planning. She did not have a clue that she and a pair of curtain rods were being weighed in his mind against the President of the United States and a rifle. Had she had any hint, not only would she have agreed to move to Dallas, she would have locked Lee in the bathroom and Ruth would have called the police. And there was another side to that evening. Lee was an expert manipulator. He knew how to get his wife back—indeed, he had done so one year before when she ran away from him and he wanted her back in time for Thanksgiving at Robert's on November 22, 1962. Had Lee, on November 21, 1963, genuinely wanted Marina back, he knew how to arrange it—the telephone call in advance, a little cajoling, believable tenderness. It seems a fair guess that, unhinged as he must have been, Lee still, on November 21, knew how to obtain the answer "Yes."

There is one other score on which Marina might have felt guilt, and that was on the matter of her former suitor, Anatoly. During our conversations Marina often spoke about her feelings for Anatoly and the President and observed that they looked alike. She had not, she said, mentioned the resemblance to Lee, and evidently it did not occur to her that by her talk of Anatoly she might unintentionally have given Lee a shove, one of a good many he had, in the direction of President Kennedy as a target. It is strange that Marina, attuned to the world of unconscious motives as she is, failed to perceive this. But there is an indication that, at some level, perhaps she did understand. Throughout our seven months of interviews, Marina was unable to recollect Anatoly's surname. Yet she had thought of marrying him, and she had written to him, surname and all, in January of 1963. A few weeks after we finished work she remembered it and telephoned from Texas to tell me the name. But her guilt feelings, if any, on this point, appear to have remained buried and unconscious to this day.

Apart from "Walker," Marina's feelings of responsibility are diffuse. She knew after April 1963 that Lee was capable of killing and was "sick," but she did not know what to do. She blamed herself for having married him when he was still too young for the responsibility. She blamed herself for treating him, during their New Orleans summer, with too much "pity" and "compassion." But from the middle of July in New Orleans until the visits of Agent Hosty in November, Lee had appeared to be getting better. Marina thought he would "outgrow his youth and trouble." Later, of course, she blamed herself bitterly for her failure to be "strict" enough with him.

George Bouhe was much gentler. He was to say later that it did not matter what Marina said or did, for "Lee did not pay the slightest attention to her anyway." And Ruth Paine, who had been a witness to the last weeks, took a still kinder view. "Marina was a rock to Lee, " she says. "She was his reality test always. Had it not been for her, he would have gone off into fantasy long before he did." A Dallas woman in whom Marina was to confide afterward agreed with Ruth that "immature" as both of them had been, Lee and Marina had their good times, and there had been "much good" in the marriage.

I have often asked Marina whether Lee might have been capable of joining with an accomplice to kill the President. Never, she says. Lee was too secretive ever to have told anyone his plans. Nor could he have acted in concert, accepted orders, or obeyed any plan by anybody else. The reason Marina gives is that Lee had no use for the opinions of anybody but himself. He had only contempt for other people. "He was a lonely person," she says. "He trusted no one. He was too sick. It was the fantasy of a sick person, to get attention only for himself."

Those who knew Lee in Dallas agree with her. "I'd have thought it was a conspiracy," one of the Russians says, "if only I hadn't known Lee." Another says, "Lee couldn't have been bought—not for love, not for money, and not for the sake of a political plot." These people think, as Marina does, that Lee acted on impulse and first thought seriously about killing the President only a day or two before he did it.

But a few of those who knew Lee have altered their sense of him over the years and, as they read about plots to kill Castro, gangland killings, and cover-ups by the FBI and the CIA, they have come to wonder whether Lee might not have been part of a conspiracy after all. Not Marina. She has kept intact her sense of Lee as she knew him. She has not heard all the conspiracy theories by any means, but she is humorous, commonsensical and nearly always incredulous at those that do come her way. She dismisses any notion that Lee knew his killer, Jack Ruby. "How could Lee have known Ruby?" she asks. "He didn't drink, he didn't smoke, he didn't go to nightclubs and, besides, he was sitting home with me all the time."

A year or so ago I told Marina about another rumor, a rumor that there had been "two Oswalds," or possibly more, one in Russia, another, or perhaps several, in America, and that some of these "Oswalds" together accomplished the assassination. Marina, who is usually quick with a retort, took a few seconds to absorb this. Then she was rather reproachful. "Really, Priscilla," she said, "with your own husband, wouldn't you know whether you were living with the same person this week as you were living with last!"

Perhaps more than anyone whose life was brushed by the assassination, Marina is encapsulated by time, her perceptions virtually unjarred by the events that happened after. Today she lives outside Dallas on a seventeen-acre farm, with cattle on it, with Kenneth Porter, whom she married in 1965. They were divorced in 1974, but they continue to live together as man and wife. Kenneth loves life on the farm, and he is an expert mechanic, "one of the best," Marina says. He is a handsome man, and a devoted stepfather, a fact which Marina, after her own difficult childhood, values greatly. Marina has retained all her old intuitiveness and candor, and these qualities mark her relationships within the family—with Kenneth, with June and Rachel, who are now fifteen and thirteen, respectively, and with whom she enjoys excellent, if not unruffled, communications, and with her eleven-year-old son, Mark Porter.

Russian that she is and remains, Marina loves nature. She has a vegetable garden, Kenneth has built her a greenhouse for her ferns, and she grows such trees and flowers as she can in the scorching Texas sun. But Marina dreams of Russia more often than she used to, and she begs Kenneth to take her some day to a place where she can see birch trees again. And, more than she used to, she thinks about her stepfather, Alexander Medvedev, who is alive and remarried and living in Leningrad. She especially misses Petya and Tanya, the brother and sister in Leningrad whom she has no hope of seeing again.

Marina grew up in hard times, and she has survived them. But her life since the assassination, as before it, has not been an easy one. Marina ascribes her discontent to her lifelong feeling that she was "special," the feeling that caused her to marry Lee. She also feels that something is missing in her life. "I came to America," Marina says, "and I lost my way." Mostly she blames herself. Some day, she says, she hopes she will feel better about herself, will feel that she is worth something. But she feels powerless to change her fate.

Moreover, no matter how obscure the lives which they try to lead, Marina, Kenneth and the children receive constant jolts from the past. Thus Marina, like many others, was shocked when, at the end of March 1977, George de Mohrenschildt committed suicide after proclaiming to a foreign journalist that he had conspired with Lee Oswald to kill the President. There was no truth to this—George and Lee had not seen one another for seven and one half months prior to the assassination and had not exchanged letters. And George himself, in a letter to a friend shortly before he died, lamented what he had written during the last year of his life as "stupidities."[2] Marina as usual put her finger on it when she remarked how odd it was that someone with so much vitality, someone who seemed to represent life, should have died by his own hand.

Marina liked the De Mohrenschildts. While she was married to Lee, it was she whom they apparently liked better at first, and later on they preferred Lee. But they never seemed critical of her until a year or so after the assassination, when during an interview on a nationally broadcast television program for which they were paid, they said that Marina had been bitchy to Lee and that her goading helped drive him to kill the President. Very soon after that, and thirteen years before De Morenschildt actually died, Marina dreamt that both George and Jeanne committed suicide.

All these years, however, Marina has praised the De Mohrenschildts. She agrees with George's friend, Samuel Ballen, that George represented sunshine and life and warmth to Lee. And while she does not go as far as Ballen, who felt that if George had been in Dallas in November 1963, the assassination might not have taken place, she does believe with Ballen that George had, on the whole, a good influence on Lee. True, she thinks that something George said prompted Lee to shoot at General Walker, but she is certain that it was not intentional. George was a "peaceful" man, she says. He had lost his own birthright by violence, and he of all men would have thought it "uncivilized" to foist his views on anybody else, much less to do so by killing. And, indeed, long after Kennedy was dead, George showed no sign of feeling guilty about his relationship with Lee. A friend who visited him in Haiti shortly after the assassination reported, "George went around planting his seed in many women. If he planted a seed, another kind of seed, in Lee Oswald, I don't think it bothers him very much."[3]

But when George returned from Haiti in the late 1960s, his life had changed once again for the worse. He had failed to pull off the big coup in sisal or oil that he had counted on. His book on his Central American adventures had been refused by several publishers. And, as always, George was feeling financial pressure. Having spent his life among tycoons, he had never been able to earn as much as he felt he needed. His relations with Jeanne became bitter. They divorced, but they went on living together, estranged from everyone they knew. Jeanne had a job, while George taught French at a small black college in Dallas. His sole remaining tie to the once-familiar world of the rich and famous was his link with the Kennedy assassination, which existed by virtue of his and Jeanne's emeritus "stray dog," Lee Oswald. A decade or so after the assassination, as his spirits sank into depression, George started to feel guilty in retrospect, his relationship with Lee apparently assuming even greater importance in his mind than it had had in reality.

Sam Ballen, who saw him in Dallas only one month before he died, found George "beating himself pretty hard." He berated himself for friendships he had lost and opportunities he had tossed aside and said that his life had been a failure. He had been an "idiot," he said, to act in a joking and cavalier fashion in his appearance before the Warren Commission. And he was worried about the people he had injured, especially Lee Oswald and the young rancher, Tito Harper.[4] But it was Lee Oswald about whose "sick mind" George was worried most. He had allowed Lee to make a hero and a father of him. He had known it, had basked in it, had tolerated it for a while. But now he thought it "frivolous" and "irresponsible" to have done so. And he was seized with guilt over whether something he had done or said, something "childish" and "sophomoric," might have influenced Lee in what he did.[5] George was "gripped by remorse."

Ballen, who had not seen De Mohrenschildt in years, came away from their meeting feeling sad. For all his faults, of which the greatest was his "utter irresponsibility," George was, Ballen believed, "one of the world's great people." He tried to reassure George. He invited him to come to Santa Fe and offered him the kind of rough, outdoor work that seemed likely to help George the most. Afterwards Ballen looked back with the feeling that he had been dining with "Hemingway before the suicide."

If De Mohrenschildt belatedly, and in illness, began to wonder what his responsibility might have been, what about Marina? She, too, has been alone for years with the question, Why? Why did Lee do it? For the overwhelming fact, the fact she mentions again and again, was that Lee liked President Kennedy. He frequently said that for the United States at this moment of its history, Kennedy was the best possible leader, just as Khrushchev was for Russia. Whenever Marina pointed out how handsome the President was, Lee agreed with her. And when she mentioned how beautiful Mrs. Kennedy was, he agreed again. He agreed, moreover, without the special edge of reserve that told her he was thinking something else. And when the Kennedys' baby died in the summer of 1963, he had been as upset as she.

Yet Lee had killed Kennedy, and Marina intuitively felt that he had done it the moment she heard the School Book Depository mentioned as the place from which the shots had originated on the afternoon of November 22. She felt it again when the rifle proved to be missing from the Paines' garage, and she saw guilt in Lee's eyes when she visited him in the Dallas police station. But she could not understand Lee's motive and it was nearly a year before she unequivocally accepted not only that Lee had killed Kennedy, but that he had intended to do so. Indeed, she came closer to accepting his intention at the beginning than she was to do later. During her first appearance before the Warren Commission in February 1964, Marina gave it as her opinion that Lee had killed the President, that his act had had a "political foundation," and also that he had wanted to make himself famous. On her second appearance, in June of 1964, she again gave it as her view that Lee had killed the President, but mentally she kept the reservation that perhaps he had meant to kill Governor Connally instead. She did not mention this because she thought that the Commission did not care to hear her speculations. Finally, in September 1964, shortly before the Warren Report was to be issued, Marina threw the Commission into confusion by testifying that Lee had liked the President so much, she thought it must have been Connally he was aiming at. (Lee's remarks about Connally had been mixed, but he had also said that he liked Connally and that he would vote for him.)

After her last appearance before the Commission, some Secret Servicemen took Marina to dinner. They told her that while President Kennedy had been sitting directly behind Connally at the moment the first shot was fired, this was no longer the case by the time of the final, fatal shot. Kennedy had been wounded by then and was leaning toward his wife. He was no longer in alignment with Governor Connally. Thus the man who fired the final shot could only have been aiming at Kennedy. Marina then accepted the fact that Lee not only had killed the President, as she had thought all along, but that for some reason which she has difficulty compassing to this day, he had actually intended to do so.

Marina did have a key that helped her to understand the reason why.

It went back to November 21, the day before the assassination, when, as she was to recall later, Lee had done everything in threes. That afternoon he tried to kiss her three times, and the third time she reluctantly acceded. But the memorable thing had been his asking her, three times, to move in to Dallas with him "soon." If she agreed, he would find an apartment "the next day." And three times Marina refused.

Marina knew that her husband attributed an altogether magical significance to the number three and was obsessed by it. She remembered that one year earlier, on November 11, 1962, when the De Mohrenschildts took her away from Lee because of his violence toward her, then, too, he had begged her three times not to leave him, but after the third time he gave up. And on the bottom right-hand corner of the Fair Play for Cuba Committee card on which he had asked her to forge the name "A. J. Hidell" the previous summer, he had written the number "33," to signify that he was the thirty-third member of his fictitious chapter—still another sign of the power he attached to the number three.[6]

Marina had known of the peculiar importance which her husband attached to the number three from the outset of their marriage when Lee often used to sneak off to see the film version of the opera based on Pushkin's short story, "The Queen of Spades." In Minsk, he played music from the opera every night and, while listening to his favorite aria ("I would perform a heroic deed of unheard-of prowess for your sake . . . "), he fell into a reverie and imagined that he was the hero, Hermann. A young Russian Guards officer during the 1820s, Hermann thought that his life was determined by the powers of fate and was obsessed by the number three. Avid for money, he obtained what he believed to be the secret of three cards which, played one after the other, would win him a fortune at the gaming table. Hermann played the three cards, staked his love and his whole life on them—and lost.

Marina believes that on the evening of November 21 Lee was again seized by the fantasy that he was Hermann. That is why he asked her three times if he might kiss her and three times if she would move in with him to Dallas. Like Hermann, he staked his life on three cards. And, like Hermann, he lost.

The more Marina thought about it, the more she had to conclude, although she came to it reluctantly and with pain, that Lee had not fully made up his mind what he was going to do when he came to see her that evening, but as a result of what passed between them—her three "no's"—he had done so by the time he left. Or perhaps he had made up his mind and was asking her to veto his decision. He was begging her to move in to Dallas with him so he would not have to go through with the terrible deed. Lee was asking Marina to save his life for him. And she, by refusing what he asked of her, failed to save him from his fate.

But Marina had no way of knowing what Lee was thinking, for he had given her no hint. It was her ignorance, and her helplessness before it, that she was to ponder afterwards. If Marina can be said to have failed Lee, it is not, as some people thought later, that she ought to have known what he was thinking and sent him frivolously to his death. It is, rather, that she, too, was fated—by her lifelong conviction that she was unworthy and by uncertainty over his affections—to refuse his request. Preoccupied by worries such as these, she failed altogether to realize what Ruth Paine called "her own great power over Lee."

The way Lee saw it, perhaps fate did have a hand. To such a man, the uncanny selection of a route that would carry the President right under his window could mean only one thing. Fate had singled him out to do the dangerous but necessary task which had been his destiny all along and which would cause him to go down in history. If Lee really felt this way, really felt the outcome was fated, then Marina's power on November 21 was not great, since he was destined to put his questions to her in such a way that she was destined to refuse.

But Lee was more than Pushkin's Hermann, playing a role marked out for him by fate. He was a Marxist, and, as a Marxist, he was also enacting a part that had been determined ahead of time. For Marxism is a determinist philosophy, which says that the course of history is decided in advance and such choices as an individual may make have little to do with the outcome. According to Marxism, it made no difference what Lee did on November 22—history would grind on and turn out in more or less the same manner anyhow. Lee was a poor Marxist in another way as well, for Marxist philosophy repudiates the kind of terroristic act he had in mind.[7] But Lee took his Marxism selectively. And, according to his Marxism, history would be moved forward by his deed and the Marxist cause would be advanced.

It is ironic, yet in keeping with Lee's rigid nature, that he had chosen not one but two determinist philosophies by which to live and to die. According to one, he was Pushkin's Hermann, who staked his life on the toss of three cards and, according to the other, he was the implacable engine of history. Both as Hermann the fatalist and as Lee Harvey Oswald the implausible Marxist, Lee had no choice but to do as he did. It happened that the two roles came together at the same moment to demand the same thing of him.

Yet accident did play a role, in the timing, for example. Lee had already attempted one assassination. But he did not go around killing every day, nor was he capable of it all the time. By chance, the President's visit came at a moment when Lee was insane enough so that he needed to kill someone and coherent enough to succeed.

And the President came to him. Compared to the route, no other determinant mattered at all. Everything that had ever happened to Lee Oswald could have happened in exactly the way it had, his whole life could have been exactly what it had been, and it would not have made any difference. President Kennedy could have come and gone from Dallas in perfect safety. But the choice of a route that would carry the President past his window could mean only one thing to Lee—fate, duty and historical necessity had come together in this time and place and singled him out to do the deed.

The tragedy of the President's assassination was its terrible randomness.

That was not the only tragedy. The death of the President was a complex thing, made up of opposites. There was the tension between determination and accident, fate and chance. And, for the assassin, there appears also to have been a conflict between love and duty. As Lee saw him, the President embodied a social and historical evil which it had become his duty to destroy. But Lee had not created his opportunity and in some respects he did not relish his task. He did not leap to a decision immediately upon learning the route and, as late as the evening before, he gave a veto power of some sort to his unknowing wife.

Yet he went ahead despite his doubts and, in so doing, he acted like another hero of his, Will Cain, the Sheriff in the movie *High Noon,* who stands up to a band of outlaws, alone, because it is his duty, even though he is risking his own life and the love of his wife, who is opposed to violence. Lee may have felt that he had something in common with Will Cain, whose song he had sung so many times in Russia, and whose refrain—"Do not forsake me, oh my darlin' "—Marina had heard again and again as Lee was writing his Diary.

> Oh, to be torn twixt love and duty
> Sposin' I lose my fair-haired beauty . . .
> I'm not afraid of death but, oh
> What will I do if you leave me? . . .[8]

Lee may have seen himself, too, as torn between "love"—Marina and his children—and "duty," which required that against his kindlier instincts and at the cost of his life, he must kill the President of the United States.

When he said goodbye to Marina at the Paine house on the morning of November 22, Lee left his wedding ring behind. It was a stunning repudiation of Marina and the family "love" she represented. And it was an act of retaliation, the sort of vengeful response to her rejection of the night before that had characterized Lee all his life. But it was much else besides. It was a way of dissociating Marina from the deed he was about to commit and the guilt he would incur for it. And it was a way of showing his scorn and relegating her, too, to the everyday herd of men and women who would be too stupid and cowardly to understand the great and heroic deed he was performing for their sakes. Lee's leaving his wedding ring was an elegant gesture of contempt, an equivalent of Will Cain's tossing his Sheriff's badge in the dust. Cain, too, is expressing his contempt. He is saying that the people for whom he has risked everything, love and life itself, are not worthy of what he has done for them. But their unworthiness did not alter his duty, and he would have been diminished as a man if he had failed to do it.

Yet Lee did not want to lose Marina, just as Cain does not want to lose Amy. In Irving on the evening of November 21 Lee in effect had asked Marina, as Cain asks Amy, "What will I do if you leave me?" Twice on the day after he shot the President, in the direst situation he was ever to know, Lee begged Marina not to forsake him, first during their brief visit in the city jail and later, that same evening of November 23, when he telephoned Ruth and virtually commanded that Marina return to her house so that she would be available to him at whatever hour he might call. If Lee saw himself as Will Cain, he may also have expected his personal drama to end the way *High Noon* does. Cain not only earns the thanks of the townspeople, he also wins back the love of his wife.

There may have been still another voice speaking to Lee before the assassination and telling him what he ought to do—that of John F. Kennedy. A few months earlier Lee had read Kennedy's *Profiles in Courage,* and since the book, like *High Noon,* was a product of the McCarthy era, it is not surprising that the message they carry is identical: a celebration of the brave and lonely hero who will stand up against the wrong-headed crowd and the climate of his time to do what he believes to be right. Kennedy's book is addressed to the ordinary citizen and its subject is political courage. When he read the book in the summer of 1963, Lee apparently took its message to heart, both as a citizen and the great man he supposed himself to be. Kennedy, in the book, defined the man of political courage as the one who will do the thing he knows in his heart to be right, whether the people understand that it is right for them or not. He cannot expect their approval. It is to history that he must look for vindication. "A man does what he must," Kennedy wrote, "in spite of personal consequences, in spite of obstacles and dangers and pressures." These words, or words very like them, may have been in Lee Oswald's head when he took aim and fired just after high noon on November 22.[9]

Oswald may also have thought that by acting as Kennedy had enjoined him to do and as his conscience told him he must, he would be achieving in life and in death a one-ness with the man he was destroying. For it is clear that Oswald's motives were not purely political. In addition to the conflict between love and duty and the polarity between accident and determinism, there was something else at work—the tension, the attraction, which the assassin felt for his victim.

Of all the bonds between this assassin and this victim the strongest, perhaps, lay in a similarity the two of them shared. Both Oswald and Kennedy were attracted to death, and both had tempted it often. Oswald had tried suicide at least once and had made a murder attempt which could easily have led to his own death. One of his fictional heroes, Will Cain, had placed himself in a position from which he could barely escape alive. Another, Hermann in "The Queen of Spades," had stabbed himself to death.

Even more frequently than Oswald, Kennedy had placed his life at hazard. He was a reckless driver, and he had often taken a risky charter flight in foul weather so as not to miss a political appointment.[10] During World War II in the Pacific he was known not merely for his bravery but for the frightening, and some said needless, risks he had taken with his own life, with his PT-boat, and perhaps with the lives of his crew.[11] As for literature, his favorite verses were said to be from a World War I poem by the American, Alan Seeger:

> I have a rendezvous with Death
> At some disputed barricade,
> When Spring comes back with rustling shade
> And apple blossoms fill the air—
>
> . . .
>
> But I've a rendezvous with Death
> At midnight in some flaming town,
>
> . . .
>
> And I to my pledged word am true,
> I shall not fail that rendezvous.[12]

Marina has said sadly of her husband that he "did not value his own life at all." And Kennedy, on the morning of his death, actually pantomimed an assassination attempt which he thought could have been carried out against him the evening before.[13] As greatly as he enjoyed life, and as much as he helped others to enjoy it, Kennedy exuded fatalism, a "come and get me" air. And Oswald, with his own fatalism, may have been peculiarly attuned to pick this up.

The Kennedy fatalism was a profound matter, with implications for others besides Oswald. Thus the President may have been attracted to death, in part, because he had already lost a beloved older sister and older brother in tragic air accidents. All of this had been publicized a good deal and had become part of the family mystique. But in becoming part of the mystique, it had also become a family taint. Already, in 1963, it was as if the Kennedys had had more than their share of untimely deaths. Each of these heightened the association in the public mind between the Kennedys and death, each made the taint greater, and each increased the vulnerability of the rest of the family, and especially of its head, the President.

To a person whose stability was as fragile as Oswald's, even a tenuous connection, such as occurred in June 1963, when President Kennedy spoke on civil rights from the White House and a black leader, Medgar Evers, was murdered a few hours later only two hundred miles from where Oswald lived, could have strengthened some half-conscious association in Oswald's mind between the President and death. And the death of the President's new-born son in August, at a time when Oswald, too, was hoping for a son, may further have strengthened the association. Marina has said that her husband was upset by the Kennedy baby's death and it was on that day that he became engaged, for the first time, in a pro-Castro street fracas and was tossed into jail, almost as if he was impelled to sidetrack his own thoughts. Lee Oswald was fascinated by death, President Kennedy was fascinated by death, and of the ties between them in Oswald's mind, this was the greatest of all.

But it was not the only one. For President Kennedy, like Lee Oswald, was a young husband and father. At the time of his election, he was handsome and in his early forties, his wife was thirty-one and beautiful, and they had been married only seven years. It was obviously true of Kennedy—as is not always the case with an older President who has been married for many years—that this President had an ongoing sex life, and there were infant children as proof. Both the President and his wife had, moreover, an extraordinary capacity to project themselves into the yearnings and fantasies of millions, and some of these fantasies were sexual. Their photographs were frequently displayed on the covers of movie magazines, which exist to exploit such fantasies. And, since the

Kennedys had close ties with Hollywood, members of the family were seen constantly with film stars and other celebrities. The symbolism surrounding such celebrities also tends to be sexual, and the presence of the Kennedys in their company contributed to a dangerous eroticization of the presidency.

Television was part of it, too, for it made the Kennedys' life in the White House more visible than that of any First Family before them. Because of these elements and, above all, because of the attractiveness of husband and wife, both of the Kennedys appealed powerfully and intimately to men and women in every age group and every walk of life, people who did not ordinarily think about politics or see their own lives reflected in any way in that of the First Family.

Far from being unusual, the Oswalds were in some respects typical. They were young, twenty-two and twenty-four years old, and they read eagerly about the Kennedys in every fan magazine they could peruse during their evening strolls past the newsstands of New Orleans. They speculated without surcease about every facet of the Kennedys' lives. Even their speculations were typical. Each seems to have yearned a little toward each of the Kennedys. Marina, for example, considered Jacqueline Kennedy a "goddess." Since she was a goddess, however, it occurred to Marina that perhaps Mrs. Kennedy was "cold," and that the President might need extra warmth in his life, warmth which a less perfect, more earthy woman such as she herself might provide. In thinking thoughts such as these, Marina seems only to have been thinking what many American women thought. She was unusual, perhaps, in that President Kennedy was a physical reminder of the suitor she wished she had married. And she was unusual in that, unlike other women whose daydreams about the President were innocuous, she was married to a man who happened to be capable of killing.

Oswald's feelings are difficult to surmise, although Marina confirms that neither he nor she had heard rumors of the President's affairs with women, nor of his Addison's disease. They thought the Kennedys were just another couple such as they were, raised to the thousandth power of beauty and success. Oswald approved of Mrs. Kennedy and knew of her troubles in having children. He was a considerate husband in one respect —he let his wife decide how many children they would have. It may be that in shooting the President, Oswald imagined that he was protecting "Jackie" from a sexually exigent Catholic husband—Oswald despised religion—who compelled her to have children no matter what the injury to her health. And it is possible, although again a matter of conjecture, that the act of assassination was enhanced, and not diminished, in its attractiveness for Oswald by the fact that Jacqueline Kennedy would be there, that *she* would see it, that *she* would witness the "deed of unheard-of prowess" which he was performing for her sake.[14]

To say that President Kennedy shared with his assassin a fatalism and perhaps a yearning toward death, and that the Kennedys were surrounded by a volatile set of symbols concerning both death and sex, may explain a phenomenon reported soon after they entered the White House by U. E. Baughman, head of the Secret Service.[15] In a book published in 1961, Baughman stated that the number of letters to the President increased by 50 percent during the early weeks of the Kennedy administration. Somewhat ominously, Baughman added that the proportion from what he called the "lunatic fringe" had increased by 300 percent, and that the number of "insane" people who tried to telephone the President or who stopped by the White House gates to threaten the President's life or the lives of members of his family had also greatly increased. Thus there was an unusually large pool of potential assassins for this particular President. John F. Kennedy was, from the outset, highly assassinable.

There was another aspect of Kennedy's special vulnerability that enhanced his appeal as a victim to Lee Harvey Oswald. It lay in the many roles he played, as a man, as a member of the Kennedy clan, as head of the First Family, and as President of the United States. Because he was vibrant and handsome, because his age gave him an across-the-board appeal and because of his ability to project himself into other people's longings, there was something in Kennedy for nearly everyone. There was scarcely any American who could not see something of himself in this President, or who did not want to. Countless men and women saw in him someone in their own lives who had been close to them, or someone they would like close to them.

Thus Kennedy had two living parents, an unusual thing for a President, and there must have been many older men and women who looked on him as a son, or as the son they wished they had had. And the children of such people could have been jealous of the President. John Kennedy was one of a large brood of brothers and sisters, and there must have been some among the population who viewed him as the fantastically successful older brother whose achievements they could not hope to match. These people, too, must have envied him.

Still others must have envied him his upbringing in a loyal and close-knit family. Oswald seems to have been one of these, for, switching things around in his mind, he told Marina that he himself would like enough children for a "whole football team." There was only one family in America which was famous for having enough children to rouse up a football game at any moment—the Kennedys.

And Oswald appears to have envied the President not only the ebullient boyhood which was in such contrast with his lonely one, but he envied him his job—a job in which the President dealt daily with Russia and Cuba—for Oswald wanted to be President, and at the very age, forty-three, at which Kennedy had attained the office. Moreover, he wanted his "son," the son he did not yet have, to be President. This, again, appears to have been a case in which Oswald identified not only with the President but with Joseph P. Kennedy, Sr., "founding father" of the dynasty.

To the man who became his assassin, Lee Oswald, President Kennedy was not an accidental victim. To the contrary, and despite the huge element of chance, Kennedy was a highly determined target and he might well have proved to be so to some other assassin than Oswald. But there was another side of the Presidency that entered into Oswald's motives and it, too, was immeasurable in its importance.

We as a nation are a family, with the President as our symbolic father, or head. What is only beginning to be understood is that the President is not only a father but to some he is a combined parent, embodying elements of the mother as well. He is therefore in a position to magnetize the emotions of those who have had particularly strong feelings about either or both of their parents.

It is perhaps a strain on the imagination to see President Kennedy, with his virile masculinity, in the role of a symbolic mother. But there was something motherly about his Presidency, for it was family lore that Kennedys are in politics to "serve," to give of themselves unstintingly and ask nothing in return. President Kennedy emphasized this by working full time for the country and giving back his salary to the Treasury. In his inaugural address he urged others to be altruistic: "Ask not what your country can do for you, ask what you can do for your country." And he created the Peace Corps, so that young Americans could devote part of their lives to helping the less fortunate. In all of these ways the President stressed the giving, caring, motherly aspect of his office.

Marina is still puzzled as to why her husband killed the President. "But he liked Kennedy!" she protests to this day. And this is the beginning of an answer, for the public figure who appeals to the good in men, who stirs in them visions of altruism and exhorts them to be better than they are, such a leader appears to touch a chord in his followers which renders him especially vulnerable to their disappointments.

And Lee Oswald's life had been rich in disappointments. He had been disappointed in the mother who, he felt, let him down so egregiously while he was growing up that he came to feel deeply wronged by her. And he had been disappointed by the father who .at him down by dying before he was born. It was not President Kennedy's fault, it was his danger, that he stood in a position to magnetize the emotions of a Lee Oswald, who had had very little love in his life and whose feelings toward both his parents were so richly compounded of hate.

President Kennedy died, then, because of his plenitude. To some, and Oswald apparently was one of them, the memories and associations which this President stirred were too deep, too charged emotionally, altogether too much to bear. President Kennedy died because he had, as man and symbol, become so many things to so many men.

Notes

PROLOGUE AND PART ONE: RUSSIA, 1941–1961

Sources

Information concerning the childhood and youth of Marina Nikolayevna Prusakova in Russia (Part One); her marriage to Lee Harvey Oswald, and their life together in Minsk (Part Two); and their life together in the United States, as well as her experiences after her husband's death (Parts Three and Four), is derived from her own recollections as Marina Oswald in personal interviews with the author in Russian from June 1964 through December 1964, and as Marina Oswald and Marina Oswald Porter in subsequent telephone conversations and correspondence in Russian and English; from Warren Commission testimony by Marina Oswald in Vols. 1, 5, and 11 (see below); from an account of her life by Marina Oswald dated January 4, 1964, written for the FBI and published in Vol. 18, pp. 596–642; and from reports on FBI and Secret Service interviews with Marina Oswald appearing in the Warren Commission Exhibits.

Hearings Before the President's Commission on the Assassination of President Kennedy (Washington, D.C.: U.S. Government Printing Office, 1964). The Testimony of Witnesses taken by the President's Commission, hereafter referred to as the Warren Commission (Vols. 1–15), and the Exhibits published by the Commission (Vols. 16–26), are cited in the Notes only by volume and page number. *Report of the Warren Commission on the Assassination of President Kennedy* (Washington, D.C.: U.S. Government Printing Office, 1964) is cited hereafter as Warren Commission Report.

1—Archangel

1. Marina was conceived in December 1940 when the worst of the purges was over and before the war with Germany began. This had made it harder for her to guess the reasons for her father's disappearance. The best estimate appears to be that he was a late victim of the Great Purges of the 1930s.

3—Death of Klavdia

1. To an outside observer, Marina does resemble Princess Mary, who was moody, intelligent and flirtacious. And Pechorin bears resemblances to the man Marina was to marry, Lee Oswald. Pechorin shunned emotional contact with other people. "How many times have I played the part of an axe in the hands of fate!" he boasted, adding that, "Fame is a question of luck. To obtain it, you only have to be nimble." (*A Hero of Our Time,* by Mikhail Lermontov, translated by Vladimir Nabokov in collaboration with Dmitri Nabokov, a Doubleday Anchor book, Garden City, New York, 1958.) An American scholar writing about Pechorin has said of him, "He is a type and an individual, and he casts a dark and ominous shadow." (*Mikhail Lermontov,* by John Mersereau, Jr., Southern Illinois Press, Carbondale, Ill., 1962.)

    Marina indignantly rejects any comparison between Pechorin and the man she married. She says that Pechorin was the much better man. He destroyed Princess Mary and others, but through his destructiveness he found himself, and she admires him for this. Oswald, on the other hand, failed to find himself through his destructiveness, and for this she holds him in contempt.

    Thinking about Marina's later life, an observer might wonder, unfairly perhaps, whether Marina married her Pechorin or created him. Did she marry Oswald sensing that he had some of Pechorin's destructive qualities or, having married Oswald, did she herself unwittingly reinforce his destructiveness?

2. For Marina, the pain of learning that she was illegitimate was in no way eased by the fact that, according to published Soviet sources, as many as 20 percent of her classmates, children born during the late 1930s and early 1940s, may also have been illegitimate.

INTERLUDE AND PART TWO: RUSSIA, 1961–1962

Sources

Warren Commission Hearings: Testimony of Richard E. Snyder, Vol. 5, pp. 260–299; Testimony of John A. McVickar, Vol. 5, pp. 299–306, 318–326; Testimony of Oswald's Marine Corps associates, Vol. 8, pp. 288–323; Testimony of Kerry Thornley, Vol. 11, pp. 82–115; Oswald's "Historic Diary," Vol. 16, pp. 94–105; Copy of handwritten notes taken by Priscilla Johnson during interview with Lee Harvey Oswald on or about November 16, 1959, Vol. 20, pp. 277–285; Copy of article submitted by Priscilla Johnson to North American Newspaper Alliance, Vol. 20, pp. 286–289; Memos of Oswald's record in U.S. Marine Corps, Vol. 23, pp. 795–798. Warren Commission Report, pp. 383–394, 681–701. *Lee: A Portrait of Lee Harvey Oswald,* by his brother Robert Oswald with Myrick and Barbara Land (New York: Coward-McCann, 1967), hereafter cited as Robert Oswald. Letters to the author from Richard E. Snyder, February 9, 1969, January 6, 1970, and December 2, 1976. Conversations with John A. McVickar, Marie Cheatham, Richard E. Snyder, and Edward L. Keenan.

1. Interview of the author with Lee Harvey Oswald in Moscow, November 16, 1959.
2. Testimony of Paul Edward Murphy, Vol. 8, pp. 319–320.

3. Interview of the author with Oswald, November 16, 1959.

4. Recently declassified documents concerning the Martin Schrand case are: Warren Commission Document No. 35, December 1, 1963; Warren Commission Document No. 492, March 11, 1964; and Warren Commission Document No. 1042, June 3, 1964.

5. Oswald first described himself as a Marxist in writing in a letter to the Young People's Socialist League dated October 3, 1956: "I am a Marxist, and have been studying socialistic principles for well over 15 months" (Warren Commission Report, p. 681). Oswald was not yet sixteen. In his interview with the author in November 1959, Oswald said that "for two years I have been waiting to do this one thing," i.e., defect to the U.S.S.R. He was stationed at Cubi Point (Subic Bay) at the beginning of those "two years," and it is not inconceivable that at this base or at one of the two other U-2 bases at which he was stationed, he did try to learn something about the super-secret aircraft that would heighten his acceptability to the Russians. (The rumor linking Oswald with Schrand's death is mentioned in an affidavit by Donald Peter Camarata, Vol. 8, p. 316, and the fact that the hangar Schrand was guarding sometimes housed a U-2 appears in testimony by Daniel Patrick Powers, Vol. 8, pp. 280–281. Both men were part of the original group, including Oswald, that had been together since Jacksonville.)

6. Conversation with Marina Oswald.

7. Testimony of John E. Donovan, Vol. 8, pp. 292 and 298–299.

8. Testimony of Nelson Delgado, Vol. 8, p. 265.

9. Robert Oswald, op. cit., p. 93.

10. Warren Commission Report, p. 688.

11. Robert Oswald, op. cit., p. 77.

12. Exhibit No. 24, Vol. 16, pp. 94–95.

13. Exhibit No. 294, Vol. 16, p. 814.

14. Oswald told many lies and was very reticent with all the Americans who spoke to him in Moscow—Snyder, Aline Mosby, and myself. As a result, we thought he had arrived in Russia shortly before the scene at the embassy, and at the time of my interview I assumed he had been in Moscow two weeks, not a month. Except for Oswald himself, Rimma Shirokova, and Soviet officials, no one knew of Oswald's suicide attempt until after he was dead and his "Historic Diary" was published.

15. I have been asked by Warren Commission lawyers and others since 1963 whether, during my brief time with Oswald, I detected any signs that he was being manipulated by outsiders. In 1959, travel arrangements to the U.S.S.R. could be time-consuming and complicated. If the would-be visitor went to the Soviet Embassy in one European capital it might take four days to obtain a visa, in another city it might take three months, and in still another there might be no reply to the request at all. Aware of this, I asked Oswald how he learned the mechanics of entering Russia and defecting, and he was either evasive or mysterious in his replies. He said that it had taken him two years to learn the mechanics but had not been "hard." He refused to name any "person or institution" that had helped him. And he added that he had never met a Communist Party member until his arrival in the U.S.S.R. and that officials there were not "sponsoring" him.

He was saying, I think, that he had no ties with the U.S. Communist Party; but he seemed also to have been trying to create an impression that he was shielding someone, when in fact he could have learned what he wanted to know from a travel agency or from the Soviet embassies in Washington or Tokyo.

My own strong impression at the time was that, far from being manipulated from the outside, Oswald was, to a degree I found shocking, responding only to signals from within. Rather than being alive to, or stimulated by, his new environment, he was at pains to seal himself off from it. At first I attributed this to a feeling of foreignness or strangeness. Then I saw that he was motivated by another kind of fear: fear that if he took a hard look at the society around him, he might question his decision. Thus the feeling he gave was that he was wholly occupied by his inner preconceptions and by promptings from within, and that he did not want to be bothered by outside forces or facts.

16. McVickar wrote a memorandum about our conversation (Exhibit No. 911, Vol. 18, pp. 106–107), which is sometimes cited as evidence that I might have been working for the State Department, even though McVickar states in the memorandum that he had to point out to me that in addition to my duty as a correspondent, I also had a "duty as an American."

In 1956, three years before my meeting with Oswald, I worked briefly for three embassies—the American, British, and Canadian—as a translator during the 20th Soviet Communist Party Congress in Moscow. The American ambassador, Charles Bohlen, tried to have my thirty-day employment extended, but the Secretary of State, John Foster Dulles, refused because I lacked a security clearance. Neither before nor since have I been employed by any agency of any government.

17. The information conveyed by Nosenko, who in 1959 was a KGB officer assigned to Intourist in Moscow, is to be found in numerous Warren Commission memoranda based on CIA and FBI interviews with him in 1964. Many of these memoranda were declassified in 1973 and 1975. Thus, according to an FBI memo dated February 28, 1964, Nosenko stated that Oswald from the time of his arrival in Moscow was regarded by the KGB as not "completely normal mentally" and not "very intelligent." The KGB's interest in Oswald was therefore "practically nil" and, when he was sent to Minsk in January, 1960, the KGB office there was merely told to keep a "discreet check" to make sure that he was not a "sleeper agent" for American Intelligence.

According to another interview with Nosenko (Commission Document No. 451, a FBI memorandum dated March 4, 1964), the KGB did not know about Oswald's Marine Corps service when he arrived in Russia and, had it known, the information would not have been of interest or significance.

18. According to a memorandum from Allen Dulles, a member of the Warren Commission, to J. Lee Rankin, its chief counsel (Commission Document No. 1345, dated July 23, 1964), Henry Brandon, Washington correspondent of the London *Sunday Times,* was told by a member of the Soviet Embassy in Washington following the assassination that it was Yekaterina Furtseva, a member of the ruling Communist Party Presidium, who heard about the Oswald case, reversed orders, and arranged for him to remain.

The rumor may have been purposely planted to discredit Khrushchev, for he was known to be personally and politically close to Furtseva, and if, through her, he could be linked to handling of the Oswald case, he might then be made to suffer political damage in the aftermath of the Kennedy assassination. Khrushchev did, in fact, fall from power less than one year after Kennedy's death. On the other hand, the rumor Brandon heard may have been true. It is not unusual for Soviet leaders to concern themselves with individual cases: on one occasion my own visa was extended through the intervention of Anastas Mikoyan, then the number two or number three Soviet leader, who was close to Khrushchev and was identified with his pro-American policy. Khrushchev may have entrusted some very high Party body, or one or more Party leaders who were especially close to him, with seeing to it that the Spirit of Camp David was implemented, or at least not sabotaged, by his own bureaucracy. If something of the sort occurred, then Mme Furtseva would have been a logical choice to have supervised the handling of "humanitarian" cases.

The dates are worth noting. Khrushchev returned from the United States in early October 1959 and quickly departed on a trip to the Soviet Far East. It would have taken a few weeks for a new policy in handling Americans to be established. Oswald was told that he would have to leave the U.S.S.R. on October 21 and he attempted suicide that day. On October 28, only one week later, he was interviewed by four new officials who, according to him, apparently knew nothing about his case. It is possible that Oswald was the beneficiary of blind luck in his timing and that that one week at the end of October, plus the suicide attempt itself, was sufficient for his case to be bucked to a higher level and decided in accordance with the new Spirit of Camp David.

19. Exhibit Nos. 294, 295, and 297, Vol. 16, pp. 814–823, 825.

6—Courtship

1. According to Soviet hospital records, Oswald was not admitted to the hospital until the next day, Thursday, March 30, and was discharged on April 11.

2. The internal passports carried by Soviet citizens for travel inside the U.S.S.R. are of three types. One is for Soviet citizens, another is for citizens of foreign countries who have permission to reside in the U.S.S.R., and the third is the so-called stateless passport, which Oswald carried, for the foreign resident who has not become a Soviet citizen but who may, or may not, have retained citizenship of another country. Confusion therefore appears to have been possible even for an official like Ilya Prusakov.

3. A small but interesting example of disarticulation of the Soviet bureaucracy may be seen here. In January, officials at OVIR, the Office of Visas and Registration, inquired whether Oswald was still interested in acquiring Soviet citizenship, and he answered no. He asked merely to have his residence permit extended for one year. Thus, OVIR in Minsk had at least a hint that he was thinking of leaving Russia. The following month, February of 1961, he wrote the U.S. Embassy in Moscow asking to have his passport back and stating his desire to go home. His Soviet "Red Cross" subsidy was immediately cut off, an indication that his letter had been intercepted and the appropriate agency in Moscow, probably the KGB, knew his intentions. Yet two months later, in April, when he applied at ZAGS, still another official agency, to marry Marina, no effort was made to dissuade either of them. Usually, when a Soviet girl applies to marry a foreigner who is not a Soviet citizen and who may leave the country some day, strong pressure is brought on the girl not to go through with the marriage and permission is very often denied. That the Oswalds were permitted to marry is a sign that it was generally supposed in Minsk that Oswald was already a citizen or was on his way to becoming one. The disarticulation was therefore a double one: what Moscow knew, Minsk did not; and OVIR in Minsk, which could have suspected Oswald's intentions, did not communicate any suspicions to ZAGS, the bureau which registers marriages—another sign that controls in the USSR, as elsewhere, are not perfect.

4. Exhibit No. 24, Vol. 16, p. 103.

5. Exhibit No. 245, Vol. 16, pp. 685–687.
6. Exhibit No. 933, Vol. 18, p. 135.
7. Exhibit No. 932, Vol. 18, pp. 133–134.
8. Exhibit No. 934, Vol. 18, p. 136.
9. Exhibit No. 251, Vol. 16, pp. 702–704.
10. Exhibit No. 1085, Vol. 22, pp. 33–34.

7—The Wedding

1. Marina's translation. Exhibit No. 108, Vol. 16, p. 476.
2. Exhibit No. 24, Vol. 16, pp. 94–105. In quoting correspondence and other writing by Oswald, spelling and punctuation have in some instances been corrected for the sake of clarity and in others, such as this one, they have been left as Oswald wrote them.
3. Pavel seems to have understood Oswald very well, for in a letter he wrote both the Oswalds on September 15, 1962, when they were in the United States, he advised Marina that it was useless to complain about Lee's lesser faults and that with some people it is a question of "remaking rather than repair." He added, enigmatically, that there "are not equal standards about important things in this world." (Unpublished Warren Commission Document No. 928, Memorandum dated May 6, 1964, by Richard Helms, Deputy Director of Plans of the CIA, titled "Contacts Between the Oswalds and Soviet Citizens, June 13, 1962, to November 22, 1963.")
4. Exhibit No. 24, Vol. 16, pp. 94–105.
5. Testimony of Marine Captain George Donabedian, Vol. 8, pp. 311–315, and Donabedian Exhibit No. 1, Vol. 19, pp. 601–605.

8—Journey to Moscow

1. Exhibit No. 252, Vol. 16, pp. 705–708.
2. Questions have been raised about the case with which Oswald traveled to Moscow without official permission, a requirement for every foreigner traveling from one city to another. How did he purchase an air ticket, or for that matter, obtain a hotel room, when Soviet citizens as well as foreigners are required to surrender their passports at the front desk? The answer seems to be that while Soviet controls are strict, they are far from perfect; Oswald was watched, but he was not under heavy surveillance. He appeared reluctant to make the trip without authorization, yet his friends may have advised him that he could do so with impunity. Any one of them might have bought his ticket. But, speaking reasonably fluent Russian and dressed in his working clothes, he probably bought it himself, and the agent for Aeroflot, the Soviet airline, simply did not bother to ask whether he had permission to travel. Foreigners often make unauthorized trips in the Soviet Union. Their success depends a great deal upon chance—who they are, where they are, and the vigilance of local officials. If they get caught, the worst that usually happens is that they are sent back to the city from which they came. Oswald also took his chances at the Hotel Berlin, where he had lived for about two weeks in 1959. The girls at the front desk remembered him and, since he presented Soviet documents instead of a foreign passport, it did not entail a great risk for them to assign him a room.

3. Letter from Richard E. Snyder to the author, February 9, 1969.
4. The Warren Commission Report states on p. 706 that Marina arrived in Moscow Sunday, July 9, citing as evidence Oswald's Diary, which is incorrect in several respects about the visit, and Marina's testimony in Vol. 1, pp. 96–97. There Marina states that Oswald left Minsk "a day early and the following morning I was to come." But Marina's subsequent account to me is so clear as to appear conclusive: on Saturday, July 8, she worked as usual at the pharmacy and had her interlude with Leonid. On Sunday, July 9, Oswald telephoned, asking her to come to Moscow, and on the morning of July 10 she went.
5. Exhibits No. 935, Vol. 18, pp. 137–139, and No. 938, *ibid.,* pp. 144–149, indicate that a Questionnaire and an Application for Renewal of Passport were executed at the embassy by Oswald on Monday, July 10, 1961.
6. Exhibit No. 935, Vol. 18, pp. 137–139.
7. Letters of Lee Oswald to Robert Oswald, May 31, 1961 (". . . if I can get the government to drop charges against me . . ."), and June 26, 1961 ("I assume the government must have a few charges against me, since my coming here like that is illegal. But I really don't know exactly what charges."), Exhibit Nos. 299 and 300, Vol. 16, pp. 827–832.
8. Exhibit No. 100, Vol. 16, pp. 436–439.
9. *Ibid.*
10. Exhibit No. 935, Vol. 18, pp. 137–139.
11. Exhibits No. 25, Vol. 16, pp. 121–122, and No. 100, *ibid.,* pp. 436–439.
12. Testimony of Richard Edward Snyder, Vol. 5, pp. 260–299, especially p. 290. See also Oswald's Diary and Exhibit No. 101, p. 440.
13. Marina laughed on hearing this particular statement of her husband's and remarked that without an ulterior purpose he would never have said any such thing.
14. Exhibit No. 935, Vol. 18, pp. 137–139.
15. Marina remembers only one visit to the embassy, on Monday, July 10, and she thinks that both sets of interviews, hers and Oswald's, were completed that day. Her memory, however, is in error, for Exhibits No. 944, Vol. 18, p. 158, and No. 959, *ibid.,* pp. 335–338, indicate that her visa petition was filled out by McVickar and executed by Lee Oswald on Tuesday, July 11, 1961.

9—Marina's Ordeal

1. Exhibit No. 1122, Vol. 22, p. 87.
2. Exhibit No. 301, Vol. 16, p. 833.
3. Exhibit No. 985, Vol. 18, p. 477
4. Oswald reported to his brother Robert: "I went hunting last weekend. . . . I shot a couple of birds with my single-barrel 15 gauge shotgun, but I couldn't find them" (Exhibit No. 303, Vol. 16, p. 836). The letter was dated Monday, August 21, so the expedition must have taken place on Saturday or Sunday, August 19 or 20, 1961.
5. "The Collective" appears in Oswald's handwriting in Exhibit Nos. 94–96, Vol. 16, pp. 347–421. For the version typed for Oswald in June 1961 by Miss Pauline Virginia Bates, a public stenographer in Fort Worth, Texas, see Exhibit No. 92, Vol. 16, pp. 285–336.
6. Later he admitted that he had actually been initiated into oral sex much earlier, by an older woman (probably a prostitute) in Japan.

10—The Long Wait

1. Letter from Robert Oswald to the author, April 26, 1965.
2. After the assassination, a fragment of the aria was found among Oswald's belongings. It is in Oswald's handwriting, in Russian, and it contains omissions, mistakes, and indecipherable phrases. It is probably an attempt to reproduce the words by listening to the recording (Exhibit No. 53, Vol. 16, p. 191). Author's translation.
3. After the assassination, when Oswald had indeed performed a deed of "unheard-of prowess," Marina again thought that he had done it to impress Rimma. It was a thought that may have been an unconscious attempt to repress the fear that he had done it to impress her. It is possible, however, that Oswald did, as Marina suspects, associate the opera, and the aria, with Rimma; it is quite likely that when he first saw *The Queen of Spades* in Moscow, Rimma went with him as his interpreter.
4. Oswald's blood was tested November 25, 1961 (Exhibit No. 1391, Vol. 22, p. 718).
5. When the Warren Commission asked Marina whether she had been hospitalized for nervous difficulty during 1961, she denied it (Testimony of Marina Oswald, Vol. 1, p. 97). Only later did she remember that she had been hospitalized because of gas fumes on a bus. Because of her denial, and because medical records handed over by the Soviet government after the assassination contained only Marina's outpatient record, not her hospital record, the Commission erroneously concluded that Marina had not been in the hospital at all and that Oswald had probably been lying (Warren Commission Report, p. 708).
6. Exhibit No. 307, Vol. 16, pp. 845–848.
7. Oswald was so impressed by the demolition of Stalin's monument in Minsk that he wrote the second of the two essays he composed in Russia. Titled "The New Era," it briefly describes the destruction of the "10 ton bronze figue of a man revered by the older generation and laughted at by the sarcastic younger generation." He ends, however, on a pessimistic note: "But Bellerussia as in Stalin's native Georgia is still a stronghold of Stalinism. and a revival of Stalinism is a very, very, possible thing in those two republics" (Exhibit No. 96, Vol. 16, p. 421).
8. In an FBI interview dated February 28, 1964 (Warren Commission document number and declassification date not legible), the defector Yury Nosenko stated that the KGB had no objection to Marina's leaving the U.S.S.R. This was a crucial determinant.
9. Report of Minsk Radio Plant Director P. Yudelevich, December 11, 1961 (Exhibit No. 985, Vol. 18, p. 433–434).

11—Birth of June

1. Exhibits No. 1124, Vol. 22, p. 90, and No. 1079, *ibid.,* p. 27.
2. Exhibit No. 256, Vol. 16, pp. 717–718.
3. Exhibit No. 247, Vol. 16, pp. 691–692.
4. On February 6, 1962, *The New York Times* ran a UPI story from Rome, citing the Italian Communist Party newspaper, *L'Unita,* which was highly reliable on Soviet affairs, as follows: "L'Unita reports today unconfirmed rumors circulating among Western correspondents in Moscow that there has been an attempt on Nikita S.

Khrushchev's life . . . the assassination attempt was reported to have taken place at Minsk, on the Soviet-Polish frontier, two weeks ago." I was in the Soviet Union the following summer and heard rumors about an attempt in Moscow, Stalingrad, Sochi, and Kislovodsk—one that Khrushchev was grazed on the arm and slightly wounded, and another that the bullet missed Khrushchev but hit the Minister of Finance, Zverev. In fact, Khrushchev left Minsk for Sochi, and did not reappear in public for three weeks, a very good sign that an attempt on his life had occurred.

5. Exhibit No. 256, Vol. 16, pp. 717–718.
6. Warren Commission Report, p. 710.
7. Exhibit No. 314, Vol. 16, pp. 865–868.
8. Exhibit No. 315, Vol. 16, pp. 870–873.
9. In a memorandum to the FBI entitled "Lee Harvey's Oswald's Access to Classified Information About the U-2," written after Kennedy's assassination, Richard Helms, the Deputy Director for Plans, conceded indirectly that Oswald may have seen the U-2: "Even if Oswald had seen a U-2 aircraft at Atsugi or elsewhere, this fact would not have been unusual nor have constituted a breach of security. Limited public exposure of the craft was accepted as a necessary risk." Helms added, however, that Oswald could have heard "rumors and gossip" but that it was most unlikely that he knew the plane's name or its mission, or that he "had the necessary prerequisites to differentiate between the U-2 and other aircraft which were similarly visible at Atsugi." This is hard to believe, since the wingspan of the U-2 was so enormous that almost anyone would have seen instantly that its mission was aerial reconnaissance. (Unpublished Warren Commission Document No. 931, dated May 13, 1964, declassified January 4, 1971.)
10. Oswald claimed in a letter to Robert that he "saw" Powers in Moscow at his trial. This is almost certainly a lie. There were American reporters and embassy officials at the trial who had seen Oswald at the time of his defection and would have recognized him had he been there. The trial was televised in Russia, and Oswald probably "saw" Powers on television in Minsk.
11. Powers was not arrested or tried when he returned to America. After lengthy interrogation by military, intelligence, and government officials, he was allowed to go back to civilian life. But in writing of his experiences in 1970, long after Oswald himself had become a *cause célèbre,* Powers suggested that Oswald, a former radar technician with access to special height-finding gear, might have betrayed the great secret, the U-2's maximum altitude, thereby enabling Russian SAMs to bring down his plane.—Francis Gary Powers and Curt Gentry, *Operation Overflight* (New York: Holt, Rinehart & Winston, 1970), pp. 375–379. In an interview with *The Times* of London on April 20, 1971, Powers noted further that Oswald at Atsugi "had access to all our equipment. He knew the altitudes we flew at, how long we stayed out on any mission, and in which direction we went."

It is impossible to say how much Oswald learned about the aircraft at the three U-2 bases at which he was stationed. It is hard to keep information narrowly confined at some bases; and Oswald later did show himself to be accomplished at picking up on his jobs extracurricular information which he was not entitled to have. It is conceivable that at least after the Philippine period (1957), he wanted to acquire classified information which he could trade for Soviet citizenship. But despite offers of radar information which he made from the moment of his arrival in Moscow, the Russians were not impressed.

At about the time of Oswald's arrival, the Russians had tried, and failed, to bring down a U-2 over Soviet territory. They tried, and nearly succeeded, on the next U-2 overflight in mid-April 1960. And on May 1 they brought down Powers. Their problem throughout this time appears not to have been lack of information about the U-2—its maximum flying altitude or its cruising altitude—but lack of the missile capacity to shoot it down.

Powers' allegations to the contrary, the best guess remains that the Russians knew all they needed to know about the U-2 from various sources, and that Oswald, a former Marine Corps private with the lowest security clearance, was at no time viewed as a possible purveyor of needed information. Indeed, all the Soviet decisions regarding Oswald appear to have been made on negative grounds—which way of handling him would be least damaging to the U.S.S.R.—and in a declassified memorandum to the Warren Commission, the CIA described five other defector cases that occurred within a year or two of Oswald's, in which all five received quicker answers and better treatment than did Oswald.

Some experts on Soviet affairs have noted that, had the Russians received information of value from Oswald, their treatment of him would have been different from the very first day. They would not have allowed him to languish in Moscow hotels—within reach of Western reporters—for two and a half months before deciding what to do with him. They would probably have accorded him slightly better treatment than he received, a chance to study full-time, for example, rather than a job as a factory hand. Lastly, and conclusively, they would not have allowed him to leave the country—ever. This they could have accomplished by granting him Soviet citizenship, which would have made him effectively their prisoner; or they could have given him a "stateless passport," as they did, and then either refused outright, or simply declined any answer at all, when he requested an exit visa. As for Oswald, he, of course, would not have dared to go home had he given the Russians information of value but would have clung to the sanctuary he had.

12. Exhibit No. 250, Vol. 16, pp. 700–701.
13. Warren Commission Report, p. 764.
14. Exhibit No. 1123, Vol. 22, p. 89.

12—Departure for America

1. Exhibit No. 317, Vol. 16, pp. 877–879.
2. Exhibit No. 1315, Vol. 22, pp. 487–488.
3. Exhibit No. 196, Vol. 16, pp. 573–574.
4. Exhibit No. 1314, Vol. 22, p. 486.
5. Exhibit No. 42, Vol. 16, pp. 171–174.
6. Exhibit No. 950, Vol. 18, pp. 276–277.
7. In Exhibit No. 994, Vol. 18, p. 615, Marina wrote, soon after the assassination, that "We lived in an apartment in Amsterdam for 3 days." As a result there has been confusion, and even speculation that the Oswalds were debriefed in a CIA "safe house" in Holland before leaving for the United States. Apart from the fact that such a procedure would have been highly unusual, the Oswalds' documents make clear that they left Moscow on a two-day train trip on June 1, 1962, crossed the border at Brest into Poland on June 2, left East Germany on June 2, entered West Germany and Holland on June 3, and sailed on the *Maasdam* June 4. Thus they could have stayed in Holland only one night, Sunday, and Marina's lament that all the shops were closed on the one day they were there fits the documentary record. (Exhibits

No. 29, Vol. 16, pp. 137–145; No. 946, Vol. 18, p. 166; and No. 1099, Vol. 22, p. 48.)

8. Exhibit No. 100, Vol. 16, pp. 436–439, especially p. 439.
9. *Ibid.,* p. 436.
10. *Ibid.,* p. 439.
11. Exhibit No. 25, Vol. 16, pp. 121–122.
12. Exhibit No. 25, Vol. 16, pp. 106–112.
13. *Ibid.,* pp. 112–116. Oswald's writings suggest he had read Lenin's *Imperialism:The Highest Stage of Capitalism,* and possibly Engels' "Anti-Dühring," or was at least familiar with their contents.
14. *Ibid.,* pp. 117–120.

INTERLUDE AND PART THREE: TEXAS, 1962–1963

Sources

Affidavit of Edward John Pic, Jr., Vol. 11, p. 82; Report of Dr. Irving Sokolow, Youth House psychologist (Exhibit No. 1339, Vol. 22, pp. 558–559); Testimony of John Carro, Vol. 8, pp. 202–214.

1. John Pic learned while he was growing up that his father did contribute to his support, although his mother told him constantly that the amount was not enough, only $18 a month. But according to Pic's father, the amount was actually $40 (Testimony of Edward John Pic, Jr., Vol. 8, p. 199). Pic was not disabused of his other illusion, that he had been the cause of his parents' divorce, until years later, after the Kennedy assassination, when he was thirty-one years old and read about his parents in *Life* magazine (Testimony of John Edward Pic, Vol. 11, p. 5).
2. Testimony of Lillian Murret, Vol. 8, p. 106.
3. Siegel Exhibit No. 1, Vol. 21, p. 491.
4. Testimony of Marguerite Oswald, Vol. 1, p. 253.
5. Testimony of John Edward Pic, Vol. 11, p. 19; Robert Oswald, *op. cit.,* p. 33; Warren Commission Report, p. 671.
6. Testimony of Marguerite Oswald, Vol. 1, pp. 254–255.
7. Testimony of John Edward Pic, Vol. 11, p. 27.
8. Testimony of Robert Oswald, Vol. 1, p. 281.
9. Robert Oswald, *op. cit.,* p. 36.
10. Testimony of John Edward Pic, Vol. 11, p. 27.
11. *Ibid.*
12. *Ibid.,* p. 29.
13. Testimony of Lillian Murret Vol. 8, p. 113.
14. Testimony of Myrtle Evans, Vol. 8, pp. 50 51 and p. 53.
15. Testimony of John Edward Pic, Vol. 11, p. 28.
16. Exhibit No. 1874, Vol. 23, p. 680.
17. When Lee Oswald got into truant difficulty in New York, Marguerite told the social worker, Evelyn Strickman Siegel, that John had also been a truant and that she allowed him to go to work until he decided to return to school (Siegel Exhibit No. 1, Vol. 21, p. 493). However, according to John, he was bitterly hurt when his mother forced him to leave school. He went back over her opposition and even had to forge her signature on his report cards, excuse slips, and other school documents (Testimony of John Edward Pic, Vol. 11, p. 33).
18. Testimony of John Edward Pic., Vol. 11, p. 73.

19. *Ibid.,* p. 77.
20. Testimony of Hiram Conway, Vol. 8, p. 89.
21. Robert Oswald, *op. cit.,* p. 42.
22. Testimony of John Edward Pic, Vol. 11, p. 73.
23. Robert Oswald, *op. cit.,* pp. 51–53.
24. Testimony of John Edward Pic, Vol. 11, p. 39.
25. After Oswald's death, Dr. Howard P. Rome of the Mayo Clinic diagnosed his difficulty from his writings and wrote a letter about it to the Warren Commission (Exhibit No. 3134, Vol. 26, pp. 812–817).
26. Exhibit No. 1339, Vol. 22, pp. 558–559.
27. Siegel Exhibit No. 1, Vol. 21, pp. 485–495.
28. *Ibid.,* p. 493.
29. Hartogs Exhibit No. 1, Vol. 20, pp. 89–90.
30. Testimony of Myrtle Evans, Vol. 8, pp. 50–51 and 55.
31. Testimony of John Edward Pic, Vol. 11, p. 49.
32. Testimony of Marguerite Oswald, Vol. 1, p. 254.
33. Robert Oswald, *op. cit.,* pp. 47–48.
34. Jean Stafford, *A Mother in History* (New York: Farrar, Straus, and Giroux, 1965), p. 106.
35. Testimony of John Edward Pic, Vol. 11, p. 80.

13—Family Reunion

1. Exhibit No. 2655, Vol. 26, p. 8.
2. *Ibid.*
3. Testimony of Martin Isaacs, Vol. 8, pp. 324–330 (esp. pp. 326 and 329).
4. Testimony of Robert Oswald, Vol. 1, p. 331.
5. Testimony of Marguerite Oswald, Vol. 1, pp. 131–132.
6. Conversations with Marina Oswald.
7. Testimony of Pauline Virginia Bates, Vol. 8, pp. 330–343.
8. Testimony of Peter Paul Gregory, Vol. 2, pp. 337–347; and conversations between Mr. Gregory and the author in August 1964.
9. Testimony of Max Clark, Vol. 8, p. 344.

14—Summer in Fort Worth

1. The report of Special Agents John W. Fain and B. Tom Carter, dictated July 2, 1962 (Exhibit No. 823, Vol. 17, pp. 728–731); Testimony of John W. Fain, Vol. 4, pp. 403–418. It does not appear to have been unusual in any way for the FBI, and not the CIA, to have interviewed Oswald on his return from the U.S.S.R.
2. Testimony of Robert Oswald, Vol. 1, pp. 315 and 389.
3. Robert Oswald, *op. cit.,* p. 119.
4. *Ibid.,* p. 121.
5. Testimony of Marguerite Oswald, Vol. 1, p. 133.
6. Exhibit No. 2189, Vol. 24, p. 872.

7. Testimony of Tommy Bargas, Vol. 10, p. 165.
8. Testimony of Marguerite Oswald, Vol. 1, p. 133.
9. Robert Oswald, *op. cit.,* p. 122.
10. Agent John W. Fain differed from Marina in his memory of how his second meeting with Oswald began (Testimony of John W. Fain, Vol. 4, pp. 420–423). He testified that he and another agent, Arnold J. Brown, staked out the house and waited down the road in a car. About 5:30 they spotted Oswald walking home from work. They moved up in front of the house. "Hi, Lee," Fain called out from the car. "How are you? Would you mind talking with us just a few minutes?" According to Fain, Lee did not object, and he climbed into the back seat of the car. Marina recalls that Fain came to their door, and that recollection seems more likely to be correct, since it was her first contact with the FBI, the effect on her husband was vivid, and she remembers it in detail. Fain, on the other hand, paid many such calls in a year and his recollection may have been fuzzy. For him the visit was routine; for Marina it was unique.

    Another point on which Fain seems to have been in error is the time at which he and Brown spotted Oswald coming home. It was probably not at 5:30, as he reported, but a few minutes after 4:30, the hour at which Oswald got out of work. The interview probably lasted, as another FBI report stated, for an hour and a quarter, from 4:45 until 6:00.
11. Exhibit No. 824, Vol. 17, pp. 736–739.
12. Testimony of John W. Fain, Vol. 4, p. 423.
13. Exhibit No. 824, Vol. 17, p. 737.
14. Exhibit No. 986, Vol. 18, p. 486. Author's italics.
15. Testimony of Marguerite Oswald, Vol. 1, pp. 136–137.
16. *Ibid.,* pp. 138–140.

15—The Émigrés

1. Testimony of Paul Roderick Gregory, Vol. 9, pp. 141–160.
2. Testimony of Peter Paul Gregory, Vol. 2, p. 341.
3. Conversation with George Bouhe, August 1964.
4. Testimony of George de Mohrenschildt, Vol. 9, p. 231.

16—Ingratitude

1. Conversation with Declan P. Ford, June 1964.
2. Conversation with Anna N. Meller, August 1964.
3. Testimony of George Bouhe, Vol. 8, p. 375.
4. *Ibid.,* p. 371.
5. Testimony of Gary E. Taylor, Vol. 9, p. 78.
6. Conversation with Anna N. Meller, August 1964.
7. Testimony of John G. Graef, Vol. 10, pp. 174–181.
8. Conversation with George A. Bouhe, August 1964.
9. *Ibid.*
10. Conversation with Anna N. Meller, August 1964.

17—Dallas

1. Testimony of Mrs. Donald Gibson (Alexandra de Mohrenschildt Taylor), Vol. 11, pp. 123–153.
2. *Ibid.*
3. *Ibid.*
4. *Ibid.*
5. Testimony of John G. Graef, Vol. 10, pp. 174–194; Testimony of Dennis Hyman Ofstein, Vol. 10, pp. 194–213.
6. Testimony of Elena A. Hall, Vol. 8, p. 396.
7. *Ibid.*, p. 395.
8. Affidavit of Alexander Kleinlerer, Vol. 11, p. 122.
9. *Ibid.*, p. 120.
10. *Ibid.*
11. *Ibid.*, p. 121.
12. Testimony of Mrs. Donald Gibson, Vol. 11, p. 141.
13. *Ibid.*, p. 131.
14. Testimony of Anna N. Meller, Vol. 8, p. 386.

18—George de Mohrenschildt

1. Testimony of George S. de Mohrenschildt, Vol. 9, p. 242.
2. De Mohrenschildt's story is taken from his testimony, Vol. 9, pp. 166–284; from the FBI file on George S. de Mohrenschildt in the National Archives, Washington, D.C.; and from conversations with Samuel B. Ballen, George A. Bouhe, and Declan and Katherine Ford.
3. Remarks of Max E. Clark, quoted in De Mohrenschildt's FBI file.
4. This account is taken from De Mohrenschildt's FBI file. Of the informants whose hearsay remarks are used in this paragraph, one was anonymous, one was known personally to the author, and the third had been governess to Dorothy Pierson de Mohrenschildt.
5. Letters from Samuel B. Ballen to the author, June 18, 1968, and February 4, 1972.
6. Jeanne de Mohrenschildt's story is taken from her testimony, Vol. 9, pp. 285–331, and from George S. de Mohrenschildt's FBI file.
7. Testimony of Max E. Clark, Vol. 8, p. 352.
8. Comment by George A. Bouhe in De Mohrenschildt's FBI file.
9. Conversation with Samuel B. Ballen, November 28, 1964.
10. Comment by Morris I. Jaffe in De Mohrenschildt's FBI file.
11. Testimony of Igor Voshinin, Vol. 8, p. 464.
12. Testimony of George A. Bouhe, Vol. 8, p. 377.
13. Testimony of Igor Voshinin, Vol. 8, p. 468.
14. The Voshinins' remarks are taken from De Mohrenschildt's FBI file.
15. Conversation with Samuel B. Ballen, November 28, 1964.
16. Testimony of Jeanne de Mohrenschildt, Vol. 9, p. 312.

17. *Ibid.,* p. 309.
18. Testimony of Samuel B. Ballen, Vol. 9, pp. 47, 52–53; and conversation with Samuel B. Ballen, November 28, 1964.

19—Reconciliation

1. Testimony of Anna N. Meller, Vol. 8, p. 387.
2. Conversations with Teofil Meller, Anna N. Meller, and George A. Bouhe.
3. Testimony of George S. de Mohrenschildt, Vol. 9, p. 238.
4. *Ibid.*
5. Testimony of Jeanne de Mohrenschildt, Vol. 9, p. 309.
6. Testimony of George S. de Mohrenschildt, Vol. 9, p. 232.
7. *Ibid.,* and testimony of Jeanne de Mohrenschildt, Vol. 9, p. 313.
8. Testimony of George S. de Mohrenschildt, Vol. 9, p. 232.
9. Testimony of Katherine N. Ford, Vol. 2, pp. 302–303; and conversations with the author.
10. Testimony of Declan P. Ford, Vol. 2, pp. 325, 333–334; and conversations with the author.
11. Exhibit No. 320, Vol. 16, p. 884.
12. Testimony of George A. Bouhe, Vol. 8, p. 377.
13. Conversation with Samuel B. Ballen, November 28, 1964.
14. Testimony of Max E. Clark, Vol. 8, p. 353.
15. Testimony of Jeanne de Mohrenschildt, Vol. 9, p. 325.
16. Testimony of John Edward Pic, Vol. 11, p. 52.
17. *Ibid.,* p. 56.
18. *Ibid.,* p. 59.

20—Lee and George

1. Testimony of Gary E. Taylor, Vol. 9, pp. 91–93.
2. Testimony of Lydia Dymitruk, Vol. 9, pp. 60–72.
3. Testimony of George S. de Mohrenschildt, Vol. 9, p. 240.
4. *Ibid.,* p. 246.
5. *Ibid.,* p. 237.
6. *Ibid.,* p. 266.
7. Testimony of Jeanne de Mohrenschildt, Vol. 9, pp. 308–309.
8. Testimony of Everett D. Glover, Vol. 10, p. 9.
9. Testimony of George S. de Mohrenschildt, Vol. 9, p. 237.
10. *Ibid.,* pp. 243, 266.
11. *Ibid.,* p. 237.
12. *Ibid.,* pp. 236–237, 242.
13. Conversations with Marina Oswald.
14. Testimony of George S. de Mohrenschildt, Vol. 9, pp. 236, 242–243.
15. Conversations with Declan and Katherine Ford.
16. Testimony of Gary E. Taylor, Vol. 9, p. 96.
17. Testimony of George S. de Mohrenschildt, Vol. 9, p. 238.
18. *Ibid.,* p. 266.

21—The Revolver

1. Testimony of Jeanne de Mohrenschildt, Vol. 9, pp. 319–321; Testimony of Katherine Ford, Vol. 2, pp. 305–307.
2. Exhibits No. 1859, Vol. 23, pp. 628–630, and Nos. 1860–1861, Vol. 23, pp. 630–632.
3. Testimony of Anna N. Meller, Vol. 8, p. 389.
4. Testimony of Mrs. Mahlon F. Tobias, Vol. 8, pp. 242–243.
5. *Ibid.*, p. 244.
6. Oswald's time sheets at Jaggars-Chiles-Stovall, Exhibit No. 1850–1856, Vol. 23, pp. 529–625.
7. Testimony of John G. Graef, Vol. 10, pp. 187–188.
8. Testimony of Dennis Hyman Ofstein, Vol. 10, p. 204.
9. This may actually have been the night Rachel Oswald was conceived. Marina's menstrual period started on January 11 and she could have been fertile on the 26th. Rachel was born on October 20, weighed nearly 7 pounds, and was said to be full term. From January 26 to October 20, 267 days had elapsed, the average length of a full-term pregnancy. Moreover, Marina remembers no other occasion around this time when she failed to take precautions.
10. Cadigan Exhibit No. 12, Vol. 19, p. 285.
11. Testimony of Alwyn Cole, documents expert of U.S. Department of Treasury, Vol. 4, pp. 375–377; Testimony of James C. Cadigan, documents expert of the FBI, Vol. 7, p. 424.
12. Exhibit No. 800, Vol. 17, p. 685.
13. Exhibit No. 12, Vol. 19, p. 579; Weinstock Exhibit No. 1, Vol. 21, p. 721.

22—The Sanction

1. Testimony of John G. Graef, Vol. 10, pp. 187–189, 193; Testimony of Dennis Hyman Ofstein, *ibid.*, p. 205.
2. Exhibit No. 93, Vol. 16, p. 346.
3. Letters from Mrs. Gladys A. Yoakum to the author, April 6 and May 6, 1973.
4. Testimony of George S. de Mohrenschildt, Vol. 9, p. 256.
5. Schmidt was never called to testify before the Warren Commission. The material in the paragraph above is all the FBI file on Schmidt in the National Archives contains about the conversation.
6. Conversation with Samuel B. Ballen, November 28, 1964.
7. Exhibit Nos. 6–7, Vol. 16, pp. 9–10.
8. Testimony of Mrs. Mahlon F. Tobias, Vol. 10, p. 243.
9. Testimony of Mahlon F. Tobias, Sr., Vol. 10, p. 256.

23—"Ready for Anything"

1. Letter from Major General Edwin A. Walker to the author, postmarked May 15, 1974.
2. Letters from Mrs. Gladys A. Yoakum to the author, April 6 and May 6, 1973, and May 24, 1975.

3. *The Militant,* March 11, 1963 (Vol. 27, No. 10), p. 7.
4. Other features that suggest the letter was written by Oswald include the tone of condescending flattery, even as the writer tells the paper what stories it ought to print; use of the term "gross error," a direct translation of a phrase used frequently in Russian; use of quotes around the word "sensational," a sarcasm characteristic of Oswald, when the writer really means that the Ortiz case was typical and not unusual or sensational; the lack of a transition between the remarks about reform politics and the story of the Ortiz case; the fact that Oswald's pretext for leaving the Marine Corps was an injury which had left his mother "unable" to work; and the writer's interest in "fundamentally transforming" the system, typical of Oswald's beliefs.

   Those who contend that Oswald did not write the letter have suggested that he would not have known or cared about reform movements in the Democratic Party, or about the campaign of H. Stuart Hughes in Massachusetts. But the handwritten document which he left behind and which is described in this chapter reflects his interest in using even elements of the Republican Party to bring about reform. In addition, the September 7, 1962, issue of *Time* magazine, to which Oswald subscribed, had a story about the Hughes campaign. Oswald could have learned about reform movements in New York and California from newspapers or from George de Mohrenschildt, whose close friend, Sam Ballen, was a New Yorker, and whose wife's daughter and son-in-law, the Keartons, were interested in politics in California.

   There are also those who concede Oswald's link to the letter but believe that he lacked the skill to write it. They think that he must have had help, and that such help points to his being part of a "conspiracy" in the spring of 1963—see Albert H. Newman, *The Assassination of John F. Kennedy: The Reasons Why* (New York: 1970), pp. 154–161. But from other writings he has left behind, there is no doubt that Oswald had the capacity to write the letter, although it would have been filled with errors of spelling and punctuation which do not appear in the published version. *The Militant* does not have the original, and the editors are unable to say whether the letter arrived in typed or handwritten form or, indeed, whether Oswald was the author. The present managing editor has, however, carefully explained the paper's policy in handling letters. Because *The Militant* has among its readers an unusually high proportion of poor people, working people, and even prisoners, it is a "long-standing policy" to edit for "syntax, grammar, spelling," as well as to add transitions. The editor commented that his paper probably edits a good deal more heavily than most. (Telephone conversation of October 29, 1975, with Larry Seigle, managing editor of *The Militant,* and letter from Larry Seigle to the author, November 17, 1975.)
5. Exhibit No. 1351, Vol. 22, p. 585, pinpoints the dates of the photographs. From the progress of the construction of a large building in the background of the photos, it was the weekend of March 9–10, and since Oswald worked Saturday until 4:00 P.M., he must have taken the photographs on Sunday, March 10.
6. Exhibit No. 2, Vol. 16, pp. 3–8.
7. Testimony of Marina Oswald, Vol. 11, p. 293.
8. Oswald's time sheet on March 12 is evidence that he probably lied sometimes about his hours. On the day he ordered the rifle, he signed in from 8:00 A.M. to 5:15 (Exhibit No. 1855, Vol. 23, p. 605). The U.S. postal inspector in Dallas, Harry D. Holmes, later testified that Oswald's money order for the rifle was issued "early on the morning of March 12." This appears to have been the case, for the order was

imprinted on Klein's cash register March 13. Since the post office window opened only at 8:00 A.M., Oswald probably lied when he signed in then. Thus the time sheets have to be used with caution.

9. Testimony of Robert Oswald, Vol. 1, pp. 391–392.

10. Exhibit No. 322, Vol. 16, pp. 886–888. Oswald had other reasons for keeping his brother at a distance. He did not want Robert to come when Marina was alone and learn from her the facts of his treatment of her. Nor did he want Robert to see the revolver on its shelf and the clutter of maps and photographs in his "office" and possibly guess his plan. Finally, Oswald had some insight into himself and may have understood that he was like a gun that is loaded, cocked, and about to go off. His target was General Walker. But if someone else came by for whom he harbored strong emotions—and he had strong feelings for both Robert and his mother—he might kill that person instead. He *had* to keep Robert away.

11. Exhibit No. 8, Vol. 16, pp. 11–12.

12. Exhibit No. 9, Vol. 16, pp. 13–20.

13. Oswald's time sheets, Exhibit No. 1855, Vol. 23, pp. 613–614.

14. Since neither weapon was sent by insured or registered mail, the dates of arrival have to be guessed at. But in a letter to the author of February 6, 1976, A. M. Temples, manager of mailing requirements of the U.S. postal service in Dallas, stated that a pistol shipped by REA Express from Los Angeles on March 20 and a rifle sent by mail from Chicago on the same day could both have arrived on the 25th, since each would have traveled at the rate of one time zone per day and each city was at a distance of five time zones from Dallas. Moreover, in another of his telltale misdatings, on his time sheets Oswald dated two successive days, Monday and Tuesday of that week, as March 25, a clue to the importance of the date.

15. REA Express no longer exists, but in 1963, the Dallas office was at 2311 Butler, near Love Field. According to former REA officials, office hours varied from city to city, depending on business. In Boston, packages could have been picked up at the REA office at Logan Field twenty-four hours a day; in certain other cities, offices were open until 8:00 P.M., and in others again, they closed much earlier.

16. Letters from Gladys A. Yoakum to the author, April 6 and May 6, 1973, May 24, 1975.

17. Exhibit No. 97, Vol. 16, pp. 422–430. This is probably the most significant document Oswald ever wrote, revealing both his emotions and his political ideas. It is striking for its apocalyptic, megalomaniacal tone, and the reader almost has to conclude that the author was possessor of the "narcissistic" personality described in Ernest Jones's famous essay "The God Complex" (*Essays in Applied Psychoanalysis* by Ernest Jones [London], pp. 204–226). Politically, the author denounces both the U.S. and Soviet systems and the U.S. Communist Party; but his primary concern appears to be destruction of the capitalist system in the United States and its future replacement. Although written before the Walker attempt, the document looks forward to Oswald's own future. It gives a better idea than anything else he wrote of what appears to have been his conscious purpose in killing President Kennedy, and of the resigned, stoical, and yet exalted spirit in which he went about it.

18. Exhibit No. 98, Vol. 16, pp. 431–434.

19. It has been stated that Sunday, March 31, 1963, was overcast, and that conditions were not bright enough for Marina to have taken the photographs of Oswald with his guns. According to weather charts supplied by the National Climatic Center, Asheville, North Carolina, which described conditions at Love Field Observatory,

5½ miles northwest of downtown Dallas, there were high thin clouds during much of that day, but there would have been no difficulty taking pictures at any time that afternoon.

24—Walker

1. Testimony of John G. Graef, Vol. 10, p. 189.
2. *Ibid.,* pp. 189–190.
3. *Ibid.,* pp. 190–191.
4. Oswald's time sheets, Exhibit 1856, Vol. 23, p. 621.
5. There is another reason why Oswald may have wanted to be fired, although there is no evidence that he thought of it. On the day after shooting General Walker, he would be the most hunted man in Dallas and it might have been dangerous for him to show up for work. On the other hand, he had never missed a day at work, and failure to show up might have been dangerous, too.
6. Testimony of Dennis Hyman Ofstein, Vol. 10, p. 203.
7. Testimony of Everett D. Glover, Vol. 10, pp. 15–30.
8. Conversation with Michael R. Paine, August 1973.
9. Testimony of Michael R. Paine, Vol. 2, pp. 393 ff.
10. *Ibid.,* p. 403.
11. Once again Oswald's timing was remarkable. He had been fired from his job and knew that he would be making his attempt on Walker within a few days. Marina and June might soon need help and, once he had been at the Paines', he saw that they were in a position to help and might be disposed to do so. Marina has said that "from the moment he met Ruth, Lee think only how to use her," and, indeed, in his "Walker note" only a few days later, Oswald told Marina that they had "friends" who would help. After the Kennedy assassination, he used the same words and made plain to his brother Robert that the friends he was referring to were the Paines (Robert Oswald, *op. cit.,* pp. 144–145).

    It is also noteworthy that from the moment he returned to the United States, Oswald always had help from outsiders when he needed it: from his mother and the Robert Oswalds, the Russian émigrés, the Paines, the Murrets. The one time he was completely on his own was, interestingly, the one time he did not need help, while he was working at Jaggars-Chiles-Stovall, October 12 to April 6. It is uncanny that the Paines should have entered his life, together, on April 2, one day after he was fired.
12. The Warren Commission investigated data about bus routes, practice sites, and places where ammunition could be bought, but did not put forward a definite theory about where or when Oswald practiced.
13. Exhibit No. 2694, Vol. 26, pp. 58–62.
14. Warren Commission Report, p. 192; Testimony of Sergeant James A. Zahm, Vol. 11, p. 308. Robert Oswald, who taught his brother how to shoot and had a similar Marine Corps record, noted that his marksmanship was only "average" when the two went small-game hunting in the summer of 1962, after Oswald's return from Russia, because he was unfamiliar with the .22 he was using. But providing his brother had enough practice, Robert believes that he was capable of the feats attributed to him. While Oswald may have practiced only on April 3 and 5, he could also have practiced all or part of April 7 to 10.

15. Conversations with Marina Oswald Porter plus Exhibits No. 2694, Vol. 26, pp. 59, 60, and No. 1156, Vol. 22, p. 197.

16. Both De Mohrenschildts remembered that this episode occurred during their visit to the Oswalds' apartment on Saturday night, April 13. (For George's recollection, see Vol. 9, p. 249; for Jeanne's, see *ibid.,* pp. 314–317.) However, the rifle was not in the apartment on April 13—Oswald dug it up only on April 14. Moreover, Jeanne remembered under cross-examination (Vol. 9, p. 315) that April 13 was not her first visit to the Oswalds' apartment. She had been there once without George. It is also extremely unlikely that Marina would have shown the rifle to anyone after her husband's attempt on Walker's life. She was afraid of him and, certainly after April 10, would not have referred to him as "my crazy husband" in his presence or his hearing, as would have been the case had the episode occurred as late as April 13.

17. Exhibit No. 1953, Vol. 23, p. 768.

18. Telephone conversation with Major General Edwin A. Walker, August 19, 1975.

19. It is possible, and even likely, that Oswald made up the story about the church announcement. E. Owen Hansen, counselor of the church, confirmed that his church had services every Wednesday from 7:30 to 9:00 P.M. and was generally empty fifteen or twenty minutes later (Exhibit No. 1953, Vol. 23, p. 763). Oswald, who had been stalking the neighborhood, may have known this already. Moreover, no announcement of the sort Oswald described has been found in either of the major Dallas dailies for that week.

20. Exhibit No. 1401, Vol. 22, p. 757.

21. Oswald could have been looking for their new apartment that night, and he could have been watching General Walker, who left Dallas on February 28.

22. Exhibit No. 1, Vol. 16, pp. 1–2.

23. All through the time that Marina was growing up in Russia, there was a law on the statute books—an infamous law of 1934—which provided that a close relative of anyone suspected of a serious crime against the state is as liable for the crime as the suspect, whether or not the relative knew of the crime either before or after it was committed. The atmosphere created by this and other laws appears to have affected Marina from the moment she learned of her husband's attempt on General Walker. Although she had neither known of his attempt in advance nor approved of it later, Marina appears to have felt that she was as guilty as he was. Her special feeling of guilt in the Walker affair lingered for months, even years, and it probably cannot be understood without knowledge of the Soviet laws of complicity which existed throughout almost the whole of her life in the U.S.S.R.

25—Legacies

Sources

Conversations with Marina Oswald Porter and her testimony in the Warren Commission Hearings, Vols. 1, 5, and 11; and conversations with Katherine Ford, Declan P. Ford, and Samuel B. Ballen.

1. Exhibits No. 1401, Vol. 22, pp. 756–757, and No. 2521, Vol. 25, p. 730.

2. Marina reports him as saying much the same *(ibid.).*

3. The Walker bullet was never traced definitely to Oswald's rifle, not even after the Kennedy assassination. (See Warren Commission Report, p. 562, and Exhibit No. 2001, Vol. 24, p. 39.)

4. Walker later denied the police theory that he moved his head at the last minute and accidentally saved his own life. Contrary to his own early testimony, he believes that Oswald fired a near-perfect shot. He was standing 120 feet away behind a stockade fence, but with a four-power sight, Walker appeared to be only 30 feet away, an easy target. Walker was not, however, sitting profiled in the window. Rather, he was well inside the room, facing out, "a side shot with a frontal angle," he explains. Firing under night-time conditions, Oswald was at the mercy of the lighting, and the angles of light and shadow, distorted by the lenses of his sight, could have thrown off his aim. He appears, however, to have had a perfect bead on his target; but with light flooding the room outside as well as in, he was unable to see the window frame. Thus the bullet was flying straight at Walker when it hit strips of window casing and was deflected. Walker at first thought that a firecracker had exploded directly above his head. Then he saw the hole in the window frame, felt bits of wood and glass in his hair, and saw bits of copper casing in his arm. (Testimony of Major General Edwin A. Walker, Vol. 11, pp. 405–410; letter from General Walker to the author, undated but postmarked May 15, 1974; and telephone conversation of General Walker and the author, August 19, 1975.)

5. Although Marina was in no way culpable for keeping silent after her husband's attempt to kill Walker, advising him to destroy evidence might, under the Texas penal code of 1974, render her culpable on two counts: accessory to attempted murder; and accomplice to the crime of destroying evidence. The present code was not in effect in 1963, however, and, indeed, the code then in effect gave a spouse immunity from being convicted for a crime committed by his or her partner.

6. Testimony of George S. de Mohrenschildt, Vol. 9, p. 249.

7. *Ibid.*, p. 250.

8. Testimony of Jeanne de Mohrenschildt, Vol. 9, pp. 317–318.

9. A description of the bundle, the way the photograph was placed in it, and the inscription was given to the author by Pat S. Russell, Jr., De Mohrenschildt's attorney, in a telephone conversation on April 21, 1977, after De Mohrenschildt's death, and a copy of the photograph, with inscriptions, was subsequently sent to the author by Mr. Russell. Some persons have questioned the authenticity of De Mohrenschildt's "find," suggesting that he placed the inscriptions there himself. There appears to be no truth to this. De Mohrenschildt immediately told friends about his discovery. In a letter of April 17, 1967, George de Mohrenschildt wrote to George McMillan, husband of the author, that he had come into possession of some "very interesting information" about Oswald since his return to the United States; and on June 22, 1968, he invited George McMillan and the author to visit him in Dallas to discuss "some interesting material on Oswald plus a *message* [De Mohrenschildt's italics] from him we discovered in our luggage."

10. On May 4, 1963, Oswald was in New Orleans and Marina was staying with Ruth Paine in Irving, Texas. Marina does not drive a car and has no recollection of returning a bundle to the De Mohrenschildts with or without Ruth. Indeed, the De Mohrenschildts were out of town. Oswald, however, had taken with him all the family's belongings to New Orleans, except for Marina's clothes and the baby's things. The package thus appears to have been mailed by Oswald from New Orleans.

11. Conversation with Samuel B. Ballen, November 28, 1964.

12. In a paper presented at the Midwestern meeting of the American Psychiatric Association in Chicago, November 15–17, 1968, Dr. James W. Hamilton, a psychiatrist at the Yale University Medical School, notes the parricidal overtones of the Walker attempt and points out that Walker's first name and initial, "Edwin A.," were the

same as those of Oswald's stepfather, Edwin A. Ekdahl, whom Hamilton described as the "paternal surrogate who disappointed him."

13. It is possible that Oswald handed out pro-Castro leaflets *before* the Walker attempt, on April 8, 9, or 10, not after, hoping perhaps to be picked up by the Dallas police before he could take Walker's life. Given his intense preoccupation with his plan, however, it is more likely that he demonstrated after the attempt. Oswald's letter to the F.P.C.C. is undated, and the only reference to time is the statement that "I stood yesterday . . ." A notation at the bottom of the letter, which was later found in the F.P.C.C.'s files, indicates that the pamphlets Oswald requested were sent on April 19. Thus it seems unlikely that he could have demonstrated any later than Monday or Tuesday, April 15 or 16 (V. T. Lee Exhibit No. 1, Vol. 20, p. 511).

14. Testimony of John R. Hall, Vol. 8, p. 409.

15. Marina later remembered that she had seen Nixon in newsreels while she was living in Leningrad and that in 1959, in Minsk, she had watched the famous Khrushchev-Nixon "kitchen debate" in newsreels or on television.

INTERLUDE AND PART FOUR: New Orleans, Mexico City, Dallas, 1963

1. Testimony of Edward Voebel, Vol. 8, pp. 5, 7, and 13. Curiously, Lee's aunt, Lillian Murret, uses identical words to explain Lee's fights in Vol. 8, p. 119.

2. Testimony of Edward Voebel, Vol. 8, pp. 9–10.

3. Exhibit No. 1386, Vol. 22, pp. 710–711.

4. *Ibid.,* p. 711.

5. Testimony of William Wulf, Vol. 8, p. 18.

6. *Ibid.,* p. 21.

26—Brief Separation

1. Testimony of Ruth Hyde Paine, Vol. 2, pp. 457–463.

2. *Ibid.,* p. 448.

3. Testimony of Michael R. Paine, Vol. 9, p. 460. Although Ruth apparently had already raised with Michael the idea of offering Marina a haven, I believe that Michael's idea, as spelled out here, actually developed during the summer, after Marina's stay at the Paines' from April 24 to May 10, 1963.

4. Exhibit No. 422, Vol. 17, pp. 140–144.

5. Testimony of Ruth Hyde Paine, Vol. 9, pp. 348–349.

6. Testimony of Lillian Murret, Vol. 8, pp. 133–135.

7. *Ibid.,* p. 128.

8. Testimony of Charles F. Murret, Vol. 8, p. 184.

9. Testimony of John Murret, Vol. 8, pp. 193–194.

10. Testimony of Marilyn Murret, Vol. 8, pp. 159, 160, 177, 178. Marilyn adds that even as a boy, Oswald always knew "he was somebody" and knew that "he was exceptionally intelligent" (*Ibid.,* p. 177).

11. Testimony of Lillian Murret, Vol. 8, p. 135.

12. Testimony of Marilyn Murret, Vol. 8, pp. 165–166.

13. Testimony of Lillian Murret, Vol. 8, p. 136.

14. Exhibits No. 1919, Vol. 23, pp. 717–718, and No. 3119, Vol. 26, p. 765.
15. Exhibit No. 1927, Vol. 23, p. 722.
16. Exhibit No. 1919, Vol. 23, pp. 717–718.
17. Testimony of Lillian Murret, Vol. 8, p. 136.
18. Exhibit No. 1945, Vol. 23, p. 745.
19. Exhibit No. 1144, Vol. 22, p. 162.
20. Testimony of Lillian Murret, Vol. 8, p. 136.
21. Testimony of Myrtle Evans, Vol. 8, p. 58.
22. Testimony of Ruth Hyde Paine, Vol. 2, pp. 446, 447.
23. Testimony of Ruth Hyde Paine, Vol. 9, p. 370.
24. Testimony of Ruth Hyde Paine, Vol. 2, p. 509.
25. *Ibid.*
26. Exhibit No. 68A, Vol. 16, p. 228.
27. Testimony of Ruth Hyde Paine, Vol. 9, p. 396.
28. Pay later Marina did. According to a letter she wrote to Ruth in July, when she and Lee were living together in New Orleans, he had reproached her bitterly for even considering driving northeast with Ruth on vacation and gave it as still another example of Marina's disloyalty to him. Marina added that it was one of the main bones of contention between them that summer.
29. In fact, Lee borrowed $30 or $40 from his uncle to make a first rental payment on his apartment. He repaid it promptly, after he had been at work a short time.

27—Magazine Street

1. Testimony of Ruth Hyde Paine, Vol. 2, pp. 470–471.
2. In a speech on April 19, 1963, President Kennedy, in what was actually an effort to soften demands for a new invasion of Cuba, predicted that "in five years' time" it was very likely Castro would no longer be the ruler of Cuba and, in the long run, the United States would be seen to have contributed to the result. In *The Militant* of April 29, 1963, a writer named William Bundy reported a statement by Robert Kennedy on April 22: "We can't just snap our fingers and make Castro go away. But we can fight for this. We can dedicate all our energy and best possible brains to that effort." Read from hindsight, with knowledge that the Kennedy administration was engaged in assassination plots against Castro, the two speeches, so closely timed together, suggest that not only Robert Kennedy and others high in the administration but also the President himself were aware of these plots. At the time, however, no one read these speeches in that light, the public question being whether there would be a second U.S. invasion. As nearly as can be ascertained, Oswald knew nothing about any U.S. assassination plots against Castro but was worried about an invasion.
3. A list of books borrowed by Oswald from the New Orleans Public Library, the main library and the Napoleon Branch, appears in Vol. 25, Warren Commission Report, pp. 929–931. A reason why Oswald borrowed the Payne biography may be another article in *The Militant,* this one by William F. Warde on p. 5 of the April 29, 1963, issue. Warde discussed the possibility that Castro had become disillusioned with the Russians, suggested that he might soon visit China, and concluded that whatever Castro's feelings about the Russians, "he has not become a Maoist either." The possibility of Castro's going to China may have kindled Oswald's desire to read

about Mao. Further, he probably identified himself with Mao, another revolutionary hero whom Payne describes as "a new kind of man: one of those who singlehandedly construct whole civilizations"—Robert Payne, *Portrait of a Revolutionary: Mao Tse-tung* (New York: Abelard, 1961). Either Oswald saw himself as that kind of man, or else he wished to become so.

4. V. T. Lee Exhibit No. 2, Vol. 20, pp. 512–513.
5. Exhibits No. 1410, Vol. 22, pp. 796–797, 798–799, and No. 2543, Vol. 25, p. 770.
6. Exhibits No. 1411, Vol. 22, pp. 800–802 (including photographs of the application forms and membership cards), and No. 2548, Vol. 25, p. 773.
7. V. T. Lee Exhibit No. 3, Vol. 20, pp. 514–516.
8. Testimony of Marilyn Murret, Vol. 8, pp. 172–173.
9. Exhibit No. 408, Vol. 17, pp. 88–91.
10. A number of things may have stimulated Oswald's interest in Castro, and his wish to travel to Cuba, among them Castro's own triumphal tour of Russia and several articles in *The Militant* which he received at about this time. They included an editorial titled "Passport Curb Revived," April 29, 1963; an unsigned story, "Travel to Cuba Arouses Inquisitors' Ire," May 13, 1963; and "HUAC Continues Anti-Cuba Smear," June 3, 1963.
11. Exhibit No. 986, Vol. 18, pp. 518–519.
12. Testimony of Marina Oswald, Vol. 5, pp. 401–402.
13. Cadigan Exhibit Nos. 23 and 24, Vol. 19, pp. 296–297.
14. Cadigan Exhibit No. 22, Vol. 19, p. 295.
15. Letter from Leo J. Kerne, Director, New Orleans Charity Hospital, to the author, March 15, 1965.
16. So close are southern Louisiana and Mississippi in geography and feeling that New Orleans is often called the southern capital of Mississippi. The closeness was evident that day, for the New Orleans *Times-Picayune* on Sunday, June 16, ran a huge front-page story on the Evers funeral, which nearly turned into a riot, and the paper also had an editorial denouncing the "senseless violence."
17. Exhibit No. 1412, Vol. 22, pp. 804–808.

28—Castro and Kennedy

1. Testimony of Nelson Delgado, Vol. 8, p. 240.
2. *Ibid.*
3. *Ibid.,* pp. 241–242.
4. *Ibid.,* p. 263.
5. *Ibid.,* pp. 243, 255.
6. John Rene Heindell was living in New Orleans during the summer of 1963, but he and Oswald did not see each other (Affidavit of John Rene Heindell, Vol. 8, p. 318).
7. Oswald's post office box number was 30061. But when he fashioned this stamp, he evidently reversed the two final numbers by mistake, so that both the leaflets and his forged vaccination certificate were printed with the wrong address. On the vaccination certificate, "Hidell" was misspelled "Hideel." Dyslexia plus Oswald's state of mind probably produced both errors.
8. Mrs. Kennedy's pregnancy was announced during the week after Easter, which was on April 14. It was Oswald who told Marina about it. Thus, between the Walker and the "Nixon" episodes and in the ten-day period before Oswald left Dallas for

New Orleans, he and Marina were looking at photographs of President and Mrs. Kennedy attending church services in Palm Beach to see if the pregnancy was visible.

9. One picture of the type Marina describes appeared in *Time* magazine, September 20, 1963. The Oswalds, who subscribed to *Time,* would have received this issue in the last days before Marina left New Orleans for Dallas. Marina says that she kept leafing through *Time,* if this was, indeed, the issue, and coming back to the photograph.

10. Exhibit No. 986, Vol. 18, pp. 520–525.

11. *Ibid.,* p. 526.

12. Unpublished Warren Commission Document No. 928, Memorandum dated May 6, 1964, by Richard Helms, Deputy Director of Plans of the CIA, titled "Contacts Between the Oswalds and Soviet Citizens, June 13, 1962, to November 22, 1963," and dated May 6, 1964.

29—Arrest

1. Testimony of Charles Joseph LeBlanc, Vol. 10, p. 214.
2. Exhibit No. 1940, Vol. 23, pp. 734–735.
3. Exhibits No. 1898, Vol. 23, p. 702, and No. 1901, Vol. 23, p. 705; Testimony of Charles Joseph LeBlanc, Vol. 10, pp. 216–217.
4. Testimony of Charles Joseph LeBlanc, Vol. 10, pp. 215 ff.
5. Exhibit Nos. 1933 and 1934, Vol. 23, pp. 727–729; Testimony of Adrian Alba, Vol. 10, pp. 221 ff.
6. Reading these and other passages of the Manchester biography after the assassination, Marina decided that, warped as her husband's mind was already, Manchester had unwittingly warped it even more. Since the country had lost its President, and she her husband, she was so angry and upset that she refused to grant an interview to Manchester, even though he was then Jacqueline Kennedy's chosen chronicler of the assassination.
7. V. T. Lee Exhibit No. 4, Vol. 20, pp. 518–521.
8. Testimony of Vincent T. Lee, Vol. 10, pp. 90, 94.
9. The F.P.C.C. was neither large nor influential, and existed so much on the fringe of American political life that it did not even dare keep a complete file of members. In December 1963, it went out of business altogether.
10. For an incomplete list, see: Burcham Exhibit No. 1, Vol. 19, p. 212; Hunley Exhibit Nos. 2, 3, and 5, Vol. 20, pp. 205–211; Rachal Exhibit No. 1, Vol. 21, p. 283; and Exhibit Nos. 1908–1911, Vol. 23, pp. 709–713. Oswald ran a real risk of being caught in the false references he gave and other lies he told on application forms. But he evidently assumed that no one would check up on him and he gave his fantasy free rein. Thus the paper trail he left behind, including his job applications and unemployment compensation forms, is helpful in any effort to understand his fantasies.
11. Testimony of Lillian Murret, Vol. 8, p. 149.
12. Exhibit Nos. 2648 and 2649, Vol. 25, pp. 919–928.
13. Exhibit No. 1145, Vol. 22, pp. 166–167.
14. V. T. Lee Exhibit No. 5, Vol. 20, pp. 524–525.
15. Testimony of Carlos Bringuier, Vol. 10, pp. 32–51; Testimony of Philip Geraci III,

Vol. 10, pp. 74–81; and Testimony of Vance Blalock, Vol. 10, pp. 81–86.

16. Testimony of Francis L. Martello, Vol. 10, pp. 51–62.

17. Testimony of John Lester Quigley, Vol. 4, pp. 431–440; Quigley's report on the interview is part of Exhibit No. 826 and appears in Vol. 17, pp. 758–762.

30—"You Understand Me"

1. In a document which was apparently written in February or March 1963, before the Walker attempt, Oswald wrote: "The Communist Party of the United States has betrayed itself!" He criticized the Party as "willing, gullible messengers" of the Kremlin, "in servile conformity to the wishes of the Soviet Union" (Warren Commission Document No. 97, Vol. 16, pp. 422–430). His anger and contempt had now given way to other feelings, and he was still trying to strengthen his links to the Party on the very last night of his life.

2. In his August 17, 1963, "Latin Listening Post" interview with William K. Stuckey, Oswald said that he had telephoned the city editor of the New Orleans *Times Picayune-States Item* before his demonstration of August 9, and had gone in person to the city room at 2:00 P.M. after the Trade Mart demonstration of August 16, and both times asked the paper to run stories about the demonstrations. Oswald claimed that both times he was refused on the grounds that the paper was unsympathetic to the F.P.C.C. (Stuckey Exhibit No. 2, Vol. 21, p. 626).

3. The transcript appears as Stuckey Exhibit No. 2, Vol. 21, pp. 621–632.

4. Letter from William K. Stuckey to the author, January 24, 1976.

5. Testimony of William K. Stuckey, Vol. 11, p. 166.

6. *Ibid.,* p. 165; and letter from William Stuckey to the author, April 16, 1976.

7. Letter from Stuckey to the author, January 24, 1976. The FBI's contact with Stuckey at this stage, while alluded to in Stuckey's testimony, does not appear in FBI reports on its surveillance of Oswald in New Orleans as published in the twenty-six Warren Commission volumes. Warren Commission Exhibit No. 826, a report filed by Special Agent Milton R. Kaack in October 1963, which summarizes most of Oswald's political activities in New Orleans, states erroneously that Stuckey's first contact with the FBI on the subject of Oswald did not occur until August 30, 1963. It is possible that Kaack's superior did not tell him of the contact with Stuckey, and thus it failed to appear in the file on Oswald in New Orleans.

8. Testimony of Carlos Bringuier, Vol. 10, p. 42.

9. Letter from Stuckey to the author, January 24, 1976. Butler, in a strange omission, was never called as a witness before the Warren Commission nor asked to give a deposition.

10. Testimony of William K. Stuckey, Vol. 11, p. 171.

11. *Ibid.,* p. 175.

12. Testimony of Charles F. Murret, Vol. 8, p. 187.

13. Exhibit No. 1145, Vol. 22, pp. 168–169. The letter raises an intriguing question. For once, Oswald had been caught in a misrepresentation and, for the moment, at least, he showed himself chastened and willing to change course. If he had been caught oftener in his lies, or if he had suffered a good scare after his attempt on General Walker, his armor of omnipotence might have suffered a dent or two, and the magic circle of invulnerability of which he believed himself the center might have been punctured briefly. If so, would this have restrained him in the future?

14. Johnson Exhibit No. 4A, Vol. 20, p. 265.
15. Exhibit No. 1404, Vol. 22, p. 787; and conversations with the author.

31—Parting

1. See, for example, remarks by Mr. and Mrs. Alexander Eames in Exhibit No. 1154, Vol. 22, p. 191.
2. Exhibit No. 1915, Vol. 23, p. 715.
3. Testimony of Mrs. Jesse Garner, Vol. 10, p. 268.
4. Many questions have been raised about Oswald's dry-firing in New Orleans, since it was the only time between the attempt on Walker in April and the shooting of Kennedy in November that he is known to have handled his rifle. One question is whether he pulled the trigger rapidly and at high speed. Marina believes the answer is No. She recalls a considerable interval between clicking sounds. Another question is whether he took the metal barrel and wooden stock apart when he cleaned the rifle. Marina does not remember. She remembers that he oiled and polished the rifle often and put it back in the closet, but she so disliked the sight of it that she watched as little as she could. Another question is whether he had a bench or some other sturdy rest to which he could clamp the rifle as he sighted it. Again, the answer is No. Marina remembers the porch as unfurnished. She thinks there was nothing on which he could have rested the gun. It might be added that, so far as is known, Oswald was then practicing to fight for Castro, not preparing for a particular murder.
5. Exhibit No. 410, Vol. 17, p. 103.
6. Testimony of Michael R. Paine, Vol. 2, p. 423.
7. Exhibit No. 421, Vol. 17, pp. 136–139; also Exhibit No. 1145, Vol. 22, pp. 169–170.
8. Exhibit No. 1145, Vol. 22, pp. 169–170.
9. Dobbs Exhibit No. 10, Vol. 19, p. 577.
10. Exhibit No. 1145, Vol. 22, p. 170.
11. Exhibit No. 93, Vol. 16, pp. 337–346.
12. In the Hearings of the House Judiciary Committee's Subcommittee on Civil and Constitutional Rights, Sessions One and Two on FBI Oversight, held on October 21, 1975, and December 11 and 12, 1975 (Serial No. 2, Part 3), it became apparent that the FBI had no regular mail cover on Oswald following his return to the United States. It therefore had no idea of the extent of his contacts either with the Soviet Embassy or with domestic organizations on the left.
13. Testimony of Marilyn Murret, Vol. 8, p. 174.
14. Testimony of Charles F. Murret, Vol. 8, p. 187; Testimony of Lillian Murret, ibid., p. 146.
15. Conversation with Ruth Paine, September 11, 1964.
16. Testimony of Michael R. Paine, Vol. 2, pp. 414–418, and Vol. 9, pp. 436–444.

32—A New Disappointment

1. The controversy arises from a statement by a woman named Sylvia Odio that a man resembling Oswald, and using the name "Leon Oswald," visited her in Dallas on the evening of Wednesday, September 25, in the company of two anti-Castro Cubans

to discuss a plot to kill President Kennedy. Her statements were taken seriously by some staff lawyers for the Warren Commission and checked extensively during the Commission's investigations and later by conspiracy theorists. The Warren Commission found no corroboration for her story. Moreover, had Oswald had any reason to be in Dallas on September 25, he could have driven there with Ruth and Marina, kept his appointment, and gone to Mexico City by bus from Dallas instead of New Orleans.

2. Warren Commission Report, Vol. 10, pp. 276–277.

3. Mrs. Twiford remembers that she received the call sometime between 7:00 and 10:00 P.M. on the evening of the 25th, and she assumes that it was a local call. Her recollection could be in error, for Oswald probably did not arrive in Houston until nearly 11:00 P.M. that evening. Or he may have made the call about 8:10 P.M. from Beaumont, Texas, a stop en route to Houston from New Orleans. There is no evidence that Oswald traveled by air either to or from Houston. (Sources include, besides the 1963 bus schedules, Affidavits of Horace Elroy Twiford and Mrs. Estelle Twiford, Vol. 11, pp. 179–180; letters to the author from Edward L. Ramsdell, Assistant Traffic Manager of Continental Trailways in Boston, Massachusetts, January 13 and 16, 1976; letter to the author from Harold E. Donovan, Public Relations Supervisor, New England Telephone Co., January 23, 1976; and conversation with Ms. Sandra Young, Public Relations Department, Southwestern Bell, Houston, Texas, January 16, 1976.) Oswald had told Ruth Paine that he had a contact who might help him find a job in Houston. Like most of his lies, this had a germ of truth in it. He did have a Houston contact, Twiford, but it was a political contact and had nothing to do with a job.

4. Affidavit of Dr. and Mrs. John B. McFarland, Vol. 11, pp. 214–215.

5. Testimony of Pamela Mumford, Vol. 11, pp. 215–224; Exhibit No. 2194, Vol. 25, pp. 20–24; and Warren Commission Document No. 78, p. 6.

6. Warren Commission Document No. 963, p. 13. The document appears to have been declassified November 5, 1973.

7. The account of Oswald's relations with the Soviet and Cuban embassies is drawn from the following sources: Warren Commission Report, pp. 733–736; Exhibit No. 2464, Vol. 25, pp. 636–637; Warren Commission Document No. 994, dated May 28, 1964, with appended translation, pp. 5–7; Warren Commission Document No. 651, March 11, 1964, declassified October 2, 1975, p. 30; Warren Commission Document No. 426, February 21, 1964, declassified January 14, 1971, p. 4; 111-page Memo to J. Lee Rankin from William T. Coleman, Jr., and W. David Slawson, February 14, 1964, entitled "Oswald's Foreign Activities: Summary of Evidence Which Might Be Said to Show that There Was Foreign Involvement in the Assassination of President Kennedy," declassified March 13, 1975, pp. 91–96.

8. On August 27, 1964, I was present when Marina came across several items of Oswald's which had not been previously confiscated. They included a portion of his return bus ticket; a booklet called "This Week—Esta Semana," a schedule of events for the week September 28–October 4 in Mexico City; and a folding guide map of the city, which included an enlarged map of the downtown area. Oswald had marked several sites on the downtown map: the bus terminals at which he arrived and from which he departed; his hotel; a travel agency; the Cuban and Soviet diplomatic establishments; the Plaza Mexico bullfight arena; and the Palace of Fine Arts. On the index beside the map he had also marked several places of historical interest, a theater, and the Anthropology and Natural History museums (Exhibits

No. 1400, Vol. 22, p. 739, No. 3073, Vol. 26, pp. 667–676, and Nos. 2488–2489, Vol. 25, pp. 689–706). And on the booklet, "Esta Semana," he had written his own name in full, both in Latin and Cyrillic, and had added a doodle, which proved on close inspection to be a tiny, fancy, old-fashioned-looking dagger, drawn very carefully in ink.

9. According to the Soviet defector Yury Nosenko, a decision was made by the KGB in Moscow to deny Oswald a reentry visa.

10. Exhibit No. 2460, Vol. 25, pp. 618–619; Warren Commission Document No. 872 (declassified November 3, 1970), pp. 4–8.

11. Exhibit No. 2541, Vol. 25, pp. 768–769.

12. Warren Commission Report, p. 737.

13. Affidavit of Theodore Frank Gangl, Vol. 11, pp. 478–479, and Gangl Exhibit No. 1, Vol. 20, p. 3. On this job application, October 4, and on another, October 10, Oswald gave the name of George de Mohrenschildt as a reference.

14. Testimony of Mary E. Bledsoe, Vol. 6, pp. 400–406.

15. Conversation with Ruth Paine, November 23, 1964.

16. Testimony of Ruth Hyde Paine, Vol. 2, p. 509.

17. Conversation with Ruth Paine, September 11, 1964.

18. Testimony of Michael R. Paine, Vol. 2, p. 422.

19. Conversation with Ruth Paine, July 11, 1964.

20. Testimony of Roy Sansom Truly, Vol. 3, pp. 213, 214. Ironically, on October 15, the Texas Employment Commission got a call for twelve to fourteen baggage handlers from Trans Texas Airways at Love Field. The job was permanent and paid $310 a month, $100 more than Oswald would earn at the depository. Oswald was considered a good prospect and the employment commission called him at the Paine house two days running, October 15 and 16. The second time, the person answering the telephone said that he had a job and he was crossed off the list. (Affidavit of Robert L. Adams, Vol. 11, pp. 480–481.) Students of the assassination have noted that if Oswald had been considering killing the President as early as mid-October, this is the job he would have taken, since the one thing sure about the President's itinerary at that date was that he would be landing and leaving at Love Field. I agree that Oswald was not thinking about killing the President at this time, but doubt that his failure to try for this job is evidence. I do not know who happened to answer the telephone at the Paine house—a neighbor or a babysitter, perhaps, certainly someone who failed to inquire about the salary and apparently did not take any message—and therefore I cannot say how Lee missed this opportunity at a higher-paying job. The affidavit of Robert L. Adams, the employment officer who called the house, makes clear that Oswald was crossed off the list for the Trans Texas job on October 17, his second day of work at the depository, and it appears that he never received any message about the employment office call. If he had, and had followed up on the Trans Texas job, it seems likely that he would have considered it even though he liked the job he had, because it paid $100 more a month and was permanent, not temporary. (Asked about the job in her testimony, Vol. 9, pp. 389–390, Ruth Paine did not know about it.)

21. Testimony of Ruth Hyde Paine, Vol. 3, pp. 39–40.

22. *Ibid.*, p. 40.

23. Audrey Hepburn, who played the role of Natasha in the Italian-American film version of *War and Peace,* one of Marina's favorite films, was in private life married to Mel Ferrer, who played her betrothed, Prince Andrei, in the same film. Marina

thought Ferrer bore a resemblance to her former suitor, Anatoly, in Minsk, and to President Kennedy.

33—Lee and Michael

1. Testimony of Mrs. Arthur Carl Johnson, Vol. 10, pp. 292–296.
2. Testimony of Roy Sansom Truly, Vol. 3, pp. 216–218.
3. Testimony of Bonnie Ray Williams, Vol. 3, p. 164; Testimony of Daniel Arce, Vol. 6, p. 364; Testimony of Roy Sansom Truly, Vol. 3, p. 218; Testimony of Billy Lovelady, Vol. 6, p. 337; and Testimony of Charles Douglas Givens, Vol. 6, p. 352.
4. In August 1964, Marina came across several of her husband's possessions which the Secret Service had accidentally failed to confiscate. Among them was an English-Russian, Russian-English dictionary inscribed, in Lee's hand, "Lee Harvey Oswald, Hotel Metropole, Moscow, November 22, 1959." The date, of course, is coincidence, yet it underlines an impression that autumn was a time of unhappy events in Oswald's life. His happier anniversaries appear to have been in the spring.
5. Conversation with Michael R. Paine, August 23, 1973.
6. *Ibid.*
7. Testimony of Michael R. Paine, Vol. 2, p. 401.
8. Conversation with Michael Paine, August 23, 1973.
9. Testimony of Ruth Hyde Paine, Vol. 2, p. 474.
10. Testimony of Michael R. Paine, Vol. 2, pp. 401, 409–410.
11. In her testimony before the Warren Commission (Vol. 5, p. 396), Marina stated that after the meeting that night Lee told her, "Paine knows that I shot at Walker." Marina later said her memory was in error. Lee made the remark, as quoted in the text, before the meeting.
12. Conversation with Michael Paine, August 23, 1973.
13. Testimony of Michael R. Paine, Vol. 11, p. 403.
14. Testimony of Michael R. Paine, Vol. 2, p. 408.
15. Testimony of Raymond Frank Krystinik, Vol. 9, pp. 465–466.
16. Testimony of Michael R. Paine, Vol. 2, p. 408.
17. Conversation with Michael Paine, August 23, 1973; Testimony of Michael R. Paine, Vol. 2, pp. 418–419.
18. Testimony of Michael R. Paine, Vol. 2, p. 409.
19. *Ibid.,* p. 401.
20. *Ibid.,* p. 419.
21. Testimony of Michael R. Paine, Vol. 2, p. 401, and Vol. 11, pp. 402–403. It is ironic that of all people it was Michael Paine—who considered himself a failure with people, and who thought his father was a genius at drawing others out but despaired of ever being able to do so himself—who better than anyone else has explained Oswald's intellectual justification for the assassination of President Kennedy. He did so, with brevity and clarity, in two of his three appearances before the Warren Commission. Had the Commission accepted Paine's summary as a true statement of Oswald's beliefs, and placed it side by side with Oswald's writings, it might have presented the American people not with the whole of his motive by any means, but with its rational component—with what Oswald *thought* he was doing.
22. Conversation with Michael Paine, August 23, 1973.
23. An extrapolation by the author from her views and those of Michael Paine.

24. Testimony of Michael R. Paine, Vol. 2, p. 410.
25. *Ibid.,* Vol. 11, p. 402.
26. *Ibid.,* p. 411.
27. Testimony of Ruth Hyde Paine, Vol. 9, pp. 351–352.
28. Testimony of Michael R. Paine, Vol. 2, pp. 414–418, and Vol. 9, pp. 437–448. Marina has been criticized for her failure to tell Ruth that Oswald had his rifle in her garage. But until mid-November, when Ruth happened to remark that she refused to buy toy guns for her children, Marina did not know Ruth's feelings about weapons. Even then she did not know that the Paines were pacifists, or exactly what this meant. But Marina did realize that Ruth would not want the gun in her garage, and she still kept her silence. Her reasoning was that it was safer, especially now that they were back in Dallas, for the gun to be with *her* than in the rooming house with her husband. She asks: "Would it really have done Ruth any good if I had told her?"

34—Agent Hosty

1. Exhibit No. 1145, Vol. 22, p. 169.
2. Exhibit No. 1145, Vol. 22, pp. 170–171. The letter, postmarked November 1, reached Mr. Johnson only on the 29th, with a line across the envelope in back suggesting that it had been opened along the way (Testimony of Arnold S. Johnson, Vol. 10, pp. 103–104).
3. I have based the account of Hosty's visits on November 1 and 5 and Oswald's reaction to them on the testimony of James P. Hosty in Vol. 4 and in the U.S. House of Representatives Judiciary Committee's Subcommittee on Civil and Constitutional Rights (Hearings on FBI Oversight, Serial No. 2, Part 3); of Marina Oswald in Vol. 1; of Ruth Paine in Vols. 3 and 9; on a conversation with Ruth Paine on November 23, 1964; and on three separate conversations with Marina Oswald. The three principals differ on such questions as the time at which the November 1 interview took place (one says 2:30, another 3:30, the third 5:00 P.M.); the duration of the second interview and where it took place; where Hosty parked the second time; on which occasion Marina talked longer with Hosty and after which occasion she gave her husband the fuller account; and whether Oswald came to Irving on Friday both weekends. I have tried to reconcile the versions with an eye to the effect of the Hosty visits on Oswald.
4. Testimony of James P. Hosty before the House Judiciary Committee's Subcommittee on Civil and Constitutional Rights, *op. cit,* p. 145. This information was not revealed in Hosty's testimony before the Warren Commission.
5. Conversation with Ruth Paine, November 23, 1964.
6. The floor plan, rear and front views, of the Paine house, are Commission Exhibits No. 430–437, Vol. 17, pp. 158–162.
7. As of this day, so many years after the assassination, Marina still does not know that the question of how she got the license number is a matter of acute debate among students of the event. They say that she could not have seen the license number from her position inside the house. In his testimony before the House Hearings (cited in note 3 above), p. 163, Hosty says he thinks he parked in the Paine driveway and that Marina could easily have taken down his number as he drove slowly up and down the street before and after the interview. Neither he nor

anybody else realizes that Marina went outside and studied the car. J. Edgar Hoover, then head of the FBI, said later that the number she took down was "incorrect in only one digit" (Testimony of J. Edgar Hoover, Vol. 5, p. 112).

8. Oswald had told Marina that, while he liked the job he had, he wanted to find another, in photography. He did not want Ruth to learn about this, because she had helped him find his job and he did not want to hurt her feelings. Still, he told Marina that one Saturday he would stay in Dallas and look for photographic work. Marina thinks that this was the weekend and that he came to Irving only on Saturday, November 9. Ruth's recollections preclude this and establish that he came on Friday, November 8. Michael Paine does not place him definitely at the dinner table on Friday, November 1, and it is barely possible that he stayed in Dallas until Saturday, November 2. But again, the weight of evidence is that he arrived in Irving about 5:30 P.M. on Friday, November 1. (No photography lab in Dallas has any record of a job application by Oswald after early October.)

Marina's confusion about the dates may result from the fact that the Hosty visits were, because of their impact on Oswald, by far the most traumatic event in her married life since Walker.

Two other points can be made. First, the fact that Oswald was thinking of another job indicates that he was not wedded to the book depository site. Second, he had been talking about coming late one weekend, and it may well be that, far from feeling angry when Marina told him not to come the November 15–17 weekend, he may actually have welcomed it.

9. Testimony of Ruth Hyde Paine, Vol. 3, pp. 101–102.
10. *Ibid.,* p. 13.
11. Testimony of Ruth Hyde Paine, Vol. 9, p. 394; and conversation with Ruth Paine, November 23, 1964.
12. Exhibit No. 103, Vol. 16, pp. 443–444. It is interesting that Oswald exonerated the Soviet Embassy in Mexico City and blamed everything on the Cuban consul. According to the defector Yury Nosenko, it was the Russians who were to blame for his troubles, the KGB in Moscow having decided to refuse him a visa. Nosenko has added that, but for the assassination, Marina and her children would probably have been granted reentry visas, although Oswald would not have been permitted to return to the U.S.S.R. Oswald's blaming the Cuban consul, however, is a clue to his frame of mind after his return from Mexico, when he turned against Cuba and resumed his old faith in the U.S.S.R. Questions have been raised about how Oswald knew that the Cuban consul in Mexico City, Señor Asque, had been replaced. On Oswald's last visit to the consulate, September 27, Asque was closeted with the man who was to replace him when Mrs. Duran called Asque out and asked him to speak to Oswald.
13. Testimony of Ruth Hyde Paine, Vol. 3, pp. 14–17.
14. Testimony of Michael R. Paine, Vol. 2, p. 412; and conversation with Michael Paine, August 23, 1973.
15. Testimony of Ruth Hyde Paine, Vol. 3, p. 17, and Vol. 9, p. 395.
16. Testimony of Ruth Hyde Paine, Vol. 3, p. 17.
17. In her testimony before the Warren Commission, Vol. 1, p. 45, Marina stated that he had to do the envelope "ten times," but in conversations with the author she said it was more like four.
18. Warren Commission Exhibit No. 986, Vol. 18, pp. 538–539.
19. Interestingly, Oswald's solution, his visit to FBI headquarters, incorporated Ruth's

advice that he go straight to the FBI. It did not, of course, incorporate the rest of her advice, that he tell them everything they wanted to know.

20. According to the Warren Commission Report, pp. 439–440, the FBI in Washington became aware of Oswald's letter to the Soviet Embassy on November 18 and routinely informed the Dallas office. Hosty learned of it only on the afternoon of November 22.

21. No one in the Dallas office of the FBI in November 1963 recalls on what day the note was delivered, although Mrs. Fenner's memory and other evidence suggest that it was delivered on the earliest possible date, November 12.

In his letter to the Soviet Embassy mailed that day, Oswald claimed that he had already made his protest to the FBI. This was false, for he knew of Hosty's second visit when he wrote the embassy and he only learned of that visit on Friday, November 8. Because of the long holiday weekend, Tuesday, November 12, was the first day Oswald could have left the note. He would have to have been severely upset to go to the FBI offices at all. In fact, he picked a time when he could be almost certain that Hosty would be out. But when he was severely upset, he had a tendency to act quickly. All of this suggests that he delivered the note on November 12. The question has arisen whether he delivered it during the week of November 18, the week of the assassination itself. It is unlikely that Oswald would have called attention to himself by going to FBI headquarters with such a note at a time when he was thinking of killing the President. Thus Mrs. Fenner's recollection that the note was delivered ten days before the assassination in itself is evidence that Oswald was not yet considering the act.

Testifying before the U.S. House Judiciary Committee's Subcommittee on Civil and Constitutional Rights (op. cit., pp. 35–59) on December 11, 1976, Mrs. Fenner created a considerable public stir by claiming that when Oswald tossed the note on her desk, it fell out of the envelope, and she read these words: "I will either blow up the Dallas Police Department or the F.B.I. office." The FBI was then severely blamed for having ignored Oswald as potentially violent.

James Hosty's description of the way the note was folded inward, with the writing inside, is in contradiction with Mrs. Fenner's description, and his account of the contents also is at variance with hers (Hearings, op. cit., pp. 129–130 and 145–147). It appears almost certain that Hosty's account is correct (interestingly, it matches that of Oswald) and that Oswald never made any threat of violence. If he had, Hosty would surely have tried to confirm the identity of the writer. But he has testified that he only became "100 percent certain" who the note was from on the afternoon of November 22 when Oswald, on meeting him in the county jail, became very upset and refused at first to speak to him (Hearings, op. cit., pp. 132 and 160).

22. On November 22, 1963, on his return from interviewing Oswald in the Dallas County Jail, Hosty was confronted at the FBI office by Special Agent in Charge J. Gordon Shanklin with the note which Oswald had left several days earlier. Shanklin, who appeared "agitated and upset," asked Hosty about the circumstances in which he had received the note and about his visits to Ruth Paine and Marina Oswald. On Shanklin's orders, Hosty dictated a two- to four-page memorandum setting forth all he knew and he gave the memorandum, in duplicate, to Shanklin.

Between two and four hours after Oswald's death on November 24, Shanklin summoned Hosty. Hosty recalls that Shanklin was standing in front of his desk and that he reached into a lower right-hand drawer and took out both the memorandum and Oswald's note. "Oswald is dead now," he said. "There can be no trial. Here, get rid of this." Hosty started to tear up the documents in Shanklin's presence. "No," Shanklin shouted. "Get it out of here. I don't even want it in this office. Get rid of it." Hosty then took the note and memorandum out of Shanklin's office, tore them up, and flushed them down a toilet at the FBI. A few days later, Shanklin asked Hosty whether he had destroyed Oswald's note and the memorandum and Hosty assured him that he had. (Hosty's testimony appears in Hearings, *op. cit.*, pp. 124–175, Shanklin's on pp. 59–129.)

Meanwhile, on November 23, Ruth Paine had given Hosty Oswald's handwritten draft of his November 9–11 letter to the Soviet Embassy (Oswald having left it on Ruth's desk when he left the house on November 12, as if he wished her to find it), and a day or so later she gave another FBI agent the copy she had made in her own hand on November 10. Hosty and the second agent, Bardwell Odum, told Shanklin about the letters and again, from his remarks, they thought he was ordering their destruction. The two agents concluded that Shanklin was on the edge of a nervous breakdown; instead of destroying Oswald's letter, they sent both copies to the FBI in Washington (Exhibit Nos. 15 and 103, Vol. 16, pp. 33–34 and 443–444).

Hosty's testimony makes it appear that his answers on an internal FBI questionnaire were subsequently falsified either by Shanklin or by someone in FBI headquarters in Washington to admit "poor investigative work" in the Oswald case. Hosty received letters of censure from J. Edgar Hoover, was placed on probation, was reprimanded for his Warren Commission testimony, and demoted to Kansas City. Years later, a promotion that was recommended for him was blocked by Clyde Tolson, chief deputy of J. Edgar Hoover. Except for Shanklin and two others, every FBI agent who had anything to do with the Oswald case in 1962 or 1963 was censured, transferred, demoted, or barred from promotion, while Shanklin received several letters of commendation from Hoover. The treatment of Hosty appears extraordinary, since it was he who saw that Oswald might warrant looking into and had recommended that the case be reopened in March 1963, after it had been closed for several months.

The statements of several witnesses before the House Judiciary Committee's Subcommittee on Civil and Constitutional Rights were at variance, particularly those of Hosty and Shanklin. Shanklin under oath denied that he had told Hosty to destroy the note and did not recall the rest of the incident as Hosty recounted it. Members of the subcommittee warned Shanklin, who is now retired, that he might be exposing himself to prosecution under federal perjury statutes. But prosecution has not been brought.

23. On April 19, 1963, President Kennedy delivered a speech on Cuba, and on April 22, Robert Kennedy made remarks in New York on Cuba which were reported in *The Militant.* Taken together, the remarks of the two men create a presumption that President Kennedy, and not just his brother, knew of plans physically to eliminate Castro. On September 9, while Oswald was still in New Orleans, the *Times-Picayune* displayed prominently an AP dispatch from Daniel Harker, in Havana, quoting Castro: "The leaders of the U.S. should think that if they are aiding in terrorist plans to eliminate the Cuban leaders, they themselves cannot be safe." There has never been any indication that Oswald put two and two together in either April or September and realized that the United States government was engaged in actual assassination attempts against Castro.

As for Castro, his interviews with Jean Daniel, Foreign Editor of the French newspaper *L'Express*, who was acting as an informal intermediary for President Kennedy and was with Castro when Kennedy died, suggest that Castro hero-worshipped Kennedy in spite of the assassination plots, of which he was aware. Castro said, "At least Kennedy was an enemy to whom we had become accustomed," and "I'm convinced that anyone else would be worse." Referring to Kennedy's Cuban policy, Castro used words similar to those Oswald used in conversation with Marina the previous summer: "He inherited a difficult situation. I don't believe a President of the United States is ever really free, and I believe Kennedy is . . . feeling the impact of this lack of freedom." (The Daniel articles appeared in *The New York Times*, November 27, 1963, and the *New Republic*, December 7 and 14, 1963.)

There is no evidence that Oswald ever felt much animus against Kennedy because of his Cuban policies or that such animus played any part in his decision to kill Kennedy. To the contrary, Oswald gave every appearance of having lost interest in Castro by November 1963, and to have shot Kennedy for totally different reasons.

35—The President's Visit

1. Conversation with Michael Paine, August 23, 1973.
2. In his testimony before the Warren Commission in 1964, Hosty said that he was carrying twenty-five to forty cases in November 1963; but in his testimony before the House Judiciary Committee's Subcommittee on Civil and Constitutional Rights in 1975, he said that he had been carrying forty to fifty cases.
3. Testimony of Ruth Hyde Paine, Vol. 3, p. 100.
4. Testimony of Ruth Hyde Paine, Vol. 2, pp. 515–516.
5. Testimony of Mrs. Arthur Carl Johnson, Vol. 10, pp. 297–298.
6. In the *Daily Texan* of May 13, 1964, the late Helen Yenne showed how, over a period of several days, news of the Barghoorn affair was printed in the Dallas papers near, or next to, stories about President Kennedy's visit. Characterizing Oswald as a "paranoid schizophrenic," Mrs. Yenne suggested that he may have hated Kennedy for "loving" Barghoorn in a way that he did not "love" him, and it was her view that the Barghoorn case could actually have triggered the assassination. So strikingly apt did Mrs. Yenne's analysis appear to the small circle of people who read her article and were also acquainted with Oswald that the weekend of November 16–17 was long afterwards known among them as "Lee's Barghoorn weekend." Mrs. Yenne, who was unaware that Oswald ever actually mentioned the Barghoorn case, was brilliant in spotting the significance of the affair.

   Publicity about Professor Barghoorn continued in newspapers, on radio, and on television through Wednesday, November 20, at which time the exact route of the Kennedy motorcade through Dallas was known. Some writers on the assassination have alleged with cruel inaccuracy that Barghoorn told Kennedy in the Oval Office following his release that he was a spy. Professor Barghoorn denies the allegation. Moreover, he never met President Kennedy and never saw him in the Oval Office—that week or any time. (Letter from Frederick C. Barghoorn to the author, August 11, 1976.)
7. Testimony of Ruth Hyde Paine, Vol. 3, pp. 43–44.

8. Warren Commission Report, p. 40.
9. Testimony of Roy S. Truly, Vol. 7, pp. 381–382; Testimony of Warren Caster, Vol. 7, pp. 387–388.
10. After the assassination, this is precisely what Oswald said about the discovery of his rifle in the Book Depository Building.
11. Exhibit No. 3009, Vol. 26, p. 536.
12. Testimony of Buell Wesley Frazier, Vol. 2, p. 222.
13. In her testimony before the Warren Commission (Vol. 1, p. 66), Marina said that it was she who asked Lee that evening to buy her a washing machine, and that after he agreed, she told him not to bother but to get something for himself instead. Thus the story arose that the Oswalds had a fight over a washing machine on the night of November 21, and that this was a pivotal event—a story which was widely circulated after the assassination among newspapermen and lawyers for the Warren Commission. But in the many interviews I have had with Marina, she says, and I believe her, that each time the subject of a washing machine came up (and it seems to have arisen three to five times in New Orleans and Irving), it was Lee who raised it, not Marina. On November 21, he apparently mentioned it as an inducement to get her to move to Dallas; and on that evening, Marina stresses, he did not say, "I'll buy a washing machine," but, "We'll buy a washing machine." Lee and Marina did not fight that evening about a washing machine. As for the car, on the long Veterans Day weekend of November 9–11, Marina and Lee had admired a second-hand car which Michael had just bought for $200. So there was a question about what the Oswalds would buy first after they had saved enough for an apartment: a car for Lee or a washing machine for Marina.
14. Testimony of Ruth Hyde Paine, Vol. 3, pp. 47–48.
15. Testimony of Ruth Hyde Paine, Vol. 3, p. 18.
16. It is possible that Oswald waited what appears to have been nine days to tell Marina in person that he had been to the FBI, because he feared the Paines' telephone was being tapped. He had not, after all, signed the FBI note, and as long as he did not mention it over the telephone, the FBI would not know for certain who it was from.
17. Testimony of Ruth Hyde Paine, Vol. 11, pp. 391–393.
18. Exhibit No. 2124, Vol. 24, p. 695.
19. Testimony of Ruth Hyde Paine, Vol. 3, p. 47.

36—November 22, 1963

1. Exhibit No. 2008, Vol. 24, p. 407.
2. Exhibit No. 2009, Vol. 24, pp. 408–409.
3. Exhibit No. 1381, Vol. 22, pp. 677–678 and 673 respectively.
4. Because he did not go in the domino room, Oswald almost certainly did not see the full-page hate group advertisement in the Dallas *Morning News* that day, which, surrounded by a heavy black border, proclaimed: "Welcome, Mr. Kennedy, to Dallas," and addressed twelve questions to the President which implied that he was helping the Communist cause.
5. Testimony of James Jarman, Jr., Vol. 3, pp. 200–201 and 210.
6. Exhibit No. 1381, Vol. 22, pp. 681–682.
7. Testimony of Charles Douglas Givens, Vol. 6, p. 350.
8. *Ibid.*, p. 349.

9. *Ibid.*, pp. 349–350.
10. Exhibit No. 723, shown in Warren Commission Report, p. 80, and in Vol. 17, p. 504.
11. Testimony of Charles Douglas Givens, Vol. 6, pp. 350–351.
12. Testimony of Bonnie Ray Williams, Vol. 3, p. 169.
13. *Ibid.*, p. 175; Testimony of Harold Norman, Vol. 3, p. 191.
14. Testimony of Bonnie Ray Williams, Vol. 3, p. 175.
15. Testimony of Harold Norman, Vol. 3, pp. 191–197.
16. Testimony of James Jarman, Jr., Vol. 3, p. 211.
17. Testimony of Bonnie Ray Williams, Vol. 3, p. 175; Testimony of Harold Norman, Vol. 3, p. 192.
18. James A. Zahm, a Marine Corps master sergeant who is expert in rifle training, testified before the Warren Commission (Vol. 11, pp. 306–310) that the four-power scope is ideal for moving targets at ranges up to 200 yards because it enhances viewing power with a minimum exaggeration of body movements. Zahm added that the fact that Kennedy's car was moving slowly away from Oswald at a downward grade of 3 degrees straightened out the line of sight in such a way as to compensate for greater distance between the first (176.9 to 190.8 feet) and last (265.3 feet) shots (15 to 22 yards as seen through the scope).

    Robert Oswald was critical of the Warren Commission for its reliance on experts and its failure to consult him about his brother's capabilities with a rifle, since he taught Oswald to shoot and was familiar with his special qualities as a marksman. Robert states that "Lee had very rapid reflexes" and was "much stronger than he looked," adding that he had "unusual strength in his hands" and that his forearms were powerful and well developed. (Robert Oswald, *op. cit.*, pp. 209–211.)

    A final point. So far as is known, Oswald never fired his rifle between April 10 and November 22. But Zahm and others have said that Oswald's dry-firing in New Orleans, working the bolt, manipulating the trigger, and aligning the sight, would have been extremely helpful, with the scope aiding him to identify any errors in trigger manipulation.
19. Testimony of Marrion L. Baker, Vol. 3, p. 252; Testimony of Roy S. Truly, Vol. 3, p. 225.
20. Testimony of Mrs. Robert A. Reid, Vol. 3, p. 274.
21. Testimony of Mrs. Mary Bledsoe, Vol. 6, pp. 409–410.
22. Warren Commission Report, pp. 161–162.
23. Testimony of Roy S. Truly, Vol. 3, pp. 226–277.
24. Testimony of Roy S. Truly, Vol. 7. p. 383.
25. Testimony of Roy S. Truly, Vol. 3, p. 230.
26. Testimony of J. W. Fritz, Vol. 4, p. 205.
27. The description broadcast on Tippit's radio was of a slender white male, about thirty, 5 feet 10 inches in height and weighing about 165 pounds (Oswald weighed between 140 and 150 pounds). The description came from a steamfitter, Howard Leslie Brennan, who watched the motorcade from a retaining wall facing, and just across the street from, the southeast corner of the book depository. Brennan twice saw a man, the same man, in the sixth-floor corner window. Once, before the motorcade's approach, Brennan watched him sit sideways on the window sill, thus seeing the man from the waist up. Brennan next saw the man as he took aim for his final shot. He appeared to be standing, resting against the window sill, holding

the gun in his left hand and against his right shoulder. Brennan estimated that he took a couple of seconds to aim and fire, then drew back and paused for a second, as if to be sure that he had hit his mark. Brennan claims to have seen 70 to 85 percent of the gun.

Immediately afterward, Brennan saw everyone, including the police, running in the wrong direction, toward the west side of the building. He went to a policeman in front of the building, and was taken to Forrest Sorrels, a Secret Service man who was parked in front in a car, and then to the sheriff's office. At 12:45 P.M., the description he gave of the man he had seen in the window went out on police car radios. It was this description that presumably caused Tippit to stop and question Oswald. That night, however, Brennan refused to identify Oswald positively in a police lineup as the man he had seen that day. He later told the Warren Commission that he refused out of fear: the shooting might be part of a conspiracy, and he and his family could be in danger if he were the sole eyewitness. Once Oswald was dead, Brennan felt the danger was over and he could safely identify him as the man he had seen in the window. (Testimony of Howard Leslie Brennan, Vol. 3, pp. 140–161, and Vol. 11, pp. 206–207.)

28. The account of Oswald's movements from the Tippit shooting to the end of the chapter is taken from the Warren Commission Report, pp. 165–180; and from David Belin's *November 22, 1963: You Are the Jury* (New York: Quadrangle Press, 1973), pp. 23–48 and 272–277. This quote appears on p. 273.

37—The Wedding Ring

1. Testimony of Ruth Hyde Paine, Vol. 9, pp. 432–433.
2. Testimony of Ruth Hyde Paine, Vol. 3, pp. 68–71.
3. *Ibid.,* pp. 69, 78–79.
4. *Ibid.,* p. 79.
5. Testimony of Michael R. Paine, Vol. 2, p. 424, and Vol. 9, p. 449; Testimony of Raymond Frank Krystinik, Vol. 9, p. 472.
6. Conversation with Michael Paine, August 23, 1973.
7. Testimony of George de Mohrenschildt, Vol. 9, pp. 274–275.
8. Testimony of Ruth Hyde Paine, Vol. 3, p. 81.
9. Testimony of Ruth Hyde Paine, Vol. 3, p. 83, and Vol. 9, pp. 371–372.
10. Testimony of Ruth Hyde Paine, Vol. 3, p. 83.

38—An End and a Beginning

1. Oswald told his brother, Robert, later that day that he considered the Paines to have been true friends to him and Marina, and that he believed the Paines would continue to care for Marina and the children (Robert Oswald, *op. cit.,* pp. 144–145).
2. Warren Commission Report, p. 200.
3. *Ibid.,* p. 601.
4. Testimony of Ruth Hyde Paine, Vol. 3, pp. 85–87.
5. Testimony of H. Louis Nichols, Vol. 7, pp. 328–330.
6. The account of Oswald's funeral is from Robert Oswald, *op. cit.,* pp. 149–165.

EPILOGUE

1. Robert Oswald, *op. cit.,* p. 169.
2. Telephone conversation with Samuel B. Ballen, May 20, 1977.
3. Conversation with Samuel B. Ballen, November 28, 1964.
4. Telephone conversation with Samuel B. Ballen, April 21, 1977.
5. Because of De Mohrenschildt's friendship with Oswald, and his acknowledged affiliation with at least one intelligence service in the past (French Intelligence during World War II), the question has arisen whether De Mohrenschildt might have been working for the CIA in Haiti, and from there, might have played a part in the assassination. The available evidence does not support either of these speculations.

    According to Warren Commission Document No. 1012, dated June 3, 1964, and declassified May 31, 1977, Richard Helms, formerly the CIA's Deputy Director of Plans, advised Lee Rankin, General Counsel of the Warren Commission, that in 1942 the Office of Strategic Services, forerunner of the CIA, considered De Mohrenschildt for employment but did not hire him because of allegations that he was a Nazi agent. According to the Helms memo, the CIA first established contact with De Mohrenschildt in December 1957, after he returned from a mission in Yugoslavia for the International Cooperation Administration. The CIA had several meetings with De Mohrenschildt at that time and maintained "informal, occasional contact" with him until the autumn of 1961.

    The rest of the memo, as well as another Helms memorandum, Warren Commission Document No. 1222, dated July 6, 1964, and declassified June 1, 1977, constitute reports on De Mohrenschildt in Dallas, Haiti and elsewhere, reports from which it appears that he could not conceivably have been a CIA employee at any time, nor have had any connection with it during the Haiti period.

    As for De Mohrenschildt's remorse over the "frivolity" of his behavior toward Oswald, to some it appeared that it was more serious, resembling that of Ivan Karamazov toward his father's murderer, Smerdyakov.
6. The number three is, indeed, conceded to have a universal symbolic meaning, since it crops up in nearly every form of human expression: in religion, mythology, folklore and literature. In psychoanalysis, the number is frequently taken to be a castration symbol. Freud called it "symbolic of the whole male genitalia." In the Christian religions, the number signifies a splitting apart, the separation of a whole into three parts and unification into one, as in the Holy Trinity, "the Three in One, the One in Three." Still another example, one closer to Oswald, perhaps, it the "thesis, antithesis and synthesis" by which the German historian Hegel, the forerunner of Marxist philosophy, believed the forward movement of history is determined.
7. *The Huey Long Murder Case,* a book by Hermann Bacher Deutsch which Oswald took out of the New Orleans Public Library on June 1, 1963, opens with the words: "Assassination has never changed the course of history."
8. Sung in the Stanley Kramer production, *High Noon,* lyrics by Ned Washington, music by Dmitri Tiomkin, copyright 1952.
9. Much of the suspense in *High Noon* is created by the ticking of a clock which hangs on the wall of a railway station. As the action proceeds, the hour hand moves slowly toward twelve noon. In *The Queen of Spades,* too, there is a clock, and the hands

move from twelve midnight to 12:25. In the Texas School Book Depository, Lee Oswald was seen at 11:55 A.M. and again at 12:10 P.M. The first shot was fired at President Kennedy a few seconds after 12:30 P.M.

10. Theodore Sorenson, *Kennedy* (New York: Harper & Row, 1965).

11. Joan and Clay Blair, Jr. *The Search for J.F.K.* (New York: Berkley-Putnam, 1976).

12. *Poems by Alan Seeger* (New York: Charles Scribner's Sons, 1916).

13. William Manchester, *The Death of a President* (New York: Harper & Row, 1967), p. 121.

14. Not only would Jacqueline Kennedy witness Oswald's act, but there was a real danger that he might hit her accidentally. When asked about this, Dr. David Rothstein, of Chicago, who has written extensively about assassinations, suggested in conversation with the author on May 4, 1971, that Oswald's willingness to risk hitting Mrs. Kennedy while aiming at her husband was an example of the "unconscious matricidal wish showing through."

15. U. E. Baughman and Leonard Wallace Robinson, *Secret Service Chief* (New York: Harper & Bros., 1961), pp. 254–255.

Selected Bibliography

BOOKS

Abel, Elie. *The Missile Crisis.* Philadelphia and New York: J. B. Lippincott Company, 1966.

Anson, Robert Sam. *"They've Killed the President!"* New York: Bantam Books, 1975.

Barron, John. *KGB: The Secret Work of Soviet Agents.* New York, Reader's Digest Press, distributed by E. P. Dutton & Co., 1974.

Baughman, E. U., and Leonard Wallace Robinson. *Secret Service Chief.* New York: Harper & Bros., 1961.

Belin, David W. *November 22, 1963: You Are the Jury.* New York, Quadrangle Press, 1973.

Blair, Clay, Jr., and Joan Blair. *The Search for JFK.* New York, Berkeley-Putnam, 1976.

Brzezinski, Zbigniew K. *The Soviet Bloc.* Cambridge, Mass.: Harvard University Press, 1967.

Chekhov, Anton. *Four Great Plays.* Translated from the Russian by Constance Garnett. New York, Bantam Books, 1958.

_____. *Sochineniya.* Tom 7. St. Petersburg: Izdateltstvo A. B. Marksa, 1901.

COINTELPRO: The FBI's Secret War on Political Freedom. New York: Monad Press, 1975.

Dostoyevsky, Fyodor. *The Brothers Karamazov.* Translated from the Russian by Constance Garnett. New York: New American Library, 1957.

Draper, Theodore. *Castroism: Theory and Practice.* New York: Praeger, 1965.

Epstein, Edward J. *Inquest.* New York: Viking Press, 1966.

Goldenberg, Boris. *The Cuban Revolution and Latin America.* New York: Praeger, 1965.

Hearings Before the Subcommittee on Civil and Constitutional Rights of the Committee of the Judiciary, U.S. House of Representatives, Ninety-Fourth Congress, First and Second Sessions on FBI Oversight, Serial Two, Part III. Washington, D.C.: U.S. Government Printing Office, 1976.

Hilsman, Roger. *To Move a Nation.* New York: Doubleday, 1967.

Holroyd, Michael. *Lytton Strachey: A Critical Biography*. New York: Holt, Rinehart & Winston, 1968.

Horney, Karen, M.D. *Feminine Psychology*. London: Routledge & Kegan Paul, 1967.

_____. *New Ways in Psychoanalysis*. New York: W. W. Norton & Co., 1939.

Hyland, William, and Richard W. Shryock. *The Fall of Khrushchev*. New York: Funk & Wagnalls, 1968.

The Investigation of the Assassination of President Kennedy: Performance of the Intelligence Agencies, Book V. Final Report of the Select Committee to Study Governmental Operations with Respect to Intelligence Activities, United States Senate. Washington, D.C.: U.S. Government Printing Office, 1976.

Jones, Ernest. *Hamlet and Oedipus*. New York, Doubleday Anchor Books, 1954.

Karol, K. S. *Guerrillas in Power*. Translated from the French by Arnold Pomerans. New York: Hill & Wang, 1970.

Kennedy, John F. *The Burden and the Glory*. New York: Harper & Row, 1964.

_____. *Profiles in Courage*. New York: Harper & Bros., 1956.

_____. *The Strategy of Peace*. New York: Harper & Bros., 1960.

_____. *To Turn the Tide*. New York: Harper & Row, 1962.

Kennedy, Robert F. *Thirteen Days: A Memoir of the Cuban Missile Crisis*. New York: New American Library, 1969.

Khrushchev Remembers: The Last Testament. Volumes One and Two. Translated from the Russian and edited by Strobe Talbott. Boston: Little, Brown & Co., 1970 and 1974.

Lermontov, Mikhail. *A Hero of Our Time*. Translated from the Russian by Vladimir Nabokov in collaboration with Dmitri Nabokov. New York: Doubleday Anchor Books, 1958.

Linden, Carl A. *Khrushchev and the Soviet Leadership, 1957–1964*. Baltimore and London: The Johns Hopkins Press, 1966.

Manchester, William. *Portrait of a President*. Boston: Little, Brown & Co., 1962.

_____. *The Death of a President*. New York: Harper & Row, 1967.

Mankiewicz, Frank, and Kirby Jones. *With Fidel: A Portrait of Castro and Cuba*. New York: Ballantine Books, 1975.

Mersereau, John, Jr. *Mikhail Lermontov*. Carbondale, Ill.: Southern Illinois University Press, 1962.

Newman, Albert H. *The Assassination of John F. Kennedy: The Reasons Why*. New York: Clarkson N. Potter, Inc., distributed by Crown Publishers, 1970.

Orton, Samuel Torrey, M.D. *Reading, Writing and Speech Problems in Children*. New York: W. W. Norton & Co., Inc., 1937.

Oswald, Robert, with Myrick and Barbara Land. *Lee: A Portrait of Lee Harvey Oswald*. New York: Coward-McCann, 1967.

Payne, Robert. *Portrait of a Revolutionary: Mao Tse-tung*. New York: Abelard-Shuman, 1961.

Powers, Francis Gary, with Curt Gentry. *Operation Overflight*. New York: Holt, Rinehart & Winston, 1970.

"The Queen of Spades," translated from the Russian by T. Keane, in *The Works of Alexander Pushkin*, selected and edited by Avrahm Yarmolinsky. New York: Random House, 1936.

Seeger, Alan, *Poems*. New York: Charles Scribner's Sons, 1916.

Sorensen, Theodore C. *Kennedy*. New York: Harper & Row, 1965.

Stafford, Jean. *A Mother in History*. New York: Farrar, Straus and Giroux, 1966.

Storr, Anthony. *Human Aggression*. New York: Bantam Books, 1968.

Tatu, Michel. *Power in the Kremlin.* Translated from the French by Helen Katel. New York: Viking Press, 1969.

Tchaikowsky, Modest. *Libretto to Pique-Dame* ("The Queen of Spades"), after text by A. S. Pushkin, English version by Boris Goldovsky. New York: G. Schirmer, Inc., 1951.

Thompson, Lloyd J. M.D. *Reading Disability: Developmental Dyslexia.* Springfield, Ill.: Charles C. Thomas, 1969.

The Trial of the U-2: Exclusive Authorized Account of the Court Proceedings of the Case of Francis Gary Powers, Heard Before the Military Division of the Supreme Court of the USSR, Moscow, August 17–19, 1960, with introductory comment by Harold J. Berman. Chicago: Translation World Publishers, 1960.

Ulam, Adam B. *Expansion and Coexistence: The History of Soviet Foreign Policy, 1917–67.* New York: Praeger, 1968.

———. *The Rivals: America and Russia Since World War II.* New York, Viking Press, 1971.

Wasiolek, Edward. *Dostoevsky: The Major Fiction.* Cambridge, Mass.: M.I.T. Press, 1964.

PUBLISHED ARTICLES

The following three articles were of special value to the author.

Freud, Sigmund. "Dostoyevsky and Patricide." *Complete Works* of Sigmund Freud, Vol. 21, pp. 222–242. Translated from the German under the general editorship of James Strachey. London: The Hogarth Press, 1961.

Jones, Ernest. "The God Complex." *Essays in Applied Psychoanalysis,* by Ernest Jones, pp. 204–226. London: The Hogarth Press, 1951.

Weissman, Philip, M.D. "Why Booth Killed Lincoln: A Psychoanalytic Study of a Historical Tragedy." *Psychoanalysis and the Social Sciences,* Vol. 5, 1958, pp. 99–115. New York: International Universities Press, 1958.

OTHER PSYCHOANALYTIC ARTICLES

Abrahamsen, David, M.D. "A Study of Lee Harvey Oswald." *Bulletin* of the New York Academy of Medicine, Vol. 43, No. 10, October 1967, pp. 861–888.

Abrahamsen, David, M.D., and Rose Palm, Ph.D. "A Rorschach Study of the Wives of Sex Offenders." *Journal of Nervous and Mental Diseases,* Vol. 119, No. 2, February 1954, pp. 167–172.

Bibring, Grete L., M.D. "Some Considerations Regarding the Ego Ideal in the Psychoanalytic Process." *Journal of the American Psychoanalytic Association,* Vol. 12, No. 3, July 1964, pp. 517–521.

Blackman, Nathan, M.D., et al. "The Hidden Murderer." *Archives of General Psychiatry,* Vol. 8, March 1963, pp. 289–294.

Bychowski, Gustav. "Psychopathology of Aggression and Violence." *Bulletin* of the New York Academy of Medicine, Vol. 43, No. 4, April 1967, pp. 300–309.

DeGrazia, Sebastian. "A Note on the Psychological Position of the Chief Executive." *Psychiatry,* Vol. 8, 1945, pp. 267–272.

Deutsch, Helena, M.D. "Some Clinical Guidelines of the Ego Ideal." *Journal* of the American Psychoanalytic Association, Vol. 12, 1964, pp. 512–516.

Freedman, Lawrence Zelic. "Profile of an Assassin." *Police,* March–April, 1966.

Gedo, John. "Thoughts on Art in the Age of Freud." *Journal* of the American Psychoanalytic Association, January 1970.

Glenn, Jules, M.D. "Sensory Determinants of the Symbol Three." *Journal* of the American Psychoanalytic Association, Vol. 13, April 1965, No. 2, pp. 422–434.

Gilula, Marshall F., and David N. Daniels. "Violence and Man's Struggle to Adapt." *Science,* April 25, 1969.

Hendrick, Ives, M.D. "Narcissism and the Prepuberty Ego Ideal." *Journal* of the American Psychoanalytic Association, Vol. 12, No. 3, July 1964, pp. 522–528.

Katz, Joseph, et al. "Lee Harvey Oswald in Freudian, Adlerian, and Jungian Views." *Journal of Individual Psychology,* Vol. 23, May 1967, pp. 19–52.

Kernberg, Otto F., M.D. "Barriers to Falling and Remaining in Love." *Journal* of the American Psychoanalytic Association, Vol 22, No. 4, pp. 486–511.

Kohut, Heinz, M.D. "Beyond the Bounds of the Basic Rule: Some Recent Contributions to Applied Psychoanalysis." *Journal* of the American Psychoanalytic Association, Vol. 8, July 1960, pp. 567–586.

———. "Forms and Transformations of Narcissism." *Journal* of the American Psychoanalytic Association, Vol. 14, April 1966, pp. 243–272.

———. "Thoughts on Narcissism and Narcissistic Rage." *Psychoanalytic Study of the Child,* Vol. 27, 1972, pp. 360–400.

Mintz, Ira L., M.D. "Unconscious Motives in the Making of War." *Medical Opinion and Review,* No. 4, April 1968, pp. 88–95.

Murray, John M., M.D. "Narcissism and the Ego Ideal." *Journal* of the American Psychoanalytic Association, Vol. 12, No. 3, July 1964, pp. 477–511.

Rothenberg, Simon, M.D., and Arthur B. Brenner. "The Number 13 as a Castration Fantasy." *The Psychoanalytic Quarterly,* Vol. 24, No. 4, 1955, pp. 545–559.

Rothstein, David A., M.D. "Presidential Assassination Syndrome (I)." *Archives of General Psychiatry,* Vol. 11, No. 3, September 1964, pp. 245–254.

Rothstein, David A. "Presidential Assassination Syndrome (II)." *Archives of General Psychiatry.* Vol, 15, No. 3, September 1966, pp. 260–266.

Shneidman, Edwin S. "Orientations Toward Death: A Vital Aspect of the Study of Lives." *International Journal of Psychiatry,* Vol 2, March 1966, pp. 167–188.

Weinstein, A., and Olga G. Lyerly. "Symbolic Aspects of Presidential Assassination." *Psychiatry,* Vol. 32, No. 1, February 1969, pp. 1–11.

Weisz, Alfred E., M.D. and Robert L. Taylor, M.D. "The Assassination Matrix," *Stanford Today,* February 1969, pp. 11–17.

ARTICLES ON READING DISABILITY

Cole, Edwin M., M.D. "The Correction of Speech and Reading Difficulties." *Rhode Island Medical Journal,* Vol. 28 (1945).

———. "Specific Reading Disability: A Problem in Integration and Adaptation." *American Journal of Ophthalmology,* Vol. 34 (1951).

DeHirsch, Katrina, M.D. "Gestalt Psychology as Applied to Language Disturbances." *Journal of Nervous and Mental Diseases,* Vol. 120 (1954).

Eustis, Richard S., M.D. "Specific Reading Disability." *The New England Journal of Medicine,* Vol. 237, No. 8 August 21, 1947.

Orton, Samuel T., M.D. "Specific Reading Disability—Strephosymbolia." *Journal* of the American Medical Association, Vol. 90, No. 14 (1928).

OTHER PUBLISHED SOURCES

Dallas Morning News, Dallas, Texas, February-April, 1963.

Dallas Times-Herald, March-April, 1963.

Daniel, Jean. "Unofficial Envoy: Talks with Kennedy and Castro." *The New Republic,* December 14, 1963.

———. "When Castro Heard the News." *The New Republic,* December 7, 1963.

McGovern, George. "A Talk With Castro." *New York Times Magazine,* March 13, 1977, pp. 20, 76–78, 80.

The Militant. Vol. 27, Nos. 1–47, January 7, 1963–December 30, 1963. New York City: The Militant Publishing Association.

National Commission on the Causes and Prevention of Violence Report to President Lyndon B. Johnson. Washington, D.C., January 1969.

Selected Issues from *The Worker,* October 28, 1962–November 24, 1963. Published in New York City.

UNPUBLISHED SOURCES

Hamilton, James W. "Some Observations on the Assassination of President Kennedy." Presented at Midwestern Meeting of the American Psychiatric Association, Chicago, Illinois, November 15–17, 1968.

Wolin, Howard. "The Kennedys: Psychological Characteristics of Leaders that Contribute to an Increased Risk of Assassination." Prepared for Meeting of the American Psychiatric Association in Washington, D.C., May 1–4, 1971, but not delivered.

ARTICLES ON BALLISTICS

Lattimer, John K., M.D. "Factors in the Death of President Kennedy." *Journal* of the American Medical Association, Vol. 198, No. 4, October 24, 1966.

———. "Observations Based on a Review of the Autopsy Photographs, X-Rays, and Related Materials of the Late President John F. Kennedy." *Resident and Staff Physician,* May 1972, pp. 34–64.

Lattimer, John K., M.D., and Jon Lattimer. "The Kennedy-Connally Single Bullet Theory: A Feasibility Study." *International Surgery,* Vol. 50, No. 6, December 1968, pp. 524–532.

Lattimer, John K., M.D., Gary Lattimer, and Jon Lattimer. "Could Oswald Have Shot President Kennedy? Further Ballistics Studies." *Bulletin* of the New York Academy of Medicine, Second Series, Vol. 48, No. 3, April 1972, pp. 513–524.

———. "The Kennedy-Connally One Bullet Theory: Further Circumstantial and Experimental Evidence." *Medical Times,* November 1974, pp. 33–56.

In addition to the above, Warren Commission documents declassified between 1965 and 1977 have been used. These include reports of the F.B.I., U.S. Department of State, U.S. Department of the Treasury, U.S. Secret Service, and the Central Intelligence Agency, most of which are numbered; and internal memoranda exchanged among members and staff members of the Warren Commission, documents and correspondence exchanged between the Warren Commission and other U.S. government agencies, photographs and other exhibits, transcripts of executive sessions of the Commission. Documents in the latter categories are unnumbered and frequently difficult to identify.

Acknowledgments

Among those who have helped me, there is one to whom I owe everything, my husband, George McMillan, for his love, his confidence, his sacrifices.

There are two other persons without whom I might not have completed this book. They are M. S. Wyeth, Jr., of Harper & Row, whose fastidiousness and gentleness I treasure. And Burton Beals, the editor's editor, a man of talent and rare grace.

I should like to thank John Leggett, who helped bring this book into being.

And Katherine N. Ford, for her wisdom and support.

I wish to thank Marion M. Johnson, of the National Archives, for help impeccably rendered over the years.

And my cousin, David C. Davenport, who gave Marina and me a haven during the unquiet weeks of September and October 1964, just after the Warren Report was issued, and who has been unflagging in his loyalty.

Others who gave Marina and me valued help in 1964 were Declan P. Ford, Jerome Hastings, Pat. S. Russell, Jr., and Bette and Bill Slack.

I should like especially to thank four persons who made themselves available over the years in interviews, telephone conversations and letters, often in a uniquely encouraging way: Samuel B. Ballen, Michael Ralph Paine, Ruth Hyde Paine, and Richard E. Snyder.

Others who were generous in answering my inquiries include Professor Frederick C. Barghoorn, David W. Bolin, Dr. Kenneth Dinklage, Dr. James W. Hamilton, Dr. John K. Lattimer, John A. McVickar, Professor John Mersereau, Robert Oswald, the late Francis Gary Powers, Edward L. Ramsdell, Dr. David A. Rothstein, Larry Seigle, William K. Stuckey and Mrs. Gladys A. Yoakum.

I should like to thank Professor John H. Mansfield of the Harvard Law School for two 1965 memoranda pertaining to Marina Oswald's deportability and to the question of her criminal liability under Texas law in 1963; Benjamin B. Sendor for a memorandum on the Texas penal code in 1963; and John B. White, formerly of the Smithsonian Astrophysical Observatory in Cambridge, Massachusetts, for his study of the March 31, 1963, photographs of Lee Oswald, and for his brilliant interpretation of *High Noon*.

Several valued colleagues in the field of Soviet affairs have helped me with questions that range from interpretation of Khrushchev's policies during the 1959–1963 period, to the light which Lee and Marina's use of Russian in conversation with each other casts on their relationship. These colleagues are Edward L. Keenan, the late Leonard J. Kirsch, and Angela Stent Yergin of the Russian Research Center at Harvard; Mervyn Matthews of the University of Surrey, England; Peter Reddaway of the London School of Economics; and Colette Shulman.

Before interviewing Marina Oswald, I consulted members of the psychoanalytic community. Since none has seen the final product, I prefer to thank them anonymously. I should, however, like to give special thanks to Dr. Sidney Isenberg, of Atlanta, Georgia, and to Dr. Irving Kaufman of Newton, Massachusetts, for their perceptiveness, their kindness, and their willingness to give even more help than I asked.

I should like to thank Brad Leithauser, Mary Jo Salter, and Carol Watson for the very special gifts they brought to this book.

And I thank Edward Crankshaw, Robert J. Korengold, Colgate S. Prentice and Strobe Talbott for their help and encouragement.

It would have been difficult for me to finish this book without Dr. Ruick S. Rolland and Dr. Doris Menzer-Benaron.

And I thank my brothers, Stuart and Coit Johnson, and my sister, Eunice Campbell, for their love.

Finally, I thank Marina Oswald Porter for her complete cooperation, for her loyalty, and for the enormous trust which she has placed in me.

Priscilla McMillan

Cambridge, Massachusetts
August 1977

Index